THE
WEST POINT
HISTORY
OF
WORLD WAR II

VOLUME 2

THE UNITED STATES MILITARY ACADEMY®

FOREWORD BY HENRY A. KISSINGER

EDITORS: CLIFFORD J. ROGERS, TY SEIDULE, AND STEVE R. WADDELL

SIMON & SCHUSTER

NEW YORK   LONDON   TORONTO   SYDNEY   NEW DELHI

Simon & Schuster
1230 Avenue of the Americas
New York, NY 10020

First Simon & Schuster hardcover edition November 2016

SIMON & SCHUSTER and colophon are registered trademarks of Simon & Schuster, Inc.

For information about special discounts for bulk purchases, please contact Simon & Schuster Special Sales
at 1-866-506-1949 or business@simonandschuster.com.

The Simon & Schuster Speakers Bureau can bring authors to your live event. For more information or to book an event,
contact the Simon & Schuster Speakers Bureau at 1-866-248-3049 or visit our website at www.simonspeakers.com.

Manufactured in the United States of America

10   9   8   7   6   5   4   3   2   1

Library of Congress Cataloging-in-Publication Data

The West Point history of World War II / The United States Military Academy ; Editors: Clifford J. Rogers, Ty Seidule, and Steve R. Waddell.
      pages cm — (The West Point history of warfare)
   Includes bibliographical references and index.
   ISBN 978-1-4767-8273-7 (vol. 1) — ISBN 1-4767-8273-3 (vol. 1) — ISBN 978-1-4767-8274-4 (ebook: vol. 1)   1. World War, 1939–1945.
   I. Rogers, Clifford J., editor.   II. Seidule, Ty, editor.   III. Waddell, Steve R., editor.   IV. United States Military Academy.
   D743. W445   2015
   940.53—dc23   2015031711

ISBN 978-1-4767-8277-5
ISBN 978-1-4767-8278-2 (ebook)

To the West Point graduates who led American soldiers and airmen to victory in World War II

*T*he West Point History of World War II, Volume 2 comprises six chapters of *The West Point History of Warfare*, completing the story of the Second World War from 1943 to 1946. *The West Point History of Warfare* is a seventy-one-chapter enhanced e-book survey of military history from ancient times through the present day, originally designed to be used by cadets in the core History of the Military Art course at West Point. George S. Patton Jr. and Dwight Eisenhower took "MilArt," as it is called, but they could never have imagined such a book or its animated maps and interactive widgets. Because we created the two projects simultaneously, we owe a debt of gratitude to all of those who have contributed to making *The West Point History of Warfare* truly groundbreaking at West Point and beyond. In particular, we want to highlight those who have helped make *The West Point History of World War II, Volume 2* the exceptional book it is.

The West Point History of World War II, Volume 2 is a product of an extraordinary public-private partnership between the Department of History at West Point and Rowan Technology Solutions. We took the best aspects of government service and paired them with the best aspects of an agile education technology start-up. The result is the book you see before you.

This project required a visionary who believed that cadets at West Point deserved the best education possible and that providing the best education required employing the latest technology. Mr. Vincent Viola not only provided the money to put together this formidable project but also realized that a bunch of historians—both in uniform and out—had no business managing a massive, high-technology endeavor. He started a company called Rowan Technology Solutions to create this book. Vinnie named the company for the famed Lieutenant Rowan from the Elbert Hubbard pamphlet *A Message to Garcia*. In 1898 President William McKinley gave Andrew Rowan, an 1881 West Point graduate, a message to deliver to the Cuban leader Calixto García. With no idea of García's exact location and no explicit instructions on how to accomplish his mission, Rowan left Washington. After a short stop in Jamaica, Rowan met García in the Oriente Mountains and delivered McKinley's message. Since then, army officers have known that "taking a message to García" is shorthand for taking initiative.

The team at Rowan lives up to his redoubtable legacy of initiative. Vinnie gave the project to his West Point classmate Anthony Manganiello to execute. Tony, as the Rowan Chief Executive Officer, gave the team focus: create the best possible product for cadets and make sure, above all, that it improves cadets' understanding of military history. Tony needed someone who could help him execute a project of immense complexity that had to straddle the divide between the army and business. We are fortunate that Tim Strabbing, Rowan President, has led this project from the beginning. His leadership, intellect, and energy infuse every aspect of this project.

Managing a project that requires the integration of business, the army, philanthropy, and academe is a difficult task. Colin Colbourn was exactly the right person for this daunting task and has done a superb job leading the Rowan project team, in addition to his duties as Rowan's in-house historian. This book is beautiful, informative, and innovative because of the extraordinary work of our cartographer, Michael

Bricknell, and our graphic designers, Terry O'Toole and Stephanie Cardenas. Chase Stone drew the soldiers that help bring the book to life.

The words needed as much care as the maps and graphics, and required editors and copy editors who had the same sense of mission and dedication. Matthew Manganiello and Christy Cefalu formed the editing team that polished the text in the main body, captions, footnotes, maps, and interactives. Danielle Viola contributed above and beyond her role as general counsel, helping to secure rights and permissions as well as skillfully helping the team navigate a myriad of challenges along the way.

Adding interactive content for the enhanced e-book version posed its own set of challenges and required world-class technologists in support. Rowan's lead technologist, Ross Harrison, created and maintains the superb digital tools that make *The West Point History of Warfare* unlike any other book ever made. Ross is the proud son of a distinguished West Point graduate—his father was a colonel who served in Afghanistan. Back-end developer Mathieu Lue worked diligently with Ross to perfect these tools.

Our senior adviser, General (Ret.) John Abizaid provided us with sage counsel at the most crucial moments and fixed problems we knew about and headed off other issues before we even knew there was a problem. Brigadier General (Ret.) Lance Betros and Colonel (Ret.) Mat Moten led the Department of History as the project was conceived and launched, and gave it their wholehearted support. Second World War historian Colonel (Ret.) Kevin Farrell, then chief of the Military History Division, also served as one of the project's volume editors (including for the WWII chapters) until his retirement. John W. Hall, the Ambrose-Hesseltine chair in military history at the University of Wisconsin, a consulting editor for the whole *West Point History of Warfare* project, read and provided valuable feedback on all the chapters.

The West Point History of World War II, Volume 2 is, of course, a history book, and we had the finest historians working on it. For each chapter we picked the best possible historian: someone who combined excellent writing ability with deep expertise about the chapter's particular topic. Thankfully, each agreed to write for us. Professors Robert Citino, Richard Overy, and Robert Love (along with co-editor Steve Waddell) provided us with invigorating text reflecting the very latest scholarship. We also needed crack historians to help us design the maps, select the images, and provide guidance for cartographers and designers. For this volume Colin Colburn was the principal Associate Editor at Rowan, though Drs. Joe Stoltz and Keith Altavilla served in that role for earlier iterations of the chapters. Professors John Stapleton and Samuel Watson and Colonel Gail Yoshitani, volume editors for other sections of *The West Point History of Warfare*, made crucial contributions to the overall design, structure, and pedagogical underpinnings of the work.

Unlike most authors and publishers, we had access to the incredible collections in the West Point Museum. Thanks to Director David Reel, Mike McAfee, Les Jensen, Marlana Cook, and Paul Ackermann. Likewise the West Point Library's Special Collections and Archives has provided us with invaluable assistance. Thanks to Director Suzanne Christoff, Casey Madrick, Susan Lintelmann, Elaine McConnell, and Alicia Mauldin-Ware.

We also owe sincere thanks for their assistance to Sarah Forgey and Charles Bowery of the U.S. Army's Center of Military History, who helped us access the incredible collection of art held by the CMH, and Lisa Crunk and Pam Overman, who helped us with images from the Navy History and Heritage Command's equally impressive image resources. Thanks also to Wendy Zieger of Bridgeman Images for her continued assistance across the whole project.

We tested *The West Point History of Warfare* with 2,400 cadets and 45 instructors over the course of two years. With feedback from cadets and instructors, we found what worked and what did not. Colonel Jason Musteen, chief of the Military History Division at West Point, ably led the faculty who taught the course over the last two years. Majors Rick Anderson and Chuck Bies and Lieutenant Colonel Casey Doss served as the course directors for the History of the Military Art, leading a group of disparate historians to embrace a new text on the new medium of a tablet. Major Greg Jenemann oversaw our vigorous assessment process to make sure we benefited from the input of faculty members who were teaching from the textbook. For the WWII chapters, the assessment team was led by Prof. John Stapleton and included Majors Chuck Bies, Nate Jennings, Dave Musick, Stu Peebles, Rocky Rhodes, and John Zdeb. Major Dave Musick took point on a variety of technology-related issues. These "iron majors" proved their mettle on this project. Every Department of History faculty member who taught using the text assisted in making the course a success. Professor Sam Watson deserves special mention for his extensive comments on the draft versions. In the Department of History, we had an impressive support team for the entire project. Ms. Deb Monks, Ms. Martha Simonnet, Lieutenant Colonel (Ret.) Ray Hrinko, Mr. Rich Stephenson, Ms. Melissa Mills, Ms. Yvette O'Neal, Ms. Loretta Woody, and Ms. Lalah Brewer helped make this project go smoothly. We also want to thank the 3,500 cadets who used the text and helped us improve it. They had no choice—the army is an obedience-based organization, after all—but they really did give us great feedback.

We were able to execute this mammoth million-word, thousand-map project only because of the support of several members of USMA's senior staff. We were lucky to work with dedicated and competent administrators who were also innovative. West Point's chief information officer, Colonel Ron Dodge, completely changed the IT landscape at West Point to ensure we could teach the text on tablets in classrooms, connected to a network. This feat took time as well as determination; the course would not have taken the shape it has without Colonel Dodge. While the technological challenges were tough, the legal challenges also proved daunting. We could not have completed this project without Lori Doughty in the Staff Judge Advocate's office. She is a superb, innovative, and creative lawyer. Thanks also to Laura Heller for her fine work.

Our friends at Apple have supported us from the beginning of this project. Apple exec Adrian Perica (USMA, 1994) gave us early support and continues to help us. Kelly Gillis provided crucial help in deploying iTunes U internally at West Point and externally through our open digital courses. Our liaison at Apple, Deirdre Espinoza, helped us negotiate that huge company.

We are grateful to have had such an excellent team at Simon & Schuster, and give special thanks to Bob Bender, our editor. Coalescing so much content into a beautiful and cohesive print product was no small task. Associate editor Johanna Li's adept guidance was invaluable at every stage. Ruth Lee-Mui, the book's designer, worked closely with the Rowan team to ensure striking visual impact. Jonathan Cox provided valuable feedback on the manuscript, and Jonathan Evans led the copyediting effort. Hilda Koparanian skillfully supervised production.

Our agent at the William Morris Endeavor agency, Eric Lupfer, was, literally, born for this job. He made his earthly debut in Keller Army Community Hospital at West Point when his father, Tim, was teaching history at West Point. He has ably led us through the publishing industry.

Finally, Cliff, Ty, and Steve would like to thank the *West Point History of Warfare* widows: our wives, Shelley Reid, Shari Seidule, and Sharon Waddell. We spent nearly every evening and nearly every weekend for the past three years on this project and we have many more months to go. Their love and patience made this book possible.

For the second time in a generation, Europe consumed itself in an inferno of blood and steel. This volume—the second in the *West Point History of World War II*—begins in 1942, by which time Germany had subdued the Continent with the power of Blitzkrieg. Only Britain remained to oppose the scourge of Nazism in the West. The desire for *Lebensraum*, or "living space," in which Adolf Hitler could fulfill what he believed to be his historical mission, had animated his efforts as much as his desire to cleanse Europe of the people he considered inferior.

In the previous volume of this set, Berlin wrestled with its options. It could launch the invasion of the British Isles it had long delayed and attempt to extinguish the last candle of democracy in Western Europe. It could seek a modus vivendi with London that would allow it to develop its European conquests. Or it could challenge the Soviet giant, opening an Eastern Front on land that it believed was destined to be subsumed by the German Reich. Hitler pursued the first two strategies—first by bombing British cities and then by offering to "guarantee" the British Empire—but Prime Minister Winston Churchill remained steadfast, staking the survival of his country on the aid and, he hoped, the armies of the United States.

Hitler invaded Russia in June 1941. Six months later, following the Japanese attack on Pearl Harbor, he declared war on America. Why he knowingly drew Washington into the European theater, when Japan might have been able to distract U.S. forces in the Pacific, remains a historical debate—one the readers of this compilation will likely conduct. What is clear, however, is that President Franklin Delano Roosevelt saw two reasons to enter the fray: to rescue a beleaguered continent and, even more ambitiously, to use what America's entrance would make a truly global war to craft a new system of international order. And with great foresight, he anticipated the American role in that new system long before the majority of the American people could.

This volume opens on the commencement of Hitler's next and perhaps most devastating decision: to divide his army and march once more on the Soviet Union. Since it was launched in the summer of 1942, the overreach of that campaign—Operation Blue—has been made an example in the strategic education of generations of soldiers. For years, it had been Hitler's instinct to push onward, but when he pushed east, it became clear that the Führer was unsure how to finish what he had so brazenly begun. Spread too thinly, his troops failed to besiege Stalingrad, reach Moscow, or master the rich oil fields but daunting geography of the Caucasus.

The tide of the war began to turn. The intensity of Blitzkrieg could not be sustained across many months or thousands of miles. And the rapacity of the German forces—their dedication to genocide and pillaging—foreclosed the possibility of their security among local populations. Like Napoleon's armies more than a hundred years prior, Hitler's Wehrmacht retreated under heavy duress.

Yet this was not the end. In the same year, the Second Battle of El Alamein saw meticulous planning and overwhelming force combine to deliver North Africa to the Allies. After a bitter and protracted struggle, U.S. Marines declared victory at Guadalcanal, halting for the first time Japanese expansion in the South Pacific. And British and American air forces took to the skies to attempt to degrade the German home front, the memory of the Blitz emblazoned in the minds of the members of the Royal

Air Force. By the end of 1943, the Allies had proven their superiority in the logistics of war—their manpower, equipment, and ability to produce and transport both to the front lines—and had adopted a system of high-level coordination that gave them a crucial advantage over the Axis powers: at a series of conferences, the heads of the Allied states coalesced around a set of strategic priorities as well as a collection of tactics to ensure their realization. They agreed in Casablanca to demand unconditional surrender of their German foes. In Cairo, they decided to impose the same requirement on the Japanese. Days later, the Big Three—Roosevelt, Churchill, and Josef Stalin—went to Tehran, Iran, where they agreed to open a second front against Germany. At Yalta, on the Crimean Peninsula, the Allies began to imagine postwar Europe; at Potsdam, Germany, they applied their organizing principles to the administration of the lands of the defeated Reich.

In the summer of 1944, America's bold landing on the beaches of Normandy reopened a front that the German forces were ill-prepared to defend. Terrible fighting lay ahead in the Pacific, but finally, in August 1945, the conflict came to an end.

World War II shaped the modern world as we have come to know and live in it. It left in its wake destruction, displacement, and uncertainty, some of which was expected—inflation and industrial dislocation were familiar to the nations of Europe that had endured the First World War—and some of which was unprecedented: from the invention of the atomic bomb came an arms race with an existential quality that the nations of the world had never before been forced to confront. America, for its part, emerged permanently changed. The imperative to rebuild Europe's economies birthed the Marshall Plan, which formed the basis of the vital transatlantic partnership that continues to shape global politics in the contemporary period. In a decades-long contest of ideas with the Soviet Union, American capitalism triumphed, claiming as its primary casualty Communism as an inspirational force. It was a new American century. Indeed, it was a new era in the history of the world.

In both conduct and consequence, World War II is a monumental story—one in which I, as a soldier in the U.S. Army, am proud to have played a very small role. These chapters, ambitious in medium as well as scope, vividly outline the conflict through annotated maps, arresting images, personal narratives, and thoroughly researched text that not only recounts events, but challenges readers to contemplate why the war ended the way it did. It is my hope that, together with its predecessor, this volume will make accessible to new generations of American military strategists the story of the world's last total war and inspire them to conduct future operations, not in the name of grandiose visions, but in the name of peace.

The

WEST POINT
HISTORY

OF

WORLD WAR II

VOLUME 2

MASTER LEGEND

⊙	Capital City
●	Major City
●	Minor City
•	Town or Village

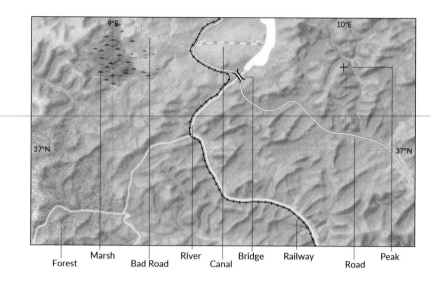

Forest   Marsh   Bad Road   River   Canal   Bridge   Railway   Road   Peak

BASE MAP

MILITARY FEATURES

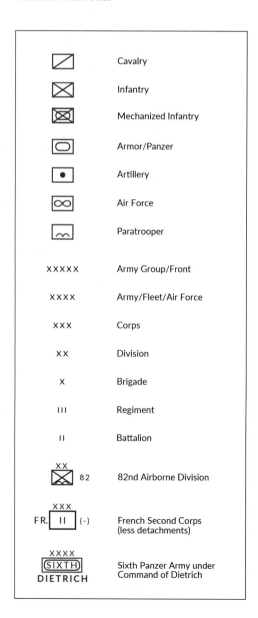

▱	Cavalry
⊠	Infantry
⊠	Mechanized Infantry
⬭	Armor/Panzer
▪	Artillery
∞	Air Force
⌒	Paratrooper
xxxxx	Army Group/Front
xxxx	Army/Fleet/Air Force
xxx	Corps
xx	Division
x	Brigade
III	Regiment
II	Battalion
⊠ 82	82nd Airborne Division
FR. II (-)	French Second Corps (less detachments)
SIXTH / DIETRICH	Sixth Panzer Army under Command of Dietrich

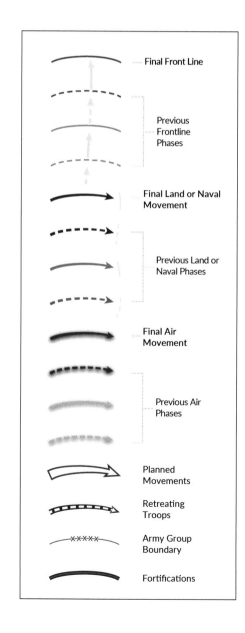

- Final Front Line
- Previous Frontline Phases
- Final Land or Naval Movement
- Previous Land or Naval Phases
- Final Air Movement
- Previous Air Phases
- Planned Movements
- Retreating Troops
- Army Group Boundary
- Fortifications

Battle / Conflict

Plane Squadron

Sunken Ship

Air-Dropped Troops

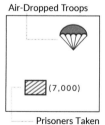

▨ (7,000)

Prisoners Taken

Airfield

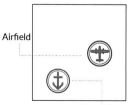

Naval Base

INTRODUCTION

No discussion of World War II would be complete without identifying its "turning point," but that can be more difficult than it sounds. A global war of this size and complexity generates many critical moments, dramatic swings in momentum, and times when victory suddenly turns to defeat. For that reason, any student of the war should be wary of using the term "turning point" too glibly.

Nevertheless, this chapter will argue that the year 1942 marked a crucial period in this protracted war. It was not so much a single turning point as a whole series of them. Of course, the Axis powers knew that a prolonged war was not likely to turn out well for them, so they bent every effort to win the war quickly. The Japanese, as we saw in chapter 5 of volume 1, rapidly conquered an immense amount of territory in the Pacific and twice tried to knock out the American battle fleet. Defeat at Midway checked their progress, but in the second half of 1942, they aimed to establish bases in the southern Solomon Islands from which they could strike at the lines of communication between America and Australia. If those could be severed, it would become practically impossible for the United States to roll back the Japanese tide.

Meanwhile, the European Axis powers, having recovered from the setbacks of the winter of 1941–42, planned to strike heavy blows against Britain and the Soviet Union. A direct attack on the United Kingdom remained impossible, so German planners identified two strategies to cut off England from the global support it needed to continue the war. The unrelenting U-boat war in the Atlantic Ocean will be discussed in the next chapter; here we will examine the German-Italian effort to drive across North Africa to capture the Suez Canal, the vital link between the British homeland and the most valuable components of the British Empire.

On an immensely larger scale, the Axis powers also planned to resume the offensive against the Soviet Union. Although they did not all agree on the best way to do it, Hitler and his military leaders did appreciate that, one way or another, they needed to land a knockout blow against Stalin's regime while they were still able to concentrate the vast majority of their strength in the East.

Depending on how successfully each side implemented its plans, 1942 could have been the year the Axis won the war, or it could have produced mixed results that deferred the real decision until 1943. But instead, it turned out to mark the high tide of the Axis push for world domination and saw that tide begin to flow backward, thanks to a series of Allied victories. The most important one took place on the Eastern Front. Operation Blue, Germany's attempt to defeat the Soviet Union before the United States could enter the war in strength, came to grief with the encirclement and destruction of an entire German field army at Stalingrad in November 1942. That same month, British Eighth Army under General Bernard Law Montgomery launched a carefully planned and lavishly supplied offensive at El Alamein in Egypt that smashed Field Marshal Erwin Rommel's *Panzerarmee Afrika*. Finally, clear across the world on the South Pacific island of Guadalcanal, a bitter struggle—in which both adversaries had to fight at the end of a long and tenuous supply line—finally ended in a victory for

THE ALLIES TURN THE TIDE

ROBERT M. CITINO

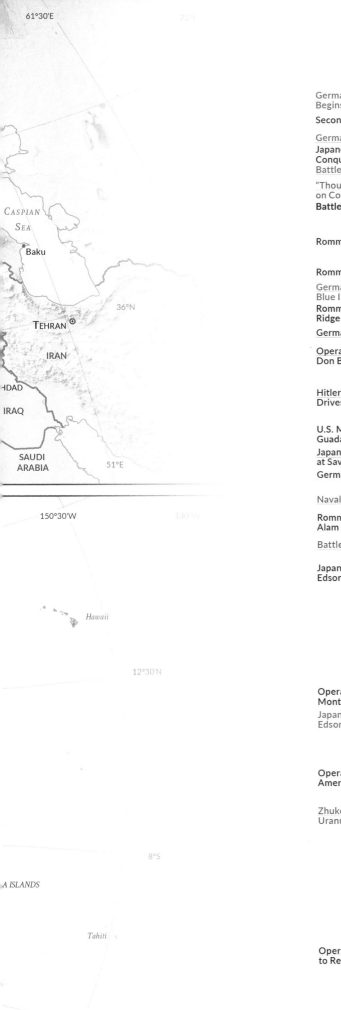

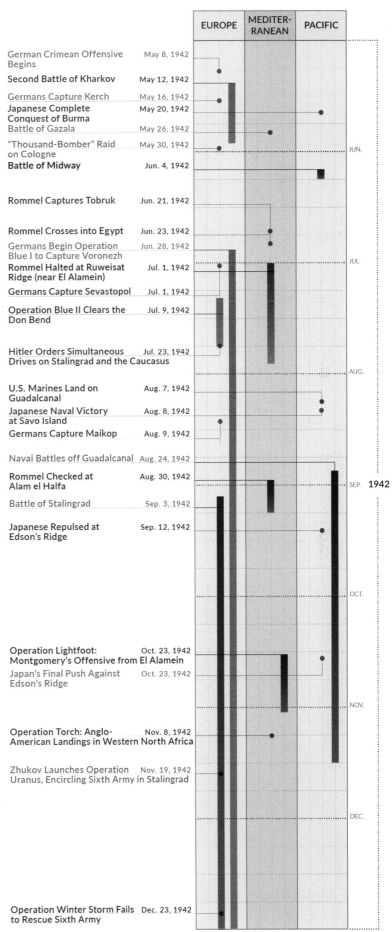

	EUROPE	MEDITER-RANEAN	PACIFIC
German Crimean Offensive Begins	May 8, 1942		
Second Battle of Kharkov	May 12, 1942		
Germans Capture Kerch	May 16, 1942		
Japanese Complete Conquest of Burma	May 20, 1942		
Battle of Gazala	May 26, 1942		
"Thousand-Bomber" Raid on Cologne	May 30, 1942		
Battle of Midway	Jun. 4, 1942		
Rommel Captures Tobruk	Jun. 21, 1942		
Rommel Crosses into Egypt	Jun. 23, 1942		
Germans Begin Operation Blue I to Capture Voronezh	Jun. 28, 1942		
Rommel Halted at Ruweisat Ridge (near El Alamein)	Jul. 1, 1942		
Germans Capture Sevastopol	Jul. 1, 1942		
Operation Blue II Clears the Don Bend	Jul. 9, 1942		
Hitler Orders Simultaneous Drives on Stalingrad and the Caucasus	Jul. 23, 1942		
U.S. Marines Land on Guadalcanal	Aug. 7, 1942		
Japanese Naval Victory at Savo Island	Aug. 8, 1942		
Germans Capture Maikop	Aug. 9, 1942		
Naval Battles off Guadalcanal	Aug. 24, 1942		
Rommel Checked at Alam el Halfa	Aug. 30, 1942		
Battle of Stalingrad	Sep. 3, 1942		
Japanese Repulsed at Edson's Ridge	Sep. 12, 1942		
Operation Lightfoot: Montgomery's Offensive from El Alamein	Oct. 23, 1942		
Japan's Final Push Against Edson's Ridge	Oct. 23, 1942		
Operation Torch: Anglo-American Landings in Western North Africa	Nov. 8, 1942		
Zhukov Launches Operation Uranus, Encircling Sixth Army in Stalingrad	Nov. 19, 1942		
Operation Winter Storm Fails to Rescue Sixth Army	Dec. 23, 1942		

JUN.

JUL.

AUG.

SEP. **1942**

OCT.

NOV.

DEC.

American forces. The fight for Guadalcanal may have been smaller than the monstrous battles of Stalingrad or Alamein, but it marked the end of Japanese expansion
and punched the first hole in Japan's Pacific defense perimeter.

Viewed together, these three battles of 1942 signal the war's turn—the point where
superior Allied operational reach, resources, and logistics began to tell. They brought
about a new phase of the conflict, transforming it from a war of lightning Axis victories into a war of attrition that could be favorable only to the Allies.

Planning and Preparing for Operation Blue, the Second German Bid for Victory in the East

Hitler was pleased with the success of his Axis allies in the Pacific, where the Americans and British had so far met defeat after defeat. Continental Europe was firmly under Nazi control, and in North Africa, Rommel was on the offensive. But the German economy was under strain, and the almost unlimited potential of American industry was worrisome. The plan to knock out the Soviet Union in a single campaign in 1941 had failed, but the immense losses of the Red Army suggested that one more really hard blow might finish the job. Stalin (disregarding intelligence reports to the contrary) expected the Wehrmacht to make another big push to capture the vital nerve center at Moscow, which despite the Soviet winter counteroffensive, was still only about a hundred miles past the front lines, and he had concentrated his forces to block that anticipated thrust. In fact, the German army commanders preferred that plan. But Hitler had something else in mind: a new Blitzkrieg—indeed, a whole series of them, but aimed to the southeast rather than toward the Russian capital.

Operation Blue would include a drive into the immense bend of the Don River, a lunge over the Don to the Volga, the seizure of the great industrial city of Stalingrad, and, finally, a wheel south into the Soviet Caucasus, home to some of the world's richest oil fields. Petroleum was the lifeblood of modern mechanized warfare, and the oil production in the Caucasus was several times greater than the total output of the German Reich. If the Germans could take that oil off the Soviet side of the ledger and add it to their own, they could win the war in the East in 1942 and then send half the forces currently deployed there to ensure victory in the West. The Germans had a long way to go before they could even begin operations into the Caucasus, and first would have to deal with the large Soviet forces pushing against them or readying offensives on the Crimean Peninsula and the Izyum salient. Hitler, however, saw these obstacles as opportunities: Red Army formations that were not expecting a major attack could be encircled and destroyed, giving him control of rich agricultural lands that could help feed the German war effort.

The decision to launch Operation Blue has garnered its share of criticism from analysts, for good reason.[1] With the final objectives lying well over a thousand miles from the start line, no one can accuse Hitler and the Armed Forces High Command (the *Oberkommando der Wehrmacht*, or OKW) of thinking small. Yet the Germans began this offensive with so many shortfalls that it is hard to say which one was the most serious. Perhaps it was the General Staff's estimate that casualties would exceed replacements by at *least* 280,000 by October—an estimate based on the assumption that all planned operations would proceed smoothly and without heavy losses.[2] The 179,000 horses lost in the Soviet Union in the first year of fighting were not going to be replaced anytime soon, and the figures for motor transport were dismal.[3] A report by the Army High Command (the *Oberkommando des Heeres*, or OKH) in May

German motorized and bicycle infantry advance past an abandoned Soviet KV-2 heavy artillery tank. The KV-2 was equipped with a massive 152-mm howitzer designed for demolishing concrete bunkers, and so heavily armored that in 1942 it was practically invulnerable to any German tank gun. But that was of no advantage if more mobile German Panzers bypassed it and cut it off from resupply of fuel.

indicated that the Wehrmacht had only 85 percent of the trucks required for the mobile divisions of the spearhead.[4] A report from the Army Organization Section warned that it was more like 80 percent, and those closer to the sharp end thought the situation was a great deal worse.[5] Field Marshal Ewald von Kleist's First Panzer Army, for example, entered the summer combat with only about 40 percent of its allotted strength in vehicles.[6]

By 1942, there were two Wehrmachts: one a high-powered strike force built around the Panzer and motorized divisions, and the other an ill-equipped infantry army, useful for little more than positional defense. An Armed Forces High Command report, written in June and entitled *War Potential 1942*, warned that the army's mobility was going to be "seriously affected" in the upcoming campaign and that "a measure of demotorization" was inevitable—dark words indeed for an army that lived and died by rapid maneuver.[7] It was an ominous sign: on the verge of its great confrontation with a revived Red Army, the Wehrmacht was in the process of reequipping its motorcycle reconnaissance battalions with bicycles. Historians often speak of the Germans scraping the bottom of the manpower barrel in 1944–45, but in fact they had already started that process by 1942. The entire class of males born in 1923 had already been drafted in April 1941, eighteen months ahead of time, and eighteen-year-olds would play a crucial role in filling out the rosters of the new divisions being formed for Operation Blue.[8]

Perhaps the best indicator of the Wehrmacht's problems was this: of the forty-one new divisions arriving in the south for Blue, twenty-one would be non-German: six Italian, ten Hungarian, and five Romanian.[9] It was a sure sign that the Germans were having difficulty with the immensity of the front, which by now stretched some 1,700 miles from Murmansk in the north to Taganrog in the south. What's worse, the Germans had to separate their own allies to keep them from fighting one another. Operation Blue had to take into account the historical animosity between the Romanians and Hungarians by slipping Italian divisions in between them, hardly a good omen for the operation's prospects. It also bodes ill when an allied commander, in this case the Italian general Giovanni Messe, states that instead of fighting alongside the Germans, he would rather "punch them in the stomach."[10]

A final problem went beyond resources. Operation Blue was based on an intelligence fiasco: a failure to draw up an accurate portrait of enemy strength. The Germans estimated available Soviet aircraft at 6,600 planes; the reality was 21,681. They estimated they were facing 6,000 tanks; the actual number was 24,446. The German estimate of Soviet artillery, 7,800 guns, was also off by a factor of four—the actual number was 33,111.[11] All in all, the German intelligence failure of 1942 was one of the worst in history, and completely missed the vast amount of war production the Soviets were generating in their relocated factories beyond the Ural Mountains.

As if all these problems were not serious enough, two events now intervened to delay Blue from its original start date of May 1942. First, the Wehrmacht had some unfinished business from the winter. Although the Germans had overrun most of the Crimean Peninsula during the initial campaigning season, Soviet forces still held the key fortress and naval base of Sevastopol.[12] They had also carried out large-scale amphibious landings in the region in January, landing most of Forty-Fourth, Forty-Seventh, and Fifty-First Armies at the eastern ports of Kerch and Feodosia. They engaged in a series of offensives against General Erich von Manstein's heavily outnumbered German Eleventh Army and its auxiliary Romanian formations.[13] The Germans could not head east without first cleaning up the Soviet threat to the Crimea.

The Crimean campaign is a classic example of the advantages of holding a "central position." Manstein had enemy armies on either side of him, but the Soviet forces in Sevastopol were focused on defense rather than offense, so he needed only minimal forces to keep them in check. Farther east, he had the advantage of defending a bottleneck where the Kerch Peninsula narrows near Parpach. Thus, he was able to hold his ground against heavy Soviet pressure from the east and simultaneously to prepare his own counteroffensive toward Kerch.[14]

Manstein noted that the Soviet offensives had ended with slight gains on the northern sector of the front, resulting in a bulge of sorts pushing out toward the German lines. German reconnaissance soon confirmed that the Soviets had deployed the mass of their forces there, leaving the southern half of this tiny front relatively weak. Spotting an opportunity, Manstein drew up a plan to break through in the south, make a very short advance of just two to three miles, and then wheel left to the coast to encircle the Soviet armies in the northern bulge.

It worked perfectly, making Manstein's strike one of the last fully successful German "cauldron battles" of the war. The infantry divisions of the German XXX Corps made the main drive on May 9, 1942, backed by one of the heaviest heavy concentrations of airpower the Wehrmacht had yet employed. The Germans concentrated

SEVASTOPOL PROPAGANDA ▶

Though the city of Sevastopol fell to the Germans in 1942, the Soviet Union promoted the desperate stand of the soldiers and sailors that defended the city. This 1957 poster commemorates the struggle, declaring Sevastopol a "Hero City."

virtually all of *Luftflotte* 4 (Air Fleet 4), whose assets usually supported the entire vast front held by Army Group South, over this tiny battlefield.[15] Working in concert with a battalion-sized amphibious landing, XXX Corps crossed an antitank ditch that the Soviets had dug as their principal defensive obstacle, opening a path for the 22nd Panzer Division to exploit. Once over the ditch, 22nd Panzer turned and headed north to the coast, cutting across the rear of Soviet Fifty-First and Forty-Seventh Armies and encircling them both, along with significant portions of Forty-Fourth Army. As the

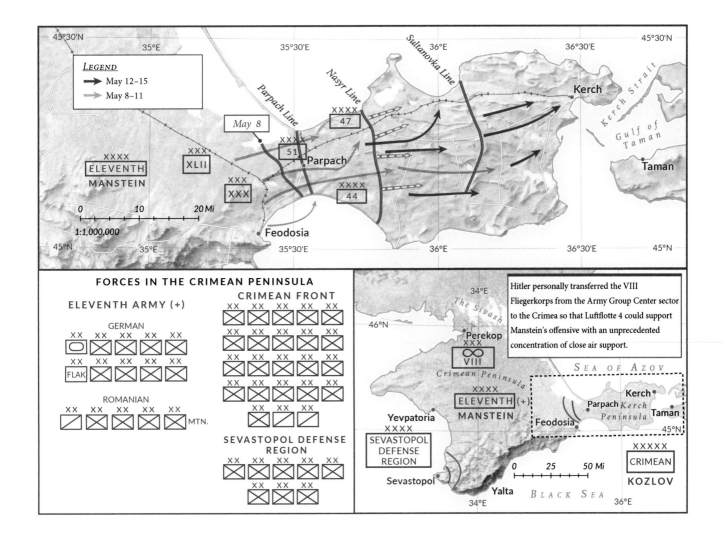

FORCES IN THE CRIMEAN PENINSULA

Germans drove eastward, Soviet command and control broke down, and the key port of Kerch fell on May 16.

Soviet losses in this campaign were colossal: 170,000 men had gone into German captivity in the vast encirclement near Parpach, and the Germans also captured 250 tanks and 1,100 guns. German casualties were just over 7,500. The operational use of the central position offers no time to rest or celebrate, however. With eastern Crimea cleared, Eleventh Army now had to countermarch back to Sevastopol. In what became a bitter campaign of positional warfare, Manstein took the city in early July, with heavy losses on both sides.[16]

Even with the Crimea finally cleaned up, a second event intervened to delay the execution of Operation Blue. This time it was a massive Soviet counteroffensive toward the large German-held city of Kharkov in May. The end of the 1941–42 winter campaign had left the Soviets in possession of a deep salient jutting over the Donets River at Izyum. For Josef Stalin and the commander of his Southwestern Front, Marshal Semyon K. Timoshenko, Izyum seemed a perfect place from which to launch an offensive. Soviet formations in the salient were already within a stone's throw of a lucrative operational target: Kharkov, a key rail hub and major industrial center. The

▲ THE KERCH OFFENSIVE

Bock wanted to focus on capturing Sevastopol first, then deal with the Soviet forces massing to the east second. But Hitler backed Manstein's view that it was better to focus on defeating the enemy's center of gravity.

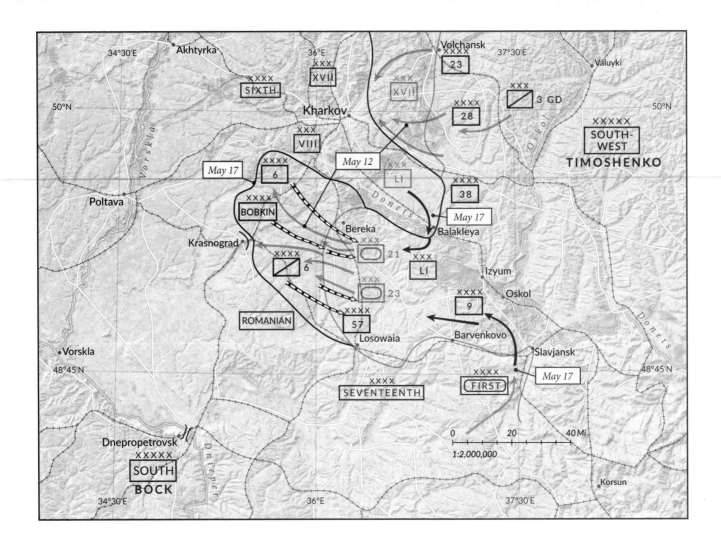

IZYUM AND KHARKOV, ▲ MAY 1942: PRELUDE TO OPERATION BLUE

Holding a salient (a bulge projecting into the enemy's front) is an opportunity and a risk. The Soviets tried to take advantage of the Izyum salient as a launching point to attack the rail hub of Kharkov, but suffered a disaster when the Germans counterattacked and pinched off the salient's narrow base.

situation looked equally tempting for Hitler and his General Staff. For an army that historically aimed at the battle of encirclement (*Kesselschlacht*), Izyum looked to be an ideal target: the Soviet formations in the salient were already encircled by German forces on three sides. At any rate, the Germans felt they had to take the salient before Blue commenced, so that they could advance to the Donets and free up the troops holding its long perimeter for the major campaign ahead. Thus, by April, both sides were planning an offensive at Izyum, with the Germans attempting to pinch off the salient, and the Soviets wanting to erupt out of it.[17]

This time it was the Soviets who struck first. Early on the morning of May 12, Timoshenko launched his offensive. Without warning, the entire front erupted in a concentrated one-hour artillery barrage, followed by a short, sharp fifteen-minute air raid. The bombardment lifted, and the Red Army attacked, striking one of the heaviest blows the Wehrmacht had sustained in this war. This Red Army was no longer the same one that the Germans had fought in 1941. It relied not on massed infantry

AIR RAID ▶

Taken during a German air raid against Soviet forces during the Battle of Kharkov, this photograph shows the firepower that air assets could now bring to the tactical level. By 1942, the Soviet Army had access to such airpower, too, making them a far more lethal opponent to the Germans than they had been in 1941.

RED ARMY SOLDIERS ▲
CAPTURED BY THE GERMANS
Since the beginning of the spring
campaign, boasts the original cap-
tion of this German propaganda
photo, "over a million Bolsheviks
have been captured on the Southeastern Front." Most of the Soviet
prisoners shown here would die in
the terrible conditions of German
POW camps on the Eastern Front.

formations but on a greatly expanded force of armor, air, and artillery, and the Germans were as surprised and shocked as the Soviet defenders had been at Kerch.

The Soviet plan called for an encirclement of German forces at Kharkov. Leading
the way was Soviet Sixth Army, led by General A. M. Gorodniansky, and an army-
sized mobile formation called "Group Bobkin." Together they blasted out of the salient
and headed west, while a second force spearheaded by Twenty-Eighth Army launched
a complementary assault farther north. Both thrusts opened up great breaches in the
German line, with Sixth Army in particular driving into the depths of the German
position and overrunning rear area installations and headquarters. Both pincers had
second echelons in place: III Guards Cavalry Corps in the north, and XXI and XXIII
Tanks Corps in the south. After a year of defensive fighting and desperate, improvised
counterattacks, this was one of the Soviet command's first opportunities to employ its
interwar doctrine of "Deep Battle," which called for multiple waves, or "echelons," of
attacks to drive relentlessly along each operational axis of assault.

Although the initial attacks had shocked the defenders, the Germans showed an
impressive ability to establish new defenses and to recover their equilibrium. They
managed to bring the Soviet push in the north to a standstill, but the southern thrust
continued unabated. And rather than try to stop it frontally, the German command
put into effect an improvised version of their own original offensive plan. First Panzer Army, which had not been heavily engaged so far, launched its attack from the
south of the salient as planned. This advance, combined with a short drive by elements of German Sixth Army from the north, pinched off the base of the salient,
leaving an immense number of Soviet divisions encircled in the resulting pocket. The

THE WEST POINT HISTORY OF WORLD WAR II

German operation was made both easier and more decisive by the Soviets' operational choices. Intelligence reports had warned that the Germans were about to strike along the Donets to cut off the advancing Soviet forces, but the Red Army commanders—apparently at Stalin's insistence—continued to push their second echelon forces forward in accordance with the Deep Battle concept instead of reacting to the threat.

By May 28, it was over. Despite the force of the initial Soviet attack, the Germans had countered and smashed another massive Soviet force. Prisoners included virtually all the survivors of Sixth and Fifty-Seventh Armies, Group Bobkin, and XXI and XXIII Tank Corps: somewhere around 240,000 men, 1,200 tanks, and 2,600 guns. German losses had been heavy in the initial assault but almost nonexistent in the encirclement.

OPERATION BLUE: THE GERMAN DRIVE TO THE CAUCASUS AND THE VOLGA

Only now, with the Crimean and Kharkov operations concluded successfully, was Operation Blue ready to proceed. The result of a protracted planning process, Blue was a complex operation that would begin in the northern Ukraine and then unroll to the south in four distinct stages.[18] The first phase, Blue I, would include the northern three armies of Army Group South (Second, Fourth Panzer, and Sixth), along with an allied

▲ GERMAN MECHANIZED INFANTRY COLUMN

German Panzer divisions included mechanized infantry forces (called *Panzergrenadiers*) provided with motorized transport so that they could keep up with the tanks. The Sd.Kfz. 251 half-track armored personnel carrier, shown here in the foreground, was introduced in 1939 for that purpose. This photograph was taken during the push into the Caucasus in 1942.

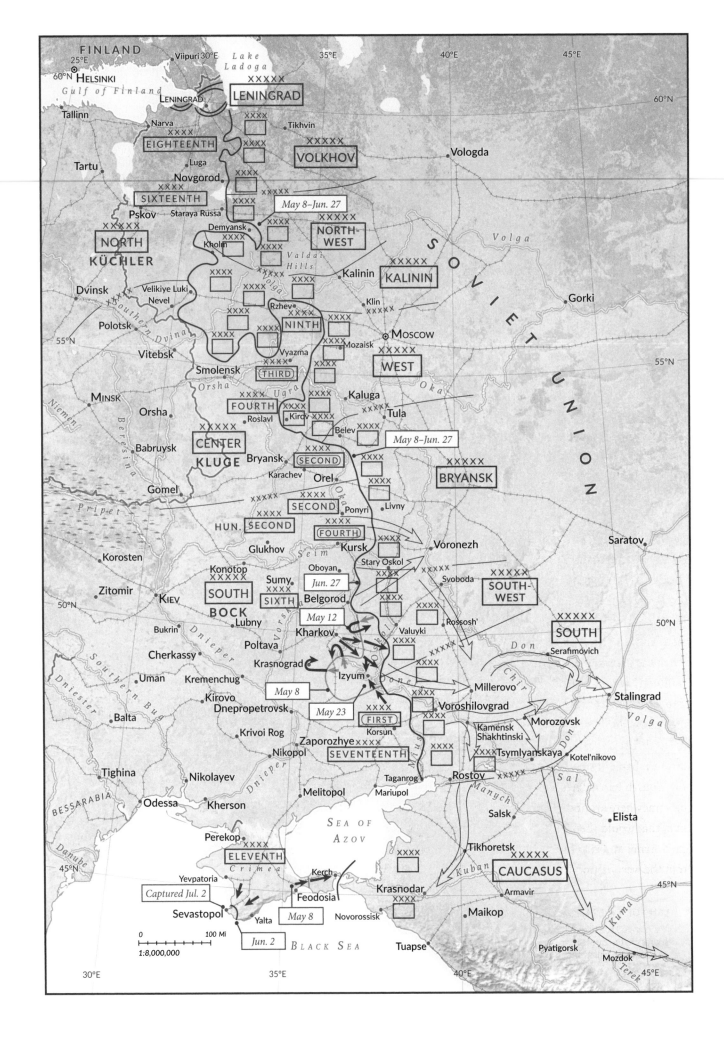

army (Second Hungarian, under General Gustav von Jany, inserted between Fourth Panzer and Sixth). Its operational objective would be the great city of Voronezh over the Don River.[19] Second, Fourth Panzer, and Second Hungarian armies would drive out of their deployment area just south of Orel, cross the Oskol River, and thrust directly east toward Voronezh. At the same time, the mechanized formations of Sixth Army, led by General Friedrich Paulus, would be coming up from the Kharkov region to the southwest. The result would be a tight encirclement, or *Kessel* (the German word for "cauldron"), of Soviet forces in front of Voronezh, close enough to be taken over quickly by the infantry, much of it Hungarian. Fourth Panzer Army, led by General Hermann Hoth, would take the city and then give way to the infantry divisions of Second Army. The Second would establish a blocking position from Orel to Voronezh, a position which would act as a kind of "roof" over Operation Blue, protecting the flank and rear of the German mobile formations as they turned south for their role in stage two of the operation: a great lunge down the right bank of the Don.

Blue II would begin ten days later. While that is a very long time in the world of modern mechanized operations, lack of transport meant that the entire German force could not be ready earlier. The next German army down the line, First Panzer, was to thrust out of its deployment area south of Kharkov, moving forward along the northern bank of the Donets. It would break through the Soviet defenses and link up with Fourth Panzer Army and Sixth Army as they came down from the north, meeting somewhere around Millerovo. The result would be another *Kessel*, a large one this time, that would then be broken up into two or three smaller ones by the infantry of Sixth Army and also by the Italian Eighth Army. Both armies would be marching in from the west behind First Panzer Army.[20]

◀ PLAN FOR OPERATION BLUE, AND PRELIMINARY OPERATIONS

   Hitler planned to strike for the Don River and then the Caucasus—partly because of the importance of the resources in the targeted area, but also partly because the ratio of forces was much better for the Germans in the southern half of the front.

▲ ROMANIAN SOLDIERS

The Soviet Union had seized two Romanian provinces in June 1940, and Romania willingly joined Hitler's anti-Bolshevik crusade in 1941. By the late summer of 1942 the Romanians had twenty-five divisions inside the U.S.S.R., but these formations generally lacked heavy artillery and antitank guns.

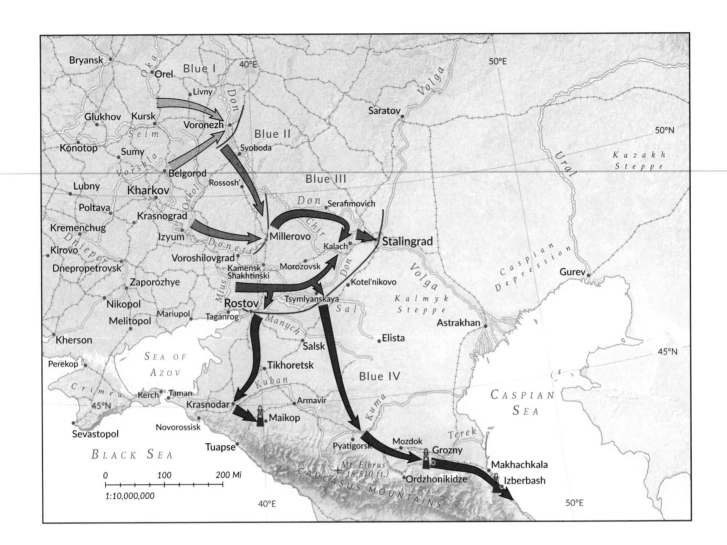

Despite the emphasis on discrete geographical objectives (Blue I heading to Voronezh and Blue II effecting a linkup at Millerovo), the real purpose of the first two portions of the maneuver sequence was much more dramatic: the destruction of the vast majority of the Soviet divisions deployed in the Don bend.

Once the Wehrmacht had smashed the Soviets west of the Don, Blue III would see Army Group South split into Army Groups A and B. Army Group A would contain Fourth Panzer Army on the left and First Panzer Army on the right, as they headed due east toward Stalingrad on the Volga, along with German Seventeenth Army, Italian Eighth Army, and Manstein's Eleventh Army out of the Crimea. Army Group B would consist almost exclusively of the infantry divisions of German Second Army, along with the Hungarians, Italians, and Romanians. Its mission was essentially defensive and static: to guard the meandering German flank from a Soviet thrust across the Don River from the north. When Blue III was completed, Army Group B would occupy a solid defensive line running from Orel through Voronezh to Stalingrad, protecting the rear of Army Group A as it prepared for its drive into the Caucasus—which would constitute the as-yet-unplanned Blue IV.

While this was a highly complex operational prospectus with far-flung and widely separated objectives in Stalingrad and the Caucasus, the campaign began favorably

▲ THE RAPID SOVIET RETREAT
This July 1942 German propaganda
photograph celebrated the immense
material losses inflicted on Red
Army forces as they pulled back to
and across the Don River. But the
destruction was not enough to constitute the knockout blow Hitler had
hoped for.

enough. Blue I opened on June 28, with Second, Fourth Panzer, and Second Hungarian Armies leading the attack toward Voronezh and breaking through Soviet defenses almost immediately. Soviet resistance was sporadic, and it was clear that the
Wehrmacht had achieved surprise. To the south, Sixth Army opened its offensive on
June 30, two days late due to rains, but it too crashed through the defenders. Soviet
forces seemed to be in utter disarray, and by July 2, the German spearheads had linked
up twenty-five miles east of Stary Oskol. As planned, Soviet Fortieth Army was now
in a neat, shallow pocket easily contained by the follow-on Hungarian infantry. Hoth's
Fourth Panzer Army reached the outskirts of Voronezh on July 4, probed it on July 5,
and entered it the next day. The Soviets still seemed befuddled, and command and
control—never the Red Army's strong suit—seemed to be breaking down again. "The
Russian is finished," Hitler told Halder at the time, and it seemed he might be right.[21]

German commanders at all levels thought they were witnessing the collapse of the
Red Army.[22] Soviet formations were not so much giving way as they were dissolving.
The opening German drives had smashed the Soviet defensive position far more easily than expected. They had broken through fortifications that the Soviets had been
preparing for six months, built upon the labor of millions of men. From one end of the
front to the other, German reconnaissance flights reported immense dusty columns of
men and vehicles scurrying to the east.

"THE SECOND-FRONT ▶
DISCUSSION"

"Hello, hello, Churchill?" asks Stalin in this cartoon of 1942. "What? You can't understand me? I should spell out my words? Damn it, by the time I spell things out it will be too late!" Like Hitler, the artist clearly hoped that the Wehrmacht would knock out Stalin's regime before the Allies could really begin to make their weight felt in the west. But less than a month after its publication, just as the German push into Stalingrad stalled, the Allies did open a second front with the Torch landings in North Africa, albeit not on the scale the Soviets wanted.

This helter-skelter retreat seems to have been ordered by Stalin and the Soviet high command as a classic means of trading space for time, traditional in Russian war making. Many historians even speak of a Soviet strategic retreat or an elastic defense. Whether or not the retreat was strategically wise, on the operational level, it proceeded ineptly, as Soviet troops abandoned one position after another without a fight, leaving behind a great deal of equipment. Having seen the high costs of the withdrawal, one month into Blue, Stalin issued his famous Order 227, entitled "Not a step back!" threatening to shoot anyone caught shirking duty or retreating without permission.[23]

A disappearing enemy is usually good news for a military operation. But the Soviet flight to the east threatened Blue's fundamental conception. The Germans knew that they had to destroy the Soviet Army, not merely push it back. The Wehrmacht could

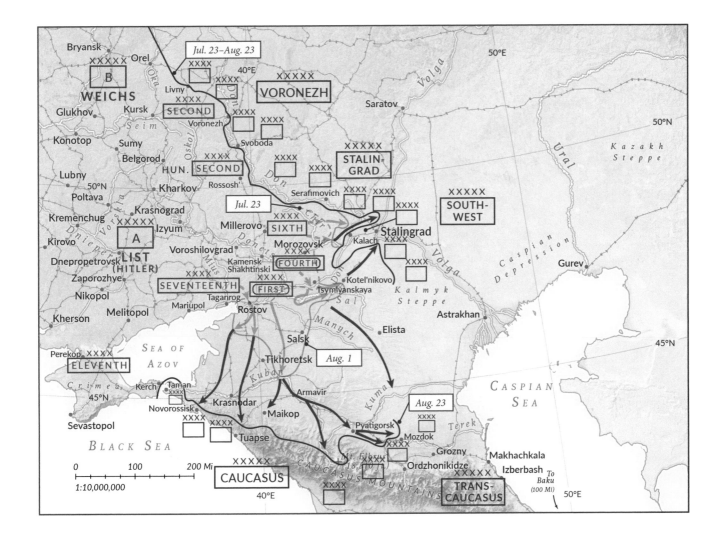

▲ GERMAN SUMMER
OFFENSIVE OF 1942,
JULY 23–AUGUST 23

So long as the German armies could
operate in reasonably good tank
country, they made rapid progress.
But armor was of limited use in the
rubble of Stalingrad or the foothills
of the Caucasus mountains.

hardly fight a great *Kesselschlacht* in the Don bend if the Soviets were no longer there. On July 9, therefore, Hitler and Halder decided to order Blue II, the great pincer attack, into action two weeks earlier than planned. Kleist's First Panzer Army entered the fray, launching its armored spearhead, General Eberhard von Mackensen's III Panzer Corps, over the Donets River. The next few days, for the Germans, were a mess. Two weeks early was too soon for them to wage the operation effectively. Entire divisions of Fourth Panzer Army were immobilized for lack of fuel, and no one was sure exactly where the Soviets were. On July 15, the spearheads of the three armies duly met near Millerovo—but they closed on next to nothing, bagging just 40,000 prisoners. Indeed, rather than destroy the Soviet Army west of the Don, as intended, the entire operational sequence had been a "blow into the air"—a misfire.[24] In any other campaign, hurtling forward hundreds of miles and seizing tens of thousands of prisoners would have constituted a victory of some sort. But compared with the needs of Germany's increasingly desperate strategic situation, and by the standards of the huge armies that the Soviets were capable of putting forth, these numbers barely registered.

Things got worse for the Germans a week later at Rostov. Sketchy intelligence reports had large Soviet forces crossing the lower Don east of the city and heading north toward the German lines. The German High Command now ordered a second, hastily

"FORTUNE FAVORS
ONLY THE BOLD" ▶

As the 1942 offensive ran into difficulties, German officers could have
taken some comfort from Clausewitz's advice that "we must have
faith in our own insight and convic-
tions. At the time this often has the
appearance of stubbornness, but in
reality it is that strength of mind and
character which is called firmness."

revised plan into action. Once again the Panzer spearheads closed on their prey, and
once again they came up with nothing. Rostov fell on July 23. The fighting was light:
the Soviets had vanished.[25] Operation Blue, which had taken the Germans so much
time and energy to plan and which had now eaten through a major portion of their
supplies on the southern end of the front, had collapsed.

At this point, with none of their options looking particularly good, the Germans
tried to pursue all of them at once—and, in doing so, made a costly error. On July 23
Hitler issued Directive No. 45.[26] The planned operational sequence for the remainder

of Blue had been a drive on Stalingrad followed by the conquest of the Caucasus. Stalingrad had to be either masked or seized in order to protect the long eastern flank of any force making the lunge into the mountain chain. Hitler and Halder now decided instead to go for both targets simultaneously, launching Army Group A into the Caucasus (Operation Edelweiss) and tasking Army Group B to seize Stalingrad (Operation Fischreiher, or "Heron").

Virtually all analysts condemn this "dual offensive," arguing that the German High Command should have gone for one target at a time. While they are correct on the surface, they ignore the fact that a conquest of either objective without the other would gain the Germans precisely nothing. Blue had been an all-or-nothing gamble from the start, and the Germans were now paying the price. Stalingrad was an important city: a key industrial center and a nexus for railroad and river communications in the southern Soviet Union. However, a historian could use the very same phrases to describe a number of other cities in the southern sector: Kharkov, Stalino, Rostov, and many others already in German hands. As important as it was, Stalingrad was not a strategic target—by no means would its fall constitute a mortal threat to the Soviet regime.[27] Likewise, a drive into the Caucasus by itself was pointless if Soviet forces could mass at Stalingrad, almost directly in the German rear.

With disaster staring the Germans in the face, they were trying to make something out of nothing. Perhaps, they hoped, one or the other of the offensive thrusts would lead to an unexpected success and to a Soviet breakdown that the Wehrmacht could exploit. It was not much of a hope, but, frankly, none of Germany's options looked favorable at this point.

Of the two elements of the dual campaign, the Caucasus campaign is nearly forgotten today.[28] But it was an epic offensive, with a quarter of the world's oil production at stake. Caucasus oil would have allowed the Germans to stretch out the war even longer than they did, and its loss would have been a material blow to Soviet operations. Involving five Axis armies—Seventeenth Army, Third Romanian Army, First and Fourth Panzer Armies, and Eleventh Army coming over from the Crimea—it was the main German effort in the original directive. With two Panzer armies acting as the spearheads, and with most of the available German transport and airpower attached, Edelweiss exploded out of the box.[29] Opening on July 26, it broke through a thin crust of Soviet forces and was soon running south at top speed. Elements of First Panzer Army took the oil city of Maikop on August 9, though the Soviets had carried out highly effective demolitions to set the city aflame before they retreated.[30] Other elements lunged due south into the high Caucasus and southeast to the Terek River, the last barrier before the even larger oil fields of Grozny. Beyond the mountains lay the fields of Baku, the richest target of all.

Despite their initially rapid advance, the Germans soon came to a screeching halt. The obvious culprit was the dual offensive itself.[31] Though the Wehrmacht at first focused much of its combat power and fuel on the Caucasus, in early July OKW had to transfer troops back to the north as the German drive on Stalingrad sputtered. The lack of fuel actually immobilized General Paulus's Sixth Army for ten full days, and, meanwhile, Soviet resistance stiffened in the eastern Don bend itself.

As the battle for Stalingrad dragged on, individual terrain formations, city blocks, and even lone buildings became the focus of the fighting. Here is a German soldier's diary entry describing the fight for one of the city's giant grain elevators.

September 16th. Our battalion, plus tanks, is attacking the elevator, from which smoke is pouring—the grain in it is burning, the Russians seem to have set light to it themselves. Barbarism. The battalion is suffering heavy losses. There are not more than sixty men left in each company. The elevator is occupied not by men but by devils that no flames or bullets can destroy.

September 18th. Fighting is going on inside the elevator. The Russians inside are condemned men; the battalion commander says, "The commissars have ordered those men to die in the elevator."

If all the buildings of Stalingrad are defended like this, then none of our soldiers will get back to Germany. I had a letter from Elsa today. She's expecting me home when victory's won.

September 20th. The battle for the elevator is still going on. The Russians are firing on all sides. We stay in our cellar; you can't go out into the street. Sergeant-Major Nuschke was killed today running across a street. Poor fellow, he's got three children.

The grind of urban combat took its toll on both sides. Here, a German officer of the 24th Panzer Division lets loose:

We have fought during fifteen days for a single house, with mortars, grenades, machine guns, and bayonets. Already by the third day, fifty-four German corpses are strewn in the cellars, on the landings, and the staircases. The front is a corridor between burnt-out rooms; it is the thin ceiling between two floors. Help comes from the neighboring houses by fire escapes and chimneys. There is a ceaseless struggle from noon to night. From story to story, faces black with sweat, we bombard each other with grenades in the middle of explosions, clouds of dust and smoke, heaps of mortar, floods of blood, fragments of furniture and human beings. Ask any soldier what half an hour of hand-to-hand struggle means in such a fight. And imagine Stalingrad: eighty days and eighty nights of hand-to-hand struggles. The street is no longer measured by meters but by corpses.[32]

As a consequence, the Germans were forced to shift troops from Army Group A to Group B. Hoth's Fourth Panzer Army went first, followed by Third Romanian Army. Manstein's Eleventh Army never made it to the Caucasus at all, instead being shifted to the Leningrad Front. It made sense, since the Germans could never hold positions in the Caucasus if their northern flank was insecure. But in the Caucasus, five attacking armies became two. There was Seventeenth Army in the west, heading for the Black Sea ports of Novorossisk and Tuapse, and First Panzer Army in the East, still halted on the Terek. Separated by three hundred miles of rugged terrain, unable to lend each other even a hint of support, the two armies slowed to a crawl in late August and then stopped altogether. The failure of the Germans to stick to any consistent plan was just the breathing space a hard-pressed Soviet army required. By late September, those two German armies in the Caucasus were facing a solid wall of eight well-supplied Soviet

STALINGRAD ▶

German gunners use a 105-mm light howitzer to clear the way for a push into Stalingrad. In the background is the famous "grain elevator," where a few dozen Soviet defenders repulsed ten attacks over four days before being overwhelmed.

STALINGRAD ▶

Red Army soldiers, well equipped for the snow, fire from a rooftop inside Stalingrad. The man in the foreground aims a mass-produced Soviet PPSh-41 submachine gun, which with its seventy-one-round drum magazine proved highly effective in close-quarters urban fighting.

By mid-September, Germans had overrun much of Stalingrad. Facing defeat, General Chuikov ordered the newly arrived 13th Guards Rifle Division (General Alexander Rodimtsev) into action, throwing it piecemeal into the path of the German advance. The following account comes from a company commander in the division:

Suddenly from behind a blank wall, from the rear, came the grind of a tank's caterpillar tracks. We had no antitank grenades. All we had left was one antitank rifle with three rounds. I handed the rifle to an antitank man, Berdyshev, and sent him out through the back to fire at the tank point-blank. But before he could get into position, he was captured by German tommy-gunners. What Berdyshev told the Germans I don't know, but I can guess that he led them up the garden path, because an hour later they started to attack at precisely that point where I had put my machine gun with its emergency belt of cartridges.

This time, reckoning that we had run out of ammunition, they came impudently out of their shelter, standing and shouting. They came down the street in a column.

I put the last belt in the heavy machine gun at the semibasement window and sent the whole of the 250 bullets into the yelling, dirty-grey Nazi mob. I was wounded in the hand but did not let go of the machine gun. Heaps of bodies littered the ground. The Germans still alive ran for cover in panic. An hour later, they led our antitank rifleman on to a heap of ruins and shot him in front of our eyes, for having shown them the way to my machine gun . . .

Again we heard the ominous sound of tanks. From behind a neighboring block, stocky German tanks began to crawl out. This, clearly, was the end. The guardsmen said good-bye to one another. With a dagger, my orderly scratched on a brick wall: "Rodimtsev's guardsmen fought and died for their country here."[33]

armies in treacherous mountain and river terrain. The drive to seize the principal oil fields of the Soviets had failed.

The other half of the dual operation, the drive on Stalingrad, started slowly, due to the early emphasis on the Caucasus. Paulus got moving when the Führer decided to prioritize the Stalingrad Front and transferred supplies from the Caucasus. By early August, the Sixth Army was moving forward again and was able to seal off an encirclement of Soviet forces at the town of Kalach-on-the-Don, destroying much of the Soviet First Tank and Sixty-Second Armies.[34] On August 23 XIV Panzer Corps thrust out of its bridgehead on the Don. The next day, Sixth Army reached the Volga and the outskirts of Stalingrad, thirty-five miles away.[35] Its arrival was heralded by a massive Luftwaffe bombing raid that smashed much of the city center and inflicted heavy civilian casualties.[36] Hoth's Fourth Panzer Army arrived in front of Stalingrad on September 3, bringing with it another great German air raid, and the Red Army withdrew into the city proper.

For the next two months, the two adversaries fought a brutal street battle for control of the city. Paulus's army tried to clear the city block by block and building by building, while the reconstituted Soviet Sixty-Second Army, led by General

◀ **STALINGRAD**
This photograph of Luftwaffe ground troops engaged in a mopping-up operation gives a good sense of the ruined landscape in which the *Rattenkrieg* ("war of the rats") took place.

◀ **STALINGRAD**
A Soviet assault group advances through the rubble in Stalingrad. Months of urban warfare reduced much of the city to a surreal postapocalyptic landscape.

▲ "THERE IS A ROCK ON THE VOLGA"

This Soviet poster from 1943 provides a good synopsis of the Battle of Stalingrad. Division after division fought to take the city on the Volga River, and the Wehrmacht did make progress, taking most of the city. However, the losses of German infantry and engineers were catastrophic and irreplaceable. Stalingrad became a symbol of Soviet tenacity and resilience.

▲ Encirclement at Stalingrad

"I've lost my ring!" The German ring around Stalingrad was trapped by a larger Soviet encirclement, and Hitler could only fret. He could neither rescue the beleaguered Sixth Army nor supply it adequately by air.

The exhausted and hungry German soldiers who surrendered at Stalingrad in early 1943 were put to work by their Soviet captors. Receiving little food and laboring under terrible conditions, half of them were dead by the spring.

Vasily I. Chuikov, held on grimly.[37] While it is possible to draw an operational map with corps and divisional designations, Stalingrad was actually a battle of squads and hastily assembled "battle groups," or *Kampfgruppen*. Much of the fire was point-blank, and the records and memoirs of both sides recall repeated moments of hand-to-hand combat. Distances were measured in yards, not miles, and individual buildings became the focus of vast battles: the Dzerzhinsky Tractor Works, the grain elevator, the vodka works, and the ancient burial mound known to the Soviets as the Mameyev Kurgan (appearing on German maps as "Hill 102").[38] In the Stalingrad inferno, even something as simple as crossing the street required careful advance planning and suppression of all known and suspected enemy positions.

Indeed, the city itself played a huge role in the fight. German skill in operational maneuver mattered here not at all, and the Soviets were quick to recognize the rubble of bombed-out buildings as a natural ally of the defenders. They also noted that even successful German assaults often left the attackers so disorganized and fragmented that they were easy prey to hastily organized counterattacks. Finally, they learned how to nullify their enemy's firepower advantage by attacking the Germans at night, or by "hugging" them, deploying as close to them as possible so that the Luftwaffe would either have to risk heavy friendly fire casualties or cease bombing altogether. In the end, the infantry on both sides bore the brunt of the damage: fighting, living, and dying in the ruins of a destroyed city. One anonymous German soldier called it a *Rattenkrieg*—a "war of the rats"—and the name seems completely appropriate, especially considering that both sides used the sewer system as a means of infiltrating enemy positions.

In operational terms, the Germans did make steady progress during those two months. But meager reinforcements brought to the city by the Volga River ferries kept Chuikov in business, and he managed to hold on to an ever-narrower strip along the steep Volga bank. By late October, the Wehrmacht had taken 90 percent of the city, but its infantry losses had been catastrophic, and the German commanders were crossing one division after another off the "capable of attacking" list.[39] They took one last shot on November 11 with Operation Hubertus, an offensive into the northern factory district spearheaded by virtually every combat engineer battalion in Army Group South. It was a desperate expedient that left the entire army group short of these precious specialist troops for months, and the gamble ultimately did not pay off. Hubertus petered out within four hundred yards of the Volga River Bank, the final Soviet defensive position in Stalingrad. In the city, four hundred yards might as well have been four hundred miles, and once again the Germans had failed.

Days later, on November 19, the Red Army launched Operation Uranus, a great counteroffensive to the north and south of Stalingrad, with the aim of encircling German forces in the city.[40] It opened with a massive assault by Fifth Tank and Twenty-First Armies against the extended front of Romanian Third Army along the Don. The Romanians were underequipped, undertrained, and undersupplied—and the Soviet offensive simply vaporized them. The next day, the same thing happened south of Stalingrad, with Fifty-Seventh and Fifty-First Armies slashing through Romanian Fourth Army to the right of Sixth Army.[41] There was not a single terrain feature on which the Romanians could base a defense in this sector. Their line simply faded out in the Kalmyk Steppe, and their resistance collapsed almost immediately.

In the face of this unexpected onslaught, the Germans were unable to formulate a response. They had one reserve formation on the entire front—the understrength XXXXVIII Panzer Corps—and Soviet attacks overwhelmed it.[42] Over the next two days, the two mobile Soviet spearheads drove hard from north and south, heading for a linkup at Kalach-on-the-Don. Making an average of thirty-five miles per day, with some units topping forty, the northern pincer reached Kalach on November 22. The southern pincer linked up with it the next day. General Paulus and his Sixth Army were now in deep trouble in Stalingrad. On the evening of November 22, Paulus wired Hitler the chilling news. His dispatch read: "Army encircled."[43]

Many of Paulus's officers recommended an immediate breakout, and historians have tended to agree that would have been Sixth Army's best option.[44] Instead, Hitler and his new chief of staff, General Kurt Zeitzler, ordered Paulus to stay put and await relief. They coupled this plan with a massive effort by the Luftwaffe to supply Sixth Army from the air. From a realistic perspective, neither breaking out nor staying put was an attractive option. The Stalingrad encirclement was enormous, trapping 246,000 men, and there wasn't an air force in the world big enough to fly in that much food on a daily basis, let alone ammunition or spare parts. While the army required

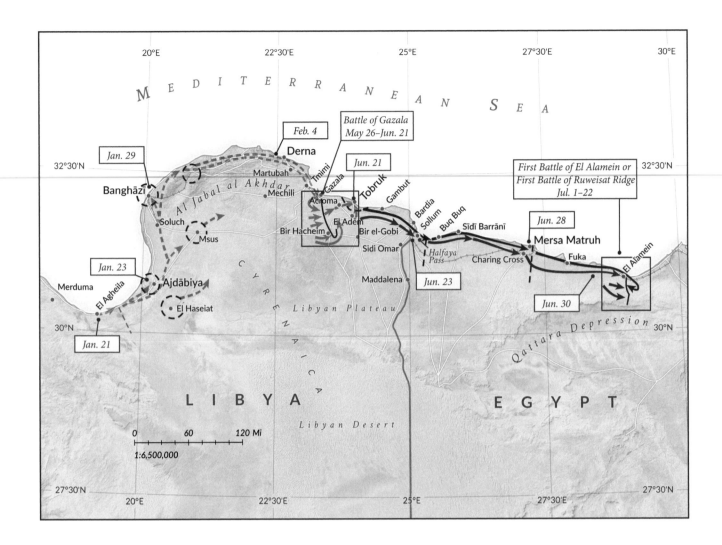

NORTH AFRICA, ▲
JANUARY 21–JULY 7, 1942

Rommel's long drive to the east was impressive but strained his logistics. At El Alamein his momentum ran out and his offensive reached its culminating point.

five hundred to seven hundred tons of supplies per day, the average brought in over the next month barely topped one hundred tons.

A breakout offensive would hardly have offered a magic solution, either. It almost certainly would have ended in disaster, if for no other reason than the army's sheer immobility. Its supply and fuel situation was catastrophic, and Paulus had long ago sent away the horses, the heart of the army's transport.[45]

And so Sixth Army sat—and waited. The Germans launched a relief offensive in December, Operation Winter Storm. But it was based around a single fresh Panzer division, all this threadbare army could afford at the moment, and the drive ultimately tapered off thirty-five miles south of Stalingrad. Meanwhile, Soviet attacks along the Stalingrad perimeter, known as Operation Kol'tso, or "Ring," shrunk the pocket steadily, herding the demoralized Germans into a smaller and smaller area. German supplies gave out—food, ammunition, and medicine—and diseases of all sorts took their toll. The Soviets made repeated surrender demands, but Paulus, who was in constant touch with Hitler via radio, refused. By the end of January 1943, resistance in the Stalingrad pocket had ceased, and Paulus finally had no choice but to surrender. From Sixth Army's initial strength of 250,000 men, just 90,000 were still alive: an entire field army, the largest in the German order of battle at the start of the campaign,

BERNARD LAW MONTGOMERY
November 17, 1887–March 24, 1976

A British field marshal of World War II, Montgomery is a controversial figure, loved and despised in equal measure. His career in the field was long and varied. He fought in imperial wars (in Ireland, Palestine, and Britain's Indian Empire) and large-scale conventional operations. He was with the first British Expeditionary Force in 1914, fighting in the desperate actions at Le Cateau and Ypres, and the second BEF in 1940, commanding the 3rd Division in both the fighting and the Dunkirk evacuation.

In all these campaigns, Montgomery learned to proceed cautiously and to develop the "infinite capacity for taking pains" that was the basis of his military art. Given command of Eighth Army in August 1942, at a time when its morale was at its lowest, he sought first to restore confidence; hence the jaunty beret, the air of sangfroid, the constant visits to the front line. But he also changed the army's doctrine. There would be no more senseless tank charges but rather a systematic approach, concentrating armor and artillery in masses behind his fortified line, waiting for Rommel to attack and "bump into it for a change." The resulting battle at El Alamein in October 1942 was the first British victory over the Germans and a signal moment in the war.

So it was with his other operations: Eighth Army in Sicily and Italy, the D-Day landings, 21st Army Group in northwest Europe. He commanded wisely, if too cautiously for his American allies, but he was acutely aware of Britain's limited resources. The one time Montgomery broke character, the bold plan for Operation Market-Garden in Holland in 1944, he paid the price in operational failure and high casualties. Otherwise, for all the complaints about him from U.S. circles, Montgomery was a winner.

had perished. It was a blow from which the Wehrmacht would never recover, giving the Soviets an advantage they would never relinquish. Hitler's gamble having failed, the German forces in the Caucasus had no choice but to withdraw from the oil fields at Maikop. The Third Reich had shot its bolt: there was no prospect that it would ever again be able to launch an offensive with even the faintest hope of knocking out the Soviet Union.

EL ALAMEIN: THE AXIS DEFEAT IN NORTH AFRICA

At virtually the same moment that the Soviets launched Operation Uranus in November 1942, disaster was also befalling Field Marshal Erwin Rommel and the Axis forces in North Africa.[46] This was almost as great a reversal of fortune as Paulus's disaster, for until then, Rommel's *Panzerarmee Afrika* had been riding high for much of the year. His offensive against British Eighth Army near the Libyan village of Gazala in May had been the high point of his career.[47] Launching a frontal feint against the British defenses, he had sent his entire main body on a wide sweep around the British southern flank, dangling far out into the desert. The maneuver surprised the British command, and Eighth Army was never able to recover its equilibrium. Hard fighting continued, and at one point, Rommel found his Panzer divisions trapped behind British lines in a position known as the Cauldron. But he managed to hold his own there and break out of the Cauldron against British forces that were always more comfortable in static, set-piece battles than in maneuver warfare. By June, he was heading east for the key

port of Tobruk in Libya, surprising and overwhelming the garrison at the tiny fortress, which had resisted his attacks in 1941. With Tobruk reduced, he continued east, crossing the wire into Egypt on June 23, with his course set for the Suez Canal.

The British now withdrew to El Alamein, where in October they would finally—more than three years into the war—make their first successful defensive stand against the German Army. They had been booted from one end of the North African theater to the other, but all that time, they had been falling back on their supply bases in Egypt, while Rommel's supply lines stretched back 1,200 miles to the Libyan capital of Tripoli. The Alamein position favored the defenders, forcing Rommel through a bottleneck between the Mediterranean Sea to the north and the Qattara Depression to the south—a salt and sand marsh that was impassable to mechanized armies. Rommel's first improvised attempt to break through at Alamein in July failed to crack the British defenses (and came to be known as the First Battle of El Alamein, or the "Battle of Ruweisat Ridge").

By now, the British high command, including Prime Minister Winston Churchill, was looking for more than successful defense. It was clear that Rommel's army was weakening, while British Eighth Army was gaining strength through vast shipments of U.S. M3 Grant and M4 Sherman medium tanks that it was receiving through the Lend-Lease program. Churchill wanted an offensive, and he appointed a new commander for Eighth Army, Montgomery, with at least implicit orders to plan and execute one. Rommel knew the British were building up forces for a major attack, and made a bid to knock out Eighth Army before reinforcements made it too strong to defeat. Striking at the end of August, he succeeded in turning the southern flank of

the British line but then was checked by the fortified rear position at Alam el Halfa and repulsed. Montgomery declined to launch an immediate counterattack, preferring to wait until preparations for his own big push were complete.

"Monty," as he was universally known, remains a controversial figure today. He is a hero and military genius to his many admirers, and an egomaniac and blowhard to his equally numerous detractors—and there may be truth in both opinions.[48] Given the British material superiority—well over two to one in tanks, and nearly two to one in manpower, with much of Rommel's manpower consisting of nonmotorized Italian infantry—Montgomery's offensive plan, Operation Lightfoot, seems rather cautious: essentially a frontal assault. We should remember, however, that caution against the Wehrmacht was something that British armies had learned the hard way. Monty's battle plan called for the infantry divisions of XXX Corps, closely supported by tanks, air, and artillery, to attack on a very narrow front and chew their way through Rommel's minefields and wire. It was what the British would call a "bite and hold" operation: an offensive with limited aims to win a lodgment in the enemy line that would then be carefully secured against enemy counterattack. Montgomery emphasized that

▲ "MONTGOMERY AFRICANUS"
Montgomery fought a cautious but victorious battle against Rommel at El Alamein. One of the war's crucial battles, the victory in Egypt secured the Suez Canal, the Middle East, and the British Empire. "Africanus" refers to Scipio Africanus, the superb Roman general who defeated Hannibal in North Africa.

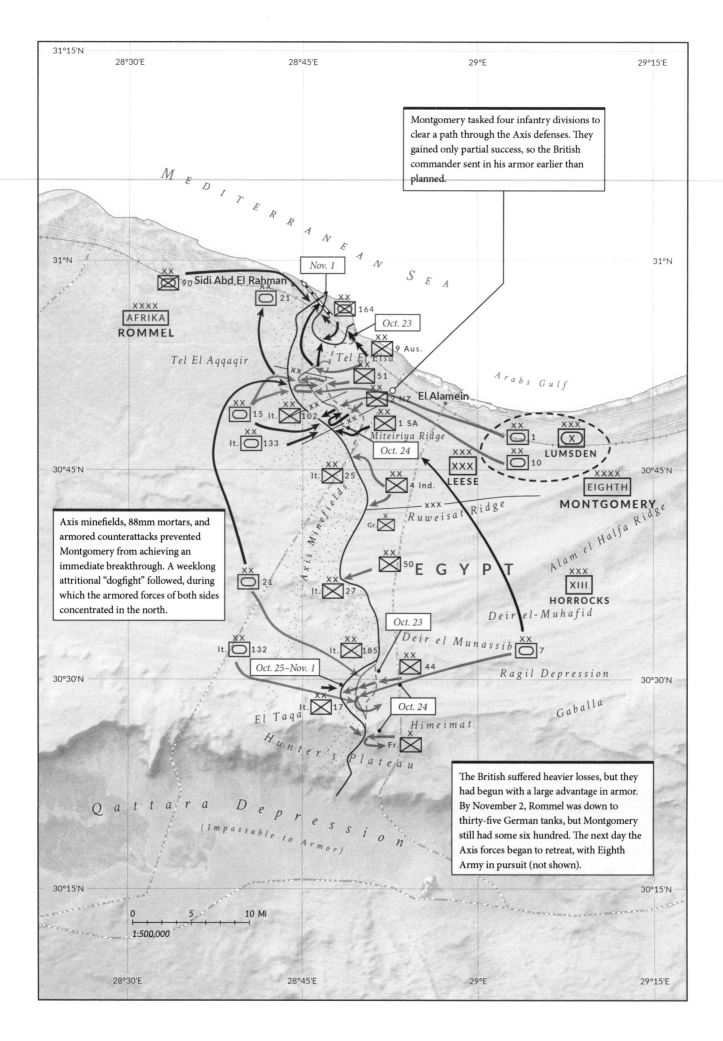

Montgomery tasked four infantry divisions to clear a path through the Axis defenses. They gained only partial success, so the British commander sent in his armor earlier than planned.

M E D I T E R R A N E A N   S E A

31°15'N

28°30'E   28°45'E   29°E   29°15'E

31°N   31°N

Nov. 1

90 Sidi Abd El Rahman

21

164

XXXX
AFRIKA
ROMMEL

Oct. 23

9 Aus.

Tel El Aqqaqir   *Tel El Eisa*   *Arabs Gulf*

51

2 NZ   El Alamein

15   It.   102

It.   133   1 SA

Miteiriya Ridge   1   X   LUMSDEN

Oct. 24   10

It.   25   XXXX
                                              EIGHT
4 Ind.   LEESE   MONTGOMERY

Axis minefields, 88mm mortars, and armored counterattacks prevented Montgomery from achieving an immediate breakthrough. A weeklong attritional "dogfight" followed, during which the armored forces of both sides concentrated in the north.

Gr.   *Ruweisat Ridge*   *Alam el Halfa Ridge*

50   *E G Y P T*

XXX
XIII
HORROCKS

21   *Deir el-Muhafid*

It.   27

Deir el Munassib

It.   132   It.   185   44   7

                                        Ragil Depression

Oct. 25–Nov. 1   *Oct. 24*   *Gaballa*

30°30'N   It.   17   30°30'N

El Taqa   *Himeimat*

Hunter's Plateau   Fr.

The British suffered heavier losses, but they had begun with a large advantage in armor. By November 2, Rommel was down to thirty-five German tanks, but Montgomery still had some six hundred. The next day the Axis forces began to retreat, with Eighth Army in pursuit (not shown).

Q a t t a r a   D e p r e s s i o n

(I m p a s s a b l e   t o   A r m o r)

30°15'N   30°15'N

0   5   10 Mi

1:500,000

28°30'E   28°45'E   29°E   29°15'E

he wanted to destroy the *Panzerarmee* not in a single blow but slowly and methodically: "crumbling" it.

Operation Lightfoot, commonly called the Second Battle of El Alamein (though since it followed two of Rommel's attacks on the British line, it was really the third), opened on October 23. At 10:40 p.m., a simultaneous thousand-gun barrage smashed the *Panzerarmee*'s headquarters, artillery batteries, and supply dumps.[49] In concert with British air attacks, Axis forces were under constant bombardment for the next six hours. Next came the great ground assault, featuring a full four British divisions along a very narrow front, merely six miles across. Despite British superiority, the going was slow, and casualties were high, and by November 2, things had stalled altogether. The attack of XXX Corps had broken into Rommel's minefields, but it had failed to penetrate the main German defensive line. To his credit, Montgomery was now able to adjust his plan on the fly, bringing in the armored divisions of X Corps to assist with the breakthrough. Rommel countered by feeding in his last reserves, but by November 3, he knew he was beaten. His armor strength was down to zero, and his infantry, consisting largely of Italian units, was abandoning discipline and drifting away from the field. Even a last-second order from Hitler, demanding that Rommel fight until "victory or death," could not reverse the verdict. Rommel's men, especially the Italians, were already voting with their feet and retreating.

Classically, the time had come for Montgomery to unleash his pursuit against the beaten enemy. Since he had already committed his armor to the breakthrough, however, he had no fresh mobile formations left to commit to the pursuit. He had mauled the *Panzerarmee*, but Rommel was able to break contact and retreat back toward the Egyptian border, and then through Libya, and finally into Tunisia. It would require another season of hard campaigning to destroy the Axis forces in Africa.

Despite an anticlimactic ending, El Alamein was one of the war's crucial battles. It succeeded in ending the Axis threat to the Suez Canal, the Middle East, and thus to the entire British Empire. In a deeper sense, it validated the entire British war effort up to this point. Again and again in the first three years of the war, the British Army had tasted defeat at the hands of the Germans, and yet the British government and people had held firm and stayed committed to the cause. In El Alamein, they had finally won a clear-cut and decisive victory. Historians who criticize the British Army's fighting qualities should remember that the British were the only power of the 1942 alliance who had opposed Hitler's war from the beginning, sticking it out at the receiving end of Germany's firepower for years by this point in the war. The United States had remained aloof for two years, and the Soviets had actually been an ally of the Third Reich as it conquered its way across Europe. If Great Britain had done likewise, Hitler would have triumphed. Its mixed combat record notwithstanding, the British Army was the indispensable force in the war against the Axis.

◀ THE BATTLE OF EL ALAMEIN: THE BRITISH BREAKTHROUGH, NOVEMBER 1–4

With a two-to-one advantage in men, tanks, guns, and planes, Montgomery knew he could win an attritional fight. The "dogfight" in the coastal zone began on October 23, and by the end of November 2 *Afrika Korps* was down to thirty-five serviceable tanks. On November 4 the British completely broke through Rommel's rearguard forces and began a months-long pursuit toward Tunis.

GUADALCANAL: THE JAPANESE DEFEAT IN THE PACIFIC

In August 1942, with the Germans driving east toward Stalingrad and British Eighth Army deploying at El Alamein, one last drama began on the other side of the globe: Operation Watchtower. On August 7 the U.S. 1st Marine Division landed on the Japanese-held island of Guadalcanal, as well as the smaller islands of Tulagi, Gavutu, and Tanambogo, all members of the Solomon Islands in the South Pacific. The landing took the Japanese garrison on Guadalcanal—naval construction troops—by surprise. The Marines got ashore without incident, established a perimeter, and overran a partially finished Japanese landing strip that they christened Henderson Field.[50]

The course of Operation Watchtower makes sense only if we realize that it was a colossal improvisation, concocted on the fly to take advantage of the recent drastic turn in the Pacific theater. In the first few months of the Pacific War, the Japanese had smashed every Allied army they faced and conquered the Western colonial empires in the Pacific Basin, occupying Burma, Malaya, the Netherlands East Indies, the Philippines, and innumerable small islands. However, recent attempts at further expansion had come to grief. The Battle of the Coral Sea, from May 4 to 8, 1942, was perhaps a Japanese tactical victory in terms of ships damaged and sunk, but it was also a strategic defeat, halting Japan's momentum and ensuring (at least temporarily) the security of Australia. One month later, from June 4 to 7, the Battle of Midway turned the tide of the naval war altogether. The Japanese lost four precious aircraft carriers—an irreplaceable loss, given Japan's gross inferiority to the United States in terms of resources, industrial base, and shipbuilding facilities.

Following Midway, the United States realized it had seized the initiative—at least momentarily—and the Joint Chiefs of Staff sought to launch a limited offensive in order to retain it. Their gaze soon landed on the Solomon Islands chain. Guadalcanal was practically the southernmost point of the Japanese conquests so far, and the Imperial Japanese Navy (IJN) was building an airfield there. Once completed, it would enable Japanese bombers and scout planes to operate against the air and sea lines of communication between America and Australia via the New Hebrides. For the Allies, capturing the island would not only eliminate that risk but also provide a base of operations from which to move up the Solomons toward the great Japanese air and naval base in the region, at Rabaul, on the island of New Britain. Admiral Ernest J. King, commander in chief of the United States Fleet, had long pushed for a more aggressive strategy in the Pacific, but he had bumped into Roosevelt's unwavering insistence on a Germany First posture. In June, however, the president made the decision to invade North Africa instead of focusing on the buildup for a 1943 invasion across the English Channel—a change in his strategy that actually made it easier to justify diverting more resources to the Pacific in the short term.

Despite general agreement that the United States needed to strike while Japan was off balance, American planners found themselves mired in a debate that reflected a

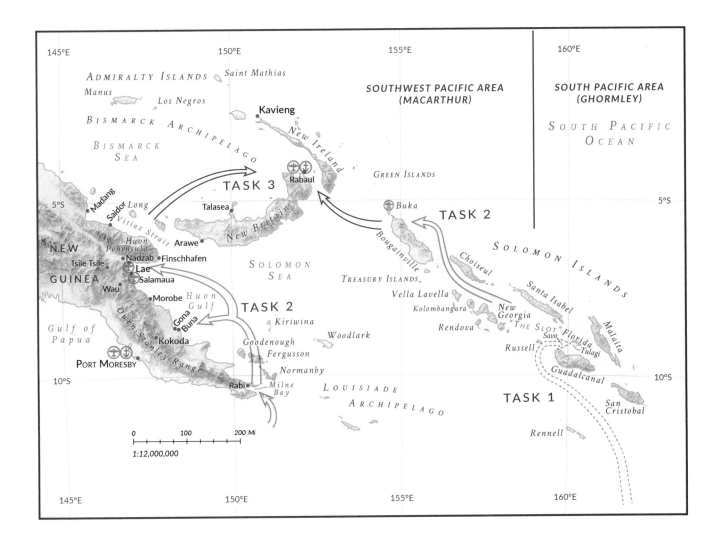

long-standing tradition of Army-Navy interservice rivalry. The Joint Chiefs had already divided the vast Pacific theater into three Pacific Ocean Areas controlled by the Navy (further subdivided into North, Central, and South) and a Southwest Pacific Area under Army command. Speaking for the Army, General Douglas MacArthur proposed a lightning drive on Rabaul. It was a target in "his" zone, in other words, and he would command the operation. Rabaul was a risky venture, however, which would require amphibious divisions that were not yet trained and two precious aircraft carriers, the scarcest asset in the fleet at the time. Admiral King wanted a safer path: a sequence of landings in the Solomon Islands and New Guinea that would gradually work their way up to Rabaul—all under naval command.[51] June saw heated debate among the Joint Chiefs until King and General George C. Marshall, the U.S. Army chief of staff, reached a compromise. The United States would indeed launch an offensive toward Rabaul, split into three phases: "Task One" was a landing in the Solomons; "Task Two" was an advance along the northeastern coast of New Guinea, paired with an advance up the Solomon chain; "Task Three" would be the attack on Rabaul. Task One would be under King's command, and both Two and Three would be under MacArthur.[52]

The orders for the operation went out in early July, but U.S. forces were not

▲ GUADALCANAL CAMPAIGN,
INITIAL LANDINGS,
AUGUST 1942

The Guadalcanal invasion proved a difficult undertaking for naval planners. In order to land Marines on the northern side of the island, amphibious vessels and their escorts had to navigate and secure "the Slot," while the Navy's aircraft carriers stayed on the south side of the island with a clear open-water escape route to Australia.

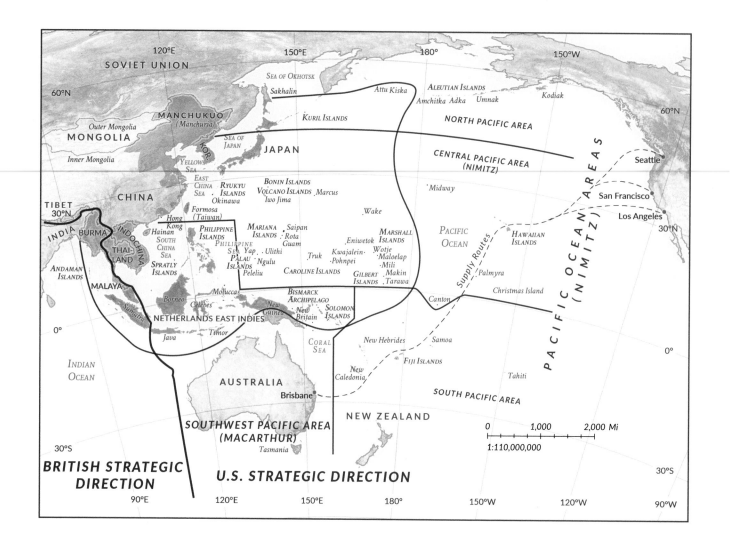

MAJOR ALLIED COMMANDS ▲ IN THE PACIFIC THEATER

As of August 1942, the Japanese still controlled a vast portion of the Pacific Ocean and the natural resources within that sphere of influence. Japanese bases in the Marianas, Solomons, and the North Pacific allowed its naval and armed forces to strike at Allied forces wherever and whenever they materialized.

particularly well prepared at that time. American commanders had organized this operation to take advantage of the enemy's momentary paralysis and seize a target of opportunity. While they showed a healthy amount of aggression and initiative, such improvised operations are rarely well planned. Maps of Guadalcanal were scarce and sketchy, and so were the charts of the tricky waters in the midst of the Solomon chain, dubbed "the Slot." The 1st Marine Division, the landing force now slated for Task One, had not only just arrived in the theater but also had departed for the Pacific with an explicit promise from Admiral King to its commander, Major General Alexander Vandegrift, that it would not have to fight before 1943.

The operational naval commander, Admiral Frank Jack Fletcher, took one look at the plan and blanched. It committed his ships to a long-term resupply mission of the Marines once they had landed, and that meant prolonged exposure of his ships to attacks by land-based aircraft. The overall naval commander for the South Pacific Forces, Rear Admiral Robert L. Ghormley, didn't like it at all, worrying about logistics and infrastructure, lack of planes and ships, and especially the lack of sufficient ports. He and MacArthur actually sent a letter to Washington calling for postponement of the operation. Admiral King's famous retort was that the Marines would go in as planned, "even on a shoestring."[53]

Admirable boldness, perhaps, and King was certainly correct to hit the Japanese while they were still reeling from Midway, but bad things happen on shoestring operations. The 1st Marines landed on the northern shore of Guadalcanal on August 7 and were able to establish a strong position. But on August 8 Admiral Fletcher, in a highly controversial decision, withdrew his carriers from the area, fearing for their safety. Japanese cruisers entered the Slot that night and inflicted a crushing defeat on the U.S. and Allied surface forces that Fletcher had left behind in the Battle of Savo Island, sinking four heavy cruisers.[54] The Japanese had trained intensively in night fighting, and both their gunnery and their torpedoes were superior to those of the Americans. With the U.S. carriers gone, and without hope of air cover for the invasion fleet, the Navy had to suspend transport of supplies and equipment, leaving the Marines temporarily stranded on Guadalcanal. Meanwhile, the Japanese were recovering from their shock and rushing reinforcements to the island from their base at Rabaul. They dispatched the 35th Infantry Brigade under General Kiyotake Kawaguchi, and part of Seventeenth Army under General Harukichi Hyakutaka.

No discussion of the fight for Guadalcanal is possible without considering all three legs of a "triphibious" campaign. At sea, the waters of the Slot were the most hotly contested in the world, with the Americans ruling during the day—once Marine aviators started flying from Henderson Field on August 20—and the Japanese at night. Virtually every day, U.S. convoys of every size and description landed men and material on the island. Then, after dark, the Japanese did the same, in the nighttime

U.S. LANDING AT GUADALCANAL

Marines disembark from a landing craft on their way ashore Guadalcanal. The front-opening landing craft designed early in the war by the United States made the numerous amphibious campaigns conducted by the Army and the Marine Corps possible.

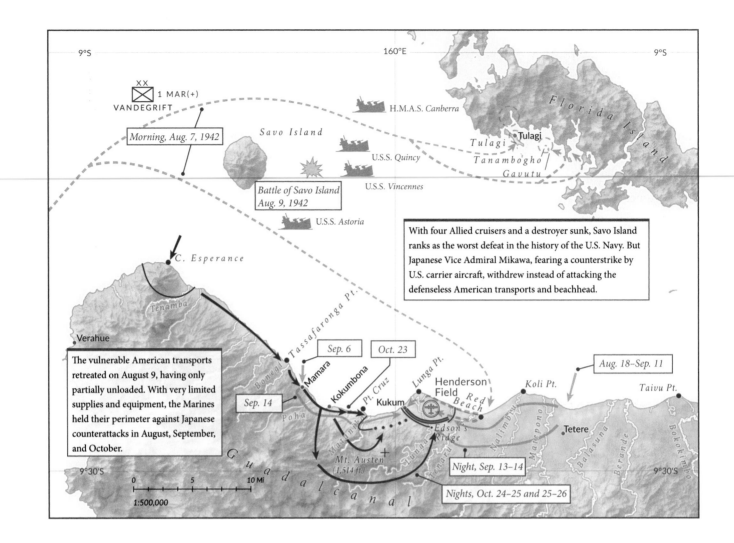

Morning, Aug. 7, 1942

Battle of Savo Island
Aug. 9, 1942

H.M.A.S. *Canberra*

U.S.S. *Quincy*

U.S.S. *Vincennes*

U.S.S. *Astoria*

With four Allied cruisers and a destroyer sunk, Savo Island ranks as the worst defeat in the history of the U.S. Navy. But Japanese Vice Admiral Mikawa, fearing a counterstrike by U.S. carrier aircraft, withdrew instead of attacking the defenseless American transports and beachhead.

The vulnerable American transports retreated on August 9, having only partially unloaded. With very limited supplies and equipment, the Marines held their perimeter against Japanese counterattacks in August, September, and October.

Sep. 6

Oct. 23

Sep. 14

Aug. 18–Sep. 11

Night, Sep. 13–14

Nights, Oct. 24–25 and 25–26

GUADALCANAL OPERATION, AUGUST 1942– FEBRUARY 1943

The fighting at Guadalcanal was concentrated around the Marine-held airfield called Henderson Field. The Marines held this ground at all costs and with little to no resupply from the endangered navy. Some of the heaviest ground combat occurred at Edson's Ridge, which was a key terrain feature that offered clear fields of fire toward Henderson Field.

runs that the Marines dubbed the "Tokyo Express." As both sides tried to protect their supply convoys, one large-scale naval action followed another: After Savo Island, there was the Battle of the Eastern Solomons (August 24), the Battle of Cape Esperance (October 11–12), the Battle of Santa Cruz (October 26), the Naval Battle of Guadalcanal (November 13–15), and more. The two sides traded losses, and so many ships sunk that the waters north of Guadalcanal became known as "Ironbottom Sound."

On land, both sides fought a general battle of attrition, but the fighting also had a definite geographical focus in Edson's Ridge, a small elevation south of Henderson Field that was named for the Marine commander in charge of the initial defense. The key to Henderson, Edson's Ridge was the target of a vigorous attack by Kawaguchi's brigade from September 12 to 14 that would immortalize the high ground with a darker name: Bloody Ridge. The Japanese came up in waves, only to be beaten back by rifle, machine gun, and mortar fire, suffering more than 700 casualties to 135 Marines. In successfully holding the ridge, the Marines had not only won a tactical encounter. They had protected their one definite advantage in the campaign. By holding Henderson Field, they enabled U.S. forces to station air assets on the island itself: a "Cactus Air Force" ("Cactus" was the Allied code name for Guadalcanal) that could respond rapidly to threats or opportunities. Japanese aircraft, by contrast, were flying in all the way from Rabaul, 550 miles away, and due to fuel limitations, they often had only a few minutes' time over their targets.

The Japanese were trading losses in men and equipment with the Americans—indeed, by the end of the campaign, each side had lost precisely twenty-four warships—but that was just the sort of contest they wished to avoid. Already the demands of Guadalcanal had forced them to halt their main offensive toward Port Moresby on New Guinea and to transfer supplies and men to the Solomons. Japan was simply not capable of fighting two sustained, matériel-intensive campaigns at once. Finding adequate shipping was the key. Even without significant losses, Japan was already short 10 percent of the tonnage required to feed its civilian population, and every transport plunging to Ironbottom Sound made the situation worse.[55]

The climax of the Guadalcanal campaign came in October. Just as planners in Tokyo considered cutting their losses, more aggressive leadership was coming to the fore on the American side. Admiral Ghormley gave way in October to Admiral William F. "Bull" Halsey.[56] The fire-breathing Halsey led a successful action at Cape Esperance off the western tip of Guadalcanal. In the aftermath, the Navy was able to land its largest troop convoy since the initial invasion, adding most of the 164th Infantry Regiment of General Alexander M. Patch's Americal Division to the fight.[57]

These soldiers arrived just in time for the last great Japanese attack of the campaign. Now reinforced by the 2nd Infantry Division and portions of the 38th Infantry Division, Japanese forces made one final thrust on successive nights, October 24 and 25. They again assaulted Bloody Ridge, in concert with an attack on the Marines' right flank along the Matanikau River. The attackers overran some U.S. outposts but came to grief again against American machine guns, mortars, and artillery, as well as a tenacious defense by the 1/7 Marines (the 1st Battalion, 7th Marine Regiment) and elements of the 3rd Battalion of the 164th. In attempting to overrun the ridge, the Japanese suffered staggering losses: perhaps as many as 3,500 men. Such was the cost of charging poorly supported infantry against modern firepower, no matter how brave the troops were. Although the fighting would drag on into 1943, never again would the Japanese come so close to Henderson Field, and in the end, the triphibious Battle of Guadalcanal boiled down to the Americans' ability to control Henderson Field.

Conclusion

The fight on Guadalcanal was nowhere near the size of the Stalingrad or El Alamein, campaigns that involved hundreds and dozens of divisions, respectively. Nevertheless, it was a major victory for the U.S. military and a great boost to American morale, demonstrating the competence and drive of U.S. forces even in a theater that was second in priority. Not only did the battle punch the first hole in Japan's Pacific defenses, it undercut the entire basis of the empire's strategy: the notion that Japanese soldiers could offset their material disadvantages through superior training, morale, and willingness to die.[58] The Japanese had shown all three in abundance on Guadalcanal, and

Dick Tregaskis was a journalist who accompanied the 1st Marine Division during the landing and operations on Guadalcanal, and wrote one of the war's first great books, *Guadalcanal Diary* (1943), which soon became a best seller in the United States. Here he describes the fight along the Tenaru River, where a massive Japanese infantry attack fell afoul of superior U.S. firepower. As always, Tregaskis got as far forward as he could.

Snipers began to range in on us from across the river. We heard the ping-ping-ping of their .25s, and bullets began to whir fairly close. I lay for a few moments while the firing continued, thinking what a wonderful target we were, gathered so close together in a small circle, and then two of the other onlookers and I got the same idea at the same moment; we headed for cover.

A pink-cheeked captain shared my coconut tree. He told me while we watched the shadowy woods across the river that it was his unit which had been doing the fighting in this particular sector. He said that his name was James F. Sherman, and that he came from Somerville, Mass. "Lots of Boston boys in the outfit," he said. Then we heard the crackling of a light .25 caliber machine gun, and it was no effort at all to duck and stop talking.

When the firing let up a little, the captain waved a hand at a point of land which marked the seaward extremity of the Tenaru's west bank. "That's Hell's Point," he said. "That's where the Japs tried their crossing. Some of our men moved up onto the point to get a better field of fire, and the Japs put up flares that were as bright as daylight. We lost some people in there. But," he added, "we stopped the Japs."

One did not have to look very hard to see that he was understating the case. I worked my way, crawling between volleys of firing, flopping close to the earth when a mortar shell or grenade burst, to Hell's Point, and looked out on hundreds of Jap bodies strewn in piles.

It was easy to see what they had tried to do. A sandbar, about fifteen feet wide and ten feet above the water level at its crest, shut off the mouth of the Tenaru from the sea.

The Japs had tried to storm our positions on the west bank of the river by dashing across the sandbar. Many of them had come close to reaching their objective. But they had run into unexpected rows of barbed wire at Hell Point, on our side of the Tenaru.

"That wire maybe saved the day," said a marine lying next to me.[59]

---

yet they had failed to retake the island from U.S. troops, who were often themselves undersupplied and dispirited. It had perhaps been a mistake to take on the clearly better supplied Americans in a major battle over five hundred miles from Rabaul, but many Japanese officers saw it differently. Wherever they fought the Americans, they were going to be at a material disadvantage. And if they could not defeat the odds and triumph on Guadalcanal, there was little reason to think they could do so anywhere else. The loss of Guadalcanal, obvious by the end of the year, was in that sense a larger strategic defeat for Japan. The year had started with the greatest victories in Japan's short history as a modern nation, at Pearl Harbor, Hong Kong, Singapore, and in the Dutch East Indies—yet now it had turned to disaster.

We might say the equivalent for the other two battles surveyed in this chapter. The campaigning season had started with some of the greatest victories in the history of

◀ GUADALCANAL

The first use of a flamethrower by U.S. forces came in January 1943 on Guadalcanal. The M1 flamethrower proved unable to spray flames far enough to be effective. The M1A1 and the subsequent M2 were far more effective. Eventually, the U.S. Army would use the M4 Sherman tank fitted with a flamethrower, but infantry, especially the Marines, would continue to use the flamethrower to good effect throughout the war. The Marine here wears a protective layer of facial cream.

the German Army. At Kerch, Kharkov, Gazala, Tobruk, and Sevastopol in the spring and early summer of 1942, the Wehrmacht had smashed every enemy army it met, reduced two crucial fortresses, and taken over 600,000 prisoners. A mere five months later, Rommel was on the run in North Africa, German Sixth Army was surrounded in Stalingrad, and an immense German force—an entire army group—was stuck eight hundred miles deep in the Caucasus with Soviet mobile formations prepared to strike deep into its rear. Germany's third great adversary, the United States, was only beginning to flex its muscles. This wasn't merely a matter of a turning point. It was a kind of decision. Thrown back on the defensive, with the material balance clearly shifting against them, the Axis powers no longer had any real prospect of *winning* the war. The question now was whether the United Nations (the Allies) could muster the skill and determination they would need to reach their avowed goal of imposing unconditional surrender on their enemies.

INTRODUCTION

Airpower and sea power were the two forces that made World War II truly global. While all the combatant states in World War II devoted a portion of their war effort to the air and sea campaigns, it was ultimately Britain and the United States that came to dominate the air-sea war. For both countries, the war was being fought overseas, and it was only by controlling the sea and the air—in Europe, the Atlantic, the Mediterranean, and the Pacific—that they were able to project their might and lay the groundwork for victory.

This chapter explores two critical strategic elements in the air-sea war: the Battle of the Atlantic—particularly the long struggle to defeat the German submarine threat to the vital Atlantic sea-lanes—and the strategic bombing offensive conducted first by Royal Air Force (RAF) Bomber Command alone, then in concert with the U.S. Eighth and Fifteenth Air Forces. Winning the convoy war in the Atlantic was a complex campaign, but it was essential for Britain and the United States: All resources for the bomber campaign and the amphibious operations in the Mediterranean and Normandy had to cross the Atlantic, as did the lifeblood of food and raw materials that the United States was sending to support the British people and the British war effort throughout the war.

In this way, the success in the sea war was an essential precondition for the success of the ground war. The Allied bombing campaign would prove to be a second precondition. The bomber offensives were designed to weaken the German war economy and reduce German airpower so that Allied offensives across the board would have a better chance of success. Although the most ambitious aims of the bomber commanders were not fully realized, since the German people did not abandon the war, nor was the German war economy brought to a halt, bombing did certainly divert Germany's military resources away from the fighting fronts and weaken the German capacity to resist the Allies' ultimate land offensives. Both the sea and air campaigns fought in the Atlantic and in the skies above the Axis were crucial elements in blunting its offensive and ultimately turning the tide in favor of the Allies.

THE MARITIME PRIORITIES

For Britain, the sea was vital for its survival and its protection. In the last year of peace, sixty-eight million tons of imports came by sea, including all of Britain's oil and its supplies of tin, copper, and rubber from the Empire.[1] Britain was a net food importer and could not adequately feed its home population from domestic production, even after the introduction of rationing during the war and propaganda encouraging people to "dig for victory" by planting their own food. Britain relied on the sea not only for food and raw materials but also for supplies of weapons and equipment that arrived from the United States and Canada throughout the war. The sea also provided Britain's security, as it had done for a thousand years. The English Channel, only

NORWAY

OSLO

STOCKHOLM

SWEDEN

DENMARK

Scapa
Flow

COPENHAGEN

BALTIC
SEA

NORTH SEA

NORTH
ATLANTIC
OCEAN

IRELAND

UNITED
KINGDOM

AMSTERDAM

NETH.

Hamburg

Jul. 27, 1943

BERLIN

Feb. 15, 19

Bombing of Dams

Dresde

Sep. 1940–May 1941

London Blitz

BRUSSELS

BELG.

Essen

Rohr   Mohne
     Sorpe

Eder

GERMANY

PRAG

Mönchengladbach

Cologne

May 30, 1942

Schweinfurt

Aug. 17, 1943

BOH

May 27, 1941

Bismarck Sunk

ENGLISH CHANNEL

Aug. 17, 1942

Rouen

LUX.

LUXEMBOURG

Rhine

Regensburg

Jun. 6, 1944

*Normandy
Invasion*

PARIS

FRANCE

BERN

SWITZ.

Alps

46°30'N

BAY OF
BISCAY

ITALY

Ape

ROM

PORTUGAL

MADRID

SPAIN

TYRRHEN
SEA

LISBON

MEDITERRANEAN SEA

36°N

TANGIER

GIBRALTAR (British)

ALGIERS

TUNIS

SP. MOROCCO

TUNISIA

Jan. 1943

Casablanca Conference

RABAT

ALGERIA

MOROCCO

0   250 Mi

12°W

1°30'W

9°E

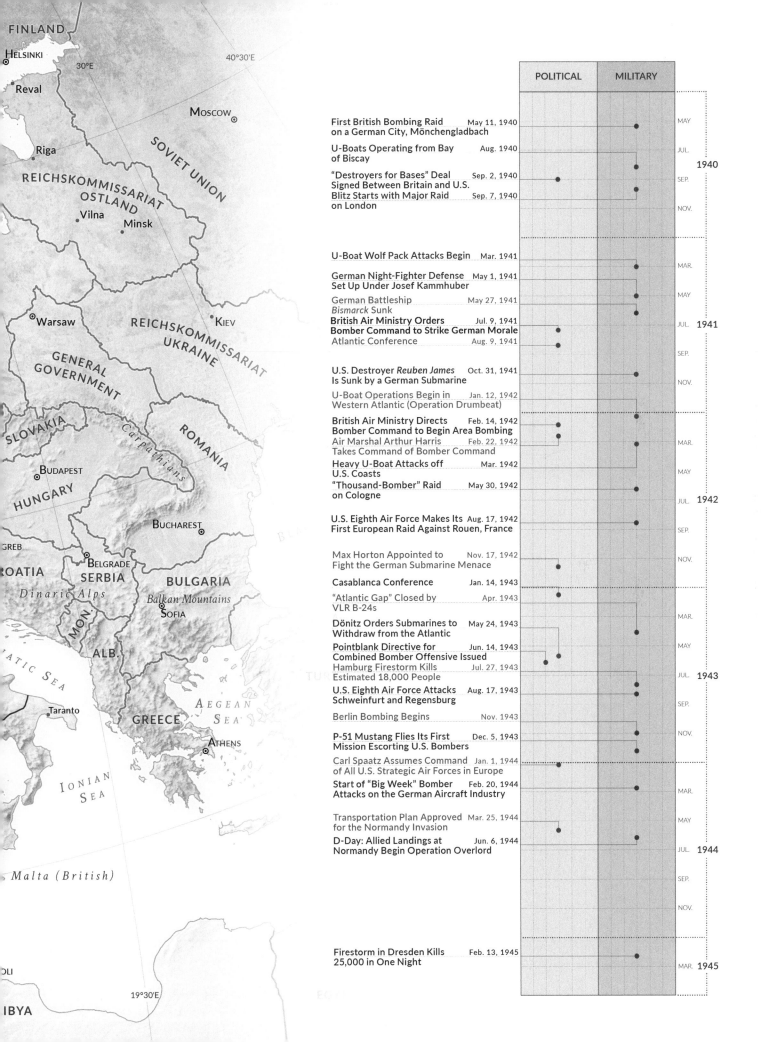

FINLAND
HELSINKI
Reval
30°E
40°30'E
Riga
MOSCOW
SOVIET UNION
REICHSKOMMISSARIAT
OSTLAND
Vilna
Minsk
Warsaw
REICHSKOMMISSARIAT
UKRAINE
KIEV
GENERAL
GOVERNMENT
SLOVAKIA
Carpathians
ROMANIA
BUDAPEST
HUNGARY
BUCHAREST
GREB
BELGRADE
ROATIA
SERBIA
BULGARIA
Dinaric Alps
Balkan Mountains
MON.
SOFIA
ALB.
ATIC SEA
Taranto
GREECE
AEGEAN SEA
ATHENS
IONIAN SEA
Malta (British)
19°30'E
IBYA
OLI

	POLITICAL	MILITARY	
First British Bombing Raid on a German City, Mönchengladbach — May 11, 1940		●	MAY
U-Boats Operating from Bay of Biscay — Aug. 1940		●	JUL.
			1940
"Destroyers for Bases" Deal Signed Between Britain and U.S. — Sep. 2, 1940	●	●	SEP.
Blitz Starts with Major Raid on London — Sep. 7, 1940		●	NOV.
U-Boat Wolf Pack Attacks Begin — Mar. 1941		●	MAR.
German Night-Fighter Defense Set Up Under Josef Kammhuber — May 1, 1941		●	MAY
German Battleship Bismarck Sunk — May 27, 1941		●	
British Air Ministry Orders Bomber Command to Strike German Morale — Jul. 9, 1941	●	●	JUL. 1941
Atlantic Conference — Aug. 9, 1941	●		SEP.
U.S. Destroyer Reuben James Is Sunk by a German Submarine — Oct. 31, 1941		●	NOV.
U-Boat Operations Begin in Western Atlantic (Operation Drumbeat) — Jan. 12, 1942			
British Air Ministry Directs Bomber Command to Begin Area Bombing — Feb. 14, 1942	●	●	
Air Marshal Arthur Harris Takes Command of Bomber Command — Feb. 22, 1942	●	●	MAR.
Heavy U-Boat Attacks off U.S. Coasts — Mar. 1942			MAY
"Thousand-Bomber" Raid on Cologne — May 30, 1942		●	JUL. 1942
U.S. Eighth Air Force Makes Its First European Raid Against Rouen, France — Aug. 17, 1942		●	SEP.
Max Horton Appointed to Fight the German Submarine Menace — Nov. 17, 1942	●		NOV.
Casablanca Conference — Jan. 14, 1943	●		
"Atlantic Gap" Closed by VLR B-24s — Apr. 1943	●		MAR.
Dönitz Orders Submarines to Withdraw from the Atlantic — May 24, 1943		●	MAY
Pointblank Directive for Combined Bomber Offensive Issued — Jun. 14, 1943	●		
Hamburg Firestorm Kills Estimated 18,000 People — Jul. 27, 1943	●		JUL. 1943
U.S. Eighth Air Force Attacks Schweinfurt and Regensburg — Aug. 17, 1943		●	SEP.
Berlin Bombing Begins — Nov. 1943		●	NOV.
P-51 Mustang Flies Its First Mission Escorting U.S. Bombers — Dec. 5, 1943		●	
Carl Spaatz Assumes Command of All U.S. Strategic Air Forces in Europe — Jan. 1, 1944	●		
Start of "Big Week" Bomber Attacks on the German Aircraft Industry — Feb. 20, 1944		●	MAR.
Transportation Plan Approved for the Normandy Invasion — Mar. 25, 1944	●		MAY
D-Day: Allied Landings at Normandy Begin Operation Overlord — Jun. 6, 1944	●	●	JUL. 1944
			SEP.
			NOV.
Firestorm in Dresden Kills 25,000 in One Night — Feb. 13, 1945		●	MAR. 1945

Airpower proved a key factor in the Allies' life-or-death struggle with the German submarines. In this 1943 painting, a three-man Avenger torpedo bomber (which was roomy enough to carry one of the bulky early antisubmarine warfare radar sets) rises after dropping a depth charge on a surfaced U-boat, while its rear machine gun rakes the crew.

twenty miles wide at its narrowest point, was still enough in 1940 to prevent Germany from invading so long as Britain had the superior navy.

The priorities for Britain's war effort were thus quite different from German priorities, since Germany relied on the army and air force as the main sources of its power and could supply most of the resources and food needed for war by conquest in Continental Europe.[2] Britain knew that its maritime strength was the key to its success, and, accordingly, in 1939 it possessed the world's largest navy and the world's largest merchant marine.

American priorities were also focused heavily on the sea. The United States had the second largest navy in the world and a substantial merchant marine. Although the United States could not easily be blockaded, any intervention in either the European or Pacific conflicts meant projecting power across oceans, which required the sea power to conduct large-scale movements of troops, equipment, and weapons. A regular army division required 144,000 tons of cargo space to cross the Atlantic, and an armored division required 250,000 tons.[3] For the United States to be able to fight at all, it was strategically essential to keep transoceanic routes open.

AIRCRAFT OF THE RAF ▶

Perhaps the most interesting element of this British poster is the map on the bottom left, which shows that already in 1941 nearly all of Europe was within range of British bombers flying from England or Egypt. The significance of that fact, however, was greatly reduced by the lack of escort fighters with comparable ranges.

AIRCRAFT OF THE R.A.F.
Some Famous Types – I.

BLENHEIM
Constant scourge of enemy shipping. "Blenheims" also made the great daylight raid on the German power-stations near Cologne.

WELLINGTON
These long-range bombers have flown from England across the Alps to hit targets at Naples in Italy.

SPITFIRE II
Britain's most famous fighter. Now armed with two cannon and four machine guns, or eight machine guns.

HURRICANE II
"Hurricanes" played a leading part in the Battle of Britain. Now armed with twelve machine guns or four 20 m.m. cannon and used for low level bombing.

BEAUFIGHTER
Armed with four cannon and six machine guns, "Beaufighters" have scored great successes against German dive-bombers in Libya.

HAMPDEN
Medium bombers, continuously used in attacking objectives in Germany. "Hampdens" cut the Dortmund-Ems Canal.

HALIFAX
Among many raids carried out by these giant long-range bombers are attacks on the German harbours of Emden and Kiel, also Berlin.

FLYING FORTRESS
Emden, Rotterdam, Kiel and shipping in the Macassar Straits are among targets attacked by "Fortresses."

SUNDERLAND
"Sunderlands" have done brilliant work in guarding British convoys and bombing German submarines. A "Sunderland" weighs 20 tons.

STIRLING
Biggest bombers in the world. "Stirlings" have dropped their immense bomb-loads on Berlin among other targets.

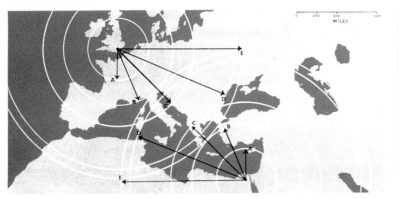

MILES
0   250   500   1000

KEY TO MAP

A   Approximate range of British "Hurricane" and "Spitfire."

B   Approximate range of British "Beaufighter."

C   Approximate range of "Blenheim," "Hampden" and Boeing "Flying Fortress" bombers.

D   Approximate range of "Wellington" bomber, and Short "Sunderland" flying boat of R.A.F. Coastal Command.

E   Approximate range of "Stirling" bomber.

Arrows represent approximate operational range of each type of plane. (Total flying distance is double.)

John Bull is pulling in his belt!

examples of food restriction in GREAT BRITAIN

PRE-WAR	NOW
SUGAR consumption in sugar confectionery	
EGGS	
LEMONS Etc. imports 1,100,000 CWTS.	NONE

PRE-WAR	NOW
WINE imports	
WHISKY production	

PRE-WAR	NOW
CREAM production 33,000 TONS	NONE
GRAPEFRUIT imports 1,300,000 CWTS.	NONE
BANANAS imports 22,000,000 BUNCHES	NONE

G.P.G./A.M./3.

For both Britain and the United States, airpower was an important adjunct to the exercise of sea power. Aircraft in World War II rapidly transformed the nature of combat at sea, since aircraft—using torpedoes or bombs—could cripple and sink even the largest vessel. Planes were just as necessary for defensive combat air patrols and for reconnaissance as they were for attack. Aircraft also had much in common with naval power for Britain and the United States, because both offered methods of inflicting damage on the enemy that overcame the problems of distance. The two forms of power projection even shared a common language: "fleets," "raids," "ships," and "crew" were part of naval vocabulary but were easily applied to the air force. In Britain, naval navigators were used to train bomber navigators for the strategic air offensive.

The Axis understood the importance of sea power and airpower to the Allies, so much so that a central element in Axis strategy—in the North Sea, the Atlantic, and the Mediterranean—was to find some way of interrupting seaborne trade routes. The German Navy was too small to challenge the Royal Navy in large-scale combat, and after the loss of five cruisers (three sunk, two damaged) and nine destroyers in the Norwegian campaign in April–May 1940, the surface fleet was reduced to a strategy of sending merchant raiders to disrupt Atlantic sea-lanes.[4] The best-known attempt at raiding, when the large new battleship *Bismarck* was sent through the Denmark Strait in May 1941, ended in disaster. After a successful engagement with British warships in which H.M.S. *Hood* was blown up and sunk, *Bismarck* was spotted making its way to

France by a Catalina flying boat (a long-range seaplane used for scouting). The battle-ship was then crippled by a torpedo bomber from the aircraft carrier H.M.S. *Ark Royal* and eventually finished off by British destroyers.[5]

Yet despite the practical neutralization of its surface fleet, Germany was able to conduct a war against Allied shipping so effective that it came close to winning the war for the Axis. That simple fact reveals how fundamentally new technologies had transformed the nature of sea power, because this naval war was not conducted by traditional warships of any sort, but rather by submarines and aircraft.

Germany began the war with only a small submarine force (fifty-seven boats) be-cause interwar planners generally believed that the invention of sonar would greatly reduce the U-boats' effectiveness. This was not enough to have much effect, especially since it was never possible to keep more than one-third of the boats engaged in opera-tions at a given time, with the rest either in port or on their way to or from patrols. But thanks to an intensive effort to ramp up production, the Germans built 750 subma-rines between 1940 and 1943. By early in the latter year, the number of subs hunting Allied merchantmen in the Atlantic reached a peak of 110 boats.[6]

The German Navy's plan was simple and, in broad terms, changed little for the first three years of the war. Once bases were secured in Norway and France in 1940, sub-marines would work in concert with aircraft to sink 750,000 tons of shipping a month. It was calculated that this would reduce Britain's merchant fleet from 22 million tons to less than 12 million over two years and thus force Britain out of the war.[7] A similar

▲ **MILITARY CONVOY**

This small convoy of five military transports, guarded by two heavy cruisers (in the right foreground and in the center of the back row), is much better protected and sail-ing in better formation than would have been normal for a merchant convoy. Overhead, on the look-out for submarines, is a Vindicator scout bomber flying from the carrier *Ranger*.

Karl Dönitz had the dubious distinction of becoming Hitler's successor as president of Germany in the closing days of the Third Reich, after the dictator had committed suicide on April 30, 1945. He rose to high office as a result of his role as commander in chief of the German submarine arm from 1939 to 1943, and his subsequent appointment as overall commander of the German Navy on January 30, 1943.

He began his career in the German Navy before World War I and was commander of a submarine in 1918 when he was captured. He claimed that in the British prison camp he worked out the tactic of using submarines in wolf packs to hunt down merchant ships. In the 1930s, he rose rapidly in the new German Navy under Hitler, whom he much admired and whose anti-Semitic sentiments he shared. As commander of submarines beginning in January 1939, he argued against large fleet engagements in favor of targeting merchant ships and tankers. Hitler supported greater submarine output and accepted Dönitz's blockade strategy, which operated over the following three years with mixed success.

In January 1943, Hitler appointed Dönitz commander in chief of the German Navy and Grand Admiral after he had sacked Erich Raeder. Dönitz struggled to find a way to bring the navy back into the war, but most of the remaining capital ships were destroyed, and the submarines were too vulnerable. On May 6, 1945, as Hitler's successor, he ordered the high command to sue for peace. Dönitz remained in office until his arrest on May 23, 1945. He was put on trial as one of the major war criminals at the Nuremberg Trials in 1945–46 and was sentenced to twenty years in prison.

calculation had been made in World War I by Admiral Alfred von Tirpitz when he campaigned for unrestricted submarine warfare in 1915–16. Yet in both cases, despite initial success, the German expectations proved far too optimistic.

THE SUBMARINE WAR

The submarine-air war in 1940 and 1941 nevertheless constituted a major threat. Churchill famously remarked in his memoirs that "The only thing that really frightened me during the war was the U-Boat peril."[8] Between 1940 and the end of 1943, the German submarine commander, Admiral Karl Dönitz, saw the number of operational submarines available increase tenfold from an average of ten to an average of one hundred. For the submarine war, the German Navy enjoyed a number of operational and tactical advantages. German cryptographers cracked British naval codes and could direct the limited number of submarines efficiently to intercept convoys rather than relying on long searches. The submarines were also directed to attack at night and on the surface, first because they would be invisible to the naval escorts around the convoy, second because the Royal Navy still relied on the ASDIC sonar device used in World

▲ GERMAN SUBMARINE, 1942

The threat posed by the U-boats was large, but the vessels themselves were not. Even the relatively big specialized subs like this Type XIV (nicknamed a *Milchkuh* or "milk cow"), designed to deliver supplies to on-station fighting boats, sailed with only about a third of the crew of a U.S. *Fletcher*–class destroyer.

◀ SINKING THE *BISMARCK*

Germany's most advanced battleship, the *Bismarck*, was still being completed when she put to sea and attempted to raid British shipping.

Schlacht der Entscheidung!

Und so greifen die deutschen U-Boote an!

Das beweisen die neuen deutschen Erfolgszahlen:
166 Schiffe mit 1035000 Bruttoregistertonnen allein im Monat November versenkt,
das ist ein weiterer furchtbarer Schlag für England, das diesen Krieg begann, nur weil die rein deutsche Stadt Danzig ins Reich zurückkehren wollte. — Churchill, einer der Hauptschuldigen an diesem Kriege, muß heute voll Angst vor der Zukunft seinen Landsleuten zurufen: „Denkt daran, daß der **U-Boot-Krieg nicht nachläßt, sondern zunimmt."**

Der englische Admiral Sir Ragnar Colvin befaßte sich in einer Rundfunkrede mit der Lage auf den Meeren. Dazu machte er folgende bemerkenswerte Eingeständnisse:
„*Alles Gerede, die U-Boot-Gefahr sei über-wunden, ist falsch. Die Schlacht auf dem Atlantik hat sich jetzt über alle sieben Meere ausgedehnt und von ihrem Ausgang hängt alles ab. Diese Schlacht hat nie ein Ende. Sie wird ununterbrochen geführt, wenn auch die Öffentlichkeit nur bemitleidenswert (!) wenig von ihr erfährt. Das U-Boot-Problem bleibt eine Frage von äußerster Wichtigkeit.*"

"THE DECISIVE BATTLE!" ▲

The figures on this German poster from late 1942 are somewhat exaggerated, but probably reflect what the OKW actually believed: the U-boats were proving so effective that they stood a good chance of winning the Battle of the Atlantic, and hence the whole war. But November 1942 turned out be the peak of the U-boat's success, and by mid-1943 the "decisive battle" had been decided—in favor of the Allies.

War I, which could only detect submarines under the surface of the sea. These advantages were enough to ensure that the groups of submarines, organized in what were called wolf packs, would find and sink their prey. In 1940, 992 ships totaling 3.4 million tons were sunk; in 1941 1,299 ships, a further 5.4 million tons.[9] British food imports fell from 14.6 million tons in 1941 to 10.6 million in 1942; and raw materials from 15 million tons in 1941 to 11.5 million the following year. Both Churchill and Roosevelt regarded the submarine menace as a major factor in Allied strategy. In May 1941 Roosevelt told Churchill that the outcome of the war "would be decided in the Atlantic."[10]

The war between Allied ships and aircraft and the German submarines was christened "the Battle of the Atlantic" by Churchill in a speech on March 6, 1941.[11] The supply lines across the ocean were vital to Britain's continued war effort. But they were also essential for Roosevelt, not only for the Lend-Lease program that was approved by Congress in March 1941, but for the eventual moment when the United States might finally find itself at war with Germany and Italy. This explains FDR's willingness to involve the United States in the Atlantic theater well before the German declaration of war on December 11, 1941. There was in effect an undeclared naval war going on in 1941 between the United States and Germany in response to the threat to American trade. In July 1941 the United States took responsibility for the military occupation of Iceland, which Britain had brought under military control in 1940 to forestall the

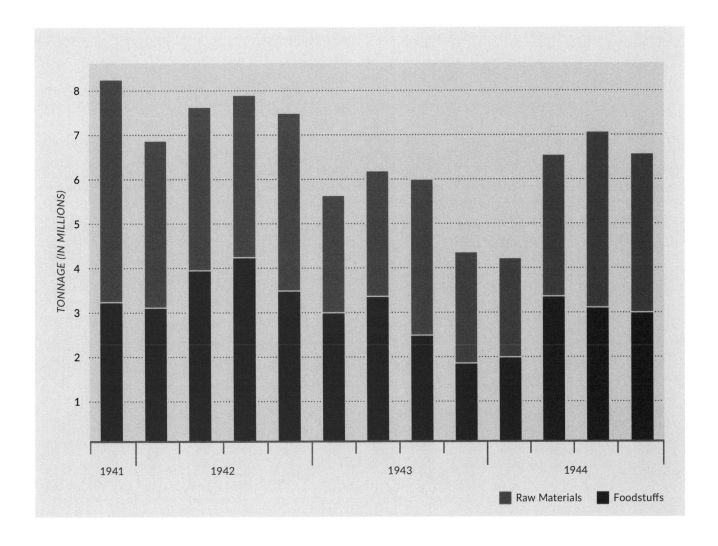

TONNAGE (IN MILLIONS)

8

7

6

5

4

3

2

1

1941   1942   1943   1944

■ Raw Materials   ■ Foodstuffs

Germans. Two modifications of American Neutrality legislation in summer 1941 allowed American merchant ships to arm themselves for voyages through the war zone, while on September 16, 1941, the first U.S. destroyers escorted a convoy to the "Mid-Ocean Meeting Point," where escort duty was handed over to British vessels.[12] The first U.S. warship lost in WWII was the U.S.S. *Reuben James*, sunk off of Iceland at the end of October 1941.

The Atlantic battle in 1941 began with heavy losses in the early months of the year, but ship and tonnage losses then declined steadily between June and November, from sixty-eight ships in June down to only ten in November. The explanation for the sudden decline in shipping losses lies partly with better escort organization for major convoys and partly with increased production of destroyers and corvettes in British shipyards. But another large factor was the changing nature of the information war between the two sides. The cryptographers of the German Navy's signals intelligence service, the B-Dienst, could already read British codes, but during the course of spring 1941, the British code and cipher center at Bletchley Park cracked enough of the German Navy's Enigma code to be able to work out where the submarine wolf packs were going to be stationed and to reroute convoys to avoid them.[13]

▲ BRITISH IMPORTS, 1941–43

▲ *Reuben James*

The sinking of the *Reuben James* by a German U-boat sparked considerable public outrage in the United States, increasing American resolve to prepare for war.

Enigma Machine ▶

The Enigma code machine was a critical component of Germany's ability to transmit orders to its submarine forces.

The intelligence war also helps to explain the sudden escalation of shipping losses again in 1942. During that year, the British, American, and Canadian merchant navies lost 7.2 million tons of shipping: 1,662 vessels in total. In the closing months of 1941, the B-Dienst cracked a new Allied code, Cipher No. 3, which all the Allied navies used. Around the same time, Admiral Dönitz grew suspicious that the Allies might be reading his navy's secret message traffic and altered the German Navy's Triton cipher by adding a new rotor wheel to the Enigma machine.[14] Thus, for ten months in 1942, the Allies could not read German messages, while Germany had access to those of the Allies.

The wolf packs could once again roam more freely, and the entry of the United States into the war in December 1941 prompted a concentrated U-boat campaign, known as Operation Drumbeat, against American coastal shipping. In a matter of weeks, 1.2 million tons of shipping was sunk off the American coast: fifty ships in four weeks sunk by only ten submarines. In response, Admiral Ernest King, the U.S. Navy chief of staff, at first refused to authorize convoys after seeing what had happened to them in the Atlantic. This was a mistaken judgment that failed to take into account that it was stragglers, sailing too slowly or out of line, that had suffered most on the ocean routes. In addition, American vessels were using radios openly and at first were conveniently silhouetted against fully lit American coastal cities, which made them easy targets. This was quickly addressed by the "dimout," which reduced lighting. These shipping losses were reduced drastically when King finally ordered ships to depart shore bases in convoys, with naval escorts and air patrols.[15] As the number of escort vessels increased and the air patrols flew farther over the Atlantic from west and east, the sphere of submarine operations was compressed into the so-called Atlantic Gap, six hundred miles wide, which aircraft could not yet reach from shore. Here Dönitz concentrated his submarines, now as many as fifty operational units, employing both the standard Type VII boat of 750 tons with eleven torpedoes, and the new Type IX, a boat of 1,100 tons and armed with twenty-two torpedoes. Here, in the heavy Atlantic seas, the two sides fought an attrition war.

Though losses were heavy, the loss of intelligence information and the increased number of submarines did not produce the disaster that Churchill feared. Recent research has highlighted the extent to which convoyed shipping survived the Atlantic run in increasing numbers. Between May 1942 and May 1943, 105 out of 174 convoys sailed without loss; out of 69 convoys that were raided by the submarines, 23 escaped without sinkings, 30 suffered minor losses, and only 10 were badly mauled.[16] Out of the 334 ships that sailed from Scotland and the United States to North Africa for the Operation Torch landings in November 1942, only one small supply vessel was lost. The U-boats, despite their greater number, operated with declining efficiency: in October 1940, submarines sank an average of 920 tons each; by August 1942, that figure had declined to a mere 149 tons.[17] During the second half of 1942, moreover, submarine losses rose sharply: sixty-five were lost between June and December 1942—four times the number lost in the first half of the year.

In 1943 the submarines' effectiveness fell even further. Exceptionally adverse weather in the first months of the year reduced the prospects for submarine attack. And even though several convoys in March were broken up and severely depleted, by May, shipping losses had declined to 160,000 tons (the lowest figure since the end of 1941), while the German submarine arm lost forty-one vessels in one month. German submariners suddenly faced suicidal conditions: in June and July 1943, another fifty-four submarines were sunk or captured. At the end of May 1943, Dönitz was forced to admit to Hitler that the Atlantic battle had for the moment been lost, and in the summer, he began to withdraw the submarines from the main Atlantic shipping lanes to rethink his strategy.[18]

VICTORY AT SEA

There are many explanations for the slowly won Allied victory in the Battle of the Atlantic. From the beginning, the Germans' chances of effectively cutting the sea lines of communication to Britain, and thereby winning the war, were diminished by the relative paucity of aviation resources they devoted to the struggle. There were seldom more than a hundred aircraft available for the mining, bombing, and reconnaissance portion of the joint operations. German planes operating in the Channel and the Atlantic were subject to increasing losses to shore-based fighters and the longer-range aircraft of RAF Coastal Command.[19] The shortage of marine aviation would prove to be a permanent disadvantage to the German blockade campaign, limiting its success and forcing it to adopt more timid strategies than it would have been able to undertake with the support of air power.

The entry of the United States into the war after Pearl Harbor expanded greatly the quantity of shipping and naval support vessels on the Allied side, making the prospect of blockade more remote. In 1941, United States shipyards launched a total of 794,000 tons of new ships, but in the next two years, they produced *27 million* tons, including 2,708 of the famous "Liberty" cargo ships, which could be mass-produced in a matter of weeks.[20] British shipyards turned out a more modest 4.7 million tons of merchant shipping by the end of 1943, but also 5,700 naval vessels, from battleships to landing craft.[21] Stronger escorts began to accompany major convoys, and by the spring of 1943, a number of escort carriers—relatively small vessels each carrying a limited number of aircraft that could search for and attack submarines—were in service. A second explanation lay in the tight system of control over shipping exercised by the Tracking Room and Trade Plot Room in London, and a U.S. Navy Tracking Room in Washington.[22] The two allies waged a real global war at sea, monitoring the flow of trade and military convoys worldwide. They were able to provide largely accurate guesses as to the whereabouts of submarines, even across a battlefield that spanned thousands of square miles, and even during the period when the Triton code could not be read.

The most important breakthrough, however, came with changes in the supporting technology, without which the antisubmarine campaign might not have been

THE U-BOAT WAR ▶
This chart, adapted from one produced in 1945 by the National Security Agency, lays out some of the main factors in the varying success of the U-boats. Another reason for the high shipping losses in the second half of 1942 and in March 1943 was the German success in cracking Allied naval codes.

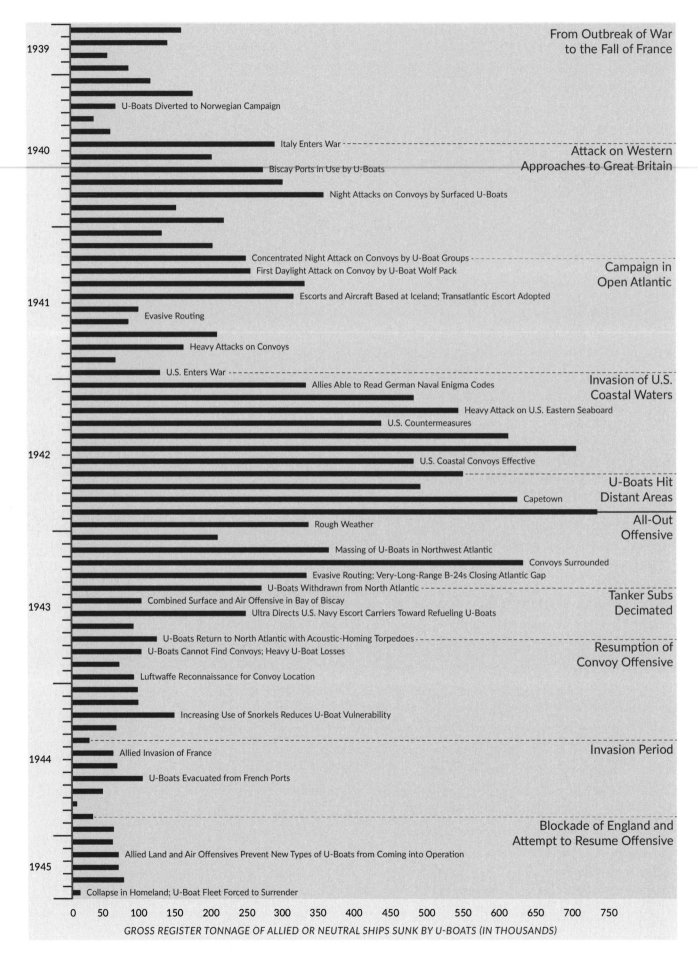

From Outbreak of War
to the Fall of France

1939

U-Boats Diverted to Norwegian Campaign

1940

Italy Enters War ----------------------

Attack on Western
Approaches to Great Britain

Biscay Ports in Use by U-Boats

Night Attacks on Convoys by Surfaced U-Boats

Concentrated Night Attack on Convoys by U-Boat Groups - - - - - - - - - -
First Daylight Attack on Convoy by U-Boat Wolf Pack

Campaign in
Open Atlantic

Escorts and Aircraft Based at Iceland; Transatlantic Escort Adopted

1941

Evasive Routing

Heavy Attacks on Convoys

U.S. Enters War - - - - - - - - - - - - - - - - -

Invasion of U.S.
Coastal Waters

Allies Able to Read German Naval Enigma Codes

Heavy Attack on U.S. Eastern Seaboard

U.S. Countermeasures

1942

U.S. Coastal Convoys Effective

U-Boats Hit
Distant Areas

Capetown

All-Out
Offensive

Rough Weather

Massing of U-Boats in Northwest Atlantic

Convoys Surrounded

Evasive Routing; Very-Long-Range B-24s Closing Atlantic Gap

U-Boats Withdrawn from North Atlantic - - - - - - - - - - -

Tanker Subs
Decimated

Combined Surface and Air Offensive in Bay of Biscay

Ultra Directs U.S. Navy Escort Carriers Toward Refueling U-Boats

1943

U-Boats Return to North Atlantic with Acoustic-Homing Torpedoes - - - - - - - - -

U-Boats Cannot Find Convoys; Heavy U-Boat Losses

Resumption of
Convoy Offensive

Luftwaffe Reconnaissance for Convoy Location

Increasing Use of Snorkels Reduces U-Boat Vulnerability

Invasion Period

Allied Invasion of France

1944

U-Boats Evacuated from French Ports

Blockade of England and
Attempt to Resume Offensive

Allied Land and Air Offensives Prevent New Types of U-Boats from Coming into Operation

1945

Collapse in Homeland; U-Boat Fleet Forced to Surrender

0   50   100 150 200 250 300 350 400 450 500 550 600 650 700 750

GROSS REGISTER TONNAGE OF ALLIED OR NEUTRAL SHIPS SUNK BY U-BOATS (IN THOUSANDS)

MAKING AMERICA STRONG

HOW AMERICAN SHIPYARDS
ARE WINNING THE RACE AGAINST TIME
TO BUILD OUR NAVY

IN NORMAL TIMES IT TOOK ABOUT
24 MONTHS TO BUILD A DESTROYER

TODAY
THEY ARE
BEING BUILT
IN
*LESS THAN
½ THAT TIME!*

BUILDING FOR VICTORY ▲

The pressing need for ships to fight a two-ocean naval war and move desperately needed supplies to America's embattled allies pushed U.S. shipyards to work harder, longer, and more efficiently.

◀ **CALSHIP BURNER**

American shipyards played a crucial role in the United States' war effort, providing the ability to build ships faster than the Germans could sink them. This painting shows one of the millions of women who went to work for the war effort.

successful. There were improvements in weaponry, including the new "Hedgehog" multiple mortar projector, which fired twenty-four small bombs from the front of the chasing ship, each one fitted with a contact fuse so that it would explode only if it hit a submarine. Depth charges, the conventional weapon against submarines, were now fitted to aircraft and, from 1942, were filled with aluminized explosive that led to a much greater blast effect. Antisubmarine aircraft received large searchlights—called Leigh Lights after their inventor, Sir Humphrey de Verd Leigh—that could be switched on to illuminate the sea where radar had indicated the presence of a submarine.[23]

The most important invention was centimetric radar, which greatly increased the chances of detecting enemy vessels. The German Navy had worked out a way of jamming the 1.7 meter (5.6-foot) air-to-surface (ASV) radar used on most search aircraft early in the war, while the same broad wavelength used on surface naval vessels was unable to detect submarines because of the action of the waves. However, in 1941, scientists at Birmingham University in England developed the cavity magnetron, a valve that permitted radar to operate at frequencies as low as ten centimeters (four inches). The new Type 271 radar, fitted to ships and aircraft in 1942, with an enhanced cavity magnetron valve added early in 1943, was able to detect any part of a submarine

▲ BUILDING FOR VICTORY

American industry was long since famous for using assembly lines to maximize production efficiency. During World War II, similar methods were applied on a massive scale to assemble cargo ships from prefabricated segments.

BUILDING FOR VICTORY ▲

This photograph shows one component of a new Liberty Ship, the *Frederick Douglass*, being lifted into place in 1943.

exposed above water—even a periscope if the sea were calm enough—and as a result greatly enhanced the accuracy of detection.[24] The German Navy failed to find a response to the centimetric sets, and a combination of radar, Leigh Lights, and enhanced weaponry contributed to the rapid increase in submarine sinkings.

The new technology and the better level of close escorting coincided with the appointment in November 1942 of Admiral Sir Max Horton as commander in chief of the Western Approaches, an area that included the eastern Atlantic Ocean, the Bay of Biscay, and the Irish Sea. He was a tough-minded commander who laid emphasis on intensive training and preparation for the submarine war.[25] In 1943 he introduced "support groups" of hard-hitting naval vessels that hovered around the convoys waiting for a sign of the submarines. He insisted that the RAF finally release numbers of

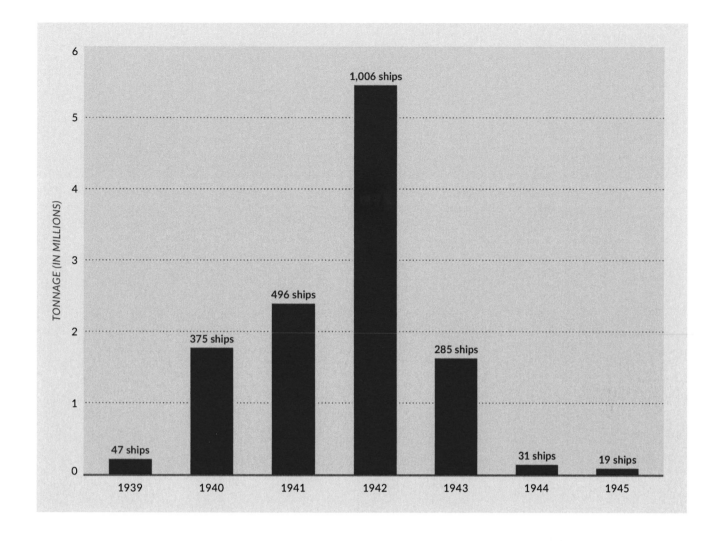

the American-built very-long-range Consolidated B-24 Liberator bombers to cover the Atlantic Gap, and thirty-seven were eventually provided. Although useful in closing the air gap over the ocean, they were just one of the many key causes of the defeat of the submarines.[26]

For example, Horton soon realized that subs were very vulnerable as they crossed the Bay of Biscay back to their bases on the French coast, and he ordered aircraft with shorter range to patrol regularly over the area, where they began to exact a steady toll of the U-boats. By early 1943, German naval Enigma could be read again, giving better indication of where the enemy was.[27] Most of the convoys Horton shepherded into British ports survived the crossing, while the high attrition of submarines made further regular combat insupportable. The combination of vanguard technology, better organization and training, and improved intelligence forced the German Navy to abandon the campaign, even though it had substantial numbers of submarines on hand, and more being produced. In June and July 1943, not one Allied ship was lost in the Atlantic. During the six months from June to December 1943, the German Navy lost 141 submarines in all areas where they still operated.[28]

The victory in the Battle of the Atlantic ensured that Britain could still be supplied

▲ LOSSES OF ALLIED MERCHANT SHIPS, 1939–45

Horton began his naval career when he joined the Royal Navy in 1898. During World War I, he commanded one of the few British oceangoing submarines and sank a German cruiser on September 13, 1914. He remained commander of submarines throughout the war, but in the interwar years commanded surface vessels, ending up as a vice admiral in command of the British Reserve Fleet in 1937.

Horton began World War II as commander of the Northern Patrol, enforcing the sea blockade of Germany. In 1940, though too senior for such an appointment, he was asked to command all British submarines in home waters because of his previous experience. He became a full admiral on January 9, 1941. His energy, insight, and knowledge of submarine warfare to fight the Battle of the Atlantic successfully led to his being named as commander in chief of the Western Approaches in November 1942. Horton introduced important operational innovations, including the allocation of naval support groups for convoys, which unlike the escorts were free to hunt the submarine in the surrounding waters. He made fuller use of long-range aircraft to bridge the Atlantic Gap, where the wolf packs waited. He had a submariner's instinct for where Dönitz would place his submarines, and even during the period without secret intelligence intercepts, which were finally available again beginning in early 1943, Horton was able to control the movement of convoys away from danger. He remained in post until the end of the war and then retired from active service.

with food and raw materials, but more importantly it ensured the safe arrival of the huge quantities of resources needed for the United States military effort in Europe. The U.S. Eighth Air Force was established in England in April 1942, and from its inception onward, all its personnel, equipment, and many of its aircraft had to be shipped across the ocean. More than 250,000 air force and service personnel were transferred by 1944.[29] The main combat theaters in North Africa, Sicily, Italy, and finally, in June 1944, in France all had to be supplied from across the Atlantic. Keeping the sea-lanes open was a critical precondition for the eventual success of Operation Overlord, the 1944 amphibious invasion of Normandy. Just how comprehensive the sea victory had been was evident when the armada of ships that crossed the English Channel to invade France suffered almost no losses to submarines, German E-boats (motor torpedo boats), or aircraft. In 1944 only thirty-one ships were lost the whole year, even though the German submarine arm now had over four hundred units available: the U-boats were bottled up in their home ports because of the success of Allied antisubmarine measures.[30]

THE CHOICE OF BOMBING

One of the many explanations given both at the time and since the war for the defeat of the submarine is the role of the heavy bomber in reducing German submarine output

THE BATTLE OF THE ATLANTIC BY FREDERICK DONALD BLAKE, 1943 ▶

Blake's poster was part of a series produced for distribution abroad in various languages, including French, Dutch, Arabic, and Portuguese. The poster shows the complexity of the air and sea war in the Atlantic.

THE BATTLE OF THE ATLANTIC

ICELAND

CONVOYS TO RUSSIA

TRONDHJEM

VAAGSÖ

NORWAY

THE FAEROES

BERGEN

CONVOYS FROM CANADA and the UNITED STATES

STAVANGER

SHETLAND ISLES

ORKNEY ISLES

DENMARK

CONVOYS AND AIRCRAFT FROM CANADA and the UNITED STATES

HAMBURG

WILHELMSHAVEN

BREMEN

THE UNITED KINGDOM

GERMANY

FRANCE

BREST

LORIENT

ST. NAZAIRE

CONVOYS TO THE MEDITERRANEAN and the EAST

A CEASELESS BATTLE IS RAGING IN THE ATLANTIC

The Axis U-boats' intention is to isolate and starve Britain. But as the U-boat offensive mounts, so do Britain's protective measures. More and more escort vessels are safeguarding convoys. The U-boats' Atlantic Coast bases are being pounded by the Allied Air Forces and the entrances to their harbours are being mined from the air. The factories where they are built are being crippled by bombs. All these counter-measures enabled Mr. Churchill to say, when reviewing the U-boat campaign in May 1943, "Our killings of the U-boats . . . greatly exceeded all previous experience and the last three months, and particularly the last three weeks, have yielded record results."

Commander William Donald was captain of the British escort vessel H.M.S. *Verdun* in 1941 at the height of the German blockade strategy against Britain using aircraft, U-boats, and fast motor torpedo boats (E-boats). In his postwar memoirs, Donald describes vividly the strains and problems facing the commanders of the small naval escort vessels trying to keep a convoy together in rough seas and to protect it against torpedo or bomb attack. He commanded his vessel until 1943 and undertook 150 operations of convoy protection before being posted to the Mediterranean theater.

The night of November 19, 1941, will live long in my memory. We had a large southbound convoy of over fifty ships, and we passed Flamborough [on the English east coast] just after sunset. It was a moonless period, with flat calm seas and not a breath of wind. Just before dark, the usual German reconnaissance machine appeared low down on the eastward horizon out to seaward, and flew up and down out of gun range. Darkness closed down on the convoy with an ominous inky black calm.

"E-Boat attack for certain tonight," I remarked to the Sub.

Extra escorts had been sent from Harwich and Humber and took station at intervals all round the convoy, and so this great collection of ships groped its way through the silent night. The suspense of waiting for the inevitable attack was unbearable, and it was almost a relief when about nine o'clock off Sheringham [Norfolk], the party started.

On that night, *Verdun* was stationed astern the convoy. The main duty of the escort was to prevent any E-boats sneaking in from the rear; a secondary duty was to deal with casualties. From the time Wolsey, the leader of the escorts, signalled the cryptic message "E-boats in the vicinity," and opened fire with star shell, there was never a dull moment for twelve hours.

At least two separate groups of E-boats, four or five to a group, started to attack simultaneously, and a general melee began as escorts moved out to drive them off. The dull glow of star shell lit up the horizon ahead; red, green, and yellow tracers crisscrossed in all directions, and the heavy boom of gunfire kept up an unceasing chorus.

All the time, the convoy plodded slowly on through the night. The first casualty was an unexpected one, as in the heat of battle, one of our destroyers, the *Campbell*, opened fire on the *Garth*, a "Hunt" class destroyer, whose smaller size and silhouette closely resembled an E-boat in the dark . . . A few minutes after this happened, there was an almighty flash and an explosion ahead.

"That'll be that that smaller tanker," said Toby . . . "Someone in trouble here, sir."

Through the darkness, we saw a ship close on our bow. She was stopped and low in the water with a heavy list. The flickering of a torch showed on the waterline, and a boat pulled away just as the ship heeled right over and slid out of sight. Only a short hiss of escaping steam, like the sigh of a dying man, broke the silence . . .

Short signals reporting the progress of the battle began to come in one after the other—"half-time scores"—as they were always referred to. Several ships had been damaged or sunk, but it was obvious the E-boats had not had it all their own way. The situation became more and more confused, and there were still several hours of darkness to get through. We pressed on through the inky night . . . The next few hours seemed like days, but at last faint signs of dawn appeared, and we were able to relax. About eight o'clock I left the bridge after a sixteen-hour spell up there, and staggered down to my sea cabin. Ten minutes later, the bell by my ear rang.

"Yes?"

"We're just passing a tug towing an oiler, sir; the latter looks in a pretty bad way."

I clambered wearily on to the bridge. The ship was a casualty from the night before, and the tug was heading for Lowestoft.

"He'll never make it."

As I spoke, the oiler took a heavy list to port. Men could be seen running along the upper deck, and a boat was turned out from its davits. At the same time, a lamp flashed from the bridge—"Am abandoning . . ."

But the signal was never finished, for the ship's list to port increased rapidly until she gave a lurch and disappeared; in the bubbling, muddy waters the ship's boat rocked and tossed about, and men's heads popped up like currants in a bun. Fortunately the tug picked up all the survivors; and after we had dropped a buoy to mark the position of the wreck, we pressed on once more to rejoin the convoy; finally we arrived at Sheerness on a cold drizzly afternoon.[31]

▲ STRATEGIC BOMBING OF GERMANY

The rate of increase may have been great, but despite the impression conveyed by this propaganda poster the damage inflicted by the RAF bombing of Germany was still quite limited in 1942—nothing like what would hit the Reich in 1943 and especially 1944.

When propaganda minister Joseph Goebbels asked Nazi delegates in 1943 "Do you want total war?" they answered with an enthusiastic "Yes!" But, warns this American leaflet, "total war" will continue until German manpower and industry are completely destroyed, unless the German people surrender and throw off Nazism and Prussian militarism. They would then be allowed to resume the normal, peaceful development of their nation.

Am 18. Februar 1943, wenige Wochen nach der Katastrophe von Stalingrad, richtete Dr. Goebbels an eine Massenversammlung im Berliner Sportpalast die Frage:

„Wollt ihr den totalen Krieg?"

Ein begeistertes „Ja" war die Antwort der Nazi-Versammlung. Heute weiss Deutschland, was „totaler Krieg" bedeutet, besser als es Dr. Goebbels und seine Ja-Schreier im Sportpalast voraussahen. Der totale Krieg, den die Nazis wollten, wird mit immer stärkerer Wucht und Wirkung fortgeführt werden, bis Deutschland bedingungslos kapituliert.

DAS DEUTSCHE VOLK MUSS SELBST WÄHLEN:

ENTWEDER Fortsetzung des totalen Nazi-Kriegs bis zur völligen Vernichtung der deutschen Arbeitskraft und Industrie — **ODER:** ➡

„Die natürliche und friedvolle Entwicklung des deutschen Volkes."

In seiner Rundfunkbotschaft vom 24. Dezember 1943 erklärte Präsident Roosevelt:

„DIE Vereinten Nationen haben nicht die Absicht, das deutsche Volk zu versklaven. Wir wünschen, die natürliche und friedvolle Entwicklung des deutschen Volkes zu einem geachteten und wertvollen Mitglied der europäischen Völkerfamilie nicht zu hemmen. Aber wir legen allen Nachdruck auf das Wort „geachtet"; denn wir sind entschlossen, das deutsche Volk ein für alle Mal vom Nationalsozialismus, preussischen Militarismus und von der phantastischen Idee zu befreien, dass das deutsche Volk eine Herrenrasse sei."

„Grossbritannien, Russland, China, die Vereinigten Staaten und ihre Verbündeten vereinigen mehr als

drei Viertel der Gesamtbevölkerung der Erde. Solange diese vier Weltmächte mit ihrer grossen militärischen Macht in ihrem Entschluss zusammenstehen, den Frieden der Welt zu bewahren, wird es keinem angriffslustigen Land mehr möglich sein, einen neuen Weltkrieg zu entfesseln. Diese vier Weltmächte müssen jedoch mit allen freiheitsliebenden Völkern Europas, Asiens, Afrikas und des amerikanischen Kontinents zusammenstehen und zusammenwirken. Die Rechte jeder einzelnen Nation, gleichgültig ob gross oder klein, müssen geachtet und so sorgsam geschützt werden, wie die Rechte jedes Einzelnen innerhalb der Vereinigten Staaten von Amerika."

Franklin D. Roosevelt

U.S.G.34

and in bombing the reinforced-concrete pens in the French Atlantic ports of Brest, Lorient, and Saint-Nazaire. The reality was rather different. Heavy bombers destroyed these towns completely in the winter of 1942–43, leaving almost nothing standing, but the submarine pens remained undamaged.[32] Bombing of submarine production along the north German coast also did little to prevent the continued construction of submarines throughout the period. These operations exposed the often wide gap between expectations from bombing and the reality—an ambiguity that lay at the heart of the whole bomber offensive.

Britain and the United States were the only combatant powers to undertake long-term and large-scale offensives from the air. Under the leadership of Reichsmarschall Hermann Göring, the Luftwaffe had prioritized supporting ground operations and failed to develop a heavy four-engine bomber comparable with the American B-17 or

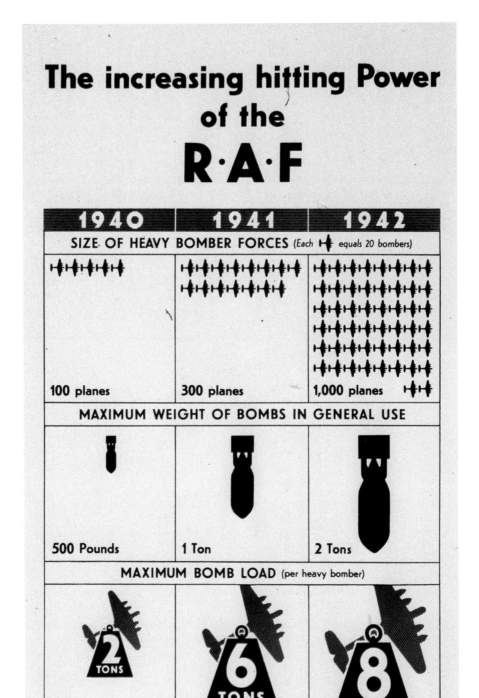

▲ GERMANY UNDER INCREASINGLY HEAVY BOMBING

The pattern from 1940 to 1942 was more bombers dropping bigger loads of more powerful bombs. Over the next two years the number of Bomber Command's planes and sorties continued to grow exponentially—from about two thousand sorties in December 1942 to a peak of more than twenty thousand in August 1944.

Allied bombing did not spare the French or Belgian civilians. Axis propaganda tried to turn that into an advantage by stirring up resentment against the British and the Americans, but the population of the occupied areas tended to blame Germany rather than the Allies for the damage incurred in a war that Hitler had initiated.

the British Lancaster. The quantity of bombs dropped in the Allied campaign utterly dwarfed the nine-month German Blitz against Britain: 1,900,000 tons throughout the war compared with 58,000 tons dropped by the German Air Force on Britain in 1940 and 1941.[33] The commitment to a bombing campaign as the principal way in which airpower should be exercised dated to the 1930s. The RAF had survived as an independent force after World War I partly because it was seen as a means to project force against a potential enemy without having to repeat the mass killings experienced in trench warfare on the Western Front. Airpower was seen as less expensive in manpower and more militarily efficient. In both Britain and the United States, the notion that the next war would be a "total war," waged between whole societies, mobilizing their economies and labor force to the full, encouraged the idea that bombing might undermine the enemy's economic fabric and create a broader social crisis. The strategic importance of the "vital centers" of the "social body" was taught at the U.S. Air Corps Tactical School in the 1930s, even though the Army Air Corps had no commitment to a strategic air force and, until 1939, no prospect of being allowed to order a fleet of strategic heavy bombers.[34]

When the threat of war became greater in Europe in the late 1930s, the RAF expected at some point to turn its bomber force against the industrial regions of Germany, and it began to plan the systematic bombardment of a range of critical industries—even though most British bomber aircraft could not even reach them from British bases.[35] When war finally came in September 1939, the RAF was impatient to begin an offensive against the German Ruhr-Rhineland area, where, so it argued, the heart of the Third Reich's war machine lay. When American air force planners were finally given the go-ahead in the summer of 1941 to contribute the air element of the Victory Program—a production and manpower plan called for by Roosevelt—they worked out a list of key targets in Germany's industrial economy on the basis that if they were all raided accurately, the campaign would critically undermine the Nazis' capacity to continue the war.[36]

In both countries, air force leaders optimistically assumed, first, that targets could actually be found and destroyed permanently, and, second, that eroding a large and complex industrial economy could be achieved within a reasonable period of time. Almost all the history written about the bomber offensive confirms that these were illusions.[37] They rested on the fact that until World War II, there had been no large-scale air war—only a great deal of exaggerated theorizing about what aircraft might be capable of achieving. Airmen were keen to defend their new service from criticism by the army and the navy, and to present a definably distinct strategic option for war making. In doing so, they embraced the total-war argument that an enemy's civilian home front was a legitimate target for attack.

This was a radical departure in the history of modern war. There had been civilian damage in World War I when both sides undertook desultory and small-scale air raids, but nothing on the scale envisaged by the two Western air forces in World War II, which would inevitably result in high levels of damage and casualties in the urban areas subject to attack.[38] The issue of whether attacks that killed civilians were legal or not has been debated often since the end of the war, but the British Air Ministry and Chiefs of Staff had no doubt in 1939. Attacks on civilians as such were declared contrary to international law, as was any bombing of military targets in populated areas that would result in "negligent harm," including bombing at night or through cloud cover.[39] Since these restrictions severely limited what the RAF could do, it required a government decision to endorse bombing. On May 15, 1940, Churchill's War Cabinet finally gave approval for raids on German targets (chiefly oil and communications) in which civilians would be at risk, since the bombing was undertaken at night.[40] Over the following year, the rules governing RAF bombing were relaxed gradually, until a directive on July 9, 1941, ordered RAF Bomber Command, led by Air Chief Marshal Sir Richard Peirse, to bomb urban centers in order to undermine the morale of industrial workers.[41]

BRITAIN'S AIR OFFENSIVE

BERLIN BY NIGHT

Britain's giant 4-engine bombers over the German capital. Military objectives in Berlin have been attacked by the Royal Air Force on more than 50 occasions.

▲ BRITISH STRATEGIC BOMBING

This was how Bomber Command wanted the British population to think of the air attacks on Berlin: surgically accurate strikes on "military objectives," including German war industries. In reality, bombs were dropped from high altitude, and more hit residential areas than factories.

Arthur Harris, known by the popular nickname "Butch," commanded RAF Bomber Command through its campaign of "area" bombing of German city centers from 1942 until the end of the war. Harris left school in England at the age of sixteen to travel to the colony of Rhodesia (now Zimbabwe), where he found work farming and mining. He returned to Britain in early 1915 to join the infant Royal Flying Corps. Harris stayed on in the recently formed Royal Air Force in 1919 and was one of the air officers responsible for introducing and operating empire "air policing" in India and Iraq. In 1939 he was made commander in chief of 5 Group, Bomber Command, but by the end of 1940, Harris had become deputy chief of staff. Churchill's dissatisfaction with the head of Bomber Command, Sir Richard Peirse, led to the decision in January 1942 to appoint Harris in his place. A man of notoriously outspoken views, Harris was a risky choice, but his early months in office showed that he was determined to expand and conserve his force for the task he had been directed to fulfill: destroying Germany's industrial cities systematically. Over the three years in which he held office, Harris persisted in this aim, even when the evidence suggested that the effects on the German economy and the morale of the German people were far less than hoped for. With great reluctance, he gave up control of his bomber force to U.S. General Dwight D. Eisenhower (the commander of the Supreme Headquarters Allied Expeditionary Force, or SHAEF) in March 1944 for the coming Normandy campaign. Starting in September 1944, Bomber Command undertook its heaviest attacks against many smaller German cities, including Dresden. Harris was criticized by many, among them Churchill, for persisting with area bombing, and he spent his long retirement after 1945 defending his record until his death almost thirty years later.

The British decision to permit operations previously regarded as illegal was defended on the grounds that the German Air Force had regularly bombed civilians and that there was no other way to bring home the war to the German population. The new strategy of city bombing was intended to contribute to the British economic warfare strategy by killing and maiming workers, destroying their housing and amenities, and forcing high levels of absenteeism. Although these aims were designed to make it look as though bombing was not indiscriminate, in practice that was the result, when whole city centers were destroyed and their populations killed.[42] Beginning in early 1942, regular attacks were also permitted on industrial targets in German-occupied Europe in the knowledge that this would kill French or Belgian or Dutch civilians, but it was approved because bombing was supposed to encourage workers in occupied areas not to labor for the Germans. As war went on, bombing civilians came to be regarded as morally expedient, to make victory more certain. American airmen seem to have been worried much less about the moral issue when the Eighth Air Force began its campaign, because it was assumed that U.S. strategic bombers could hit industrial targets with sufficient precision and at the risk of only limited civilian collateral damage. American bombing directives, unlike British, never specified German civilian workers and the civilian milieu as the intended targets.[43]

There were many problems confronting the early bombing campaign. Despite the central commitment to bombing Germany's industrial cities to undermine production and morale, RAF Bomber Command found itself compelled to undertake a wide range of other operations in response to requests from the War Cabinet or the Chiefs of Staff. Bombers were asked to help with the Battle of the Atlantic in the spring of 1941 and again in the winter of 1942–43, diverting aircraft away from Germany. Churchill, keen to use bombing as a political instrument, approved attacks on Italy beginning in June 1940, because Italian morale was considered to be much more fragile than that of the German people.[44] Bombing Germany was also supposed to bring a possible political dividend by creating unrest against the Hitler regime, though there was no evidence to support this expectation.

The absence of a consistent strategy was exacerbated by operational and technical deficiencies. Until the summer of 1942, Bomber Command was equipped largely with medium bombers, with a limited range and bomb load. They had no electronic navigation aid until the spring of 1942, an ineffective bombsight, and bombs that often failed to detonate. An investigation of bombing accuracy carried out in August 1941 resulted in the so-called "Butt Report," named after the economist who carried out the survey, which showed that only one in five of all bombers came within *five miles* of the assigned target.[45] The Air Ministry responded by abandoning any pretense of precision and ordering aircraft to carry a high proportion of incendiaries to drop on the crowded residential areas of cities; accuracy was less of an issue here, since aircraft could simply drop bombs on the fires ahead of them. This policy greatly increased damage to city areas, but it did not greatly reduce the productive performance of German industry in 1942–43.[46]

It is often argued that two factors in early 1942 made a real difference to the campaign: the appointment of Air Marshal Arthur Harris as commander in chief of Bomber Command on February 22, and the arrival in Britain of the first units of the USAAF Eighth Air Force in April.[47] Harris, however, did not originate the policy of making the German working-class population the principal target. That decision was made in a directive issued on February 14, 1942, just before he took over. He stuck to this idea for the rest of the war, resisting every effort to divert his force to other targets or to work out a more strategically coherent set of objectives. The only measure of success became the acreage of city area burnt out by the bombers, though there was no way of knowing how much this affected the German war economy.[48] Similarly, Harris did oversee the implementation of a "Pathfinder" scheme in which a dedicated group of skilled pilots used flares to mark the target for the oncoming bomber stream to ensure that the right city could be found. But this improvement was imposed on Bomber Command over Harris's strong objections, not something he championed. (He preferred the idea of using the best pilots in each bomber group to guide the rest of the unit onto the target, rather than creating a special elite force.) On the other hand, Harris does deserve credit for changing the tactics employed on operations by insisting on greater concentration of the bomber force in space and time so that it could deliver its incendiary load rapidly and overwhelm German defenses. This increased the level of devastation inflicted and also helped reduce losses to his crews.[49]

All this time, the German Air Force was constantly improving its air defenses.

BRITISH NIGHT BOMBING ▶

Like the British during the London Blitz, German civil defense officials used propaganda posters to aid public awareness. Here, a Wagnerian scene reminds Germans to keep their blackout shades closed to hinder British night bombers.

GENERAL CARL "TOOEY" SPAATZ
1891–1974

Carl Spaatz was the highest-ranking American air force officer in the European theater of World War II, and the architect of the U.S. Army Air Forces' bomber campaign against the Axis powers. He worked on the staff of Frank Andrews, commander of the GHQ (General Headquarters) Air Force in the late 1930s, where he was exposed to ideas on the value of strategic bombing promoted by the Air Corps Tactical School. It was during this period that the Pennsylvania native changed his surname from the German-sounding Spatz by adding an "a."

He joined General Arnold's staff in October 1940 and became chief of staff of the Air Corps in July 1941. In January 1942 Spaatz's wide experience made him an obvious choice to lead Air Force Combat Command. In May 1942 he assumed command not only of the Eighth Air Force based in England but also of other U.S. air forces in the theater. In December he was transferred to the Mediterranean to support Eisenhower as commander of the Allied Northwest African Air Forces and then of the renamed Mediterranean Allied Air Forces. In January 1944 Spaatz was finally restored to full command of all U.S. Strategic Air Forces in Europe and able to coordinate the bombing of Axis targets from Italy and from England.

Spaatz believed that destroying the Luftwaffe was an essential precondition for a successful invasion. He ordered the bombing of the German aircraft industry and oil, while U.S. fighter aircraft destroyed German airpower over German soil. At the end of the war in Europe, he was transferred to the Pacific. In February 1946 Spaatz became the commanding general of the Army Air Forces, succeeding Henry Arnold, and in September 1947 President Harry Truman named him the first chief of staff of the new U.S. Air Force.

As in Britain during the Blitz, defense against night bombing was not easy. General Josef Kammhuber was given the task of setting up a line of searchlights, antiaircraft guns, and night fighters across northern Europe—from Denmark, to northern France, and eventually as far south as the Swiss border—which took a rising toll of attacking bombers. German radar was used to pinpoint a night fighter onto a bomber, and over the following years, an electronic war was fought out between the Allied radio scientists and the German communications research establishment, as each side tried to break the other's electronic guidance system.[50]

The arrival of the Eighth Air Force also made little difference at first. The USAAF commander in chief, General Henry "Hap" Arnold, was able to get approval for an American air offensive against the Axis powers consistent with air force ideas about attacking the "vital centers." Unlike the British, the American air force's Air War Plans Division (AWPD) drew up a detailed strategic program in August 1941, AWPD-1, and then a second plan in September 1942, AWPD-42.[51] The object was to undertake high-level "precision" daylight bombing using the Boeing B-17 Flying Fortress and the Consolidated B-24 Liberator against a series of target systems deemed vital to Germany's military-economic war effort: the aircraft industry, rubber, chemicals, ball bearings, submarines, and vehicle manufacturers. Neither Arnold nor the first commander of the Eighth, General Carl Spaatz, realized how long it would take to create a major strategic air force. Training, supplying aircraft, building air bases, and gaining experience all took time.

The first U.S. raid took place on August 17, 1942, pitting a handful of aircraft against a target in the French town of Rouen. But no German target was raided until

January 27, 1943, and heavy raids on industrial objectives developed only in the late summer and autumn of 1943.[52] It was soon found that accuracy was difficult to achieve from high levels in a geographical region in which cloud was much more common than clear weather, and where planes were under constant danger from antiaircraft fire and defending fighters. American airmen had assumed that flying by day and using the advanced Norden bombsight would make it possible to bomb with a precision that was impossible for British bombers flying at night, which sometimes found it hard to identify an entire city. But in the end, operational conditions made it inevitable that American airmen would have to bomb through cloud and haze and from high altitude to avoid antiaircraft fire. By late 1944, over 75 percent of all U.S. bombing was done blind, using the H2X radar navigation aid. This was a modification of the British H2S radar, introduced in 1943, which helped Bomber Command to find and concentrate on a large city area. But it still left 50 percent of the bombs outside the three-mile target zone, even by 1944.[53]

▲ AVRO LANCASTER

The four-engine Lancaster was the workhorse of the RAF's night-bombing campaign. British factories churned out more than seven thousand of these large planes, each of which was capable of delivering a bomb load of up to fourteen thousand pounds. Specially modified Lancasters were used to drop twenty-two-thousand-pound "Grand Slam" bombs on hard targets like fortified submarine pens.

THE COMBINED BOMBER OFFENSIVE

Bombing became more effective only when the two air forces were given clear strategic guidelines. At the Casablanca Conference—held in Morocco among Churchill,

Roosevelt, and the combined chiefs of staff from January 14 to 24, 1943—a directive was drawn up for the bombing campaign to undertake the progressive dislocation of the German military-economic home front, and to undermine the morale of the workforce.[54] Although the Casablanca Directive reinforced strategies that were already in operation, the purpose of the bombing was linked directly to the Allied plans for the invasion of mainland Europe. The object was to limit Germany's military capability so that the ground forces could invade occupied and Axis Europe with a better chance of success. Only on this basis could the armies and navies of the two Allies be persuaded to support a bombing offensive at all, since Allied leaders were skeptical that airpower alone could deliver victory. The chiefs of staff insisted that the attack on Germany should be a joint effort, despite the differences between day and night bombing, and the strategy became the Combined Bomber Offensive (CBO).

In June 1943 the offensive was finally given a detailed set of instructions known as the "Pointblank Directive." It permitted Harris to carry on the area bombing of people and houses, while the new commander of the U.S. Eighth Air Force, Lieutenant General Ira Eaker (who replaced Spaatz in November 1942), was to attack industrial target systems and the "intermediate" target of the German Air Force and its support structure.[55] A second offensive, separate from the CBO, was to be conducted against Italy, partly because it was believed—correctly, in this case—that the Fascist political

system was in crisis, and partly because the Allies agreed at Casablanca that they would invade Sicily and Italy first before launching what became Operation Overlord in 1944. Bomber Command carried out area raids on northern Italian industrial cities (Milan, Turin, and Genoa), while the U.S. Twelfth (later Fifteenth) Air Force attacked ports and communications. Italy had poor air defenses, no effective radar, few night fighters, and limited civil defense preparations. As a result, the bombing had a more damaging material and psychological impact than it had against Germany.[56]

The CBO was in truth a "parallel" offensive rather than a "combined" offensive. Bomber Command and the Eighth Air Force rarely collaborated. Harris undertook a separate Battle of the Ruhr in spring and early summer 1943; and then a Battle of Hamburg in late July and early August (to which the Eighth contributed two small raids); and, finally, a Battle of Berlin, starting in November 1943.[57] Bomber Command was now a much larger force, able to put up to a thousand bombers in the air, most of them the heavy four-engine Avro Lancaster, which could carry up to eighteen thousand pounds of bombs. The bomber stream was led by Pathfinder forces armed with the new, fast Mosquito bomber, which used flares and incendiaries to light up the city center to be bombed; the main force would then follow up with larger bombs, such as the four-thousand-pound blockbuster or large oil-based incendiaries. Harris persisted with heavy area bombing because he still hoped that it might end the war before Overlord, thus validating his argument that airpower was decisive. He tried to use the destructive raids on Hamburg in late July 1943, where an estimated 37,000 people were killed, to strengthen his case for city bombing as the key to victory.[58] Nevertheless it was difficult to evaluate the effects of the damage to war production or to civilian morale, and although Bomber Command raids became more accurate and destructive, the impact on the German enemy remained speculative.

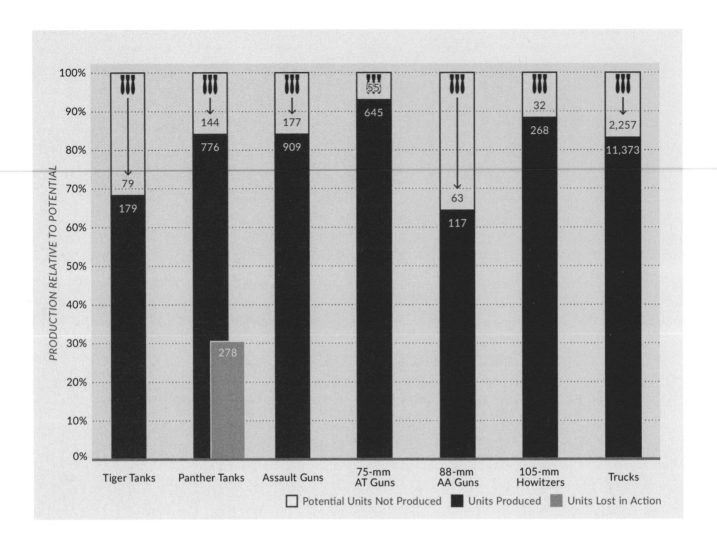

| | Potential Units Not Produced | Units Produced | Units Lost in Action |

THE EFFECT OF BOMBING ▲ ON GERMAN WAR PRODUCTION

It was and is impossible to measure precisely how much more productive German factories would have been if they had not been subject to the Combined Bomber Offensive. Allied bombing reduced output in many ways beyond direct damage to factories: air raids and even false alarms deprived workers of sleep and made them less efficient, injuries and damage to homes increased absenteeism, and damage to parts suppliers or to the transportation system could idle a factory. Nonetheless, the German Army did conduct a study to estimate how much armaments production had been reduced by Allied bombing during the last quarter of 1943. The results (shown above) were intended to reflect the minimum losses to production, but even so they total enough to equip an entire new Panzer Army. Note the especially large reductions to production of the vital 88-millimeter guns and Tiger tanks.

Eighth Air Force was less ambitious, but as the force grew in size, American air force commanders hoped that it could inflict decisive damage on key industries. In August 1943 and again in October, Eighth conducted major raids against German ball bearing production at Schweinfurt, which had been identified as a key bottleneck industry serving all the German armaments firms. The raids, however, took exceptional losses, with the August 17 raid alone costing 31 percent of the force. Eaker was compelled to suspend major operations at just the time that Harris was facing loss rates of 8 percent to 10 percent each night.[59] German defenses had improved substantially over the course of 1943, and the defending fighter and night-fighter force was larger than ever, with around three-quarters of all fighters now stationed to combat the raids and concentrated belts of antiaircraft guns around vulnerable industrial targets. Although the Allies could not know it, war production in Germany expanded almost threefold between 1941 and 1944, despite the bombs. By the end of 1943, it seemed unlikely that

ESCORT FIGHTER RANGES ▶

Before the arrival of the P-47 and P-51, losses to RAF and USAAF bomber aircrew were becoming intolerably high. The new American planes turned the tables on the German fighter force and practically drove it from the skies.

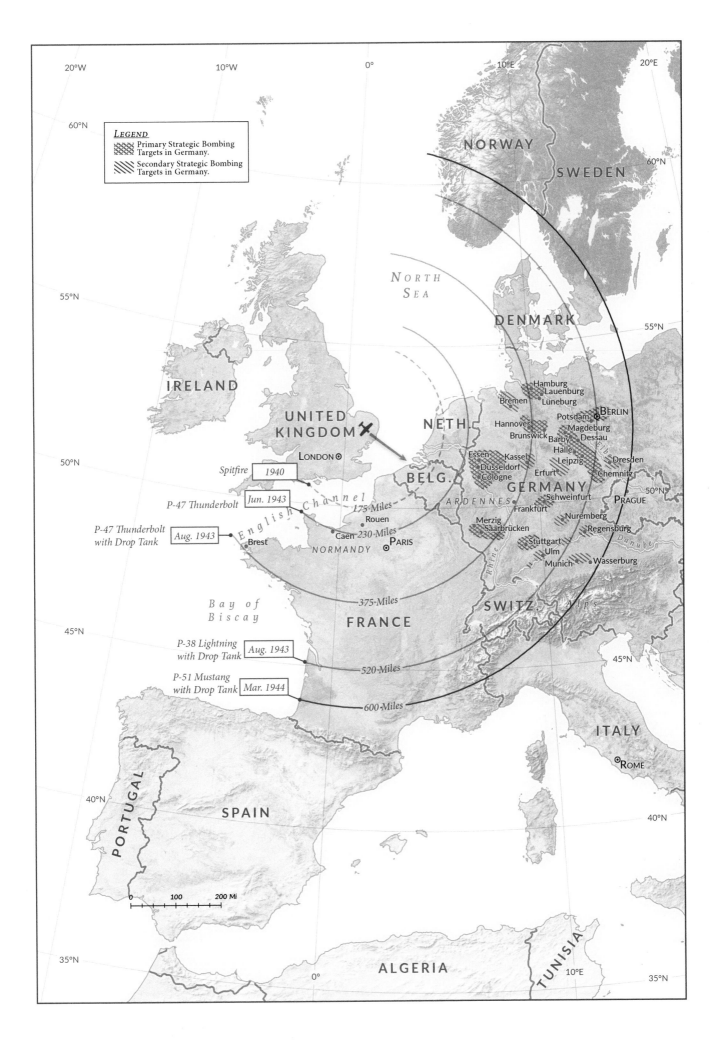

20°W
10°W
0°
10°E
20°E

60°N
55°N
50°N
45°N
40°N
35°N

NORWAY
SWEDEN
DENMARK

NORTH SEA

IRELAND

UNITED KINGDOM

LONDON

NETH.

BELG.

Hamburg
Lauenburg
Lüneburg
Bremen
BERLIN
Potsdam
Hannover
Magdeburg
Brunswick
Barby
Dessau
Halle
Essen
Kassel
Leipzig
Dresden
Dusseldorf
Cologne
Erfurt
Chemnitz
Schweinfurt
PRAGUE
Frankfurt

GERMANY

ARDENNES

175 Miles

Rouen
230 Miles
Caen
PARIS
NORMANDY

Merzig
Saarbrücken
Nuremberg
Regensburg
Danube
Stuttgart
Ulm
Munich
Wasserburg

Spitfire 1940
P-47 Thunderbolt Jun. 1943
P-47 Thunderbolt
with Drop Tank Aug. 1943
Brest

English Channel

375 Miles

SWITZ.
Alps

Bay of
Biscay

FRANCE

P-38 Lightning
with Drop Tank Aug. 1943
520 Miles

P-51 Mustang
with Drop Tank Mar. 1944
600 Miles

ITALY

ROME

PORTUGAL

SPAIN

0   100   200 Mi

ALGERIA

TUNISIA

0°
10°E

One of the few survivors of the Luftwaffe's defeat to write his postwar memoir, Heinz Knoke was commander of 11 Fighter Wing (II/JG.11) in the spring of 1944 when the U.S. Eighth Air Force launched its concentrated attack on the Luftwaffe using long-range fighters and bomb attacks on the aircraft industry. Knoke witnessed firsthand the attrition of German airpower in the face of large numbers of American fighters. His memoir is based on a diary he kept during the war years, and this extract comes from an entry in April 1944.

April 29, 1944

1130 hours: off to the west and below I spot the first vapour trails. They are Lightnings [P-38]. In a few minutes, they are directly below, followed by the heavy bombers. These are strung out in an immense chain as far as the eye can reach. Thunderbolts [P-47s] and Mustangs [P-51s] wheel and spiral overhead and alongside.

Then our Focke-Wulfs [Fw190s] sweep right into them. At once, I peel off and dive into the Lightning below. They spot us and swing round towards us to meet the attack. A pack of Thunderbolts, about thirty in all, also come wheeling in towards us from the south. This is exactly what I wanted . . . Then we are in a madly milling dog-fight. Our job is done; it is a case of every man for himself. I remain on the tail of a Lightning for several minutes. It flies like the devil himself, turning, diving, and climbing almost like a rocket. I am never able to fire more than a few pot-shots.

Then a flight of Mustangs dives past. Tracers whistle close by my head. I pull back the stick with both hands, and the plane climbs steeply out of the way. My wingman, Sergeant Drühe, remains close to my tail.

Once again I have a chance to fire at a Lightning. My salvoes register at last. Smoke billows out of the right engine. I have to break away, however. Glancing back, I see that I have eight Thunderbolts sitting on my tail. The enemy tracers again come whistling past my head.

Evidently my opponents are old hands at the game. I turn and dive and climb and roll and loop and spin. I use the methanol emergency booster, and try to get away in my favourite "corkscrew climb." In only a few seconds, the bastards are right back on my tail. They keep on firing all the time. I do not know how they just miss me but they do . . . My fuel indicator needle registers zero. The red light starts to flicker its warning. Ten more minutes only, and my tank will be empty. I go down in a tight spiral dive. The Thunderbolts break away . . . Suddenly the wingman beside me flicks his aircraft round and vanishes into the cloudbank.

So what the hell? . . .

In a flash I glance round, and then instinctively duck my head. There is a Thunderbolt sitting right on my tail, followed by seven more. All eight open fire. Their salvoes slam into my plane. My right wing bursts into flames.

I spiral off to the left into the clouds. A shadow looms ahead: it is a Thunderbolt. I open fire. Its tail is soon in flames . . . The ground comes up with a rush. Too late for me to bail out now. I cross some large fields. Down goes the nose, and the plane settles. The flames come up reaching for my face. Earth flies into the air. There is a dull, heavy thud. The crate skids along in a cloud of dust, then digs its own grave in the soft earth. I throw up my arms to cover my face, and brace my legs against the rudder bar. It is all over in a split second. Something crashes with stunning force on to my head.

So this must be the end! It is my last thought before losing consciousness . . .[60]

Pointblank would be able to deliver the kind of damage that the army and navy would need if Overlord was to work.

THE "BATTLE OF GERMANY"

A solution was found by the USAAF, now under the supreme command of General Spaatz, who had been made commander in chief of all American strategic and tactical air forces in Europe in January 1944.[61] The American strategy had always insisted that the defeat of Germany's Air Force was a precondition for the success of Pointblank, and therefore of Overlord. Spaatz realized that this had not been achieved by early 1944 and made it a priority for the Eighth Air Force, in the months running up to the invasion of France, to take the battle for air supremacy into German airspace and inflict a decisive defeat on the German Air Force. Under the new commander of the Eighth Air Force, Lieutenant General James Doolittle, an extensive campaign was launched from February 1944 onward to destroy the German fighter force and the Luftwaffe's supply chain in time for the invasion, using the fighter wing of the Eighth Air Force and the Ninth Tactical Air Force to inflict the damage. Historians seeking to highlight the contribution of airpower to the success of Operation Overlord have often focused on the importance of the so-called Transportation Plan, approved in March 1944, which diverted temporarily the Allied bombing efforts to focus on rail communications in northern France and the Low Countries rather than industrial targets in Germany. But there is a compelling argument to be made that it was not the bombers that made the most important air contribution to the defeat of Germany but rather the Eighth Air Force Fighter Command, under the fiery and audacious General William Kepner, together with the Ninth Tactical Air Force, which from February to June 1944 kept up a relentless attrition of German airpower over the Reich.[62] What might be called the "Battle of Germany"—the mirror image of the "Battle of Britain" in 1940—was about establishing air superiority in enemy airspace by destroying the German fighter force, German air bases, and the supply of aircraft. It would be, as Spaatz told Doolittle, the "critical deciding factor in Germany's defeat."[63]

The primary factor that allowed the American air forces to overwhelm German air defense was the long-range fighter. Although Arnold had identified the lack of such an aircraft as the key gap in Allied air armament in 1942, the option of fitting additional fuel tanks to American fighter planes took a long time to be realized. Eaker was convinced that large fleets of B-17s and B-24s were armed heavily enough to defend themselves. But the mauling given to American raids in the autumn of 1943 finally made it clear just how badly the Allies needed fighter support over Germany. The Republic P-47 Thunderbolt and the Lockheed P-38 Lightning were both given drop tanks that could at last take them deep into German airspace. The aircraft that really transformed American airpower, however, was the North American Aviation P-51 Mustang fighter. Fitted with a British Rolls-Royce Merlin engine in 1943, its performance outdid any other fighter available, and in 1944, extra fuel tanks extended its combat range beyond Berlin. A crash production program was pushed through, and the P-51 began to appear in large numbers by the early spring. Even without the Mustang, the longer escort made possible by the P-47 and P-38 transformed the air battle.[64] The first bombing raids accompanied by long-range fighters, in December and January of 1943, confirmed that enemy fighters were best fought by fighters, not by massed bombers. Kepner told fighter pilots to adopt a tactic of "Free Lance," which allowed them to pursue German aircraft at will rather than tie themselves to the bomber stream, and had them strafe any air bases they passed on the return leg. Even when there was no bombing raid, Kepner began sending out long-range fighters on combat missions against German air force targets.

The outcome of the "Battle of Germany" was not a foregone conclusion. The

One of many bomber pilots who experienced damaging fighter attacks, Lieutenant Graves served with the 94th Bombardment Group, Eighth Air Force, in 1944. Here he describes a mission over French territory after the landings in Normandy in June 1944 to drop not bombs but resources for the French Resistance fighters. By this stage, the Luftwaffe in the West was very weak but still able to inflict damage. Graves was fortunate to survive the loss of two engines in his B-17 Flying Fortress.

Everything is the same. You lie there half asleep, half awake, expecting it to happen but hoping it will not. Then it happens, the crunch of footsteps in the gravel coming closer and closer, the door of the quanset opens, a voice calls out "Graves," and you know you're on for today's mission. Rise and shine at 0100 hours and go through the routine of shower, shave, dress. Trying not to think too much of what the day might hold for you. Emerge into the dark English morning and continue the routine.

The scene in the briefing room this morning is the same as many others. A lot of nervous small talk and private thinking. A call to attention, and things start moving. Immediately we are made aware that this one is different. No bombs today. Today we are flying supplies and munitions to the Free French in southern France. A mission of mercy instead of destruction. A "piece of cake," since the invasion was already in progress [Normandy Invasion, June 1944], having been launched 20 days ago, and part of the mission will be over occupied territory... Briefing over, watches synchronized, equipment checked out, and a short jeep trip to the hard stand, where the mighty B-17 Flying Fortress stands at the ready, thanks to the ground crew having spent much of yesterday and most of the night healing her wounds and coaxing her back to good health after yesterday's mission into Germany...

Take off at 0345 hours into the first light of dawn over the English countryside. Form into a flight of three, meld into position with three other flights to form a squadron, always in a gradual climb to altitude, and in time to join forces with two other squadrons to form the group. Other groups, having formed in like manner, will follow at intervals to complete the Wing. This operation must rate high on the list of well-orchestrated, finely coordinated mass efforts of all times... As we leave the south coast of England and head out over water, the signal is given to test fire the guns, after which we settle down to staying in position in the formation and keeping all eyes on the sky for "Bandits."

We cross the French coast at 0723 hours. Beyond Caen, and the relative safety of being over Allied occupied territory, the group is hit by German fighters, one of which seems to have a fascination for our position in the formation. It is hypnotic to watch a plane closing in on you with its guns winking at you as it comes closer and closer. You are drawn to it, you must ignore it. Stay in formation. Let the gunners worry about that. Suddenly the plane is rocked by the force of an explosion. A shell has detonated between Nos. 1 and 2 engines, putting them both out of commission—a split-second difference, and the wing could have been gone.

The procedure is well known. Feather the propellers to reduce drag, increase power on the good engines to compensate for the loss of half of your power, stabilize the 'plane, drop out of formation, and call for a crew check to assess damage to crew and plane. With the realization that we are still flyable comes the decision to chuck anything we can spare to reduce weight and help maintain altitude. This is done in record time, and includes unbolting the ball turret and dropping it on the French landscape... Freed of this weight, and having decided we would not try the long trip back to base over water, we head in search of a fighter strip we can land on.[65]

German aircraft industry was turning out more than 1,500 fighters a month in 1944; the air defense units in the west had more than 1,000 operational fighters; and there were 5,325 heavy and 9,359 light antiaircraft guns pointing skyward in Germany, aided by a sophisticated radar network.[66] Yet these figures disguise some important weaknesses. Shortages of fuel and training resources cut the number of practice hours for German trainee pilots from 210 hours in 1942 to 112 in 1944, and operational training with the combat squadrons was reduced 50 percent.[67] Around one-quarter

of the German fighters were twin-engine Messerschmitt Me110s and Me410s, armed with cannon designed to hit the bombers. Against fast single-engine fighters, they were easy prey. The German single-engine force was ordered by General Adolf Galland, the general of fighters, to attack the American raids with up to 150 aircraft. But not only did this mean losing time while the groups assembled, it also played into Allied hands. American escorts, now numbering as many as 700 to 800 fighters, were looking for large-scale air combat so as to impose insupportable attrition levels, and intelligence intercepts allowed them to arrive in large numbers over the German assembly points.[68]

Spaatz also ordered a campaign against the aircraft industry, undertaken in what was called "Big Week" from February 19 to 26, 1944, but its effects were limited because much of the aircraft industry had already been dispersed to safer sites. In March Spaatz wanted to attack oil as a primary target to cut the output of aviation fuel. And though many of his planes were occupied by the Transportation Plan at the time, Spaatz was able to get the Fifteenth Air Force (stationed by then in Italy, following that country's surrender on September 8, 1943) to attack oil targets in Romania and southern Germany. He was eventually allowed to do the same from bases in England.[69] These bombing campaigns certainly made some difference to German Air Force performance, but the real impact was made by the fighter force. American fighter groups

▲ THE AFTERMATH
OF BOMBING

The Combined Bomber Offensive had a devastating effect on Germany's urban centers and civilian population. Civilian deaths as a result of strategic bombing mounted into the hundreds of thousands.

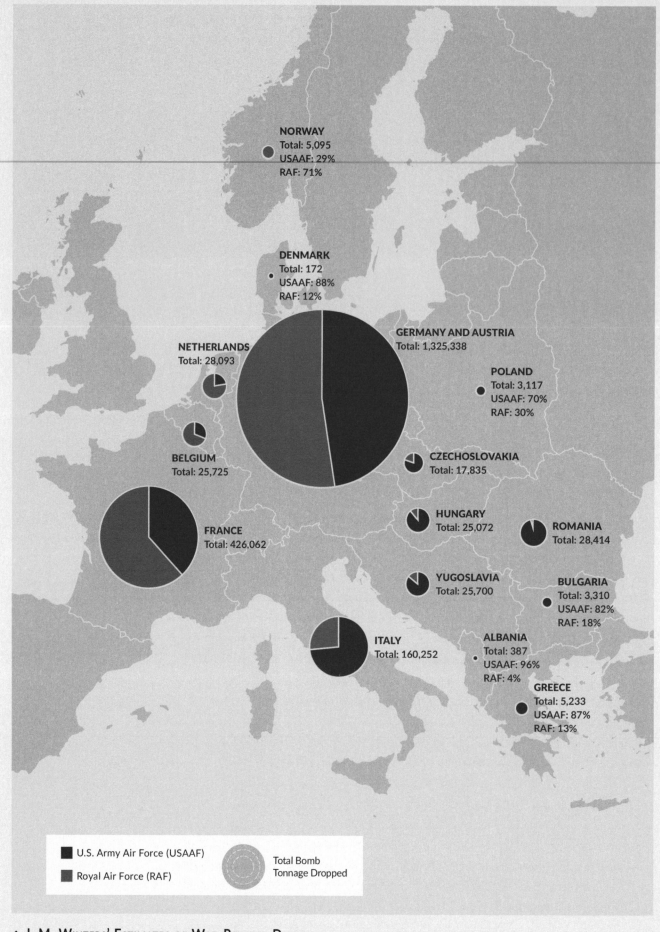

NORWAY
Total: 5,095
USAAF: 29%
RAF: 71%

DENMARK
Total: 172
USAAF: 88%
RAF: 12%

GERMANY AND AUSTRIA
Total: 1,325,338

NETHERLANDS
Total: 28,093

POLAND
Total: 3,117
USAAF: 70%
RAF: 30%

BELGIUM
Total: 25,725

CZECHOSLOVAKIA
Total: 17,835

HUNGARY
Total: 25,072

ROMANIA
Total: 28,414

FRANCE
Total: 426,062

YUGOSLAVIA
Total: 25,700

BULGARIA
Total: 3,310
USAAF: 82%
RAF: 18%

ITALY
Total: 160,252

ALBANIA
Total: 387
USAAF: 96%
RAF: 4%

GREECE
Total: 5,233
USAAF: 87%
RAF: 13%

■ U.S. Army Air Force (USAAF)

■ Royal Air Force (RAF)

Total Bomb
Tonnage Dropped

▲ J. M. Winters' Estimates of War-Related Deaths

It is impossible to calculate even *military* war-related deaths accurately, and different historians and demographers give quite different numbers. Estimates for civilian deaths must be even more approximate. Nonetheless, this data visualization gives at least a rough idea of the relative costs of the war for the belligerent nations.

suffered high losses because of the scale of combat, but the German fighter force was decimated, losing some 43 percent of its strength in April 1944 and 50.4 percent in May. Between January and June 1944, the German Air Force lost 9,867 aircraft, most of them fighters defending in Western Europe, more than the total of 9,400 produced.[70] This rate of attrition could not be supported, and new production was simply sucked into a downward spiral. For the rest of the war, American long-range fighters and fighter-bombers roamed far and wide over Germany and occupied territory, destroying bases, runways, and thousands of aircraft caught on the ground.

The defeat of the German Air Force over German territory immediately eased the pressure exerted by German forces on all three major fighting fronts. The diversion of aircraft and guns to protect against the bombing had already denuded the Russian and Italian fronts of air units. And the defeat of the fighter force ensured that Overlord would be carried out with minimum intervention from German aircraft.[71] When the bombing offensive resumed in September 1944, after Eisenhower released the bomber forces from the direct control he had exercised during the campaign in France, the German air defense system was no longer able put up a fight. Bomber Command reestablished its bombardment of German cities, and the Eighth and Fifteenth Air Forces established continuous daytime bombing of oil, air force, and transportation targets in Germany and across Eastern Europe. The German jet aircraft, the Messerschmitt Me262 and the Heinkel He162, came into service in the last weeks of 1944, too late and in quantities too small to make any difference.[72]

In the last eight months of the war, British and American air forces dropped almost three-quarters of the wartime bomb total on Germany and killed around half of the Germans who died in the bombing. The USAAF had over 5,000 heavy bombers and 5,000 fighters in the European theater; Bomber Command had around 1,400 aircraft.[73] The result was that strategic bombing began at last to have serious effects on Germany's war effort. Oil supply fell by 65 percent over the course of the year. Between September 1944 and January 1945, German rail freight traffic fell by almost half.[74] Gradually the raids merged with the operations of the tactical air forces in support of the advancing Allied fronts. The devastating RAF raid on Dresden on February 13–14, 1945, in which a firestorm killed 25,000 people, was undertaken at Churchill's insistence to help the advancing Red Army.[75] On the Western Front, heavy bombers hit German Army troop concentrations and transportation until they were simply churning up the ruins. By this stage, all bombing produced diminishing returns.

THE BOMBING ACHIEVEMENT

There has been persistent argument ever since the bombing ended over its strategic worth. Postwar surveys by the Americans and the British concluded that area bombing by Bomber Command contributed relatively little to undermining the German military effort, though it did lead to the diversion of German resources for defense

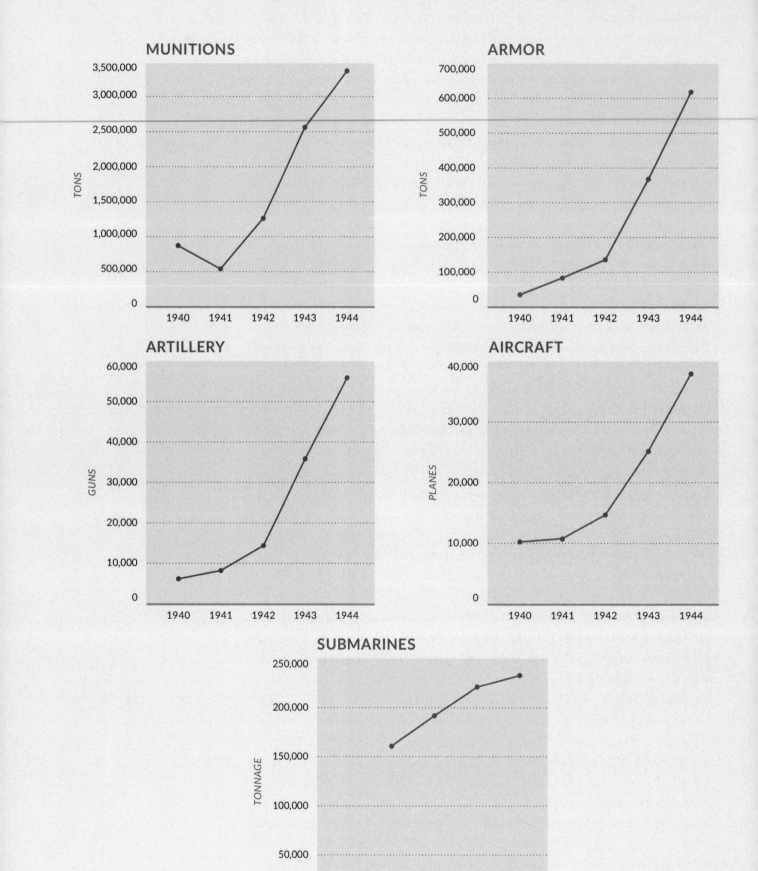

MUNITIONS

TONS

3,500,000
3,000,000
2,500,000
2,000,000
1,500,000
1,000,000
500,000
0

1940 1941 1942 1943 1944

ARMOR

TONS

700,000
600,000
500,000
400,000
300,000
200,000
100,000
0

1940 1941 1942 1943 1944

ARTILLERY

GUNS

60,000
50,000
40,000
30,000
20,000
10,000
0

1940 1941 1942 1943 1944

AIRCRAFT

PLANES

40,000
30,000
20,000
10,000
0

1940 1941 1942 1943 1944

SUBMARINES

TONNAGE

250,000
200,000
150,000
100,000
50,000
0

1940 1941 1942 1943 1944

and forced German industry to adopt dispersal policies, which had at least some effect on productive performance.[76] Overall loss of potential production was assessed at just 2.7 percent in the heavily bombed cities, though some recent literature has challenged this largely negative judgment on the effectiveness of bombing. When American bombing of target systems was added in, the loss was calculated at 9 percent of potential planned output in 1943 and 17 percent in 1944.[77] Nevertheless, German military output continued to expand until September 1944, reaching a level more than three times greater than in 1941. All the senior German officials and officers interrogated in 1945 confirmed that attacks on oil, the fighter force, and transportation were the three critical factors in the air war against Germany, and modern research has confirmed these conclusions.[78] The diversion of resources to combat the Allied bombing was also an evident drain on Germany's military effort, absorbing one-fifth of all ammunition and one-third of all electronic and optical equipment.

At the political level, however, it is evident that German morale was not broken in the way that the bomber commanders had hoped it would be. Germans were demoralized by the destruction of more than half the country's urban area and more than 350,000 deaths, but this did not produce social protest or political crisis. The longer the bombing went on, the more dependent the population became on the German state, and the less willing it became to challenge the National Socialist German Workers' Party's monopoly on power.[79]

In terms of Allied strategy, the effects of the bombing are open to question. Bombing certainly contributed to the decision of the Italian military leadership to overthrow Fascist Premier Benito Mussolini on July 25, 1943, and to surrender on September 8. But many other factors influenced the decision, including the Allies' successful invasion of Sicily.[80] In the case of Germany, it was not bombing as such but the successful fighter assaults on the Luftwaffe that eroded German airpower. It was also the fighters and fighter-bombers of the tactical air forces that disrupted German transportation in France prior to D-Day and then played a key role in the whole subsequent ground campaign. It can safely be said that without bombing, German resistance would certainly have been firmer, but if there had been no bombing, the Allied resources devoted to the CBO could have been diverted elsewhere. More vessels could have been produced to speed up the timetable of the cross-Channel invasion, as well as more army equipment and even more tactical aircraft to defeat the German Air Force at the front line rather than over Germany.

What is evident is that Bomber Command's ambitious idea—that the enemy could be defeated by paralyzing the civilian home front—did not work in Germany any more than it had worked in Britain during the Blitz. The enormous civilian cost in the loss of lives, serious injuries, and the destruction of homes did little to hasten German defeat. In the end, the bomber forces found there was no substitute for defeating the enemy's armed forces, a perennial truth in all modern wars. The bombers remained vulnerable to insupportable levels of attrition until the point when the strategic fighter

◀ Output of Main Classes of Weapons in Germany

The U.S. Strategic Bombing Survey, completed in 1946, argued that the "final breakdown of civilian morale in Germany was strategic bombing." Allied air forces killed and injured more than a million civilians, yet at the political level the bombings did not lead to social protest or political crisis in Germany. This chart shows how Allied air commanders saw the problem of morale.

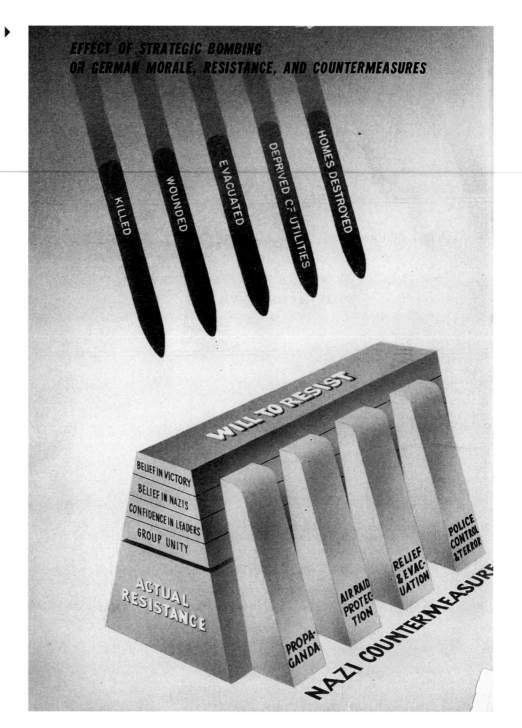

could escort them, like the naval vessels that escorted the merchant ships across the Atlantic.

The analogy of the aerial convoy and the marine convoy suggests that there was much in common between the naval and air strategies pursued by the United States and Britain. Both campaigns, in the air and at sea, were conducted in the most difficult combat conditions and exacted high casualties from the forces involved. German submariners were doomed when their vessels were hit, and out of 39,000 of them, 28,000 perished—a loss rate of 72 percent. Merchant seamen had to set out time after time across the ocean knowing that a single torpedo could plunge them into the icy Atlantic

water. Even in a lifeboat, survival was a matter of luck. Of the 55,800 crew members whose ships were sunk, 25,000 drowned.[81] Loss rates in the strategic air war were also high, both from accident and from combat. Flying was dangerous and uncomfortable, with flights often undertaken in poor weather or visibility, and in freezing cold at high altitudes. Like submariners, aircrews were often doomed once their ship was hit. Bomber Command lost 55,000 crew in all operations, 55 percent of all RAF dead during the war, with 8,195 of those losses coming from accidents. The American strategic air forces in Europe lost 30,099 in the European theater.[82] Both the sea and air campaigns demanded exceptional courage from those who fought in them.

The bombing of Germany was a dangerous business for the aircrew of the Eighth Air Force. A tour of duty for airmen flying heavy bombers was normally limited to twenty-five to thirty missions: General Ira Eaker considered that policy necessary to avoid "leaving clearly in the mind of the combat crewman the belief that he must go on until he cracks up and becomes a jibbering idiot or an admitted coward, or until he is killed." But that still represented a very high risk rate for aircrews, considering that (according to data collected in the summer of 1944) each time a B-17 flew out on a mission over Germany it had a one percent chance of not coming back. And even if a plane survived twenty-five missions, the odds were that at least one of its ten crewmen would first have been killed or wounded by enemy fire.

M2 Flak Vest with M4 Apron

About half of the heavy bombers shot down in the European theater were brought down by anti-aircraft fire, but flak also caused over 90 percent of the aircrew casualties on planes that made it home. Losses would have been even higher without the introduction of armor like the M2 flak vest with M4 apron that this aviator carries slung over his shoulder. Small manganese steel plates sewn between layers of canvas reduced the number of torso wounds by around 40 percent.

Electrically Heated Gloves

B-17 bombers flew at twenty to thirty thousand feet, and it got cold up there. Airmen commonly endured temperatures as low as negative 50 degrees Fahrenheit. In the early days of the Combined Bomber Offensive, frostbite of the hands accounted for one third of all Eighth Air Force casualties. By the end of 1943, improved equipment greatly reduced the problem: aircrew wore shearling mittens over electrically heated gloves over silk or rayon glove inserts.

West Point Class Ring, 1941

In the 1930s, graduates of the United States Military Academy had first call on the limited number of active-duty flying assignments in the Army Air Corps. As America rapidly expanded its military prior to entering the war, reserve officers came to outnumber those with Regular Army commissions in the USAAF—but in the top ranks, West Pointers like Hap Arnold, Joseph T. McNarney, Carl Spaatz, and Hoyt Vandenberg predominated.

Cold Weather Boots

In the piercing cold of high altitude, layering was key. It took two layers of wool socks, heated slippers, and rubber-treated, shearling-lined outer boots to keep feet warm.

The second factor that links the two campaigns was the necessity of finding some way of reducing the military threat posed by submarines and German air defenses. For all the talk of "total war" against the home front, military combat was decisive, and military solutions had to be found. Defeating the submarine wolf packs and smashing the German fighter forces would prove to be the two essential preconditions for the success of Allied ground armies in Europe, from Torch to Overlord. These campaigns eventually succeeded because of the depth of industrial capacity and the degree of scientific and technological ingenuity enjoyed by both the United States and Britain. But neither sea power nor airpower could win the war on its own. They were permissive elements in Allied strategy, making it possible for the armies to invade and defeat first Italy and then Germany. Only against Japan (as we will see in chapter 5) did the American air forces and Navy play a more decisive role in victory.

◀ U.S. Bomber Pilot

INTRODUCTION

Though the precise turning point to World War II may be difficult to pin down, there is little doubt that the Allies were winning the war by 1943. By this point, the Grand Alliance of the United States, Great Britain, and the Soviet Union enjoyed a decisive superiority over its Axis adversaries in every measure: manpower, natural resources, industrial production.

The Allied powers had one other crucial advantage: their increasing skill at coalition warfare, one of the most difficult of all military activities. In the course of 1943, the Allies (especially the Anglo-Americans) worked out policies and procedures that resulted in a relatively smooth cooperative effort. While not without their occasional flare-ups and disputes, the Allies managed to hold firm through difficult times, a process that was eased along by a series of high-level diplomatic conferences at Casablanca, Cairo, and Tehran.[1]

The first of these, at Casablanca in January 1943, was crucial to the events of the following year. Here the U.S. and British air forces agreed to prosecute a Combined Bomber Offensive against Germany, with the Americans bombing industrial targets by day and the British bombing German cities by night. Even more importantly, President Franklin D. Roosevelt and Prime Minister Winston Churchill announced to the world press that the Allies were fighting for nothing less than the "unconditional surrender" of the Axis powers. It was as clear a statement of war aims as military history has ever seen. It also stood in stark strategic contrast to the situation in the Axis camp. Never a particularly cohesive alliance in the first place, it fell apart altogether in the course of 1943 with the defection of Italy.[2]

Unconditional surrender was the goal, but how to get there was the problem. Casablanca saw the Allies agree to wrap up the ongoing Tunisian campaign and to clear North Africa of German and Italian forces. After that came question marks. Both the United States and Great Britain were committed to a cross-Channel invasion to strike directly into the heart of German power, but where, how, and exactly when they would land that blow were all still in the air. The Americans wanted it sooner rather than later; the British, just the opposite. Churchill in particular was wedded to a strategy of striking around the periphery of Axis-occupied Europe, and was already seeking to influence Roosevelt and U.S. military commanders in the same direction. Further campaigning in the Mediterranean—an invasion of the island of Sicily followed by a leap onto the Italian mainland—seemed to him to be the best options once the fighting in North Africa was over. U.S. strategists such as General George C. Marshall, by contrast, had no desire to devote any more resources than necessary to the Mediterranean. Marshall wanted to get to the main event as soon as possible: an amphibious invasion of Western Europe.

While historians often take sides in the debate, both Allied partners had solid reasons for their respective positions. The British were already becoming strapped for resources and manpower. They wanted to avoid a risky operation that might degenerate into a bloodbath of the sort they had suffered all too frequently in World War I.

Top map (Europe, North Africa, and Western Soviet Union):

57°N · 12°W · 1°30'W · 9°E · 19°30'E · 30°E · 51°

OSLO · NORWAY · STOCKHOLM · SWEDEN · ESTONIA · *Volga* · Demyansk · *Oct. 1943*

Moscow Conference · Moscow · LATVIA · Riga · LITHUANIA · Polotsk · Smolensk

NORTH SEA · DENMARK · Copenhagen · BALTIC SEA · REICHSKOMMISSARIAT OSTLAND · Vilna · Minsk · *Jul. 1943* · *Operation Citadel* · SOVIET UNION · Voronezh · Kursk

IRELAND · UNITED KINGDOM · *Hamburg* · AMSTERDAM · NETH. · BERLIN · GERMANY · Warsaw · GENERAL GOVERNMENT · *Nov. 6, 1943* · Belgorod · *Don* · *Stalingrad* · Kharkov · Kiev · Voroshilovgrad

LONDON · BRUSSELS · BELG. · LUX. · *Jul. 27, 1943* · REICHSKOMMISSA... UKRAINE · *Dnieper* · *Donets* · *Feb. 1943*

NORTH ATLANTIC OCEAN · ENGLISH CHANNEL · PARIS · Prague

46°30'N · FRANCE · Vienna · BUDAPEST · HUNGARY · ROMANIA · BUCHAREST · *Caucasus M...*

BAY OF BISCAY · Berne · SWITZ. · Alps · Zagreb · CROATIA · Sarajevo · BELGRADE · SERBIA · BLACK SEA

Pyrenees · ITALY · Apennines · ADRIATIC SEA · ...ON · ALB. · BULGARIA · SOFIA · ANKARA

SPAIN · MADRID · ROME · Naples · *Salerno* · *Sep. 9, 1943* · IONIAN SEA · GREECE · AEGEAN SEA · TURKEY

PORTUGAL · TYRRHENIAN SEA · *Palermo* · *May 7, 1943* · *Bizerte* · *Tunis* · Sicily · *Messina* · *Operation Husky* · ATHENS · SYRIA

LISBON · *Operation Torch* · *Nov. 8, 1942* · ALGIERS · *Kasserine Pass* · *Jul. 1943* · Crete

TANGIER · Gibraltar (Br.) · SP. MOROCCO · Oran · *Feb. 1943* · Malta (British) · MEDITERRANEAN SEA · PALESTINE

RABAT · Casablanca · ALGERIA · TUNISIA · TRIPOLI · *Nov. 13, 1942* · *Tobruk* · TRANS JORDAN

Casablanca Conference · *Jan. 1943* · LIBYA · CAIRO · EGYPT

MOROCCO · 0 · 500 Mi · 9°E · 19°30'E · Suez · 30°E

12°W · 1°30'W

Bottom map (Asia and Pacific):

IRAN · 66°E · 86°30'E · 107°E · PEKING · 127°30'E · SEA OF JAPAN · KOREA · 148°E · 168°30'E · 17

0 · 500 · 1,000 Mi · YELLOW SEA · JAPAN · TOKYO

NEPAL · BHUTAN · CHUNGKING · Shanghai · CHINA · EAST CHINA SEA · RYUKYU ISLANDS · BONIN ISLANDS

INDIA · BURMA · Okinawa · Iwo Jima · VOLCANO ISLANDS · Wake Island · NORTH PACIFIC OCEAN

Formosa (Taiwan) · Hong Kong · BABUYAN ISLANDS · PHILIPPINE SEA · MARIANA ISLANDS

RANGOON · SIAM · BANGKOK · Hainan Island · Saipan · Guam Island

12°30'N · ANDAMAN ISLANDS · FRENCH INDOCHINA · MANILA · PHILIPPINE ISLANDS · Yap Island · Eniwetok

SPRATLY ISLANDS · SOUTH CHINA SEA · Truk · Kwajalein · MARSHALL ISLAN... · Pohnpei

MALAYA · Singapore · CELEBES SEA · PALAU ISLANDS · CAROLINE ISLANDS

Sumatra · Borneo · GILBERT ISLA... · *Tarawa*

Cape Gloucester Landing · *Dec. 26, 1943* · *Nov. 194...*

BATAVIA · Java · Moluccas · NETHERLANDS EAST INDIES · Rabaul · SOUTH PACIFIC

INDIAN OCEAN · Celebes · New Guinea · New Britain · SOLOMON ISLANDS

Timor · Port Moresby · *Guadalcanal*

8°S · Darwin

CORAL SEA · New Hebrides

AUSTRALIA · FIJI · New Caledonia

127°30'E · 148°E · Brisbane · 168°30'E

86°30'E · 107°E

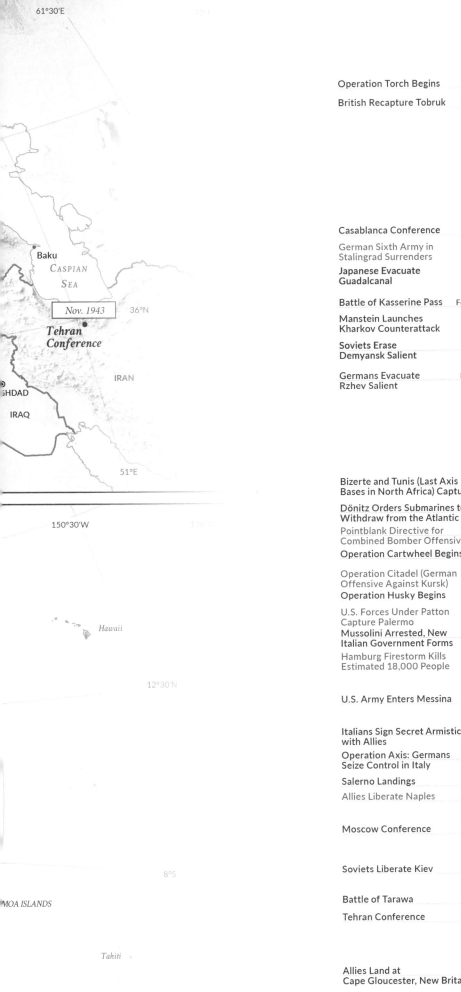

61°30'E

Baku

CASPIAN
SEA

Nov. 1943

36°N

Tehran
Conference

IRAN

GHDAD

IRAQ

51°E

150°30'W

Hawaii

12°30'N

8°S

MOA ISLANDS

Tahiti

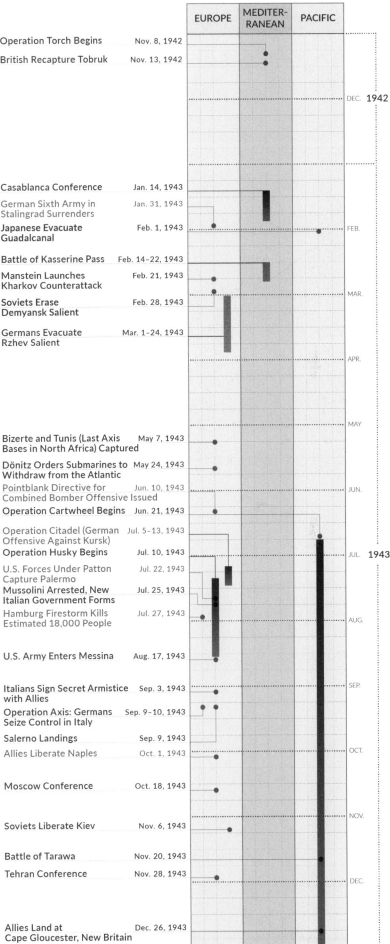

	EUROPE	MEDITER-RANEAN	PACIFIC

Operation Torch Begins — Nov. 8, 1942

British Recapture Tobruk — Nov. 13, 1942

DEC. **1942**

Casablanca Conference — Jan. 14, 1943

German Sixth Army in Stalingrad Surrenders — Jan. 31, 1943

Japanese Evacuate Guadalcanal — Feb. 1, 1943

FEB.

Battle of Kasserine Pass — Feb. 14–22, 1943

Manstein Launches Kharkov Counterattack — Feb. 21, 1943

Soviets Erase Demyansk Salient — Feb. 28, 1943

MAR.

Germans Evacuate Rzhev Salient — Mar. 1–24, 1943

APR.

MAY

Bizerte and Tunis (Last Axis Bases in North Africa) Captured — May 7, 1943

Dönitz Orders Submarines to Withdraw from the Atlantic — May 24, 1943

Pointblank Directive for Combined Bomber Offensive Issued — Jun. 10, 1943

JUN.

Operation Cartwheel Begins — Jun. 21, 1943

Operation Citadel (German Offensive Against Kursk) — Jul. 5–13, 1943

Operation Husky Begins — Jul. 10, 1943

JUL. **1943**

U.S. Forces Under Patton Capture Palermo — Jul. 22, 1943

Mussolini Arrested, New Italian Government Forms — Jul. 25, 1943

Hamburg Firestorm Kills Estimated 18,000 People — Jul. 27, 1943

AUG.

U.S. Army Enters Messina — Aug. 17, 1943

Italians Sign Secret Armistice with Allies — Sep. 3, 1943

SEP.

Operation Axis: Germans Seize Control in Italy — Sep. 9–10, 1943

Salerno Landings — Sep. 9, 1943

Allies Liberate Naples — Oct. 1, 1943

OCT.

Moscow Conference — Oct. 18, 1943

NOV.

Soviets Liberate Kiev — Nov. 6, 1943

Battle of Tarawa — Nov. 20, 1943

Tehran Conference — Nov. 28, 1943

DEC.

Allies Land at Cape Gloucester, New Britain — Dec. 26, 1943

"One Down, Two to Go" ▶

This picture was taken by a U.S. Army signal corps photographer on September 3, 1943. The invasion of Sicily led to the overthrow of Il Duce, Benito Mussolini. Corporal Janesk knew that there were still two tough foes to face.

The much wealthier and better supplied Americans wanted to follow a more direct approach. The problem was that Churchill's proposed strategy offered no hope for a quick end to the war, while Marshall did not yet have the military forces, equipment, or plans to do what he think needed to be done.

Without question, 1943 also saw the Axis lose the initiative, especially on the European Eastern Front. While the year would open with Field Marshal Erich von Manstein's successful counterstroke in present-day Ukraine, which managed to restore a front torn open by the debacle at Stalingrad, it would be the Wehrmacht's last victory. The failure of the German Kursk offensive (Operation Citadel) in July placed the initiative firmly in the hands of the Red Army, which remained on the offensive for the rest of the war.

The situation was the same on the other fronts. In the air and on the sea, as the last

Snipping Will Never Save the House . . *You Gotta Smash Those Pots!*

chapter discussed, 1943 witnessed the defeat of the U-boats in the Atlantic and a geometric increase in the tonnage of bombs dropped by the RAF and the U.S. Army Air Forces on Germany, the practical destruction of Hamburg in July, and heavy blows struck against Berlin itself in November and December. In the Mediterranean, Field Marshal Erwin Rommel's blow against the Americans at Kasserine Pass in February 1943, for all its shock value, marked the beginning of the end for the Axis in North Africa. For the rest of the year, the Allies would be moving forward—to Tunis, to Sicily, and thence to mainland Italy. We see a similar pattern in the Pacific, although the fighting there was of a different character, with both sides battling the jungle as much as they battled each other. There would be no more operational offensives by Japan after 1942. Instead, the Japanese adopted a strategy of holding on grimly to the islands that made up their empire's defensive perimeter in the Pacific, hoping that they could

▲ "SNIPPING WILL NEVER SAVE THE HOUSE," DR. SEUSS, 1942

The idea of unconditional surrender was clear and powerful. The Allies felt that the only way to end the threat was to defeat the Germans and the Japanese completely. Dr. Seuss, Theodor Seuss Geisel, joined the army in 1942 and served as the commander of the Animation Department of the First Motion Picture Unit of the United States Army Air Forces.

"It takes a goddamned lot of good
American construction material to
build this road to Tokyo," says Uncle
Sam in this German cartoon. The
Axis leaders hoped that the Allies
would ultimately prove unable or
unwilling to pay the human and fi-
nancial costs of fighting through to
complete victory.

inflict so many casualties on the advancing American forces that the United States
would accept some sort of compromise peace. On the operational level, virtually all
decisions in the Pacific were American ones: which islands to attack, which to screen,
and which to bypass entirely.

This chapter details the array of difficulties that both sides faced in 1943. The Axis
powers had tried to win the war quickly, before their opponents could muster superior resources, and they had failed. Even so, they had already driven well forward in
their initial offensives, and they held powerful defensive positions almost everywhere.
From the Allied front lines at the end of 1942, it was a still a very long way to Rome,
Berlin, and Tokyo. And the ferocity of the fighting in 1943 indicated that it was going
to be a hard and bloody road. In that sense, the year might well have been the most
difficult of the war for all participants.

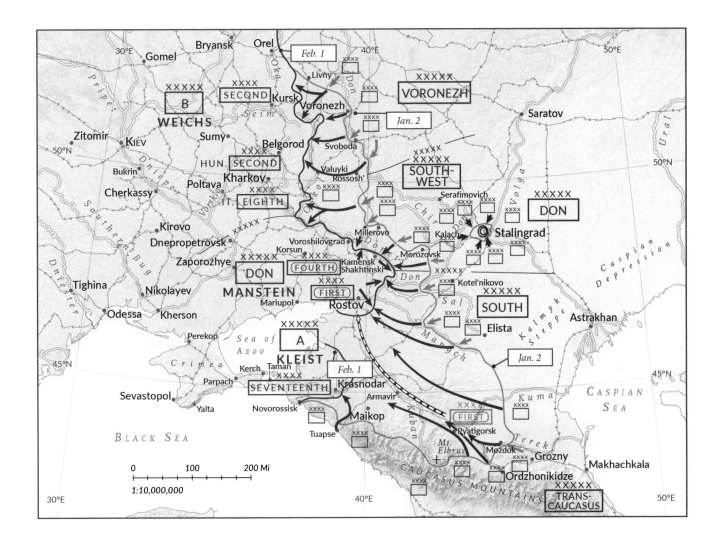

THE EASTERN FRONT IN 1943: KHARKOV

At the close of 1942, the German forces in the Soviet Union were reeling from the catastrophe at Stalingrad. As chapter 1 explained, the Wehrmacht's summer offensive of 1942, Operation Blue, had run out of steam by mid-November. Army Group A had failed to capture the key oil fields and facilities of the southern Caucasus, while far to its north, Army Group B had ground to a halt in the intense urban fighting at Stalingrad. Before the end of 1942, a massive Soviet counteroffensive (Operation Uranus) had transformed the German situation from bad to disastrous, with Sixth Army encircled and slowly starving in Stalingrad, the rest of Army Group B fighting for its life, and Army Group A in danger of being cut off in the Caucasus. Faced with a gaping hole between the two army groups, on November 20 the OKH formed a new Army Group Don to restore the situation. One of the shrewdest and most aggressive commanders in the Wehrmacht, Field Marshal Erich von Manstein, took command.

Army Group Don had the dual task of reopening a supply path to Stalingrad and regaining the territory lost to Operation Uranus—but neither part was going to be easy. While Soviet attacks continued unabated, the German front consisted of ad hoc "groups" (*Gruppen*): formations of various size thrown together hastily from the

▲ MANSTEIN IN DANGER

The successful offensives by Southwest and Voronezh Fronts in January 1943, and further advances in February that carried the Red Army as far west as Sumy, left the German forces north of the Sea of Azov in danger of being encircled and destroyed.

flotsam and jetsam of the defeated forces along the Don River. These groups would eventually coalesce into "provisional armies": multicorps formations short of staff, heavy weapons, and transport. The dire situation saw virtually all of the soldiers normally assigned to those roles handed rifles and ordered into battle as infantry. Given the difficulty the Germans had even in forming a cohesive defensive front, it is not surprising that their attempt to relieve Stalingrad, known as Operation Winter Storm, made very little headway. It consisted of little more than a single Panzer division—all that a threadbare Wehrmacht could spare at the moment—and faced Soviet defenders who outnumbered the German attackers many times over.[3]

The situation grew still more dire as the Red Army unleashed a series of great winter offensives. Operation Little Saturn in December smashed Italian Eighth Army holding the northern shoulder of the Don River's southern bend. The Ostrogozhsk-Rossosh Operation in January 1943 encircled and practically destroyed Hungarian Second Army a little farther north. Operation Gallop took the Red Army all the way across the Donets River in late January. February's Operation Star mauled German Second Army on the right flank of Army Group Center.[4] In the course of the winter, the Red Army lunged forward 350 miles and opened up a 300-mile-wide gap between the German Army Group Center and the tattered remnants of Army Group B to its south.[5] With Soviet armies driving toward the Dnieper River and the crossing points at Dnepropetrovsk and Zaporozhye, the Germans were facing disaster. If the Soviets got over the Dnieper while the Germans still lay far to the east of it, the result would be a "super-Stalingrad": an encirclement that would result in the destruction of the entire German southern wing: Army Group A, Army Group B, and Army Group Don alike.

Field Marshal Manstein's generalship in the ensuing campaign is still worthy of study.[6] He successfully managed chaos, shifting his meager reserves hither and yon to respond to emergencies while also pleading for reinforcements from the high command. These soon arrived in the form of the II SS Panzer Corps, three full-strength mechanized divisions. He had to struggle to convince the Führer, Adolf Hitler, and chief of the General Staff, General Kurt Zeitzler, to recall Army Group A from its lonely perch in the Caucasus, but he ultimately succeeded. Finally, Manstein began planning a counterstroke to hit just when the time was right. What he had in mind was a "castling maneuver," in the language of chess.[7] Using all available rail transport, he would rapidly shift the armies on his far right, First Panzer and Fourth Panzer, to his extreme left. Once they were arrayed, facing north, they would be in an ideal position to smash deep into the left flank of Soviet forces heading west.

Manstein's moment soon arrived. The Red Army had begun its latest operational sequence on the Volga River in November 1942. It had retaken the immense bend of the Don before the end of that year, driven across the Donets in January–February 1943, and was now heading for the Dnieper. In the course of this long drive, however, the offensive was reaching what Carl von Clausewitz, the renowned nineteenth-century Prussian military theorist, called the "culminating point": the moment at which the gradual wearing down of the attacker's strength brings it into balance with

the defense, and vulnerable to a devastating counterthrust.[8] Supplies of all sorts were running low, and actual fighting strength was probably half of what it had been at the start of the winter offensives.[9]

Despite the warning signals, however, the Soviets drove on. By now, intelligence was flowing into front and army headquarters alike of a massive German shift: formations moving to the west, roads choked with men and vehicles. It was Manstein's castling maneuver in action. Stalin and the Soviet high command alike, however, misread these signs as indications of a wild and desperate German flight to the Dnieper, and urged their army commanders to drive onward with redoubled urgency.[10]

Surprise was total, then, when Manstein launched his counterattack on February 21. Two convergent thrusts, one from the south by Fourth Panzer Army and one from the northwest by the II SS Panzer Corps, caught the spearheads of the Soviet Sixth and First Guards Armies by surprise. The Germans struck the Soviet forces in front and on the flanks, scattering them. Wehrmacht casualties were minimal; Soviet losses nearly total. And no wonder: one Soviet formation after another was quite literally running out of fuel at the very moment of Manstein's attack.

For the next month, the Germans had the Soviets on the run, with First Panzer Army on the right and Fourth Panzer Army on the left. Leading the way for the latter

▲ STREET FIGHTING IN KHARKOV
A German armored personnel carrier makes its way through the streets of Kharkov. The city changed hands four times during the war.

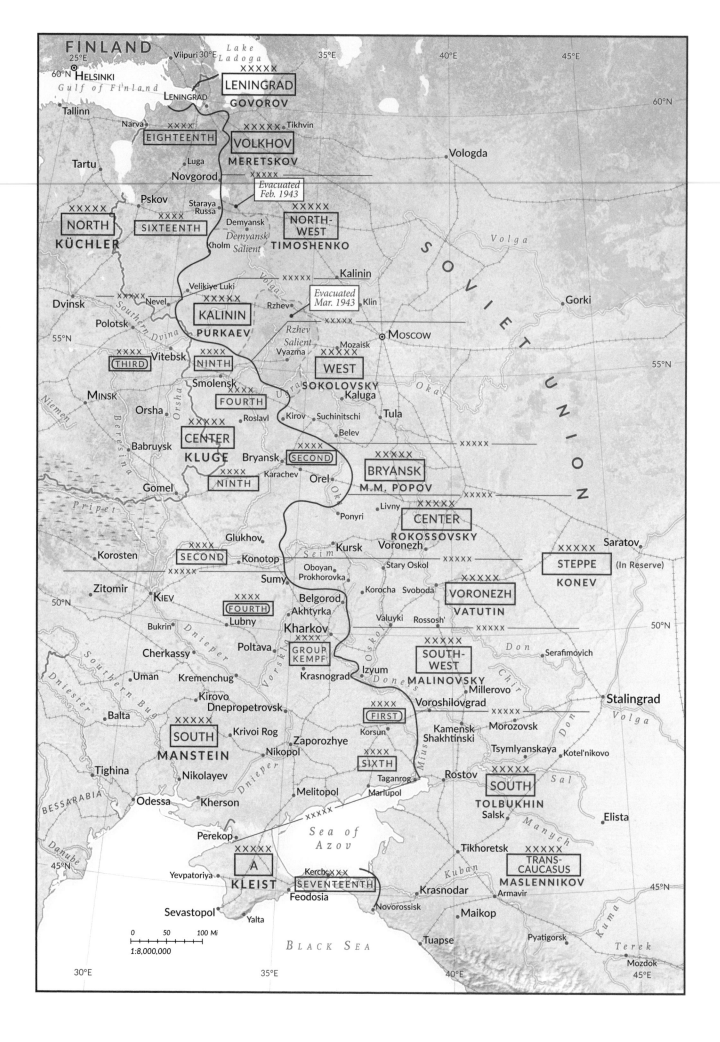

was II SS Panzer Corps, which fought its way into Kharkov, the fourth largest city in the Soviet Union, and cleared it after three days of bloody street fighting from March 12 to 14. Then the thaw came, the mud arrived, and large-scale operations had to cease.

KURSK

In the course of the Kharkov campaign, the Germans had done what seemed impossible just a few months before: they had reformed their front in the south after it had been torn open by the debacle at Stalingrad. Even more remarkable, Manstein's counterblow had restored the front to approximately where it had stood at the start of the 1942 campaign.[11]

But even giving Manstein his due, the victory at Kharkov had solved nothing. In the course of their offensive, the Germans had advanced up to a long, meandering line along the Donets River. But they did not have enough strength to hold such an extended position in the coming year. Manstein knew it, as did Hitler and the high command, and the end of the campaign in the spring of 1943 would find them all

◀ **THE EASTERN FRONT, JANUARY–JULY 1943: PRELUDE TO OPERATION CITADEL**

By voluntarily withdrawing from the salients (eastward bulges) at Demyansk and Rzhev, the Germans reduced the length of the perimeter they had to defend, freeing up forces for offensive action against the Soviets' salient around Kursk.

▲ **PANZER VI "TIGER" TANK**

In 1941 the Soviet T-34 proved superior to any German tank. In 1942, however, the Wehrmacht deployed the Tiger, which was much more heavily armored and equipped with an extremely powerful 88-mm gun. From eight hundred to five hundred meters, the Tiger could shoot through even the frontal armor of the T-34, practically without danger to itself. The manual for Tiger crewmen included a ditty to emphasize the importance of engaging within the "mealtime" zone: "This is the moral of the story / I can kill you, you can't kill me."

ALLIES

WESTERN (xxxxx)
- FIFTIETH (xxxx)
- ELEVENTH GUARDS (xxxx)
- FIRST ∞ (xxxx)

□ x2   ⊡ x1   ⊠ x20

BRYANSK (xxxxx)
- THIRD (xxxx)
- SIXTY-FIRST (xxxx)
- SIXTY-THIRD (xxxx)
- FIFTEENTH ∞ (xxxx)

Corps/Division Summary
□ x1   ⊡ x2   ⊠ x24

CENTRAL (xxxxx)
- THIRTEENTH (xxxx)
- FORTY-EIGHTH (xxxx)
- SIXTIETH (xxxx)
- SIXTY-FIFTH (xxxx)
- SEVENTIETH (xxxx)
- SECOND (xxxx)
- SIXTEENTH ∞ (xxxx)

□ x4   ⊡ x1   ⊠ x40

VORONEZH (xxxxx)
- THIRTY-EIGHTH (xxxx)
- FORTIETH (xxxx)
- SIXTY-NINTH (xxxx)
- SIXTH GUARDS (xxxx)
- SEVENTH GUARDS (xxxx)
- FIRST (xxxx)
- SECOND ∞ (xxxx)

□ x4   ⊠ x1   ⊠ x37

SOUTHWESTERN (xxxxx)
- FIFTY-SEVENTH (xxxx)
- SEVENTEENTH ∞ (xxxx)

□ x1   ⊠ x8

STAVKA RESERVE
- THIRD GUARDS (xxxx)
- FOURTH (xxxx)
- ELEVENTH (xxxx)

□ x6   ⊠ x2   ⊠ x8

STEPPE (xxxxx)
- FOURTH GUARDS (xxxx)
- TWENTY-SEVENTH (xxxx)
- FORTY-SEVENTH (xxxx)
- FIFTY-THIRD (xxxx)
- FIFTH GUARDS (xxxx)
- FIFTH GUARDS (xxxx)
- FIFTH ∞ (xxxx)

□ x4   ⊠ x4   ⊠ x41

Soldiers
2,759,701
1,036,907

Tanks and Assault Guns
8,540
3,033

AXIS

CENTER (xxxxx)
- SECOND (xxxx)
- SECOND (xxxx)
- NINTH (xxxx)
- SIXTH ∞ (xxxx)

Under SECOND:
- LV (xxx)
- LIII (xxx)
- XXXV (xxx)

Division Summary
□ x2   ⊠ x2
⊠ x16

Under SECOND:
- XIII (xxx)
- VII (xxx)

⊠ x8

Under NINTH:
- XX (xxx)
- XXIII (xxx)
- XLI (xxx)
- XLVI (xxx)
- XLVII (xxx)
- VIII Hungarian (xxx)

□ x6   ⊠ x1
⊠ x20

SOUTH (xxxxx)
- FOURTH (xxxx)
- KEMPF (xxxx)
- FOURTH ∞ (xxxx)

Under FOURTH:
- LII (xxx)
- XLVIII (xxx)
- II SS (xxx)

□ x2
⊠ x4
⊠ x4

Under KEMPF:
- XI (xxx)
- XLII (xxx)
- III (xxx)

□ x3
⊠ x6

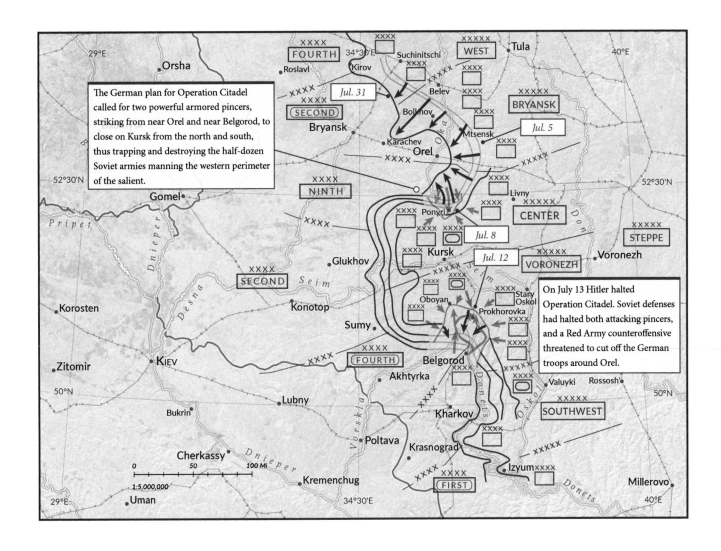

The German plan for Operation Citadel called for two powerful armored pincers, striking from near Orel and near Belgorod, to close on Kursk from the north and south, thus trapping and destroying the half-dozen Soviet armies manning the western perimeter of the salient.

On July 13 Hitler halted Operation Citadel. Soviet defenses had halted both attacking pincers, and a Red Army counteroffensive threatened to cut off the German troops around Orel.

pondering just how they might retain the initiative in the East in the face of a vast Soviet superiority in men and matériel.

One obvious target for the next German attack was the Kursk salient, a great westward bulge in the line on the operational border between Army Group South and Army Group Center.[12] An assault on Kursk was originally Manstein's idea, envisioned as an immediate follow-on to the victory at Kharkov. The generally exhausted state of the German Army at the end of the winter campaign rendered it impossible, however.[13] While planning went forward under the code name Operation Citadel, Germany postponed execution repeatedly.

The reasons were all good ones. The Germans waited for the ground to dry. They needed time for reinforcements and replacements to come up. Above all, having been handled roughly by the superb Soviet T-34 tanks, they were waiting for new tanks to join their arsenal, many of which were just coming into production: the Mark V Panther with its sloped armor and high-velocity 75-mm gun; the Mark VI Tiger, which married the very successful 88-mm gun to a heavy tank; and a monstrous tank

▲ OPERATION CITADEL
The Soviets were ready for the German attempt to pinch off the Kursk salient, and Operation Citadel was a costly failure.

◀ ORDER OF BATTLE FOR THE BATTLE OF KURSK, JULY 4–AUGUST 1, 1943

GERMANS ATTACKING ▶
AT KURSK

At Kharkov the Germans had briefly regained the initiative. Manstein hoped Operation Citadel would turn the tide of the war on the Eastern Front, but instead the attack failed completely—at a cost of half a million casualties.

destroyer (a vehicle with main-gun armament but no turret) called "Ferdinand," carrying a fixed 88-mm gun and a full 100-mm of frontal armor.

These repeated postponements, stretching out for months, did allow the Wehrmacht to recuperate. But the Soviets benefited also and gained strength at a much faster pace. All told, the Germans were able to build up a force of 650,000 men in three armies, supported by some 2,600 tanks and assault guns and 1,800 planes, directed against a salient that was only 160 miles from north to south.[14] But the Soviet concentration dwarfed the German one: three complete army groups (called "fronts") comprising sixteen armies, backed by masses of artillery and support troops. The Soviets managed to pack some 1.8 million men into the Kursk salient, with more than 5,000 tanks and 20,000 guns and mortars.[15] They were equally well provided with airpower. Indeed, the weeks before the offensive saw repeated Soviet air attacks on German installations, airfields, and troop concentrations, and the Luftwaffe was never able to win air superiority over the battlefield, let alone the air supremacy that had fueled the Wehrmacht's early campaigns.[16]

The climax of the battle of Kursk came near the village of Prokhorovka, where the Fifth Guards Tank Army crashed into the II SS Panzer Corps on July 12, 1943. While Soviet commander Pavel Rotmistrov later wrote a highly colored version of the battle, his description of the start of the fight is accurate enough. As he readies his counterstroke at Prokhorovka, Rotmistrov has a visitor to his command post: Marshal Aleksandr Vasilevsky, chief of the Soviet General Staff. Here is Rotmistrov's account:

Although it was toward evening, the bombings by German aircraft did not stop. Riding in a jeep, we crossed a grove and saw the buildings of a state farm on the right. Ahead of us, about one half mile away, dozens of tanks were moving along the road. Vasilevsky ordered the driver to pull up at the edge of the road and, looking at me sternly, asked me in an unexpectedly sharp voice, for he was usually even-tempered, "General Rotmistrov, what's happening? Why are the tanks moving ahead of time?"

I looked through my binoculars. "They are German tanks."

"Then they may deprive us of our foothold and, what's more, they may capture Prokhorovka."

I said that we would not let this happen and immediately radioed two tank brigades to advance west of Prokhorovka to disrupt the German action. This was soon accomplished.

The morning of July 12 came. I was at my command post in an orchard southwest of Prokhorovka. The trunks of apple trees were pitted by fragments of bombs and shells. The rods of aerials were protruded from holes dug behind currant bushes.

The quiet of the morning was broken by the roar of Messerschmitts. Columns of smoke soared into the sky from the German bombers. Over 200 advancing Panzers appeared in the northeast.

At 8:00 a.m. a cyclone of fire unleashed by our artillery and rocket launchers swept the entire front of German defenses.

After fifteen minutes of artillery and air bombardment, Soviet tanks left their cover. The 5th Guards Tank Army rushed forward to meet the attacking enemy columns.

Hundreds of vehicles met head-on on a narrow front bound by the Psel River on the one side and a railway embankment on the other.

That was how the famous battle of Prokhorovka began.[17]

When Operation Citadel began on July 5, therefore, it went nowhere. The plan was a simple one. General Walter Model's Ninth Army would attack the northern face of the salient, and General Hermann Hoth's Fourth Panzer Army and a provisional army under General Karl-Adolf Hollidt would attack the southern face. Together they would carry out a gigantic pincer maneuver, linking up east of Kursk and trapping all Soviet forces inside the salient.

Both drives fizzled completely, and it is hard to see how it could have been otherwise. The Soviets were hunkered down behind eight concentric defensive lines, with nearly 3,100 miles of trenches and over a million mines sown in the likely path of the German advance. Every village and hill was fortified, and the Soviet high command had guessed correctly the main German sectors of attack.[18] While a tactical analysis might show this or that company or battalion managing to get forward, the overall result, on the operational level, was something akin to a dead stop. Hoth advanced barely ten miles the first week, and Model even less.[19]

Despite the lack of maneuver on either side, the sheer number of men and tanks on both sides made Kursk an extraordinarily destructive battle. Nearly seven thousand armored fighting vehicles took part on both sides, and the fighting was intense. The climax came early on the morning of July 12, just south of the village of Prokhorovka.

Heading north, General Paul Hausser's II SS Panzer Corps crashed into the Soviet Fifth Guards Tank Army, led by General Pavel Rotmistrov. The Germans had the edge in training and equipment, particularly at longer ranges, so Soviet tanks had to close as rapidly as possible in order to get their T-34s within effective fighting distance. Some accounts speak of tanks ramming one another, and while it is not easy to verify such claims, Prokhorovka was a point-blank melee. Soviet losses were heavy, but Hausser's SS never did manage to break through.[20] As much progress as he was making to his front, he had to deal constantly with Soviet forces lapping around both flanks, a threat that tied up most of his infantry by the end of the day's fighting.

In the final analysis, even if the Germans had broken through at Prokhorovka, they would have still been in deep trouble at Kursk. The Soviets had vast unengaged reserves in the salient. Indeed, on the very day of Prokhorovka, they launched a giant offensive of their own against German forces in the Orel salient, north of Kursk.[21] It threw the divisions of the northern German wing back onto the defensive and then into retreat. A few weeks later, a second Soviet offensive smashed into the German positions south of Kursk, overrunning Belgorod and continuing on to Kharkov.[22]

On July 13 Hitler called off Operation Citadel altogether. It had been a disaster for the Wehrmacht. Of seventy German divisions engaged, the fighting had chewed up thirty, and the Germans had suffered 500,000 casualties. As always in this war, these were massive casualties compared with the minimal losses the Germans were suffering against the Western Allies. Operation Barbarossa had begun in 1941 as a high-risk

OPERATION TORCH ▼
(NOVEMBER 8) AND
MONTGOMERY'S PURSUIT
AFTER EL ALAMEIN
(NOVEMBER 5–23, 1942)

The American Joint Chiefs were hesitant to support the Torch landings, not wanting to divert resources away from preparations for the cross-Channel invasion of France. But FDR insisted that substantial numbers of American troops be fighting Germans in 1942, partly to answer Soviet demands for a second front, and partly to head off political pressure to depart from the "Germany First" strategy.

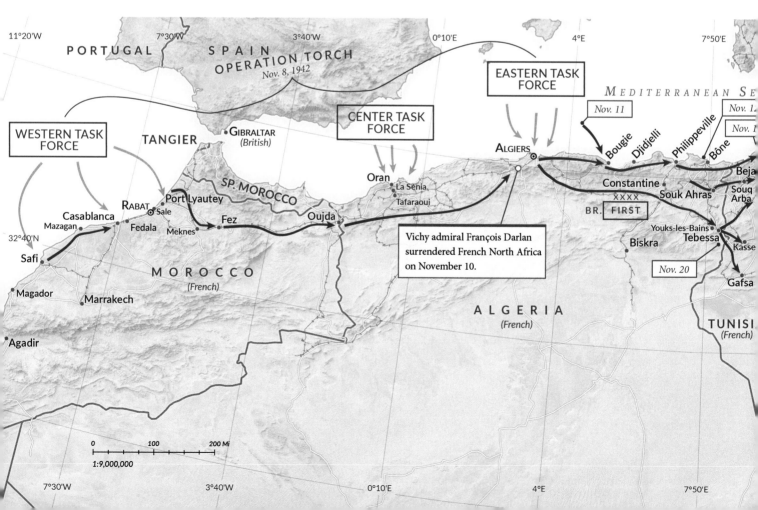

gamble for a quick victory in the Soviet Union. But by now, it had devolved into a war of attrition against superior forces that enjoyed qualitative parity or near parity with the Wehrmacht, a nearly hopeless task for the Germans. In strategic terms, the Wehrmacht had permanently lost the initiative on the Eastern Front. The post-Kursk Soviet ripostes threw the Germans onto the defensive in the East, and there they would remain for the rest of the war.

TUNISIA AND THE KASSERINE PASS

Besides Soviet resistance, Hitler had one other reason for calling off Citadel: the Mediterranean Front had suddenly erupted into flames.

The Allies had landed in North Africa back in November 1942 in Operation Torch.[23] They overran the French colonies of Morocco and Algeria, but their drive on the port of Tunis had sputtered in December. The Germans were able to rush reinforcements to North Africa by air, leaving the Allies no choice but to conduct a long and difficult campaign in early 1943 to dig Axis forces out of Tunisia.

The situation at the start of 1943 was a textbook representation of the advantages of interior lines, in which a centrally located force can try to mass first against one opposing army, defeat it, and then do the same to the second. The Germans and their Italian allies—specifically General Hans-Jürgen von Arnim's Fifth Panzer Army and

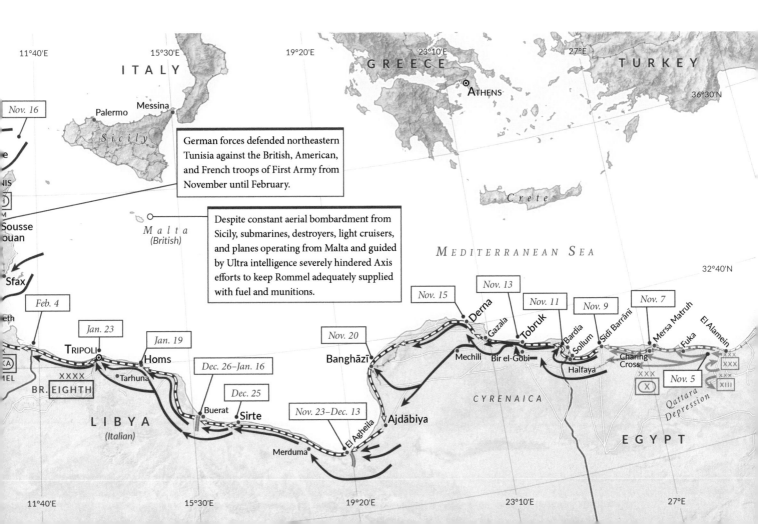

German forces defended northeastern Tunisia against the British, American, and French troops of First Army from November until February.

Despite constant aerial bombardment from Sicily, submarines, destroyers, light cruisers, and planes operating from Malta and guided by Ultra intelligence severely hindered Axis efforts to keep Rommel adequately supplied with fuel and munitions.

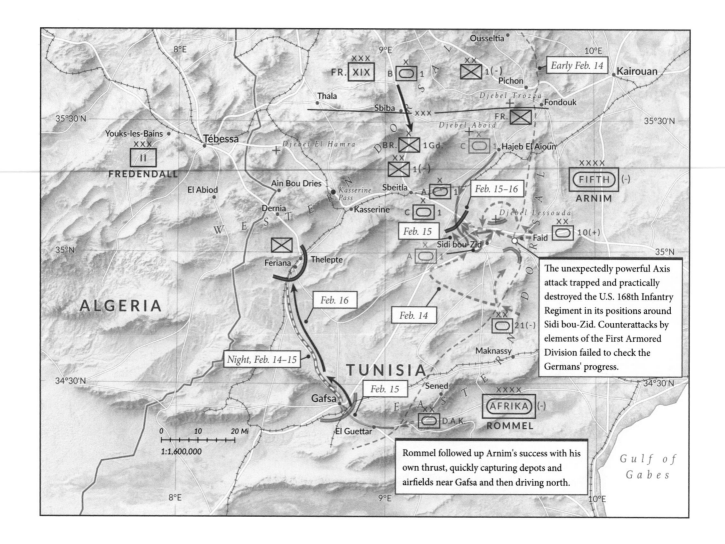

The unexpectedly powerful Axis attack trapped and practically destroyed the U.S. 168th Infantry Regiment in its positions around Sidi bou-Zid. Counterattacks by elements of the First Armored Division failed to check the Germans' progress.

Rommel followed up Arnim's success with his own thrust, quickly capturing depots and airfields near Gafsa and then driving north.

THE GERMAN OFFENSIVE, ▲
FEBRUARY 14–16, 1943
The first phases of the Battle of Kasserine Pass amounted to a stinging defeat of the U.S. II Corps.

Field Marshal Erwin Rommel's German-Italian Panzer Army—sat between powerful Allied armies that vastly outnumbered them. British First Army (composed of American and French soldiers as well as British ones), led by General Richard Anderson, was moving in from the west, and General Bernard Law Montgomery's British Eighth Army was advancing slowly from the east.[24] The Germans, therefore, had a chance to concentrate their forces and smash the first army to come within reach before the Allied forces could unite and triumph through sheer numbers.

In February they did just that, with Arnim and Rommel launching a combined operation against the southern flank of First Army, at positions held by U.S. Army's II Corps, led by General Lloyd Fredendall.[25] The first operation, Frühlingswind ("Spring Breeze"), opened with a powerful drive by two Panzer divisions out of the Faïd Pass against exposed American positions at Sidi bou-Zid, Tunisia. It was a Panzer attack in the grand style, spearheaded by more than two hundred tanks (including a dozen new Mark VI Tiger giants), and it overwhelmed the defenders, encircling and destroying the entire U.S. 168th Infantry Regiment before continuing westward. With U.S. attention diverted to this sector, a second operation (Morgenluft, "Morning Air") now began. Rommel's Panzers struck at Gafsa far in the south, catching American

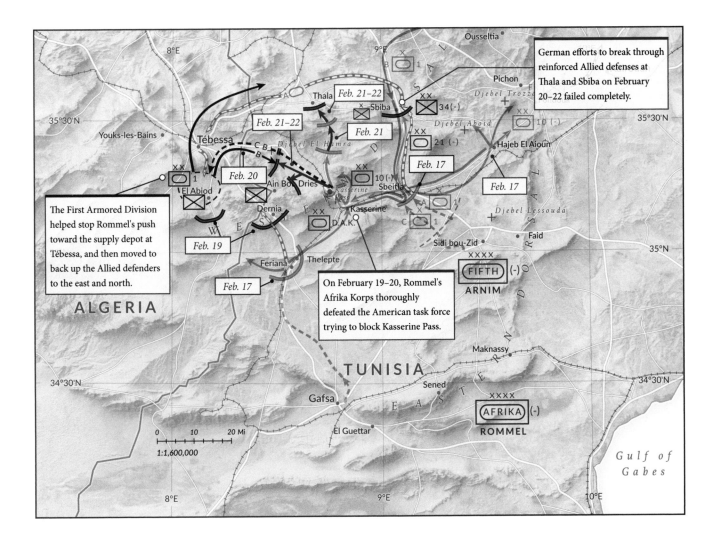

German efforts to break through reinforced Allied defenses at Thala and Sbiba on February 20–22 failed completely.

The First Armored Division helped stop Rommel's push toward the supply depot at Tébessa, and then moved to back up the Allied defenders to the east and north.

On February 19–20, Rommel's Afrika Korps thoroughly defeated the American task force trying to block Kasserine Pass.

defenders completely unprepared and overrunning U.S. supply depots, airfields, and formations alike before pushing north.

These two concentric drives met at the Kasserine Pass, which sat astride the last defensible position in Tunisia: the so-called Western Dorsal.[26] If the U.S. soldiers could not hold here, the entire Allied strategic position in Africa would be in danger. On February 19–20, Rommel's mobile spearhead the *Afrika Korps* (composed of the 15th Panzer Division and the Italian *Centauro* armored division) attacked the pass and smashed a motley collection of U.S. defenders designated Task Force Stark. It included a handful of infantry, engineer units rushed to the front with only rudimentary tactical training, and two batteries of French artillery.[27] German and Italian armor attacked frontally, fixing the defenders in place, while Axis infantry methodically worked its way up the heights overlooking the pass. Counterattacks by U.S. tanks ran into the fire of German 88-mm antitank guns, and by the evening of February 20, the U.S. defenses in the Kasserine Pass had collapsed. Survivors streamed away in confusion, and the wrecks of two hundred U.S. tanks littered the battlefield.[28] Fredendall, protected in an underground bunker 100 miles to the west of Sidi bou-Zid, had lost control of the situation, and perhaps of himself. "They have

▲ THE BATTLE OF KASSERINE PASS, FEBRUARY 17–22, 1943

In the end Kasserine was a strategic victory for the Allies. The U.S. Army had not lived up to its own expectations, but nevertheless did succeed in preventing the Germans from delivering the knockout blow their operational situation demanded.

Soldiers of the 33rd Field Artillery Regiment prepare to fire their 105-mm howitzer in the defense of Kasserine Pass.

broken through, and you can't stop them," he told one of his commanders at the time.[29]

For all these reasons, what happened over the next few days is surprising. With Fredendall's II Corps driven from position after position, the Western Dorsal pierced, and disaster looming, U.S. defenses finally stiffened. Seeing the Americans on the run, Rommel ordered three simultaneous thrusts. The first, a northward drive on the pass at Sbiba by the 21st Panzer Division, failed completely, screeching to a halt against four full U.S. and British infantry regiments and an artillery battalion. A second thrust, toward Thala, ran into a similar wall. Here the British 26th Armoured Brigade held the front, backed by the newly arrived artillery of the U.S. 9th Infantry Division, which had been stationed 800 miles away in Oran, Algeria, just four days before.[30] Rommel's third drive was the crucial one, targeting Tebéssa, the principal U.S. supply depot in Tunisia—well stocked with gasoline, which Axis forces had nearly run out of. But it

too failed. The U.S. 16th Infantry Regiment blocked the way, supported by counter-attacks of the 1st Armored Division and, once again, highly accurate American artillery fire.

The Kasserine offensive—an attempt to destroy First Army, or at least to set back its operational timetable—had failed, and had cost the Wehrmacht dearly in manpower, ammunition, and matériel. Rommel had taken heavy losses, and his supplies had dwindled to a mere four days' worth of rations and 155 miles' worth of fuel. Worst of all, the advance guard of Montgomery's Eighth Army was beginning to close in from the east. On February 23 Rommel ordered his battered formations out of the Kasserine Pass and back to their original positions.

Kasserine Pass presents a mixed picture. Certainly it showed a U.S. Army that was not yet ready for high-intensity combined-arms warfare. British forces, who had seen action against the Germans for years and who knew the difficulties, were appalled at the amateurishness of U.S. planning and field operations, as well as the behavior of higher commanders such as Fredendall. They took to referring to their U.S. allies by the insulting moniker of "Alice."[31] Many American officers, too, viewed Kasserine as a humiliation, a notion that was difficult to shed. Indeed, Kasserine appears to be a classic example of U.S. military unpreparedness.

The problem with this point of view is that it dwells only on the opening fiasco.

KEY

British Eighth Army

British First Army, United States Second Corps, and General Giraud's North African French forces

Fighting French force, led by General Leclerc

On May 13th. 1943. General Alexander reports to the Prime Minister:

"Sir,—It is my duty to report that the Tunisian campaign is over. All enemy resistance has ceased. We are masters of the North African shores."

MAY 7th, 1943

TUNIS AND BIZERTA CAPTURED

EGYPT TO TUNISIA
1,700 Miles in 28 weeks

THE AFRICAN CAMPAIGNS HAVE COST THE AXIS:

950,000 Troops Killed or Captured,
8,000 Aircraft Destroyed,
6,200 Guns Captured or Destroyed,
2,550 Tanks Captured or Destroyed,
70,000 Trucks Captured or Destroyed,
And Vast Quantities of Military Equipment.

NOVEMBER 8th, 1942. British First Army and United States forces land at Algiers.
NOVEMBER 26th, 1942. British First Army captures Medjez el Bab, jumping-off ground for final assault, and holds it against continued enemy pressure for five months.
FEBRUARY 20th, 1943. Under the supreme command of General Eisenhower, General Alexander assumes command of Eighteenth Army Group including British First and Eighth Armies, Second American Corps and Nineteenth French Corps.

APRIL 7th, 1943

The British Eighth Army made contact with the United States Second Corps. The ring of Allied forces was now drawn tight around the doomed Axis armies. Within a few days the final annihilation began.

Advance **1,700** miles

MARCH 28th, 1943

The powerful fortifications of the Mareth Line fell to a fierce frontal assault by the British Eighth Army and a swift flanking attack which threatened the rear of the Axis forces at El Hamma. Once more the enemy had to retreat to avoid the destruction of the remaining forces.

Advance **1,375** miles

JANUARY

The British Eighth Ar two-and-a-half years armies in North Afric French column led which had advance Lake Chad area, British Eighth Army.

Advance **1,**

▲ THE END IN NORTH AFRICA

For British Eighth Army, the linkup with the Allied forces coming in from the west and the final push to capture Tunis and Bizerte were only the capstones of a long, hard push that began half a year earlier with the victory at El Alamein.

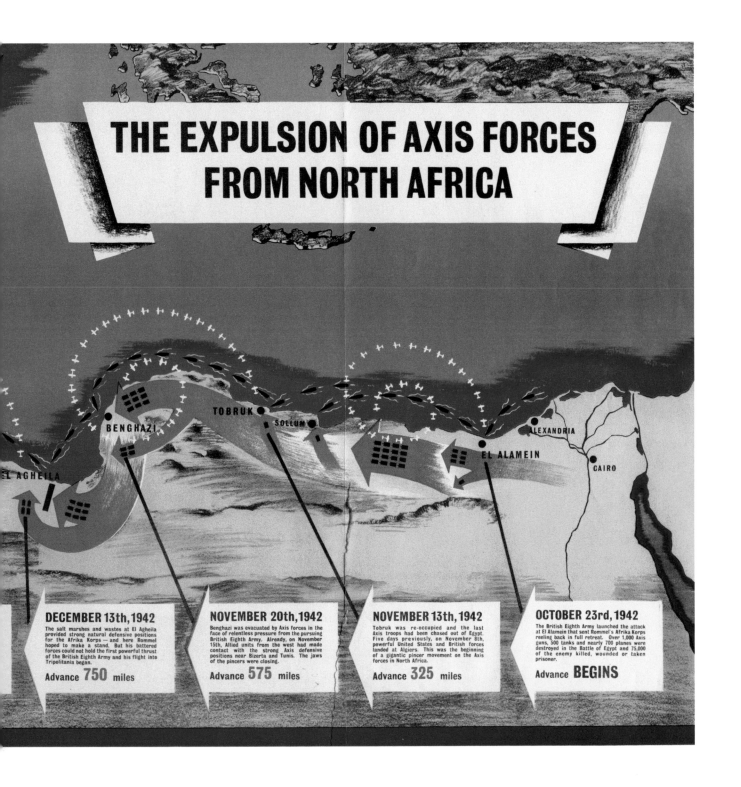

THE EXPULSION OF AXIS FORCES FROM NORTH AFRICA

DECEMBER 13th, 1942

The salt marshes and wastes at El Agheila provided strong natural defensive positions for the Afrika Korps — and here Rommel hoped to make a stand. But his battered forces could not hold the first powerful thrust of the British Eighth Army and his flight into Tripolitania began.

Advance 750 miles

NOVEMBER 20th, 1942

Benghazi was evacuated by Axis forces in the face of relentless pressure from the pursuing British Eighth Army. Already, on November 15th, Allied units from the west had made contact with the strong Axis defensive positions near Bizerta and Tunis. The jaws of the pincers were closing.

Advance 575 miles

NOVEMBER 13th, 1942

Tobruk was re-occupied and the last Axis troops had been chased out of Egypt. Five days previously, on November 8th, powerful United States and British forces landed at Algiers. This was the beginning of a gigantic pincer movement on the Axis forces in North Africa.

Advance 325 miles

OCTOBER 23rd, 1942

The British Eighth Army launched the attack at El Alamein that sent Rommel's Afrika Korps reeling back in full retreat. Over 1,000 Axis guns, 500 tanks and nearly 700 planes were destroyed in the Battle of Egypt and 75,000 of the enemy killed, wounded or taken prisoner.

Advance BEGINS

A British field marshal of World War II, Alexander was a key figure in the Anglo-American coalition. Respected equally by British colleagues and U.S. allies, he was the very embodiment of coalition warfare. While no one considered him a great intellect, his disdain for personal danger was legendary, and he had an undeniable ability to charm the most obstreperous Allied subordinate.

Alexander's success was due largely to a simple fact: when the coalition first formed, he was one of its most experienced officers. He had been a battalion commander at the Somme in World War I, a division commander in France in 1940 (he commandeered his own small boat in the Dunkirk evacuation), commander in chief of British Forces in Burma in February 1942, and commander in chief of Middle East Command in August. By the time the Allies needed to choose their theater commanders, there was a small list of potential candidates.

Alexander proved adept at army group command, which is concerned less with brilliant maneuver than it is with administration, logistics, and people skills. He imposed order on the Tunisian theater as commander of 18th Army Group (First and Eighth British Armies), and then presided over the invasion of Sicily as commander of 15th Army Group in Operation Husky (U.S. Seventh and British Eighth Armies), and Italy (U.S. Fifth and British Eighth Armies). As commander of Allied armies in Italy in March 1944, he oversaw the breakout of Allied forces from the Anzio-Cassino stalemate.

Alexander was on the short list for the ground forces commander in the D-Day invasion, but the post went eventually to General Bernard Law Montgomery. Alexander's career, therefore, unfolded in the Mediterranean, with its peripheral status and low priority in manpower and supplies. His record of victory, therefore, is all the more impressive.

The end of the battle, by contrast, showed the U.S. Army finally pulling itself together. It had assembled a fighting package that included vast material resources, enabling a sustained level of logistics that no one else in the world could match; immense levels of firepower, especially from the artillery; and most important, solid field-grade leadership from the officers who were actually leading formations in battle. It was a combination that the Germans would find more and more difficult to counter as the war went on. "The Americans," Rommel wrote later, "had fought brilliantly." [32] More than anyone, he ought to have known.

The conclusion to the Tunisian fighting was predictable. [33] The Germans were outmanned and outgunned, and they had shot what little logistical bolt they had at Kasserine. Both Allied armies were now operating side by side, forming 18th Army Group under Field Marshal Harold Alexander. The Allies had already won the battle in the air, with three thousand Allied aircraft confronting just three hundred Axis planes. They had also won the battle of supply, building up stocks of equipment and ammunition at will while choking off Axis transports from mainland Europe through naval and air forces that were guided by invaluable Ultra intelligence. During the course of April, a solid ring of Allied formations caved in the German defensive perimeter and overran the last Axis position in Africa. The same U.S. troops maligned for their performance at Kasserine were in on the kill, with II Corps (now under the able command of General Omar Bradley) spearheading the drive toward Mateur and then the key port of Bizerte.

Both Bizerte and Tunis fell on May 7, bringing the fighting in Africa to a close. A huge number of German and Italian prisoners fell into Allied hands, perhaps as many as 200,000. [34] It was a complete victory and a satisfying end to a very tough fight. Losses had not been light, however. The Allies sustained 70,000 casualties: 36,000 British, 16,000 French, and 18,000 American. If anyone in the Allied command had any illusions about how easy it was going to be to invade Europe and to smash the Wehrmacht once and for all, Tunisia dispelled them.

THE INVASION OF SICILY

With the Tunisian campaign finally over, the Allies decided to invade Sicily in what would be called Operation Husky.[35] The decision was logical. The cross-Channel invasion of France was still in the planning state, huge Allied forces were in the Mediterranean, and they weren't going to be fighting the Germans anywhere else that summer. Sicily was a perfect target of opportunity.

The Allied leaders planning for Husky had to deal with a number of complex issues. The first was the choice of a landing site. Enemy intentions were unclear. Many in the Allied camp expected the Italians to fold, but German divisions were also going to be present, and they would certainly fight. The plan, therefore, came down in the middle between dispersion and concentration. The Allies would hurl a massive force at southeastern Sicily: Field Marshal Harold Alexander's 15th Army Group, which contained two armies, the British Eighth under Montgomery and U.S. Seventh under General George S. Patton Jr. Seven divisions would land on day one, making Husky the largest amphibious operation of the war, but the landings would be dispersed at twenty-six sites along 110 miles of coastline. The aim was to take advantage of Italian weakness and to protect against German strength at the same time, perhaps an impossible task.[36]

A second thorny issue was that of interallied distrust. Husky gave British Eighth Army the starring role. It would land near the port of Syracuse, advance north over the plain to Catania, and drive on Messina, trapping Axis forces on Sicily. Patton's Seventh Army would land to the west, its mission to protect Montgomery's flank.[37] The Americans would not even have their own major port, relying instead on the much smaller ports of Gela and Licata, as well as beach maintenance. Not a few U.S. officers felt slighted by the plan.

Husky began in the early morning hours of July 10, 1943, just a few days after Germany had launched its great offensive at Kursk. A series of airborne landings led off, but they went bad early. As the British 1st Airlanding Brigade flew to the Ponte Grande Bridge south of Syracuse, the gliders scattered badly en route, and most of them dropped into the sea, losing all of their men. Likewise, elements of the 82nd Airborne Division, attempting a drop on the Piano Lupo, a hill mass behind the U.S. beaches, scattered all over southeastern Sicily, and fewer than 200 men reached the objective.[38]

The seaborne landings, by contrast, went very smoothly. Aided by a new generation of specialized landing craft such as the LCVP (an abbreviation for landing craft, vehicle, personnel), or Higgins Boat, most of the landing force got ashore according to plan. The British landed XXX Corps around the Pachino Peninsula in the south and southeast, and XIII Corps along the eastern coast. Resistance was spotty, and by early afternoon, XIII Corps had seized Syracuse and began pushing north. U.S. II Corps

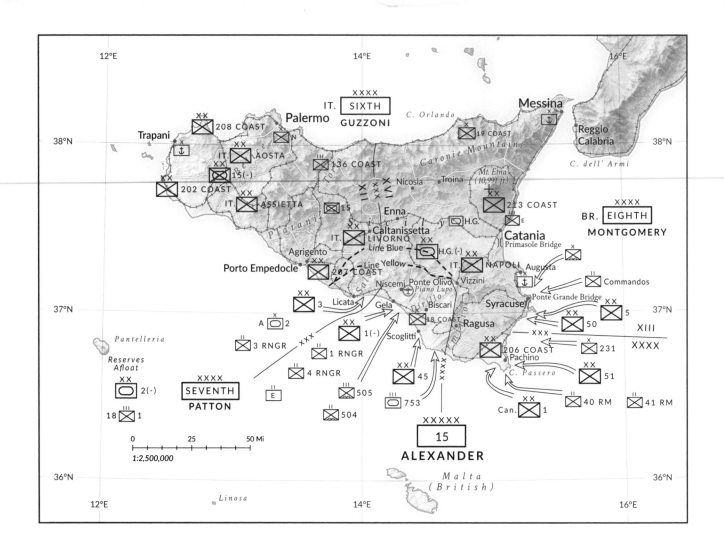

OPERATION HUSKY ▲

The Allied plan for Operation Husky, the landings on Sicily in 1943, was in some ways even more complex than the plan for the Normandy landings the following year.

(under General Bradley) came ashore at Licata, Gela, and Scoglitti, and likewise faced little hard fighting. While there was a massive Axis force on the island—300,000 men of Italian Sixth Army along with two German mechanized divisions—most of the former soon deserted.

The Germans fought, as expected. Within hours of the landing, the Hermann Göring Parachute Panzer Division had launched a counterattack against the U.S. beaches.[39] However, it was late getting started, the victim of bad roads, worse terrain, and nonstop Allied air strikes. Elements of the 1st Infantry Division, U.S. Army Rangers, and a sprinkling of airborne infantry halted the German attack at Niscemi and Biscari, five miles from the beach. The Allies had successfully established at least a temporary position on the island and had survived day one.[40]

The Germans came back the next day, however, in the most serious threat the Allies would face in the Sicilian campaign. Some sixty German Panzers launched a counterattack, driving forward in two columns. They penetrated the U.S. frontline positions and by noon were less than a mile from the sea, raking American supply dumps

GOING IN ▶

Almost a year before the more famous D-Day in Normandy, there was another, even larger, D-Day in Sicily.

Hermann Göring was born in Bavaria in 1893 into a family of soldiers and bureaucrats. He joined the Prussian Army as a cadet and during the First World War became a fighter pilot in the fledgling German Air Force, eventually rising to command the famous Richthofen squadron and winning Germany's highest honor, Pour le Mérite. After the war, Göring found it hard to settle into civilian life. In 1922 he met Adolf Hitler, joined the National Socialist Party, and became leader of its storm troopers (SA). Wounded in the Hitler Putsch in November 1923, Göring went into exile. He returned later in the 1920s and was one of the party leaders to help engineer Hitler's appointment as chancellor in January 1933. In the first years of the dictatorship, he helped set up the Gestapo (political police force). Already air minister in 1933, in 1935 he was appointed commander in chief of the German Air Force, a position he held until 1945. He oversaw the massive expansion of German air power while at the same time, as plenipotentiary for the Four-Year Plan (1936), he also took a commanding position in the German military economy. His air force was developed chiefly to provide close air support for ground operations. In the Battle of Britain (1940) and the Blitz (1940–41), his air force struggled to wage a strategic air war over British soil. The failure contributed to the gradual decline of Göring's political influence. In 1943 his promise to supply the besieged German Army at Stalingrad was a complete failure, and from then on Hitler marginalized him in the German war effort. In April 1945, with Hitler blockaded in his Berlin bunker, Göring attempted to become Führer in his place. Hitler ordered his arrest and execution, but he was saved by loyal air force troops. He was arrested as a major war criminal, found guilty on all counts at the Nuremberg Trials, and committed suicide in October 1946 on the eve of his hanging.

and landing craft with direct main gun and machine-gun fire. U.S. personnel ashore began burning papers and destroying equipment lest it should fall into enemy hands. The beachhead itself was at stake, but the timely arrival of U.S. reinforcements— elements of the 32nd Field Artillery Battalion—saved the day. Within minutes, they were pouring rounds point-blank into the German Panzer columns, and soon U.S. naval vessels joined in. This hurricane of fire brought the German attack to a halt and rescued Operation Husky in the process.[41]

With the landing phase complete, the campaign proper now began. It took place under three operational dynamics, shaped by the attitudes of the campaign's three main contingents. First, British commanders, specifically Alexander at 15th Army Group and Montgomery of Eighth Army, had no confidence at all in the fighting qualities of their American allies. Second, the U.S. Army leadership—Eisenhower as supreme commander, Patton of Seventh Army, Bradley of II Corps—knew how the British felt, and saw Husky not simply as a chance to conquer the island but also as a way to prove their worth and outdo the British. Finally, after some early vacillating, the German supreme commander in the Mediterranean, Field Marshal Albert Kesselring, had decided that holding Sicily was impossible and had begun preparations to evacuate the island.[42]

These systemic factors—rather than any individual command decisions—governed the fighting. Alexander's operational plan relied almost exclusively on British fighting strength, allotting most of the road space to British tanks and transport. Montgomery

PARATROOPER OF THE 82ND AIRBORNE DIVISION ▶

Helmet

The helmet was the same as that worn by other American military personnel except that it included a heavy chinstrap, similar to that found on a football helmet, designed to keep the helmet in place through the shock of the parachute's deployment. Once on the ground, however, soldiers frequently left their chinstraps unbuckled or folded the strap over the helmet's peak, as this soldier has done.

Tommy Gun

Because paratroopers were expected to fight without support, airborne platoons and companies in all armies had significantly more firepower than their counterparts in the infantry. This trooper carries the M1A1 Thompson submachine gun, a weapon popular with the paratroops. With a twenty- or thirty-round box magazine, the .45-caliber Thompson had serious hitting power and was especially useful for street fighting in Europe's many towns and villages. With each thirteen-man squad equipped with a .30-caliber M1919A4 machine gun and a mix of M1 Garand rifles, M1 carbines, and submachine guns, the U.S. paratrooper squad epitomized the idea of light infantry.

Uniform

Paratroopers' uniforms were designed for soldiers who needed to carry on their persons everything they needed to fight. The M42 jumpsuit worn by this soldier was made of cotton twill, and had four angled pockets on the jacket and a number of interior pockets (including one in the collar designed to hold a switchblade), while the trousers had two cargo pockets with ties, two slash pockets on the waist, and two on the rear: enough pocket space to carry loose ammunition, magazines, grenades, rations, or other miscellaneous items. This trooper's uniform has been reinforced on the knees and elbows with canvas.

The 82nd was originally a "straight-leg" infantry division, serving on the Western Front during the First World War. Germany's employment of airborne troops during its invasion of Holland in 1940 led most of the world's militaries to develop their own airborne troops, and the U.S. Army was no exception. In August 1942, the 82nd was reconstituted as the "82nd Airborne Division." It served with distinction in North Africa, the Mediterranean and Northwest Europe, participating in more combat jumps than any other airborne division in the U.S. Army.

Boots

Paratroopers wore high Corcoran jump boots, designed to provide additional ankle support during landing.

Journalist Dick Tregaskis, who had described the 1st Marine Division's fight in the Solomon Islands in *Guadalcanal Diary*, also landed with U.S. forces in Sicily. In this excerpt from his 1944 book *Invasion Diary*, Tregaskis is with a U.S. infantry platoon driving for the Sicilian town of Nicosia, and, as always, he is as far forward as he can get.

Then the German artillery began to fire at us. We heard the screech of the approaching shell, but it was so quick that we did not have time to hit the deck. I saw a splash of earth forty or fifty yards away, and then the blast of the explosion came almost directly over us. By that time, I was lying down, and I found myself next to a sergeant. Almost immediately we heard the crying of a wounded man, a bubbling sort of attempt at "Help, help," which had the strangely liquid sound of a voice under water. I had heard similar cries of the wounded in the Pacific.

A man hobbled down the hill with his hands over his face, blood running down his shirt. The sergeant called out, "Jimmy, you hit?" Jimmy nodded, made no sound. Another man sat on the ground, one hand holding his back. The captain called, "Medics here!"

I suddenly realized that the burst must have gone off just over my head, for two men had been hit, one on each side of me, neither more than fifteen feet away. Then I, too, began to feel the increasing breathlessness, that almost unbearable tension of waiting for the next shell.

Then it came. We heard the rustling of a shell suddenly swelling into a screech, then bursting with a blast that shook the air and filmed our vision over with concussion. Again there was the breathless moment of waiting for the cries of the wounded, wondering if you, too, had been hit, thinking that you should look and see, not daring for a moment to make the effort. Again the wounded screamed, and we looked up higher on the hill where, apparently, the shell had done most damage. Up there someone cried out, "medics, medics!" It was the same desperate sound I had heard on Guadalcanal, only there the word was "corpsman."[43]

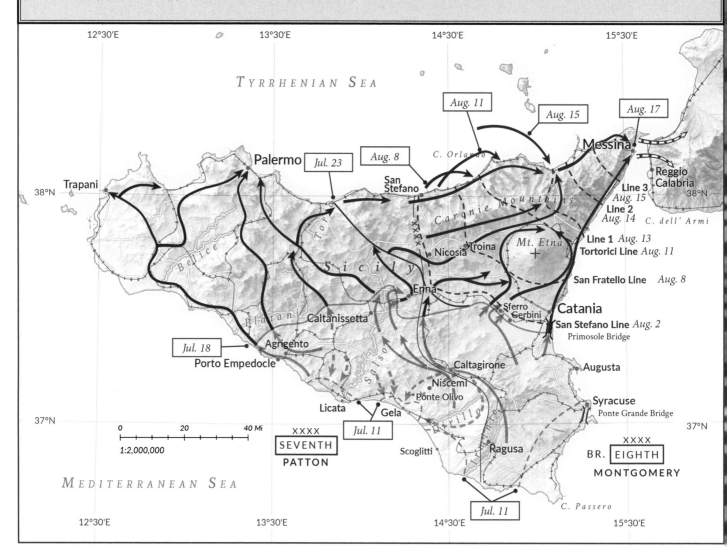

▲ RACE TO MESSINA

Both British and American forces raced across the island to reach Messina, on the northeast coast. Patton's Seventh U.S. Army beat the British (seen here in Catania) by a day, a point of pride for the American forces.

◀ THE CONQUEST OF SICILY

Eisenhower chose wisely when he picked the bold and energetic Patton to lead Seventh Army's sweeping left hook north to Palermo and then east to Messina.

The Germans often blocked the roads in Sicily by blowing up buildings, thus forcing American vehicles to make their way down narrow side streets, where they sometimes hit mines or booby traps.

would launch a frontal assault up the Catania road by XXX Corps, supported by a wide swing west of Mount Etna, the tallest mountain in Sicily, by XIII Corps. That left U.S. Seventh Army with little to do except clear western Sicily. It did so in style, with Patton launching his entire army on July 18 on a high-speed dash to the north and west. Towns fell in a rush, 50,000 prisoners (almost all Italian) fell into U.S. hands, and Patton overran western Sicily in a week with minimal casualties. The climax of his sweep was the fall of Palermo, Sicily's capital, on July 23. It was the first European city conquered by the U.S. Army in World War II.[44]

Patton would later call it a "glorious chapter in the history of war," but in light of the third dynamic of this operation, his ride was almost completely insignificant.[45] While the Germans were fighting hard and defending themselves tenaciously, their overall strategy was to evacuate the island. The end of July saw them retreating into an ever-tighter ring around Messina to the northeast. The U.S. and British press would describe the rest of the campaign as a race for Messina, with Patton and Montgomery vying for honors. But it wasn't much of a race. With two Allied armies

Lieutenant General George S. Patton Jr., and Brigadier General Theodore Roosevelt Jr., consult in Cerami, Sicily, prior to the drive on Messina. Patton did not think highly of Roosevelt's military skills, but recognized him as "one of the bravest men I have ever known." Roosevelt would later be the only general officer to go ashore with the first wave of troops on D-Day in 1944.

abreast (Seventh on the left and Eighth on the right) facing three German divisions in some of the most forbidding mountain terrain in Europe, it was a very slow grind, with a great deal of hard fighting. At Troina, for example, the U.S. 1st Infantry Division suffered heavy losses against fierce German resistance.[46] The mountains limited the effectiveness of U.S. artillery and air strikes, and attempts to flank the town to the north and south came to naught. The Germans were able to successfully break contact and withdraw.

Trying to get things moving in the north, Patton launched frontal assaults in concert with a series of amphibious end runs: small-scale landings behind the German

THE FALL OF ▶
MUSSOLINI'S ITALY

Hitler may have sometimes felt that his alliance with Italy was more trouble than it was worth, but the toppling of Mussolini's regime and the occupation of the lower half of the Italian boot gave an important morale boost to the Allies.

„СОЮЗНИК С ВЕСОМ"

Гитлеровская печать пытается создать шумиху вокруг встречи Гитлера с Муссолини, заявляя в связи с этой встречей, что „Италия снова приобретает военный вес".

(Из газет)

lines. But the Germans were quick enough to slip the traps and kept falling back on Messina. Heavy concentrations of German antiaircraft assets canceled out Allied air-power, and no one in the Allied naval command wished to risk an action in the confined waters of the Straits of Messina, less than two miles wide at the narrowest point. In the end, Patton won the race against Montgomery, entering Messina on August 17, one day before the British. The city was empty, however. The Germans were already safely back on the Italian mainland.

Analysis of Husky almost always calls it a disappointment for the Allies—a "bitter victory."[47] But if it was bitter, it was definitely a victory: the Allies overran the huge island at a cost of only 20,000 casualties, caused the overthrow of Benito Mussolini's regime, and brought one of the three main Axis powers to the brink of collapse. The Allies did fail to halt the German evacuation, but once the Germans decided to leave, it is hard to see what the Allies could have done to stop them.

THE INVASION OF ITALY

The invasion of the Italian peninsula in September 1943 arose from the same factors that had led to Husky.[48] Massive Allied forces—land, sea, and air—were present in the Mediterranean, the direct invasion of Western Europe was still in the planning stages, and there were no prospects of fighting the Germans anywhere else at the moment.

Despite its forced origins, the Italian campaign was a monumental struggle in its own right. In Italy, the Americans and British encountered some extraordinarily tough fighting—not against a logistically starved forlorn hope or a rapidly withdrawing rear-guard action, as in Tunisia and Sicily, respectively, but against a skilled and determined German foe fighting on favorable terrain who at times managed to halt the Allied offensive dead in its tracks. To win the war, the American and British ground forces had to demonstrate that they could pair their quantitative superiority with tactical and operational competence on a par with the German Army's—the same requirement that Soviet armies were in the process of mastering. It was in the course of the fighting on mainland Italy that the Allied armies really showed they were up to the task.

Italy was one of the Axis powers the Allies had committed to driving to unconditional surrender, and Churchill and Roosevelt knew that the Italian leaders had little enthusiasm for continuing the struggle after losing so many men in North Africa. Indeed, the new Italian government of Marshal Pietro Badoglio had already secretly expressed willingness to surrender. Knocking out one of the three main enemy belligerents would be a huge morale booster for the Allies' home fronts, as well as the accomplishment of a principal war aim. It would also constitute real progress toward defeating the Third Reich. It was obvious that the Germans would not simply pull out of the peninsula and allow the Allies to reach their southern border simply because the Italians had given up and asked them to leave, but Allied planners calculated that if they struck rapidly and in conjunction with Italy's surrender announcement, they could occupy at least the southern half of the Italian boot at relatively low cost. Because of the Allied superiority at sea, the expectation was that the Germans would not defend the lower half of the Italian boot, south of Rome. That included the modern Italian airfield complex at Foggia in southern Italy, which would allow Allied bombers to reach the Romanian oil fields at Ploeşti, on which the German war machine depended.

As is often the case in war, things did not go according to plan. The Italians did

Another amphibious operation, the attack at Salerno was far more difficult than the landings in Sicily. The Allies met fierce resistance, but their overwhelming advantage in firepower ultimately assured the success of the landings.

agree to surrender terms, but they handled the surrender ineptly, with Badoglio and King Victor Emmanuel III fleeing Rome as Allied troops landed. Their flight left units of the Italian Army without clear orders.[49] The Germans reacted to news of the surrender with their customary vigor. They launched Operation Axis, a rapid and brutal occupation of key points in the peninsula that involved disarming Italian troops and imprisoning or killing those who resisted.[50]

The first Allied landing took place on September 3, with Montgomery's Eighth Army landing in Calabria, on the toe of the boot, after an immense 630-gun artillery barrage. That display of firepower proved to be wholly unnecessary. The Germans did not contest the landing and were already pulling back to the north.[51] On September 9 U.S. Fifth Army, led by General Mark Clark, landed near Salerno, 150 miles up the western coast and 40 miles south of Naples. Called Operation Avalanche, it was the first return of the U.S. Army to the European mainland since 1918.

Clark had two corps in the initial Salerno landing: British X on his left and U.S. VI on his right. The British would bear the main burden, as they had to land, establish themselves, and then wheel northwest on the great city of Naples. The American mission was to guard the inland flank of the British maneuver. To do so, they would land

General Mark Clark's Fifth Army landed at Salerno south of Naples on September 9, 1943, and ran into trouble almost immediately. U.S. troops were unsteady, coordination with the British was tenuous, and German mechanized and Panzer divisions ringed the beaches. Operation Avalanche was, in Clark's memorable phrase, a "near disaster." Here he describes the battle's crisis point:

In the center of the beachhead heavy fighting swung back and forth around the Tobacco Factory, and elements of the 45th Division, which had been pushed back from the Ponte Sele, were in danger of being isolated. It was becoming obvious that General Ernest J. Dawley had not been fully aware of the strength of the enemy on his left flank and had not taken steps or been able to take steps to protect himself from counterattack in that sector after the failure of our thrusts toward Ponte Sele and Battipaglia. Furthermore, as the counterattacks developed, it was disclosed that all the troops had been committed in a cordon defense, leaving none in reserve to meet an enemy breakthrough. We were getting into a very tight place.

I recall that about this time I had to consider the possibility that we would be driven back to the sea. . . . I went down to look over the vast piles of supplies on the beach and to recall the stern admonitions that had been drilled into us in school about taking precautions to prevent stores from falling into the hands of the enemy. I knew that if I were involved in a theoretical problem at the War College, I would at this point get hell from some instructor if I failed to issue orders to be prepared for possible destruction of those supplies; but this wasn't a theoretical problem, and I couldn't see how I'd do anything but damage morale if I issued such orders at Salerno. I thought it over carefully as I walked along the beach. I was dirty and tired and worried, and, finally, I said to hell with the theory. I'm not going to issue any such orders. Furthermore, I decided, the only way they're going to get us off this beach is to push us, step by step, into the water.[53]

near Paestum and advance into the high ground overlooking the beaches. The Salerno landing, however, ran into major trouble from the start.[52] The main operational obstacle was the Sele River, which bisected the Salerno plain, blocking contact between the two corps.

Closing the Sele gap before the Germans could take advantage was a priority, but it proved to be a problem. Avalanche met fierce German opposition from the outset, with just three Allied divisions fighting elements of six German divisions. Seeking surprise, U.S. troops went in at 3:00 a.m. on September 9 without a preliminary bombardment but nonetheless found themselves under heavy fire the moment they landed. As Clark himself admitted, it came very close to disaster.[54] By the twelfth, the Germans identified the Sele gap and launched a major thrust against it the next day. The target was the Tobacco Factory, a small group of stone warehouses overlooking the Sele.[55] U.S. defenders were badly strung out, with the 36th Infantry Division holding a thirty-five-mile front that was nothing more than an outpost line, and the 45th Division still not completely ashore. The Panzers broke into the clear and by dusk were just half a mile from the sea. In a replay of Sicily, all that stood in their way was a U.S. gun line (elements of two artillery battalions), along with a handful of tank destroyers. A few hundred yards behind them was the Fifth Army's command post, defended by a hastily formed line of "cooks, clerks, and drivers."[56] If the Germans could punch through it, the beachhead was doomed. What saved the day was a burned bridge over

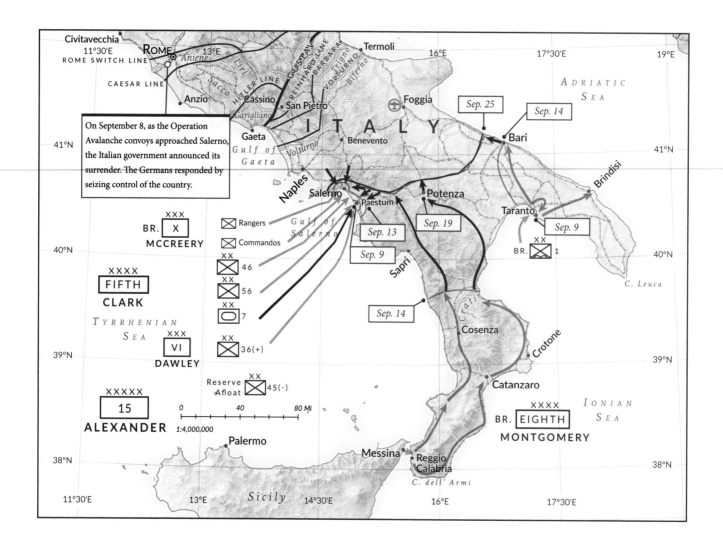

On September 8, as the Operation Avalanche convoys approached Salerno, the Italian government announced its surrender. The Germans responded by seizing control of the country.

OPERATION AVALANCHE ▲

The Germans anticipated an Allied amphibious operation at Salerno, which was near the limits of the range of fighter aircraft flying from Sicily. Realizing that they lacked the strength to halt a landing at the beaches, the defenders held the high ground and bought time for reinforcements to arrive.

the Calore River, a tributary to the Sele, that halted the Germans just long enough for the U.S. guns to open up and pour on a destructive barrage of fire.[57]

In the end, the margin of survival on the Salerno Beach contained two elements. The first was determination. The Americans did not crumple from the shock of the attack as they had at Sidi bou-Zid in Tunisia. The second was well-coordinated firepower: land, air, and sea. While still in the mountains, the Germans were fairly safe. But once they came down onto the plain, they were nothing but a vulnerable target. During the fighting on the thirteenth, U.S. artillery fired 3,650 rounds in just four hours, and every German commander at Salerno mentioned the unequal fight against naval bombardment. Steaming just off the mouth of the Sele, the cruiser U.S.S. *Philadelphia* fired some one thousand 6-inch rounds at point-blank ranges, and the U.S.S. *Boise* came close to that figure.[58] Joining them were USAAF B-17 Flying Fortress bombers used in a tactical role against exposed attacking forces crowded around a very small bridgehead. Wehrmacht losses were terrific, with the 16th Panzer Division losing two-thirds of its tanks on the first day alone. Under such an onslaught, German pressure on the beachhead began to slacken. A last-ditch attack on September 16 suffered crippling losses and went nowhere. The battle for Salerno was over, and with Montgomery finally coming up out of Calabria, the German divisions attacking

◀ MOUNTAINOUS TERRAIN
IN ITALY

Taken near Prato in 1945, this photograph gives a good sense of the
difficulty of the Apennine terrain
through which Allied forces had to
fight their way north.

the bridgehead had no choice but to retreat from the whole area. Clark took Naples,
southern Italy's largest city, on October 2.

Often overlooked is the impact that Salerno had on the plans of the German High
Command. Hitler had first thought of abandoning southern Italy and defending
higher up, near the top of the boot. He wanted to hold the Po River Valley, Italy's
population and resource center, and had created a new Army Group B under Field
Marshal Erwin Rommel to defend it. But Kesselring argued for a line much farther
south—even south of Rome if possible. It would be a shorter line and would therefore require a much smaller force than Rommel would need in the north. The lack-
luster Allied showing at Salerno, where the Germans had come close, once again,
to crumpling an unsteady American beachhead, brought Hitler around: the Wehrmacht would defend Italy south of Rome, establishing a defensive position along the
Volturno River.[59]

This decision fundamentally changed the campaign. Rather than a rapid drive up

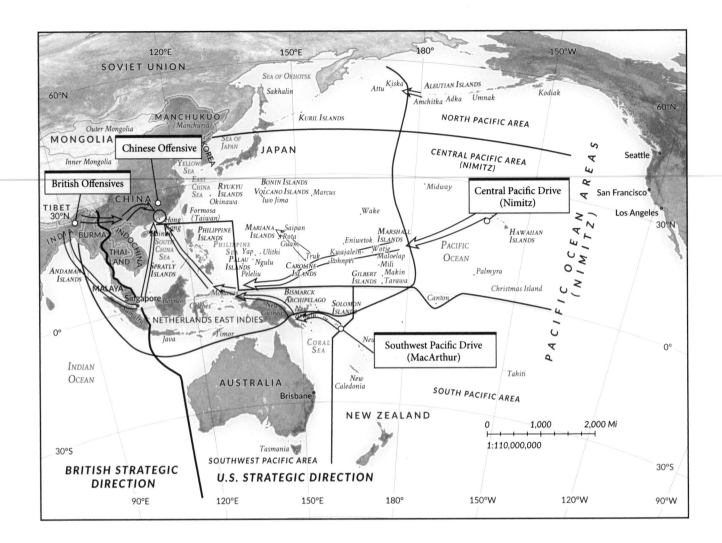

the peninsula, the Allies now had to claw their way inch by inch up the boot. The fighting was hard and bloody, consisting of one Allied frontal assault after another. Italy has a rocky spine in the Apennine Mountains, and hundreds of rivers, gullies, and gorges radiate out to either coast, each one an ideal defensive position. Repeatedly, the Germans would make a stand on one line, prepare another to the rear, and then retreat when the Allies had penetrated. By December 1943, the Allies were still hung up in front of the Gustav Line, the main German defensive position, eighty miles south of Rome. Positioned just behind the swift Rapido River, anchored on the town and monastery of Monte Cassino, and then running to the Sangro River on the Adriatic Sea, the position was impossible to flank and difficult to crack. The Allies tried repeatedly and failed, and the dismal weather only made it worse. It remained an unsolved problem as 1944 dawned.

THE PACIFIC IN 1943: SEIZING THE INITIATIVE

Just as the Germans were now on the defensive, so it was with the Japanese. In the course of 1943, a vast Allied coalition would pose a series of operational challenges

that the Japanese would find increasingly difficult to counter. The Imperial Japanese Army was now facing multiple foes: there were the U.S. forces in the Solomon Islands, New Guinea, and the Central Pacific, supported ably by their Australian and New Zealand allies; in the China-Burma-India (CBI) theater, the Japanese met increasingly well-supported British, American, Indian, and Chinese forces; and in mainland China, Generalissimo Chiang Kai-shek's massive *Kuomintang* (Nationalist) Army. The Japanese would have had some chance against any one of these enemies, but all of them together posed an insurmountable problem. As a result, the Allies would seize the initiative in 1943. They were able to choose the time and place to attack, forcing the Japanese to respond to diverse blows from multiple directions. With the Japanese spread even more thinly than the Wehrmacht in Europe, that would prove to be a war-winning formula, stretching Japan's already inferior resources well beyond the safety point. As in Europe, nothing particularly decisive would happen during this difficult year, but the Allies would demonstrate an increasing superiority over their enemies in qualitative as well as quantitative terms, and set themselves up to strike mortal blows against the Japanese Empire the following year.

▲ MacArthur and Nimitz

General Douglas MacArthur and Admiral Chester Nimitz (with President Roosevelt between them) operated independent commands in the Pacific, regularly arguing over supplies and strategies.

By 1943, the main outlines of U.S. Pacific strategy were in place. The Joint Chiefs of Staff had organized the Pacific Ocean into two gigantic commands—the Southwest Pacific Area and the Pacific Ocean Area—and further subdivided the latter into North, Central, and South Pacific Areas. General Douglas MacArthur commanded the Southwest Pacific Area, leaving operations in these areas largely in the hands of the army. Admiral Chester Nimitz commanded the Pacific Ocean Area, making it a navy theater.[60]

As a result, there was no single, overall military commander for the U.S. war against Japan. Analysts both then and since have been highly critical of this arrangement. Unity of command is a universally recognized principle of war; yet in the Pacific war, virtually every American decision had to come before the Joint Chiefs, to be thrashed out by representatives of the various services, and sometimes even by the president. One respected historian of the war called this system a "monstrosity,"[61] and even the U.S. Army's official history regretted the "duplication of effort and keen competition for the limited supplies of ships, landing craft, and airplanes."[62]

Even so, the case for divided command was a convincing one. The Pacific Ocean is not merely a "military theater." It is one-third the surface of the globe. Operations required for a drive across the Central Pacific, with vast expanses of open ocean and its tiny islands and atolls, would necessarily be of a different character than those in the Southwest Pacific, where giant islands abound and a great deal of ground fighting would be necessary. New Guinea, for example, is almost four times the size of Great Britain, and operations there were not "island warfare" so much as a major land campaign. Placing operations there under naval command would have been as senseless as placing the South and Central Pacific drives, where the intricacies of naval warfare and carrier operations were dominant, under the command of an army officer.

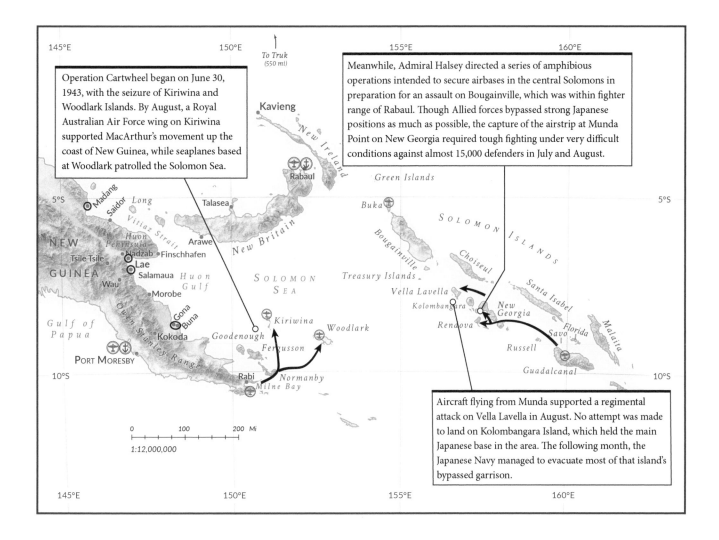

Operation Cartwheel began on June 30, 1943, with the seizure of Kiriwina and Woodlark Islands. By August, a Royal Australian Air Force wing on Kiriwina supported MacArthur's movement up the coast of New Guinea, while seaplanes based at Woodlark patrolled the Solomon Sea.

Meanwhile, Admiral Halsey directed a series of amphibious operations intended to secure airbases in the central Solomons in preparation for an assault on Bougainville, which was within fighter range of Rabaul. Though Allied forces bypassed strong Japanese positions as much as possible, the capture of the airstrip at Munda Point on New Georgia required tough fighting under very difficult conditions against almost 15,000 defenders in July and August.

Aircraft flying from Munda supported a regimental attack on Vella Lavella in August. No attempt was made to land on Kolombangara Island, which held the main Japanese base in the area. The following month, the Japanese Navy managed to evacuate most of that island's bypassed garrison.

▲ OPERATION CARTWHEEL, JUNE–AUGUST 1943

Despite the tensions built into the Pacific command structure, with army and navy each demanding priority for their respective sectors, operations were not hampered to any significant degree. The year opened with U.S. forces engaged at a number of locations in the South and Southwest Pacific Areas. Most notable were two already nearly completed campaigns: in Guadalcanal, where the protracted U.S. effort to seize the island was finally coming to an end, and New Guinea, where a Japanese attempt to cross the Owen Stanley Mountains and seize the key base of Port Moresby in the summer of 1942 had come to grief against tough Australian resistance and inadequate Japanese logistics. A combined Australian-American counteroffensive then pushed the Japanese back over the forbidding mountain range in horrible conditions of rain and mud, and drove them back to their original bridgeheads at Buna, Gona, and Sanananda. Here a series of bloody Allied assaults brought Japanese resistance to an end by January 1943.[63]

With the Japanese exhausted by their twin defeats, MacArthur was thinking big, with a plan called Operation Cartwheel. The objective was the principal Japanese air and naval base in the Southwest Pacific: the vast fortress complex of Rabaul on the island of New Britain. Since assaulting it frontally would be costly and bloody, MacArthur drew up a plan for a complex series of preliminary landings that would

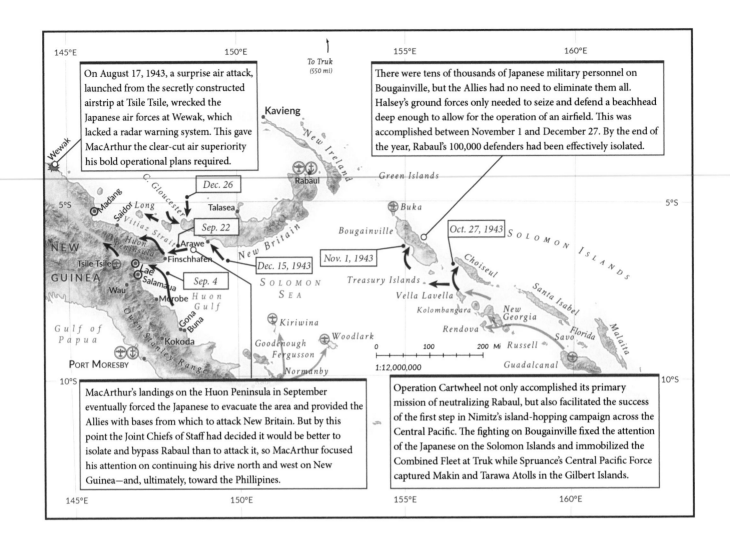

On August 17, 1943, a surprise air attack, launched from the secretly constructed airstrip at Tsile Tsile, wrecked the Japanese air forces at Wewak, which lacked a radar warning system. This gave MacArthur the clear-cut air superiority his bold operational plans required.

There were tens of thousands of Japanese military personnel on Bougainville, but the Allies had no need to eliminate them all. Halsey's ground forces only needed to seize and defend a beachhead deep enough to allow for the operation of an airfield. This was accomplished between November 1 and December 27. By the end of the year, Rabaul's 100,000 defenders had been effectively isolated.

MacArthur's landings on the Huon Peninsula in September eventually forced the Japanese to evacuate the area and provided the Allies with bases from which to attack New Britain. But by this point the Joint Chiefs of Staff had decided it would be better to isolate and bypass Rabaul than to attack it, so MacArthur focused his attention on continuing his drive north and west on New Guinea—and, ultimately, toward the Phillipines.

Operation Cartwheel not only accomplished its primary mission of neutralizing Rabaul, but also facilitated the success of the first step in Nimitz's island-hopping campaign across the Central Pacific. The fighting on Bougainville fixed the attention of the Japanese on the Solomon Islands and immobilized the Combined Fleet at Truk while Spruance's Central Pacific Force captured Makin and Tarawa Atolls in the Gilbert Islands.

OPERATION CARTWHEEL, ▲
AUGUST–DECEMBER 1943

flank Rabaul to the west and the east, establish air bases closer and closer to the complex, and eventually attack it. Cartwheel called for no fewer than thirteen separate landings within eight months along the northern coast of New Guinea and up the Solomon Islands chain.[64] Southwest Pacific command would begin by landing on Woodlark and Kiriwina Islands, protecting the northeastern flank of New Guinea, followed by a series of landings on the northern coast of New Guinea itself to secure the Huon Peninsula. Meanwhile, forces of the South Pacific Area, led by Admiral William F. Halsey, would advance up the Solomon chain from the south, landing first on New Georgia and Bougainville. The point of all these maneuvers was, as MacArthur put it, "to advance our bomber line towards Rabaul."[65] Once sufficient air bases were available, the pincers would close on Rabaul, culminating in a landing on New Britain.

Cartwheel opened on June 30, 1943, and the months-long plan proceeded just as MacArthur had hoped. Halsey's pincer landed on New Georgia in July, Vella Lavella in August, and Bougainville in November, feinting toward some islands and bypassing others. MacArthur handled his part of the operation with skill. Building a secret airstrip in a grassy valley at Tsile Tsile, sixty miles west of the Japanese positions at Lae and Salamaua on the Huon Gulf, he launched a series of bomber raids on the Japanese air base at Wewak that destroyed much of Japanese Fourth Air Army. The Australian

9th Division conducted amphibious landings east of Lae, which, in concert with an airdrop at Nadzab, to the west of Lae, boxed in the Japanese defenders. By September, both Lae and Salamaua were in Allied hands. Another amphibious landing by Australian troops secured Finschhafen, and by November, the Allies had overrun the Huon Peninsula. The final act of 1943 was a landing at Cape Gloucester on western New Britain, on December 26.

The pincers were closing on Rabaul, but they never did close completely. Massive raids by U.S. carrier aircraft in November pummeled the base and succeeded in breaking the backs of Japanese air and naval power in the Southwest Pacific. Japanese naval units evacuated Rabaul for the Truk Islands, eight hundred miles to the north. Japanese troop strength in Rabaul still topped 90,000, but the remaining garrison was isolated, undersupplied, and increasingly irrelevant in a strategic sense. Ultimately, the U.S. Joint Chiefs decided to bypass the fortress altogether. Cartwheel had triumphed, in other words, without actually taking its primary objective.[66]

None of it had been simple, however. Every fight in the Pacific was difficult. Both the Solomons and New Guinea were covered by tropical rain forest, with razor-sharp grasses, crawling vines, tangled roots, and giant hardwood trees that blocked out the sun. It was a world of giant ants, three-inch wasps, spiders, leeches, and mosquitos that carried malaria. As bad as all these things were for the Americans, they were that much harder for the Japanese infantry, whose supplies of equipment, ammunition, and food were far inferior. The imbalance was often crucial in battle, and recent research suggests that more Japanese soldiers may have died from starvation than from combat. In this light, the Japanese soldier's continued resolve, in defense and then in vigorous counterattack, is all the more impressive.[67]

▲ ISLAND FIGHTING

A column of Marines trudges forward to the fighting lines on Bougainville in this 1944 charcoal drawing by war artist Kerr Eby, a World War I veteran who accompanied frontline troops in the Pacific as a member of the combat artists program.

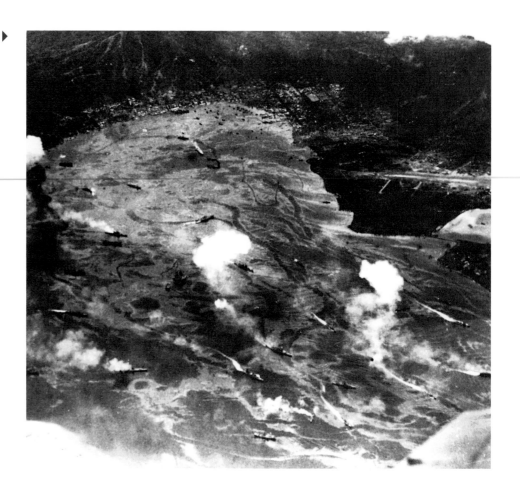

RAID ON RABAUL ▶

Japanese ships disperse off the coast of Rabaul during an American raid on November 5. The photographer was Paul Barnett of the U.S. Navy, and he was killed by Japanese fire moments after taking this picture.

THE GILBERTS

As 1943 drew to an end, one last key battle took place. On November 20 the second great American drive across the central Pacific began under Admiral Nimitz, with elements of the 27th Infantry and 2nd Marine Divisions assaulting the relatively minor islands of Makin and Tarawa in the Gilbert Islands.[68] Though a small operation in the scheme of things, the landing was nevertheless crucial in setting a pattern for much of the Pacific War. When dug in, the Japanese had all the tactical advantages that come with a well-planned defensive position, multiplied by the inherent difficulties an attacker meets in any amphibious landing. Their defenses formed an interwoven network of bunkers, pillboxes, and dugouts, with machine guns, coastal artillery, and mortars sited for mutual support. On Makin and Tarawa, Japanese forces had created positions as strong as any professional military could have devised in 1943.

Countering these tactical advantages, however, the Americans were able to leverage their strengths on the strategic and operational levels. The Battle of Midway had given them the initiative in this vast theater, allowing them to choose their target in the Gilberts and to assemble overwhelming strength for the assaults on Tarawa and Makin. They could also afford to concentrate much of their considerable firepower in the Central Pacific—both air and naval—against the Gilberts. In the end,

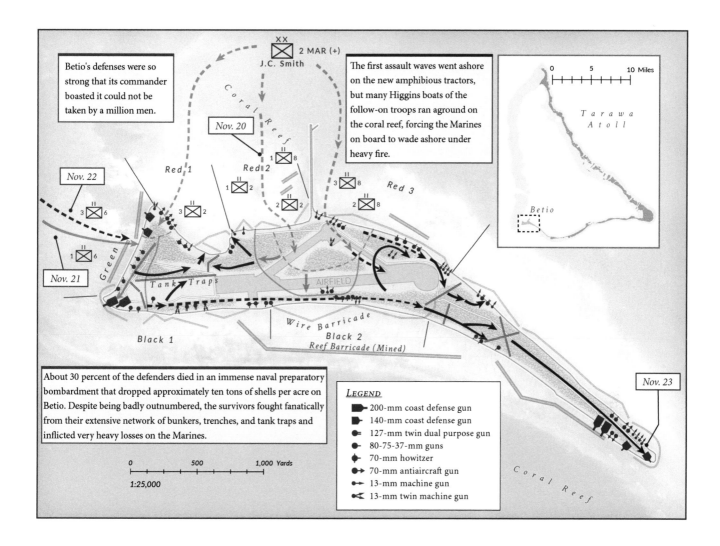

Betio's defenses were so strong that its commander boasted it could not be taken by a million men.

The first assault waves went ashore on the new amphibious tractors, but many Higgins boats of the follow-on troops ran aground on the coral reef, forcing the Marines on board to wade ashore under heavy fire.

About 30 percent of the defenders died in an immense naval preparatory bombardment that dropped approximately ten tons of shells per acre on Betio. Despite being badly outnumbered, the survivors fought fanatically from their extensive network of bunkers, trenches, and tank traps and inflicted very heavy losses on the Marines.

LEGEND
- 200-mm coast defense gun
- 140-mm coast defense gun
- 127-mm twin dual purpose gun
- 80-75-37-mm guns
- 70-mm howitzer
- 70-mm antiaircraft gun
- 13-mm machine gun
- 13-mm twin machine gun

0   500   1,000 Yards

1:25,000

two U.S. divisions—some 30,000 men in all, supported heavily from the sea and air—confronted about 5,000 isolated Japanese defenders.

Though U.S. forces had the clear advantage in terms of both manpower and firepower, the fighting was still far from easy. On Makin atoll, a U.S. regimental combat team of the 27th Division had a very tough time rooting out a mere 400 Japanese defenders, suffering 200 casualties in the process. Even worse was in store for the Marines storming tiny Betio Island—part of the Tarawa Atoll, 110 miles south of Makin. Enough Japanese defenders, protected in deep bunkers, survived the preliminary U.S. bombardment to shoot the first assault waves to pieces. Uncertain intelligence also played a role here. Planners had thought U.S. amphibious landing craft would be able to get over Betio's coral reef, but they were wrong. The Marines therefore had to wade hundreds of yards to the shore, holding their rifles aloft and dodging enemy fire the entire time. Offshore, torpedoes from the Japanese submarine *I-175* also sank the American carrier *Liscome Bay* off of Makin, killing more than 600 crewmen. While U.S. forces did manage to secure both objectives, they took extremely high casualties for such brief fighting: nearly 1,000 dead and 2,000 wounded. The price paid for such a tiny objective shocked the American public, as did the grisly casualty photos published in the press.[69]

▲ THE BATTLE OF TARAWA, NOVEMBER 20–23, 1943

While there were fewer than five thousand Japanese defenders on Betio Island, they were well entrenched in reinforced concrete bunkers. American Marines suffered heavy casualties and took four days to clear the island.

As they came close to the shore, the Marines reached another barrier—barbed wire. Japanese machine guns were sited to lay enfilading fire along these obstacles.

TARAWA ▶

Unlike the Higgins boats, the amtracs (amphibious tractors) were able to cross the reefs and carry their passengers up to the shore, but many of them were knocked out on the beaches.

TARAWA ▶

The LVTs used at Tarawa were unarmored, but they could still provide at least some protection (and covering machine gun fire) for Marines trying to push off the beaches.

TARAWA

Japanese bunkers made with coconut logs, sand, and coral proved surprisingly resistant to the Americans' preliminary air and naval bombardment, and enough Japanese soldiers survived to inflict heavy losses on the landing force.

TARAWA

The sea wall that had prevented many of the amtracs from moving inland also provided some shelter for the Marines. As the invasion force moved ahead, the wounded were brought back to aid stations set up behind it.

TARAWA

As the high tide ebbed, it uncovered men who had died on the Japanese wire. Kerr Eby, the World War I veteran and combat artist whose sketches are presented here, wrote that "in two wars, I think this is the most frightful thing I have seen."

TARAWA LANDING ▲

The American capture of Tarawa was a crucial strategic victory. It demonstrated both Japan's resolve to hold the Pacific islands that were the stepping stones toward the Japanese homeland, and the American ability to capture them despite strong defenses.

The possession of an insignificant island such as Tarawa was obviously not worth the human losses on either side, and even the victorious Americans could see how far they still were from Tokyo and ultimate victory. Nevertheless, the battle for Tarawa, like Guadalcanal, was crucial on the strategic level. The Japanese were unlikely to fortify any position in the Pacific more heavily than they had fortified Tarawa, and a mere four days of fighting had utterly destroyed them. Their entire Pacific strategy—based on the notion that the Americans lacked the stomach to fight their way across the entire Pacific Ocean island by island and atoll by atoll—now lay in ruins.

CONCLUSION

By the end of 1943, the global war was in full swing, and it would have been difficult to find a spot on earth that was not affected by it in one way or the other. From Soviet antitank gunners grimly holding the line at Kursk, to Allied transport pilots in the CBI trying to manage the difficult flight over the Himalayan "Hump" into China, to civilians in many lands trying only to survive their ordeal, the world was in arms.

It was precisely the vast expanse of the global conflict, however, that conveyed a decisive advantage to the Allied powers. They controlled a large majority of the earth's

resources and industrial production, had relatively secure lines of seaborne communication for shifting forces from one spot to the next, and were in the process of winning firm control of the air. Both Germany and Japan were now trapped in a war of attrition against vastly superior foes.

Beyond Allied superiority in numbers and logistics, however, one last fact emerges from the 1943 fighting. The Allied armies had by now recovered from their early difficulties and were planning and executing their operations with a great deal of skill. The tough fighting in the Solomons; MacArthur and Eisenhower's skillful use of amphibious mobility in the Southwest Pacific and the Mediterranean, respectively; the ability of U.S. forces to storm even the most heavily fortified positions, such as Tarawa; and, above all, the development of the Red Army into the world's dominant land power—these were the hallmarks of 1943.

At sea, too, 1943 was a big year for the Allies, as we saw in chapter 2. They finally seemed to have gotten the German U-boat menace under control. May was the crucial month in the Battle of the Atlantic—called "Black May" by the Germans—in which improved Allied convoy tactics sent no fewer than forty-one submarines to the bottom of the ocean, or about 25 percent of Germany's total number of operational boats.

▲ TEHRAN CONFERENCE
The first official meeting of the Big Three Allied leaders (Stalin, Roosevelt, and Churchill) in November 1943 led to an agreement for the opening of a second European front in the coming year.

Likewise, in the air, the American Eighth Air Force had arrived in the European theater, and while it would experience a slow start, it too began to present Germany with yet another challenge to its limited resource base. From here until the end of the war, the Axis would be under siege across the full spectrum of operational domains.

While all of the battles of 1943 had been fierce and bloody, the Allies had managed to win every one of them, and that surely was no accident. The initiative was now firmly in their hands. But the ferocity of the fighting on land, sea, and air had dispelled any illusions that the war would be over soon or that victory over the Axis was going to come cheaply.

INTRODUCTION

The climax of the war in the European Theater of Operations came in the final two years of fighting, in 1944 and 1945. A series of great campaigns and battles engulfed the Continent, each seemingly larger and more lethal than the one before. When this convulsion of violence was over, the Allies had smashed the German war machine—and much of Europe in the process.[1]

On the Eastern Front, the Soviet Army conducted three vast offensives in this period: In June 1944 the Byelorussian offensive, Operation Bagration, smashed an entire German army group, an unprecedented event. In January 1945 the lunge from Warsaw to the Oder River on Germany's eastern border brought Soviet forces into the heart of the Reich, from East Prussia to Silesia. Finally, in April 1945, the Battle of Berlin was perhaps the most bitter city fight of the war, leading to Hitler's suicide and the end of the war in Europe. In all these victories, the Red Army showed that its military qualities went well beyond sheer numbers: it now had tested commanders at all levels, impressive skills at combined mechanized warfare, and a sophisticated operational doctrine of Deep Battle.

While the Western Allies opened 1944 still trying to get themselves moving in Italy, they too wound up landing heavy blows. Operation Overlord, the landing in Normandy, and the subsequent drive across Western Europe showed that British and U.S. armies had finally learned how to fight high-intensity warfare. This chapter will look at the planning and execution of the D-Day landings; the very difficult fighting in the *bocage* country of Normandy; the Operation Cobra breakout and the Allied drive across Europe; the last German offensive in the Ardennes (the Battle of the Bulge); and finally, the hard fighting of 1945 and the drive into the heart of Germany.

The battles mentioned above form only a partial list. With the economies of all the participants now fully mobilized for war, the campaigns of 1944–45 dwarfed anything seen before or since. Moreover, all of the military forces involved in the fighting had honed their skills to a high degree and were much more efficient killing machines than they had been at the outset. For that very reason, the last year of the war would be the bloodiest in the entire conflict.

THE EASTERN FRONT IN 1944

The end of 1943 saw Soviet armies on the move in the southern sector of the Eastern Front, harrying the depleted formations of Army Group South to the Dnieper. It is a sign of the toll taken on the Germans in the hard fighting of 1943 that they were unable even to hold their line at that mighty river. Soviet forces crossed the Dnieper at numerous places: first at Bukrin, south of Kiev; and then at Cherkassy, Kremenchug, and Dnepropetrovsk, eventually linking up to form an immense fortified position on the western bank.[2] Calling it a bridgehead, the usual designation for such a position, is a considerable understatement: it was as big as some European countries.

FINLAND
HELSINKI
Leningrad

Tallinn
Riga
Vilna
Begins Jun. 19, 19
Operation
Bagration

NORWAY
OSLO
STOCKHOLM

SWEDEN

NORTH SEA

DENMARK
COPENHAGEN

BALTIC SEA

UNITED
KINGDOM
LONDON

NETH.
AMSTERDAM
Operation
Market
Arnhem   Sep. 17, 1944
Operation
Garden
Antwerp
BRUSSELS   Aachen   Mar. 7, 1945
BELG.   Remagen
Ardennes
LUXEMBOURG

Berlin
Torgau   Apr. 25, 1945

POLAND
Warsaw   Kowel
Lublin

GERMANY

Lvov
Tarnopol

PRAGUE
PROTECTORATE
OF
BOHEMIA AND MORAVIA

SLOVAKIA

HUNGARY

Jun. 6, 1944
Operation
Overlord

Caen

Falaise   Aug. 25, 1944

Paris

Dec. 25, 1944

Danube

VIENNA

Budapest
Feb. 13, 1945

FRANCE

Loire   Seine

47°30'N

BERN
SWITZ.   Alps

ZAGREB

YUGOSLAVIA   ROMAN

BELGRADE
Danu

ITALY

Apennines

SARAJEVO
Dinaric Alps

Pyrenees

42°N

Operation
Dragoon

Aug. 15, 1944

ADRIATIC SEA   BU
Sofia

ALB.

SPAIN

Rome
Jun. 5, 1944
Anzio   Monte Cassino
Operation
Shingle
Jan. 22, 1944

GREECE

TYRRHENIAN SEA

MEDITERRANEAN SEA

Sicily

ATHE

ALGIERS

TUNIS

ALGERIA   TUNISIA   Malta

1°30'W   9°E   19°30'E   30°E

58°30'N

53°N

9°E   19°30'E

Niemen   Bug   Carp

Rhine

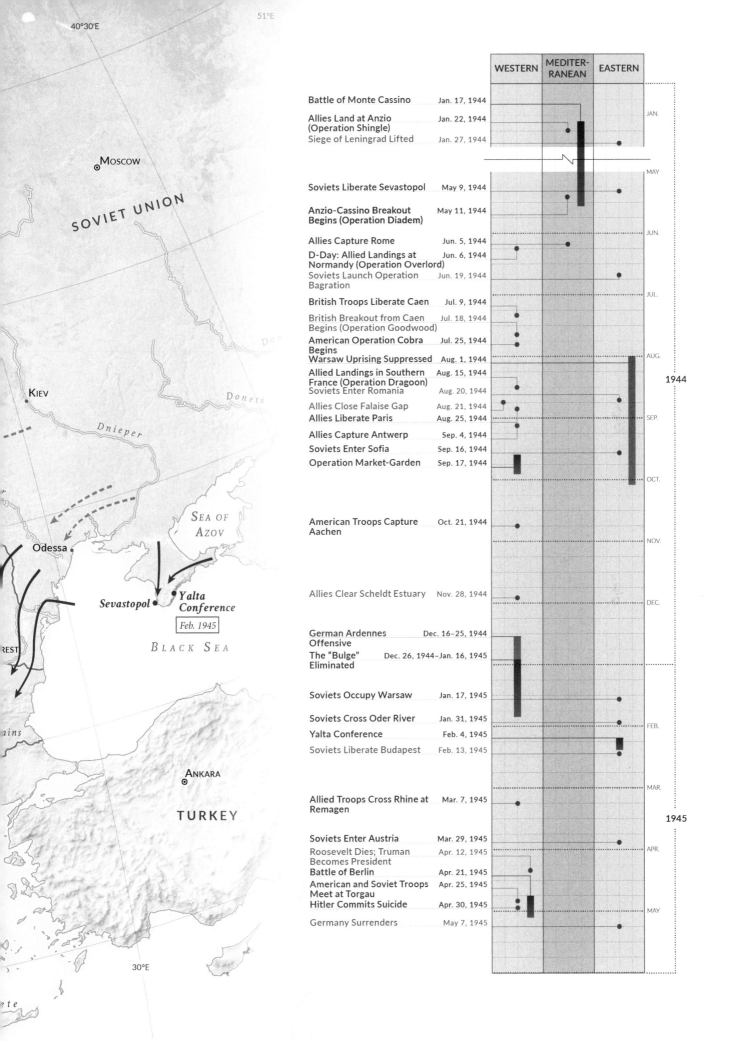

	WESTERN	MEDITER-RANEAN	EASTERN	
Battle of Monte Cassino	Jan. 17, 1944			
Allies Land at Anzio (Operation Shingle)	Jan. 22, 1944			
Siege of Leningrad Lifted	Jan. 27, 1944			
Soviets Liberate Sevastopol	May 9, 1944			
Anzio-Cassino Breakout Begins (Operation Diadem)	May 11, 1944			
Allies Capture Rome	Jun. 5, 1944			
D-Day: Allied Landings at Normandy (Operation Overlord)	Jun. 6, 1944			
Soviets Launch Operation Bagration	Jun. 19, 1944			
British Troops Liberate Caen	Jul. 9, 1944			
British Breakout from Caen Begins (Operation Goodwood)	Jul. 18, 1944			
American Operation Cobra Begins	Jul. 25, 1944			
Warsaw Uprising Suppressed	Aug. 1, 1944			
Allied Landings in Southern France (Operation Dragoon)	Aug. 15, 1944			
Soviets Enter Romania	Aug. 20, 1944			
Allies Close Falaise Gap	Aug. 21, 1944			
Allies Liberate Paris	Aug. 25, 1944			
Allies Capture Antwerp	Sep. 4, 1944			
Soviets Enter Sofia	Sep. 16, 1944			
Operation Market-Garden	Sep. 17, 1944			
American Troops Capture Aachen	Oct. 21, 1944			
Allies Clear Scheldt Estuary	Nov. 28, 1944			
German Ardennes Offensive	Dec. 16–25, 1944			
The "Bulge" Eliminated	Dec. 26, 1944–Jan. 16, 1945			
Soviets Occupy Warsaw	Jan. 17, 1945			
Soviets Cross Oder River	Jan. 31, 1945			
Yalta Conference	Feb. 4, 1945			
Soviets Liberate Budapest	Feb. 13, 1945			
Allied Troops Cross Rhine at Remagen	Mar. 7, 1945			
Soviets Enter Austria	Mar. 29, 1945			
Roosevelt Dies; Truman Becomes President	Apr. 12, 1945			
Battle of Berlin	Apr. 21, 1945			
American and Soviet Troops Meet at Torgau	Apr. 25, 1945			
Hitler Commits Suicide	Apr. 30, 1945			
Germany Surrenders	May 7, 1945			

1944

1945

VICTORIA

EJERCITOS DE LAS NACIONES UNIDAS QUE DERROTARON A ALEMANIA

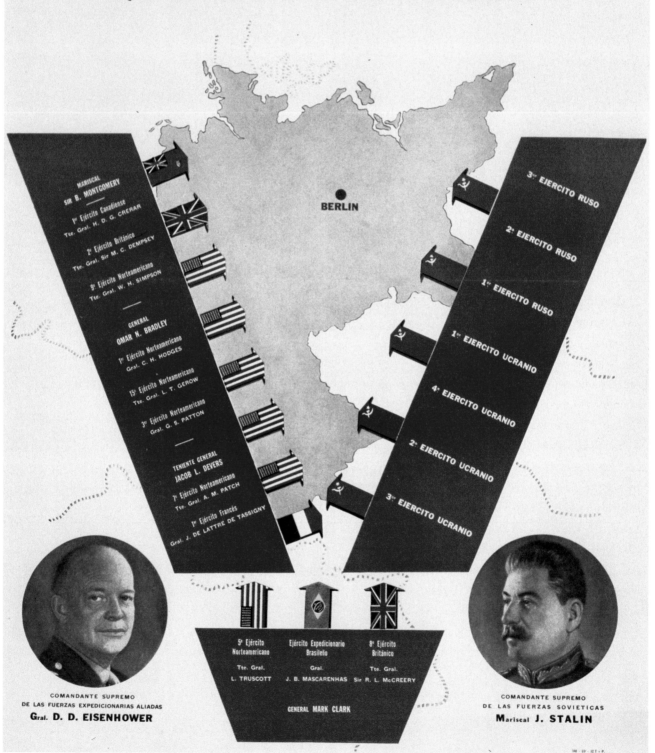

◀ Soviet T-34
By 1944, the Soviet Army had made substantial strides in both personnel and material resources. Veteran tank crews operating T-34s plagued the Wehrmacht soldiers who had invaded Russia.

The fighting never stopped as winter arrived. By now, the Soviets had four fronts (army groups) on line in the south: the 1st through 4th Ukrainian. These contained all six of the Red Army's tank armies—the most powerful formations in the order of battle.[3] Soviet numerical superiority in Ukraine was three to one, although it was much higher in designated breakthrough sectors. In those areas, the Germans were often outnumbered by ten to one or more in armor, artillery, and aircraft.[4]

More important than numbers, however, was the increasing quality of the Red Army on all levels. The concept of Deep Battle, first theorized in the 1930s, was now coming to full fruition. Assault forces concentrated against extremely narrow sectors of the German line, with entire armies deployed along a mere ten miles of front. Behind them, Soviet commanders deployed in depth with a second and even a third echelon of reserves, preparing to feed them in along the same axis of attack after the first wave had achieved a breakthrough.[5] A gifted and now experienced officer corps was handling operations, and it was backed by a much-improved logistical network.

It is easy to equate Soviet operational doctrine with the simple application of mass, but that is unfair. Rather than a simple reliance on brute force, Soviet commanders from division on up had mastered the art of fighting the German Army. They invariably employed "forward detachments" as their attack spearheads.[6] Powerful forces of

◀ V for Victory
By early 1945, the end of Hitler's "thousand-year Reich" was in sight.

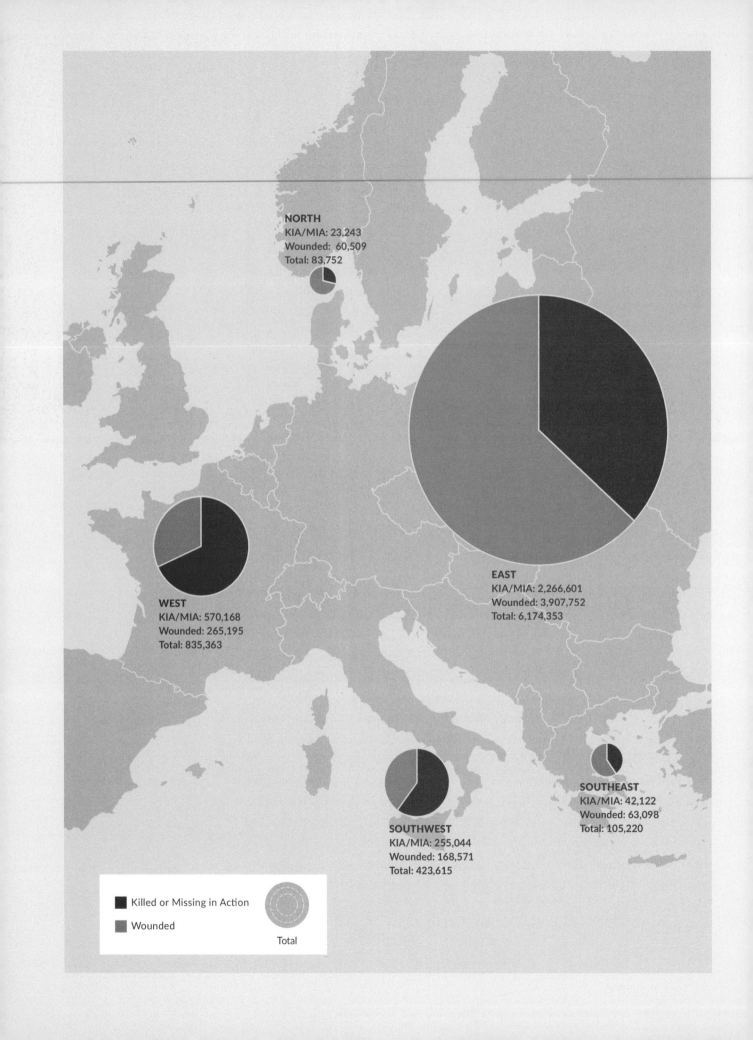

NORTH
KIA/MIA: 23,243
Wounded: 60,509
Total: 83,752

EAST
KIA/MIA: 2,266,601
Wounded: 3,907,752
Total: 6,174,353

WEST
KIA/MIA: 570,168
Wounded: 265,195
Total: 835,363

SOUTHWEST
KIA/MIA: 255,044
Wounded: 168,571
Total: 423,615

SOUTHEAST
KIA/MIA: 42,122
Wounded: 63,098
Total: 105,220

■ Killed or Missing in Action
■ Wounded

Total

A marshal of the Soviet Army in World War II, Konstantin Rokossovsky joined the Red Army in 1919 and fought in the Russian Civil War. In the interwar era, he was one of the military progressives who argued for mechanization of the army. Arrested during Stalin's purges in 1937, he was imprisoned for three years and suffered the full range of torture and beatings. But then Rokossovsky was released suddenly and without explanation or apology in March 1940. With the rapidly expanding Red Army in desperate need of experienced officers, he received command of the V Cavalry Corps, and then the IX Mechanized Corps, and eventually the Sixteenth Army.

During the Great Patriotic War, he fought at Smolensk and Moscow in 1941, commanded the Bryansk Front in summer 1942, and then the Don Front that spearheaded the Soviet offensive at Stalingrad (Operation Uranus) and the reduction of the German pocket in the city itself. At Kursk, he commanded the Central Front, facing the German pincer coming down from the north (General Walter Model's Ninth Army) and stopping it cold. Renamed 1st Byelorussian Front, Rokossovsky's command took the lead in Operation Bagration. Smashing through the German line in the Pripet Marshes, he lunged all the way to the Vistula River opposite Warsaw in two months of classic Deep Battle. And there he sat, even as the Polish Home Army rose in revolt. Soviet inactivity while the Germans suppressed the revolt and destroyed much of Warsaw is controversial, but it almost certainly emanated more from Stalin than Rokossovsky. He ended the war commanding the 2nd Byelorussian Front, driving through East Prussia and eventually linking up with British forces at Wismar on May 3, 1945.

Though still virtually unknown in the West, Rokossovsky was one of the greatest generals of the war, especially skilled in the handling of large mechanized formations.

all arms, they preceded the main body by twelve to thirty miles. They were responsible for maintaining the momentum of the advance, overrunning installations in the German rear and breaking up counterattacks before they began. They paved the way for the much larger Soviet tank and mechanized armies that followed. In concert with an increasingly sophisticated Soviet tactical air doctrine, based above all on the lethal Sturmovik Il-2 ground attack aircraft, the Soviets had learned how to neutralize the previous superiority of the German Army at the point of contact.

An increasingly dilapidated Wehrmacht was unable to resist. This or that defensive position might hold out, but Soviet commanders learned to respond by shifting the direction and center of gravity of their approach. Sooner or later, even the bravest German stand turned into a hasty retreat, due to a defensive collapse on one or both flanks. For the Wehrmacht, the final phase of the war in the East was a dreary procession of rearguard fights through what one staff officer later called "a bunch of towns with unpronounceable names."[7]

Hitler and the high command had no real answer to the Soviet offensive. In each battle, the Führer's solution was almost always the same: a stand-fast order to hold a given position to the last man, a naive expectation that only increased casualties.[8] The professional officers around him almost always recommended a type of

◀ GERMAN CASUALTIES BY FRONT

The data represented on this graphic comes from German wartime documents. OKW appreciated at the time what Anglo-American audiences sometimes forget: the Red Army did most of the work wearing down the German ground forces.

By 1944, the German armies fighting the Soviet Union were not the well-equipped veteran formations they had been in 1941.

warfare based on rapid maneuver, shock, and surprise, but this was equally unrealistic, given the Wehrmacht's lack of mechanized formations by this point in the war.[9] Hitler won the argument, as always, and in the process he dismissed gifted operational commanders such as Army Group South's field marshal, Erich von Manstein, and the Fourth Panzer Army's General Hermann Hoth. In their place, he put firm-jawed commanders like General Ferdinand Schörner, who was appointed to command Army Group South Ukraine in October 1943, and General Walter Model, designated to lead Army Group North Ukraine in March 1944. The point is not that Hitler was appointing bunglers. These new men were competent enough. What really recommended them to Hitler, however, was that they were "standers": men who would stay put where they were ordered to.[10] They weren't "operators," a word that Hitler had come to despise. They were men of will and determination who considered retreat a personal insult and were willing to fight to the last German soldier in a hopeless war. Schörner, for example, would eventually shoot hundreds, perhaps thousands, of his own soldiers to prevent the collapse of discipline on his front.[11]

Standing fast, however, meant surrendering the initiative to the Soviets, and the Red Army spent the last eighteen months of the war launching one great offensive after another. The winter of 1943–44 saw the four fronts in the south clear Ukraine: they encircled two German corps at Korsun in February 1944, overran the vast German tank and supply depot at Uman in March, and reconquered the Crimea in April and May.[12] The going was rougher on other sectors of the front, especially since the Soviets had concentrated most of their armor in the south. But in the north, too, the Red Army had its successes, most notably breaking the German siege of the starving city of Leningrad in February 1944.[13]

While Germany's Army Group Center emerged from the Soviet winter offensive relatively unscathed, that very fact posed grave dangers. With Soviet progress on both its northern and southern flanks, the army group now lay in a gigantic bulge toward the east, with Soviet forces threatening it from the Baltic region in the north and the Pripet Marshes in the south. The four component formations of Army Group Center (from north to south, Third Panzer Army, and then Fourth, Ninth, and Second Armies) were not only holding extended fronts but also were weak in armor. Furthermore, partisan activity to their rear—once a mere nuisance—had now grown into a serious problem requiring manpower-intensive patrolling. Typically consisting of the remnants of previously smashed Soviet formations, the partisans by this point numbered an estimated 143,000 men and women and controlled 60 percent of the territory of Byelorussia.[14]

Realizing the opportunity that beckoned, the Soviets aimed their main offensive for summer 1944 at Army Group Center. Operation Bagration was the greatest Soviet offensive yet, involving four fronts (1st Baltic and 3nd, 2nd, and 1st Byelorussian), which contained 15 armies, 118 infantry divisions, and 43 tank divisions.[15] Some 5,800 tanks, 8,000 combat aircraft, and 32,000 guns took part.[16] The last two numbers were critical. In the run-up to Bagration, the Red Air Force was able to establish air superiority for the first time in the war, and the preparatory artillery barrage was one of the greatest in history.

Bagration commenced on the night of June 19–20, with a wave of partisan attacks in the German rear, followed two nights later by massive air attacks deep behind German lines. The ground assault, begun on June 23, met success everywhere. Preliminary probes by Soviet reconnaissance detachments penetrated the German front

SOVIET LENINGRAD AND ▶ UKRAINE OFFENSIVES, DECEMBER 2, 1943– APRIL 30, 1944

In late 1943 and early 1944 the Soviets broke the long and horrific siege of Leningrad and launched the immense offensive that would carry the Red Army to and past the Dniester during the spring.

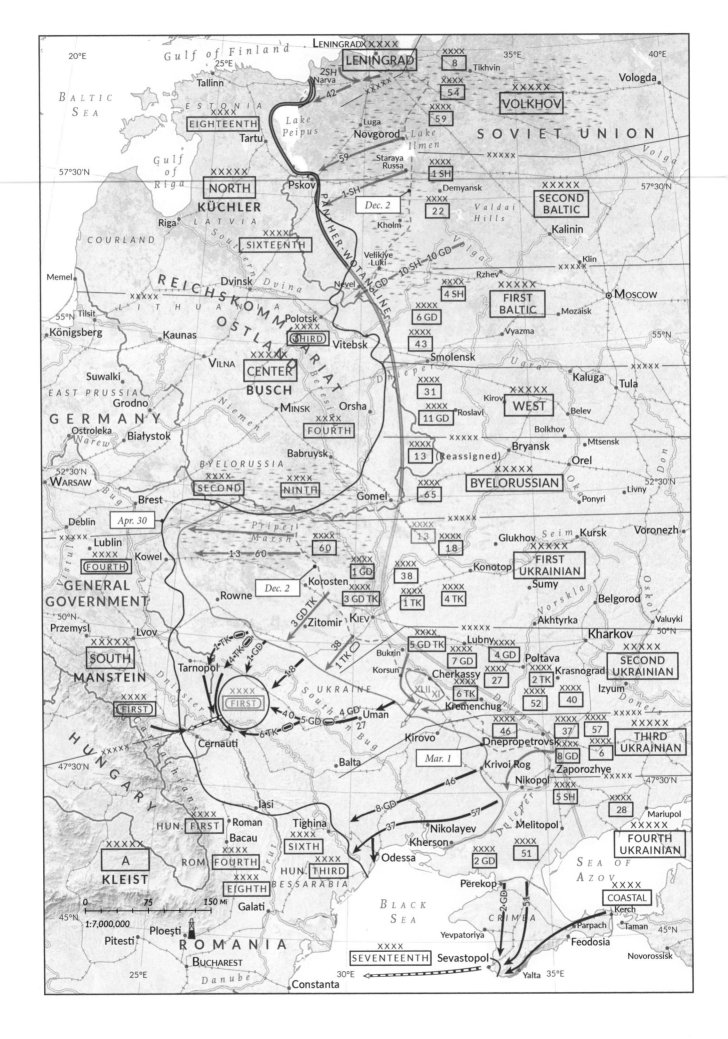

Gulf of Finland

20°E   25°E   35°E   40°E

LENINGRAD XXXX
LENINGRAD
2SH
Narva
42

XXXX
8   Tikhvin

Vologda

Tallinn

ESTONIA
Lake Peipus
Luga
Novgorod
Lake Ilmen

EIGHTEENTH
Tartu

XXXX
54

XXXX
59

VOLKHOV

SOVIET UNION

BALTIC
SEA

Gulf of Riga

57°30'N

NORTH
KÜCHLER
Pskov

XXXXX

59

Staraya Russa

XXXXX

Dec. 2   1-SH

XXXX
1 SH

Demyansk

Valdai Hills

SECOND BALTIC

Kalinin

57°30'N

Riga

LATVIA

Southern Dvina

Kholm

XXXX
22

COURLAND

SIXTEENTH

XXXX

Velikiye Luki
10-SH-10 GD

Memel

REICHSKOMMISSARIAT

Dvinsk   Dvina

Nevel

1 GD

Rzhev

Klin

Vologda

XXXX
4 SH

FIRST BALTIC

Moscow

55°N

Tilsit

LITHUANIA

Polotsk

OSTLAND

THIRD   Vitebsk

XXXXX

Mozaisk

55°N

Königsberg

Kaunas

VILNA

Niemen

CENTER
BUSCH

XXXXX

Smolensk

Uvra

XXXX
6 GD

XXXX
43

Vyazma

EAST PRUSSIA

Suwalki

Grodno

Orsha

XXXX
FOURTH

Kirov

WEST

Kaluga   Tula

GERMANY

Ostroleka

Białystok

Narew

MINSK

XXXX
31

Roslavl

XXXX
11 GD

Belev

Bolkhov

Mtsensk

Warsaw

BYELORUSSIA

Babruysk

XXXX
13 (Reassigned)

Bryansk

Orel

Don

52°30'N

Bug

Brest

SECOND

XXXX

NINTH

XXXX

Gomel

BYELORUSSIAN

XXXXX

Oka

Ponyri

Livny

52°30'N

Deblin

Apr. 30

Pripet Marsh

XXXX
65

Glukhov

Seim   Kursk

Voronezh

Lublin

XXXX
FOURTH

Kowel

1-3   60

XXXX
60

Rowne

Dec. 2   Korosten

XXXXX
13

XXXX
18

FIRST UKRAINIAN

Konotop

Sumy

GENERAL GOVERNMENT

50°N

Przemysl

Lvov

XXXX
1 GD

XXXX
38

Vorskla

Belgorod

Oskol

Valuyki

50°N

3 GD TK

Zitomir

3 GD TK

XXXX
3 GD TK

XXXX
1 TK

XXXX
4 TK

KIEV

1 TK

Akhtyrka

Kharkov

SOUTH MANSTEIN

XXXXX

48

38

Bukrin

XXXX
5 GD TK

Lubny

XXXX
7 GD

XXXX
4 GD

Poltava

SECOND UKRAINIAN

XXXXX

1-TK

4-TK

1-GD

FIRST

Korsun

UKRAINE

XXXX
27

Krasnograd

XXXX
2 TK

Izyum

Donets

XXXX
FIRST

Tarnopol

Dniester

Cherkassy

XLII XI

XXXX
6 TK

Kremenchug

XXXX
52

XXXX
40

4 GD

Southern Bug

Uman

5-GD

40

27

6-TK

Cernauti

Kirovo

Mar. 1

Dnepropetrovsk

XXXX
46

XXXX
37

XXXX
57

XXXX
6

THIRD UKRAINIAN

Balta

Krivoi Rog

XXXX
8 GD

Zaporozhye

HUNGARY

Carpathians

Iasi

Nikopol

Dnieper

47°30'N

HUN. FIRST
Roman

46

8 GD

Nikolayev

XXXX
5 SH

Melitopol

XXXX
28

Mariupol

47°30'N

Bacau

Tighina

37

Kherson

A
KLEIST

ROM. FOURTH

Prut

SIXTH

XXXX

Odessa

XXXX
2 GD

XXXX
51

Perekop

SEA OF AZOV

EIGHTH

HUN. THIRD

BESSARABIA

BLACK SEA

2-GD

CRIMEA

51

COASTAL

Kerch

45°N

Galati

0   75   150 Mi

1:7,000,000

Yevpatoriya

Parpach   Taman

45°N

Ploesti

ROMANIA

SEVENTEENTH   Sevastopol

30°E

Yalta   35°E

Feodosia

Novorossisk

Pitesti

BUCHAREST

Danube

25°E

Constanta

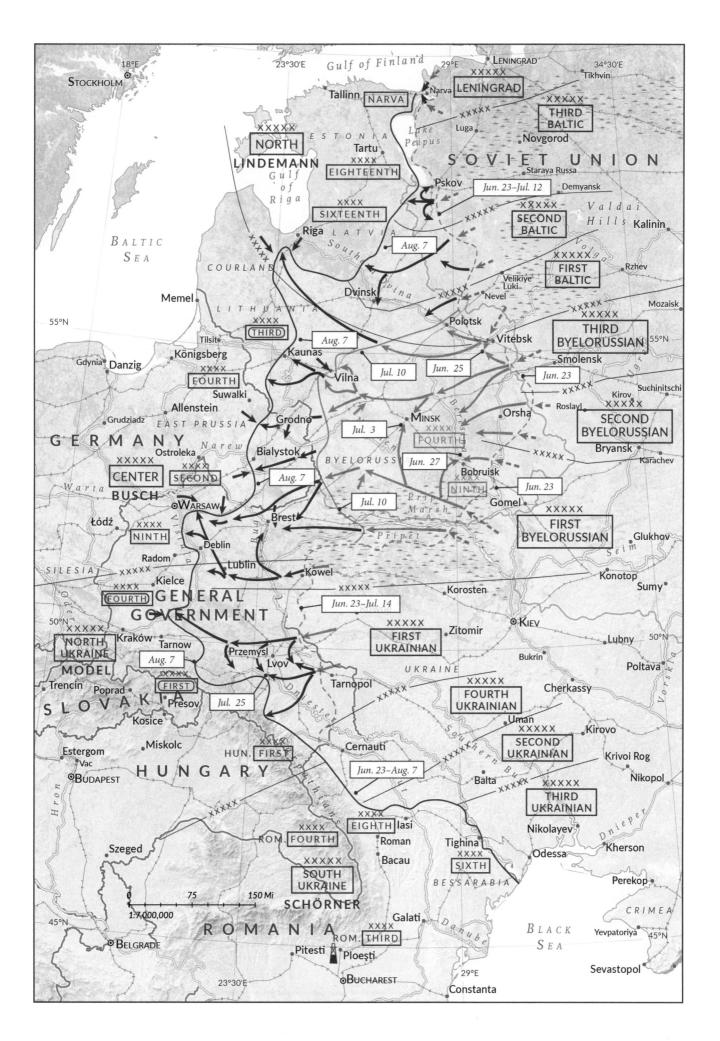

Gottlob H. Bidermann was a company commander in the Wehrmacht. Wounded five times and awarded numerous decorations for valor, he saw action in the Crimea and the siege of Sevastopol, participated in the vicious battles in the forests south of Leningrad, and ended the war trapped in the Courland Pocket. Here his company has been ordered out on patrol to protect the open southern flank of Army Group North, uncovered by the Soviet offensive in Byelorussia in June 1944, Operation Bagration.

The landsers [German soldiers] prepared for action, securing chin straps to their steel helmets, checking canteens of water, ensuring that magazines were fully loaded, and that weapons were once again functioning faultlessly. Canvas sacks of hand grenades were distributed, and the infantrymen shared the burden of reserve machine-gun ammunition. Suddenly a Kübelwagen sped by our position, and from the front passenger seat of the vehicle, Oberstleutnant Katzmann called above the clatter of the Volkswagen's air-cooled engine, "Leutnant Bidermann! Now show us what you can do!" I brought my hand to the rim of my helmet in acknowledgment as he disappeared in a cloud of dust.

We struck south without artillery support, penetrated the blocking fire of a Soviet howitzer battery, and shortly thereafter came under a concentrated mortar barrage, but miraculously we suffered no casualties. I led the company forward at a run, and as we cleared a small rise, we suddenly found ourselves on a road occupied by Russian engineers busily engaged in laying box mines in the evening twilight. The Russians scrambled for cover while opening fire with submachine guns in an attempt to protect themselves, but the detachment was raked by a machine-gun burst Aigner fired from the hip.

The enemy attempted to scatter, and we took two pony carts and a truck under fire with our small arms and hand grenades. Within seconds, the incident was over, and the guns had fallen silent... Of more importance to the hungry grenadiers for the moment, they had discovered several pasteboard boxes marked in English in black-stenciled letters, and they enthusiastically stuffed their pockets and bread bags with the tinned meat found in the containers...

We deprived the enemy the use of the road for the remainder of the night, and the next morning, we again moved toward the south and arrived at the location of an abandoned Soviet howitzer battery position. Dozens of spent shells lay scattered among piles of empty and discarded tins marked "Oscar Mayer—Chicago."[17]

line with ease.[18] The assault proper first smashed the German anchoring positions on the northern face of the bulge (at Vitebsk) and then the southern (at Babruysk), and quickly peeled open a 250-mile-wide gap in the German front. Soon the second and third echelons were motoring in the open, just as Soviet Deep Battle doctrine prescribed, never giving the Germans time to recover or reconsolidate. Amid scenes of panic in the German rear, powerful Soviet armored pincers converged on Minsk, the headquarters of Army Group Center, on July 3, day eleven of the offensive.[19] The onslaught surrounded some German formations, such as LIII Corps at Vitebsk and much of Fourth Army east of Minsk, but it pulverized many more. In effect, Army Group Center, responsible for one-third of the German defensive line on the Eastern Front, had ceased to exist. With no fewer than thirty divisions lost, it was "a far worse catastrophe than Stalingrad."[20]

Realizing the severity of the blow it had just landed, Soviet headquarters now ordered a general westward advance by all four fronts, combined with a drive by the 1st Ukrainian Front south of the Pripet.[21] Although the Germans rushed in the few reserves they could spare, the Soviet drive continued unabated. Over the course of July, Soviet armies advanced to the old prewar border, crossed into Poland and the Baltic states, and charged all the way to the Vistula River by the first week of August.

◀ Operation Bagration

The scale of Operation Bagration dwarfed that of the near-simultaneous Operation Overlord in Normandy.

It was a moment of high drama. As the Soviet armies approached the Vistula, Pol-ish resistance forces inside Warsaw took up arms against the German occupiers.[22] The rising was only partially successful, freeing much but not all of the central city, and the Germans soon went into action to crush it. Soviet forces stood just over the river to the east and the south but did nothing to help. Over sixty-three days, the Wehrmacht destroyed both the Polish resistance and much of the historic core of Warsaw. Many Poles at the time, and many historians since, have accused Stalin of cynically allowing the Germans to quell the uprising, since he had no interest in having Poland liberated by its own people.[23] Indeed, he clearly intended to install a Communist regime and would soon establish one in the liberated city of Lublin.

But there is also another story to be told. In the course of their 350-mile drive to the Vistula, Soviet forces had taken heavy losses, outrun their logistics, and generally exhausted themselves. The force that reached the river opposite Warsaw was a sin-gle understrength rifle army, the Forty-Seventh. Its three corps were spread out over nearly fifty miles, and its kinetic energy was spent.[24] Like most decisions that inspire

▲ WARSAW UPRISING

The Poles hoped to independently liberate their capital, Warsaw, in order to improve their chances of avoiding Soviet domination after the war. After insurgents gained control of much of the city, Him-mler responded by ordering that all Poles be shot out of hand. The Ger-mans killed 40,000 Poles before that order was rescinded, and then began to take large numbers of prisoners.

Finland accepted an
armistice on September 19.

OSLO

SWEDEN

STOCKHOLM

COPENHAGEN

BALTIC
SEA

BERLIN

GERMANY

Poznań

Łódź

Breslau

PRAGUE

BOHEMIA

VIENNA

SOUTH
FRIESSNER

Trieste

Zara

ADRIATIC
SEA

FINLAND

Lake
Ladoga

Viipuri

HELSINKI

LENINGRAD

Tikhvin

LENINGRAD

SOVIET
UNION

Gulf of Finland

Narva

Tallinn

ESTONIA

Luga

xxxxx

Novgorod

XXXXX

THIRD
BALTIC

Staraya Russa

Tartu

Demyansk

Gulf
of
Riga

Pskov

Valdai
Hills

XXXXX

NORTH
SCHÖRNER

COUR
LAND

Riga

LATVIA

Kholm

Volga

XXXXX

SECOND
BALTIC

Velikiye Luki

Rzhev

Oct. 15–Dec. 15

LITHUANIA

Dvinsk

XXXXX

FIRST
BALTIC

Nevel

Southern Drina

Polotsk

Memel

XXXXX

Vyazma

55°N

Vitebsk

Smolensk

Tilsit

Sep. 15

Kaunas

THIRD
BYELORUSSIAN

Ugra

Dnieper

Roslavl

Kirov

THIRD

Königsberg

VILNA

Orsha

Danzig

Nov. 1–Dec. 15

Suwalki

MINSK

Bryansk

XXXXX

CENTER
REINHARDT

Allenstein

FOURTH

EAST PRUSSIA

Ostroleka

Grodno

Narew

Bialystok

SECOND
BYELORUSSIAN

Babruysk

BYELORUSSIA

Berezina

Gomel

Vistula

Warta

SECOND

Glukhov

WARSAW

XXXXX

FIRST
BYELORUSSIAN

Oder

NINTH

Deblin

Aug. 8

Brest

Pripet
Marshes

Pripet

Konotop

Neisse

Radom

Sep. 15–Dec. 15

Kowel

Korosten

Seim

Elbe

XXXXX

Lublin

XXXXX

Kielce

GENERAL

Lvov

FIRST
UKRAINIAN

Rowne

KIEV

50°N

A

HARPE

SILESIA

FOURTH

GOVERNMENT

Zitomir

Lubny

Moravska
Ostrava

Kraków

Przemysl

Lvov

FOURTH
UKRAINIAN

Dnieper

SEVENTEENTH

Ternopol

URKAINE

Cherkassy

Zilina

FIRST

Dniester

Kremenchug

Poprad

Uman

Kirovo

SLOVAKIA

Presov

Kosice

SECOND
UKRAINIAN

Carpathians

Cernauti

EIGHTH

Miskolc

Iasi

Baltax XXXX

THIRD
UKRAINIAN

Nikolayev

Estergom

Vac

HUNGARY

Roman

Tighina

Kherson

BUDAPEST

Bacau

Dec. 15

Lake
Balaton

Oct. 12

Sep. 15

BESSARABIA

Odessa

SIXTH

Szeged

Aug. 26

Galati

45°N

ZAGREB

ROMANIA

Prut

45°N

YUGOSLAVIA

F

Pitesti

Ploeşti

BLACK
SEA

Aug. 31

SARAJEVO

Oct. 14

BELGRADE

WEICHS

BUCHAREST

Constanta

Danube

BULGARIA

On September 8, Bulgaria
switched to the Allied side.

XXXX

BUL.

Balkan Mountains

0   75   150 Mi

1:8,000,000

SOFIA

polemical debates, the Soviets' choice not to fight into Warsaw probably emerged from a variety of factors.

With the Germans nursing their wounds in the center, Soviet attention turned to the flanks. The rest of 1944 would see the Red Army overrun the Baltic states and drive the remnants of Army Group North into a small enclave in the Courland Peninsula in Latvia, where its twenty divisions would remain for the duration of the war.[25] To the south, 2nd and 3rd Ukrainian Fronts blasted into Romania in August and smashed Army Group South Ukraine. In September they overran the Ploești oil fields—crucial to German prosecution of the war. In October and November, they pushed into Hungary and, by Christmas 1944, had encircled Budapest, trapping IX SS Mountain Corps and two Hungarian divisions.[26]

Through all these vast offensives, the Red Army inflicted massive casualties on the Wehrmacht: over 500,000 in Bagration, another 200,000 in the drive to the Vistula, at least that many more in the punishing drive through Romania and into the Balkans. In total, it was roughly a million men. They also drove Germany's allies Finland and Romania out of the war—the loss of the latter robbing the Third Reich of its major oil supplier.[27] Enjoying both quantitative and qualitative superiority by this point, and having a firm grasp on the initiative, the Red Army had by January of 1945 entered the endgame in its long struggle with the Wehrmacht.

▲ **THE RED ARMY CROSSES THE VISTULA RIVER, JULY 31, 1944**

The Soviets held a position on the west side of the Vistula but did not help the uprising in Warsaw against the Nazis. The reason the Soviets failed to help the uprising has been the subject of much debate. Some historians contend that Stalin cynically allowed the Germans to destroy the uprising, though others argue that the Soviets were unable to help. The latter camp cites the Soviets' recent four-hundred-mile move and depleted forces and logistics as insurmountable barriers to attempting an urban attack in Warsaw.

◀ **SOVIET BALKAN AND BALTIC OFFENSIVES, AUGUST 19–DECEMBER 31, 1944**

The Soviet drive into Hungary, Romania, Bulgaria, and Yugoslavia not only hastened the collapse of Germany, it helped shape the Cold War that followed.

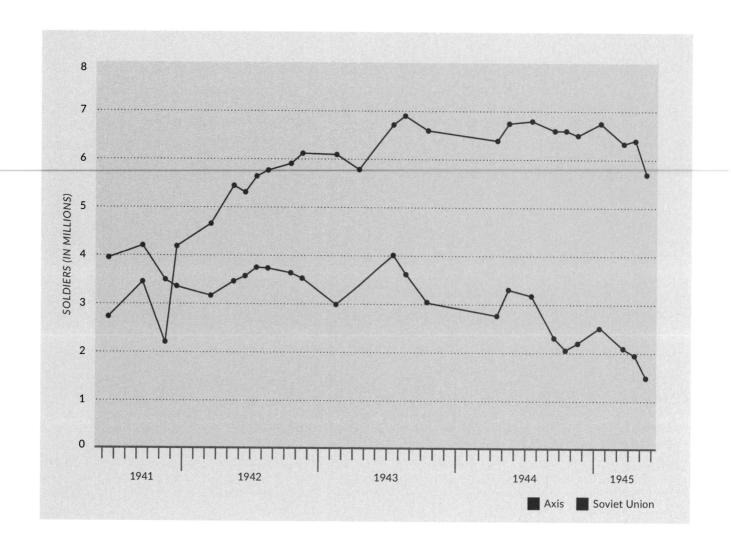

SOLDIERS (IN MILLIONS)

1941   1942   1943   1944   1945

■ Axis   ■ Soviet Union

**CORRELATION OF ▲
COMBAT FORCES ON THE
SOVIET-GERMAN FRONT**

The numbers suggest that if the Axis ever had a chance of achieving victory on the Eastern Front, that chance was gone by mid-1943.

WAR IN THE WEST: ITALY IN 1944

In contrast to the Soviet Union, the Western Allies had still not struck anything resembling a decisive blow by early 1944. Despite all the investment of wealth, resources, and industry, their returns so far had been modest. They had overrun North Africa and Sicily, ended the Axis threat to the Suez Canal, and knocked Italy out of the fight. The campaign in Italy had stalled seventy-eight miles south of Rome against determined German defenders, however, and getting things moving again was the first Allied operational problem as 1944 dawned.[28]

The German defensive position in Italy, the Gustav Line, straddled the peninsula from sea to sea. Anchored on the town and monastery of Cassino behind the Rapido River in the southwest, it ran to the Sangro River and then to the Adriatic Sea in the northeast. All attempts by General Mark Clark's U.S. Fifth Army and Montgomery's Eighth to crash through it in 1943 had failed ignominiously, and there was no possibility of outflanking it on land.[29] By now, however, the Allies had a great deal of experience at amphibious landings.

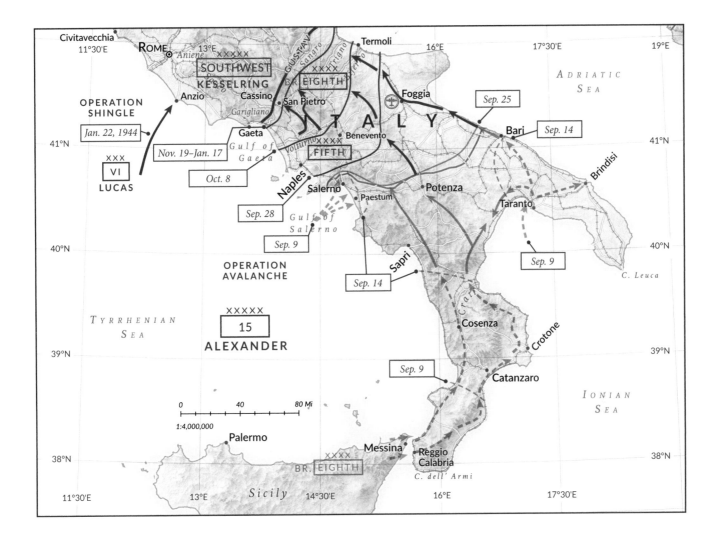

Operation Shingle was formulated as an attempt to outflank the Gustav Line by landing at Anzio, fifty miles in the German rear.[30] But from the start, it was an ill-fated operation. By January 1944, men, supplies, and equipment were departing the Mediterranean in preparation for the great landing planned in Normandy, and Italy was becoming the sideshow it had always been destined to be. Rather than a full-scale landing in the manner of Operation Husky, this one employed only a single corps: the U.S. VI under General John Lucas. Rather than a deep strike, Shingle was a relatively shallow turning movement, and the Germans—as always in Italy—would be able to reinforce the sector far more rapidly than the Allies could.

Although the landing on January 22 was unopposed, Lucas made no immediate move to strike into the interior. Historians blame him for excessive caution, but the memory of Salerno, where U.S. troops had barged into the interior and almost been thrown back into the sea, was still fresh. "Don't stick your neck out, Johnny," Clark had warned Lucas. "I did at Salerno and got into trouble."[31] The Germans in turn reacted with customary vigor, rushing reinforcements to the area, and soon VI Corps was facing the German Fourteenth Army under General Eberhard von Mackensen. Although the Germans lacked the strength or logistics to push VI Corps into the sea, they held the high ground all around a very shallow bridgehead, every inch of which

▲ Anzio Landings

A landing at Anzio had been considered in the fall of 1943, but at that time there were no Allied airbases within fighter range. By early 1944 that was no longer a problem, making Anzio an obvious target for an amphibious turning movement that would force the Germans out of the Gustav Line.

The fortified town of Monte Cassino helped anchor the Gustav Line, blocking the Allied forces trying to move north to relieve the Anzio beachhead and capture Rome. After the first attack on the position failed, the Allies bombed a sixth-century Benedictine abbey, which they wrongly believed the Germans were using above the town as part of their defenses, into rubble.

was under German observation and artillery fire. It was a demoralizing situation for the Allies, and they did what armies often do in such circumstances: they fired the general. The indecisive Lucas was thrown out, and the more determined General Lucian K. Truscott Jr. was brought in, but the overall situation hardly changed.[32]

In an ironic twist, the only solution to this operational problem was for the Fifth Army to break through the Gustav Line and rescue the force at Anzio. It was a complete reversal of the original mission, in which the Anzio landing was supposed to unlock the Gustav Line. In January, February, and March, the Allies launched three corps-level assaults in the Cassino sector, but a gritty defense by the German 1st Airborne Division beat back each one with heavy Allied losses.[33] Critics again have charged U.S. commanders with mishandling the battle, this time by being overly profligate with their use of bombardment: they essentially turned Cassino into rubble and in doing so impeded the progress of their own attack.[34] It is hard to see what might have been gained by assaulting Cassino with less fire support, however.

Not until May did General Harold Alexander, commanding the Allied 15th Army Group, devise a solution to the Anzio-Cassino mess. He concentrated both his armies,

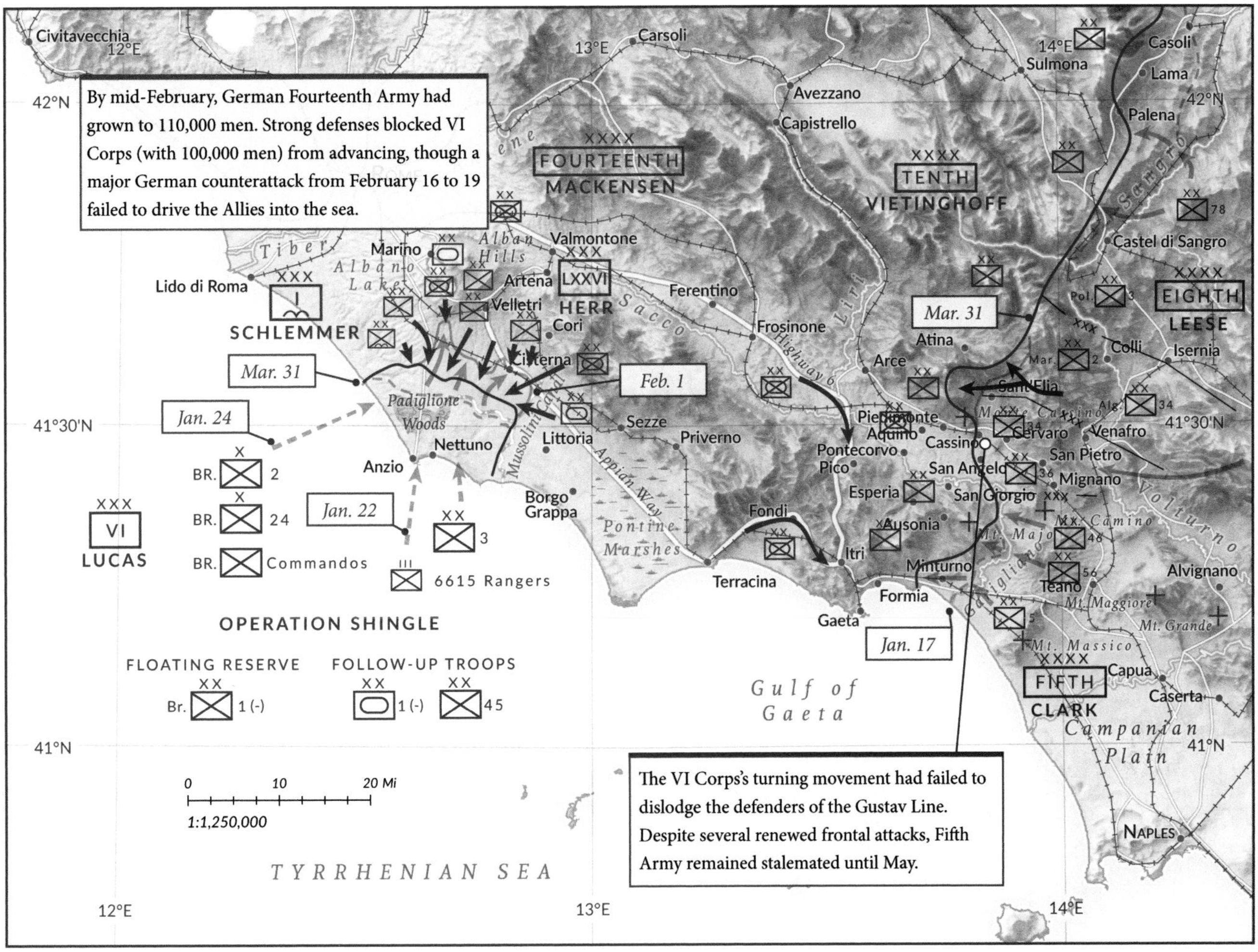

By mid-February, German Fourteenth Army had grown to 110,000 men. Strong defenses blocked VI Corps (with 100,000 men) from advancing, though a major German counterattack from February 16 to 19 failed to drive the Allies into the sea.
The VI Corps's turning movement had failed to dislodge the defenders of the Gustav Line. Despite several renewed frontal attacks, Fifth Army remained stalemated until May.
FOURTEENTH
MACKENSEN
TENTH
VIETINGHOFF
EIGHTH
LEESE
FIFTH
CLARK
VI
LUCAS
LXXVI
HERR
SCHLEMMER
OPERATION SHINGLE
FLOATING RESERVE
FOLLOW-UP TROOPS
Commandos
6615 Rangers
Mar. 31
Jan. 24
Jan. 22
Feb. 1
Jan. 17
Civitavecchia
Carsoli
Avezzano
Capistrello
Sulmona
Casoli
Lama
Palena
Castel di Sangro
Isernia
Colli
Venafro
San Pietro
Mignano
Alvignano
Capua
Caserta
Naples
Lido di Roma
Marino
Alban Hills
Albano Lake
Valmontone
Artena
Velletri
Cori
Cisterna
Ferentino
Frosinone
Atina
Arce
Aquino
Piedimonte
Cassino
Sant'Elia
Cervaro
Pontecorvo
Pico
Esperia
San Angelo
San Giorgio
Ausonia
Minturno
Teano
Formia
Gaeta
Itri
Fondi
Terracina
Priverno
Sezze
Littoria
Borgo Grappa
Anzio
Nettuno
Padiglione Woods
Mussolini Canal
Appian Way
Pontine Marshes
Highway 6
Sacco
Liri
Tiber
Sangro
Volturno
Garigliano
Mt. Majo
Mt. Camino
Mt. Maggiore
Mt. Grande
Mt. Massico
Campanian Plain
Gulf of Gaeta
TYRRHENIAN SEA
1:1,250,000
0 10 20 Mi
12°E
13°E
14°E
42°N
41°30'N
41°N

▲ **Anzio-Cassino: Operation Diadem, the Gustav Line, and Anzio Breakout**

The Anzio landings were meant to break the deadlock on the Gustav Line, but in the end the Allies had to push through at Cassino in order to break VI Corps out of its beachhead.

Clark's Fifth and the British Eighth, on the western sector opposite Cassino in order to launch a massed attack on a narrow twenty-mile front. He also reinforced the Anzio bridgehead, shipping in the U.S. 34th and 36th Divisions. Soon the bridgehead was bulging with seven Allied divisions—150,000 men in all. Alexander's plan, Operation Diadem, called for twin offensives: one through Cassino and one out of Anzio, to catch the German Tenth and Fourteenth Armies between two fires and destroy them both.[35]

The opening of Diadem on May 11, 1944, struck like a thunderbolt. Months of grinding mountain combat with a materially superior enemy had worn down the Germans on the Cassino line, and the Allies had finally learned how to apply their overwhelming combat strength. Clark's main body finally took Cassino, driving northwest toward Anzio. On May 22 Truscott's VI Corps blasted out of the beachhead. The two forces linked up just three days later near the bombed-out village of Borgo Grappa.[36] German forces were then in full flight across the front, and it looked like Diadem would go on to achieve its larger aim: the destruction of the German armies in Italy.

It did not, for reasons that are still controversial. On May 26 Clark ordered Truscott to shift the axis of his advance almost 90 degrees to the left. Rather than continuing

his drive eastward toward Valmontone, which would cut off Highway 6 and block the retreat of the German Tenth Army, Truscott was to wheel northwest and seize Rome as rapidly as possible. For this decision, Clark has been accused of botching the mission in his eagerness to make headlines by seizing a great city.[37] It is fair to point out, however, that encircling the Tenth Army was never a high probability: it was already in full retreat, and there are many roads north besides Highway 6.[38] Encircling a field army is a swirling, even chaotic enterprise, and the Anglo-American armies had already proven many times in this war that they operated best in a controlled, set-piece environment, with clear sector lines and phased advances. In the end, Clark headed for Rome rather than for a linkup in Italy's rocky interior with U.S. forces coming from the opposite direction, and Diadem had to be satisfied with mauling the Germans, rather than destroying them. The Allies pursued the beaten enemy all summer before finally coming to a halt in early August on the Gothic Line, just above Florence. They were more than 250 miles north of where they had been in May, but they still had a long way to go.[39]

WAR IN THE WEST: OVERLORD AND THE ETO IN 1944

On June 6, 1944, the Allies made their long-awaited cross-Channel invasion.[40] Operation Overlord was an epic, massive, and complex undertaking involving 3 million Allied personnel, 5,000 naval vessels, and over 11,000 aircraft. It was the product of more than a year of intensive planning by an Anglo-U.S. staff called COSSAC (Chief of Staff to the Supreme Allied Commander) under British general Frederick Morgan. COSSAC had been working since April 1943, long before General Dwight D. Eisenhower was appointed supreme commander of Operation Overlord in January 1944.[41] The result of all that planning, involving hundreds of officers and hundreds of thousands of man-hours, was a fairly simple frontal assault in the fairly safe location of Normandy. The choice of landing site was something of a trade-off: a riskier option than Brittany, but safer than the Strait of Dover. A landing at the latter would have put Allied armies closest to Germany, but for that reason, German defenses there were the strongest. Confirming the Germans in their decision to place the weight of their defenses in the Strait of Dover was an elaborate Allied deception plan, Operation Fortitude. Fortitude created a fictional "First U.S. Army Group" (FUSAG) in Great Britain, with dummy camps and equipment, false radio messaging, and even a commander, General George S. Patton Jr., who was supposedly going to lead FUSAG in a cross-Channel landing across the Strait of Dover.

The Allies would actually land two armies abreast: the U.S. First, led by General Omar N. Bradley, on the right; and the British Second, commanded by General Miles

◀ ROME LIBERATED
American troops captured Rome on June 5, 1944, though the event is overshadowed in American memory by the Normandy landings, which took place the next day.

FUSAG TANK ▲

Aided by Ultra intelligence (which enabled Allied deception officers to determine which of their tricks were working and which were not), SHAEF's Operation Fortitude convinced the Germans that the Allies would feint at Normandy before landing their real main effort near Boulogne. Dummy landing craft, inflatable tanks, fake guns, and radio operators sending messages from one nonexistent headquarters to another created the illusion of a "First U.S. Army Group" that Patton would lead across the Channel to the Pas de Calais.

Dempsey, on the left. Together the two armies made up the 21st Army Group under Montgomery. Bradley had VII Corps on his right, landing at the beach designated Utah, and V Corps on his left, at Omaha. Dempsey had XXX Corps landing at Gold Beach and I Corps, the extreme left of the Allied line, landing at both Juno and Sword Beaches. Securing the flanks would be airborne drops: the 101st and 82nd Airborne Divisions landing behind Utah and the British 6th Airborne Division seizing the bridges over the Orne River, the anchor of Overlord's left flank. Once landed, I Corps was expected to push inland and take the key crossroads city of Caen on day one. The U.S. Army would turn west and drive on the port of Cherbourg, since gaining a port early was crucial to the plan's logistics.

The plan was essentially a prudent one, landing close enough to Germany to facilitate future operations but far enough away to be safe. Still, some of the decisions were problematic. The choice to go in at "half-light," forty minutes after dawn, was a compromise between the need for surprise (with the assault forces approaching the beaches under cover of darkness) and what the planners saw as a need for massive bombardment from the air to soften up the defenders (which required daylight). The time frame was tight, with Allied aircraft essentially having only a single quick pass over the beaches before the assault.[42]

The Wehrmacht, too, had faced some tough choices in arranging its defensive positions. The overall deployment was standard: General Johannes Blaskowitz's Army Group G was stationed in southern France, and Field Marshal Erwin Rommel's Army Group B was in the north, both under the authority of Field Marshal Gerd von Rundstedt, commander in chief West. Some of their decisions were simple: for instance the Pas de Calais presented the most obvious beach for invasion, so it would have the

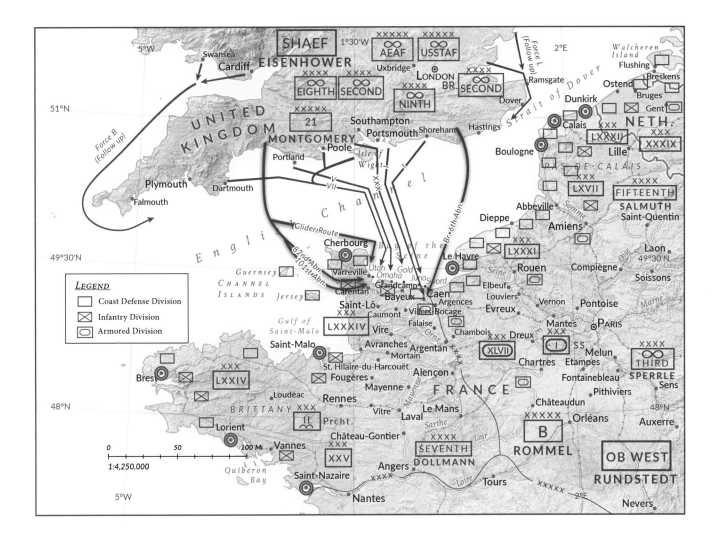

largest and best supplied force, Fifteenth Army, to defend it.[43] Other problems, however, were thornier, such as the placement of the Panzer divisions. Rommel knew how hard it was to operate under Allied air attacks and wanted them close to the water's edge. This, he felt, would be the only chance of smashing the landing: hitting the Allies in their most vulnerable moment, as they were wading ashore. Rundstedt wanted a more orthodox solution, grouping the Panzer divisions into a strong, centrally located reserve. To Rommel, that meant they might never get into the battle at all, since Allied control of the skies would severely curtail their movement.[44] But Rommel's approach had its own weaknesses: he had to guess right as to the Allied landing site, and up to the night before the invasion, no one in the German camp was able to anticipate the beach with any certainty. As in all such debates, there was no ideal solution. Rundstedt outranked Rommel and won the argument; at the time of the landing, most of the Panzers were formed into "Panzer Group West" and deployed far enough back to give coverage to both the Normandy and Pas de Calais sectors.

Overlord began on June 6, 1944—D-Day—and went smoothly overall. At Utah, the U.S. 4th Infantry Division overcame sparse resistance and penetrated inland. Utah had been added at the last second when planners had a fit of nerves about the beachhead being too cramped for the follow-on waves of men and matériel. At Gold, Juno,

▲ Operation Overlord

The core advantage of the offensive is the ability to use the initiative to concentrate against a dispersed defender.

and Sword Beaches, British and Canadian forces came ashore with strong support from the specialized tanks ("funnies") of the 79th Armoured Division, including DD (duplex drive) amphibious tanks, which could literally swim ashore. Of these three beaches, there was resistance only at Juno, where the first Canadian assault waves took heavy casualties. Bad weather held up the landing till 0800 (ninety minutes behind the other landings), and the local sea wall proved to be a tough obstacle. Here, too, the Canadians managed to push inland, though at a cost of 1,200 casualties.

The bloodiest beach was Omaha.[45] The landing by V Corps ran into a full-strength,

There is no more iconic day in the history of the U.S. Army than D-Day, June 6, 1944, and no more iconic place than Omaha Beach. A landing plan that promised a tremendous preliminary bombardment from sea and air went bad early, and German fire shot the first assault waves to pieces. Here is the testimony of two of the thousands of men who were there:

NORMAN GROSSMAN

Company L, 116th Infantry, 29th Division
As we neared the shore, I heard the clatter of machine guns and the explosions of artillery and mortar fire. Before I knew it, I heard someone yell, "The ramp is down! Everyone out!" We dashed into waist-deep water and ran the 300 yards to clear the beach. I remember a burst of machine-gun fire landed about ten yards from me, but I kept going, for we had instructions to get off the beaches as fast as we could. At the end of the beach was a sand dune covered with rocks, behind which we took refuge . . . I asked my platoon sergeant what to do, and I could see by his face he did not know. I then got the funniest feeling I have ever experienced. I felt like the young soldier who said, "A guy could get killed here!" I wanted to run—I didn't know where—but I wanted to get out of there.

LIEUTENANT COLONEL LAWRENCE MEEKS

Commander, 3rd Battalion, 116th Infantry, 29th Division
I had my hand on Capt. Gaffney's shoulder when there was an incredibly loud explosion, blowing the ramp off the landing craft. Capt. Gaffney and some of his men who were up front on the craft were killed. The captain's head slumped on my shoulder, and I noticed he had blood oozing from his nose and mouth. I could see he was dead. This was our first battle casualty, and the first person I saw killed. Water gushed into the landing craft, sinking it in shoulder deep water. We shed our equipment—about 60 pounds—and keeping low in the water, waded ashore. It was probably fate that saved us, because if we hadn't sunk, we would have touched down in front of a machine gun emplacement and probably would have been killed.[46]

nine-battalion Wehrmacht infantry division, the 352nd. Murderous German fire tore up the initial assault waves, and the DD tanks ran into difficulty due to the heavy surf. The 741st Tank Battalion launched twenty-nine tanks that morning, and twenty-seven of them sank in the course of the landing. By midmorning, U.S. infantry were huddled under a tiny rock ledge on the beach, caught in machine-gun cross fire, and desperately trying to find cover. When the second wave arrived, it only added to the chaos—and following it came headquarters, antitank guns, and artillery elements that were completely useless for the moment. For Bradley, it was a morning of bad news all across the board: "Obstacles mined, progress slow . . . DD Tanks . . . for Fox Green [Beach] swamped."[47]

Saving the day on the beach were local commanders such as General Norm "Dutch" Cota, assistant commander of the 29th Division. He and others rallied the men in their immediate vicinity and began to lead them up off the beach. The initial U.S. plan had been to drive for the "draws": the gaps in the hills. But the Germans had them so well defended that U.S. forces eventually decided to scale the bluffs themselves. The terrain was rougher, but the decision allowed the Americans to avoid the worst of the German fire.[48] It was an impressive example of improvisation under fire and a sign of how far the U.S. Army had come in its leadership and training. They were still in danger and held only a shallow bridgehead, but by evening, V Corps had secured a foothold at Omaha at a cost of 3,000 casualties.

Though the Allies were safely ashore, a hard road lay ahead of them. The first and

most obvious problem was the terrain. Normandy was an ancient land of small farms, each separated from the next by hedgerows, or *bocage*: earthen embankments topped by thick, twisted hedges ten to fifteen feet high. They formed ideal protection for the defenders, and U.S. troops soon learned that charging a hedgerow without a careful prior reconnaissance was suicide.

A second problem was the enemy. While the Wehrmacht had been content simply to slow down the Allies in their invasions of Sicily and Italy, the terms were different now. The Germans were in Normandy to stay and seeking a decisive defensive battle: the destruction of the Allied invasion. Along with the benefit of terrain, the German Army held a number of advantages over the Allies: more powerful tanks, more aggressive infantry, and more ruthless commanders. Moreover, most of its elite units were here, including the well-equipped mechanized formations of the Waffen-SS.[49] Even at bay, the Wehrmacht was a dangerous adversary.

Solving all these problems and more was the decisive Allied advantage: absolute control of the air. By now, a new generation of aircraft had come into service. The P-51 Mustang was the best fighter of the war in speed, range, and maneuverability. The P-47 Thunderbolt was the fighter-bomber par excellence, and even when loaded for bear with a full range of heavy machine guns, bombs, and rockets, it was still maneuverable enough to take on German fighters. These were superb aircraft, produced in overwhelming numbers, and Panzer units soon found that movement by day was simply suicide.

All through June and July, the U.S. Army ate its way slowly through the *bocage*, with heavy casualties. In the east, meanwhile, British forces pounded against a solid wall of German armor in front of Caen. Montgomery first tried a pair of right hooks

◀ AMERICAN INGENUITY

The Allies in Normandy had plenty of tanks, but the bocage terrain made it difficult to use them to root out the German infantry defending the hedgerows. Sergeant Curtis G. Culin of the 2nd Armored Division improvised the first "Rhino," using scrap steel to add "tusks" to a Sherman tank. These tusks enabled the Rhinos to dig into and break up the hedgerows.

west of the city, with the 7th Armoured Division's attack at the village of Villers-Bocage on June 13, followed by a larger effort by VIII Corps, Operation Epsom, starting on June 26. The latter succeeded in pushing across the Odon River and threatening the rear of the Germans at Caen before being checked by two newly arrived Panzer divisions. Next he tried an immense frontal assault spearheaded by I Corps. Operation Charnwood, as it was called, featured the first use of "carpet bombing" in the theater, using heavy strategic bombers, designed to smash entire enemy cities, in a tactical role: that is, flying in close support of the ground troops. Nonetheless, the attack gained only limited success, with the Germans still managing to hold on to the southern half of Caen.[50]

By mid-July, both Allied armies knew that time and manpower were being wasted, and that their current situation—tucked into a small corner of northwestern France—was untenable. Both were already planning a new set of offensives that they hoped would finally crack the German line. The first was Operation Goodwood, with Montgomery's 21st Army Group attacking to the east of Caen. Two complete armies, the Canadian First and the British Second, would strike on a narrow front with hundreds of tanks, massive carpet bombing, and lavish artillery support.[51]

The other offensive was the brainchild of the U.S. First Army commander, Omar Bradley. Operation Cobra was a departure for the U.S. Army: rather than a frontal assault all along the line, it aimed for a breakthrough on a carefully chosen sector.[52] Leading off would be a massive carpet bombing attack: 1,500 heavy bombers ranged against a four-mile stretch of the road from Saint-Lô to Périers. Defending the sector was a single understrength German division, Panzer Lehr. Following the bombing, an

Camouflage

Although Waffen-SS units were integrated into the normal military chain of command for operations, their recruitment, equipment, promotion, and other personnel matters remained separate. The development of printed camouflage smocks and helmet covers was an SS initiative, and through 1942 they were issued only to the Waffen-SS. Numerous different patterns were designed for use in different terrain. Worn over normal uniforms, the smocks were reversible, with a spring-summer pattern on one side and a fall-winter pattern on the other. This grenadier is attired for service on the Western Front.

Sturmgewehr 44

The familiar term "assault rifle" originated as a translation of the German *Sturmgewehr*, and the StG 44 was the first mass-issue weapon of the type. During the early years of World War II, the Wehrmacht found that few firefights took place at more than three hundred yards. That meant there was little advantage to the thousand-yard range made possible by the powerful cartridges used in bolt-action rifles. The StG 44 used a new short rifle round that gave the weapon much better reach than a submachine gun (which used pistol cartridges) but also allowed fully automatic fire, with a cyclic rate of five hundred rounds per minute. The detachable magazine held thirty rounds.

Adolf Hitler organized the *Schutzstaffel* ("Protection Squad") or SS as his personal "muscle" within the Nazi Party in 1925. In the decade before the outbreak of war, Heinrich Himmler expanded the SS into a massive paramilitary force with hundreds of thousands of members who were selected for racial purity and Nazi fervor and organized into a strict hierarchy similar to a monastic order. In addition to running the concentration camps and the German national security police, starting in 1939 the SS organized combat divisions of Waffen-SS ("Armed-SS") soldiers. Initially they were elite units; by the end of the war, many were second-rate formations including Eastern Europeans and other foreigners who lacked the ideological motivation of the early volunteers.

No part of Operation Cobra received more attention from planners than the carpet-bombing attacks that began it. Here is General Bradley, commanding U.S. First Army, receiving some bad news from the front:

> By 11:30, a heavy cloud cover still obscured the target. At 11:40, just 20 minutes before H Hour for the heavy bombers, a radio signal instructed them to turn back over the Channel. The attack was to be postponed 24 hours more.
>
> It was not until I had returned to my Army CP that I was told a box of heavies had crossed the coast and tripped its bombs through the cloud cover on the target. They had fallen short on the 30th Division, more than a mile behind the carpet.
>
> "Short?" I cried, "but how could they? These bombers were to come in on the Périers road parallel to our lines."
>
> "That's not that way they came in, sir," G-3 replied, "they came in on a perpendicular course."
>
> Leigh-Mallory [Trafford Leigh-Mallory, the commander of the air forces supporting the Normandy operations] arrived at the CP a few minutes after. Although the casualty count had not yet come in, he was as distressed as I over the accidental bombing . . . He promised to check immediately with the Eighth Air Force on the direction of air attack . . .
>
> All morning long on July 25, the air throbbed with heavy bombers while I fidgeted in Collins's CP within easy reach of the telephone. Once again Eisenhower had come across the Channel to be with us on the breakout. After three days of postponement and the previous day's bad bombing, our nerves were tight and stringy.
>
> The thunder had scarcely rolled away when casualty reports began trickling in.
>
> Thorson [Colonel Truman Thorson, Bradley's operations officer] handed me a TWX [teletype message]. "They've done it again," he said.
>
> "Oh Christ," I cried, "not another short drop?"
>
> He nodded and sifted the messages he still held in his hand. Air had hit the 9th and 30th Divisions a punishing blow. Both units had been rocked off balance, and as the bombers floated serenely away, reserves were rushed into the gaps.[53]

entire U.S. corps (VII Corps, under General J. Lawton Collins) would drive through the German line and open a hole for a huge mobile force in the second echelon: the 1st Infantry Division along with the 2nd and 3rd Armored Divisions. At this point, VIII Corps on the right, led by General Troy Middleton, would join in and drive south, trapping German forces between itself and VII Corps. Then, with the activation of Third Army, under General George S. Patton Jr., on First Army's right, Bradley would move upstairs to command the new, all-U.S. 12th Army Group. General Courtney Hodges would take over First Army.

Goodwood opened on July 18 and stalled, despite Montgomery's many advantages in numbers and matériel. To be fair, the operation did attract virtually all of the German armor in Normandy. As a result, when Cobra finally opened on July 25, it went close to plan. The carpet bombing caused some significant friendly fire losses, but it vaporized Panzer Lehr division—and potential German reinforcements were already tied up by Goodwood.[54] U.S. forces blasted their way through the line in two days, reached Coutances, turned the corner at Avranches, and finally broke out of Normandy.

This was Patton's moment, as Third Army now set out on a rapid pursuit march, driving simultaneously west into Brittany to secure the ports there and east toward the German border.[55] Heading in two opposite directions, Third Army was at one

◀ WAFFEN-SS PANZERGRENADIER

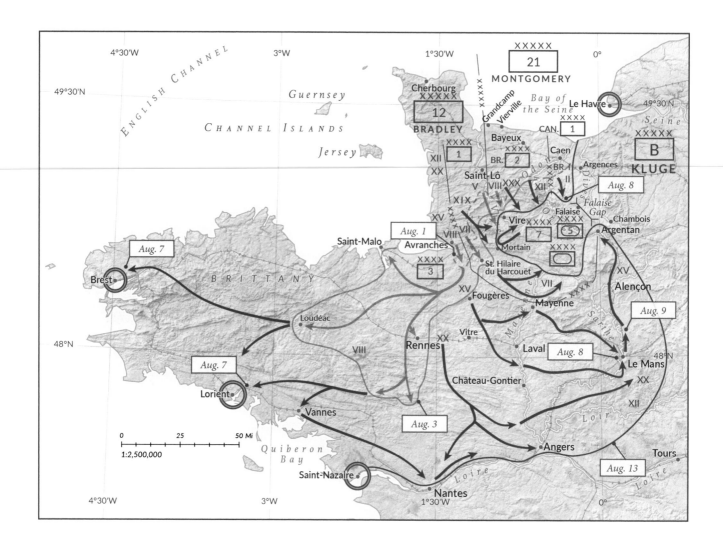

THE NORMANDY BREAKOUT ▲

Patton's careful study of military history and the art of war gave him an exceptionally strong appreciation for the importance of energy and audacity in military operations. He was the perfect person to lead Third Army's charge through the gap opened by Operation Cobra.

point spread out over six hundred miles. With virtually no Germans in front of him, Patton was in high gear. Often forgotten, but churning right alongside, was Hodges's First Army.[56] He had the inner line, as it were, and was thus in actual contact with German forces and heavy resistance the entire time.

Cobra had led to an impressive breakout, and suddenly it looked like there might be an opportunity to smash the Wehrmacht in the western theater in a single seamless campaign. The German High Command's response to Cobra was a counterattack by all available Panzer formations toward Mortain and the sea, seeking to cut off Patton's spearheads from the rest of the Allied invasion force. Launched on August 6, it quickly ran into a brick wall outside of Mortain, which was defended by elements of the U.S. 30th Infantry Division.[57] The real hero here was the U.S. mechanized infantry, which raced forward to seize positions on the Mortain Heights. Soon forward observers were in position, calling down deadly artillery fire on the German Panzers advancing in the plain below. The U.S. Army was mastering its own form of combined-arms warfare, utilizing high mobility and heavy firepower in equal measure.

The Germans were now in deep trouble. Had they made a quick breakthrough, Patton undoubtedly would have been recalled to deal with it. As it was, Patton's Third Army was already far to the east. Virtually every Panzer in the West had inadvertently raced into an Allied noose, and by August 12, that noose was closing near the town of

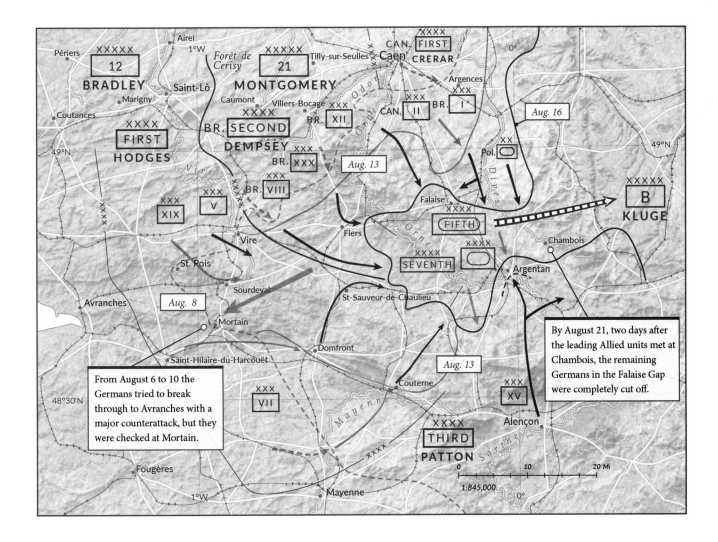

Within the map:

12 BRADLEY · Airel 1°W · Périers · Forêt de Cerisy · Tilly-sur-Seulles · CAN. FIRST CRERAR · 0° · 21 MONTGOMERY · Caen · Argences · Saint-Lô · Marigny · Caumont · Villers-Bocage · BR. XII · CAN. II · BR. I · Aug. 16 · 49°N · Coutances · FIRST HODGES · BR. SECOND DEMPSEY · BR. XXX · Odo · Orne · Pol. · XXXXX B KLUGE · 49°N · Vire · BR. VIII · Aug. 13 · Falaise · Dives · FIFTH · Chambois · XIX · V · Flers · Orne · SEVENTH · Argentan · Vire · St. Pois · Sourdeval · St-Sauveur-de-Chaulieu · Aug. 8 · Avranches · Mortain · Domfront · Aug. 13 · Couterne · By August 21, two days after the leading Allied units met at Chambois, the remaining Germans in the Falaise Gap were completely cut off. · Saint-Hilaire-du-Harcouët · 48°30'N · VII · Mayenne · XV · Alençon · From August 6 to 10 the Germans tried to break through to Avranches with a major counterattack, but they were checked at Mortain. · Fougères · THIRD PATTON · Sarthe · 0 · 10 · 20 Mi · 1°W · Mayenne · 1:845,000 · 0°

Falaise. All that was needed to seal the pocket was a quick attack by Montgomery and a rapid drive south, matched by an American thrust north. Both Allies moved a bit too slowly, however, and 40,000 Germans, including precious cadre and headquarters units, managed to escape through the "Falaise Gap" before the ring was closed on August 21.[58]

Historians often describe Falaise as an unsatisfying victory, or even a failure.[59] In reality, it represented a crushing defeat of the Wehrmacht. Those who escaped the encirclement had to run a gauntlet of Allied fire, especially air attack, and Allied airmen were licking their chops at such tightly packed targets. The immense destruction included the loss of 700 tanks and thousands of vehicles of all sorts—the cream of the Panzer armies in the West.[60] Overall, the Battle of Normandy destroyed forty German divisions and inflicted 450,000 casualties, and the defeated survivors now had to beat a hurried and general retreat back to Germany.

The last week of August saw the Allies restart their forward drive. The French 2nd Armored Division of Hodges's First Army liberated Paris on August 25. Patton's Third Army was still motoring east, and by August 31, it had crossed the Meuse River at Verdun, just seventy-five miles from Germany. By now, fuel supply had become the most pressing issue in continuing the advance. Patton pleaded with Bradley: four hundred thousand more gallons and he would be in Germany in two days. Fuel allocation was

▲ THE FALAISE GAP

The "double pincer" maneuver creating a "cauldron battle" was commonly employed by the Germans in their early victories of 1939–41. In August 1944 the Allies aimed to give the Germans a taste of their own medicine, but the Wehrmacht managed to keep the jaws from closing at Falaise until 40,000 soldiers had escaped the pocket.

**AN AMBUSHED ▲
GERMAN CONVOY**

The Germans suffered a crushing defeat in the Falaise Gap. As Montgomery and Bradley squeezed a salient shut, Allied airmen conducted bombing and strafing runs at the tightly packed German troops trying to escape the trap. The Wehrmacht lost over seven hundred tanks and a thousand other vehicles like the one pictured here.

Eisenhower's call, however, and a perpetual problem for the Allied armies in France. The Allies had 2.25 million mouths to feed, along with 450,000 vehicles (including 5,000 battle tanks) to fuel. With the unexpected success of the breakout, there simply was not enough fuel to go around. Until now, Eisenhower had avoided the issue by following a broad-front strategy of equal supplies for all: Montgomery's armies (British Second and Canadian First Armies), Hodges's First Army, Patton's Third, and General Alexander Patch's U.S. Seventh Army, which had landed only recently in southern France, on August 15 (Operation Anvil) and was driving north to link up with Patton. With the German border in sight and logistics strained to the maximum, Eisenhower now had to make a choice: whether to continue the broad-front advance or change to a single-thrust strategy in which one of the forces would get priority, and the others would just have to wait.

With Eisenhower mulling his options, Montgomery approached him with an uncharacteristically daring plan. Operation Market-Garden would begin with Operation Market, which would drop three full airborne divisions, including over 35,000 paratroopers in the initial wave, to seize a series of river crossings in the Netherlands—bridges over the Wilhelmina Canal, the Maas River, the Waal River, and the Lower Rhine, along with dozens of smaller ones. As that was taking place,

the armored formations of British XXX Corps would launch an overland thrust—Operation Garden—to link up with them, driving over a narrow, sixty-mile-long airborne-cleared carpet to and over the Rhine River. The Rhine was the last major terrain barrier in the West. Once across it, the Allies would be on the doorstep of Germany's industrial heartland, the Ruhr, and would also have bypassed the fortifications the Germans were preparing on their western border, the Siegfried Line, known better to the Allies as the West Wall.[61]

It was a complex plan, and as events indicated, perhaps too complex: Operation Market opened on September 17. The Allies launched in broad daylight, a benefit of having complete air superiority over the battle space, and virtually all the units dropped on time and on target. Nevertheless, German opposition was fierce from the start. The 101st Airborne dropped north of Eindhoven and successfully seized its bridges, opening the gate for XXX Corps. That same day, the ground forces quickly pushed through toward their linkups with the 82nd and the British paratroopers. But they stalled at Zon, where a Bailey bridge had to be thrown up to replace one destroyed

▲ NEW AMERICAN FIGHTERS

The aptly named P-47 Thunderbolt delivered impressive firepower, with eight .50-caliber machine guns in its wings and the ability to carry ten 5-inch "Holy Moses" high-velocity rockets for use against ground targets. American factories produced more than fifteen thousand P-47s—more than any other fighter—and P-47 pilots flying in Europe claimed to have destroyed more than 160,000 trucks, rail cars, and locomotives, as well as some 6,000 armored fighting vehicles and 7,000 enemy planes.

A division, corps, army, and army group commander in the U.S. Army in World War II, Bradley was one of the most recognizable American faces of the war, eclipsed only perhaps by Generals Eisenhower above him and Patton below him.

Bradley served Eisenhower as a troubleshooter and personal representative to the front in Tunisia, he recommended the dismissal of General Lloyd Fredendall after the fiasco at Kasserine Pass, and then he commanded U.S. II Corps through the capture of Tunis and the invasion of Sicily. He then moved on to London to become commander of U.S. ground forces for the upcoming Overlord invasion. Bradley's U.S. First Army landed at Utah and Omaha Beaches (the former uneventfully; the latter a near disaster). He wrote later that he briefly considered evacuating Omaha in the course of that terrible morning, but thought better of it. This decision at Omaha Beach may well have been his defining moment of the war. His army bashed its way through the *bocage* up to Saint-Lô, and Bradley played a key role in planning the Cobra breakout, especially the carpet-bombing attacks that began it. He ended the war commanding the U.S. 12th Army Group. With over 1.3 million men, it was the largest U.S. force in history under a single field commander.

Bradley was known in popular media as "the G.I.'s general" and portrayed to have an aw-shucks demeanor and plebeian manner, though this was largely the invention of journalists such as Ernie Pyle. Many who knew him did not find this popular reputation to reflect his true nature. Bradley remains one of the U.S. Army's great captains. He was much more a manager and a skilled administrator than a fierce battlefield operator or tactical innovator, but this was a war that demanded management and administration above all.

by the Germans. That left both the 101st behind them and the two airborne divisions in front of them locked in bloody fights to keep control of the bridges in their sectors.

The British 1st Airborne, landing at Arnhem over the Rhine, had it worst. Unknown to Allied intelligence, the entire 9th SS Panzer Division had recently deployed there. Although elements of the 1st Airborne managed to reach the bridge, they were fighting for their lives from the moment they hit the ground, as attacks by German armor gradually drove in their perimeter. On day five, reinforcements arrived in the form of the Polish 1st Independent Parachute Brigade. But it too dropped into a bloodbath; the fully alerted defenders soon had the Poles hemmed in to a narrow enclave along the south bank of the Rhine.[62] Both the Poles and the British paratroopers were doomed if Operation Garden did not reach Arnhem soon.

But XXX Corps had run into all sorts of problems. Since British tanks could not deploy off road in this sector, due to the soft Dutch ground, they had to drive along one elevated road, exposing them to German gunners from both sides like ducks in a shooting gallery. "Hell's Highway," the tank crews called it. As always, Allied airpower and artillery helped them fight forward, and XXX Corps did manage to reach the first three crossings. But all along, the drive took heavy casualties, and it petered out altogether on September 25, still a few thousand yards south of Arnhem. The failure not only left British 1st Airborne Division to its fate but also more generally shattered any hopes of a quick German collapse in 1944.[63]

This was a depressing reality for the Allies. They now had massive force in the theater. Montgomery's 21st Army Group had two armies: First Canadian and Second British.[64] Bradley's 12th Army Group had three: U.S. First, Ninth, and Third. And

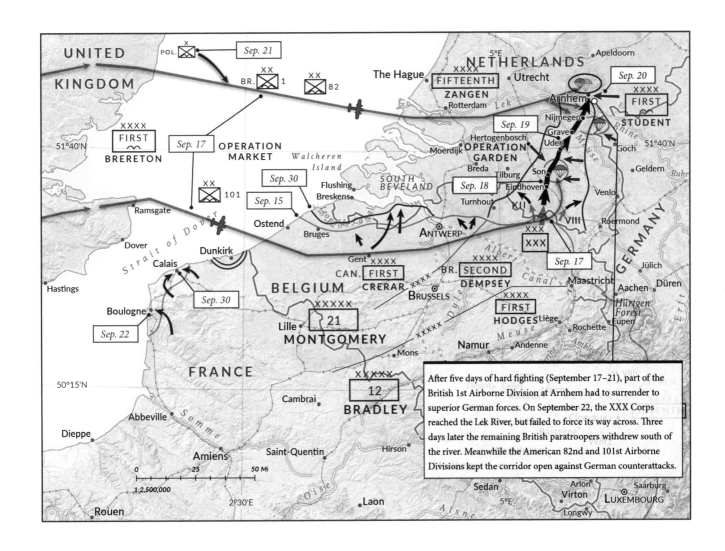

After five days of hard fighting (September 17–21), part of the British 1st Airborne Division at Arnhem had to surrender to superior German forces. On September 22, the XXX Corps reached the Lek River, but failed to force its way across. Three days later the remaining British paratroopers withdrew south of the river. Meanwhile the American 82nd and 101st Airborne Divisions kept the corridor open against German counterattacks.

▲ OPERATION MARKET-GARDEN

The problem with Operation Market-Garden was in the hyphen. The northernmost airborne drop of Operation Market was at Arnhem, which proved just a bit too far for Operation Garden (the northward drive of XXX Corps) to reach the paratroopers before they were overwhelmed.

◀ AIRBORNE DROP, OPERATION MARKET-GARDEN

Members of the 82nd Airborne Division parachute into Holland during Operation Market-Garden. The Allied attacks on Holland and Belgium were the largest airborne operations in the history of the world.

American soldiers parade through the Arc de Triomphe and down the Champs-Élysées. Their faces reflect stolid determination rather than jubilation; they know there will be much hard fighting to come on the long road to Berlin.

another U.S. Army Group had formed under General Jacob L. Devers, whose 6th Army Group contained U.S. Seventh Army and French First Army. Although Eisenhower had all seven of these armies battering forward, they weren't getting far. The lightning drive across France had stalled along Germany's western border, in front of the Siegfried Line's pillboxes, bunkers, and concrete tank traps. The slowdown had allowed the Wehrmacht to do what had seemed impossible in the wake of Cobra: recover its balance and its cohesion.

As a result, the autumn fighting was a firepower-intensive grind rather than maneuver warfare. Hodges's First Army took the city of Aachen in October after hard, block-by-block fighting: the first city in Germany to fall to the Allies. There were heavy casualties on both sides, including the city itself, which was almost completely destroyed. To the south, Patton's Third Army was stuck in Lorraine, struggling with bad roads, mud, and above all, fierce German resistance in front of the French fortress city of Metz. Patton opened his offensive into Lorraine on September 27, but did not take Metz until November 22, nearly two months later.[65]

Montgomery, meanwhile, was having an equally hard time opening Europe's greatest port: Antwerp, Belgium. It fell easily enough on September 4, but Antwerp is an inland port. Knowing that the Allies desperately needed Antwerp's docks to

resolve their logistical problems, the Germans stubbornly defended the city's seaward approaches in the Scheldt Estuary, which Montgomery could not clear until November 28. The worst fighting of this period was Hodges's drive into the Hürtgen Forest just south of Aachen: fifty square miles of dense fir and pine, winding trails, and Germans.[66] Hodges assaulted it frontally, and it took ten weeks of bitter fighting to clear completely.

For all these reasons, it was an exhausted Allied force that reached the German border in December: the very moment that the Wehrmacht chose to launch its last great offensive of the war. On December 16 three German armies—Sixth SS Panzer, Fifth Panzer, and Seventh—struck Hodges's First Army in the Ardennes Forest.[67] The defenders consisted of six divisions of the U.S. V and VIII Corps, strung out along a hundred miles of meandering front. Most of the men had made the exhausting lunge from Normandy or had fought in the Hürtgen and were here resting and refitting.

The main defenses of the West Wall (as the Siegfried Line was also called) were concrete pillboxes constructed from 1936 to 1938 and sited for mutual support by fire. The defenses were not intended to stop an attacker cold, but rather to buy time for counterattack forces to concentrate and strike back.

Others were green, new units being introduced to the rigors of life in the field in a supposedly quiet sector.

Hitler viewed this counterattack, Operation Wacht am Rhein, as a potential war winner. The Panzers would smash through the weak U.S. line in the Ardennes, cross the Meuse River, and then drive on Antwerp. With American forces mauled and the British cut off from their main port, he believed the Western alliance might even unravel. Others weren't so sure. In fact, not one ranking general believed that Wacht am Rhein would work: not Rundstedt; not Model, the commander of Army Group B; not Generals Hans Krebs or Siegfried Westphal, the staff officers, who actually had to draw up the orders. In Model's opinion, the plan didn't "have a damn leg to stand on." If the Panzer forces were stopped before the Meuse, he said, "the only result will be a bulge in the line." Rundstedt felt the same way. "Antwerp!" he exclaimed at the time. "If we even get to the Meuse, we should get down on our knees and thank God!" [68]

Mirroring these varied opinions, the Ardennes offensive was a curious mix of power and weakness. The Wehrmacht assembled as complete a package as it could by this point of the war. There was force aplenty: twenty-four divisions in all, including

ten Panzer. The assault formations were elite: the 1st SS Panzer Division, the best armored formation left in the order of battle; the 150th Panzer Brigade, equipped with
captured U.S. vehicles; the von der Heydte Parachute Battalion, which carried out the
last German drop of the war; even *Einheit Stielau* commando teams, made up of German soldiers fluent in the peculiarities of American English, who donned U.S. Army
uniforms and spread a great deal of confusion in the opening hours by misdirecting
traffic.

At the same time, it was clear that the Germans were scraping the bottom of their
manpower pool for this operation. The offensive featured a mass of *Volksgrenadier*
divisions in the assault force: units made up of men combed out of rear areas, or remnants of units destroyed in Russia, or lightly wounded soldiers convalescing inside
Germany. Hastily thrown together, given rudimentary training, and underequipped,
they fought about as well as could be expected—that is to say, not quite well enough
for a major offensive.

Despite the scale of their preparations, the Germans achieved almost total secrecy.
By now, a certain overconfidence had crept into the Allied command. After inflicting

▲ CAPTURE OF AACHEN

The Americans took the city of
Aachen in October 1944 after hard
block-by-block fighting. Aachen was
the first city in Germany to fall to the
Allies.

CLOSE QUARTERS ▲

In the Hürtgen Forest, as in the street fighting in Aachen, the Allied command of the air was of very limited value.

massive defeats on the Wehrmacht in the last five months, American and British leaders believed the Germans incapable of a large-scale offensive. That had been a main reason Eisenhower had continued attacking all fall: to prevent the Wehrmacht from accumulating a reserve large enough to mount a counterstrike.

As a result, the initial attacks on December 16 achieved complete surprise and were highly successful. The Germans struck hard, and with bad December weather grounding the Allied air forces, they made good progress. One green U.S. division, the 106th, melted away almost completely, with two of its three regiments, 8,000 men, surrendering. It had arrived in France on December 6 and had reached the Ardennes only on December 16—a few short days before it was destroyed.

Elsewhere, however, American forces offered tough resistance. Perhaps it is best to judge an army by its reaction to adversity—how it fights when its front is torn open, or when it is out of communication, or lacking all air support. The U.S. Army fought through all of these problems in the Ardennes. The 7th Armored Division distinguished itself in the defense of Saint-Vith, holding the critical road junction for five crucial days. Likewise, the 101st Airborne, rushed up from Eisenhower's tiny SHAEF reserve, got to the town of Bastogne just before the Germans did, and then hung tough after being completely surrounded. The presence of these two divisions along the main

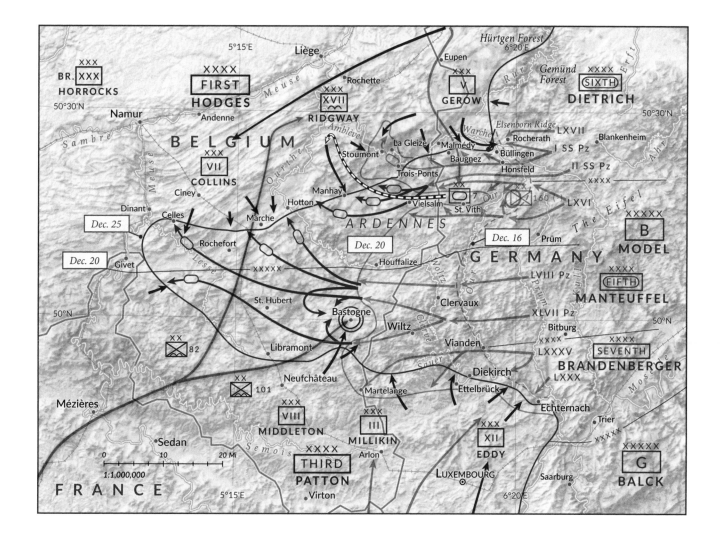

east-west roads through the forest was a serious brake on German progress. U.S. forces on both flanks also managed to contain the offensive. The German Seventh Army got nowhere in the south, and Sixth SS Panzer Army in the north came up against stiff U.S. resistance on the Elsenborn Ridge. The failed counterattack is remembered less for its operational significance than for a series of massacres of U.S. prisoners of war by SS soldiers: 19 were killed at Honsfeld, 50 at Büllingen, and 86 at Malmédy.[69] In each case, victims were taken into open fields and machine-gunned en masse.

In general, the main difference between the 1944 and 1940 offensives in the Ardennes was that the Germans were now trying to *fight* their way through the wooded hills, not merely drive through them. They did form a great salient in the U.S. line, giving the Battle of the Bulge its name, and German spearheads came within six miles of the Meuse. But they never did make a complete breakthrough. By late December, the weather had cleared, and Allied aircraft, the scourge of the Panzers, once again filled the skies. In January 1945 a vigorous counterthrust by Patton's Third Army—whose speed of response was yet another sign of increased American operational proficiency—relieved Bastogne and began the thankless task of rolling back the Germans from their initial gains.[70] Wacht am Rhein—Hitler's last throw of the dice—had failed.

▲ THE BATTLE OF THE BULGE, DECEMBER 16–26, 1944

In planning Operation Wacht am Rhein, Hitler hoped for a replay of 1940. While the spearheads of the German attack quickly overran many of the Allied frontline troops, mechanical problems and fuel shortages stunted the progress of the Nazi Panzers enough to allow U.S. forces to regroup.

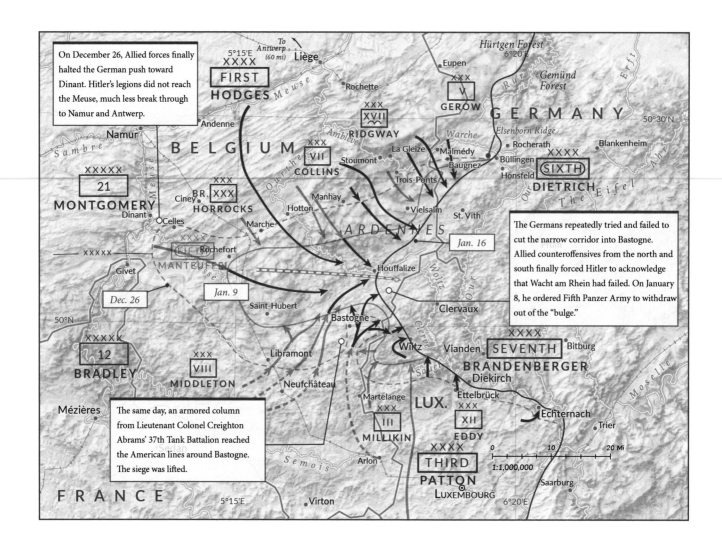

On December 26, Allied forces finally halted the German push toward Dinant. Hitler's legions did not reach the Meuse, much less break through to Namur and Antwerp.

The Germans repeatedly tried and failed to cut the narrow corridor into Bastogne. Allied counteroffensives from the north and south finally forced Hitler to acknowledge that Wacht am Rhein had failed. On January 8, he ordered Fifth Panzer Army to withdraw out of the "bulge."

The same day, an armored column from Lieutenant Colonel Creighton Abrams' 37th Tank Battalion reached the American lines around Bastogne. The siege was lifted.

THE BATTLE OF THE BULGE, DECEMBER 27, 1944–JANUARY 16, 1945 ▲

As the weather cleared in late December, the Allies managed to leverage massive airpower in their own counterattack to the German offensive. On the ground, American forces battled forward on the southern flank, reinforced by Patton's Third Army in the struggle for the Bastogne corridor. Renewed assaults by Allied forces to the north and south finally forced the Germans into a fighting withdrawal.

THE END: 1945 IN THE ETO

By the new year, the end really was in sight. The Allied air forces had bombed Germany's cities into rubble. The Bulge had eaten up the Wehrmacht's last reserves. The German Army was filled with hastily formed units: old men and boys given crude training, handed *Panzerfaust* antitank weapons, and sent out to die. These were the *Volkssturm*, yet another downhill slide in the quality of German personnel.[71] Nonetheless, both army and home front were still holding firm—whether out of faith in Hitler, fear of Allied reprisals, or simple inertia, it is difficult to say. Most likely it was a combination of all three.[72]

With the military issue no longer in doubt, the Allies were already looking forward to the shape of postwar Europe. The Grand Alliance of the United States, the Soviet Union, and Great Britain was a marriage of convenience, with the relationship between the Anglo-Americans on the one hand and the Soviets on the other particularly tense. Stalin suspected that the Western powers were sitting off to the side and using the Red Army to bleed Germany; the West suspected Stalin of a plan to use victory to install Communist regimes in Eastern Europe, perhaps even in Germany. Wartime diplomatic conferences failed to end this mistrust.

Here soldiers of the 7th Armored Division patrol a village recently captured during the American counterattack during the Battle of the Bulge.

The most important took place at the Soviet Crimean resort of Yalta in February 1945. Here the Allies reaffirmed the unconditional surrender of Germany as their war aim, finalized the division of postwar Germany into four occupation zones (American, British, Soviet, and French), and jointly signed a Declaration on Liberated Europe, promising "free elections" in the occupied territories to establish "governments responsive to the will of the people." Thorny issues remained, however. After the German invasion of 1939, for example, the Polish government had fled to London, declared itself the "government in exile" of the Polish Republic, and had won the recognition of Great Britain and the United States. When the Red Army entered Poland in 1944, however, the Soviets set up a Communist committee in the city of Lublin, which declared itself to be Poland's legitimate government. At Yalta, the United States and Great Britain recognized the Lublin committee, ensuring a Communist government (and Soviet domination) in postwar Poland. In return, Stalin agreed to join the new United Nations, one of President Roosevelt's key policy aims, and to declare war on Japan within three months of German surrender. While the Allies had reached a modus vivendi for the immediate postwar era, they had also laid the foundations for the future Cold War.

As the Allies deliberated at Yalta, the war in Europe entered its endgame. In 1945,

On the morning of December 22, 1944, German soldiers waving truce flags delivered a message addressed "To the U.S.A. Commander of the encircled town of Bastogne." "There is only one possibility to save the encircled U.S.A. troops from total annihilation," it read. "That is the honorable surrender of the encircled town . . ." Brigadier General Anthony McAuliffe returned the following typed response:

> December 22, 1944.
> To the German Commander,
> N U T S!
> The American Commander

gigantic offensives broke over Germany from east and west. In January the Soviets struck out of their Vistula River bridgeheads, lunging from Warsaw to the Oder River in three weeks—another three hundred miles of forward progress and a classic example of mature Deep Battle.[73] After spending February overrunning East Prussia, the Red Army prepared its final offensive: the drive on Berlin. On April 16 two Soviet fronts—1st Byelorussian under Georgy Zhukov and 1st Ukrainian under Ivan Konev, together including more than 2 million men and 6,500 tanks—crashed through German defenses on the Oder. Konev snaked around Berlin from the south, linking up with U.S. forces at Torgau on the Elbe River on April 25 and cutting Germany in half, while Zhukov passed north of the city, swinging round and surrounding it.[74]

Now it was all over but the dying. The German defenders—an uneven mix of divisional remnants, partially trained *Volkssturm*, and elite Waffen-SS—were outnumbered and fighting in a hopeless cause. But if the Wehrmacht fought any battle "fanatically," Berlin was the one.[75] Indeed, SS squads roamed the streets of the central districts throughout the fighting, checking papers and identities, shooting or hanging anyone suspected of desertion. It was slow going, and Soviet losses were high. By April 28, Zhukov's men were on the Spree River in the northern outskirts, and Konev was near the city center, in the park known as the Tiergarten. Their two spearheads

were less than a mile apart, but it would take them four full days of fierce house-to-house combat to cross that final distance.

Realizing that all was lost, Hitler shot himself on April 30. Later that day, Soviet infantry hoisted the hammer-and-sickle flag over the Reichstag building. On May 2 resistance in Berlin ceased after a horrific city fight that cost Soviet forces no fewer than 360,000 casualties. German losses were at least that many, plus another 400,000 prisoners.

On the Western Front, the Anglo-American war machine went into gear in February, overrunning the Rhineland and closing up to the river itself.[76] Crossing the Rhine posed a serious challenge, requiring careful planning, cooperation between infantry and engineers, and a great deal of time. The problem solved itself on March 7, however, when U.S. First Army had the good fortune to seize an intact bridge over the Rhine at Remagen. "Hot dog!" Bradley exclaimed when he heard the news.[77] Suddenly the Allies were over the Rhine. Patton, too, found a way, forcing his own crossing over the river at Oppenheim, south of Mainz, on March 22. In this short campaign, the Allies inflicted heavy casualties and took more than 250,000 German prisoners.

The Wehrmacht was falling apart. Within a week, both Hodges and Patton had

The First Wave

The *Volkssturm* was organized into four waves to be called up in succession as the enemy approached their home areas. The men of the first wave averaged fifty-two years of age, and included many veterans of the First World War. Only first-wave battalions could be used outside their immediate home areas.

"Uniform"

Many members of the *Volkssturm* had old uniforms from previous military service, or uniforms issued to members of Nazi Party organizations, but many others had only their civilian clothes. Armbands marked *Deutscher Volkssturm Wehrmacht* ("German People's Storm of the Armed Forces") served, barely, to meet the Geneva Convention requirement that combatants be recognizable as members of military units.

Panzerfaust

A cheaper, more easily manufactured relative of the American bazooka, the *Panzerfaust* ("Armored Fist") consisted of a simple launch tube and a rocket projectile with a shaped-charge warhead. Unlike the bazooka, it was designed to be operated by a single person. The most widely used model had an effective range of just sixty meters (sixty-six yards). It thus required real bravery, though not much training, to use against enemy tanks—its main intended purpose. The weapon could also be used against infantry sheltering behind walls.

Established in late 1944 as the Allied armies closed in on Germany from both east and west, the *Volkssturm* (People's Storm) reflected Hitler's determination that the Third Reich would fight a total war to the bitter end. All fit men from sixteen to sixty not already in the armed forces were called up for service, organized by Nazi Party local and regional leaders, and given four hours of training per week. *Volkssturm* battalions and companies secured rear areas and prepared fortifications in German towns and cities. The number of its members who saw combat in the final defense of the Reich is unknown, but probably rose into the millions, with casualties in the hundreds of thousands by May 1945.

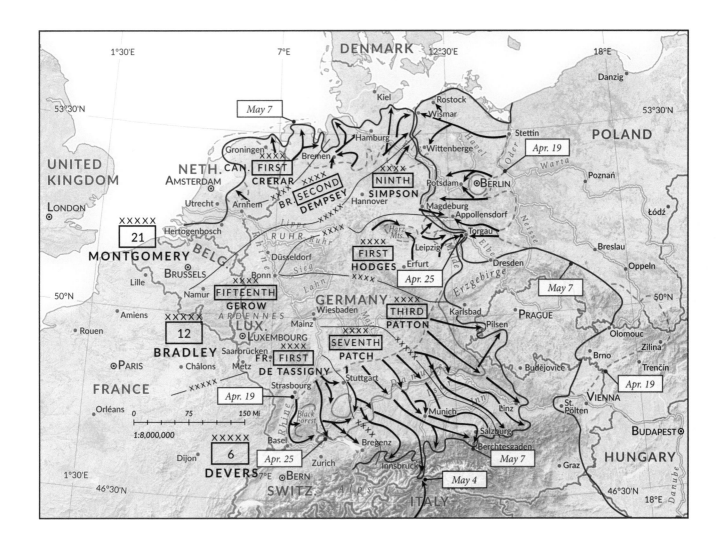

Map labels:
DENMARK • POLAND • UNITED KINGDOM • NETH. • GERMANY • FRANCE • LUX. • BELG. • SWITZ. • ITALY • HUNGARY

Kiel • Rostock • Wismar • Stettin • Danzig • Hamburg • Wittenberge • Potsdam • BERLIN • Magdeburg • Appollensdorf • Poznań • Łódź • Torgau • Leipzig • Dresden • Breslau • Oppeln • Erfurt • Karlsbad • Pilsen • PRAGUE • Olomouc • Zilina • Brno • Trenčín • Budějovice • Linz • St. Pölten • VIENNA • Munich • Salzburg • Berchtesgaden • Innsbruck • Bregenz • Graz • BUDAPEST • Stuttgart • Strasbourg • Basel • Zurich • BERN • Dijon • Orléans • PARIS • Rouen • Amiens • Lille • BRUSSELS • Namur • Bonn • Düsseldorf • Hannover • Bremen • Groningen • Amsterdam • Utrecht • Arnhem • Hertogenbosch • LONDON • Wiesbaden • Mainz • Saarbrücken • Metz • Châlons • LUXEMBOURG

Army boxes: XXXXX 21 MONTGOMERY • XXXXX 12 BRADLEY • XXXXX 6 DEVERS • XXXX FIRST CRERAR • BR. SECOND DEMPSEY • XXXX NINTH SIMPSON • XXXX FIRST HODGES • XXXX FIFTEENTH GEROW • XXXX THIRD PATTON • XXXX SEVENTH PATCH • FR. FIRST DE TASSIGNY

Date boxes: May 7 • Apr. 19 • Apr. 25 • May 7 • Apr. 19 • Apr. 19 • Apr. 25 • May 7 • May 4

Scale: 0 75 150 Mi 1:8,000,000

Coordinates: 1°30'E, 7°E, 12°30'E, 18°E, 53°30'N, 50°N, 46°30'N

advanced seventy-five miles out of their bridgeheads. Montgomery, too, made it over the Rhine on March 23–24. The assault crossing, Operation Plunder, was a huge set-piece battle involving thousands of tanks, 3,500 guns, and even two airborne divisions.[78] Once over the river, he and Hodges turned and encircled all of Army Group B in the Ruhr in April.[79] The Allies took 317,000 prisoners, including two dozen generals. Model, the army group commander, shot himself. With the fall of Berlin, Hitler's death, and the junction of all the Allied armies, the war in Europe was over. On May 6 General Alfred Jodl, the Wehrmacht's chief of operations, flew to SHAEF headquarters in Rheims, France, where he signed the surrender document on May 7, 1945.[80]

CONCLUSION

The Allied victory in Europe was a complex event, resulting from many factors, and anyone seeking a single cause is embarking on a fool's errand. Certainly numbers, resources, and production had all tilted dramatically in favor of the Allies, especially

▲ FINAL OPERATIONS

Facing Allied demands for unconditional surrender, the Nazi regime kept fighting to the bitter end. The war continued until Anglo-American forces advancing from the west met with Red Army soldiers driving east.

◀ VOLKSSTURM

ALLIED HANDSHAKES ▲

American and Soviet troops greet each other over the rubble of Germany.

from 1942 on. Hitler and the German High Command had known that from the start, but they still hoped they could win enough early victories to make continuing the war an unpalatable option for the Allies. It was an illusion that lasted for a long time, even after the invasion of the Soviet Union had stalled and the United States had entered the war. At any rate, numbers alone have never guaranteed victory.

In fact, the Allies won for a simple reason: they learned how to fight World War II; that is to say, how to conduct combined-arms warfare on a massive scale. Their early stabs at it—the British in France, the Soviets in the first phase of Barbarossa, the U.S. Army at the start of the fighting in Tunisia—had all been equally inept. Germany had been the one European country preparing in earnest for war during the 1930s, and the early campaigns showed it. Dashing and aggressive commanders, tough and disciplined troops, skill in combined-arms warfare: the Wehrmacht had it all early in the war.

But these things have a way of evening out, and once Germany's adversaries began

THE WAR'S END ▶

Each of the combatant nations responded differently to the end of the war. Here, a French poster triumphantly depicts the fall of the German eagle.

THE WEST POINT HISTORY OF WORLD WAR II

to gain experience under fire, the course of operations changed dramatically. The Allied forces improved their performance across the board. Commanders found wanting in combat were replaced by those who had proven themselves. It usually took place more gently in the Western armies than in the Soviet, but the result was much the same. Cooperation and combination of the arms, between air and ground forces or between artillery and the mobile arms, improved rapidly, seemingly by the month. When wedded to an advanced operational doctrine such as Deep Battle, expertise at combined-arms warfare made the Soviet Army the most formidable land force in the world. Jointness—the cooperation between services, the smooth interplay of land, sea, and air—was a special hallmark of the Anglo-American coalition. If Operation Overlord was any indication, there might not have been a spot on the West European coast, either Normandy or the Pas de Calais, that the Germans could have defended successfully.

In both cases, the Soviet or the Anglo-American, the science of logistics came to the fore during the final year of the war. Combined-arms warfare and amphibious invasions alike are hugely complex and supply intensive—not just for the forces in the first wave but also for the follow-on echelons. As General Eisenhower came to realize, logistics was an absolute prerequisite for any vast operation. In the end, the Allies were able to seize and hold a decisive superiority in this crucial area, and to generate enormous combat power as a result. On the beaches in Normandy, for example, before they had seized any ports, the Allies simply created them. The famous "Mulberry" prefabricated harbors were a gigantic engineering and construction project that was utterly beyond German capabilities at any point in the war. The Allies were not merely richer in material terms. They spent a great deal of time and effort figuring how to convert that wealth into battlefield strength, how to produce weapons on an enormous scale, how to ship those weapons to the front, and how to keep supplying them to sustain the advance. In World War II, the Allied powers invented the art and science of logistics, viewing the supply of armies, air forces, and fleets as a vast and seamless chain that began on the factory floor and ended in the ruins of the Third Reich.

Nevertheless, it is erroneous to see the Allied victory solely in terms of superior resources. No military outcome is inevitable. War is the domain of chance and uncertainty, as Carl von Clausewitz wrote in the nineteenth century. Every war—every battle—is a sort of gamble; a game of probability and chance. The decisive victory of the Allied powers over Germany was no exception. Both sides made blunders, but in the end, the Allies were able to overcome them in a way that the Germans were not. Studying the question "why the Allies won"[81] yields fruitful lessons not only in the area of resource management but also in military flexibility, adaptability, and a willingness to learn the hard lessons of war on the battlefield itself.

INTRODUCTION

Disarray and folly characterized not only Japan's prewar economic and military preparations but also its prosecution of the conflict with the English-speaking powers. American outrage at the attack on Pearl Harbor precluded a negotiated settlement; the early Japanese offensive overran too many indefensible, far-flung outlying positions; and its subsequent strategy of resisting every enemy advance reduced the forces available to defend more vital sites.

True, there was also some disarray in Allied strategy, reflecting not only the partners' differing war aims but also divisions within the American higher command. China sought the eviction of the Japanese from the Asian mainland and the recovery of Manchuria, Mongolia, and Formosa (Taiwan). The British intended to regain Burma, Malaya, and Hong Kong and to restore Indochina to the French and the Netherlands East Indies to the Dutch. America sought to liberate the Philippines, recover Guam and Wake Island, and replace Japan with China as the foremost power in the Far East. The Allies agreed on the need to impose "unconditional surrender" on Japan and to occupy the country to reshape its politics.

Their "Germany First" strategy notwithstanding, the Allies, from 1942 on, conducted simultaneous campaigns in the South Pacific, Southwest Pacific, Central Pacific, and the China-Burma-India (CBI) theaters. American officials agreed on supporting China so as to tie down Japanese troops on the Asian mainland, but disagreed about strategy elsewhere. For personal and political reasons, General Douglas MacArthur, the Southwest Pacific commander, favored a drive north from New Guinea to liberate the Philippines. General "Hap" Arnold, chief of the U.S. Army Air Forces (effectively an autonomous service) identified these islands and China as sites from which to conduct a long-range bombing campaign against Japan. He argued that strategic bombing, supplemented by an air-sea blockade, would defeat Japan. Admiral Ernest King, the chief of naval operations, did not wholly disagree, but he focused more on eliminating the enemy fleet, seizing advanced air bases and fleet anchorages, and conducting a commerce-raiding campaign against Japanese shipping. He preferred to bypass the Philippines in favor of a direct approach to Japan via the Central Pacific archipelagos and the Chinese coast. Because strategy and command were linked, neither King nor General George C. Marshall, the Army chief of staff, would yield, so all three efforts were pursued in parallel.

As outlined in chapter 3, in 1943 Operation Cartwheel leapfrogged up the Solomons and along the New Guinea coast, while Admiral Chester Nimitz's Pacific Fleet seized Tarawa and Makin in the Gilberts. This chapter focuses on 1944–45, as the Allies advanced in the Southwest Pacific, the Central Pacific, and Burma.

The Pacific Fleet took the Marshalls early in 1944 and defeated the Japanese fleet at the Battle of the Philippine Sea that summer. The capture of the Mariana Islands and the arrival of long-range B-29s allowed large-scale strategic bombing of Japan's Home Islands, which along with a highly effective submarine campaign against merchant shipping practically wrecked the Japanese war economy. When MacArthur

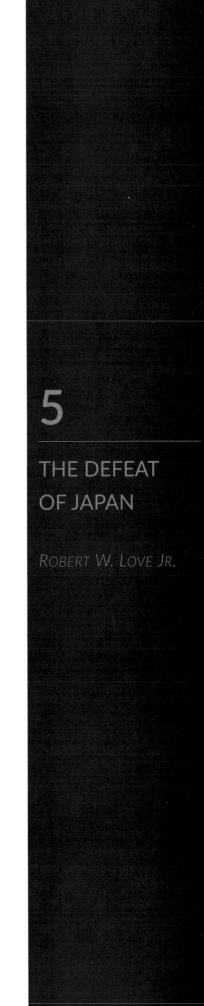

5

THE DEFEAT OF JAPAN

ROBERT W. LOVE JR.

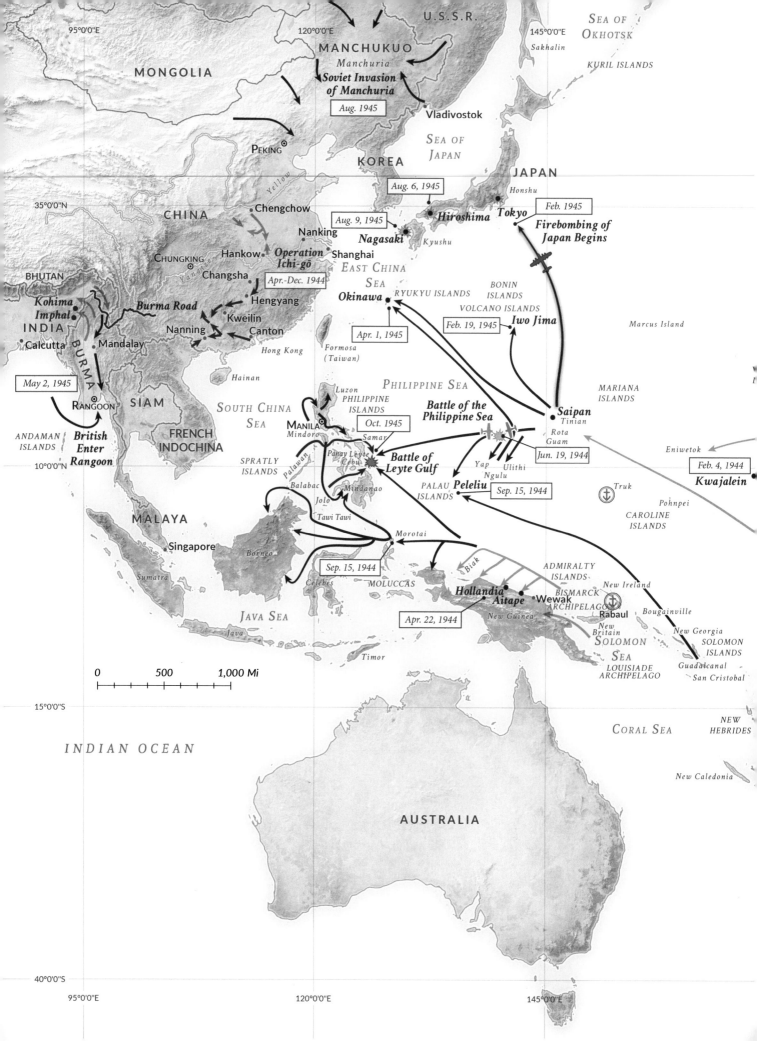

U.S.S.R.

SEA OF
OKHOTSK

MONGOLIA

MANCHUKUO
Manchuria
**Soviet Invasion
of Manchuria**
Aug. 1945

Sakhalin

KURIL ISLANDS

PEKING◎

Vladivostok

SEA OF
JAPAN

KOREA

JAPAN

Honshu

CHINA

Chengchow

Aug. 6, 1945

Hiroshima **Tokyo**

Feb. 1945
**Firebombing of
Japan Begins**

Nanking

Aug. 9, 1945

CHUNGKING◎
Hankow **Operation
Ichi-gō**
Changsha *Apr.-Dec. 1944*

Nagasaki *Kyushu*

Shanghai

Yangtze

EAST CHINA
SEA

BHUTAN

*Kohima
Imphal* **Burma Road**

Hengyang

Okinawa RYUKYU ISLANDS

BONIN
ISLANDS

Marcus Island

INDIA

Kweilin

Apr. 1, 1945

VOLCANO ISLANDS

Feb. 19, 1945 **Iwo Jima**

Calcutta

Nanning Canton

Mandalay

Hong Kong

Feb. 19, 1945

MARIANA
ISLANDS

BURMA

SIAM

Hainan

*Formosa
(Taiwan)*

PHILIPPINE SEA

May 2, 1945

RANGOON◎

Luzon

**Battle of
the Philippine Sea**

SOUTH CHINA
SEA

PHILIPPINE
ISLANDS

Saipan
Tinian

ANDAMAN
ISLANDS

**British
Enter
Rangoon**

FRENCH
INDOCHINA

MANILA
Mindoro

Oct. 1945

Samar

*Rota
Guam*

Eniwetok

Jun. 19, 1944

Feb. 4, 1944

Panay *Leyte*
Cebu **Battle of
Leyte Gulf**

Yap
Ngulu

Kwajalein

SPRATLY
ISLANDS

Palawan

Balabac

Mindanao

PALAU
ISLANDS **Peleliu**

Ulithi

⚓ Truk

MALAYA

Jolo

Tawi Tawi

Sep. 15, 1944

Pohnpei

CAROLINE
ISLANDS

Singapore

Borneo

Morotai

Sep. 15, 1944

Biak

ADMIRALTY
ISLANDS

Sumatra

Celebes

MOLUCCAS

Hollandia
Aitape Wewak

New Ireland

BISMARCK
ARCHIPELAGO

JAVA SEA

Apr. 22, 1944

New Guinea

Rabaul

Bougainville

Java

Timor

*New
Britain*

SOLOMON

New Georgia SOLOMON
ISLANDS

0   500   1,000 Mi

SEA

Guadalcanal

LOUISIADE
ARCHIPELAGO

San Cristobal

15°0'0"S

CORAL SEA

NEW
HEBRIDES

INDIAN OCEAN

New Caledonia

AUSTRALIA

40°0'0"S

95°0'0"E   120°0'0"E   145°0'0"E

95°0'0"E   35°0'0"N   120°0'0"E   10°0'0"N   145°0'0"E

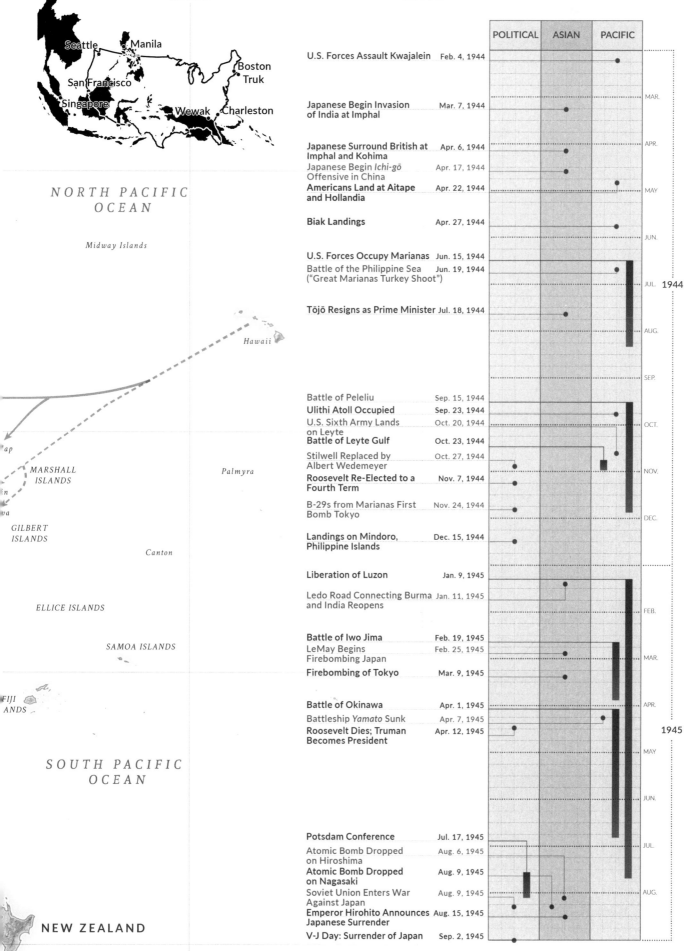

	POLITICAL	ASIAN	PACIFIC
U.S. Forces Assault Kwajalein Feb. 4, 1944			●
Japanese Begin Invasion Mar. 7, 1944 of India at Imphal		●	
Japanese Surround British at Apr. 6, 1944 Imphal and Kohima		●	
Japanese Begin *Ichi-gō* Apr. 17, 1944 Offensive in China		●	
Americans Land at Aitape Apr. 22, 1944 **and Hollandia**			●
Biak Landings Apr. 27, 1944			●
U.S. Forces Occupy Marianas Jun. 15, 1944			●
Battle of the Philippine Sea Jun. 19, 1944 ("Great Marianas Turkey Shoot")			●
Tōjō Resigns as Prime Minister Jul. 18, 1944		●	
Battle of Peleliu Sep. 15, 1944			
Ulithi Atoll Occupied Sep. 23, 1944			●
U.S. Sixth Army Lands Oct. 20, 1944 on Leyte			●
Battle of Leyte Gulf Oct. 23, 1944			●
Stilwell Replaced by Oct. 27, 1944 Albert Wedemeyer	■		
Roosevelt Re-Elected to a Nov. 7, 1944 **Fourth Term**	●		
B-29s from Marianas First Nov. 24, 1944 Bomb Tokyo	●		
Landings on Mindoro, Dec. 15, 1944 **Philippine Islands**	●		
Liberation of Luzon Jan. 9, 1945		●	
Ledo Road Connecting Burma Jan. 11, 1945 and India Reopens			
Battle of Iwo Jima Feb. 19, 1945			
LeMay Begins Feb. 25, 1945 Firebombing Japan		●	
Firebombing of Tokyo Mar. 9, 1945		●	
Battle of Okinawa Apr. 1, 1945			
Battleship *Yamato* Sunk Apr. 7, 1945			●
Roosevelt Dies; Truman Apr. 12, 1945 **Becomes President**	●		
Potsdam Conference Jul. 17, 1945			
Atomic Bomb Dropped Aug. 6, 1945 on Hiroshima			
Atomic Bomb Dropped Aug. 9, 1945 **on Nagasaki**	■		
Soviet Union Enters War Aug. 9, 1945 Against Japan	●	●	
Emperor Hirohito Announces Aug. 15, 1945 **Japanese Surrender**	●	●	
V-J Day: Surrender of Japan Sep. 2, 1945	●		

1944

1945

165°0'0"W   140°0'0"W

MAR.
APR.
MAY
JUN.
JUL.
AUG.
SEP.
OCT.
NOV.
DEC.
FEB.
MAR.
APR.
MAY
JUN.
JUL.
AUG.

Seattle   Manila
San Francisco
Singapore
Wewak   Charleston
Boston
Truk

NORTH PACIFIC
OCEAN

Midway Islands

Hawaii

ap

MARSHALL
ISLANDS

n

va

GILBERT
ISLANDS

Palmyra

Canton

ELLICE ISLANDS

SAMOA ISLANDS

FIJI
ANDS

SOUTH PACIFIC
OCEAN

NEW ZEALAND

165°0'0"W   140°0'0"W

▲ AVENGE PEARL HARBOR!

The Japanese had planned to build an "iron wall" around the Southern Resource Area and "defeat America and Britain." But American fury over the attack on Pearl Harbor, kept hot by government propaganda, helped sustain American determination to crush Japan at any cost.

▲ "CHINA CARRIES ON"

Americans had long sympathized with the Chinese victims of Japanese aggression, and FDR envisioned a postwar world in which China would play a prominent role as a U.S. ally in the region.

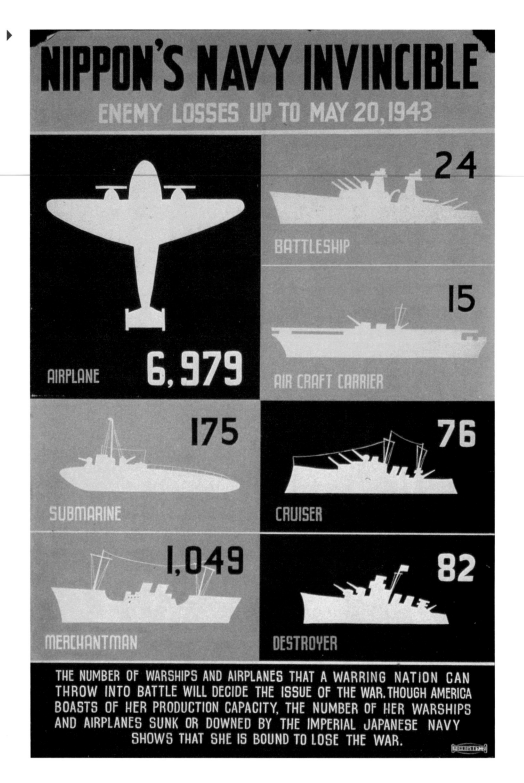

returned to the Philippines in October, the Japanese made another bid for a decisive naval victory but met complete defeat in the Battle of Leyte Gulf. Meanwhile, on the Asian mainland, a Japanese thrust into India was repulsed by the British, who then advanced into Burma and Malaya. China absorbed the body blow of the Japanese Ichi-gō offensive, but resisted despite heavy losses.

The efficient use of material superiority allowed the Allies to advance rapidly on all fronts against Japan while simultaneously prosecuting the struggle in Europe.

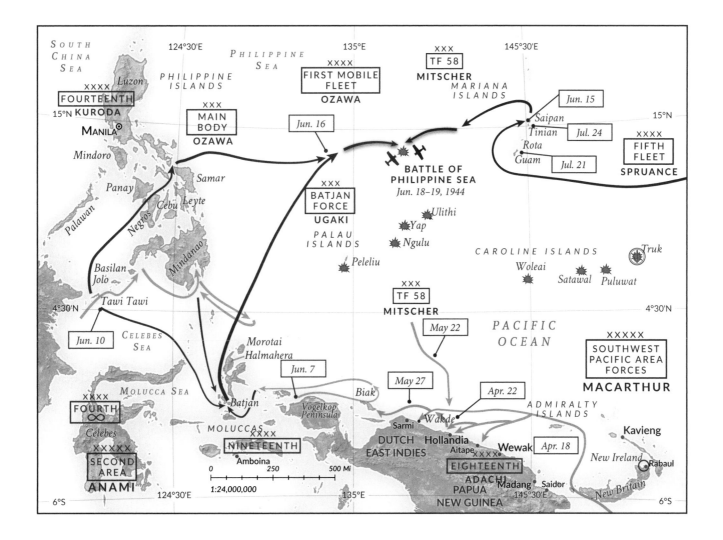

Advance to the Mariana Islands, April 1– August 10, 1944

In the Central Pacific, Admiral Nimitz and the Navy's Fast Carrier Task Forces relentlessly raided Japanese-held territory from the Volcano Islands to Palaus, as well as the main harbor at Truk. From June to August 1944, the U.S. captured the islands of Saipan, Tinian, and Guam in the Marianas, leading some Japanese leaders to finally conclude that they would lose the war.

Gross Japanese miscalculations helped. Already short of raw materials and skilled manpower, and nearly bankrupt even before they engaged the Western powers, the Japanese sent ships and aircraft without adequate defensive characteristics into battle; appointed indecisive and ill-informed generals and admirals to important commands; and deployed armies composed of poorly armed, semiliterate peasants whose main battlefield advantage was a fanatical willingness to die in large numbers. Not only did they misuse the Type 93 torpedo and their few other superior weapons, but also even their few tactical innovations—such as the kamikaze suicide plane and the inland defenses on Iwo Jima and Okinawa—reflected the fatalism of Japanese tactics. From Pearl Harbor to Hiroshima, they clung to the belief that they could avoid complete defeat by winning a "decisive battle" that would undermine the Allies' will to continue the struggle. This unrealistic expectation warped their wartime diplomacy and strategy and made two atomic bombings necessary to convince the Tokyo regime that the only alternative to capitulation was national destruction.

America and Britain made substantial efforts to support Chiang Kai-shek's government, but getting the Nationalists the supplies they needed to turn the tide against the Japanese Army proved extremely difficult. "I'm sorry, sirs," says "the hungry dragon of Chungking" in this German cartoon. "But it's impossible to breathe fire on an empty stomach!"

„Tut mir leid, meine Herren, mit leerem Magen kann man nicht Feuer speien!"

THE CENTRAL PACIFIC

The second stage of Admiral Nimitz's Central Pacific drive erupted in January–February 1944, when Admiral Raymond Spruance's Fifth Fleet entered the central Marshalls and the Marines overcame stiff opposition to occupy the islands of Kwajalein, Roi-Namur, and Eniwetok.[1] A simultaneous carrier-battleship raid on the large naval base at Truk in the Caroline Islands forced the Japanese fleet to withdraw to the Philippines. This and subsequent carrier and land-based bomber raids on enemy air bases in the Central Pacific paved the way for the third stage: the descent on the Marianas, which brought the Americans within B-29 range of Japan.[2]

The invasion of the Marianas in June 1944 was an undertaking on a scale never contemplated by prewar strategists.[3] The seven carriers and eight light carriers of

THE FLYING TIGERS ▶

Claire Chennault's Flying Tigers of the 1st American Volunteer Group were not in the U.S. Army Air Corps when the war began. During the early months of the war, they struck the first blows against the Japanese. In 1942 they were absorbed into the regular military, forming the core of the Fourteenth Air Force, commanded by Chennault.

Fifth Fleet, designated Task Force 58 (or TF 58), isolated the archipelago, deprived the defenders of air support, and provided close air support to the landing forces. Five divisions went ashore, and despite difficult terrain and numerous and determined defenders, the islands of Saipan, Tinian, and Guam were taken by August 2. On each island, the fighting culminated in suicidal "banzai" charges by the last defenders.[4]

Meanwhile, Admiral Soemu Toyoda, the new commander of the Japanese Combined Fleet, moved to defend the Marianas by luring the Fifth Fleet carriers into a killing zone between hundreds of land-based aircraft on Guam, Yap, and Rota, as well as Admiral Jisaburō Ozawa's battleship-carrier fleet, which operated 473 aircraft.[5] This strategy would have made sense if the rival air forces were equal, but the Japanese now faced superior enemy numbers, superior planes, aircrews with superior training, and lethal ship-based air defenses.[6] Moreover, Admiral Spruance, forewarned of Toyoda's plans, had already badly damaged the Marianas' airfields, reducing one Japanese advantage.

Submarines warned Spruance that Ozawa's ships were steaming into the Philippine Sea, flights of Japanese planes from the Marianas and Truk did little damage, and four waves of attacking carrier aircraft were detected by American radar and shattered by the defending combat air patrol (CAP) and the Fifth Fleet's antiaircraft batteries.[7] The Battle of the Philippine Sea, fought June 19–20, 1944, was so one-sided that U.S. Navy aviators nicknamed it the "Great Marianas Turkey Shoot." The Japanese lost 633 planes, and 3 carriers they could not replace; the Americans lost just 123 planes, which could easily be replaced. Moreover, the Japanese inner defense line had been breached, and the Americans would soon be able to operate B-29 bombers against the

Home Islands. The Japanese military could no longer keep the war away from Japan. The defeat led to Prime Minister Hideki Tōjō's resignation on July 18.[8]

CHINA-BURMA-INDIA THEATER

Since 1937, the Japanese had committed huge numbers of soldiers to fighting in China. American support for the Chinese government led by President Chiang Kai-shek had contributed greatly to the tensions that led to Pearl Harbor. In 1942, in addition to money and military supplies, Army Chief of Staff George C. Marshall sent General Joseph "Vinegar Joe" Stilwell to China, charging him to advise Chiang, to oversee the training of the Chinese Army, and to command American forces in the China-Burma-India (CBI) theater.[9] Keeping China fighting was both an important political goal and also a means to ensure that a large fraction of the Japanese Army remained tied down on the mainland.

The Japanese conquest of Burma in the spring of 1942 led to the closure of the Burma Road and the beginning of Allied efforts to restore a land route to China. Until that could be done, supplies for the Chinese had to be transported over the twenty-one-thousand-foot-high Hump of the eastern Himalayas by transport planes based in northeast India—an expensive and inefficient method. In August 1943 the Allies activated the combined South East Asia Command (SEAC) to oversee the war effort in the theater. British Admiral Lord Louis Mountbatten became the supreme commander, with Stilwell as his deputy. Stilwell concentrated his efforts on opening a new overland supply route to China: the Ledo Road. His persistent call for more Chinese troops for use in Burma caused friction with Chiang, who was more concerned with husbanding his forces for future use against the Japanese and the Communist Chinese than with aiding the British, whom he distrusted.

Partly in response to Stilwell's efforts and the growing damage inflicted by General Claire Chennault's China-based Fourteenth U.S. Air Force, and partly in recognition that time was not on their side and that only rapid, aggressive action could bring decisive results, the Japanese high command planned two land offensives in early 1944. First, Lieutenant General Renya Mutaguchi's Fifteenth Army would advance from Burma into India to isolate the British rail junction at Imphal, severing the flow of supplies to the Chinese. Then Japan's half-million-man China Expeditionary Force would launch operation Ichi-gō, aiming to establish a rail line of communications from North China to occupied Indochina, to eliminate the American air bases in South China and ultimately to compel Chiang to capitulate. Victory in China would then allow substantial forces to be redeployed in the Pacific, to resist the American advance toward Japan. Events proved, however, that Japan's goals for its immense dual offensive were unrealistically ambitious.

The Japanese drive into India was successful initially. Despite being outnumbered, Mutaguchi's aggressive troops pushed ahead to surround Imphal in April. But the Japanese lacked the support units and logistical infrastructure to sustain their troops

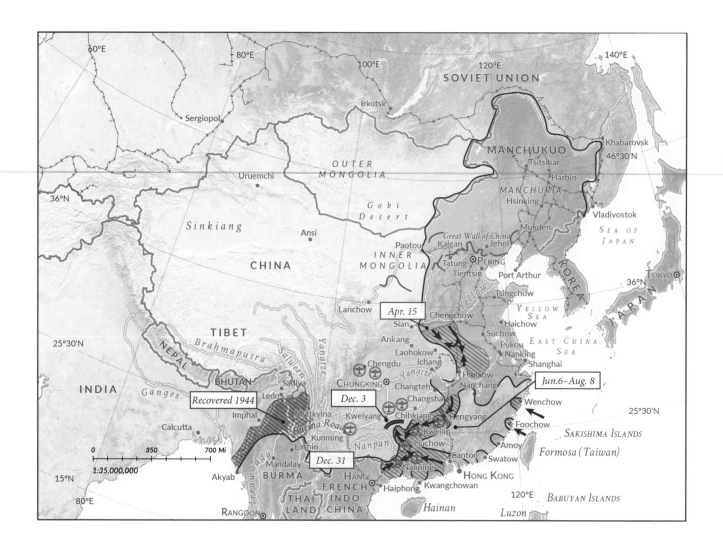

OPERATION ICHI-GŌ, ▲ APRIL–DECEMBER 1944

The last great Japanese offensive of the war succeeded in opening a continuous line of rail communication to Indochina and overran airbases from which American planes were causing all sorts of trouble. But the Japanese did not capture the Nationalist capital at Chungking or knock the KMT Army out of action.

inside India, and tough resistance by the veteran Indian IV Corps bought time for British Major General William Slim to complete his preparations for a major counterattack. When Slim struck in June 1944, his now-seasoned Fourteenth Army possessed large numerical superiority and plenty of air support, artillery, and armor; his opponents were worn out, starving, and desperately low on all sorts of supplies. Mutaguchi nonetheless delayed his withdrawal, allowing Slim to pursue and destroy the retreating Japanese by September, and ultimately recover all of Burma by mid-1945.[10]

In its second operation, Ichi-gō, Japan fared better but still fell short of its objectives. In China, Japanese forces still had numerical and qualitative superiority, and were operating close to their bases. They pushed south starting in April, overrunning seven of Chennault's twelve bases by September and reaching the border with Indochina by year's end.[11] The American B-29s pushed out of China simply redeployed to the Mariana Islands and resumed operations. The Japanese, moreover, were unable to sustain service on their newly captured rail lines. And although the Chinese Army was repeatedly defeated and China's entire position imperiled, Chinese troops avoided encirclement, manned new defensive lines, and at length held the enemy in Szechuan in early 1945. Ichi-gō was an operational victory but accomplished nothing at the strategic level.[12]

6

Moving Up: On Utah Beach the Americans met less German resistance. The troops moved up the beach, overwhelmed the German defenders, and moved inland to link up with the airborne forces that had dropped into Normandy the night before.

5

Fighting Inland: As the battle for Omaha Beach raged through the morning, the commanders afloat looked for signs that the troops had gotten off the beach. First as individuals and then in small groups, American soldiers worked their way up the bluffs between the German strongpoints despite enemy fire. The first soldiers arrived at the top of the bluff around 8:00 a.m. By 11:00 a.m., large numbers of Americans were moving off the beach and inland.

3

Going In: Although the Royal Navy and the U.S. Navy had the main responsibility for getting the troops ashore, many of the landing craft were operated by the U.S. Coast Guard, which manned well over a hundred large and small landing craft during the operation.

On the Beach: The first several **4** hours on the beach were the most difficult. Intense German defensive fire killed or wounded many Americans as they struggled to get off their landing craft, across the beach, and up the bluff.

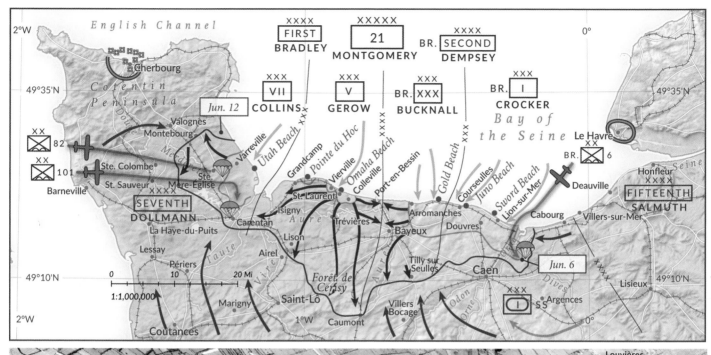

English Channel

2°W

49°35'N

Cotentin Peninsula

Cherbourg

xxxx
FIRST
BRADLEY

xxxxx
21
MONTGOMERY

xxxx
BR. SECOND
DEMPSEY

0°

49°35'N

xx 82

xx 101

Barneville

xxx
VII
COLLINS

Jun. 12

xxx
V
GEROW

xxx
BR. XXX
BUCKNALL

xxx
BR. I
CROCKER

Bay of the Seine

Le Havre

BR. xx 6

Valognes
Montebourg
Ste. Colombe
St. Sauveur
Ste. Mère-Eglise
Varreville
Utah Beach
Grandcamp
Pointe du Hoc
Vierville
Omaha Beach
Colleville
Port-en-Bessin
Courseulles
Juno Beach
Gold Beach
Arromanches
Sword Beach
Lion-sur-Mer
Deauville
Honfleur
Seine

xxxx
FIFTEENTH
SALMUTH

SEVENTH
DOLLMANN

La Haye-du-Puits

Lessay

Périers

Marigny

Coutances

Carentan
Lison
Airel
Isigny
St. Laurent
Trévières
Bayeux
Douvres
Cabourg
Villers-sur-Mer
Lisieux

Forêt de Cerisy

Saint-Lô

Caumont

Villers Bocage

Tilly sur Seulles

Caen

Jun. 6

xxx
I SS

Argences

49°10'N

2°W

1°W

0°

49°10'N

0   10   20 Mi

1:1,000,000

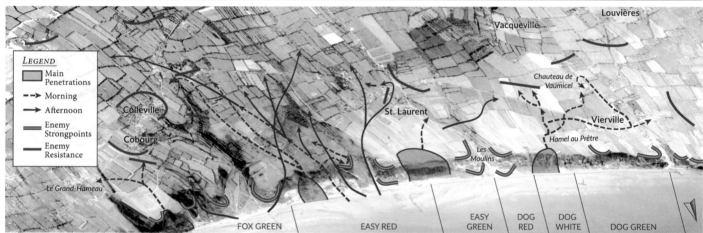

LEGEND
- Main Penetrations
- Morning
- Afternoon
- Enemy Strongpoints
- Enemy Resistance

Louvières
Vacqueville
Chateau de Vaumicel
Vierville
Hamel au Prêtre
St. Laurent
Les Moulins
Colleville
Cobourg
Le Grand-Hameau

FOX GREEN   EASY RED   EASY GREEN   DOG RED   DOG WHITE   DOG GREEN

D-DAY, JUNE 6, 1944

D-Day, June 6, 1944

The Americans landed at Omaha and Utah Beaches while the British and Canadians landed at Gold, Juno, and Sword Beaches. Supported by massive air and sea forces, the Allied ground forces overcame the German defenses and established a bridgehead from which they could launch future operations to liberate Western Europe and defeat Nazi Germany. In line with John Steinbeck's view that "total war would require the use not only of all of the material resources of the nation but also the spiritual and psychological participation of the whole people," the U.S. military considered that art could provide "material for reflection and inspiration [that] is an essential contribution to a nation's total effort." The Army, Navy, and Marine Corps, as well as the private company Abbott Laboratories, supported uniformed and civilian combat artists charged with capturing "the essence and spirit of war" for the American people. The artworks reproduced here evoke the human experience of D-Day in a different way from the more familiar work of combat photographers. Many additional images can be found on the websites of the U.S. Army Center of Military History and the U.S. Naval History and Heritage Command.

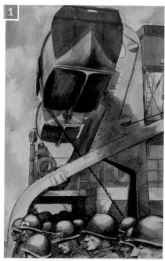

Heading Out: Operation Neptune—the Allied amphibious assault landings on the beaches of Normandy—involved the movement of massive numbers of troops, vehicles, and supplies. After a day's delay due to bad weather General Eisenhower gave the order to go, and the invasion fleet of nearly seven thousand ships and small craft (most of them British) sailed for France. The hour for the landing was 6:30 a.m., June 6, 1944.

Clearing the Way: Before the first assault wave hit the beach, Allied planes and warships hit the defenders with intense air and naval bombardment, including direct fire by the powerful 12-inch guns of the old battleship *Arkansas*. Naval demolition teams went ashore with the first landing craft and used explosive packs to destroy the beach obstacles emplaced by the Germans, clearing lanes for the subsequent waves.

Meanwhile, the quarrel between Stilwell and Chiang reached a climax in October 1944, when Marshall and Stilwell convinced Roosevelt to propose that Stilwell command the entire Chinese Army.[13] Chiang, deeply insulted, responded by insisting that Stilwell be sacked, forcing Marshall to replace Vinegar Joe with General Albert Wedemeyer.[14] More able than Stilwell, Wedemeyer persuaded Chiang to send some of his best troops to Burma, reopening the Ledo Road in January 1945, and helped to contain Ichi-gō. But Chiang's inability to get Roosevelt to honor his many vague promises and the failure of the Chinese Army to prevent Japanese wartime depredations discredited the Nationalist regime in the eyes of its people, and China was too fatigued for more exertions.[15]

▲ THE JAPANESE ADVANCE

This painting by army combat artist Sergeant Samuel D. Smith records the Japanese push that captured the American airfield at Liuchow, China, in November 1944. A Chinese counterattack recovered the town in June 1945.

SUBMARINE COMMERCE RAIDING

Even had Ichi-gō succeeded completely, the Japanese lacked enough freighters to supply the Home Islands with raw materials or enough transports to redeploy troops to
threatened bases in the Pacific. This was a result of the commerce-raiding campaign
conducted by American submarines.

The Japanese and American navies adopted different approaches toward submarine construction and strategy. Design and shipyard shortcomings not only kept the
number of Japanese submarines small, but also undermined their plan to prevail over
greater American numbers with ships and weapons of superior quality. About the
only superior weapon Japan deployed was the lethal submarine-launched Type 93 torpedo, with more than double the range of Allied equivalents.[16] The inability to exploit
this advantage in pursuit of a practical strategy characterized Japanese submarine operations. Like the Americans, prewar Japanese strategists envisioned using their boats
to attack capital ships rather than merchantmen or tankers. Unlike the Americans,
they continued to adhere to this approach even after it failed. When Pearl Harbor was
attacked, American shipping between the West Coast and Hawaii was exposed to a
half dozen submarines, but Japanese skippers reserved their torpedoes for battleships
and carriers, which they could not overhaul.[17] Then, just before Midway, all Japanese
submarines were withdrawn permanently from the eastern Pacific, immunizing the
American sea lines of communications thereafter. Despite the German example, the
Japanese never mounted a concerted submarine commerce-raiding campaign.

The Americans, however, did. The Japanese 1942 offensives had created forty-seven
new sea lines of communication between the Home Islands and outposts from Burma
to the Central Pacific, but Japanese shipyards—focused on constructing the capital
ships that would contribute to winning a "decisive battle"—were unable to build large

See Action Now

★ **JOIN THE SUBMARINE SERVICE**

▲ THE SUBMARINE SERVICE

Submarine service was dangerous and cramped, so the U.S. Navy had to actively recruit for volunteers. But the results were clearly worth the effort: the 288 boats of the service collectively sank 8 aircraft carriers, 1 battleship, 11 cruisers, and close to 1,300 enemy merchant ships.

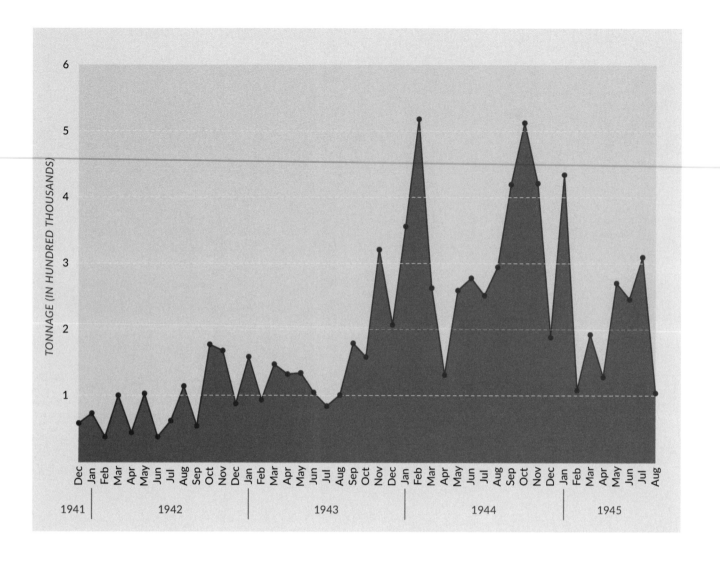

JAPANESE LOSS OF ▲
MERCHANT SHIPPING,
DECEMBER 1941–
AUGUST 1945

numbers of freighters or escorts, and the fleet devised no efficient escort-of-convoy strategy or tactics.[18] An escort command was organized in April 1942, but it adopted the wrongheaded practice of assigning one or two escorts to defend small convoys of ten or fewer ships, as opposed to the Allied practice of many more escorts guarding much larger convoys.[19] Not only were military and civilian shipping uncoordinated, but also Japanese antisubmarine offensive tactics were generally ineffective.[20]

Consistent with the prewar design for the defeat of Japan, War Plan Orange, the U.S. Navy had ordered large numbers of heavy, fast submarines.[21] In December 1941 the fleet operated one hundred boats, with over seventy more under construction.[22] Most were fifteen-hundred-ton vessels with long eleven-thousand-mile ranges. Knowing that well-defended convoys could defeat commerce raiding, interwar planners intended to employ their submarines to support the battle fleet as escorts, scouts, and skirmishers.

Some boats were deployed to Australia in 1942, but most Pacific Fleet submarines were based at Pearl Harbor until early 1943, when Rear Admiral Charles Lockwood took command of the Submarine Force and established a forward base at Midway. He appointed more aggressive skippers, remedied problems with malfunctioning torpedoes, and shifted strategy by launching a vigorous campaign against Japanese

shipping.[23] Lockwood deployed some boats to intercept convoys in midocean and, to greater effect, stationed others off ports of arrival and departure. More submarines, better torpedoes, ruthless skippers, and the concurrent amphibious drive—which brought land-based American aircraft within range of the critical sea-lanes—led to a massacre of Japanese shipping during the last two years of the war. Lockwood's boats, intermittently diverted to support major invasions, also often disrupted Japanese fleet operations. For instance, submarines on station off Borneo in mid-1944 prevented Ozawa from training his carrier squadrons, which contributed to the one-sided nature of the Battle of the Philippine Sea.[24] Following Nimitz to his forward headquarters on Guam in January 1945, Lockwood and the Australia-based commands flooded the South China Sea with submarines to stanch the flow of oil to the Home Islands. At times, more than half the tankers inbound to Japan were sunk.[25]

The recklessness of Japan's leaders was illustrated by their failure to appreciate the danger that Allied submarines could pose to their merchant shipping, the Achilles heel of their war effort. When Pearl Harbor was attacked, the Japanese merchant marine amounted to only about six of the ten million tons of shipping the country required to supply its 1940 level of imports. Over the course of the war, in addition to 8 carriers, 1 battleship, 11 cruisers, and 200 other warships, Pacific Fleet submarines sank 1,560 tankers and freighters totaling 5.3 million tons, at a cost of just 48 boats. Aircraft, surface ships, and mines accounted for almost 3 million more. The reduction

▲ TORPEDOED JAPANESE DESTROYER *YAMAKAZE* PHOTOGRAPHED THROUGH THE PERISCOPE OF U.S.S. *NAUTILUS*, JUNE 25, 1942

American submariners sank more than two hundred warships and many hundreds of merchant ships at a cost of forty-eight U.S. boats lost. The U.S. Navy's submarine force was one of the most effective branches of any military in World War II and one of the least publicized.

Halsey was born in New Jersey into a Navy family. He graduated from the Naval Academy in 1904 and served for many years on torpedo boats and destroyers, earning a Navy Cross in World War I for his command of the destroyer *Shaw*. After tours as a naval attaché and on battleships, Halsey earned his wings at the age of fifty-two in 1935 and commanded the carrier *Lexington* and carrier divisions of the Battle Force. First to implement Admiral Ernest J. King's blocking and raiding strategy in 1942, Halsey on the U.S.S. *Enterprise* attacked Japanese bases in the Gilberts and Marshalls in February and Wake in March. These operations culminated in the Tokyo Raid in April.

Forced by illness to miss the Battle of Midway, Halsey returned in October to command in the South Pacific during the struggle for Guadalcanal. Risking his limited naval forces, he adopted an aggressive strategy that gutted the enemy's air and naval arms and compelled the abandonment of the island in January 1943.

The subsequent campaign, which evicted the enemy from the Solomon Islands and Bougainville, was capped by a devastating carrier raid on the Japanese fleet base at Rabaul. In May 1944 King shifted Halsey to command of the Third Fleet, which participated in the invasion of the Philippines, the complex Battle of Leyte Gulf, and the seizure of the Palau Islands. After a few months ashore, Halsey resumed command of the Third Fleet for a final "Victory Cruise" off the enemy coast. Though King was unhappy with Halsey for driving his ships into two typhoons in 1945, he chose Halsey over Raymond Spruance as the last of the four five-star fleet admirals.

of the merchant fleet to three-fifths of its prewar level by December 1, 1944, deprived Japan's overseas forces of supplies, caused fuel shortages that limited pilot training and fleet operations, and starved Japanese industry, already short of many necessities.[26]

APPROACHING THE PHILIPPINES

Among the Japanese forces deprived of supplies and support by the loss of so much shipping were the defenders of New Guinea and the Philippines. By early 1944, MacArthur and Admiral William Halsey had already bypassed New Britain and its major naval base on Rabaul and completed its isolation by seizing the Admiralty Islands.[27] MacArthur held that New Guinea was too large to be bypassed entirely, but the early phases of Operation Cartwheel had already demonstrated that the main Japanese forces along the coast might be similarly outflanked and isolated by amphibious operations. He prepared to leap five hundred miles past the eighty thousand Japanese at Hansa Bay and Wewak to land at Hollandia and Aitape. Then he would advance to the Vogelkop Peninsula on the northwestern tip of the island, where he planned to establish airfields within range of the Philippines.[28] General George Kenney's Fifth Air Force bombers from Australia and fighters from the Admiralties practically eliminated Japanese air forces in the landing area.[29] Then on April 22 Lieutenant General Robert Eichelberger's three-division Alamo Force landed at Aitape, and also at Hollandia, one hundred twenty-five miles farther west.[30] Spruance's twelve Fifth Fleet carriers, designated Task Force 58, having supported the Hollandia landings, withdrew on April 26, when Australian fighters flying from Aitape took over.[31] The bypassed

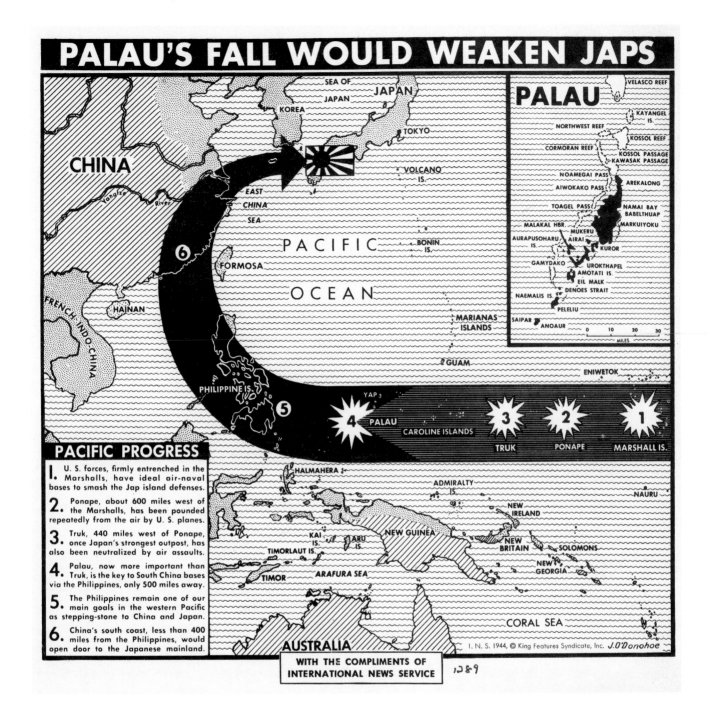

PALAU'S FALL WOULD WEAKEN JAPS

PALAU

VELASCO REEF
KAYANGEL IS.
NORTHWEST REEF
KOSSOL REEF
CORMORAN REEF
KOSSOL PASSAGE
KAWASAK PASSAGE
NOAMEGAI PASS
AREKALONG
AIWOKAKO PASS
TOAGEL PASS
NAMAI BAY
BABELTHUAP
MALAKAL HBR.
MARKUIYOKU
MUKERU
AURAPUSOHARU IS.
AIRAI
KUROR
GAMYDAKO
UROKTHAPEL
AMOTATI IS.
EIL MALK
NAEMALIS IS.
DENOES STRAIT
PELELIU
SAIPAR
ANOAUR
0 10 20 30
MILES

CHINA

SEA OF JAPAN
JAPAN
KOREA
TOKYO
VOLCANO IS.

EAST CHINA SEA

PACIFIC OCEAN

Yangtze River

FORMOSA
BONIN IS.

FRENCH INDO-CHINA
HAINAN

MARIANAS ISLANDS

GUAM

PHILIPPINE IS.

YAP
PALAU
CAROLINE ISLANDS
TRUK
PONAPE
MARSHALL IS.

ENIWETOK

PACIFIC PROGRESS

1. U. S. forces, firmly entrenched in the Marshalls, have ideal air-naval bases to smash the Jap island defenses.

2. Ponape, about 600 miles west of the Marshalls, has been pounded repeatedly from the air by U. S. planes.

3. Truk, 440 miles west of Ponape, once Japan's strongest outpost, has also been neutralized by air assaults.

4. Palau, now more important than Truk, is the key to South China bases via the Philippines, only 500 miles away.

5. The Philippines remain one of our main goals in the western Pacific as stepping-stone to China and Japan.

6. China's south coast, less than 400 miles from the Philippines, would open door to the Japanese mainland.

HALMAHERA
ADMIRALTY IS.
NAURU
NEW IRELAND
KAI IS.
ARU IS.
NEW GUINEA
NEW BRITAIN
SOLOMONS
TIMORLAUT IS.
NEW GEORGIA
TIMOR
ARAFURA SEA
CORAL SEA
AUSTRALIA

I. N. S. 1944, © King Features Syndicate, Inc. J.O'Donohoe

WITH THE COMPLIMENTS OF INTERNATIONAL NEWS SERVICE

1289

Japanese Eighteenth Army attempted a desperate counterattack against Aitape, but it was completely shattered by the Americans' defensive firepower. One of the more audacious strokes of the war, MacArthur's Hollandia operation underscored the formidable American advantages in firepower, mobility, and generalship.[32]

What would be the next major target? Marshall supported MacArthur's plan to recover the Philippines, but King and Nimitz still preferred to bypass the islands and occupy Formosa, which would bring American land-based air forces closer to Japan's Home Islands. In the midst of his third reelection campaign, Roosevelt visited Pearl Harbor and got photographed listening to both sides, but, as usual, the president remained aloof from disputes over military strategy. King agreed to support MacArthur's

▲ APPROACHING THE PHILIPPINES

MacArthur wanted the Palaus neutralized to protect his right flank as his forces moved north from New Guinea to liberate the Philippines. Capturing Peleliu, at the southern end of the archipelago, required some of the toughest fighting of the war.

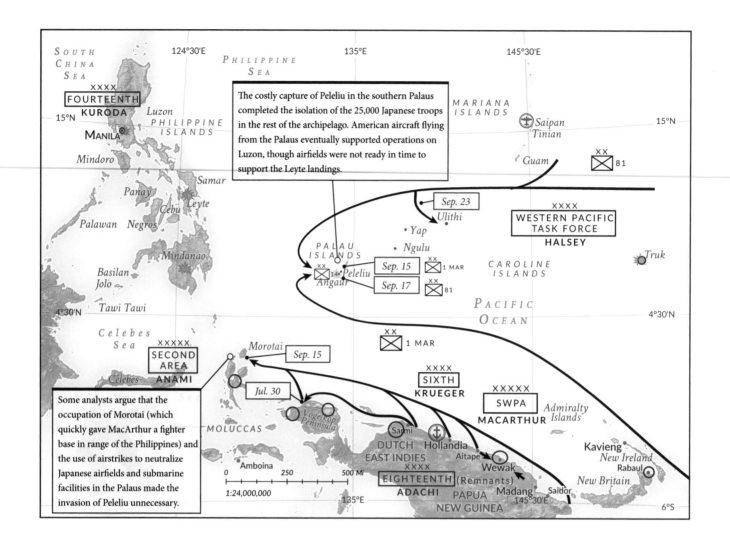

The costly capture of Peleliu in the southern Palaus completed the isolation of the 25,000 Japanese troops in the rest of the archipelago. American aircraft flying from the Palaus eventually supported operations on Luzon, though airfields were not ready in time to support the Leyte landings.

Some analysts argue that the occupation of Morotai (which quickly gave MacArthur a fighter base in range of the Philippines) and the use of airstrikes to neutralize Japanese airfields and submarine facilities in the Palaus made the invasion of Peleliu unnecessary.

ADVANCE TO THE ▲
PHILIPPINES, JULY 30–
SEPTEMBER 22, 1944

The leaders of the dual offensives in the Pacific (MacArthur and Nimitz) initially had differing strategic objectives. Admiral Nimitz wanted to seize Formosa (Taiwan) and from there launch the invasion of the Japanese Home Islands. MacArthur, however, considered it a top priority to liberate the Philippines. The general won the argument, and by fall 1944 the two drives were positioned to converge on Leyte.

plan to skip past the southern Philippine island of Mindanao, landing instead on the more central island of Leyte; in return, Marshall assented to Nimitz's operations against the outlying Japanese islands of Iwo Jima and Okinawa. Halsey's Third Fleet (the same ships as Fifth Fleet, but given a different designation when Halsey rather than Spruance was in command), including the fast battleships and heavy carriers of TF 38, was to cover the landings, but Nimitz made it clear that Halsey's primary mission was to meet the Japanese fleet should it seek an engagement. Vice Admiral Thomas Kinkaid's Seventh Fleet, consisting of an amphibious force, old battleships, submarines, and eighteen light escort carriers, was to provide offshore bombardment, land the Sixth Army, provide close air support, and defend the entrances to the gulf.[33] Whereas Halsey was subordinate to Nimitz, Kinkaid reported to MacArthur. These arrangements seemingly conflicted with the nostrum of "unity of command," and, after the event, engendered considerable controversy.[34]

On September 6 Halsey flung strikes against Japanese airfields on Yap, Ulithi, and the Palaus, and then steamed up the southern Philippines to prevent Japanese land-based air from disrupting the invasion. Nine days later Kinkaid's Seventh Fleet landed troops on Morotai Island, where an airstrip was established within fighter range of the southern Philippines.[35] That same day, Third Fleet carriers covered the landing of

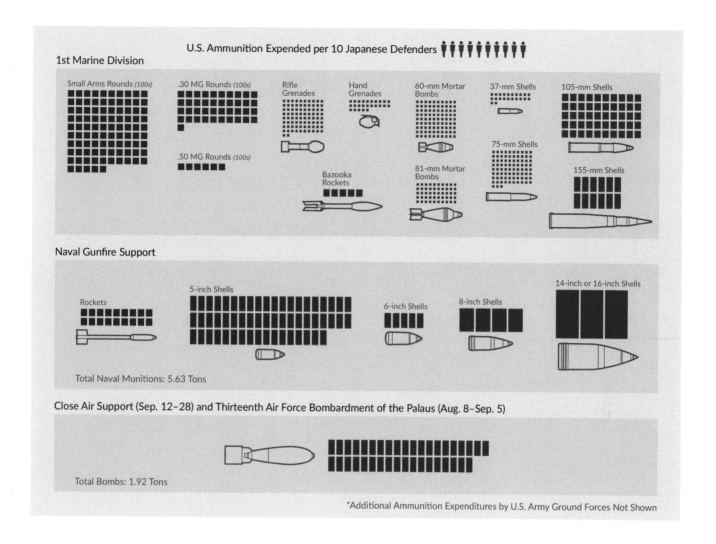

U.S. Ammunition Expended per 10 Japanese Defenders

1st Marine Division

Small Arms Rounds (100s)

.30 MG Rounds (100s)

.50 MG Rounds (100s)

Rifle Grenades

Hand Grenades

Bazooka Rockets

60-mm Mortar Bombs

81-mm Mortar Bombs

37-mm Shells

75-mm Shells

105-mm Shells

155-mm Shells

Naval Gunfire Support

Rockets

5-inch Shells

6-inch Shells

8-inch Shells

14-inch or 16-inch Shells

Total Naval Munitions: 5.63 Tons

Close Air Support (Sep. 12–28) and Thirteenth Air Force Bombardment of the Palaus (Aug. 8–Sep. 5)

Total Bombs: 1.92 Tons

*Additional Ammunition Expenditures by U.S. Army Ground Forces Not Shown

Marines on Peleliu, another small island with airfields in fighter range of the Philippines. What was supposed to be a quick operation turned into a brutal monthlong struggle. Instead of defending the beaches to the last man, the Japanese on Peleliu retreated to dug-in positions on high ground, from which they had to be chiseled out at high cost.[36] Meanwhile, an army division overcame much lighter resistance to capture Ulithi Atoll, which Halsey needed as a fleet anchorage. Within a month, Naval Construction Battalions (Seabees) transformed the lagoon into a massive advance base featuring a floating dry dock to service capital ships and other replenishment and repair facilities.[37] Finally, in mid-October Halsey's efforts to neutralize the Formosa airfields led to another "turkey shoot," with more than five hundred Japanese planes lost, compared with fewer than a hundred American aircraft.

▲ MARINE, NAVY, AND AIR FORCE MUNITIONS EXPENDITURES FOR THE PALAUS OPERATION, AUGUST–OCTOBER 1944

When they relied on defense-in-depth tactics, as they did at Peleliu, Japanese defenders commonly inflicted about one American casualty each before being killed. Considering the mind-boggling weight of matériel the United States military employed against them, that ratio testifies to the Japanese Army's tactical skill and discipline.

▲ Hard Going on Peleliu

Major General William H. Rupertus, commander of the 1st Marine Division, knew the assault on Peleliu would be tough, but he also expected it to be quick. Apparently he expected the Japanese to destroy themselves in banzai counterattacks after his Marines secured a beachhead. Instead the island's defenders, after inflicting heavy damage on D-Day, fell back into the incredibly complex and difficult terrain of the coral rises inland. Fighting from pre-pared positions that were well protected, well concealed, and well sited to provide mutual support by fire, the roughly 11,000 Japanese servicemen on Peleliu inflicted over 9,000 casualties on the American attackers.

THE BATTLE OF LEYTE GULF

The Allies returned to the Philippines on October 17, 1944, when Allied forces assaulted the small island of Suluan, off Samar, to clear the way for the much larger landing on Leyte three days later. The Japanese navy's response triggered the largest and most complex naval battle of the Second World War: the Battle of Leyte Gulf, comprising the individual engagements known as the Battle of the Sibuyan Sea, the Battle of Surigao Strait, the Battle of Cape Engaño, and the Battle off Samar. It is worth studying in detail because it exemplifies both the weaknesses of Japanese naval operations and the strengths of the Pacific Fleet, two of the most important factors in explaining the overall Allied victory over Japan.

Having failed to inflict a decisive defeat on the Pacific Fleet at Midway or in the Philippine Sea, the Japanese calculated that Leyte Gulf would be their last chance for a clash of fleets they could still hope to win. If they allowed the Americans to recover the Philippines, then the oil supply from Borneo, without which the Combined Fleet could not operate, would inevitably be cut. To prevent this from happening, Admiral Toyoda devised a typically complex operational plan.[38]

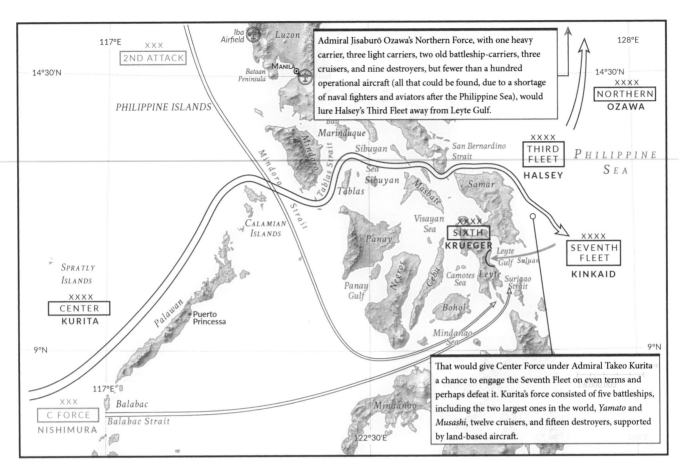

Admiral Jisaburō Ozawa's Northern Force, with one heavy carrier, three light carriers, two old battleship-carriers, three cruisers, and nine destroyers, but fewer than a hundred operational aircraft (all that could be found, due to a shortage of naval fighters and aviators after the Philippine Sea), would lure Halsey's Third Fleet away from Leyte Gulf.

That would give Center Force under Admiral Takeo Kurita a chance to engage the Seventh Fleet on even terms and perhaps defeat it. Kurita's force consisted of five battleships, including the two largest ones in the world, *Yamato* and *Musashi*, twelve cruisers, and fifteen destroyers, supported by land-based aircraft.

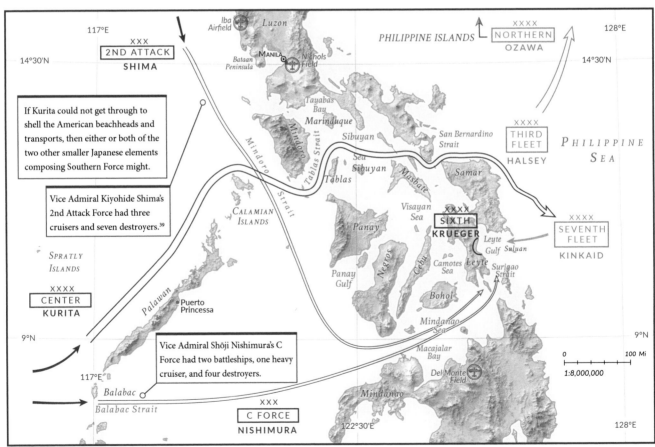

If Kurita could not get through to shell the American beachheads and transports, then either or both of the two other smaller Japanese elements composing Southern Force might.

Vice Admiral Kiyohide Shima's 2nd Attack Force had three cruisers and seven destroyers.[39]

Vice Admiral Shōji Nishimura's C Force had two battleships, one heavy cruiser, and four destroyers.

ORDER OF BATTLE FOR THE BATTLE OF LEYTE GULF, OCTOBER 23–26, 1944 ▶

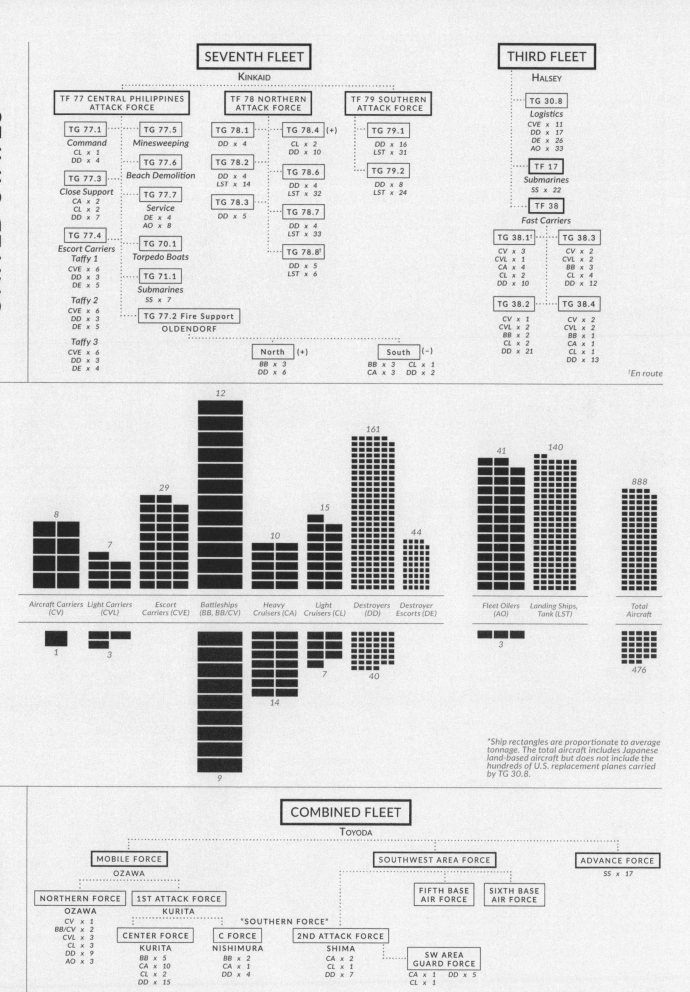

UNITED STATES

SEVENTH FLEET
Kinkaid

TF 77 CENTRAL PHILIPPINES ATTACK FORCE

TG 77.1
Command
CL x 1
DD x 4

TG 77.3
Close Support
CA x 2
CL x 2
DD x 7

TG 77.4
Escort Carriers
Taffy 1
CVE x 6
DD x 3
DE x 5

Taffy 2
CVE x 6
DD x 3
DE x 5

Taffy 3
CVE x 6
DD x 3
DE x 4

TG 77.5
Minesweeping

TG 77.6
Beach Demolition

TG 77.7
Service
DE x 4
AO x 8

TG 70.1
Torpedo Boats

TG 71.1
Submarines
SS x 7

TG 77.2 Fire Support
OLDENDORF

North (+)
BB x 3
DD x 6

South (−)
BB x 3   CL x 1
CA x 3   DD x 2

TF 78 NORTHERN ATTACK FORCE

TG 78.1
DD x 4

TG 78.2
DD x 4
LST x 14

TG 78.3
DD x 5

TG 78.4 (+)
CL x 2
DD x 10

TG 78.6
DD x 4
LST x 32

TG 78.7
DD x 4
LST x 33

TG 78.8[†]
DD x 5
LST x 6

TF 79 SOUTHERN ATTACK FORCE

TG 79.1
DD x 16
LST x 31

TG 79.2
DD x 8
LST x 24

THIRD FLEET
Halsey

TG 30.8
Logistics
CVE x 11
DD x 17
DE x 26
AO x 33

TF 17
Submarines
SS x 22

TF 38
Fast Carriers

TG 38.1[†]
CV x 3
CVL x 1
CA x 4
CL x 2
DD x 10

TG 38.2
CV x 1
CVL x 2
BB x 2
CL x 2
DD x 21

TG 38.3
CV x 3
CVL x 2
BB x 3
CL x 4
DD x 12

TG 38.4
CV x 2
CVL x 2
BB x 1
CA x 1
CL x 1
DD x 13

[†]En route

8	7	29	12	10	15	161	44	41	140	888

Aircraft Carriers (CV) — Light Carriers (CVL) — Escort Carriers (CVE) — Battleships (BB, BB/CV) — Heavy Cruisers (CA) — Light Cruisers (CL) — Destroyers (DD) — Destroyer Escorts (DE) — Fleet Oilers (AO) — Landing Ships, Tank (LST) — Total Aircraft

1 — 3 — 9 — 14 — 7 — 40 — 3 — 476

Ship rectangles are proportionate to average tonnage. The total aircraft includes Japanese land-based aircraft but does not include the hundreds of U.S. replacement planes carried by TG 30.8.

JAPAN

COMBINED FLEET
Toyoda

MOBILE FORCE
OZAWA

SOUTHWEST AREA FORCE

ADVANCE FORCE
SS x 17

FIFTH BASE AIR FORCE

SIXTH BASE AIR FORCE

NORTHERN FORCE
OZAWA
CV x 1
BB/CV x 2
CVL x 3
CL x 3
DD x 9
AO x 3

1ST ATTACK FORCE
KURITA

"SOUTHERN FORCE"

CENTER FORCE
KURITA
BB x 5
CA x 10
CL x 2
DD x 15

C FORCE
NISHIMURA
BB x 2
CA x 1
DD x 4

2ND ATTACK FORCE
SHIMA
CA x 2
CL x 1
DD x 7

SW AREA GUARD FORCE
CA x 1   DD x 5
CL x 1

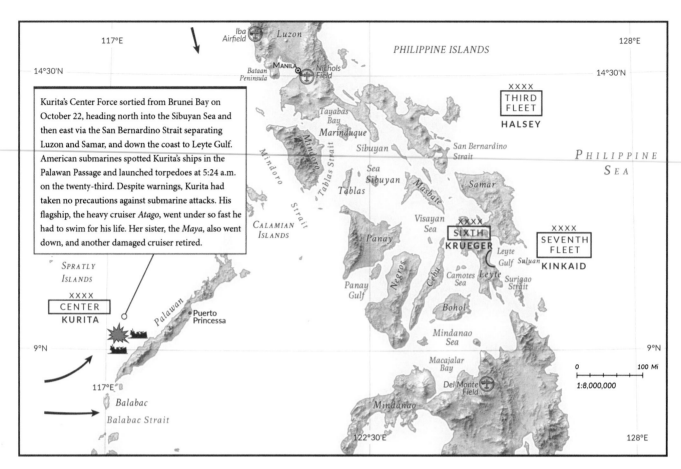

Kurita's Center Force sortied from Brunei Bay on October 22, heading north into the Sibuyan Sea and then east via the San Bernardino Strait separating Luzon and Samar, and down the coast to Leyte Gulf. American submarines spotted Kurita's ships in the Palawan Passage and launched torpedoes at 5:24 a.m. on the twenty-third. Despite warnings, Kurita had taken no precautions against submarine attacks. His flagship, the heavy cruiser *Atago*, went under so fast he had to swim for his life. Her sister, the *Maya*, also went down, and another damaged cruiser retired.

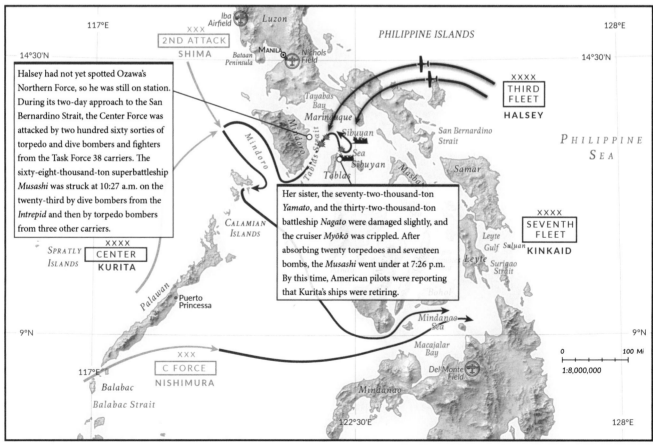

Halsey had not yet spotted Ozawa's Northern Force, so he was still on station. During its two-day approach to the San Bernardino Strait, the Center Force was attacked by two hundred sixty sorties of torpedo and dive bombers and fighters from the Task Force 38 carriers. The sixty-eight-thousand-ton superbattleship *Musashi* was struck at 10:27 a.m. on the twenty-third by dive bombers from the *Intrepid* and then by torpedo bombers from three other carriers.

Her sister, the seventy-two-thousand-ton *Yamato*, and the thirty-two-thousand-ton battleship *Nagato* were damaged slightly, and the cruiser *Myōkō* was crippled. After absorbing twenty torpedoes and seventeen bombs, the *Musashi* went under at 7:26 p.m. By this time, American pilots were reporting that Kurita's ships were retiring.

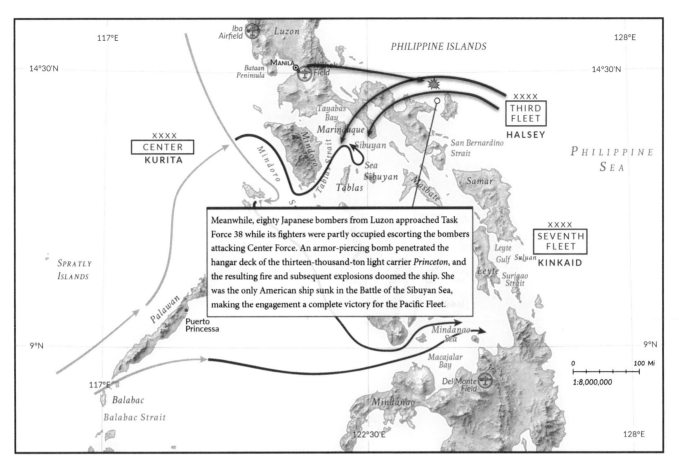

Meanwhile, eighty Japanese bombers from Luzon approached Task Force 38 while its fighters were partly occupied escorting the bombers attacking Center Force. An armor-piercing bomb penetrated the hangar deck of the thirteen-thousand-ton light carrier *Princeton*, and the resulting fire and subsequent explosions doomed the ship. She was the only American ship sunk in the Battle of the Sibuyan Sea, making the engagement a complete victory for the Pacific Fleet.

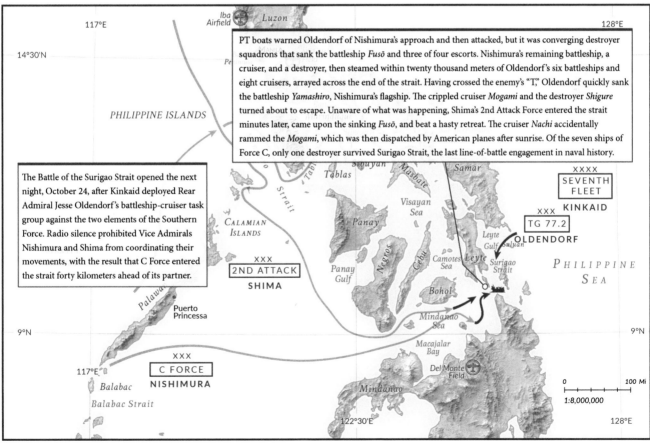

PT boats warned Oldendorf of Nishimura's approach and then attacked, but it was converging destroyer squadrons that sank the battleship *Fusō* and three of four escorts. Nishimura's remaining battleship, a cruiser, and a destroyer, then steamed within twenty thousand meters of Oldendorf's six battleships and eight cruisers, arrayed across the end of the strait. Having crossed the enemy's "T," Oldendorf quickly sank the battleship *Yamashiro*, Nishimura's flagship. The crippled cruiser *Mogami* and the destroyer *Shigure* turned about to escape. Unaware of what was happening, Shima's 2nd Attack Force entered the strait minutes later, came upon the sinking *Fusō*, and beat a hasty retreat. The cruiser *Nachi* accidentally rammed the *Mogami*, which was then dispatched by American planes after sunrise. Of the seven ships of Force C, only one destroyer survived Surigao Strait, the last line-of-battle engagement in naval history.

The Battle of the Surigao Strait opened the next night, October 24, after Kinkaid deployed Rear Admiral Jesse Oldendorf's battleship-cruiser task group against the two elements of the Southern Force. Radio silence prohibited Vice Admirals Nishimura and Shima from coordinating their movements, with the result that C Force entered the strait forty kilometers ahead of its partner.

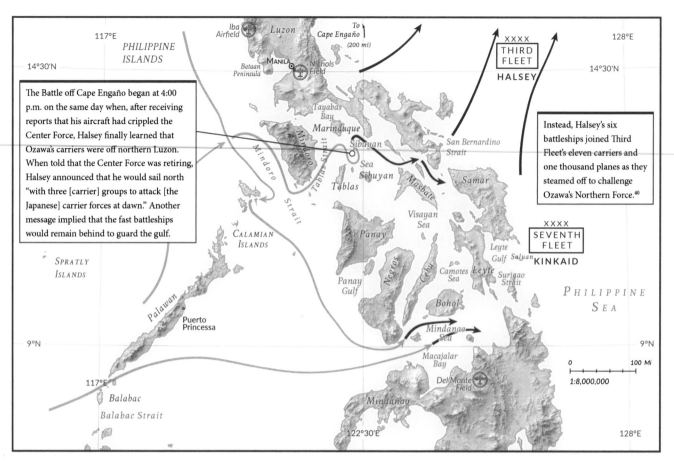

The Battle off Cape Engaño began at 4:00 p.m. on the same day when, after receiving reports that his aircraft had crippled the Center Force, Halsey finally learned that Ozawa's carriers were off northern Luzon. When told that the Center Force was retiring, Halsey announced that he would sail north "with three [carrier] groups to attack [the Japanese] carrier forces at dawn." Another message implied that the fast battleships would remain behind to guard the gulf.

Instead, Halsey's six battleships joined Third Fleet's eleven carriers and one thousand planes as they steamed off to challenge Ozawa's Northern Force.[40]

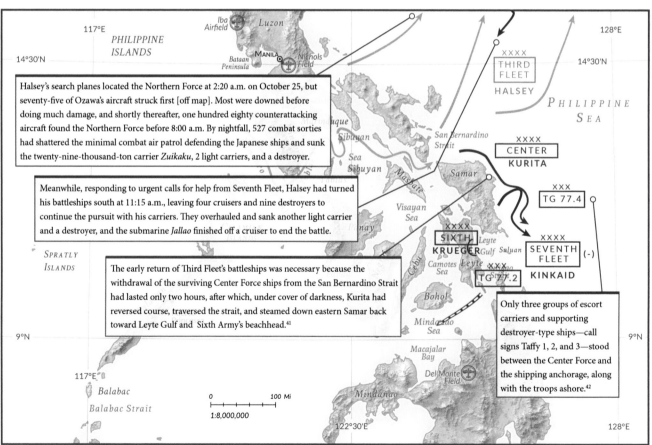

Halsey's search planes located the Northern Force at 2:20 a.m. on October 25, but seventy-five of Ozawa's aircraft struck first [off map]. Most were downed before doing much damage, and shortly thereafter, one hundred eighty counterattacking aircraft found the Northern Force before 8:00 a.m. By nightfall, 527 combat sorties had shattered the minimal combat air patrol defending the Japanese ships and sunk the twenty-nine-thousand-ton carrier *Zuikaku*, 2 light carriers, and a destroyer.

Meanwhile, responding to urgent calls for help from Seventh Fleet, Halsey had turned his battleships south at 11:15 a.m., leaving four cruisers and nine destroyers to continue the pursuit with his carriers. They overhauled and sank another light carrier and a destroyer, and the submarine *Jallao* finished off a cruiser to end the battle.

The early return of Third Fleet's battleships was necessary because the withdrawal of the surviving Center Force ships from the San Bernardino Strait had lasted only two hours, after which, under cover of darkness, Kurita had reversed course, traversed the strait, and steamed down eastern Samar back toward Leyte Gulf and Sixth Army's beachhead.[41]

Only three groups of escort carriers and supporting destroyer-type ships—call signs Taffy 1, 2, and 3—stood between the Center Force and the shipping anchorage, along with the troops ashore.[42]

Early in the Battle off Samar, when (as Vice Admiral Clifton Sprague reported) "it did not appear that any of our ships could survive another five minutes of the heavy-caliber fire being received," his destroyers and destroyer escorts created a smokescreen that, in combination with a sudden rain squall, gave his escort carrier fifteen minutes of cover. In this interval Sprague ordered his screening vessels to conduct the desperate torpedo attacks that bought time for the escape of his "baby flattops."

Rear Admiral Clifton Sprague, commanding Taffy 3, was unsettled when, at 6:47 a.m. on the twenty-fifth, a patrol plane sighted Kurita's formation approaching from the west-northwest, just seventeen miles from his position.[43] Although Sprague ordered Taffy 3 to turn south, his ships were slow, and the Japanese were closing fast. The carriers dodged shells under squalls and smokescreens while their planes, joined by aircraft from Taffy 2 and Taffy 1, attacked. Armed mostly with high-explosive munitions for close air support rather than antiship armor-piercing bombs, the aircraft did little damage. Desperately, Sprague threw his completely outclassed escort vessels against the Japanese fleet. The skipper of the destroyer escort *Samuel B. Roberts* warned his crew that they faced "a fight against overwhelming odds from which survival could not be expected, during which time we would do what damage we could."[44] And so they did, until the *Roberts* was sunk. The destroyer *Hoel* kept fighting through forty hits—some of which passed through her without exploding because the shells were meant for bigger targets—before sinking. The destroyer *Johnston* managed to badly damage the much larger heavy cruiser *Kumano*, but then was struck by six big shells, including three 14-inchers, and went under.[45] Meanwhile, aviators who had run out of bombs made dry runs through antiaircraft fire to distract Japanese gunners or strafed the enemy decks with machine-gun fire. The Japanese, though slowed and distracted by these attacks and blinded by smoke, ultimately steamed within range. At 8:20 a.m., an 8-inch shell fired by the cruiser *Chikuma* struck the escort carrier *Gambier Bay*, which was finished off by the *Yamato's* 18-inch batteries, the only U.S. carrier ever lost to enemy gunfire. In return, attacks by American planes and destroyers had sunk three Japanese cruisers.

Although four Japanese battleships and three heavy cruisers were closing on the

Had Kurita's warships made it past Taffy 3 to shell the crowded beaches of the American landing area, they could have wreaked absolute havoc. Shown here are two of the LSTs (landing ships, tank) that even when afloat were referred to, with grim humor, as "large, slow targets."

fleeing American escort carriers, and Kurita was on the cusp of victory, at 9:15 a.m. he suddenly ordered his ships to retire, a decision he never satisfactorily explained, ending the Battle off Samar.[46] Breast-beating about a "decisive battle" masked a lack of moral courage. When faced with risk to achieve victory, Japanese admirals commonly shrank from decision, fearful of the "loss of face" that defeat would entail.[47]

The ordeal of the escort carriers was not over, however. At 7:40 a.m. on the twenty-fifth, the first flight of the Special Attack Unit of explosive-packed kamikaze suicide planes had attacked Taffy 1 off northern Mindanao, damaging the escort carriers *Santee* and *Suwannee*. And at 10:50 a.m., after Kurita retired, nine Zeros flying from Luzon approached Taffy 3. Some damaged the escort carriers *Kitkun Bay*, *White Plains*, and *Kalinin Bay*; others were splashed by antiaircraft gunfire, but one crashed onto the *St. Lo's* flight deck and sank the ship. When the kamikaze attacks ended at nightfall on the twenty-sixth, fifty-five suicide planes had sunk one escort carrier and five smaller vessels and damaged thirty-three others.

The Battle off Samar had been a costly victory for the Americans, who lost more sailors killed than in the 1942 Battles of the Coral Sea and Midway combined. Still, the defeat of Kurita's powerful Center Force by Kinkaid's small escort carriers—which were never intended to participate directly in fleet actions—spelled the end of the largest naval engagement of the century.

At the Battle of the Leyte Gulf, the Japanese again sought a "decisive battle," but the decision once more went against them. The loss of four carriers, three battleships, and eighteen smaller combatants meant that the Combined Fleet could no longer provide sea-based air defense to its remaining capital ships or defend its sea lines of

TAKEO KURITA
1889–1977

A veteran battleship skipper, Kurita lost a cruiser off Midway but took command of the 3rd Battleship Division during the struggle for Guadalcanal and successfully shelled Henderson Field in October 1942. He continued to lead battleship-cruiser forces in the Solomon Islands campaign until, in late 1943, he assumed command of the Second Fleet, which saw action in the Battle of the Philippine Sea.

Kurita's battleships were initially intended to operate with the Mobile Fleet carriers to defend the central Philippines in late 1944, but this was upended when the Americans landed on Leyte earlier than expected. In addition, the deployment of carrier aircraft to Formosa and their destruction there by Halsey's Third Fleet, the lack of replacements, and a fuel shortage, led Admiral Toyoda to deploy the Mobile Fleet as a decoy in the north and rely on the Southern Force and Central Force to disrupt the American landing. Kurita was apparently unhappy with this strategy: if his ships transited the San Bernardino Strait and reached Leyte Gulf, their only targets would be empty transports. After American submarines and aircraft attacked the Central Force in the Sibuyan Sea, Kurita ordered his ships to retire, only to be countermanded by Toyoda, who insisted on continuing the attack.

The progression of the Central Force through the San Bernardino Strait at night was disrupted both by Seventh Fleet destroyers and planes from six escort carriers. By allowing his flagship to fall to the rear, Kurita lost sight of the action and forfeited command of the battle, with the result that he issued several wrongheaded orders. Impressed by the damage that his ships were absorbing, he mistook the inferior enemy escort carriers for the mighty Third Fleet heavy carriers. After an engagement lasting slightly over two hours, Kurita, on the cusp of victory, ordered a general retreat.

Criticized for his failure to press home the attack, Kurita was sent ashore soon afterward. He was reluctant to discuss the battle in retirement, and his few but contradictory explanations mostly suggested that he viewed the entire operation as pointless and wasteful.

communication to Japan. Despite this one-sided outcome, the Battle of Leyte Gulf effected no change in the war aims or military strategy of either belligerent.[48]

THE RECOVERY OF THE PHILIPPINES

The American landings on Leyte that sparked the naval Battle of Leyte Gulf had surprised General Tomoyuki Yamashita, commander of the Fourteenth Area Army in the Philippines. He directed the 16th Division to delay the invaders and deployed reinforcements from Luzon to the Thirty-Fifth Army on Leyte. He was throwing everything he could at the Americans, hoping to destroy the landing forces before they could establish airfields or receive reinforcements. The Japanese navy's typically exaggerated reports of the damage done to the U.S. fleet in recent actions had encouraged him in this course.[49]

Many of the troops sent by Yamashita got through, but General George Kenney's medium bombers revisited the Luzon airfields, and Halsey's carriers sank dozens of transports—severing interisland communications by early December and crippling the Japanese airpark. Burdened by inferior weapons and logistical support, the Japanese on Leyte exploited the rough terrain, especially the treacherous central mountain ridge, and tropical storms, which hindered the movement of General Walter Krueger's

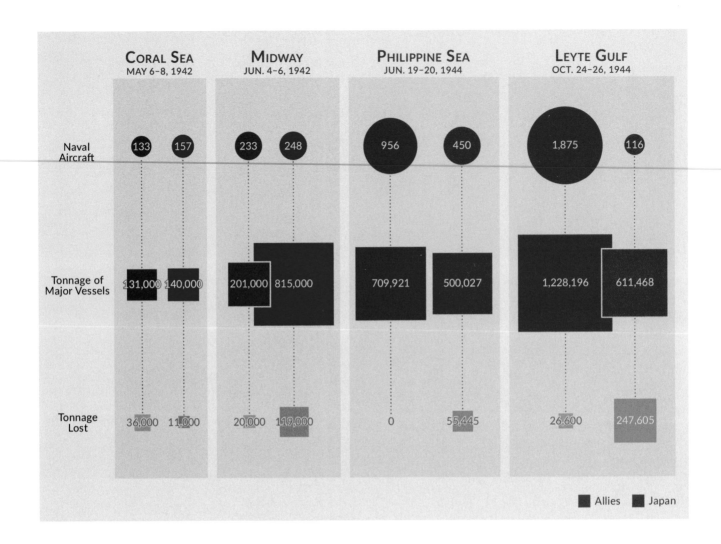

	CORAL SEA MAY 6–8, 1942	MIDWAY JUN. 4–6, 1942	PHILIPPINE SEA JUN. 19–20, 1944	LEYTE GULF OCT. 24–26, 1944
Naval Aircraft	133 / 157	233 / 248	956 / 450	1,875 / 116
Tonnage of Major Vessels	131,000 / 140,000	201,000 / 815,000	709,921 / 500,027	1,228,196 / 611,468
Tonnage Lost	36,000 / 11,000	20,000 / 119,000	0 / 55,445	26,600 / 247,605

■ Allies ■ Japan

PRINCIPAL NAVAL BATTLES ▲ OF THE PACIFIC WAR

Before Pearl Harbor, Admiral Yamamoto noted that if the war lasted two or three years, the Imperial Japanese Navy could not be confident of victory. By 1944, the U.S. Navy was qualitatively better than the Japanese, but even had that not been the case, the huge American advantage in quantity would have sufficed to guarantee U.S. victories at sea.

Sixth Army. The Sixth Army's X Corps, on the right, slogged overland toward the stronghold of Limon, with Rear Admiral Daniel Barbey's Seventh Fleet Amphibious Force lifting assault units around the opposing lines. And XX Corps, on the left, moved against the hills overlooking the port of Ormoc. On December 7, after reinforcements arrived, Krueger organized a double envelopment featuring an amphibious landing behind the southernmost enemy line and frontal assaults in the north; these wings occupied Limon and Ormoc and encircled the surviving defenders on the twentieth.[50]

The next major target was the island of Luzon, including the Philippine capital, Manila. As a preliminary, MacArthur ordered the seizure of the island of Mindoro, from which Kenney's fighters could reach Luzon. Covered by Halsey's carrier aircraft, two regimental combat teams landed on December 15. Two weeks later, two airstrips were operational.[51]

MacArthur devised a three-phase operational plan for the subsequent Luzon campaign. First, Krueger's Sixth Army would land on Lingayen Gulf on the northwestern coast. Second, General Robert Eichelberger's newly established Eighth Army would go ashore north and south of Manila, thus placing American troops astride roads and rail lines from the capital to the central plains. Third, after recovering Manila, the Sixth Army would push the Japanese into the hinterlands.[52]

◀ LEYTE

After landing on Leyte south of Tacloban on October 20, 1944, troopers of the 1st Cavalry Division had to wade through a deep swamp in order to reach and gain control of Highway 1. Getting their equipment across sometimes required three passages through waist-high water.

Although Yamashita's 260,000-man Fourteenth Area Army outnumbered the invaders, his soldiers were short of tanks, transport, weapons, fuel, and ammunition, and the Americans controlled the air. The general divided his command into three groups to defend the island: the 150,000-man Shobu Group to defend northern Luzon, the 80,000-man Shimbu Group to screen Manila and southern Luzon, and the 30,000-man Kembu Group to guard both the western coast and the Bataan Peninsula.

Oldendorf's battleships began shelling the landing zones at Lingayen Gulf on January 6, 1945, while fighters from Mindoro hit the Japanese air bases on Luzon. Kamikazes appeared over the fleet nonetheless, sinking the escort carrier *Ommaney Bay* and damaging dozens of other vessels.[53]

When assault units of Sixth Army went ashore on the ninth, they met scant opposition. Within days, 208,000 troops had debarked and secured a beachhead 25 miles long. They then pushed southward, reaching Clark Field on the twenty-third. Meanwhile, the ships that had carried Sixth Army had returned with new Eighth Army units that encircled Manila and cut it off from Yamashita's main body between January 30 and February 3.

Led by Major General Robert S. Beightler, the 37th Infantry Division entered the outskirts of Manila on February 4 and advanced rapidly to the outskirts of the old Intramuros, or "Walled City." Yamashita had withdrawn from the city and ordered that it not be defended, but the base commander, Rear Admiral Mitsuji Iwabuchi, cobbled together an 18,000-man garrison and organized a tenacious defense of static positions. The GIs of the 37th Infantry Division, without air support due to MacArthur's desire to minimize civilian casualties, used tanks and field artillery to blast their way from one building to the next. A month of fierce close-in street fighting cost the lives

THE LIBERATION OF LUZON, ▶
JANUARY–FEBRUARY 1945

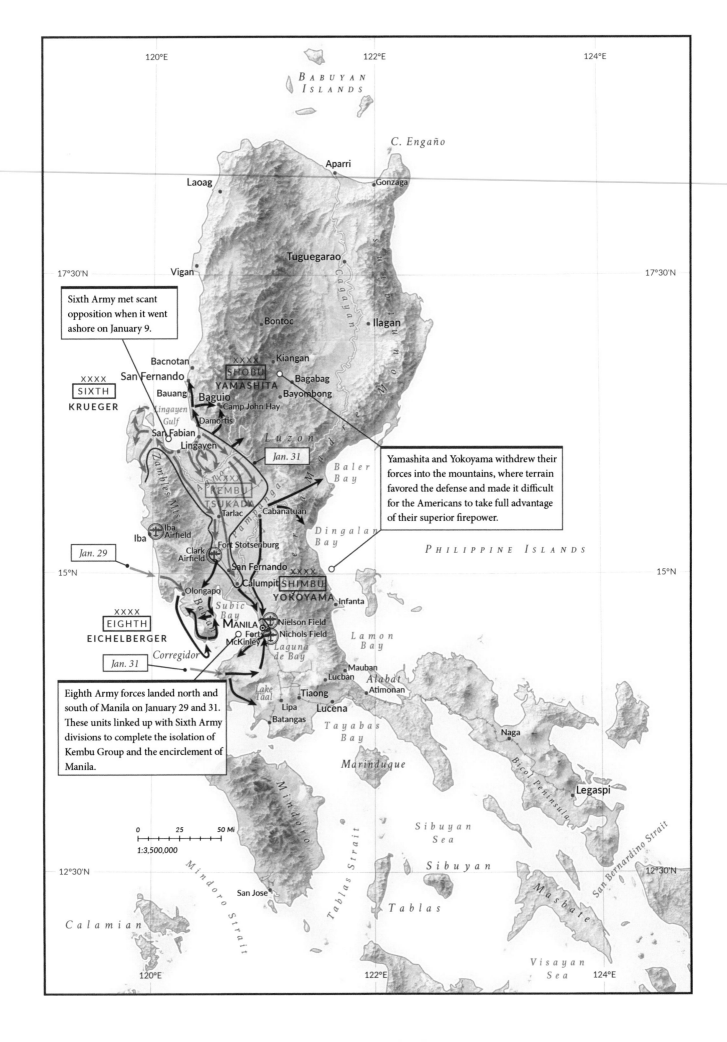

120°E   122°E   124°E

B A B U Y A N
I S L A N D S

C. Engaño

Aparri

Laoag

Gonzaga

Vigan

Tuguegarao

17°30'N   17°30'N

Bontoc

Ilagan

Sixth Army met scant
opposition when it went
ashore on January 9.

Kiangan

Bacnotan

XXXX
SHOBU
YAMASHITA

Bagabag

San Fernando

Bayombong

Bauang

Baguio

XXXX
SIXTH

Camp John Hay

KRUEGER

Lingayen Gulf

Damortis

San Fabian

Lingayen

L u z o n

Jan. 31

*Baler
Bay*

Yamashita and Yokoyama withdrew their
forces into the mountains, where terrain
favored the defense and made it difficult
for the Americans to take full advantage
of their superior firepower.

Tarlac

Cabanatuan

Iba
Airfield

Iba

*Dingalan
Bay*

Jan. 29

Fort Stotsenburg

Clark
Airfield

P H I L I P P I N E   I S L A N D S

15°N

San Fernando

Calumpit

15°N

XXXX
SHIMBU
YOKOYAMA

XXXX
EIGHTH

Olongapo

*Subic
Bay*

Infanta

EICHELBERGER

MANILA

Nielson Field

Fort
McKinley

Nichols Field

*Lamon
Bay*

Jan. 31

Corregidor

*Laguna
de Bay*

Eighth Army forces landed north and
south of Manila on January 29 and 31.
These units linked up with Sixth Army
divisions to complete the isolation of
Kembu Group and the encirclement of
Manila.

*Lake
Taal*

Mauban

Lucban

Alabat

Tiaong

Atimonan

Lipa

Lucena

Batangas

Naga

*Tayabas
Bay*

Marinduque

Bicol Peninsula

0   25   50 Mi

1:3,500,000

Legaspi

12°30'N

Mindoro Strait

Tablas Strait

*Sibuyan
Sea*

San Bernardino Strait

12°30'N

San Jose

Sibuyan

Masbate

Calamian

Tablas

*Visayan
Sea*

120°E   122°E   124°E

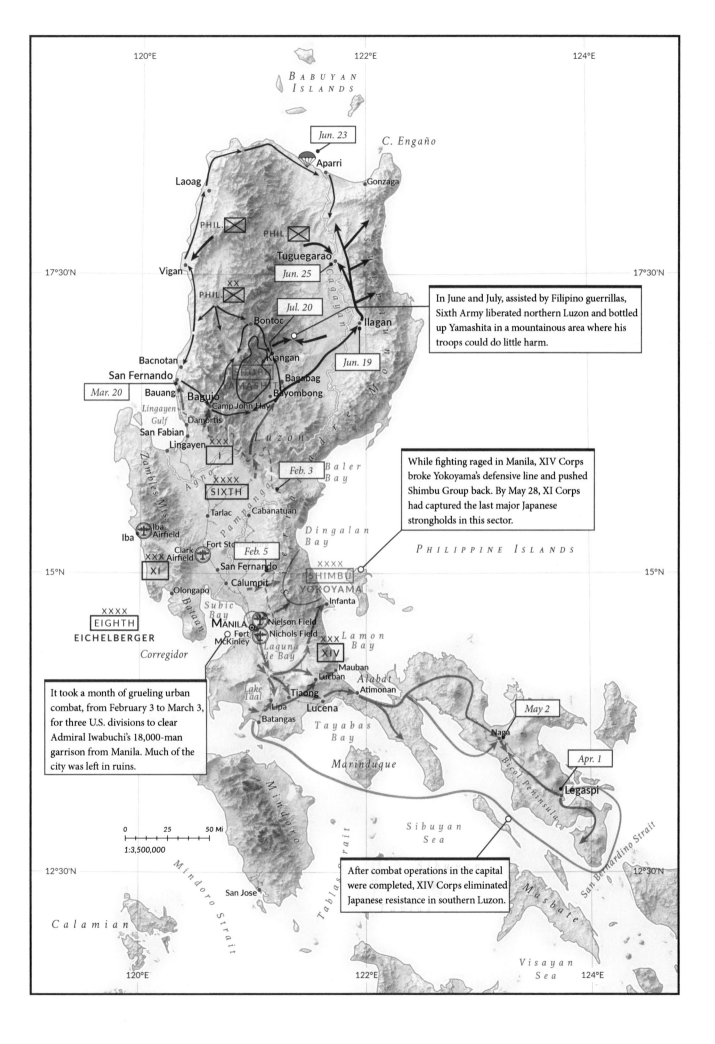

B A B U Y A N
I S L A N D S

C. Engaño

Jun. 23

Aparri

Gonzaga

Laoag

PHIL. ⊠

PHIL. ⊠

Tuguegarao

Vigan

Jun. 25

17°30'N   17°30'N

PHIL. ⊠

Jul. 20

Bontoc

In June and July, assisted by Filipino guerrillas,
Sixth Army liberated northern Luzon and bottled
up Yamashita in a mountainous area where his
troops could do little harm.

Ilagan

Bacnotan

Kiangan

Jun. 19

San Fernando

SHO YAMASHI

Bagabag

Mar. 20

Bauang

Bayombong

Baguio

Camp John Hay

Lingayen
Gulf

Damortis

San Fabian

Lingayen

XXX
1

While fighting raged in Manila, XIV Corps
broke Yokoyama's defensive line and pushed
Shimbu Group back. By May 28, XI Corps
had captured the last major Japanese
strongholds in this sector.

Feb. 3

Baler
Bay

XXXX
SIXTH

Tarlac

Cabanatuan

Dingalan
Bay

Iba
Airfield

Iba

Clark
Airfield

Feb. 5

San Fernando

PHILIPPINE   ISLANDS

15°N   15°N

XXX
XI

Calumpit

SHIMBU
YOKOYAMA

XXXX

Olongapo

Subic
Bay

Infanta

XXXX
EIGHTH

EICHELBERGER

MANILA

Fort
McKinley

Nielson Field

Nichols Field

Laguna
de Bay

Lamon
Bay

Corregidor

Bataan

XXX
XIV

Mauban

It took a month of grueling urban
combat, from February 3 to March 3,
for three U.S. divisions to clear
Admiral Iwabuchi's 18,000-man
garrison from Manila. Much of the
city was left in ruins.

Lake
Taal

Tiaong

Lipa

Lucena

Lueban

Alabat

Atimonan

May 2

Batangas

Tayabas
Bay

Naga

Apr. 1

Marinduque

Bicol Peninsula

Legaspi

Mindoro

Sibuyan
Sea

0   25   50 Mi

1:3,500,000

San Bernardino Strait

12°30'N   12°30'N

Mindoro Strait

San Jose

After combat operations in the capital
were completed, XIV Corps eliminated
Japanese resistance in southern Luzon.

Tablas Strait

Masbate

Calamian

Visayan
Sea

120°E   122°E   124°E

▲ MacArthur Returns
Douglas MacArthur and his staff inspect troop dispositions in the Philippines.

◀ The Liberation of Luzon, February–August 1945

Walter Krueger was a Prussian immigrant who enlisted during the Spanish-American War and then earned his commission in the Philippines in 1901. Krueger served with General John J. Pershing during the punitive operations in Mexico in 1916, fought in France in World War I, and turned down a chance to be chief of staff in 1939. Notwithstanding Krueger's age, MacArthur chose him for command in the Southwest Pacific in 1943, where he led the Alamo Force during the difficult attack on New Britain and the Sixth Army in a series of amphibious leaps along the northern coast of New Guinea in early 1944. His handling of the Hollandia operation, although controversial, was eminently successful.

In October 1944, Krueger's Sixth Army landed on Leyte in the Philippines and, after reducing the enemy there, liberated the large island of Luzon beginning in January 1945. While his conduct of the battle for Manila was inspired, he was victimized by poor intelligence about his enemy's order of battle during the pursuit of the Japanese into the island's interior.

Often trapped between MacArthur's overly ambitious strategies and his subordinates' reservations, Krueger was as frequently criticized for excessive caution as for ill-informed zeal. Nonetheless, he was so uniformly successful that MacArthur rated him with Patton and chose him to lead the Allied Ground Forces in the aborted invasion of Kyushu, Japan.

---

of 100,000 Filipino civilians and 1,010 American soldiers before the historic city was cleared.[54]

Pushed eastward by converging landings on the island's western and northern shores, Yamashita retired to the mountains of the northeast and the south. Pinioned by the Sixth Army and Filipino militia, and short of rations and medicines, the Shobu force was reduced to fewer than 50,000 survivors by war's end. In total, over 190,000 Japanese died in the Battle for Luzon, from disease, hunger, and enemy actions. By contrast, around 10,000 Americans perished, a disparity reflecting vastly superior U.S. firepower, medical services, and supply lines.[55]

After recovering Manila, MacArthur instructed Eichelberger's Eighth Army to liberate the southern Philippines from Admiral Kantorō Suzuki's 100,000-man Thirty-Fifth Army. Because the Japanese forces there had been effectively bypassed, these operations were militarily unnecessary, but MacArthur understood that ending the enemy occupation would help restore the frayed political ties between Filipinos and Americans. Between February and July, elements of the Eighth Army landed on over fifty beaches, capped by three landings on the southern, eastern, and northern coasts of Mindanao, which were held by two Japanese divisions. Eichelberger's converging forces trapped Suzuki's command in the center of the island, where the survivors held out until September.[56] Long before, MacArthur had transported the surviving members of the Philippine Assembly to Manila to reconstitute the Commonwealth government. This, and his encouragement of the Filipinos to participate in their own liberation, helped to reestablish the long-standing bond with Washington, a tie that later proved vital to the American conduct of the Cold War in Asia.

Tasked by General MacArthur with clearing the port of Manila while the fighting raged in the city in January 1945, Rear Admiral William A. Sullivan recalled his first harrowing visit to the harbor and the monumental difficulties his salvage command faced.

The Japanese were still holding out in the Intramuros and in the areas between the Intramuros and the South Harbor [inside the second breakwater]. They occupied the left bank of the Pasig [river] and as far as the Luneta [battery] on the other side. The buildings ... on the waterfront of Manila's North Harbor were completely demolished. The piers in this section did not appear badly damaged, but we couldn't get near enough to see much, for if we tried we would be visible to the Japanese on the other side of the river. We could see, though, that the slips between the piers were almost chock-full of sunken barges, interisland ships, harbor craft, and the like. The river itself was dammed up in a number of places with wrecks ... We could see larger ships that had been sunk ... just outside the breakwater forming South Manila Harbor.

Some army personnel were on the scene with a bulldozer and some trucks ... trying to clear away some of the debris in the area, but as soon as they began work, snipers on the breakwater off North Harbor opened fire and killed the bulldozer operator. The truck drivers then opened up with rifle fire, but only drove the Japanese to cover on the side of the breakwater. So a Cub plane was obtained, and a man was sent up to toss grenades on the open breakwater. The grenades drove the Japs off the breakwater, but they swam to a sunken ship about fifty feet offshore. Five or six men reached the wreck. The army then called for some mortars to open up on the wreck. The engineers got to work but were soon under fire again. So finally the assault party got into an LCVP and were covered overhead by a couple of planes with men in them tossing grenades. When they got to the wreck offshore, they used a flamethrower and with this killed the Japanese on board.[57]

THE STRATEGIC BOMBING OF JAPAN

A secondary reason for the drive toward the Philippines was that General Arnold early on envisioned establishing one bomber command on Luzon and another in China, to conduct a strategic bombing campaign against Japan's Home Islands.[58] In mid-1943, however, Admiral King convinced Arnold that the new long-range B-29 Superfortresses could be deployed in large numbers in the Marianas—only fifteen hundred miles from Tokyo—and supplied by shipping directly from the American West Coast. Marshall, who had opposed the Central Pacific approach, relented, and the offensive got under way with the invasions of the Gilberts, Marshalls, and Marianas. There was little secret as to what strategic bombing was intended to achieve. "Flying Fortresses will be dispatched immediately to set the paper cities of Japan on fire," Marshall had warned in November 1941. "There won't be any hesitation about bombing civilians—it will be all out."[59]

The first B-29 arrived in India only days after the headquarters of XX Bomber Command opened there in April 1944—months before bases on Saipan and Luzon became available. Airfields near Calcutta were enlarged, more planes appeared, and the first raid of ninety-eight bombers attacked railroad yards in Bangkok, Thailand, on June 5. However, the Superforts could reach targets in Japan only by flying from four forward bases around Chengdu in China, which were converted for the heavy aircraft by 350,000 Chinese laborers. Supply was the main shortcoming; all fuel and

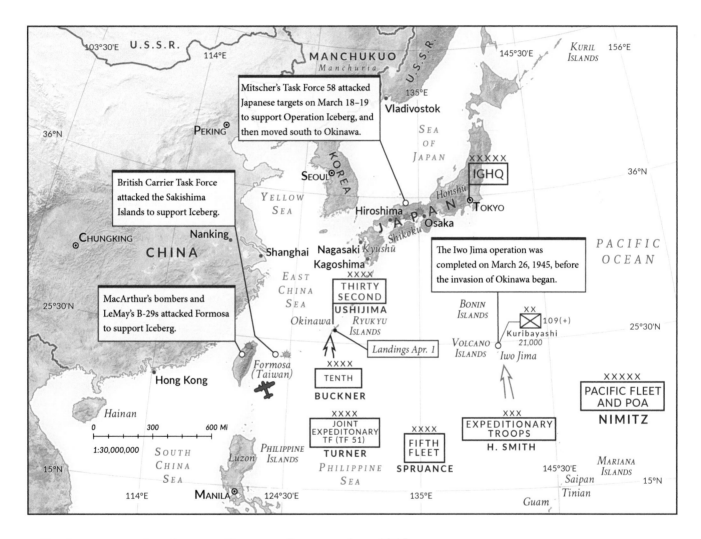

Mitscher's Task Force 58 attacked Japanese targets on March 18–19 to support Operation Iceberg, and then moved south to Okinawa.

British Carrier Task Force attacked the Sakishima Islands to support Iceberg.

MacArthur's bombers and LeMay's B-29s attacked Formosa to support Iceberg.

The Iwo Jima operation was completed on March 26, 1945, before the invasion of Okinawa began.

Landings Apr. 1

THIRTY SECOND
USHIJIMA

TENTH
BUCKNER

JOINT EXPEDITONARY TF (TF 51)
TURNER

FIFTH FLEET
SPRUANCE

EXPEDITIONARY TROOPS
H. SMITH

109(+)
Kuribayashi
21,000

PACIFIC FLEET AND POA
NIMITZ

IGHQ

0   300   600 Mi
1:30,000,000

▲ The Invasions of Iwo Jima and Okinawa, February–June 1945

The invasions of Iwo Jima and Okinawa were two of the costliest battles in the Pacific War for American forces. While some historians question Iwo Jima's strategic importance, the morale boost the U.S. gained from the flag-raising on Iwo Jima helped to completely fund the Seventh War Loan Drive.

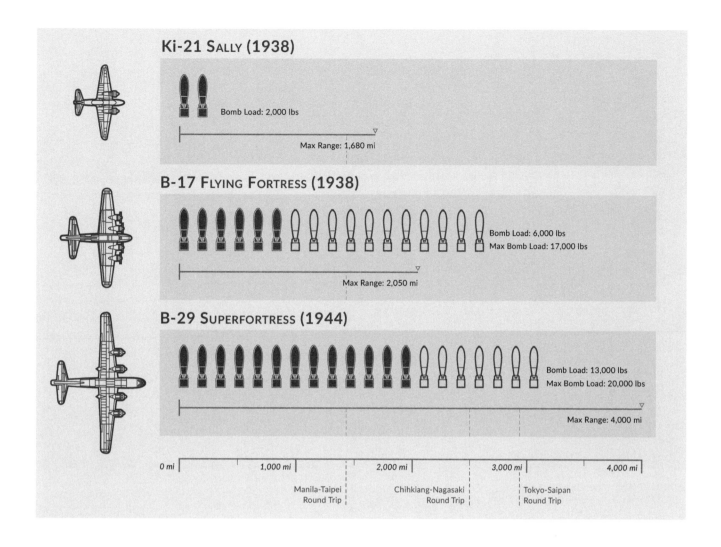

Ki-21 Sally (1938)

Bomb Load: 2,000 lbs

Max Range: 1,680 mi

B-17 Flying Fortress (1938)

Bomb Load: 6,000 lbs
Max Bomb Load: 17,000 lbs

Max Range: 2,050 mi

B-29 Superfortress (1944)

Bomb Load: 13,000 lbs
Max Bomb Load: 20,000 lbs

Max Range: 4,000 mi

0 mi	1,000 mi	2,000 mi	3,000 mi	4,000 mi

Manila-Taipei
Round Trip

Chihkiang-Nagasaki
Round Trip

Tokyo-Saipan
Round Trip

munitions had to be flown over the Hump to South China, and it took six round-trip cargo flights to prepare for one combat mission. Still, enough was delivered by June 14 to mount the first raid against the Home Islands since the Halsey-Doolittle Raid of 1942. This mission targeted a steelworks on Kyushu. All but one bomb missed the target, leaving the plant unscathed. For this meager result, five bombers were lost. Furious, Arnold ordered Major General Curtis LeMay, an innovative tactician, to take command of XX Bomber Command in late August.[60] LeMay realized that Arnold's strategy was flawed, that supplying the Chengdu bases from India was impractical, and that XX Bomber Command's effort should be abandoned. One searches in vain for another high-ranking officer on either side of the conflict who not only condemned his chief's strategy but also asked that his own command be dismantled.

Once the Marianas were occupied that summer, Navy Seabee construction battalions built huge bases for the B-29s of XXI Bomber Command under Brigadier General

▲ The Wings of Progress

The development of the revolutionary B-29 bomber, with double the range and double the standard bomb load of the B-17, reflects the extraordinary rapidity of technological progress under the urgent pressure of "total war."

◄ "We'll Finish the Job!"

Americans had few qualms about the devastation of Japanese cities from the air. Anger over the sneak attack at Pearl Harbor and the Japanese treatment of American POWs, fueled by racially charged propaganda, remained so fierce that a poll in December 1944 found 13 percent of Americans in favor of the literal extermination of the entire Japanese population.

Curtis LeMay was an Ohio State University graduate who entered the Army Air Corps in 1929. He became a pursuit plane pilot and an early expert in air navigation, and participated in several highly publicized exercises navigating bombers. Even as a junior officer, LeMay was known as an advocate of relentless training, although then and later he resisted the Air Corps's sporadic obsession with aircrew "cross training."

In October 1942, his first command, the 305th Bomb Group, joined the Eighth Air Force in Britain and flew some of the first combat missions against Germany. Partly responsible for the adoption of the innovative "box formation," LeMay personally led his group on several harrowing missions beyond the range of fighter escorts. Although he was promoted to command the new 3rd Air Division, LeMay's deep operations were too costly and he was restricted to targets within range of the fighters until early 1944, when the arrival of squadrons of long-range P-51 Mustang escorts made possible the long-awaited

implementation of the Combined Bomber Offensive that laid Germany low.

After briefly heading XX Bomber Command in the China-Burma-India theater, he convinced General Arnold to abandon the effort. Instead, Arnold ordered LeMay to assume command of XXI Bomber Command in the Marianas; his radical strategy and novel tactics led to the destruction of the Japanese economy before the atomic bombings.

LeMay was the most influential military officer of the Cold War. He organized the 1948–49 Berlin Airlift, molded the Strategic Air Command into an effective strategic nuclear force, and served as Air Force vice chief of staff during Dwight Eisenhower's second term and chief of staff during the presidencies of John F. Kennedy and Lyndon Johnson. Hardworking, straightforward, and highly intelligent, LeMay was feared by his generals but revered by most airmen. He was known as "Big Cigar" for the stogie that he typically clasped between his teeth to prevent a facial twitch, which was a symptom of his Bell's palsy.

Haywood Hansell. He adopted the same high-level, tight-formation, precision bombing tactics so successful in Europe. During training flights, starting in November, however, the results were discouraging. Planes failed to keep formation, navigation was poor, and few bombs struck their targets.[61] Nonetheless, these tactics were employed in an attack on the Nakajima Aircraft Plant in Tokyo on November 24. Flying at 30,000 feet over Tokyo, where they were safe from Japanese fighters, 111 Superforts encountered jet stream winds of more than 185 miles per hour that disrupted formations and scattered bombs. Few planes located the factory, most bombed the docks, and little damage was done. Despite the arrival of more B-29 wings and the construction of three 2,600-yard runways on Tinian, the results of further attacks on Tokyo, Nagoya, and Kobe were similarly unimpressive.

Furious, Arnold directed LeMay to relieve Hansell.[62] Starting in January 1945, LeMay devised a different strategy and new tactics. Rather than focusing on precision attacks against manufacturing sites, he emphasized area bombing to destroy the

**PERCENTAGE OF PRINCIPAL JAPANESE CITIES DESTROYED ▶
BY B-29 INCENDIARY ATTACKS**

In order to bring home to American policymakers how much damage the B-29s had done to Japan, the Air Force compiled this list of comparisons to U.S. cities.

JAPANESE CITY	PERCENTAGE OF CITY AREA DESTROYED	U.S. POPULATION EQUIVALENT (1940)

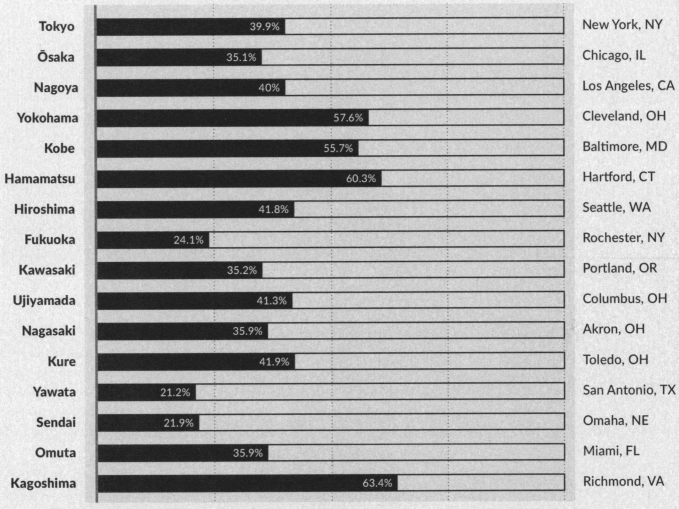

Japanese City	% Destroyed	U.S. Population Equivalent (1940)
Tokyo	39.9%	New York, NY
Ōsaka	35.1%	Chicago, IL
Nagoya	40%	Los Angeles, CA
Yokohama	57.6%	Cleveland, OH
Kobe	55.7%	Baltimore, MD
Hamamatsu	60.3%	Hartford, CT
Hiroshima	41.8%	Seattle, WA
Fukuoka	24.1%	Rochester, NY
Kawasaki	35.2%	Portland, OR
Ujiyamada	41.3%	Columbus, OH
Nagasaki	35.9%	Akron, OH
Kure	41.9%	Toledo, OH
Yawata	21.2%	San Antonio, TX
Sendai	21.9%	Omaha, NE
Omuta	35.9%	Miami, FL
Kagoshima	63.4%	Richmond, VA

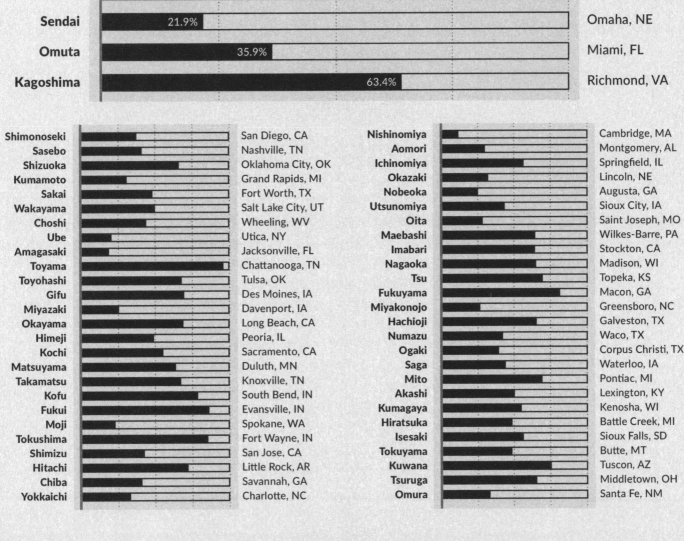

Japanese City	U.S. Equivalent	Japanese City	U.S. Equivalent
Shimonoseki	San Diego, CA	Nishinomiya	Cambridge, MA
Sasebo	Nashville, TN	Aomori	Montgomery, AL
Shizuoka	Oklahoma City, OK	Ichinomiya	Springfield, IL
Kumamoto	Grand Rapids, MI	Okazaki	Lincoln, NE
Sakai	Fort Worth, TX	Nobeoka	Augusta, GA
Wakayama	Salt Lake City, UT	Utsunomiya	Sioux City, IA
Choshi	Wheeling, WV	Oita	Saint Joseph, MO
Ube	Utica, NY	Maebashi	Wilkes-Barre, PA
Amagasaki	Jacksonville, FL	Imabari	Stockton, CA
Toyama	Chattanooga, TN	Nagaoka	Madison, WI
Toyohashi	Tulsa, OK	Tsu	Topeka, KS
Gifu	Des Moines, IA	Fukuyama	Macon, GA
Miyazaki	Davenport, IA	Miyakonojo	Greensboro, NC
Okayama	Long Beach, CA	Hachioji	Galveston, TX
Himeji	Peoria, IL	Numazu	Waco, TX
Kochi	Sacramento, CA	Ogaki	Corpus Christi, TX
Matsuyama	Duluth, MN	Saga	Waterloo, IA
Takamatsu	Knoxville, TN	Mito	Pontiac, MI
Kofu	South Bend, IN	Akashi	Lexington, KY
Fukui	Evansville, IN	Kumagaya	Kenosha, WI
Moji	Spokane, WA	Hiratsuka	Battle Creek, MI
Tokushima	Fort Wayne, IN	Isesaki	Sioux Falls, SD
Shimizu	San Jose, CA	Tokuyama	Butte, MT
Hitachi	Little Rock, AR	Kuwana	Tuscon, AZ
Chiba	Savannah, GA	Tsuruga	Middletown, OH
Yokkaichi	Charlotte, NC	Omura	Santa Fe, NM

matrix of wood-built cottage industries forming the backbone of Japan's industrial activity. He increased range by off-loading guns and skipping formation assembly, armed the planes with incendiaries rather than high-explosive bombs, and told the aircrews to deliver them during low-level runs at night, to avoid defending fighters. LeMay expected a large number of small fires to combine into very large fires that would overwhelm Japan's firefighting establishment.

On March 9 more than three hundred Superforts took off and flew toward Tokyo. Guided by pathfinders that marked the aiming points, 279 bombers reached their targets that night and dropped 1,500 tons of bombs. Only 16 aircraft were lost, and the mission created a firestorm that consumed 25 square miles of the city, destroyed 1 million dwellings, and killed 100,000 Japanese. Osaka was devastated four days later, Kobe on the sixteenth, and Nagoya on the twentieth. Once provided with long-range P-51 Mustang escort fighters, LeMay also mounted daytime B-29 missions. In June his bombers struck sixty smaller cities and selected industrial sites, mostly refineries, using the same tactics. By July, XXI Bomber Command was almost out of targets. That month, Halsey's Third Fleet steamed along Japan's east coast, sinking the fishing fleet and destroying interisland barge traffic. Industry was at a standstill. By the time Japan surrendered, bombing had destroyed its 5 largest cities, left 86 others in shambles, killed or injured about 700,000 Japanese, and rendered over 9 million homeless. Transportation stood still, and famine haunted the islands.[63]

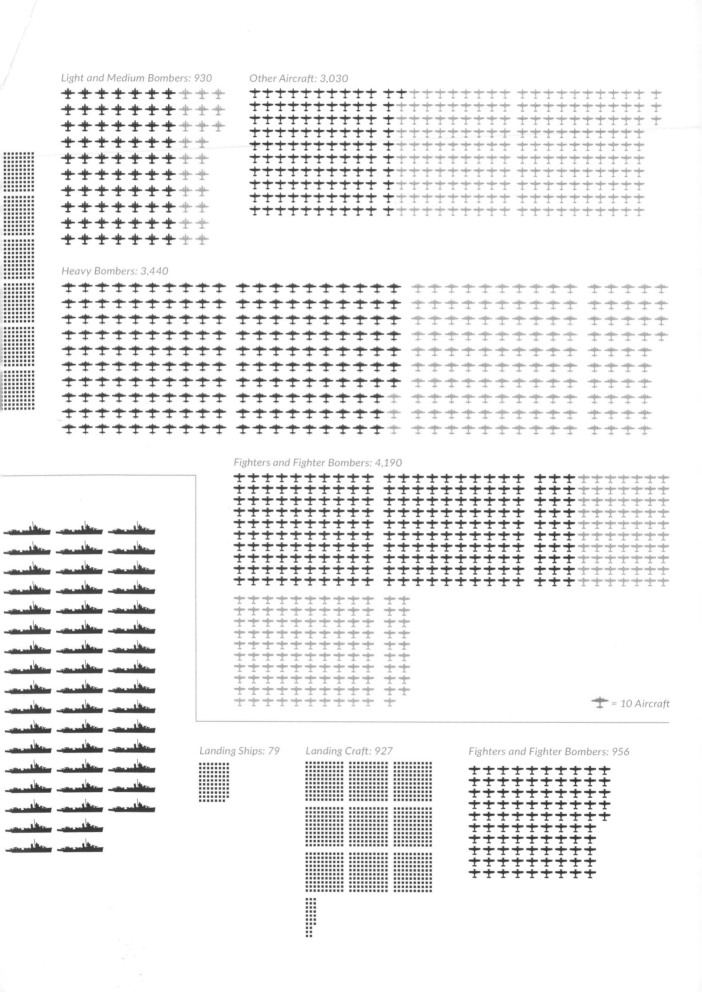

Light and Medium Bombers: 930

Other Aircraft: 3,030

Heavy Bombers: 3,440

Fighters and Fighter Bombers: 4,190

= 10 Aircraft

Landing Ships: 79

Landing Craft: 927

Fighters and Fighter Bombers: 956

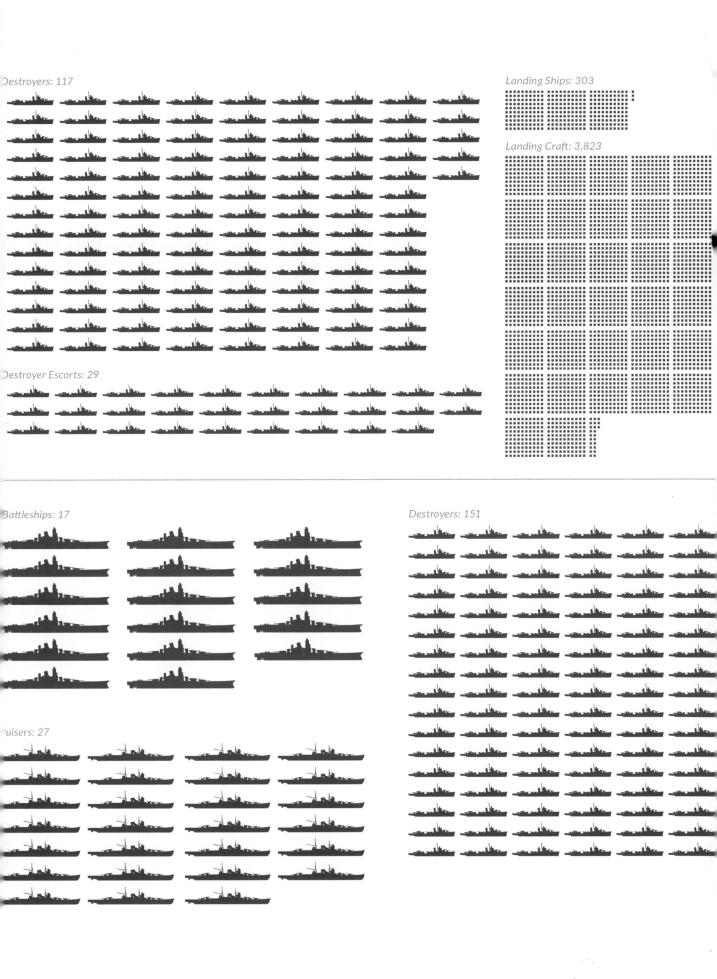

Destroyers: 117

Destroyer Escorts: 29

Landing Ships: 303

Landing Craft: 3,823

Battleships: 17

Cruisers: 27

Destroyers: 151

MAJOR ALLIED OPERATIONS, JUNE 1944

MAJOR ALLIED OPERATIONS, JUNE 1944

OPERATION OVERLORD

Ground Forces: 156,115

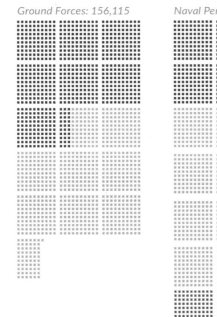

Naval Personnel: 195,701

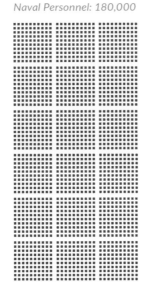

Escort Carriers: 3 *Batteships: 7*

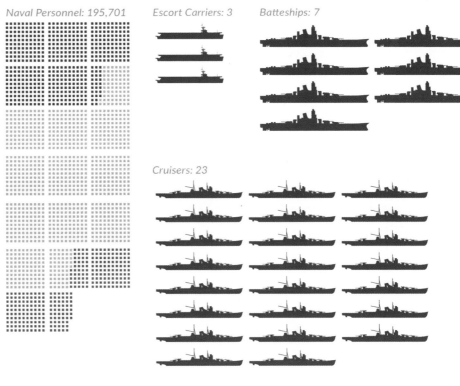

Cruisers: 23

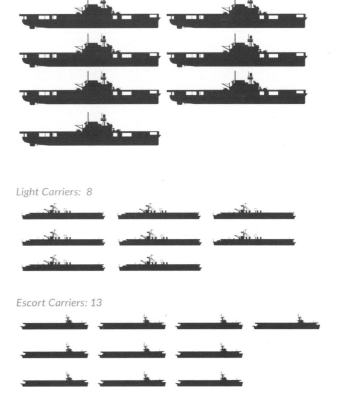

■ *U.S.* ■ *U.K.* ■ *Allies*

OPERATION FORAGER

Ground Forces: 120,000

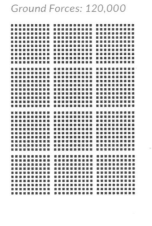

Naval Personnel: 180,000

Aircraft Carriers: 7

Light Carriers: 8

Escort Carriers: 13

◀ TOKYO ERASED

In the downtown business district there were some modern edifices constructed with steel, stone, and concrete that survived the incendiary bombings, but the homes and businesses built of wood and paper were reduced to less than rubble.

THE APPROACH TO JAPAN

King had long urged Nimitz to prepare one operation while another was under way, and a month after the invasion of Luzon, the Pacific Fleet landed a Marine amphibious corps on Iwo Jima in the Bonin Islands to deny its airstrips to the enemy and to seize airfields within P-51 fighter range of Japan.[64] The defenders of the island, which was considered part of Japan proper, recognized they were doomed but were determined to impose heavy casualties on the Americans. Well-prepared beach defenses cost the Marines 2,400 casualties on day one, February 19, 1945, and thousands more were lost advancing inland and up Mount Suribachi, a volcanic cone that completely dominated the flatlands below, through a honeycomb of caves, tunnels, and pillboxes. At sea, the kamikazes reappeared. Most were splashed, but several ships were damaged, and one plane crashed into the carrier *Saratoga*, killing 123 sailors and destroying 42 aircraft; another sank the escort carrier *Bismarck Sea*.

After the island was secured, Seabees extended two airfields on the island so that they could receive B-29s, and more than twenty-two hundred Superforts eventually made emergency landings on Iwo Jima, saving thousands of airmen. Controversy still remains as to whether the Iwo Jima operation, which took five weeks and cost the lives of 6,900 Marines and nearly 19,000 of the 22,000 defenders, was necessary.[65]

Preparatory operations were already under way for the invasion of the island of Okinawa, which had been part of Japan since 1872 and was defended by the 97,000 men of Lieutenant General Mitsuru Ushijima's Thirty-Second Army.[66] His mission

was to inflict such staggering losses on the invaders as to discourage further operations. Ushijima's plan was to count on kamikazes to disrupt the invasion, as Okinawa was beyond the range of American land-based fighters, and to deploy a weaker force to the northern Mobutu Peninsula and a stronger force to shield the port of Naha in the south.

In preparation for the landings, B-29s from the Marianas bombed targets on Formosa, TF 58 carriers struck air bases on Kyushu, and recently arrived British flattops attacked the nearby Sakishimas.[67] The kamikazes struck back. Only 24 of 193 suicide planes got through improved air defenses, but these caused over 1,000 casualties, crippled the new 27,000-ton carrier *Franklin*, and damaged the carriers *Yorktown* and *Wasp*—though all were saved with improved firefighting gear. In all, before

Marine Corporal Ruby Ottis Buchanon Jr. served in the head-quarters company of the 3rd Battalion, 1st Marines, 1st Marine Division during the invasion of Okinawa. The Japanese defenders were divided into two bastions: a weaker formation in the north and a far stronger body to the south. After clearing the northern end of the island, the division redeployed to the southern line, where the enemy lay in wait.

We had, for a day or two, fairly easy going. And then we hear "crack," and a Marine would fall. And we could look at these things. There would be a hill up there. And a tunnel came straight up from a lower tunnel. Came straight up. And a bush was right over there. He'd pop, come up, out of that little hole, shoot, put his bush back. And all you could see was a hillside. And, so we got to watching those things pretty close...

Picture a big, big gully, maybe half mile long. Up here, you start at the crest, up on the edge... And you look down, and it's about two or three hundred feet deep. And not exactly straight... And the sides are po[ck]marked with, well, it was just limestone rocks and caves. Caves in all those rocks... We really couldn't figure out a way to get those jokers out of there. And we didn't want to by-pass them, because you don't need them behind you... Back at that time, we used napalm, a lot. In bombing and in the flamethrowers. It was about the only way you could get those jokers out of those caves... Captain [Lawrence K.] Hennessy told me to take eight men up this [draw] and try to get those guys... So we went in there and... it seemed like there were machine guns coming out of every crevice all around that little valley. And we got pinned down, almost before we got started... We never did get the weather we needed to napalm that place and... the lines were supposed to move on, so we bypassed that thing. I don't know what ever happened to the Japs that were in there. I don't know how they came, but they got behind us and caused us a lot of trouble.[68]

the occupation of Okinawa was completed, kamikaze attacks claimed 36 Allied ships and landing craft, damaged 368 more, killed nearly 5,000 sailors, and injured another 4,800.[69]

The invasion of Okinawa was the most complex ship-to-shore operation ever undertaken. After a five-day naval bombardment, Lieutenant General Simon Bolivar Buckner's Tenth Army of 60,000 men landed on April 1, 1945. The assault troops initially encountered unexpectedly light opposition and quickly overran the nearby airfields. Two Marine divisions then rapidly cleared the northern peninsulas against fierce but shallow resistance.

Meanwhile, Tokyo organized a coordinated counteroffensive, code-named *Ten-go* ("Operation Heaven"), featuring attacks on the amphibious shipping off Okinawa by seven hundred kamikazes and a sortie by the remnants of the Combined Fleet. Lacking air cover, a decent screen, or sufficient fuel, Admiral Seiichi Itō's superbattleship *Yamato* put to sea heading for Okinawa on April 6. Forewarned by Navy code breakers, Spruance's carriers and battleships scurried north, and, on the morning of the seventh, four deck-load strikes of 280 planes drilled the *Yamato* with eleven torpedoes and six bombs before she capsized, drowning Itō and most of his 2,700-man crew.[70]

Ashore, Buckner, moving south, ran into the Shuri Line: a carefully prepared maze of cave-riddled artillery and machine gun sites immune to naval gunfire or aircraft attack. These defenses, combined with monsoon rains that turned the battlefield into mud, slowed the American advance to a crawl. Buckner, ignoring advice to outflank

Chief Petty Officer Dwight DeHaven served in the Engineering Department of the fabled destroyer escort *England* from her commissioning in December 1943 until after she was badly damaged by Japanese planes off the coast of Okinawa in May 1945.

For me, the toughest part of the war was off Okinawa. We were out there for nineteen days on what they called the "ping line," looking for submarines. We were actually a radar picket ship. We didn't have any problem with the submarines, but there were a lot of suicide planes out there—kamikazes. The Japs sent out 320 planes on one raid. They were all over the place. Our captain liked to turn the stern of the ship to the kamikazes as soon as one made a dive at us, and try to turn out from under it.

One made a dive on us within a few days of our first going on station. He came down at about a 70-degree angle. Just before he got to us, the captain turned, sidestepping him, and only a wheel, a wing, and a few gallons of gasoline hit us. The kamikaze had a delayed-action bomb, but by the time it went off, he was in the water and well astern of us.

During general quarters, we had way too many people down in the engine room—people who really weren't needed to operate the machines. To give them as much protection as I could during these kamikaze raids, I had them lie down on the floor plates between the main motor and the main alternator, which were two pieces of heavy machinery. I laid them out like cordwood, figuring that would be their best protection from shrapnel. The only thing they wouldn't be protected from would be superheated steam if the steam lines were ruptured.

We were on station for nineteen days before we finally got hit. The kamikaze that did hit us almost missed us. We were in a high-speed turn to port. The captain had just called for a full astern on the port screw. The kamikaze caught a wing on the boat divot on the starboard side, and that turned the plane into the side of the ship—into the superstructure. The men on the 20 mm gun back there, and the crew of the 3-inch gun, were all killed.

The plane had a delayed-action bomb on board that entered the wardroom area. It exploded and killed everyone in the number one repair party that was in the forward mess hall, which was just below the wardroom. The shrapnel came down on them from above . . . All the men in the radio shack were burned to death. They didn't have an escape route. We lost 34 men out of 180 to 200 men on the ship.[71]

---

the Japanese with amphibious landings, adopted costly frontal assault tactics. The Japanese conducted what one Marine officer called a "magnificent" fighting withdrawal, but the Americans responded with "a tremendous weight of metal [poured] in on those positions, not only from artillery but from ships at sea. It seemed nothing could possibly be living in that churning mass where the shells were falling and roaring, but when we next advanced, [the Japanese] would still be there, even madder than they had been before."[72] After Ushijima burned off much of his remaining strength in a ferocious but ineffective counterattack on May 4, the Americans finally outflanked the Shuri Line and took Naha on the twenty-seventh, but resistance continued for another month. One count listed 130,000 Japanese dead—although for the first time in the war, a significant number (nearly 11,000) surrendered. About 12,500 Americans died, including General Buckner, and another 50,000 were wounded, making Okinawa the costliest battle of the Pacific War for the United States.[73]

THE BATTLE OF OKINAWA, APRIL 1–JUNE 22, 1945 ▶

The Battle of Okinawa was an enormously complex amphibious invasion involving both U.S. Army and Marine Corps ground forces. The Japanese drew the American forces into a strong defense in depth, causing devastating casualties. All told, the Battle of Okinawa cost the U.S. over 12,500 killed in action.

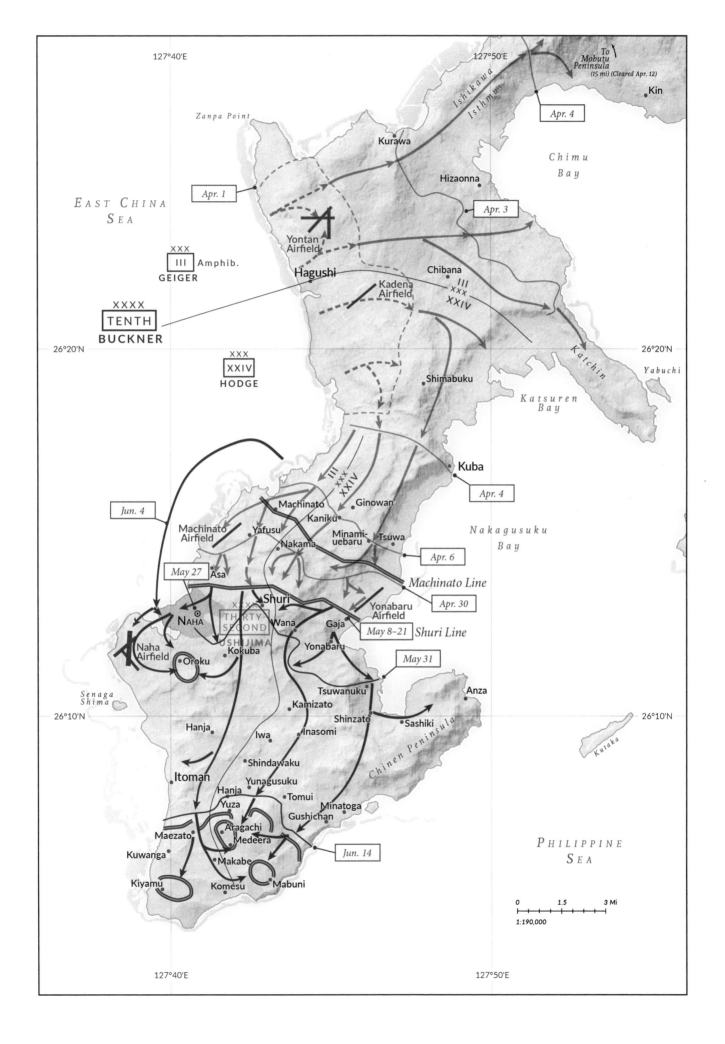

127°40'E   127°50'E

To
Mobutu
Peninsula
(15 mi) (Cleared Apr. 12)

Kin

Ishikawa Isthmus

Zanpa Point

Kurawa

Hizaonna

Apr. 4

C h i m u
B a y

E A S T C H I N A
S E A

Apr. 1

Yontan
Airfield

Hagushi

Chibana

Kadena
Airfield

III
xxx
XXIV

Apr. 3

xxx
III Amphib.
GEIGER

xxxx
TENTH
BUCKNER

Katchin

26°20'N

26°20'N

Yabuchi

xxx
XXIV
HODGE

Shimabuku

K a t s u r e n
B a y

Kuba

Apr. 4

N a k a g u s u k u
B a y

Jun. 4

Machinato

Kaniku

Ginowan

III
xxx
XXIV

Machinato
Airfield

Yafusu

Nakama

Minami-
uebaru

Tsuwa

Apr. 6

May 27

Asa

Machinato Line

Apr. 30

Shuri

Wana

Gaja

Yonabaru
Airfield

May 8–21 *Shuri Line*

NAHA

xxx
THIRTY
SECOND
USHIJIMA

Kokuba

Yonabaru

Naha
Airfield

Oroku

Tsuwanuku

May 31

Anza

Senaga
Shima

Kamizato

Shinzato

Sashiki

26°10'N

Chinen Peninsula

26°10'N

Hanja

Iwa

Inasomi

Kutaka

Shindawaku

Itoman

Yunagusuku

Hanja

Tomui

Yuza

Gushichan

Minatoga

P H I L I P P I N E
S E A

Maezato

Aragachi

Medeera

Jun. 14

Kuwanga

Makabe

Kiyamu

Komesu

Mabuni

0   1.5   3 Mi

1:190,000

127°40'E   127°50'E

▲ Destruction of the *St. Lo*

The escort carrier *St. Lo* was the first American ship to be destroyed by a kamikaze attack. The *St. Lo* had formerly been the *Midway*, but lost that name in October 1944 to a more prestigious fleet carrier under construction. In naval lore, renaming a ship is bad luck, and many of the *St. Lo*'s older sailors were quite concerned.

Prewar studies never envisioned American operations beyond the recovery of the Philippines, and wartime planning for the invasion of Japan's Home Islands, code-named Downfall, languished until late 1944.[74] King preferred seizing Formosa and a base on the Chinese coast before approaching the Home Islands, but the partial success of the Japanese *Ichi-gō* offensive in China undermined this strategy, and Nimitz disliked the Formosa operation.[75] Arnold asserted that strategic bombing and a blockade would compel Tokyo to surrender, whereas Marshall, worried that domestic support would flag if the war continued too long, backed MacArthur's plan to assault Kyushu, the southernmost Home Island, and then invade Honshu, Japan's main island. King favored the blockade-bombardment strategy but agreed to the Kyushu operation and to MacArthur's assumption of overall command on the condition that Nimitz, who distrusted MacArthur, might appeal the latter's orders to the Joint Chiefs, giving King an effective veto.[76]

Army and AAF units totaling one million men were already designated for redeployment from Europe to the Pacific to participate in Downfall.[77] MacArthur's plan, code-named Olympic, provided that Spruance's immense Fifth Fleet—composed of forty-two carriers, twenty-four battleships, and over four hundred cruisers, destroyers, and destroyer escorts—would cover the landing of fourteen divisions of Krueger's Sixth Army on thirty-five beaches on southern Kyushu. Thousands of aircraft, operating from the carriers and Iwo Jima and Okinawa, would interdict enemy reinforcements and provide close air support. After establishing beachheads, Krueger's III corps would converge and advance northward until the southern third of the island was occupied. Captured airstrips would then provide close air support for the Sixth Army and cover for the subsequent invasion of Honshu.

Because everything had to be shipped across the Pacific, this would be by far the most complicated amphibious invasion that had even been attempted, so the Olympic plan was understandably imperfect.[78] Indeed, Admiral Nimitz found it so flawed that he confided to King in July that the operation, scheduled for November 1, 1945, could not be undertaken.[79] Nimitz's unhappiness with MacArthur's Olympic plan was reinforced by intelligence about the Japanese plans for the defense of Kyushu.[80] First, Japan's reserve of five thousand suicide planes would be committed to "saturate the invasion fleet with as many kamikazes in three hours as they sent against Okinawa in three months."[81] Second, nearly a million troops—three times as many as anticipated in the Olympic planning process—were scheduled to be deployed on Kyushu by November.[82] Japanese soldiers were preparing fixed positions inland of the beaches and honeycombing southern Kyushu's mountains with well-concealed artillery, mortar, and machine-gun sites.[83] The Japanese, intending to exceed the American tolerance for casualties, sought to compel Washington to negotiate a compromise and at least to avert the occupation of the Home Islands, the deposition of the emperor, and the wholesale restructuring of Japan's political system. "If we hold firm," explained the new prime minister, Admiral Kantorō Suzuki, "they will yield before we do."[84]

ERNIE PYLE ▲

Famed war correspondent Ernie Pyle (third from the left) died not long after this photograph was taken of him on Okinawa. After his death, private citizens paid to have a B-29 built in his honor and with his face drawn on as nose art. "The Ernie Pyle" served from May 27, 1945, to the end of the war. The base commander ordered the nose art removed, fearing it would make the crew a prime target for Japanese fighters.

Some Japanese leaders had long since been thinking along these lines. Soon after the setback at Midway, Emperor Hirohito leaned on his ministers to negotiate, but they refused until the invasion of Okinawa caused a cabinet shake-up. Prohibited from discussing terms directly, Prime Minister Suzuki and his foreign minister secretly instructed Japan's ambassador to ask Moscow to act as an intermediary—an inexplicable folly.[85] Stalin, wanting to eliminate Japanese obstruction to Communist expansion in the Far East, predictably declined.[86] When the Big Three met at the Potsdam Conference in July 1945, the Americans, British, and Chinese issued a declaration warning of the "utter destruction of the Japanese homeland" unless Tokyo capitulated, a threat the Japanese ignored.[87]

Before this declaration was issued, the Allied leaders had learned that they would be able to make good on their threat without paying the huge cost in lives that the planned invasion would have entailed. At a tête-à-tête with Stalin at Potsdam, Harry S. Truman (president of the United States since Franklin D. Roosevelt's sudden death in April) revealed that the Americans possessed an atomic bomb, clueless that the Soviet dictator knew more about the device than he did.[88] Every major belligerent attempted to construct a nuclear weapon, but only the British and the

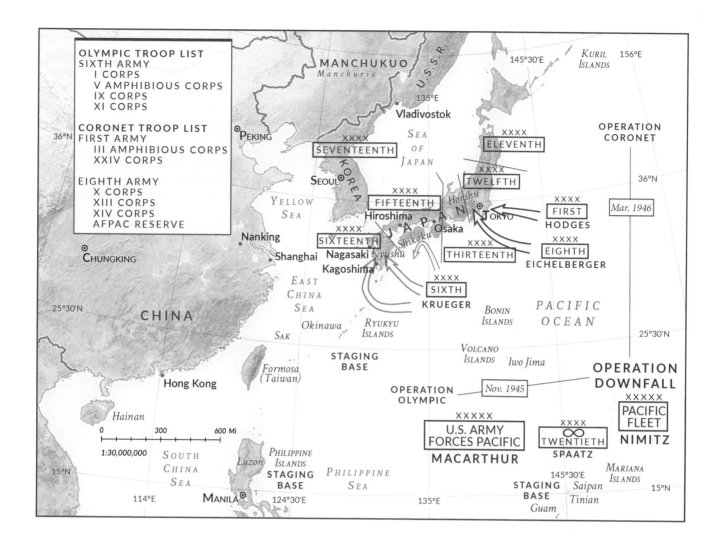

OLYMPIC TROOP LIST
SIXTH ARMY
 I CORPS
 V AMPHIBIOUS CORPS
 IX CORPS
 XI CORPS

CORONET TROOP LIST
FIRST ARMY
 III AMPHIBIOUS CORPS
 XXIV CORPS

EIGHTH ARMY
 X CORPS
 XIII CORPS
 XIV CORPS
 AFPAC RESERVE

Americans made much headway. Physicist Albert Einstein had urged the effort on FDR in 1939, but three years elapsed before the War Department was given the task. The British project, vulnerable to the Luftwaffe's bombing, was shipped to the United States, which pledged to share the results, another discarded obligation.[89] Directed by a dynamic engineer, Major General Leslie Groves, the Manhattan Project constructed facilities costing $2 billion and employing 120,000 workers at thirty sites in the United States and Canada.[90] Two devices were constructed: a simpler bomb named "Little Boy" and a more complex device called "Fat Man." In the first test, a Fat Man bomb created a shock wave heard one hundred miles away and left a thirty-foot-diameter crater in the New Mexico desert.[91]

Three staggering blows that upended Tokyo followed. First, on July 24 Truman approved Arnold's order to employ the atomic bombs "as made ready" once the conferees left Potsdam. Fifteen B-29s configured to carry the ten-thousand-pound weapons had been ready since December 1944. On August 6, six took off from Tinian at 2:45 a.m. and flew nearly seven hours before reaching Hiroshima, one of the few cities still untouched by LeMay's firebombing. There one of the special Superforts, the *Enola Gay*, released Little Boy. "About 80 percent of the city was wiped out, destroyed,

▲ OPERATION DOWNFALL

The invasion of the Japanese home islands had the potential to be the costliest battle fought in American history. Operation Downfall was broken into two successive landings. The first, Operation Olympic, called for the invasion of Japan's southern island, Kyushu, by the U.S. Sixth Army, backed by thousands of ships and aircraft. The second, Operation Coronet, called for the invasion of Honshu by two more U.S. armies.

THE MOST POWERFUL FLEET ▲
IN HISTORY

This photograph shows just part of the Fifth Fleet in the protected waters of Majuro anchorage in the Marshall Islands in 1944. In the foreground five fleet carriers, three light carriers, and three battleships are visible.

or burned" and "casualties have been estimated at 100,000," the Kure Naval Station reported to Tokyo.[92]

Some Japanese officials discounted these reports, "because Japan's top scientists deemed the production of atomic weapons impossible."[93] But Truman announced that Japan faced a "rain of ruin from the air, the like of which has never been seen on this earth" until it surrendered.[94] Suzuki proposed to accept the Potsdam Declaration, but General Korechika Anami, the army chief of staff, objected. The plans to defend the Home Islands, he insisted, would inflict horrendous casualties on invaders and force Washington to compromise, preserving the monarchy and avoiding occupation. The cabinet remained deadlocked on the morning of the ninth.

Another blow fell on August 9. The Soviets declared war, and the Red Army launched an immense triple-pincer movement featuring 1.6 million troops, more than two thousand tanks, and four thousand aircraft against Japanese-occupied Manchuria and northern Korea. Tokyo, alert since the Neutrality Pact had lapsed in April, was confident that its armies could resist for weeks, but superior Soviet weight, mobility, and firepower quickly overwhelmed the defenders.

The final blow also landed on the ninth, when a Fat Man bomb destroyed the city of Nagasaki, killing about 70,000. General Anami remained unyielding, so Prime Minister Suzuki asked Hirohito to attend a midnight cabinet session. The emperor broke the

your **BATTLESHIP**
And Her Requirements

TO BUILD A BB ➡ 2,500,000 man hours for design—30,000,000 man hours for construction | Up to 6,250 ship-builders for 3½ years | 348,000 lbs. blue-print paper 30" strips 5,808,000 ft. long

1,135,000 rivets—4,300,000 ft. of welding | Electrical plant for all needs of a city of 20,000 | 1,220,000 ft. of electrical cable | 422,000 ft. of piping | 9½ acres or 404,000 sq. ft. of decks and platforms

More than 900 electric motors | 5,300 electric lighting fixtures | 1,091 telephones for internal communication | 84,480 ft. of airducts for ventilation | **TO OPERATE A BB (PER YEAR)** ➡ 1,500,000 lbs. of vegetables

600,000 lbs. of fruit | 9,000,000 gals. of fuel oil | 10,000 lbs. of wheat, 4,500 lbs. of cotton produces powder for one 16" broadside | 800,000 lbs. of meat | 60,000 lbs. of butter and 900,000 eggs | 300,000 bars of candy | 60,000 qts. of ice cream | 100,000 bars of soap | 75,000 lbs. of coffee

deadlock, instructing his ministers to surrender. On August 10 Tokyo broadcast an offer conditional on the Allies' assurance that the emperor would continue to reign.[95] Only Moscow questioned Truman's decision, on August 12, to allow the emperor to remain as nominal sovereign.[96] Hirohito broadcast the surrender on August 15. Imperial princes conveyed the order to overseas commands, and the formal ceremony took place on the deck of the battleship *Missouri* in Tokyo Bay on September 2.

CONCLUSION

Having failed to deter Japan in 1941, the United States and the British Empire faced a new struggle in Asia demanding attention despite their Germany First strategy. These Allies, endowed with impressive advantages in industrial production, raw materials, technology, and the management of large enterprises, absorbed early setbacks and counterattacked in late 1942 in the South Pacific and in 1943 in the Central Pacific. In 1944 and 1945, as described in this chapter, American forces isolated Rabaul, evicted the Japanese from New Guinea, overran the Marianas—exposing Japan's Home Islands to strategic bombing by long-range B-29s—liberated the Philippines, and seized

▲ WEALTH AT WAR

This poster highlights the immense investment of resources it took to build a capital ship—30 million work-hours, 420,000 feet of pipes, and so on—and the equally immense logistical effort that went into sustaining one in action for a year, including the provision of 9 million gallons of fuel and 60,000 quarts of ice cream.

"Suicide in Pairs" ▲

Depicted here is an early kamikaze attack during the Philippines campaign. A Japanese pilot streaks down toward an LST that has already been hit by one plane. Several hundreds of Allied vessels were damaged or sunk by kamikaze aircraft.

Iwo Jima and Okinawa. The British ejected the Japanese from Burma. And China, despite reverses, refused to capitulate.

Japan went to war with the United States and the British Empire to isolate China and to compel the Western powers to compromise, but the Chinese resistance persisted, the Allies were unwilling to negotiate, and Tokyo lacked the means to check the Anglo-American counterattack. Folly characterized Japanese leadership, which continually sought a "decisive battle" that would compel Japan's enemies to seek peace—although every decision went against them, from the Philippine Sea, to Leyte Gulf, to Okinawa. Instead of withdrawing from indefensible positions, they chose to defend every far-flung outpost, thus allowing the Americans to bypass important enemy strongpoints. Even novel tactics such as banzai charges, carefully prepared inland defenses, and kamikaze planes reflected the fatalism of Japan's military culture. Japan's leaders devised neither a useful strategy for their submarines, nor a successful defense of their own shipping against the Pacific Fleet's submarine commerce-raiding campaign, nor an adequate air defense of their Home Islands. The Allies' task was made easier by such self-defeating lapses.

Major General Leslie Groves (USMA, 1918), the head of the Manhattan Project, and Professor J. Robert Oppenheimer, director of Los Alamos National Laboratory, pose at the base of the steel tower used to hold the atomic device used in the Trinity test.

Allied war aims, although scarcely compatible, were at least realistic, but Japan's war aims were beyond its grasp. Although Japanese industry was laid low by strategic bombing and an invasion of the Home Islands was imminent, two atomic bombs were needed to convince Tokyo's leaders that they had lost the last "decisive battle."

◭ Warning Leaflet

Although the action increased the risk to American aircrew, USAAF bombers dropped a million warning leaflets over thirty-five Japanese cities prior to the atomic bomb attacks. "In the next few days," the leaflets read, "some or all of the cities named on the reverse side will be destroyed by American bombs. These cities contain military installations and workshops or factories which produce military goods. We are determined to destroy all of the tools of the military clique which they are using to prolong this useless war. But, unfortunately, bombs have no eyes. So, in accordance with America's humanitarian policies, the American Air Force, which does not wish to injure innocent people, now gives you warning to evacuate the cities named and save your lives. America is not fighting the Japanese people but is fighting the military clique which has enslaved the Japanese people."

The Japanese Surrender ▶

Captain Sidney Simon, a U.S. Army war artist, was on the deck of the *Missouri* when the Japanese surrendered. This painting, which is remarkably somber and free of triumphalism, now hangs in the Pentagon.

INTRODUCTION

With Japan's formal surrender on September 2, 1945, the Second World War officially ended. An estimated 50 million people had died. While peace silenced the guns, it did not put an end to the work of the armed forces. The Allies had to create military governments and oversee the occupation of Germany, Italy, and Japan. Millions of displaced persons (DPs) and refugees needed aid. Liberated Allied prisoners of war (POWs) and millions of enemy POWs had to be cared for and processed. The armed forces were also responsible for accounting for all dead and missing service personnel, and establishing tribunals to hold perpetrators accountable for war crimes. The victors also set out to determine what could be learned from their wartime experience to make their militaries more effective in the future.

All of these postwar tasks had to be accomplished while the Allies demobilized their military forces. The men and women serving their countries wanted nothing more than to return home to their loved ones and to lives that had been interrupted by the war. As the Allies demobilized, undertook their occupation duties, and confronted the new reality of an emerging Cold War, historians began to study the Second World War, to assess what had happened and why and to explain why the Allies won.

Historians and military analysts have come to agree that the Allies won the Second World War not just because of their greater resources but also for a number of other essential reasons: they used those resources more efficiently; they conducted coalition warfare much more effectively; they better managed their people's will to win; and throughout the fighting, they steadily improved their tactical ability to defeat enemy forces on the battlefield.

OCCUPATION

As World War II progressed and the defeat of Nazi Germany and Imperial Japan grew more certain, the question of what would come after the defeat of the Axis became more important. As the Allied leaders looked back on the end of the Great War and the apparent failure of the Treaty of Versailles, they were determined to avoid repeating the same mistakes. President Franklin Roosevelt took an important first step with his announcement, at the Casablanca Conference in January 1943, that the Axis would have to surrender unconditionally.[1] Although the Allies thereafter could picture how the war would end—with the Axis countries occupied and their governments fundamentally reshaped—many questions remained. Who would provide the occupying forces? How would the European economy be restored? How would the German and Japanese people be fed? How would Germany be denazified and Japan freed from militarists' control? How would new democracies be created in the former Axis nations? And perhaps most importantly, how effectively would the politically and ideologically disparate Allied powers cooperate once the primary unifying forces—Adolf Hitler and Nazi Germany—were defeated? It made sense to work out as many of the

6

OCCUPATION, DEMOBILIZATION, AND ASSESSING VICTORY

STEVE R. WADDELL

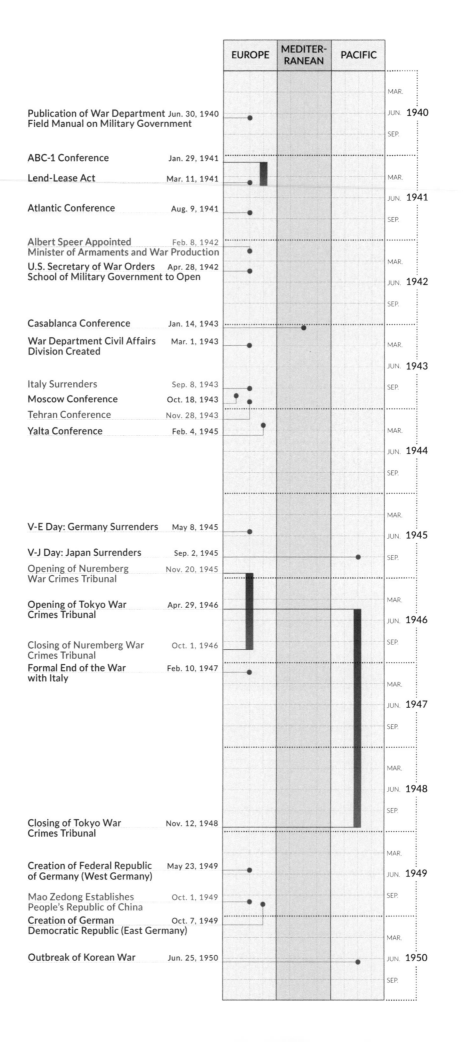

		EUROPE	MEDITER-RANEAN	PACIFIC	

Publication of War Department Jun. 30, 1940
Field Manual on Military Government

ABC-1 Conference   Jan. 29, 1941

Lend-Lease Act   Mar. 11, 1941

Atlantic Conference   Aug. 9, 1941

Albert Speer Appointed   Feb. 8, 1942
Minister of Armaments and War Production

U.S. Secretary of War Orders   Apr. 28, 1942
School of Military Government to Open

Casablanca Conference   Jan. 14, 1943

War Department Civil Affairs   Mar. 1, 1943
Division Created

Italy Surrenders   Sep. 8, 1943

Moscow Conference   Oct. 18, 1943

Tehran Conference   Nov. 28, 1943

Yalta Conference   Feb. 4, 1945

V-E Day: Germany Surrenders   May 8, 1945

V-J Day: Japan Surrenders   Sep. 2, 1945

Opening of Nuremberg   Nov. 20, 1945
War Crimes Tribunal

Opening of Tokyo War   Apr. 29, 1946
Crimes Tribunal

Closing of Nuremberg War   Oct. 1, 1946
Crimes Tribunal

Formal End of the War   Feb. 10, 1947
with Italy

Closing of Tokyo War   Nov. 12, 1948
Crimes Tribunal

Creation of Federal Republic   May 23, 1949
of Germany (West Germany)

Mao Zedong Establishes   Oct. 1, 1949
People's Republic of China

Creation of German   Oct. 7, 1949
Democratic Republic (East Germany)

Outbreak of Korean War   Jun. 25, 1950

MAR.
JUN. 1940
SEP.

MAR.
JUN. 1941
SEP.

MAR.
JUN. 1942
SEP.

MAR.
JUN. 1943
SEP.

MAR.
JUN. 1944
SEP.

MAR.
JUN. 1945
SEP.

MAR.
JUN. 1946
SEP.

MAR.
JUN. 1947
SEP.

MAR.
JUN. 1948
SEP.

MAR.
JUN. 1949
SEP.

MAR.
JUN. 1950
SEP.

GEORGE C. MARSHALL
1880–1959

A graduate of Virginia Military Institute, Marshall gained a reputation as a first-rate staff officer during World War I, having coordinated the movement of nearly 600,000 troops from the Saint-Mihiel salient to the Meuse-Argonne in two weeks. General John J. Pershing made Marshall his chief aide from 1919 to 1924. In the interwar years, he served at the U.S. Army Infantry School at Fort Benning, Georgia, and then became chief of the War Plans Division of the General Staff in 1938. In recognition of Marshall's exceptional competence, President Roosevelt reached thirty-four places down the seniority list to pick him as the next Army chief of staff.

Starting September 1, 1939, Marshall took over an army of 190,000 troops and oversaw its expansion to 8.267 million soldiers by the end of the war. He orchestrated the mobilization of the National Guard and the implementation of the first peacetime draft in September 1940, and also helped guide the mobilization of American industry to supply the growing army. After the United States entered the war, Marshall was a strong supporter of the Germany First strategy and argued for an invasion of Western Europe as soon as possible. In March 1942 he implemented a major reorganization of the Army into the Army Ground Forces, Army Service Forces, and Army Air Forces. The changes contributed to his reputation as the organizer of victory. He provided the president with advice regarding strategy and accompanied him to, or attended for him, most of the Inter-Allied Conferences during the war. FDR picked Eisenhower rather than Marshall to command the invasion of Europe because Marshall was indispensable where he was. On December 5, 1944, he was promoted to general of the army (five stars).

After the war, Marshall retired from the military, served as President Truman's special representative to China, and from 1947 to 1949 was secretary of state, authoring the Marshall Plan. After a short stint as secretary of war, 1950–51, Marshall retired from public life at the beginning of the Korean War. He received the Nobel Peace Prize in 1953.

details of the occupation prior to the war's end, because as victory approached, the underlying tensions between the Soviet Union and the West were already moving the two sides ever closer to a Cold War.[2]

The U.S. Army as an institution had entered World War II already possessing an appreciation for the importance of military government and occupation plans. American forces had participated in the occupation of the Rhineland following the armistice in 1918, and as Colonel Robert I. Hunt of the occupation forces concluded in his 1920 report *Military Government of Occupied Germany, 1918–1920*: "The American army of occupation lacked both the training and organization to guide the destinies of the nearly one million civilians whom the fortunes of war had placed under its temporary sovereignty."[3] Over the course of the interwar years, Army War College committees studied the issues of occupation and military government and shared their conclusions with Army leaders. Despite the distractions of more pressing doctrinal concerns, the Army paid sufficient attention to the subject to authorize the creation of Field Manual 27-5, *Military Government*.[4] Published on July 30, 1940, with Western Europe under Nazi control and the Battle of Britain just beginning, FM 27-5 included a statement of purpose, policies, and procedures. Colonel Hunt had stressed that administering occupied territory involved more than just stationing troops there; it required lengthy preparation to effectively administer a territory and to establish a military government. The intellectual groundwork laid prior to U.S. entry into the war thus

BUY WAR BONDS

▲ HOMECOMING

For years the U.S. government urged the people at home to work and save in order to end the war and bring their boys home. After V-J Day, that promise had to be kept, even though the occupation of the defeated Axis nations imposed heavy responsibilities on the armed forces.

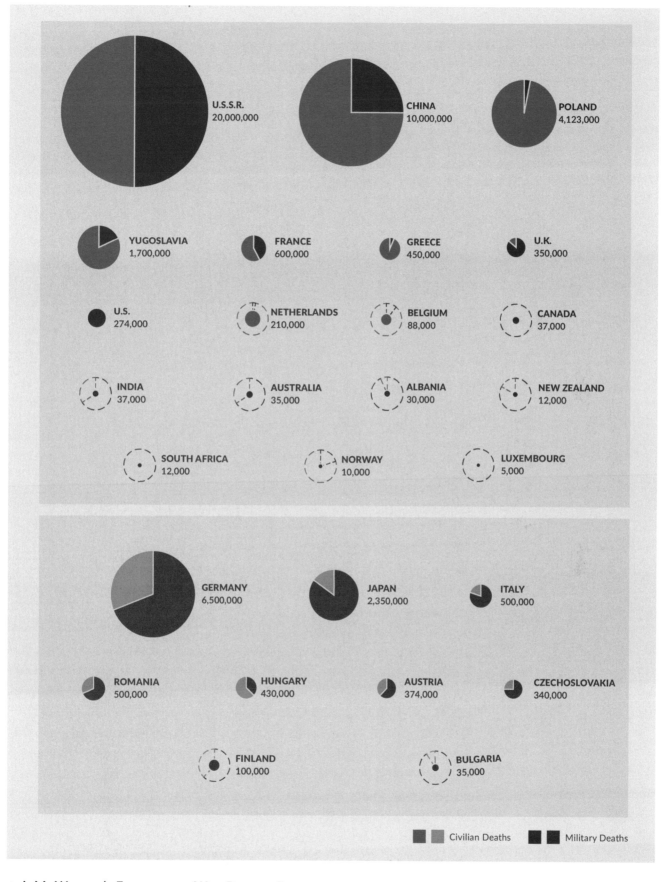

U.S.S.R.
20,000,000

CHINA
10,000,000

POLAND
4,123,000

YUGOSLAVIA
1,700,000

FRANCE
600,000

GREECE
450,000

U.K.
350,000

U.S.
274,000

NETHERLANDS
210,000

BELGIUM
88,000

CANADA
37,000

INDIA
37,000

AUSTRALIA
35,000

ALBANIA
30,000

NEW ZEALAND
12,000

SOUTH AFRICA
12,000

NORWAY
10,000

LUXEMBOURG
5,000

GERMANY
6,500,000

JAPAN
2,350,000

ITALY
500,000

ROMANIA
500,000

HUNGARY
430,000

AUSTRIA
374,000

CZECHOSLOVAKIA
340,000

FINLAND
100,000

BULGARIA
35,000

Civilian Deaths   Military Deaths

▲ J. M. Winters's Estimates of War-Related Deaths

It is impossible to calculate even *military* war-related deaths accurately, and different historians and demographers give quite different numbers. Estimates for civilian deaths must be even more approximate. Nonetheless, this data visualization gives at least a rough idea of the relative costs of the war for the belligerent nations.

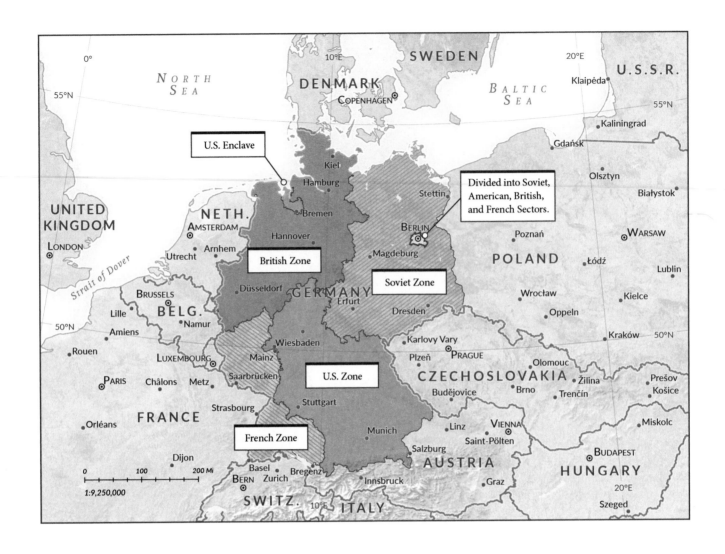

Map labels:

U.S. Enclave

Divided into Soviet, American, British, and French Sectors.

British Zone

Soviet Zone

U.S. Zone

French Zone

NORTH SEA · SWEDEN · U.S.S.R. · DENMARK · COPENHAGEN · Klaipėda · BALTIC SEA · Kaliningrad · Gdańsk · Olsztyn · Białystok · Kiel · Hamburg · Stettin · Poznań · WARSAW · UNITED KINGDOM · NETH. · AMSTERDAM · Bremen · Hannover · BERLIN · Magdeburg · POLAND · Łódź · Lublin · LONDON · Arnhem · Utrecht · Düsseldorf · GERMANY · Erfurt · Wrocław · Kielce · Strait of Dover · BRUSSELS · BELG. · Dresden · Oppeln · Kraków · Lille · Namur · Karlovy Vary · Amiens · Wiesbaden · Plzeň · PRAGUE · Olomouc · Prešov · Rouen · LUXEMBOURG · Mainz · CZECHOSLOVAKIA · Žilina · Košice · PARIS · Châlons · Metz · Saarbrücken · Budějovice · Brno · Trenčín · FRANCE · Strasbourg · Stuttgart · Miskolc · Orléans · Linz · VIENNA · Munich · Saint-Pölten · Salzburg · BUDAPEST · Dijon · Basel · Bregenz · AUSTRIA · HUNGARY · BERN · Zurich · Innsbruck · Graz · SWITZ. · ITALY · Szeged

0   100   200 Mi
1:9,250,000

THE ALLIED OCCUPATION ▲
OF GERMANY

provided the Army with an immensely helpful head start in its preparations for the eventual occupation of liberated territories and the Axis homelands.

Recognizing that any future victory over the Axis would require the U.S. Army to occupy foreign territory, Army leaders established a School of Military Government in April 1942 at the University of Virginia.[5] Although it soon became clear that the school could not graduate nearly enough officers to meet future needs, it represented a move in the right direction.[6] A central question early on was which organization would be responsible for any military governments created. The Allied landings in North Africa in November 1942 and the resulting difficulties managing the newly liberated regions settled the ongoing turf war.[7] The combat forces had realized quickly that they needed to hand off civil affairs to someone else. They could not both fight the war at the front and manage the occupied territory in the rear areas for which they were responsible. In response, the Joint Chiefs created the War Department Civil Affairs Division on March 1, 1943, stating that the new organization was the "logical staff to handle civil affairs in nearly all occupied territory."[8]

The new General Staff Division proved its worth rapidly and became a vital part of U.S. Army planning. For example, Civil Affairs officers provided input into planning for Operation Overlord, and the final plan provided for a civil affairs component

The last major Allied conference saw Clement Attlee replace Churchill, and Harry Truman replace Roosevelt. Though they continued to work with Stalin on the war effort, the victory in Europe began to expose previously ignored differences.

to the invasion force and a substantial allocation of shipping space for civil affairs supplies to ensure that the liberated French population had sufficient food and fuel to survive until a stable supply system could be established.[9] Although most of the personnel actually executing the civil affairs missions around the world had to learn their business on the job, that task was facilitated greatly by the substantial leavening of School of Military Government graduates among their ranks, especially in senior positions. The combination of professional education and wartime experience then ensured that the U.S. Army had the large number of competent personnel needed to confront and overcome the great challenges imposed by the postwar occupation of Germany, Italy, and Japan.

When the Big Three (Roosevelt, Churchill, and Stalin) met at Yalta in February 1945, they discussed a plan for the occupation of Germany. They agreed that they would create a four-member Allied Control Council, including France. Each of the four occupying powers would have an occupation zone, including a slice of Berlin. The Soviet Union agreed to a French zone provided that the territory came from the American and British sectors. Each Allied power would establish a military government for its zone, and the council would address any issues that crossed zone boundaries.

In front of a bullet-pocked wall, a German official, with a U.S. public safety officer looking on, interviews civilians for a job. The sign in the background reads "Bread-Cutting Room—Entry Forbidden."

The Yalta Conference thus settled two important issues: it established an agreed-upon plan for the occupation of Germany before the end of the war and the onset of the Cold War further complicated matters, and it ensured that the end of World War II would be different from the end of World War I. There would be no German army marching home having signed an armistice. The war would end with a thoroughly defeated and occupied Germany. If German citizens had any doubts about whether they had lost in 1918, they would have none in 1945.[10] The people of Italy and Germany would likewise be left with no room to doubt the completeness of the defeat to which their militaristic governments had led them.

Space does not allow a comprehensive treatment of the differing policies and experiences of each of the occupying powers, but all faced many of the same problems and issues. The best approach, therefore, is to treat the American occupation in some detail, which will also give a general sense of developments in the other zones. With the advent of V-E Day, the organization of American forces in Europe evolved to meet the changing situation. General Eisenhower became the commander in chief, U.S.

Forces European Theater, and represented America on the Allied Control Council. The actual task of governing fell to General Lucius D. Clay, Eisenhower's deputy for military government.[11] To make the task more manageable, Eisenhower divided the American zone into Eastern and Western districts, with the U.S. Third Army and the U.S. Seventh Army in charge, respectively. The Allied armies in Germany faced daunting tasks: to establish a government, get Germany on its feet politically and economically, and ensure that it was denazified in the process.

The decision to occupy Germany meant that the Allies were responsible for everything. Germany had suffered from years of strategic bombing, and the heavy fighting on the ground in the last months of the war had only compounded the destruction. Berlin and all the major cities of Germany were largely in ruins, with wrecked electrical, water, sewer, and transportation systems. Shortages of housing, food, fuel, and medical supplies existed everywhere. The occupying forces had to provide security for themselves and the German people, while also ensuring that the population had sufficient resources and services to not only survive but also to begin rebuilding.

▲ CARE PACKAGES

The Allied armies were responsible for feeding the population of occupied Axis countries, but the home front helped. Millions of CARE (Cooperative for American Remittances to Europe) packages were purchased by individual Americans for ten dollars each, and the CARE charity arranged for their delivery to Europe or Japan, either to specified individuals or for general distribution.

CONFRONTING THE TRUTH ▲

Outside Nammering, Germany, there was a mass grave of some 800 slave laborers from the concentration camp at Flossenbürg. American GIs forced the townsfolk to dig up the bodies, witness the terrible emaciation of the victims, and reinter the bodies in individual graves. The Allies wanted to ensure that the German people understood what the Nazi government had done in their name.

The U.S. Army, meanwhile, implemented a comprehensive plan for the denazification of the American zone.[12] The experience of liberating the many German concentration camps and witnessing the treatment of Allied POWs in the last months of the war underlined the importance of this task—but the removal of Nazi Party members and anyone closely associated with the Nazi regime greatly complicated the task of restoring public services and the economy overall.[13] Whereas the British and French were inclined to keep the local power plant operator on the job, even if he had been a low-level Nazi Party member, U.S. policy demanded that he be fired and replaced—even if that left no one to run the plant. When the need to restore services trumped denazification, American newspapers often expressed their displeasure. For example, when General George Patton kept Nazi Party members on the job rather than firing them, arguing that "it is no more possible for a man to be a civil servant in Germany and not have paid lip service to Nazism than it is for a man to be a postmaster in America and not have paid lip service to the Democratic Party or the Republican Party when it is in power," he found himself in deep trouble.[14] The

American political leaders and public expected Germany to be denazified, but those on the ground in Germany soon realized that the issue was much more complicated than anyone imagined.[15]

Europe faced a massive humanitarian disaster at the end of the war, and the occupying powers had to do much more than just disarm the German Army, round up some Nazi leaders, and go home. They had to restore order in Western Europe and do it with an increasing awareness that the process could not take forever, especially with a Cold War beginning with the Soviet Union. The Paris Peace Treaties, signed February 10, 1947, officially ended the war with Italy and restored Italian sovereignty.[16] Italy's surrender in September 1943 and subsequent help in defeating Nazi Germany made it easier to end the occupation and return control to the Italian government. The occupation in Germany did not begin to transition to civilian control until May 1949, with the creation of the Federal Republic of Germany, known as West Germany. The Soviet Union followed in October 1949, with the creation of the German Democratic Republic, known as East Germany. Military forces of the occupying powers remained

▲ DENAZIFICATION

Suspected Nazis fill in a questionnaire about their political activities. Figuring out the extent of denazification necessary to run postwar Germany was a constant struggle for the occupying powers.

Douglas MacArthur governed postwar Japan, punishing war criminals
while maintaining the emperor as a
passive observer of military leadership.

as the two Germanies became symbols of the Cold War—and likely front lines if that Cold War should heat up into World War III.[17]

The occupation forces in Japan faced similar challenges.[18] One key difference, however, was that the United States was the sole occupying power. General Douglas MacArthur assumed command of the Japanese occupation and set about rebuilding the nation. Japanese cities had been spared an American invasion but had been devastated by strategic bombing—including, in the case of Hiroshima and Nagasaki, the use of two atomic weapons. The Japanese people needed housing, food, fuel, and medical services as much as, if not more than, the Germans and the Italians.

Although Japan surrendered unconditionally, the United States allowed the Japanese to keep their emperor, Hirohito. The decision, made for political and administrative reasons, simplified the occupation of Japan, ensured a peaceful Japanese citizenry, and helped the country return to some sense of normalcy as rapidly as possible. For

the emperor to remain on the throne, it became important that he not be seen as a war criminal: in the aftermath, Hirohito was thus portrayed as a puppet of the militarists; a figurehead who had not been in control during the war. Only in the last twenty years has the view of the wartime emperor begun to shift from innocent puppet to involved leader.[19] With Mao Zedong's Communist victory in China in 1949, the outbreak of the Korean Conflict in June 1950, and the growing Cold War tensions, the importance of a strong, friendly Japan became ever greater. The occupation ended on April 28, 1952, with Japan emerging as a firm ally of the United States.[20]

▲ "RUBBLE WOMEN"

It has been estimated that war damage left Germany with over five hundred million cubic yards of debris that needed to be cleared before the country could be rebuilt. Enough women contributed to the work that the German language acquired a new word to describe them: *Trümmerfrauen*, "rubble women."

OCCUPATION CHALLENGES

Occupation involved much more than just establishing military governments to oversee the administrations of Germany, Italy, and Japan. The occupying forces worked diligently to deal with a number of major issues. These included three core tasks: (1) addressing the refugee and displaced persons crisis, as millions of people sought to get home; (2) caring for the surviving, dead, and missing soldiers on both sides, which entailed liberating and repatriating Allied POWs, receiving and feeding the millions of German and Japanese POWs who were taken in the final days of the war,

FREIBURG IN RUINS ▶
Destroyed by the RAF in December 1944, the German city of Freiburg was still a burned-out shell in the summer of 1945 or 1946, when this photograph was taken.

and accounting for all the dead and missing service personnel; and (3) ensuring that war criminals would face justice. All of these responsibilities took considerable assets and had to be accomplished in the midst of a massive demobilization of forces.

REFUGEES AND DISPLACED PERSONS (DPs)

At the end of the war in Europe, upward of fourteen million people were displaced persons or refugees.[21] Many had been taken to Germany as forced laborers to work in German factories and mines. Others had fled their homes to escape the fighting when it arrived on their doorstep. Vast numbers of former POWs from countries across Europe were eager to go home. Still others were former concentration camp inmates—survivors of the Holocaust and the vast German camp system—happy to be alive but sick and hungry and not sure of what to do next. Many of these people, mainly those from Eastern Europe, had no home to return to or were uncertain whether they would be welcome if they did.[22]

Many of the refugees were Germans who had fled eastern Germany to escape the

advancing Soviets. Roughly fourteen million more Germans were forcibly evicted from Soviet-occupied areas immediately after the war.[23] The Poles and the Czechs did not want any ethnic Germans to remain in their territory. With the Soviet occupation of Eastern Europe and the Holocaust preventing millions from returning home, the need for humanitarian assistance was great. DP camps, often former German military camps, provided short-term relief (food, shelter, and medical care) for many, but they were crowded, and the people didn't want to be there—they wanted to go home, or to somewhere new, where they could start over. Humanitarian groups stepped up to help, and the recently formed United Nations created the United Nations Relief and Rehabilitation Administration (UNRRA) to help resettle the DPs.[24] The camps, meant to be temporary homes for those with no place to go, were gradually closed as the DPs found governments that would take them in. The process took much longer than anticipated, with the last DP camp not closed until 1959. In the end, Germany and Austria accepted the remaining DPs.

The ultimate solution to the refugee and DP problems was the economic recovery of Europe—a recovery made all the more urgent with the beginning of the Cold War,

▲ **GERMAN PRISONERS OF WAR BOARDING A TRAIN IN BOSTON**

Millions of prisoners of war needed repatriation after the war ended, including 425,000 German POWs in the United States in more than seven hundred detention facilities. An additional 51,000 Italian POWs were brought to the United States.

as the unemployed and hungry often looked to the Socialists and the Communists for leadership. The execution of the Marshall Plan—a mammoth package of economic aid from the United States—helped restore the European economy, putting people back to work and enabling millions to provide themselves with food, shelter, and hope for the future.

In the Pacific, after V-J Day, the main concern of American authorities relating to DPs was the repatriation of Japanese citizens—over seven million of them—from the far-flung areas they had occupied during the war. This vast undertaking was left as much as possible to the management and resources of the Japanese government, under the supervision of MacArthur's administrators.

MARSHALL·PLAN

◀ THE MARSHALL PLAN

THE MARSHALL PLAN

The European Recovery Program or ERP (the official name of the Marshall Plan) was intended to be the wind in the sails propelling the nations of the war-ravaged continent back toward prosperity. The United States had pragmatic reasons to help former foes as well as friends: America wanted strong trading partners in Europe, and worried that poverty and despair might lead to the spread of communism there. But support for the program also reflected genuine humanitarian compassion for the suffering people of Europe.

ACCOUNTING FOR THE LIVING, THE DEAD, AND THE MISSING

Allied leaders understood that as their forces entered Germany, they would begin liberating POWs and encountering displaced persons. In February 1945 the Western Allies and the Soviet Union signed an agreement detailing how liberated citizens of each nation were to be treated and repatriated.[25] The Allies agreed to identify foreign nationals, ensure their safety, and return them to the appropriate jurisdiction. With

More than one hundred battalions of Soviet citizens volunteered to serve in the German-organized "Russian Liberation Army," despite the anti-Slavic racism of the Nazi regime. Many were captured Red Army soldiers who were desperate to escape the terrible conditions of the German POW camps. They faced grim prospects if they were returned to Stalin's control, but nonetheless most of those captured by the western Allies were repatriated to the U.S.S.R. after the war.

many of the German POW camps located in the East, the Western Allies wanted assurance from the Soviet Union that their liberated servicemen would be properly treated. Conversely, many Soviet civilians, POWs, and Soviets in German service came into the possession of the Western Allies, and Stalin wanted them all returned. This led to the problem of what to do with individuals who did not want to return home; who feared for their safety. Despite some hesitation by the GIs who actually had to carry out the policy, many Soviet citizens were forcibly turned over to Soviet authorities, only to be sent to the gulag or shot for treason.

The United States devoted a great deal of time and energy during the war to accounting for all its personnel. By war's end, 124,079 U.S. Army personnel had become POWs or were interned by neutral countries. Of these, 111,426 returned to Army control either by escaping or being liberated at the war's end.[26] Those who had fallen into the hands of the Germans or the Italians fared much better than those captured by the Japanese.[27] Of the 27,465 personnel captured and interned in the Pacific theater, 40.4 percent died, compared with only 1.2 percent of those captured in the European and Mediterranean theaters. The Japanese military did not abide by the Geneva Convention and often mistreated and executed POWs, as on April 1942's notorious Bataan Death March, for instance.[28] In the Pacific and Asia, the Japanese moved most POWs out of the way of advancing Allied forces, or in some cases executed them to prevent

their rescue.[29] Most Allied POWs had to wait for the end of the war to be liberated. Once freed, however, all Allied POWs received the best care possible and were repatriated home as soon as medically feasible.

A bigger POW issue involved taking care of millions of German and Japanese prisoners of war. The sheer number of POWs who fell into Allied hands in the final days of the war—along with the difficulty of organizing them and providing shelter, food, and medical care, while the Allies were still concluding combat operations and dealing with DPs—taxed the capabilities of the Army. This led to some instances of hungry German POWs and even accusations of abuse or war crimes, but such claims of systematic abuse have been found baseless.[30] The United States had taken 2,057,138 prisoners of war before Germany surrendered and received another 4 million "disarmed enemy personnel" after the surrender.[31] Complicating matters further was the large number of Soviet soldiers (estimates are over a million) who had volunteered to serve in the German Army—many as a means of escaping the POW camps and likely death.[32] The U.S. Army returned those captured in the West to Soviet control, though many were subsequently imprisoned or executed for having surrendered to or served the Germans, or for being ideologically "tainted" by exposure to Western ideas.

While all the nations involved in World War II expressed concern in accounting for their dead and missing, none put as much effort into accounting for its service personnel as the United States. This effort has continued to the present day.[33] At war's end, the United States had 78,976 servicemen listed as missing in action.[34] Graves Registration Units followed behind the advancing front, locating the dead, attempting to identify them, and seeing that they were interred in temporary cemeteries. It was

◀ Unrecoverable

There was no way to recover the bodies of aircrew lost in the depths of the ocean.

undoubtedly one of the toughest jobs of the war. Despite their best efforts, they could not identify 18,641 of the approximately 325,000 recovered dead.[35] In an era before DNA testing, decomposition and lost dog tags and papers often made identification impossible. When the search teams were finally free to move about the former enemy territories, they scoured the countryside looking for any aircraft crash sites and burial locations they could find. The Cold War increasingly limited the ability to search for American dead in Eastern Europe, while the dense jungles of the Pacific made locating lost aircraft and ground personnel nearly impossible. Although unable to account for everyone, the search effort brought comfort to thousands of loved ones back home and to the comrades of those lost.

The task of the Graves Registration Units did not end with the location, identification, and interment of the dead in a cemetery in Europe or the Pacific. Families had the choice of whether or not to bring their loved ones home for burial. After the war, 233,181 American dead were transported home to their families in the United States. Those who remained in Europe rested in permanent U.S. military cemeteries similar to the one overlooking Omaha Beach in Normandy. Due to the remote locations of the battles in the Pacific, the Army attempted to disinter all the dead there in the years immediately after the war, either returning them home to their families or reinterring them in the National Memorial Cemetery of the Pacific in Hawaii.[36] The American effort to account for its dead and missing after World War II was unprecedented, and only a nation with the unparalleled resources of the United States could have undertaken it.[37]

◀ German POWs

Shown here is a column of German prisoners in Aachen, Germany. Note the badly damaged homes in the background. The desire to shift resources to reconstruction as quickly as possible encouraged the Allied governments to move quickly to release captured Axis soldiers.

The Normandy American Cemetery is enormous, covering 172 acres. Buried there are 9,387 soldiers, sailors, and airmen. Additionally, the cemetery lists the 1,557 names of those whose bodies were never recovered.

WAR CRIMES TRIBUNALS

As word of Axis atrocities, the Holocaust, and the mistreatment of prisoners of war reached the Allies during the fighting years, the call for justice after the war grew louder.[38] Following the meeting of the foreign ministers of the Big Three at the Moscow Conference of October 1943, Roosevelt, Stalin, and Churchill issued the Moscow Declaration stating that the Axis leaders would be held accountable for their actions.[39] The decision represented an early effort to define the protection of human rights as part of international criminal law.[40] When Germany and then Japan surrendered, the hunt for war criminals commenced, and prosecutors throughout Europe and Asia began preparing their cases.[41] The number of total cases tried throughout the world is unknown, and new ones continue to be added to the total. It is known that by the end of the war, the United Nations War Crimes Commission had compiled a list of 36,529 war crimes suspects.[42]

The best-known International War Crimes Tribunals took place in Nuremberg, Germany, from 1945 to 1946 and in Tokyo from 1946 to 1948.[43] Although Adolf Hitler did not live to face justice, having shot himself in his bunker as the Red Army overran Berlin, the prosecutors at Nuremberg released their indictments of twenty-four key Nazi leaders on October 6, 1945. The military tribunal indicted all the defendants on at least two of the following four counts: (1) common plan or conspiracy, (2) crimes

against peace, (3) war crimes, and (4) crimes against humanity. Of twenty-two brought to trial, twelve were sentenced to hang, three received life sentences, four received lengthy prison terms, and three were acquitted.[44] The similar Tokyo War Crimes Tribunal tried senior Japanese officials responsible for the war in the Pacific; six were sentenced to hang, including Prime Minster Tōjō.[45]

The prosecution—and in many cases execution—of the senior living German and Japanese leaders represented a stark departure from past norms. British prosecutor Hartley Shawcross summed up the significance of the postwar trials by saying they made it clear that "to initiate a war of aggression is an international crime; that the individuals who lead their countries into such a war are personally responsible; [and] that individuals therefore have international duties which transcend the National duty of obedience imposed by particular states where to obey would constitute a crime against the Nations."[46]

The trials were not without controversy. The defense lawyers noted that the defendants were being tried for crimes that did not exist when they were supposedly committed. The war crimes trials of World War II represented an early experiment in international justice. A major undertaking for the occupation authorities, they had a lasting impact on war—and on the concept of international law and international justice—that continues to evolve through the work of the International Criminal Court.[47]

▲ WAR CRIMES

These are a few of the thousands of prisoners who died of ill-treatment at the Ebensee labor camp in Austria. When the 3rd Armored Cavalry Regiment arrived in May 1945, the inmates were starving to death at the rate of three hundred per day. The Americans requisitioned food from nearby towns to keep the survivors alive until more regular arrangements could be made.

WAR CRIMES TRIBUNALS ▲

Nazi leaders Hermann Göring, Rudolf Hess, Joachim von Ribbentrop, and Wilhelm Keitel (front row) at the Nuremberg Trials. Hess was the only one not sentenced to death, but he and Göring both committed suicide in prison.

DEMOBILIZATION

"We wanna go home!" became the objective for millions of men and women serving in the military when the war ended. They had been drafted or volunteered to serve for the duration of the war, and now it was over. The major powers began to demobilize rapidly. For example, the U.S. Army included 8,290,000 men and women on May 12, 1945; 8,020,000 on September 1, 1945; 4,228,936 at the end of 1945; and just 1,889,690 by the end of fiscal 1946. In the first nine months, the Army discharged 6,133,614 soldiers. Demobilization ended officially on June 30, 1947, with the Army's strength down to 989,664.[48] By mid-1946, the Army had not a single combat-ready division; not even among the occupation forces. Not only did the personnel go home, but also fleets of aircraft were sold and scrapped, and much of the greatest navy ever assembled was either put into mothballs or likewise sold for scrap. In a matter of months, the United States dismantled the mightiest military machine ever assembled.[49]

How did the U.S. Army accomplish such a feat? Planning for the demobilization began long before the war ended. Even as the armed forces faced some of their

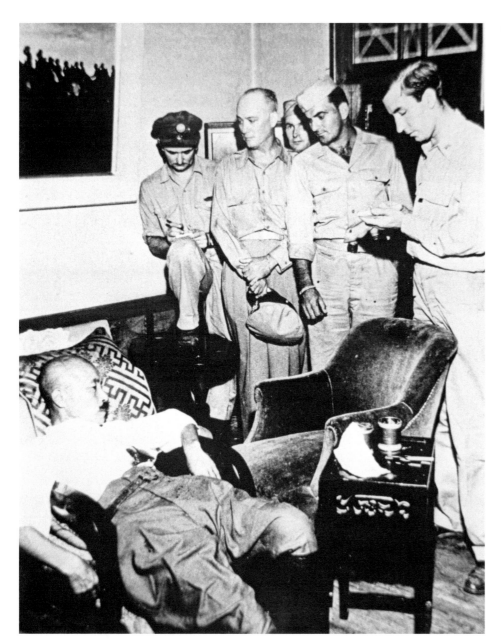

toughest fighting of the war in the summer and fall of 1944, the War Department and the War Production Board issued statements regarding demobilization and the conversion back to a civilian economy.[50] When victory in Europe arrived in May 1945, the war with Japan remained to be won, but it seemed clear that some of the forces in Europe could be safely demobilized.[51] Some troops would remain to perform occupation duties, while others would be shipped to the Pacific to help defeat Japan.

Who would stay? Who would head for the Pacific? Who would go home? A system to make these decisions had to be created, and it had to be as fair as possible. The Army issued each soldier an Adjusted Service Rating Card. Utilizing a point system, the Army determined which soldiers were going home. Each received one point for each month served in the Army, one point for each month served overseas, and five points for each service award received, starting September 16, 1940. Twelve points were given

for each minor child, up to a limit of three. The objective of the system was fairness, to reward those with the longest overseas service who had fought in the most campaigns and faced the greatest danger. The credit for children ensured that more fathers made it home, but it wasn't popular with the single men. Fortunately for everyone, the war in the Pacific ended before the troops from the European Theater ever reached the Pacific.

ASSESSING VICTORY AND SEEKING LESSONS LEARNED

With the war officially over and the occupations and demobilization well under way, the armed forces of each nation began seeking lessons to be learned as they looked ahead to future conflicts.[52] In the summer and fall of 1945, the U.S. Army sought to capture the experiences and lessons of the war quickly, before they were forgotten or lost to demobilization, and to begin a long-term effort to record the history of the war. The U.S. armed forces began producing a massive collection of official histories to preserve the record of the war for future generations.[53] The general histories established the basic narrative of the war, while individual unit histories, of varying quality and thoroughness, preserved a record of each unit's wartime service.[54] The officers preparing the Army and Army Group Reports of Operations produced useful documents detailing the scope of operations undertaken by those units.[55]

While all of these endeavors captured raw data and established the basic wartime narrative, other reports identified important lessons of the war: what worked, what didn't, and what should be changed, The General Board of the European Theater produced the most important of these documents. A series of committees, each composed of experts in the topic examined, studied everything from unit organization to psychological warfare. They produced 131 reports,[56] each of which included an overview of the issue studied, conclusions reached, and recommendations for future action. For example, the committee studying the use of tank destroyers, after highlighting the strengths and weaknesses of the force, advised that the "tank destroyers as a separate force be discontinued."[57] The U.S. Army Air Forces undertook the Strategic Bombing Survey to assess the effectiveness of the bombing campaign against Germany and Japan.[58] Investigators studied the many targets from the ground and used large quantities of captured enemy documents to determine the impact of the bombing campaign on the enemy economies, morale, and overall war effort. While criticized by some as overstating the effectiveness of strategic bombing, the methodologies developed and the data collected have proven useful to analysts and historians studying bombing since the war.[59]

Whether they consisted of short chronologies and lists of unit members, or detailed accounts of individual units at war, these histories and reports represented the immediate response to the question, What had the U.S. Army just experienced? The initial effort at history lacked much of the *why* behind what had happened and left out some material (such as the Ultra intelligence, because the information remained classified), but with time and reflection, the deeper questions and issues became clearer.

V-E DAY ▲
V-E Day in New York, May 8, 1945.

Ever since, historians, both military and civilian, have studied the Second World War in depth and breadth. Their work makes it possible to explain why the Allies won World War II.

WHY THE ALLIES WON

Why had the Allies won? Why had the Axis lost? These are two of the most-asked questions about the Second World War, and the answers are complex and often debated. Most historians would now agree, however, that the Allies' victory was not pre-ordained. The Allies ultimately won because they did what was necessary to win. They

MORE OF EVERYTHING ▶

Playing on the fact that the Allied victory symbol "V" was also a Roman numeral, this poster listed five reasons to be confident that the Axis would eventually be defeated. All five, however, are variations on just one: the Allies had more "stuff." Historians now put more emphasis on qualitative as well as quantitative advantages enjoyed by the Allies.

5 REASONS WHY THE ALLIES WILL WIN

1. The Allies have greater man-power.

2. The Allies have greater air-power.

3. The Allies have greater sea-power.

4. The Allies have greater machine-power.

5. The Allies have greater resources.

THIS IS THE SIGN OF V VICTORY FOR THE ALLIES

"VICTORY OR BOLSHEVISM!" ▶

By 1943, it was becoming increasingly evident that the war on the Eastern Front was not going well for the Axis. But if the prospect of permanently acquiring land, slaves, and resources for the Reich was fading, the fear of Soviet domination of Europe remained a powerful motivator.

maximized the production of war materials not just because they had more secure access to vital natural resources but also through the efficient and effective use of labor and industrial capacity. Despite conflicting national self-interests the Allies exercised unprecedented cooperation among themselves to formulate realistic strategies to defeat the Axis. The Axis powers' own actions made it relatively easy for the Allies to portray the war as one of good versus evil, but Churchill, Roosevelt, and Stalin must be given their share of credit for mobilizing and maintaining their countries' will to win throughout the war. Finally, the Allies created large land, air, and naval forces adequately supported by extraordinarily robust logistical systems that defeated the Axis forces on the battlefield.[60]

The Allies also had enemies who, for the most part, didn't do what they did—who sought another path to victory that ultimately failed. The Axis powers, of course, did not start the war intending to lose; they sought to achieve their national objectives individually through the rapid, decisive use of military force. For a time, it seemed to many that the Axis would triumph, but it eventually became clear that Germany, Italy, and Japan had started a conflict that they increasingly could not win. Nonetheless, the Axis forces fought to the bitter end. Even after the Allies had survived the early campaigns, fully mobilized, and brought to bear huge material superiority, they had to battle Axis forces for every inch of ground and had to maintain their focus on the final objective of unconditional surrender all the way to the end. The Allied victory was neither preordained nor easy to achieve.

RESOURCES AND PRODUCTION

The Axis powers began the war fully aware that they lacked the strategic natural resources to fight a long, drawn-out conflict.[61] Both Germany and Japan chose to start wars in large part to acquire access to resources before it became impossible to do so. Whether to gain *Lebensraum* ("living space") in Eastern Europe or to create the Greater East Asian Co-Prosperity Sphere in Asia, they counted on quick victories to obtain the resources they would need in the future. In the end, they were wrong on two counts: their quick victories on the battlefield didn't prevent the long war they feared most, and the resources they captured proved more difficult to extract and ship than they had expected.

Chief among the decisive resources was oil. Modern war demanded vast quantities of it. Industrial production and mechanized warfare depended upon the internal combustion engine, and it required oil for lubrication and fuel. While the Allies had access to most of the world's supply of this extremely vital resource, the Axis powers increasingly found their naval, mechanized, and air units unable to move due to fuel shortages.[62] The Allies had a similar advantage with nearly every strategic resource needed to support a large modern war, whether it was iron ore, copper, strategic metals for steel production such as tungsten or nickel, or foodstuffs. The Allies dealt with shortages of natural rubber, quinine, and other strategic materials by producing synthetic replacements. The challenge for the Allies was how to transport vast quantities of material from mines and wells all over the world to their factories, and then move finished goods to the front. The mass production of Liberty Ships and trucks and massive infrastructure projects all played major roles in the Allied victory.

Take, for instance, the Big Inch pipeline from East Texas to the Northeast: 1,330 miles long and built in a single year, from August 1942 to August 1943, it was able to

Drawn up before the start of Operation Barbarossa, this graphic puts the resources of the U.S.S.R. in a position that suggests they were available to the Axis powers—but even so shows that the United States and Britain effectively controlled a large majority of the world's strategic raw materials.

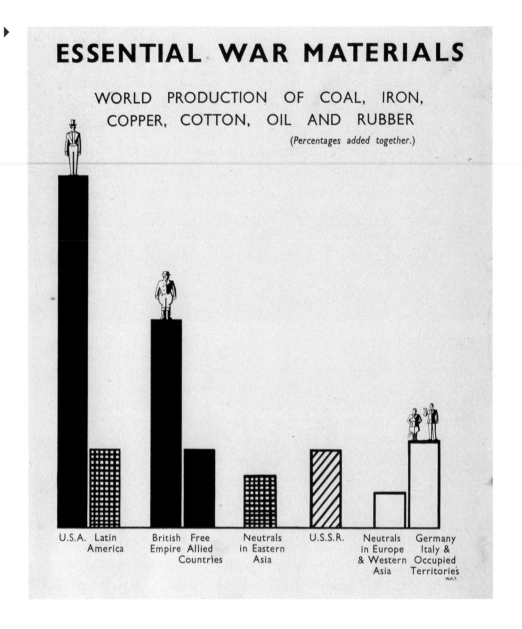

ESSENTIAL WAR MATERIALS

WORLD PRODUCTION OF COAL, IRON, COPPER, COTTON, OIL AND RUBBER

(Percentages added together.)

| U.S.A. Latin America | British Empire Free Allied Countries | Neutrals in Eastern Asia | U.S.S.R. | Neutrals in Europe & Western Asia | Germany Italy & Occupied Territories |

deliver more oil per day than was produced by all Axis refineries combined.[63] The Allies most certainly had to manage their resources by prioritizing production, but they had sufficient resources to allow for the occasional production mistake or inefficiency. The Axis nations, by contrast, had to manage their resources much more carefully and had no room for error. Any diversion of resources from the main war effort, such as producing V-weapons or jet aircraft—or exterminating millions of Jews—ultimately proved too costly for the Axis.

The Allies proved much more effective in managing their wartime economies. While the Axis powers had prepared primarily for a short, intense conflict, the British, Soviets, and Americans entered the war with a clear understanding that they had to fully mobilize their economies for the long haul if they hoped to win. As a result, they took steps to organize production, to maximize the size of the available workforce, and to stress quantity as well as quality.

Safe from Axis bombing, the workers of the United States awoke from their Great Depression slumber and went to work. The American gross domestic product (GDP) increased by 72 percent from 1939 to 1944.[64] The British GDP had increased by 26 percent by 1943.[65] The Americans accomplished such a feat despite putting nearly sixteen million people, or approximately 10 percent of the population, into uniform. They not only increased the size of the workforce by ensuring all men who could work were working, but also succeeded in moving women into the workforce—and into jobs they had not traditionally occupied. The image of women welding on ships and riveting aircraft became symbols of this effort to expand the workforce. The number of hours worked increased as plants ran twenty-four hours a day, seven days a week. Although racism and sexism existed in America, official U.S. government policy stressed that Americans were all one team, all working for victory. The United States truly became the arsenal of democracy during the war.

While the United States let the forces of capitalism work to maximize production, the Soviet Union moved in another direction. The Soviets' command economy transitioned rapidly to a full wartime footing following the German invasion in 1941. Unlike the United States, safe behind two oceans, the Soviet Union found itself a battleground with many of its most productive areas occupied by German forces. In

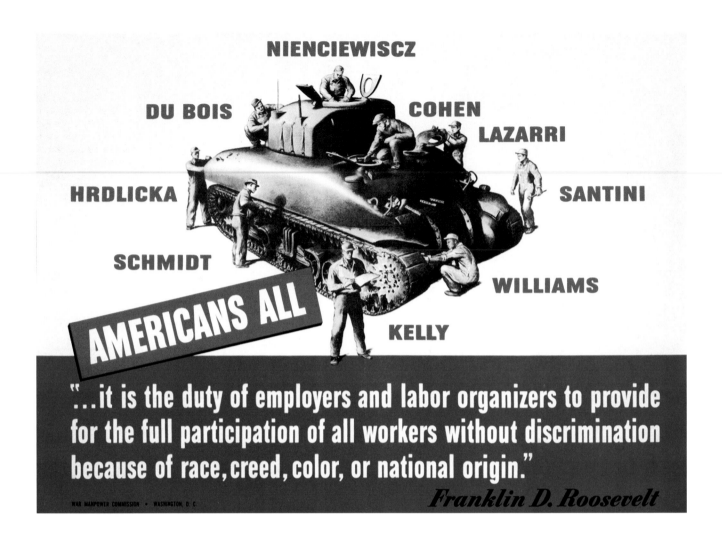

NIENCIEWISCZ

DU BOIS

COHEN

LAZARRI

HRDLICKA

SANTINI

SCHMIDT

WILLIAMS

AMERICANS ALL

KELLY

"...it is the duty of employers and labor organizers to provide for the full participation of all workers without discrimination because of race, creed, color, or national origin."

Franklin D. Roosevelt

WAR MANPOWER COMMISSION • WASHINGTON, D. C.

AMERICANS ALL ▲

The U.S. government promoted unity in the war effort with posters, like the one shown here, that emphasized national diversity and working together toward a common goal.

response, the Soviets devoted their entire economy to the war effort, at levels much higher than those of the other Allies. They all but ceased production of consumer goods and focused exclusively on war materials. They succeeded to an astounding degree in getting the most out of every pound of steel and ton of coal.[66] Despite the fact that Germany produced nearly three times as much steel as the Soviet Union did during the war, the Soviets outproduced Germany in tanks, guns, and ammunition from 1942 onward. Although Germany built more aircraft and trucks, Allied Lend-Lease shipments helped even the playing field in those areas. On the battlefields of the Soviet Union, the quantity and quality of the Soviet weapons mattered.

Germany ramped up military production once the war began, but in the early years of the war, the Third Reich lacked the sense of urgency exhibited by the Allies. The victories of 1939 to 1941 enabled the German economy to exploit the newly conquered territories for resources and labor to meet immediate wartime requirements. Only with the failure of Operation Barbarossa in the fall of 1941 did it become evident that the war would not end soon and that a greater effort had to be made in the area of production. Hitler appointed Albert Speer as Minister of Armaments and War Production in February 1942 to maximize production and optimize the German

◄ "STRONGER FROM
YEAR TO YEAR!"
In response to Allied propaganda
trumpeting the United Nations' advantage in material resources, the
Germans emphasized that the Axis
conquests of 1939–1942 went a
long way toward evening the score.
But occupied areas and populations
subjected to forced labor could not
be harnessed to a war effort as effectively as free nations fighting in
a just cause.

economy for war. His efforts proved successful, and war production increased significantly from 1942 to 1944 even though German GDP increased by only 13.8 percent
from 1939 to 1944.[67] However, as the manpower losses at the front required more and
more German men to enter the military, Germany struggled to find workers. By 1944,
some 7,128,000 forced or foreign laborers had been put to work alongside 36,210,000
German workers.[68] The productivity of these workers, often hungry and sick, remained
low throughout the war. As the strategic bombing campaign intensified and the front

Pictured here are victims of the concentration camp at Buchenwald who survived long enough to be liberated by the U.S. 80th Division. Germany's wartime production depended on working hundreds of thousands of Jews, POWs, homosexuals, Roma (Gypsies), Communists, and others literally to death.

lines moved ever closer to Germany, depriving it of valuable resources and destroying its transportation network, the German economy ultimately collapsed.

The Japanese experience mirrored Germany's, with a few exceptions. Whereas Germany failed to gain the expected quantities of resources from Eastern Europe and Russia, the Japanese did acquire access to rich resources with their early conquests. They gained control of Southeast Asian oil, rubber, tin, and rice. However, transporting the resources to Japan to support the production of war materials proved increasingly difficult. American submarines took an ever-increasing toll on Japanese shipping over the course of the war. With the seizure of the Mariana Islands in June 1944, the commencement of the strategic bombing of Japanese cities practically destroyed Japan's ability to produce war materials. The Japanese had chosen to go to war knowing they could not match the industrial might of the United States. When the Allies chose to fight on rather than accept initial Japanese success, Japan's odds of victory decreased dramatically.[69]

As important as resources and production were to victory, they did not by themselves assure victory. Fighting powers can compensate for economic limitations by making better use of resources and what they produce. In coalition wars, this requires allies to cooperate to minimize their individual weaknesses. In the Second World War, the United States, Great Britain, the British Commonwealth, and the Soviet Union worked together much more effectively than the Axis powers did.

A SUCCESSFUL COALITION

"There is only one thing worse than fighting with Allies," Churchill once quipped, "and that is to fight without them."[70] The Allies benefited greatly from their ability to cooperate and formulate a combined strategy for defeating the Axis.[71] The relationship forged between Franklin Roosevelt and Winston Churchill and their ability to work with Josef Stalin to accomplish a common goal played a major role in the defeat of the Axis. These three resourceful and determined leaders and their military advisors met regularly throughout the war and discussed, debated, and argued over strategy. The willingness of the Big Three to subordinate their separate national interests to defeating the Axis enabled them to achieve victory.

From the beginning of American involvement in the war, the Allied leaders shared an understanding of the Axis threat and of the need to cooperate to achieve victory. It began with the Big Three and extended throughout all the levels of command.[72] From the earliest talks between the American and British chiefs of staff at the ABC-1 Conference of January–March 1941, to the decision to create a Combined Chiefs of

▲ OSAKA, 1945

Before the dropping of the atomic bombs on Hiroshima and Nagasaki, B-29s loaded with incendiaries caused comparable destruction in dozens of Japanese cities. About 300,000 civilians were killed in the strategic bombing campaign.

▲ THE BIG THREE

The Soviets recognized that the invasion of Italy and especially the Combined Bomber Offensive took some pressure off them in 1943, but it was not until the cross-Channel invasion in 1944 that they were really satisfied with the British and American contribution to the defeat of Hitler.

THE UNITED NATIONS FIGHT FOR FREEDOM

UNITED STATES · GREAT BRITAIN · SOVIET RUSSIA · CHINA
AUSTRALIA · BELGIUM · BRAZIL · CANADA
COSTA RICA · CUBA · CZECHOSLOVAKIA · DOMINICAN REPUBLIC
EL SALVADOR · ETHIOPIA · GREECE · GUATEMALA
HAITI · HONDURAS · INDIA · LUXEMBOURG
MEXICO · NETHERLANDS · NEW ZEALAND · NICARAGUA
NORWAY · PANAMA
PHILIPPINES · POLAND
SOUTH AFRICA · YUGOSLAVIA

RADAR ▲

The most important innovation in radar technology during World War II was the British invention of the cavity magnetron. The U.K. quickly shared the design with the U.S., and MIT engineers helped develop the centimetric radar sets that made a vital contribution to Allied antisubmarine warfare and strategic bombing efforts. Naval centimetric radar sets that could spot enemy battleships twenty-nine miles away, or incoming bombers at twice that range, gave the Allies a key advantage in the later battles of the Pacific War.

◀ **THE UNITED NATIONS FIGHT FOR FREEDOM**

The coalition that defeated the Germans and the Japanese represented more than the great powers. Brazil, for instance, sent a 25,000-man expeditionary force to fight in Italy. The threat posed by Nazi Germany—and, to a lesser extent, Japan—bound the Allies together despite their ideological differences.

Staff (CCS) in December 1941 at the Arcadia Conference, the American and British military leaders worked toward success despite frequent disagreements.

Cooperation trumped division. When General Eisenhower took command, he warned his staff that he would not tolerate any disrespect toward the British, and some American officers were sent home following inappropriate anti-British comments. Officers were expected to present their positions, debate, even argue, but it was to be done in a civilized fashion. Individuals such as General Patton and Field Marshal Montgomery never became the best of friends, but there was an understanding by all involved that defeating Hitler and the Axis powers remained the top priority.

Roosevelt and Churchill met repeatedly during the war. In Newfoundland in August 1941, they issued the Atlantic Charter that defined the Allied postwar goals. At Casablanca in January 1943, they decided that the Battle of the Atlantic should receive top priority, that they would conduct a Combined Bomber Offensive against Germany, and that they would insist upon unconditional surrender by Germany and Japan. The Big Three met at Tehran in November 1943 and set the date for the invasion of Western Europe.

▲ THE BIG FOUR

The Big Three (Roosevelt, Churchill, and Stalin) had the predominant voices in planning for the postwar world, but the American president hoped that after Japan's defeat Generalissimo Chiang Kai-shek would lead a free and friendly Republic of China to become a force for stability in East Asia.

The Axis held no such significant meetings. Strategic coordination between Germany or Italy and the Japanese was practically nonexistent. Adolf Hitler and Benito Mussolini did meet occasionally, but even they never met to compare goals, decide upon a combined Axis strategy, or coordinate their efforts. Each fought his own war, hoping his allies would assist as needed, and believing that his individual national interests took precedence over any kind of cooperative efforts. Neither they nor Tōjō saw any need to agree on a unified Axis strategy for a long war, which none of them intended to fight. Unfortunately for the Axis powers, the short decisive campaigns that were supposed to bring them victory ended up growing into a long, drawn-out war.

The Axis nations' failure to coordinate their actions resulted in missed opportunities. Mussolini's desire to gain some of the spoils of the war led to his unilateral decision to invade Greece in October 1940; this, combined with the pro-British military coup in Yugoslavia, forced Hitler to invade the Balkans, and ended up delaying the start of Operation Barbarossa in 1941.[73] Although one cannot say that the addition of a week or two of good campaigning weather would have ensured German victory, the Wehrmacht did come within twenty miles of Moscow by December 1941, and any extra summer campaigning time could have only improved its chances of achieving victory in the East that year. At that same crucial point in the war, the Japanese considered declaring war on the Soviet Union but chose not to do so. A 1941 German-Japanese "Russia First" strategy analogous to the Germany First strategy agreed upon by the United States and Britain probably represented the best chance for an overall Axis victory in World War II, but instead, Japan decided to turn south, bringing the United States into the war.[74]

In addition to opportunities to coordinate strategy, the Axis powers had technology they could have shared. For example, Germany possessed radar, missile, and jet engine technology it could have shared with Japan and Italy. The Japanese had the best torpedo of the war, technology which German U-boat forces could have used to improve their chances of success in the crucial Battle of the Atlantic. Viewing each other as future competitors, however, they chose not to share technology when it might have mattered. When Germany and Japan did attempt to exchange technological information near the end of the war, it was too late to make a difference.

The Allies, on the other hand—especially the United States and Great Britain—viewed each other as postwar partners and shared technologies in radar, atomic energy, and jet engines, among others. They also shared intelligence, the most important being the Ultra intelligence obtained by breaking the German Enigma codes. The Allies did everything in their power to keep their partners fighting, even when it threw off their own plans and preferences. The best example may be Roosevelt's insistence on an invasion of North Africa in 1942 in order to support the British forces in the Mediterranean and to create a "second front," however limited, to take some of the pressure off the Soviets—even though his own military advisors would have preferred to focus on building up forces in England for a 1943 cross-Channel invasion, and the American public wanted more emphasis on the war against Japan. Other pertinent examples include the dispatch of large quantities of scarce matériel to Britain and the

Soviet Union from America under the Lend-Lease program, and the aid laboriously ferried by aircraft over the Himalayan Hump to the Nationalist Chinese.

When the tide shifted against the Axis, the Allies could have drifted apart, but they instead continued to work together, shifting their focus from staving off defeat to ensuring victory and planning for a postwar world. Meetings at Bretton Woods and Dumbarton Oaks in the summer and fall of 1944 led to the formation of the United Nations and plans for postwar economic cooperation.[75] In 1945 Big Three meetings at Yalta and Potsdam dealt with the final defeat of the Axis and occupation plans. Although tensions among the Allies increased as victory neared, the coalition stayed focused. The Cold War would erupt only after the defeat of the Axis powers. The Allies, to varying degrees, effectively shared resources, technology, intelligence, and war plans, while the Axis for the most part did not.[76] The Allies' successful practice of coalition warfare played a major role in the Allied victory.

GOOD VS. EVIL AND THE WILL TO WIN

Both sides engaged in propaganda wars to motivate their own populations and to break the morale of those on the other side. The Allied advantage in the struggle of ideas was that the war was ultimately about the Axis powers' attempts to advance their own interests by conquering large parts of the world and subjugating the people living there. It was easier for the Allied governments to motivate their people—to convince them that the war was necessary—than for the Axis governments to justify to their citizens the war they had started. Allied propaganda didn't have to push the boundaries of truth nearly as far as Axis propaganda did, and it seemed that each Axis invasion and atrocity only increased the Allies' determination to win.

The primary motivation of the Allied powers differed based upon national circumstances, with the British fighting to restore the balance of power in Europe and preserve their empire, and the Soviet Union mobilizing its people to save Mother Russia, preserve Communism, and prevent the annihilation or enslavement of the Slavic peoples. The Americans fought for values such as the "Four Freedoms"—freedom of speech, freedom of worship, freedom from want, and freedom from fear—and to liberate people being oppressed by the Axis.[77] They also fought to avenge Pearl Harbor and to preserve the American way of life by preventing the spread of Nazism and fascism. Whereas the Axis powers invaded their neighbors with the intent of staying, the Western Allied forces fought to liberate those conquered by the Axis and then go home.[78] The world envisioned by each proved to be very different: the Axis powers imagined a world with little room in it for anyone who wasn't Germanic ("Aryan") or Japanese, while the Allies—even the average Soviet citizen—imagined a world, very idealistically, of peace and freedom.[79]

Although global peace and freedom proved difficult to achieve—with the Soviet Union "liberating" most of Eastern Europe, the colonial powers returning to Asia after the war, and the onset of a Cold War—that didn't change the fact that during the war the Allies had a vision of a postwar world that trumped anything the Axis could

BUCHENWALD ▲
CONCENTRATION CAMP

Artist Gary Sheahan described what he saw when American troops liberated the immense Buchenwald concentration camp (which at peak held over 100,000 prisoners) in April 1945: "thousands of walking, stinking skeletons, crowding around me as I worked at a simple pencil sketch, others standing, vacantly staring. Many lying sprawled on the ground, dead or alive, I was unable to tell."

offer. The Allies successfully cast themselves as the forces of good, which helped them garner the support of the neutral nations of the world, rally resistance forces in occupied territory, and weaken the Axis coalition.[80] While the Axis powers had the opportunity to turn various ethnic groups into allies in their fight against the Soviet Union and the European colonial powers, the racist views of the Germans and the Japanese—and their cruel and often barbaric occupation policies—won them few friends.[81]

The Allied and Axis approach to "time" also differed and affected their ability to maintain their peoples' will to win. Convinced that the war to defeat the Axis would take years, the Allied leadership understood the need to maintain the will to win, to keep their people informed and motivated to continue the struggle however long it might take. The Allies' message that the war represented a struggle between good and evil proved relatively easy to believe and made it clear that they fought not strictly for national gain but to eliminate a threat to world peace. Such a message became clearer to everyone as the scope of Axis atrocities and war crimes became known.

In contrast, the Axis leadership approached the war with a short time horizon. Lacking the resources and production capacity to challenge the combined economic might of Britain, the Union of Soviet Socialist Republics, and the United States, and fearful of putting too much pressure on their societies, they sought to accomplish their national objectives with short, intense campaigns that caught their opponents unaware and unable to stave off defeat. Such an approach worked in the early years of the war, against weak or inexperienced neighbors close at hand. Maintaining a strong

THE Atlantic Charter

THE President of THE UNITED STATES OF AMERICA and the Prime Minister, Mr. *Churchill*, representing HIS MAJESTY'S GOVERNMENT IN THE UNITED KINGDOM, being met together, deem it right to make known certain common principles in the national policies of their respective countries on which they base their hopes for a better future for the world.

1. *Their countries seek no aggrandizement, territorial or other.*

2. *They desire to see no territorial changes that do not accord with the freely expressed wishes of the peoples concerned.*

3. *They respect the right of all peoples to choose the form of government under which they will live; and they wish to see sovereign rights and self-government restored to those who have been forcibly deprived of them.*

4. *They will endeavor, with due respect for their existing obligations, to further the enjoyment by all States, great or small, victor or vanquished, of access, on equal terms, to the trade and to the raw materials of the world which are needed for their economic prosperity.*

5. *They desire to bring about the fullest collaboration between all nations in the economic field with the object of securing, for all, improved labor standards, economic advancement and social security.*

6. *After the final destruction of the Nazi tyranny, they hope to see established a peace which will afford to all nations the means of dwelling in safety within their own boundaries, and which will afford assurance that all the men in all the lands may live out their lives in freedom from fear and want.*

7. *Such a peace should enable all men to traverse the high seas and oceans without hindrance.*

8. *They believe that all of the nations of the world, for realistic as well as spiritual reasons, must come to the abandonment of the use of force. Since no future peace can be maintained if land, sea or air armaments continue to be employed by nations which threaten, or may threaten, aggression outside of their frontiers, they believe, pending the establishment of a wider and permanent system of general security, that the disarmament of such nations is essential. They will likewise aid and encourage all other practicable measures which will lighten for peace-loving peoples the crushing burden of armaments.*

FRANKLIN D. ROOSEVELT

WINSTON S. CHURCHILL

August 14, 1941

▲ THE ATLANTIC CHARTER

The Axis powers began the war with the expressed intent of gaining territory and control over "inferior" peoples; the Western Allies fought defensively, hoping to free "all men in all lands" from "fear and want," and expressly forswore any intent to profit from victory. It is normal in war for both sides to claim to be "the good guys," but in this case it was perfectly clear that right and justice were with the Allies.

Although the Four Freedoms are commonly associated with the famous paintings by Norman Rockwell, the underlying idea came from President Roosevelt's 1941 State of the Union address. After the United States entered the war, the Four Freedoms provided Americans with a clear and simple vision of a future worth fighting and sacrificing for.

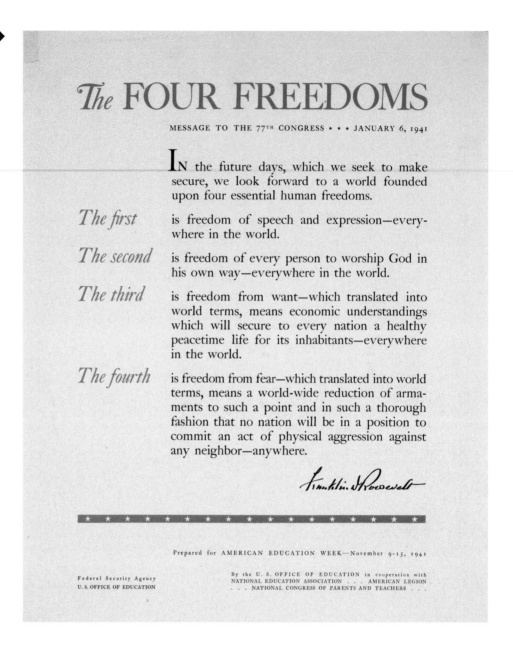

national will to win was a low priority if victory came quickly. When the Axis leaders discovered that they could not defeat Great Britain, the Soviet Union, or the United States in rapid military campaigns, and that the Allies' citizens were not as weak-willed as expected, they found themselves in deep trouble.

DEFEATING THE ENEMY ON THE BATTLEFIELD

Even the combination of superior resources, more efficient production, active coalition cooperation, and a strong will to win did not ensure victory. The Allied military forces had to meet the formidable Axis forces on the field of battle—on land, in the air, and at sea—and defeat them. They had to drive them back to their homelands and obtain their unconditional surrender.

▲ THE AXIS CAUSE
"The USA will rescue European culture from destruction," says this poster in ironic juxtaposition to images of American "decadence." This was a favorite theme of Axis propaganda, but how much could Germans, much less the Dutch audience targeted in this version, be expected to sacrifice to a fight against jazz, money, and bad taste?

SACRIFICE
THE PRIVILEGE OF FREE MEN

WINNER INTERNATIONAL BUSINESS MACHINES CORP. AWARD—NATIONAL WAR POSTER COMPETITION
HELD UNDER AUSPICES OF ARTISTS FOR VICTORY, INC.—COUNCIL FOR DEMOCRACY—MUSEUM OF MODERN ART

▲ SACRIFICE

German propaganda was mostly negative—focused on the need to defeat the threat posed by the "Jewish-Bolshevik world conspiracy"—but the Allies could take heart from the idea that their sacrifices would contribute toward a positive good: the spread of freedom and the creation of a better, more peaceful world order.

In the European theater, the Allies halted the German advance in 1941–42, regained the initiative in 1943, and began the relentless drive to Berlin in 1944–45. After the fall of France, the key battles and campaigns were won by the Allied forces. The forces of Great Britain, standing nearly alone, won the Battle of Britain in 1940. The soldiers of the Red Army survived Operation Barbarossa in 1941, regained the initiative at Stalingrad in 1942 and Kursk in 1943; and then they outfought the German forces all the way to Berlin.

In the Pacific, the Allied forces halted the Japanese threat to Australia, crippled the Japanese fleet at Midway, and wrestled the initiative from the Japanese in a six-month campaign on and around Guadalcanal from August 1942 to February 1943. Then they succeeded in launching twin drives to the Philippines and eventually Japan itself.

Allied forces defeated German and Italian forces in North Africa in 1942, landed in Italy, and forced Italy out of the war in 1943 before fighting a long campaign against German defenders up the Italian peninsula. The Allies meanwhile won the Battle of the Atlantic, and then in 1944 executed a massive amphibious operation to land in France and drove across Western Europe into the heart of Germany by early 1945.

Starting in late 1942, Allied forces defeated their Axis enemies on all the battlefields that mattered. In the end, the quality of individual German soldiers or their tactical prowess did not bring them victory; it merely prolonged their agony and cost many soldiers and civilians their lives. Once American, British, and Russian soldiers

▲ "Two Hundred Flags and Banners of the Defeated German Army are Brought to the Feet of the Heroes"

Throughout 1945, each nation had victory parades to thank the men and women of Allied services for defeating the Axis forces on battlefields on land, on sea, and in the air all over the globe. The biggest parade was held in Moscow on June 24, 1945, and featured Marshals Georgy Zhukov and Konstantin Rokossovsky riding into Red Square on stallions to start the festivities. At the end of the parade, Red Army soldiers carried the banners of Nazi Germany and threw them down next to Lenin's mausoleum.

gained combat experience and proved more than capable of defeating their German opponents, it didn't matter how good a Tiger tank or an Me262 jet fighter may have been.[82] Too few were built, they had too many teething problems due to being rushed into production, and they lacked the fuel to operate. The Allies built well-rounded military forces, trained and equipped them with quality weapons, sustained them with logistical and intelligence systems the Axis could only dream about, and used them capably in joint and combined operations to slowly and steadily crush the Axis forces. The heroes of this effort were the millions of men and women who served in the Allied armed services and defeated the Axis forces on the countless battlefields of World War II.[83]

Conclusion

The end of hostilities did not end the work of the Allied armed forces. They faced a variety of postwar challenges that had to be dealt with under difficult conditions. They occupied Germany, Italy, and Japan, and established military governments. Responsible for restoring some semblance of order to devastated nations, the occupying powers set about providing assistance to millions of displaced persons and refugees. Allied forces liberated their POWs and worked to ensure their rapid return home; they processed and cared for large numbers of Axis POWs; and they worked with extraordinary diligence to account for all their war dead and missing in action. They undertook all these tasks at the very time the Allies were demobilizing their military forces. The duties of the Allied armies went well beyond signing the peace terms; they found themselves responsible for beginning to pick up the pieces of a shattered Europe and Asia.

The victors and defeated alike also began assessing what had happened. Why had the Allies won? What lessons could be learned from the Second World War experience? These questions continue to generate debate, and the Allied victory in World War II does not provide a simple solution for winning all wars. But it does provide valuable insight into what helps achieve victory. The Allies won World War II because they had access to necessary resources; efficiently converted those raw materials into military power; created and maintained a successful coalition; understood the importance of maintaining the will to win; and created military forces capable of defeating the enemy in combat. The Axis chose another path, one in which "racial superiority" and high-quality forces were supposed to achieve rapid battlefield victories, redressing the material balance against them, and leading to overall victory. Such a path did not ensure their defeat, but it left little leeway for error. The Allies could survive their errors, the Axis could not—and it is the Allies who emerged victorious.

CHAPTER 1: THE ALLIES TURN THE TIDE

1. The battle for the city of Stalingrad itself has had a huge body of literature devoted to it, and the Soviet offensive that ended it has not done badly, either. The campaign that led up to it, however (Operation Blue), has been underserved, rarely rating more than a clichéd sentence or two in the general histories. For those with German-language reading skills, see the German official history, *Das Deutsche Reich und der Zweite Weltkrieg*, vol. 6, *Die Ausweitung zum Weltkrieg und der Wechsel der Initiative, 1941–1943* (Stuttgart: Deutsche Verlags-Anstalt, 1990), hereinafter *GOH*, pt. 6, "Der Krieg gegen die Sowjetunion, 1942–43," authored by Bernd Wegner. Preeminent in the English-language literature is Joel S. A. Hayward, *Stopped at Stalingrad: The Luftwaffe and Hitler's Defeat in the East, 1942–1943* (Lawrence: University Press of Kansas, 1998), a book that is ostensibly about air operations but is in reality a careful analysis of the interplay between land, air, and sea, as well as David M. Glantz with Jonathan M. House, *To the Gates of Stalingrad: Soviet-German Combat Operations, April–August 1942* (Lawrence: University Press of Kansas, 2009).

2. Wegner, *GOH*, "Der Krieg gegen die Sowjetunion, 1942–43," 779.

3. Earl Ziemke and Magna Bauer, *Moscow to Stalingrad: Decision in the East* (Washington, D.C.: Center of Military History, 1987), 293.

4. See George E. Blau, *The German Campaign in Russia—Planning and Operation, 1940–1942*, Department of the Army Pamphlet No. 20-261a (Washington, D.C.: Department of the Army, 1955), 137. The book is part of the German Reports Series. Blau based his text on manuscripts written by the German generals in captivity, among them General Franz Halder, chief of the General Staff until 1942, General Gotthard Heinrici, "and others" (*iii*). It is very good on the preparations for the offensive (the German authors apparently had use of their planning memoranda in preparing the manuscript), but very general on the actual course of operations.

5. Ibid., 138.

6. Ibid., 149–50.

7. Walter Warlimont, *Inside Hitler's Headquarters 1939–45* (Novato, CA: Presidio, 1964), 239–40. Warlimont was deputy chief of operations for the OKW from 1939 to 1944.

8. Ziemke and Bauer, *Moscow to Stalingrad*, 294; Warlimont, *Inside Hitler's Headquarters*, 240.

9. Blau, *The German Campaign in Russia*, 126.

10. Richard L. Dinardo, *Germany and the Axis Powers: From Coalition to Collapse* (Lawrence: University Press of Kansas, 2005), 136.

11. See the table entitled "Die deutsche Einschätzung der sowjetischen Industrieproduktion des Jahres 1942," in Wegner, *GOH*, "Der Krieg gegen die Sowjetunion, 1942–43," 806.

12. On the Crimea, one must start with the principal primary source, Erich von Manstein, *Lost Victories* (Novato, CA: Presidio, 1982), especially 204–59. It has become axiomatic in the historical profession to advise caution in using the memoir literature generated by the German officer corps. This is particularly important with regard to the tendency of the authors to blame Hitler for everything that went wrong in the war, to exculpate themselves, and to invent disagreements with him, even to the point of describing bogus face-to-face arguments. There is, likewise, nary a word in any of them about "donations"—large grants of money and land from the Führer to his loyal commanders—which certainly puts a new spin on their determination to hold out to the last man. Manstein's memoir is no exception. However, all these books are arguably at their most reliable when they are actually discussing operations: orders of battle, troop movements, operational maneuvers, and the like. Two other essential primary sources are General Friedrich Schulz, *Battle for Crimea*, part of the *Foreign Military Studies* series, manuscript T-20, and General Hellmuth Reinhardt, *Selected German Army Operations on the Eastern Front (Operational)*, manuscript P-143a, 187–212. A copy of each of these reports, along with the rest of this immense series, is on file in the U.S. Army Military History Institute at Carlisle Barracks in Carlisle, Pennsylvania. Both Wegner, *GOH*, and Hayward, *Stopped at Stalingrad*, contain much useful analysis.

NOTES

13. The principal source on the Soviet offensive in the Crimea is David M. Glantz, "Forgotten Battles of the German-Soviet War (1941–45), pt. 6: The Winter Campaign (December 5, 1941–April 1942): The Crimean Counteroffensive and Reflections," *Journal of Slavic Military Studies*, 14, no. 1 (March 2001): 121–70. It is part of a long-term and very ambitious project in which Glantz painstakingly reconstructs a historical narrative of numerous battles and campaigns that ended disastrously for the Red Army, and that were then systematically tossed down the Stalinist memory hole in the postwar years. His book *Zhukov's Greatest Defeat: The Red Army's Epic Disaster in Operation Mars, 1942* (Lawrence: University Press of Kansas, 1999) is part of the same effort.

14. The operation was named "Bustard Hunt." The bustard is the harmless black game bird that inhabits the Crimea in great numbers. "Bustard hunt" might be reasonably rendered as "turkey shoot" in English. For Manstein's Kerch offensive, see Robert M. Citino, *Death of the Wehrmacht: The German Campaigns of 1942* (Lawrence: University Press of Kansas, 2007), 69–77.

15. Hayward, *Stopped at Stalingrad*, 68–69. Nearly seven hundred German aircraft took part in the Kerch operation.

16. For the Sevastopol campaign, see Citino, *Death of the Wehrmacht*, 77–81. For the German casualties in the fighting, see Hayward, *Stopped at Stalingrad*, 117, who gives a figure of 75,000; for the 100,000 figure, see Gerhard Weinberg, *A World at Arms: A Global History of World War II*, 2nd ed. (Cambridge: Cambridge University Press, 2005), 413; for 25,000 German dead, see Wegner, *GOH*, "Der Krieg gegen die Sowjetunion, 1942–43," 851 ("allein auf deutscher Seite fielen fast 25,000 Soldaten").

17. There is no scholarly monograph dealing solely with the Battle of Kharkov. It is no doubt a matter of timing: with Stalingrad looming just around the corner, Kharkov will probably always suffer in comparison. The researcher should begin with the few primary sources available. Pride of place goes to the Soviet Staff Study, edited and translated by the omnipresent David M. Glantz, *Kharkov 1942: Anatomy of a Military Disaster Through Soviet Eyes* (Shepperton, Surrey, UK: Ian Allan, 1998). Glantz presents this 1951 account warts and all, and then brackets it with his own informed commentary. For the German side, there is the postwar account by the chief of the General Staff for the LI Corps, Hans Doerr, "Der Ausgang der Schlacht um Charkow im Frühjahr 1942," *Wehrwissenschaftliche Rundschau* 4, no. 1 (January 1954): 9–18. Doerr was the chief of the General Staff for the German LII Army Corps during the battle. Fedor von Bock, *Generalfeldmarschall Fedor von Bock: The War Diary, 1939–1945* (Atglen, PA: Schiffer Military History, 1996), is essential in tracing the difficult birth and triumphant course of the battle.

Within the secondary literature, Kharkov usually receives brief treatment. Begin with the pertinent sections in John Erickson, *The Road to Stalingrad* (New York: Harper & Row, 1975), which are indeed short (343–47) but typically excellent. For those of a certain scholarly generation, it was Erickson's prose that first captured the drama of the Russo-German War. Indeed, it will be tough for any future author to top passages like this one: "On the morning of 12 May, preceded by an hour of artillery and air bombardment, Timoshenko's northern and southern prongs jabbed into Paulus's Sixth Army which for three days and nights rocked and lurched in a highly dangerous situation as waves of Soviet riflemen and slabs of Soviet armour crashed down on it . . ." (345).

See also the very useful sections in Ziemke and Bauer, *Moscow to Stalingrad*, 269–82.

18. For Directive 41, see Walther Hubatsch, *Hitlers Weisungen für die Kriegführung 1939–1945* (Koblenz, Ger.: Bernard & Graefe, 1983), 183–91.

19. There was later a dispute within the German high command over the exact operational intent, but the language of Directive 41 seems clear: "The goal of this breakthrough is the occupation of Voronezh itself." See Directive 41, "Die Hauptoperation an der Ostfront," Hubatsch, *Hitler's Weisungen*, 186.

20. Hayward, *Stopped at Stalingrad*, 22–25, contains an extremely lucid explanation of this extraordinarily complicated operation; also helpful is Ziemke and Bauer, *Moscow to Stalingrad*, 286–90.

21. Quoted in Geoffrey Roberts, *Victory at Stalingrad* (London: Longman, 2002), 60.

22. Entry for July 6, 1942, in Franz Halder, *Kriegstagebuch*, 3:475, *War Journal* (SHAEF: A. G. EUCOM, 2007), 7.

23. Particularly good on the order is Richard Overy, *Russia's War: A History of the Soviet War Effort, 1914–1945* (New York: Penguin, 1998), 158–61.

24. As Field Marshal Bock put it, "we're trying to surround an enemy who is no longer there" [*Einen Gegner einzukesseln, der nicht mehr da ist*]. Entry for July 7, 1942, in Bock, *War Diary*, 520. See also Wegner, *GOH*, "Der Krieg gegen die Sowjetunion, 1942–43," 881.

25. For an openly contemptuous look from within the German officer corps, complete with "air quotes," see "Die 'Kesselschlacht' von Rostow," Hans Doerr, *Feldzug nach Stalingrad: Versuch eines operativen Überblickes* (Darmstadt, Ger.: E. S. Mittler, 1955), 22–24. Doerr was a German staff officer involved in the campaign.

26. For Directive 45, see Hubatsch, *Hitlers Weisungen*, 196–200, and Doerr, *Feldzug nach Stalingrad*, 124–26. A translation of the latter is available online via Stalingrad.net, http://web .archive.org/web/20120406075705/http://www.stalingrad.net/german-hq/hitler-directives /dir45.html.

27. It has been suggested that Hitler also hoped to benefit from the psychological impact of the capture of "Stalin's city," but there is little evidence to support this idea. His main purpose was to protect the flank of the drive into the Caucasus.

28. For a campaign of such earthshaking importance—indeed, the first war for oil—the literature on Operation Edelweiss is quite thin. The geography is remote, the campaign lacks the distinguishing feature of a great, culminating battle, and the entire undertaking lives in the shadow of the dramatic events unfolding to the north at Stalingrad. It is, in the parlance of military history cliché, the "forgotten war." The entire campaign receives only a single paragraph in John Keegan, *The Second World War* (New York: Penguin, 1989), for example. Far and away the best current source in English is Hayward, *Stopped at Stalingrad*, 152–82. Also essential is the short chapter 18, "Operation Edelweiss," in Ziemke and Bauer, *Moscow to Stalingrad*, 366–81, as well as Erickson, *Road to Stalingrad*, 376–81. Wilhelm Tieke, *The Caucasus and the Oil: The German-Soviet War in the Caucasus, 1942–43* (Winnipeg, Can.: J. J. Fedorowicz, 1995), is big, sprawling, detailed, and, unfortunately, far too disorganized to be the definitive work on the topic.

29. For the dazzling opening of the Caucasus campaign, see Citino, *Death of the Wehrmacht*, 227–33.

30. Ziemke and Bauer, *Moscow to Stalingrad*, 370–71, describe First Panzer Army "guided night and day by sheets of flame thousands of feet high."

31. For the sudden halt in the Caucasus, see Citino, *Death of the Wehrmacht*, 233–43.

32. Clark, *Barbarossa*, 229, 238.

33. Ibid., 228.

34. For maps and narrative of the Kalach Kessel, see "Die Schlacht im Don-Bogen westlich Kalatsch," in the popular magazine *Die Wehrmacht* 6, no. 18 (September 2, 1942): 19. For what Doerr calls Sixth Army's "last victory in the open field," see Doerr, *Feldzug nach Stalingrad*, 40–41.

35. For the lunge to the Volga, see Hayward, *Stopped at Stalingrad*, 187–88; Doerr, *Feldzug nach Stalingrad*, 44–45; and Ziemke and Bauer, *Moscow to Stalingrad*, 384.

36. The first great air raid on Stalingrad features prominently in every source on the battle. For the dramatic impact, see Alan Clark, *Barbarossa: The Russian-German Conflict, 1941–45* (New York: Quill, 1985), 216–17: "The effect was spectacular. Nearly every wooden building— including acres of workers' settlements on the outskirts—was burned down, and the flames made it possible to read a paper forty miles away." For the operational details, see Hayward, *Stopped at Stalingrad*, 188–89. The numbers of civilian dead, however, continues to be controversial. Many popular sources continue to say 40,000 dead. But this figure is harder and harder to sustain, especially in our modern environment, when the casualty statistics from

Allied bombing raids on German cities—a thousand plane raids by B-17 and B-24 bombers—are being routinely revised downward. We have now reached a point where civilian deaths during the fiery destruction of the great city of Dresden are said to be "just" 25,000. If that is so, then it is hard to imagine a much smaller German air force dropping a fraction of the payload of Allied bombers actually generating 40,000 civilian casualties in Stalingrad.

37. There is a vast literature on the fighting within Stalingrad. Soviet primary sources, which should be read and consulted with care, include the testimony of Marshal G. K. Zhukov, *Marshal Zhukov's Greatest Battles, Edited with an Introduction and Explanatory Comments by Harrison E. Salisbury* (New York: Harper & Row, 1969), and General V. I. Chuikov, *The Battle for Stalingrad* (New York: Holt, Rinehart and Winston, 1964). The latter is one of the most widely quoted books on the battle. See also Louis Rotundo, ed., *Battle for Stalingrad: The 1943 Soviet General Staff Study* (Washington, D.C.: Pergamon-Brassey's, 1989), although many readers, even quite well-informed ones, will find it tough going. For the Germans, neither Hitler nor his generals ever wrote a full narrative account, for obvious reasons. Walter Görlitz, ed., *Paulus: "Ich stehe hier auf Befehl!"* (Frankfurt, Ger.: Bernard & Graefe, 1960), is far more the work of editor Görlitz than of Paulus, although the former did have access to Paulus's "Nachlass, Briefen, und Dokumentation," as well as the cooperation of the field marshal's family. Nevertheless, it does print many of the pertinent documents and is worthwhile for that reason alone.

The journalistic and popular histories continue to be read. Begin with Alexander Werth, *The Year of Stalingrad: An Historical Record and a Study of Russian Mentality, Methods and Policies* (London: Hamish Hamilton, 1946), in particular, the "six main reasons" why the Germans were unable to take the city (196–97). Its analog from the German side is Heinz Schröter, *Stalingrad* (New York: E. P. Dutton, 1958), by a correspondent accredited to Sixth Army during the battle. It is a gritty and realistic account, so much so that Nazi propaganda minister Joseph Goebbels forbade its publication during the war. A recent addition to the journalistic literature is Antony Beevor and Luba Vinogradova, eds., *A Writer at War: Vasily Grossman with the Red Army, 1941–1945* (New York: Pantheon, 2005), which restores Grossman to his rightful place as one of the most passionate eyewitnesses to the "ruthless truth of war" on the Eastern Front. For his accounts of the Stalingrad fighting, see 110–212.

The popular literature is massive. William Craig, *Enemy at the Gates: The Battle for Stalingrad* (New York: Reader's Digest Press, 1973), is still a fine and readable work, episodic rather than thematic or chronological. More useful, yet still necessarily classified as popular literature due to the insufficiency of citation and bibliography are the works by V. E. Tarrant, *Stalingrad: Anatomy of an Agony* (London: Leo Cooper, 1992), and, the most recent word on the battle, Antony Beevor, *Stalingrad* (London: Viking, 1998). The latter will remain the standard narrative of the battle for many years.

38. Doerr, *Feldzug nach Stalingrad*, 52, writes, "The meter replaced the kilometer as a measure of distance."

39. For the 90 percent figure, which comes from a speech by General Alfred Jodl, see Wegner, *GOH*, "Der Krieg gegen die Sowjetunion, 1942–43," 994. Hitler went Jodl one better: "We have as good as got it," he told a group of his "old fighters" at the annual Bürgerbräukeller speech on November 8, the anniversary of the Beer Hall Putsch. "There are only a couple of small bits left." The army could be moving faster, Hitler added, but he wanted to avoid "a second Verdun." See Beevor, *Stalingrad*, 213.

40. Along with the street fighting, the Soviet counteroffensive has been the star of the show in the Stalingrad historiography. Until quite recently, however, very few scholars had access to the Soviet documents. For that reason alone, even the relatively short account in David M. Glantz and Jonathan House, "Operation Uranus: The Destruction of 6th Army," 129–47, in *When Titans Clashed: How the Red Army Stopped Hitler* (Lawrence: University Press of Kansas, 1999), was a signal event in the literature and is still the place to start. One awaits a larger study from Glantz on Stalingrad, to take its rightful place next to his works on Leningrad and Kursk.

Two readily available primary sources from the Soviet side, still worth consulting, are Zhukov, *Greatest Battles*, 105–94, and Marshal Andrei Yeremenko, "Battle of Stalingrad," in *Battles Hitler Lost: First-Person Accounts of World War II by Russian General on the Eastern Front* (New York: Richardson & Steirman, 1986), 62–75.

41.   For the impact of coalition warfare on the Battle of Stalingrad, see DiNardo, *Germany and the Axis Powers*, 136–57.

42.   The tanks of XXXXVIII Corps had been parked outdoors in frigid temperatures for months. Mice had nested in the tanks of the 2nd Panzer Division in order to escape the cold, and they had chewed through the insulation of the electric cables, thus preventing a number of tanks from starting. See Beevor, *Stalingrad*, 231, and Hayward, *Stopped at Stalingrad*, 227–28.

43.   Paulus's chilling dispatch is reprinted in its entirety in the appendices to Manfred Kehrig, *Stalingrad: Analyse und Dokumentation einer Schlacht* (Stuttgart, Ger.: Deutsche Verlags-Anstalt, 1974).

44.   Preeminent among them was the commander of LI Corps, General Walther von Seydlitz-Kurzbach. For Seydlitz's tortured story, see his memoir, Walther von Seydlitz, *Stalingrad: Konflikt und Konsequenz: Erinnerungen* (Oldenburg, Ger.: Stalling, 1977).

45.   The principal primary source here is Manstein, *Lost Victories*, especially chapter 12, "The Tragedy of Stalingrad," 289–366, who blamed Hitler above him and Sixth Army beneath him for the destruction of the *Kessel*. Paulus, especially, comes in for heavy fire for refusing to take the decision to cooperate with the relief offensive. Not everyone has been satisfied with Manstein's explanation. See Joachim Wieder, *Stalingrad und die Verantwortung des Soldaten* (Munich, Ger.: Nymphenburger, 1962), as well as the expanded and updated edition, Joachim Wieder and Heinrich Graf von Einsiedel, eds., *Stalingrad: Memories of Hell* (London: Arms and Armour, 1993). Wieder survived the battle and Soviet captivity to write his memoirs in 1962; Einsiedel, a Luftwaffe lieutenant, was taken prisoner and joined the anti-Nazi *National-komitee Freies Deutschland*. He helped edit a new edition of the book in 1993, which spends a great deal of time haranguing Manstein.

46.   The sixtieth anniversary of El Alamein in 2002 triggered a wave of new literature on the battle. See, for example, Jon Latimer, *Alamein* (Cambridge, MA: Harvard University Press, 2002); John Bierman and Colin Smith, *Battle of Alamein* (London: Viking, 2002); and Stephen Bungay, *Alamein* (London: Aurum, 2002). See also the extremely sophisticated operational history in Niall Barr, *The Pendulum of War: The Three Battles of El Alamein* (Woodstock, NY: Overlook, 2005), which will likely be the standard work on British arms in the desert for some time to come. There is still a very fine body of older literature to consult, however. See, for example, Fred Majdalany, *The Battle of El Alamein: Fortress in the Sand* (Philadelphia: Lippincott, 1965), and Correlli Barnett, *The Desert Generals* (Bloomington: Indiana University Press, 1989). Also essential is the German-language memoir, Erwin Rommel, *Krieg ohne Hass* (Heidenheim, Ger.: Verlag Heidenheimer Zeitung, 1950). B. H. Liddell Hart, ed., *The Rommel Papers* (New York: Harcourt, Brace, 1953), is the English translation.

47.   For Gazala, see Rommel, *Krieg ohne Hass*, 109–74, and the parallel passages in Hart, *Rommel Papers*, 189–232. See also F. W. von Mellenthin, *Panzer Battles: A Study of the Employment of Armor in the Second World War* (New York: Ballantine, 1956), 107–37. Mellenthin was Rommel's intelligence chief.

48.   For a solid biographical profile, see Michael Carver, "Montgomery," in *Churchill's Generals*, ed., John Keegan (New York: Grove Weidenfeld, 1991), 148–65, as well as Robert M. Citino, *Armored Forces: History and Sourcebook* (Westport, CT: Greenwood, 1994), 258–61. Nigel Hamilton, *Monty*, 3 vols. (London: Hamish Hamilton, 1981–86), is still the standard work.

49.   In Anglophone histories, this is usually termed the Second Battle of El Alamein, though the Germans normally call it the "Third," counting the Battle of Alam el Halfa as the "Second." For operational details, see the best currently available account of the battle in Barr, *Pendulum of War*, 307–405. The accounts by both Barrie Pitt, *The Crucible of War: Year of Alamein, 1942* (London: Jonathan Cape, 1982), 297–453, and Barnett, *Desert Generals*, 249–313, are still

extremely useful, the latter being highly critical of Montgomery's generalship at Alamein, which is the book's principal thesis. Michael Carver participated in the battle, and both his *Dilemmas of the Desert War: a New Look at the Libyan Campaign, 1940–1942* (London: Batsford, 1986) and *El Alamein* are valuable, the former for the matrix of factors that generated Alamein and the latter for its reminder to be wary of "wisdom after the event" (195–205).

50. Major Lofton Henderson was a U.S.M.C. aviator killed in action at the Battle of Midway. A student seeking the overall shape of a campaign as long and as complex as Guadalcanal, which stretched from August 1942 to February 1943, should start with the volume in the U.S. Army's Green Book series *The U.S. Army in World War II*: John Miller Jr., *Guadalcanal: The First Offensive* (Washington, D.C.: Center of Military History, 1949). From here, see the relevant portions of Samuel Eliot Morison, *History of the United States Naval Operations in World War II*, 15 vols. (Boston: Little, Brown, 1947–62). This work is not only a useful history but also a priceless gem of American literature, written by an experienced naval officer and a brilliant stylist. Those seeking a shorter summary will turn to Morison's *The Two-Ocean War: A Short History of the United States Navy in the Second World War* (Boston: Little, Brown, 1963), 164–214. For incisive criticism of the U.S. war in the Pacific, see Ronald H. Spector, *The Eagle Against the Sun: The American War with Japan* (New York: Free Press, 1985), 184–219. No one knows the documents in greater detail, and no one understands how to level the most severe criticism of the wartime actors in a more judicious way. See also Richard B. Frank, *Guadalcanal: The Definitive Account of the Landmark Battle* (New York: Random House, 1990). Historians often speak of "making a case" in their books, but few do it as well as Frank. He is a lawyer by trade, as well as a meticulous historian.

51. For a clear explanation of these arguments, based both on strategic constraints and interservice rivalry, see Spector, *Eagle Against the Sun*, 184–87. Spector is explicit in going beyond merely personalist arguments, painting MacArthur not merely as a thoughtless egotist but also as a figure who understood the theater in which he is operating: "The general must have known all along that he could not launch a quick campaign against Rabaul, even given all the troops and warships he had asked for" (187). The real issue, Spector notes, was to win a "bureaucratic success" in a brutal—even Darwinian—war for limited resources.

52. Still the clearest discussion of the strategic decisions involved here is Miller, *Guadalcanal*, 1–21. In order to place the entire Task One target area (Guadalcanal, Tulagi, and Florida Islands) completely within the Navy's zone, the Joint Chiefs moved the boundary between the South Pacific Area (Navy) and Southwest Pacific Area (Army) 1 degree to the west on August 1, 1942.

53. Spector, *Eagle Against the Sun*, 206.

54. For an overview of the U.S. disaster at Savo Island, see Morison, *Two-Ocean War*, 167–77. For a meticulous accounting of details of "the most humiliating defeat suffered by the United States Navy in World War Two," see Frank, *Guadalcanal*, 83–123.

55. It is a fact that very few scholars in the English-speaking world who analyze Japanese strategy actually read Japanese. For one scholar who can actually read what Japan was trying to do in World War II, see Edward J. Drea, *Japan's Imperial Army: Its Rise and Fall, 1853–1945* (Lawrence: University Press of Kansas, 2009). For the critical shipping issue, see 229–30.

56. See the comment by an air intelligence operator on Guadalcanal: "Then we got the news that the Old Man had been made COMSOPAC . . . ! One minute we were too limp with malaria to crawl out of our foxholes; the next, we were running around whooping like kids." Quoted in Evan Thomas, *Sea of Thunder: Four Commanders and the Last Great Naval Campaign, 1941–1945* (New York: Simon & Schuster, 2006), 69.

57. Miller, *Guadalcanal*, 141–42.

58. For discussion of the cultural origin of the Japanese army's infantry doctrine, especially its sense of a "romanticized imperial past," the way it "ritualized death," and "popularized the concept of death before dishonor," see Drea, *Japan's Imperial Army*, 46, 48, and 119.

59. Richard Tregaskis, *Guadalcanal Diary* (New York: Random House, 1943), 229 and 238.

1. The best account of Britain's trade patterns is in C. B. A. Behrens, *Merchant Shipping and the Demands of War* (London: HMSO, 1955), 190–97.

2. The problems of wartime food supply are covered ably in Lizzie Collingham, *The Taste of War: World War Two and the Battle for Food* (London: Allen Lane, 2011); on Britain, see chapter 5; on Germany, chapter 8.

3. R. W. Coakley, and R. M. Leighton, *Global Logistics and Strategy*, 2 vols. (Washington, D.C.: Center for Military History, 1955–68), 1:638.

4. The most comprehensive account of the Norway campaign is in Bernd Stegemann, "Operation Weserübung," in *Germany and the Second World War*, vol. 2, *Germany's Initial Conquests in Europe*, ed. Klaus Maier (Oxford: Oxford University Press, 1991), 206–19. See too Anthony Martienssen, ed., *Fuehrer Conferences on Naval Affairs 1939–1945* (London: Greenhill Books, 1990), 91. The documents reproduced in the latter provide a very full account of the naval war from the German side.

5. For the account of the battle, see Holger Herwig and David Bercuson, *Bismarck* (London: Hutchinson, 2002).

6. Details on submarine building and operational strength can be found in David F. White, *Bitter Ocean: The Battle of the Atlantic, 1939–1945* (New York: Simon & Schuster, 2006), 297–98.

7. The best account of the German air-sea war is Sönke Neitzel, *Der Einsatz der deutschen Luftwaffe über dem Atlantik und der Nordsee 1939–1945* (Bonn, Ger.: Bernard & Graefe Verlag, 1995). For this material see pt. 6, 121–49.

8. Winston Churchill, *The Second World War*, vol. 2 (London: Cassell, 1951), 529.

9. Details in Friedrich Ruge, *Der Seekrieg: The German Navy's Story 1939–1945* (Annapolis, MD: U.S. Naval Institute, 1957), 43–44; losses in Stephen Roskill, *The War at Sea, 1939–1945*, 3 vols. (London: HMSO, 1961), 3: pt. 2, 479. On German decrypts, the best account is David Kahn, *Hitler's Spies: German Military Intelligence in World War II* (London: Macmillan, 1978), 218–19. The German B-Dienst (serving Naval Intelligence) lost access to British naval codes in August 1940, but after seven weeks, the new codes were broken and were read regularly, down to the middle months of 1943.

10. Elliot Roosevelt, ed., *The Roosevelt Letters*, vol. 3, *1928–1945* (London: George G. Harrap, 1952), 364, Roosevelt to Churchill, May 4, 1941.

11. Churchill, *Second World War*, 3:107–9. For Churchill's views on the vital nature of the sea war, see his personal secretary John Colville's *The Fringes of Power: Downing Street Diaries, 1939–1955* (New York: Norton, 1986), 358, 372. Colville is an excellent primary source for observing Churchill at work during 1940 and 1941.

12. White, *Bitter Ocean*, 132–33.

13. In the early postwar histories of the battle, this was a secret that could still not be told; not until the late 1970s were the details of British intelligence successes revealed fully and the explanation for the sudden reprieve in the Atlantic explained. Two very good accounts written after the secret of Enigma had been revealed are Patrick Beesly, *Very Special Intelligence: The Story of the Admiralty's Operational Intelligence Centre, 1939–1945* (New York: Doubleday, 1978), 88–95, and John Winton, *Ultra at Sea* (London: William Heinemann, 96–101. The official histories written by Stephen Roskill in the 1950s and 1960s have excellent detail on all aspects of the tactical and operational war but could say nothing about Enigma/Ultra (online versions of vol. 1 and vol. 2 are available at Hyperwar.org).

14. Winton, *Ultra at Sea*, 103–7; David Kahn, *Seizing the Enigma: The Race to Break the German U-Boat Codes* (Boston: Houghton Mifflin, 1991), 214–17. More recently Michael Smith, *Station X: The Codebreakers of Bletchley Park* (London: C4 Books, 1998), 108–23.

15. Details of Operation Drumbeat (*Paukenschlag*) in Ruge, *Der Seekrieg*, 252–55. There is good detail in Michael Hadley, *U-Boats Against Canada* (Toronto: McGill-Queens University Press, 1990), 52–55, and in Marc Milner, "Anglo-American Naval Co-operation in the Second

World War," in *Maritime Strategy and the Balance of Power*, ed. John Hattendorf and Robert S. Jordan (London: Macmillan, 1989), 252–54. On intelligence issues, see Beesly, *Very Special Intelligence*, 102–10.

16. Jürgen Rohwer, *The Critical Convoy Battles of March 1943* (London: Ian Allen, 1977), 36; Beesly, *Very Special Intelligence*, 182. Rohwer's book is an excellent introduction to the convoy system and the German operational approach to submarine warfare.

17. Beesly, *Very Special Intelligence*, 148–51; Karl Dönitz, *Memoirs: Ten Years and Twenty Days* (London: Cassell, 1959), 253, 315.

18. *Fuehrer Conferences on Naval Affairs*, 331–32, Conference of 31 May 1943. Operational submarine losses were running at 30 percent a month.

19. The standard book on RAF Coastal Command is Christina Goulter, *Forgotten Offensive: Royal Air Force Coastal Command's Anti-Shipping Campaign, 1940–1945* (London: Frank Cass, 1995). Goulter argues a convincing case that Coastal Command, once it was armed with enough effective aircraft, played an important but unacknowledged role in the war against German submarines and coastal vessels. See too John Buckley, *Air Power in the Age of Total War* (London: UCL Press, 1999), 137–38, who shows that German submarine losses due to Coastal Command increased from 3 percent in 1941 to 35 percent in 1943.

20. The "Liberty Ship" began life as a small cargo vessel capable of carrying ten thousand tons, ordered by the British in 1940 to replace merchant ship losses. By late 1941, there was a program for 2,700 ships. They were mass-produced in U.S. shipyards using prefabricated sections that were welded together. The first ships took 355 days to build, but by 1943, production time was down to an average of 41 days. See Francis Walton, *Miracle of World War II* (New York: Macmillan, 1956), 75–79.

21. British output can be found in *What Britain Has Done: 1939–1945* (London: Atlantic Books, 2007), reprinted from the Ministry of Information original, 105–6. American figures are from White, *Bitter Ocean*, 201–4; Frederic C. Lane, *Ships for Victory: A History of Shipbuilding under the US Maritime Commission in World War II* (Baltimore: Johns Hopkins Press, 1951), 5–7; Morison, *History of United States Naval Operations*, vol. 15, *Supplement* (Boston: Little, Brown, 1962).

22. Milner, "Battle of the Atlantic," 46, 54–55; B. B. Schofield, "The Defeat of the U-Boats During World War II," *Journal of Contemporary History* 16 (1981): 120–24.

23. John Buckley, "Air Power and the Battle of the Atlantic," *Journal of Contemporary History* 28 (1993): 146–50; Brian Johnson, *The Secret War* (London: BBC Books, 1978), 237–38.

24. For a good introduction to the radar story, see Guy Hartcup, *The Effect of Science on the Second World War* (Basingstoke, UK: Palgrave, 2003), 18–34; the most detailed account is in Derek Howse, *Radar at Sea: The Royal Navy in World War II* (London: Macmillan, 1993), 99–109, 132–43

25. The best book on Horton is Rear Admiral W. S. Chalmers, *Max Horton and the Western Approaches* (London: Hodder & Stoughton, 1954), though the author is hardly impartial in his assessment of Horton's worth.

26. On the role of aircraft and other tactical changes, see Chalmers, *Max Horton*, 186–94; Buckley "Air Power," 155; Roskill, *War at Sea* (London: HMSO, 1961), 2:363–64, 366–67. A good account of the problems faced by the maritime air forces against the submarine is in Brereton Greenhous, Stephen Harris, William Johnston, and William Rawling, *The Crucible of War 1939–1945: The Official History of the Royal Canadian Air Force*, vol. 3 (Toronto: University of Toronto Press, 1994), 389–99.

27. Ralph Bennett, *Behind the Battle: Intelligence in the War with Germany 1939–1945* (London: Sinclair-Stevenson, 1994), 168–202. Bennett considers the breakthrough in 1943 as "decisive" (182).

28. White, *Bitter Ocean*, 293, gives a figure of 77 losses of submarines in Atlantic waters from June to December 1943.

29. Air Force Historical Research Agency, Maxwell AFB, CD A5835, Eighth Air Force, Growth, Development and Operations, December 1942–December 1943, Personnel Status, exhibit 1.

30. Roskill, *War at Sea*, vol. 3, pt. 2 (London: HMSO, 1961), 442–45, appendix ZZ, "Annual Allied Merchant Ship Losses"; submarines in White, *Bitter Ocean*, 298. The German submarine arm had 437 boats in April–June 1944.

31. William Donald, *Stand by for Action: The Memoirs of a Small Ship Commander in World War II* (Barnsley, UK: Seaforth Publishing, 2009), 93–96.

32. On destruction of French towns, see Andrew Knapp and Lindsey Dodd, " 'How Many Frenchmen Did You Kill?': British Bombing Policy Towards France (1940–1945)," *French History* 22 (2008): 474–80; prepublication version available online, http://centaur.reading.ac.uk/27959/1/DoddKnappBombFrance070708a.pdf.

   Air Marshal Sir Arthur Harris had his own views on the pointless character of raids on the pens. See Arthur Harris, *Bomber Offensive* (London: Collins, 1947), 136–37.

33. Richard Overy, *The Air War, 1939–1945* (New York: Potomac Books, 2007), 120.

34. Tami Davis Biddle, *Rhetoric and Reality in Air Warfare: The Evolution of British and American Ideas About Strategic Bombing* (Princeton, NJ: Princeton University Press, 2002), 162–70; Richard Overy, "Allied Bombing and the Destruction of German Cities," in *A World at Total War: Global Conflict and the Politics of Destruction*, ed. Roger Chickering, Stig Förster, and Bernd Greiner (Cambridge: Cambridge University Press, 2005), 277–80; Williamson Murray, "Strategic Bombing: The British, American and German Experiences," in *Military Innovation in the Interwar Period*, ed. Murray and Allan Millett (Cambridge: Cambridge University Press, 1996), 116–27.

35. The best account is Neville Jones, *The Beginnings of Strategic Air Power: A History of the British Bomber Force, 1923–1929* (London: Frank Cass, 1987).

36. Hayward Hansell, *The Air Plan That Defeated Hitler* (Atlanta: Higgins McArthur, 1972), 298–307; Robert Futrell, *Ideas, Concepts, Doctrine: A History of Basic Thinking in the United States Air Force* (Maxwell AFB, AL: Air University Press, 1971), 59–61.

37. Among the recent crop of critical histories, see Randall Hansen, *Fire and Fury: The Allied Bombing of Germany 1942–1945* (New York: NALCaliber, 2009); Martin van Creveld, *The Age of Airpower* (New York: Public Affairs, 2011). A more positive view can be found in Mark Clodfelter, *Beneficial Bombing: The Progressive Foundations of American Air Power, 1917–1945* (Lincoln: Nebraska University Press, 2010)

38. On bombing in World War I, see Richard Overy, "Strategic Bombing Before 1939: Doctrine, Planning and Operations," in *Case Studies in Strategic Bombardment*, ed. R. Cargill Hall (Washington, D.C.: Air Force History Program, 1998), 13–24, and Biddle, *Rhetoric and Reality*, 35–48, 53–56.

39. The best account of the moral problem that bombing presented between the wars is Joel Hayward, "Air Power, Ethics, and Civilian Immunity During the First World War and Its Aftermath," *Global War Studies* 7 (2010): 102–30. For a contrary view, see too Peter Gray, "The Gloves Will Have to Come Off: A Reappraisal of the Legitimacy of the RAF Bomber Offensive against Germany," *Air Power Review* 13 (2010): 9–40; a prepublication version is available online, ccadd.org.uk/uploads/International%20Conference/11paperGrayW.doc.

40. Martin Gilbert, *Finest Hour: Winston S. Churchill 1939–1941* (London: Heinemann, 1983), 329–30, 334, 342–47; the cabinet discussions are in Martin Gilbert, ed., *The Churchill War Papers*, vol. 2, *May 1940–December 1940* (London: Heinemann, 1994), 17–18, 25, 38–41.

41. The directive can be found in Charles Webster and Noble Frankland, *The Strategic Air Offensive Against Germany*, 4 vols. (London: HMSO, 1961), 135–40.

42. For a critical analysis of RAF intentions, see Richard Overy, " 'The 'Weak Link'? Bomber Command and the German Working Class, 1940–1945," *Labour History Review* 77 (2012): 11–34.

43. There are several ways of interpreting American views of the ethics of bombing. Conrad Crane, "Evolution of U.S. Strategic Bombing of Urban Areas," *Historian* 50 (1987): 14–39; Ronald Schaffer, "American Military Ethics in World War II: The Bombing of German Civilians," *Journal of American History* 67 (1980): 318–34. For a more polemical view, see Douglas

P. Lackey, "The Bombing Campaign of the USAAF," in *Terror from the Sky: The Bombing of German Cities in World War II*, ed. Igor Primoratz (New York: Berghahn Books, 2010), 41–45. On the search for precision, the standard book is Stephen McFarland, *America's Pursuit of Precision Bombing, 1910–1945* (Washington D.C.: Smithsonian, 1995), 165–90.

44. Claudia Baldoli and Andrew Knapp, *Forgotten Blitzes: France and Italy Under Allied Air Attack, 1940–1945* (London: Continuum, 2012), 20–25.

45. On problems of accuracy, see Randall Wakelam, *The Science of Bombing: Operational Research in RAF Bomber Command* (Toronto: Toronto University Press, 2009), 19–23, and Robert Ehlers, *Targeting the Reich: Air Intelligence and the Allied Bombing Campaign* (Lawrence: University Press of Kansas, 2009), 116–18. David Bensusan Butt was on the staff of the Cabinet statistical section.

46. See the estimates in United States Strategic Bombing Survey, *Over-all Report: European Theater* (Washington, D.C.: Government Printing Office, September 30, 1945), 25–26, 37–38, 73–74.

47. The standard biography of Harris is now Henry Probert, *Bomber Harris: His Life and Times* (London: Greenhill Books, 2006). On his assumption of command, 126–40. On the initiation of the Eighth Air Force, James Parton, *"Air Force Spoken Here": General Ira Eaker & the Command of the Air* (Bethesda, MD: Adler & Adler, 1986), 128–34; Richard G. Davis, *Carl A. Spaatz and the Air War in Europe* (Washington D.C.: Smithsonian, 1992), 67–71.

48. The best account of the acreage strategy is Tami Davis Biddle, "Bombing by the Square Yard: Sir Arthur Harris at War, 1942–1945," *International History Review* 21 (1999): 626–64.

49. On the development of the target marking force, the standard account is Hugh Melinsky, *Forming the Pathfinders: The Career of Air Vice-Marshal Sydney Bufton* (Stroud, UK: History Press, 2010). See too Wakelam, *Science of Bombing*, 75–79.

50. The standard book on electronic warfare is Alfred Price, *Instruments of Darkness: The History of Electronic Warfare 1939–1945* (London: Greenhill Books, 2005), which focuses principally on the bombing and air defense aspects. By far the best book on the German defensive system is Edward Westermann, *Flak: German Anti-Aircraft Defenses, 1914–1945* (Lawrence: University Press of Kansas, 2001).

51. The official history has a full account of AWPD-42. See Wesley Craven and James Cate, *The Army Air Forces in World War II:* vol. 2 (originally published Chicago: University of Chicago Press, 1949; reprint Washington, D.C.: Office of Air Force History, 1978), 277–93. AWPD stands for Air War Plans Division.

52. For details of all Eighth Air Force raids, see Roger Freeman, *The Mighty Eighth War Diary* (London: Jane's, 1981).

53. On American bombing compared with British, see the pioneering article by W. Hayes Park, " 'Precision' and 'Area' Bombing: Who Did Which, and When?," *Journal of Strategic Studies* 18 (1995): 145–74. See too Robert Ehrhart, "The European Theater of Operations, 1943–1945," in *Piercing the Fog: Intelligence and Army Air Forces Operations in World War II*, ed. John Kreis (Washington D.C.: Air Force History Program, 1996).

54. Casablanca Directive reproduced in Webster and Frankland, *Strategic Air Offensive*, 4, 153–54.

55. Pointblank Directive in ibid., 158–60, and Biddle, *Rhetoric and Reality*, 215–22. On the switch to the "intermediate" targets, see Stephen McFarland and Wesley Newton, "The American Strategic Air Offensive Against Germany in World War II," in *Case Studies in Strategic Bombardment*, ed. Cargill Hall, 192–96.

56. Baldoli and Knapp, *Forgotten Blitzes*, 20–22, 130–33. A good summary of the effects of bombing is Claudia Baldoli and Marco Fincardi, "Italian Society Under Allied Bombs: Propaganda, Experience, and Legend, 1940–1945," *Historical Journal* 52 (2009): 1017–38. On establishment of the Fifteenth U.S. Air Force, see Richard Davis, *Bombing the European Axis Powers* (Maxwell AFB, AL: Air University Press, 2006), 198–201.

57. For details of all Bomber Command raids, see Martin Middlebrook and Chris Everitt, *The Bomber Command War Diaries* (Leicester, UK: Midland Publishing, 2000).

58. The most recent and balanced account of Operation Gomorrah is Keith Lowe, *Inferno: The Devastation of Hamburg, 1943* (London: Viking, 2007). The impression is often given that all 37,000 victims died on the night of the firestorm, but this is the total over the week of bombing. The first major raid, on July 24–25, killed 10,289 people; the firestorm on the night of July 27–28 killed 18,474; and the July 29–30 bombing claimed an additional 9,666. The remaining deaths came from smaller RAF and USAAF operations.

59. On the stalemate in autumn 1943, see McFarland and Newton, "American Strategic Air Offensive," 193–204. On Schweinfurt, Davis, *Bombing the European Axis*, 158–60, 182–84, and Donald Miller, *Eighth Air Force: The American Bomber Crews in Britain* (London: Aurum, 2007), 194–205, 208–13.

60. Source: Heinz Knocke, *I Flew for the Führer* (London: Evans Brothers, 1953), 155–57.

61. On the shakeup in command, see Davis, *Carl A. Spaatz*, 267–80. On Eaker's disappointed reaction to his transfer to the Mediterranean, Parton, *"Air Force Spoken Here,"* 335–46.

62. The finest account of the counter-air campaign is Stephen McFarland and Wesley Newton, *To Command the Sky: The Battle for Air Superiority over Germany, 1942–1944* (Washington D.C.: Smithsonian, 1991). A profile of Kepner is on 117–18.

63. Library of Congress, Spaatz Papers, Box 84, Spaatz to Doolittle, January 26, 1944.

64. Charts on aircraft ranges from 1943–44 can be found in Davis, *Carl A. Spaatz*, 362–63; on the new escort tactics, see 358–61. Changes in tactics for escort are also discussed in McFarland and Newton, *Command the Sky*, 140–42.

65. Ian McLachlan and Russell J. Zorn, *Eighth Air Force Bomber Stories* (Yeovil, UK: Patrick Stephens, 1991), 95–96.

66. Westermann, *Flak*, 234–35.

67. Figures from AFHRA, CD A5835, Eighth Air Force tactical development, 1942–1945, 99.

68. There is good detail on German combat tactics in Library of Congress, Eaker Papers, Box I:35, "Decline of the G.A.F." There is a very useful set of essays by Luftwaffe commanders on the campaign in 1944 in David Isby, ed., *Fighting the Bombers: The Luftwaffe's Struggle Against the Allied Bomber Offensive* (London: Greenhill Books, 2003).

69. On the arguments over transportation versus oil, see Walter W. Rostow, *Pre-Invasion Bombing Strategy: General Eisenhower's Decision of March 25, 1944* (Aldershot, Hants, UK: Gower, 1981). See too Solly Zuckerman, *From Apes to Warlords: The Autobiography of Solly Zuckerman* (London: Hamish Hamilton, 1978), 216–45. Zuckerman was the chief architect of the Transportation Plan. On Spaatz's reaction, see Davis, *Carl A. Spaatz*, 345–55.

70. An excellent account of the decline of Luftwaffe fighting power can be found in Williamson Murray, *Luftwaffe* (London: George Allen & Unwin, 1985), 211–19.

71. On June 6 German Air Fleet 3 in northern France had just 176 serviceable aircraft against around 12,000 in the Allied air forces. Air superiority was ensured, though the conquest of northern France still took much longer than had been hoped.

72. On the development of jets and other German scientific developments, see Ulrich Albrecht, "Military Technology and National Socialist Ideology," in *Science, Technology and National Socialism*, ed. Monika Renneberg and Mark Walker (Cambridge: Cambridge University Press, 1994), 95–125.

73. Figures in Davis, *Carl A. Spaatz*, appendix 8; Probert, *Bomber Harris*, 305–6.

74. For a detailed account of the impact of bombing on rail transportation, see Alfred Mierzejewski, *The Collapse of the German War Economy: Allied Power and the German National Railway* (Chapel Hill, NC: North Carolina University Press, 1988), appendices A3–A4, figure A1, 191–92, 198. On oil, see the detailed tables in Webster and Frankland, *Strategic Air Offensive*, 4:507–11.

75. Although just one among many damaging raids, the Dresden operation continues to stir fierce debate. The best introduction is Paul Addison and Jeremy Crang, eds., *Firestorm: The Bombing of Dresden, 1945* (London: Pimlico, 2006). The most controversial essay is by Donald Bloxham, "Dresden as a War Crime," 180–208. For two essays that deal with Dresden

and are critical of the ethics of bombing, see Ronald Schaffer, "The Bombing Campaigns in World War II: The European Theater," and Robert Moeller, "The Bombing War in Germany, 2005–1940: Back to the Future?," in *Bombing Civilians: A Twentieth-Century History*, ed. Yuki Tanaka and Marilyn Young (New York: New Press, 2009), 30–76. On the Dresden raid itself, the standard work is Frederick Taylor, *Dresden: Tuesday 13 February 1945* (London: Bloomsbury, 2004). Taylor argues that Dresden was an entirely legitimate target.

76. The best account of the work of the bombing survey is Gian Gentile, *How Effective Is Strategic Bombing? Lessons Learned from World War II to Kosovo* (New York: New York University Press, 2000). On the British survey, the best account is Zuckerman, *Apes to Warlords*, 324–44. There is a useful introduction in Gordon Daniels, *A Guide to the Reports of the United States Strategic Bombing Survey* (London: Royal Historical Society, 1981). The British overall report has been reproduced in Sebastian Cox, ed., *The Strategic Air War Against Germany: The Official Report of the British Bombing Survey Unit* (London: Frank Cass, 1998).

77. United States Strategic Bombing Survey, *Over-All Report (European War)* (Washington D.C.: Government Printing Office, September 30, 1945), 25–26, 37–38, 73–74. See too Gentile, *How Effective Is Strategic Bombing?*, 55–56. There is an interesting case made for bombing as a matter of diminishing returns. See Jürgen Brauer and Hubert van Tuyll, *Castles, Battles and Bombs: How Economics Explains Military History* (Chicago: University of Chicago Press, 2008), 211–3, 217–19.

78. On the interrogation material, see Library of Congress, Spaatz Papers, Box 68, USSTAF HQ, "The Allied Offensive Against Germany and Principal Criticisms by the Enemy Leaders."

79. On the impact of bombing on German society, there is a great deal of literature. An older but still useful history is Earl Beck, *Under the Bombs: The German Home Front, 1942–1945* (Lexington: Kentucky University Press, 1986). There is a good summary in Richard Evans, *The Third Reich at War* (London: Allen Lane, 2008). The best recent analysis is Stephan Glienke, "The Allied Air War and German Society," in *Bombing, States and Peoples in Western Europe, 1940–1945*, ed. Claudia Baldoli, Andrew Knapp, and Richard Overy (London: Continuum, 2011), 184–205.

80. There is still much dispute about whether the bombing of Rome on July 19 contributed directly to the overthrow of Mussolini six days later. On the debate, see Claudia Baldoli, "Bombing the Eternal City," *History Today* 62, no. 5 (May 2012): 11–15.

81. Behrens, *Merchant Shipping*, 178.

82. British losses found in the National Archives (London), AIR 20/2025, Casualties of RAF, Dominion and Allied Personnel, 31 May 1947; Canadian losses in Greenhous et al., *Crucible of War*, 864; U.S. losses in Davis, *Carl A. Spaatz*, appendix 4, appendix 9.

Chapter 3: Waging Global War

1. The pertinent volume in the U.S. Army's Green Book series *The U.S. Army in World War II* continues to be indispensable: Maurice Matloff, *Strategic Planning for Coalition Warfare, 1943–1944* (Washington, D.C.: Center of Military History, 1959).

2. The best book on military relations between the Wehrmacht and its allied armies is DiNardo, *Germany and the Axis Powers*.

3. For the weak state of the German front after Stalingrad, with special attention to the "groups" (*Gruppen*), see Horst Scheibert, *Zwischen Don und Donez* (Neckargemünd, Ger.: Kurt Vowinckel Verlag, 1961), 25–29.

4. The indispensable work on all the Soviet winter offensives of 1942–43 (Little Saturn, the Ostrogozhk-Rossosh operation, Operation Gallop, and Operation Star) is David M. Glantz, *From the Don to the Dnepr: Soviet Offensive Operations, December 1942–August 1943* (London: Frank Cass, 1991). Glantz and House, *When Titans Clashed*, continues to be useful as an operational précis.

5. Carl Wagener, *Heeresgruppe Süd: Der Kampf im Süden der Ostfront, 1941–1945* (Bad Neuheim, Ger.: Podzun, 1967), 215.

6. The primary source on the winter counteroffensive of 1943 is Erich von Manstein, *Verlorene Siege* (Bonn, Ger.: Athenaeum Verlag, 1955). The English translation is *Lost Victories*. There are two indispensable English-language works: Dana V. Sadarananda, *Beyond Stalingrad: Manstein and the Operations of Army Group Don* (Mechanicsburg, PA: Stackpole, 2009), and Glantz, *From the Don to the Dnepr*. See also Theodor Busse, "Der Winterfeldzug 1942/1943 in Südrussland," in *Nie ausser Dienst: Zum achtzigsten Geburtstag von Generfeldmarschall Erich von Manstein* (Köln, Ger.: Markus Verlagsgesellschaft, 1967).

7. For the *Rochade*, see Manstein, *Verlorene Siege*, 405. The term is translated, badly, as "leap-frogging" (*Lost Victories*, 374).

8. The standard English translation is Carl von Clausewitz, *On War*, edited and translated by Michael Howard and Peter Paret (Princeton, NJ: Princeton University Press, 1984), with introductory essays by Paret, Howard, and Bernard Brodie. See book 7, chapter 4, "The Diminishing Force of the Attack," 527; chapter 5, "The Culminating Point of the Attack," 28; and chapter 22, "The Culminating Point of Victory," 566–73.

9. Glantz, *From the Don to the Dnepr*, 146.

10. Colonel V. P. Morozov, "Warum der Angriff im Frühjahr im Donezbecken nicht zu Ende geführt wurde," *Wehrwissenschaftliche Rundschau* 14 (1964): 429.

11. See, among hundreds of references, Sadarananda, *Beyond Stalingrad*, 146: "Manstein's counterstroke had regained the initiative for the German aside and brought German forces back to the approximate line they held in the summer of 1942."

12. The Battle of Kursk has generated an enormous literature, although it is of uneven quality and has been badly shaken by a recent wave of long-overdue revisionism. A good place to start is Manstein, *Verlorene Siege*, 473–507. The version of events found in the English translation, *Lost Victories*, 443–49, is completely different and wholly inadequate, embracing a mere seven pages. Read Manstein's account in conjunction with Heinz Guderian, *Erinnerungen eines Soldaten* (Heidelberg, Ger.: Kurt Vowinckel, 1951), 253–84; the English translation is *Panzer Leader* (New York: Ballantine, 1957), 215–51. Mellenthin, *Panzer Battles*, 258–83, an account by the chief of staff of the XXXXVIII Panzer Corps during Citadel, only further muddies the waters; even basic questions—for example, which officers were present at the famous Munich Conference planning session in May 1943—receive different answers. See also Stephen H. Newton, ed., *Kursk: The German View: Eyewitness Reports of Operation Citadel by the German Commanders* (New York: Da Capo, 2002). Literature in English is copious, and runs the gamut from high scholarship to the more popular variety. Without a doubt, the leading scholarly work in English is David M. Glantz and Jonathan M. House, *The Battle of Kursk* (Lawrence: University Press of Kansas, 1999). On all counts—depth of operational detail, research, organization, engagement with the scholarly controversies—it is a towering achievement. Mungo Melvin, *Manstein: Hitler's Greatest General* (London: Weidenfeld & Nicolson, 2010), 347–81, is critical of the field marshal and concludes that "Manstein's memoir surely would have been all the better had he, just the once, acknowledged that he had been outfought at Kursk by a superior enemy" (381). Earl Ziemke, chapter 7, "Operation Zitadelle," in *Stalingrad to Berlin: The German Defeat in the East* (Washington, D.C.: Center of Military History, 1968), 118–42, still forms the standard scholarly narrative. Timothy P. Mulligan, "Spies, Ciphers and 'Zitadelle': Intelligence and the Battle of Kursk," *Journal of Contemporary History* 22, no. 2 (April 1987): 235–60, and David Thomas, "Foreign Armies East and German Military Intelligence in Russia 1941–45," *Journal of Contemporary History* 22, no. 2 (April 1987): 261–301, read together, effectively re-create the battle for intelligence in and around Kursk, like the operation itself, a decisive victory for the Soviet military. See also the pertinent portions of the German official history, *Das Deutsche Reich und der Zweite Weltkrieg* (hereafter *DRZWk*), vol. 8, *Die Ostfront 1943/44* (Munich, Ger.: Deutsche Verlags-Anstalt, 2007), pt. 1, Bernd Wegner, "Von Stalingrad nach Kursk," 1–79; pt. 2, Karl-Heinz Frieser, "Die Schlacht im

Kursker Bogen," 81–208; and pt. 3, Bernd Wegner, "Die Aporie des Krieges," 209–74. Together these three sections add up to a major scholarly monograph on Kursk, its origins, course, and aftermath, written by two of the deans of operational military history in Germany.

Three final works deserve mention. Walter S. Dunn Jr., *Kursk: Hitler's Gamble, 1943* (Westport, CT: Praeger, 1997), reminds us that a great deal of very fine military history emerges from outside the traditional academy. As in everything he writes, Dunn displays meticulous scholarship here. M. K. Barbier, *Kursk: The Greatest Tank Battle, 1943* (Saint Paul, MN: MBI, 2002), is a true rarity: a profusely illustrated volume that contain serious and erudite scholarship. Dennis E. Showalter, *Hitler's Panzers: The Lightning Attacks That Revolutionized Warfare* (New York: Berkley Caliber, 2009), 253–73, combines sophisticated analysis of both the Wehrmacht and the Red Army—its "density, redundancy, management, movement" (273)—with writing so vivid that it makes you feel as if you were there. Showalter has been doing it so long and so successfully that we sometimes forget how gifted he is.

13. Manstein was still confident in 1943 about carrying out "offensives with far-flung goals" ("Offensiven mit weitgesteckten Zielen," *Verlorene Siege*, 481), while Hitler maintained that "we cannot carry out a great operation this year" ("Wir können in diesem Jahr keine grossen Operationen machen"). See *DRZWk*, vol. 8, pt. 1, Wegner, "Von Stalingrad nach Kursk," 61. For the context of Hitler's words, see the "Lagebesprechung vom 18.2.1943," reprinted verbatim in Eberhard Schwarz, *Die Stabilisierung der Ostfront nach Stalingrad: Mansteins Gegenschlag zwischen Donez und Dnjepr im Frühjahr 1943* (Göttingen, Ger.: Muster-Schmidt, 1986), Anlage C 1, 255.

14. See the tables in Glantz and House, *Battle of Kursk*, 65, and Piekalkiewicz, *Operation Citadel*, 111.

15. Glantz and House, *Battle of Kursk*, 61.

16. According to Piekalkiewicz, *Operation Citadel*, 110–11, the Luftwaffe concentrated about two-thirds of its total strength on the Eastern Front for the Kursk offensive.

17. *Battles Hitler Lost*, 92–93.

18. *DRZWk* vol. 8, pt. 2, Frieser, "Die Schlacht im Kursker Bogen," speaks both of "the hopeless initial situation" ("die aussichtlose deutsche Ausgangslage," 83) and a "frontal attack without surprise" ("Frontalangriff ohne Überraschungseffekt," 84).

19. See the account, for example, in Mellenthin, *Panzer Battles*, 271.

20. Glantz and House, *Battle of Kursk*, 193.

21. The successful Soviet operation known as Kutuzov has received scant attention from English-language historians compared with what they have lavished on the failed German Operation Citadel. Books on the German offensive toward Kursk number in the double digits, while Kutuzov has not a single dedicated scholarly monograph. It is easy to list the reasons: lack of Russian-language skills in the American scholarly community, tendency to identify with the Germans, difficulty in accessing the Russian-language sources and archives. Even the usually reliable Ziemke, *Stalingrad to Berlin*, rushes through Kutuzov in a few pages, 136–42. The scholar seeking sources will have to start with individual secondary works on the German-Soviet war, or on the Battle of Kursk, the best of which offer a chapter or two on the Soviet offensives toward Orel and Belgorod-Kharkov. See, for example, the seminal works by S. M. Shtemenko, *The Soviet General Staff at War, 1941–1945* (Moscow: Progress Publishers, 1981); John Erickson, *The Road to Berlin: Continuing the History of Stalin's War with Germany* (Boulder, CO: Westview, 1983), which offers a chapter on "Breaking the Equilibrium: Kursk and Its Aftermath" (87–135); Glantz and House, *Battle of Kursk*, 225–25; and David M. Glantz, "Soviet Military Strategy During the Second Period of War (November 1942–December 1943): A Reappraisal," *Journal of Military History* 60, no. 1 (January 1996): 115–50. Geoffrey Jukes, *Kursk: The Clash of Armor, July 1943* (New York: Ballantine, 1969), offers good coverage of Kutuzov, as does Barbier, *Kursk*.

22. Like Operation Kutuzov, the Belgorod-Kharkov operation (Operation Rumiantsev) is nearly missing in the English-language historiography. All the same sources listed in note 21, above,

are pertinent here as well. In this case, however, there is something nearly akin to a dedicated monograph: Glantz, "Operation 'Polkovodets Rumyantsev': The Belgorod-Khar'kov Operation, August 1943," in *From the Don to the Dnepr*, 215–365.

23. The volume in the U.S. Army's Green Book series *The U.S. Army in World War II* continues to be indispensable: George F. Howe, *Northwest Africa: Seizing the Initiative in the West* (Washington, D.C.: Center of Military History, 1957).

24. For Rommel's retreat after El Alamein, see the primary source: Rommel, *Krieg Ohne Hass*, 287–343. For the English translation, see the analogous sections in Hart, *Rommel Papers*, 337–96. For analysis from the British side, begin with the primary source, Bernard Law Montgomery, *Memoirs of Field-Marshal the Viscount Montgomery of Alamein* (London: Collins, 1958), 140–69, and then move on to the British official history volume, I.S.O. Playfair and C. J. C. Molony, *Destruction of the Axis Forces in Africa*, 215–38; Robin Neillands, *Eighth Army: The Triumphant Desert Army That Held the Axis at Bay from North Africa to the Alps, 1939–45* (New York: Overlook, 2004), 173–89; and C. L. Verney, *The Desert Rats: The 7th Armoured Division in World War II* (London: Hutchinson, 1954), 127–61.

25. General Lloyd R. Fredendall's father had been the sheriff of Laramie, Wyoming. See Douglas Porch, *The Path to Victory: The Mediterranean Front in World War II* (New York: Farrar, Straus and Giroux, 2004), 383. Rick Atkinson, *An Army at Dawn: The War in North Africa, 1942-1943* (New York: Henry Holt, 2002), 273, calls Fredendall père the "scourge of cattle rustlers" in the Wyoming Territory. Robert H. Berlin, *U.S. Army World War II Corps Commanders: A Composite Biography* (Fort Leavenworth, KS: U.S. Army Command and General Staff College, 1989), notes that twenty-four of the army's thirty-four wartime corps commanders attended West Point, and that twenty-three of them graduated. "The twenty-fourth, Lloyd R. Fredendall, was dismissed in both 1902 and 1903 for failing mathematics" (4–5).

26. The Battle of the Kasserine Pass has had its fair share of attention in the literature, far more than is typical for what amounted, in the end, to little more than a corps-sized encounter. For the voice of the manager, calm, orderly, and detail-oriented, start with Dwight D. Eisenhower, *Crusade in Europe* (Garden City, NY: Doubleday, 1948), 141–48. For the war fighter and operator seeking the knockout blow, see Rommel, *Krieg ohne Hass*, 347–62, which should be read in tandem with Albert Kesselring, *Soldat bis zum letzten Tag* (Bonn, Ger.: Athenäum, 1953), 202–6. Next, turn to the official histories on both sides. The four full chapters in Howe, *Seizing the Initiative in the West*, have enough operational detail to satisfy even the purist, but as always in the Green Books, there are moments when the narrative fails to cohere. From the German side, we turn now to *Das Deutsche Reich und der Zweite Weltkrieg*, vol. 8, *Die Ostfront: Der Krieg im Osten und an den Nebenfronten*, pt. 6, "Der Krieg an den Nebenfronten," especially Gerhard Schreiber, "Das Ende des nordafrikanischen Feldzugs und der Krieg in Italia 1943 bis 1945," 1100–62. Schreiber is a fine historian, known for his work on German relations with Italy, but he devotes barely two pages (1105–6) to the military encounter at Kasserine and, indeed, covers the entire vast war from Kasserine to the Po River Valley in just sixty. The operational detail is minimal throughout, certainly when compared with other entries in the *DRZWk* series (and other portions of this very volume) and must be considered a disappointment. Likewise, Tunisia is all but missing in action in both of the standard German-language histories of the General Staff: Walter Görlitz, *Der deutsche Generalstab: Geschichte und Gestalt, 1657–1945* (Frankfurt am Main, Ger.: Verlag der Frankfurter Hefte, 1950), and Waldemar Erfurth, *Die Geschichte des deutschen Generalstabes von 1918 bis 1945* (Berlin: Musterschmidt, 1957).

    For the professional literature, see Kurt E. Wolff, "Tank Battle in Tunisia," a reprint of a German article originally published in *Das Reich*, in *Military Review* 23, no. 6 (September 1943): 61–63; George F. Howe, "Faid—Kasserine: The German View," *Military Affairs* 13, no. 4 (Winter 1949): 216–22, a very useful abridgment of one of his Green Book chapters; George F. Ashworth, "Interior Lines in Tunisia," a reprint of a British analysis published in *Military Review* 23, no. 5 (August 1943): 30; Herman W. W. Lange, "Rommel at Thala," *Military Review*

41, no. 9 (September 1961): 72–84. A very fine unpublished work from the U.S. military community is the master's thesis by Mark T. Calhoun, "Defeat at Kasserine: American Armor Doctrine, Training, and Battle Command in Northwest Africa, World War II" (Fort Leavenworth, KS: U.S. Army Command and General Staff College, 2003). Calhoun rightly identifies the problems of the U.S. Army in Tunisia as "inferior equipment and illogical doctrine" (81).

And finally, for the story from the inside by a very fine U.S. Army officer who saw his command destroyed and was taken prisoner by the Germans, see the interview with John K. Waters, part of the Senior Officers Oral History Program, Project 80-4 (1980), 617–19. A copy is on file at the U.S. Army Heritage and Education Center (USAHEC) in Carlisle, Pennsylvania.

The monographic literature in English is copious. Pride of place goes to Macksey, *Crucible of Power*, 140–78; Watson, *Exit Rommel*; Martin Blumenson, *Kasserine Pass: Rommel's Bloody, Climactic Battle for Tunisia* (New York: Cooper Square Press, 2000); and of course, Atkinson, *Army at Dawn*. The author's writing in chapter 9 ("Kasserine") alone, 338–92, is worth the Pulitzer Prize. Other works to be read with profit include the sturdy operational account in Liddell Hart, *History of the Second World War* (Old Saybrook, CT: Konecky & Konecky, 1970), 402–10; Carlo D'Este, *World War II in the Mediterranean* (Chapel Hill, NC: Algonquin Books, 1990), 13–21; Porch, *Path to Victory*, 384–90; and Orr Kelly, *Meeting the Fox: The Allied Invasion of Africa, from Operation Torch to Kasserine Pass to Victory in Tunisia* (New York: John Wiley & Sons, 2002), 227–58.

27. For the confused state of U.S. defenses in the pass, see Howe, *Seizing the Initiative in the West*, 447–48, and Atkinson, *Army at Dawn*, 371–73.

28. For the battle in the pass, with good order of battle information for the Germans, see Watson, *Exit Rommel*, 91–93.

29. Quoted in Atkinson, *Army at Dawn*, 375.

30. Howe, *Seizing the Initiative in the West*, 466.

31. Atkinson, *Army at Dawn*, 183.

32. Rommel, *Krieg ohne Hass*, 357: "Die Amerikaner hatten sich vorzüglich geschlagen." See also his praise for the U.S. Army's "stubborn defense of the Kasserine Pass" ("die zähe Verteidigung des Kasserinepasses durch die Amerikaner"), 362.

33. For the post-Kasserine fighting in Tunisia, see Robert M. Citino, *The Wehrmacht Retreats: Fighting a Lost War, 1943* (Lawrence: University Press of Kansas, 2012), 98–104.

34. Most historians place the number of Axis POWs at Tunis somewhere around 275,000: Howe, *Seizing the Initiative in the West*, 510; Omar N. Bradley, *A Soldier's Story* (New York: Holt, 1951), 99 (more than "a quarter-million, more than half of whom were Germans"); *DRZWk* vol. 8, pt. 6, Schreiber, "Das Ende des nordafrikanischen Feldzugs," 1109 (267,000–275,000). Blumenson, *Kasserine Pass*, 313, observes "the defeat exceeded the disaster at Stalingrad." Hart, *History of the Second World War*, 431, is skeptical of such figures, pointing out that the ration strength of the Army Group Africa in late April was 170,000 to 180,000, "so it is hard to see how the number of prisoners taken could have exceeded this strength by nearly 50 percent." See also the very fine discussion of the casualty and prisoner count and the significance of Axis losses in Porch, *Path to Victory*, 412–14.

35. For Operation Husky, begin, as always, with the volume in the U.S. Army's Green Book series *The U.S. Army in World War II*: Albert N. Garland and Howard McGaw Smyth, assisted by Martin Blumenson, *Sicily and the Surrender of Italy: United States Army in World War II, The Mediterranean Theater of Operations* (Washington, D.C.: Center of Military History, 1965).

36. The best account of the tortuous Allied planning process for Operation Husky, including the decision to go ahead with the invasion in winds that were estimated as a Force V gale—a precursor to Overlord—is the primary source, Eisenhower, *Crusade in Europe*, 159–72. Equally indispensable is Montgomery, *Memoirs*, especially 170–84, and Arthur Bryant, *Turn of the Tide: A History of the War Years Based on the Diaries of Field-Marshal Lord Alanbrooke, Chief of the Imperial General Staff* (New York: Doubleday, 1957), 543–46. The Green Book

chapter by Garland and Smyth, *Sicily and the Surrender of Italy*, 52–68, and 88–111, still impresses with its depth of detail, and the pertinent chapter in the British official history, C. J. C. Molony, *The Mediterranean and Middle East*, vol. 5, *The Campaign in Sicily, 1943 and the Campaign in Italy, 3rd September 1943 to 31st March 1944* (London: Her Majesty's Stationery Office, 1973), 1–34, more than meets the high standard for scholarship, documentation, and analysis set earlier in the series by I. S. O. Playfair. Andrew J. Birtle, *Sicily* (Washington, D.C.: Center of Military History, n.d.), is a very useful précis, part of *The U.S. Army Campaigns of World War II* series. Within the literature, see also Rick Atkinson, *The Day of Battle: The War in Sicily and Italy, 1943–1944* (New York: Henry Holt, 2007), 1–72, vol. 2 of *The Liberation Trilogy* and a worthy companion to his very fine *Army at Dawn*; and Carlo D'Este, *Bitter Victory: The Battle for Sicily, 1943* (New York: Harper Perennial, 1988), 17–126. See also the pertinent sections from the Sicily chapter in Hanson Baldwin, *Battles Lost and Won: Great Campaigns of World War II* (New York: Harper & Row, 1966), 187–96; Porch, *Path to Victory*, 415–21; and Charles B. MacDonald, *The Mighty Endeavor: The American War in Europe* (New York: Da Capo, 1992), 150–54. Perhaps the most sharply argued work on Sicily is the pertinent portions of Adrian R. Lewis, *Omaha Beach: A Flawed Victory* (Chapel Hill, NC: University of North Carolina Press, 2001), 79–83.

37. The plan went through various iterations, none of them satisfactory to all parties. The final plan was essentially what Montgomery presented to the Husky planners in a bravura briefing on May 2. See Montgomery, *Memoirs*, 177–82.

38. Both the British and American airborne drops on Sicily are analyzed capably in William B. Breuer, *Drop Zone Sicily: Allied Airborne Strike, July 1943* (Novato, CA: Presidio, 1983). For the U.S. landings, and the airborne component of Husky in general, see the exciting account by James M. Gavin, at the time the still-boyish commander of the 505th Parachute Infantry Regiment, *On to Berlin: Battles of an Airborne Commander, 1943–1946* (New York: Viking, 1978), 14–50.

39. For German defenses and order of battle on Sicily, see the pertinent reports in the Foreign Military Studies series, especially T (for "Thema")-2, an omnibus including the following reports: Walter Fries, "Der Kampf um Sizilien" and "Der Kampf der 29. Panzer-Grenadier-Division auf Sizilien"; Bogislaw von Bonin, "Betrachtungen über den italienischen Feldzug 1943/1944," pt. 1, "Kampf um Sizilien, 10.7.-16.8.43"; Helmut Bergengruen, "Der Kampf der Panzer Division 'Hermann Goering' auf Sizilien"; and Wilhelm Schmalz, "Der Kampf um Sizilien im Abschnitt der Brigade Schmalz." Fries was the commander of the 29th Panzergrenadier Division; Bergengruen, the chief of staff for the Panzer Division Hermann Göring; and Bonin, the chief of staff of the XIV Panzer Corps. See also the reports by Eberhard Rodt, "15th Panzer Grenadier Division in Sicily," C-077, and Paul Conrath, "Der Kampf um Sizilien," C-087. All of these reports are available in both German and English at the U.S. Army Heritage and Education Center (USAHEC) in Carlisle, Pennsylvania. For the German counterattack on day one, see Conrath, "Der Kampf um Sizilien," 8–10, and Bergengruen, "Der Kampf der Panzer Division 'Hermann Goering' auf Sizilien," 1–4. Garland and Smyth, *Sicily and the Surrender of Italy*, 147–62, are—as should be expected—very useful for the U.S. side; less so for the German.

40. Richard Tregaskis, *Invasion Diary* (Lincoln, NE: Bison Books, 2004), 37–38.

41. Still the best operational account of the German counterattack on D+1 is D'Este, *Bitter Victory*, 290–309. See also Atkinson, *Day of Battle*, 91–105, and Garland and Smyth, *Sicily and the Surrender of Italy*, 164–74. The account in James Scott Wheeler, *The Big Red One: America's Legendary 1st Infantry Division from World War I to Desert Storm* (Lawrence: University Press of Kansas, 2007), 228–36, emphasizes the role of the divisional artillery in halting the German attack.

42. For the initial German optimistic judgment about holding Sicily, as well as the rapid disillusionment, see Kesselring, *Soldat bis zum letzten Tag*, 222–24.

43. Richard Tregaskis, *Invasion Diary* (Lincoln, NE: Bison Books, 2004), 37–38.

44. Garland and Smyth, *Sicily and the Surrender of Italy*, 244–57, is still the place to start for Patton's "western sweep" and the "pounce on Palermo." See also Atkinson's description of "an army unrefined" in *Day of Battle*, 129–35, and D'Este's account of "the Palermo venture" in *Bitter Victory*, 412–27.

45. See "U.S. 7th Army: General Order No. 18," reprinted in George S. Patton Jr., *War as I Knew It* (New York: Bantam, 1981), 61–62.

46. For Troina, see Bradley, *Soldier's Story*, 144–57. For Allen and Roosevelt's dismissal, see 154–57.

47. D'Este, *Bitter Victory*.

48. The same historiographical dynamic we observed in the Sicilian campaign is at work when studying operations in Italy: Anglo-American historians have dwelt on it to the point of obsession, while the Germans have barely noticed it. The official histories bear out this point. The Green Book series devotes two complete volumes to the subject: Garland and Smyth, *Sicily and the Surrender of Italy*, and Martin Blumenson, *Salerno to Cassino* (Washington, D.C.: Center of Military History, 1969). The U.S. Navy's official history is also indispensable: Samuel E. Morison, *History of United States Naval Operation in World War II*, vol. 9, *Sicily—Salerno—Anzio, January 1943–June 1944* (Boston: Little, Brown, 1954). The official British point of view is almost as well represented in Molony, *Mediterranean and Middle East*, vol. 5, *The Campaign in Sicily and Italy*. The German official history, as already noted in the discussion of the Sicilian campaign, devotes a relatively brief amount of space to the fighting in Italy. See *DRZWk*, vol. 8, *Die Ostfront 1943/44: Der Krieg im Osten und an den Nebenfronten*, pt. 6, "Der Krieg an den Nebenfronten," especially Gerhard Schreiber, "Das Ende des nordafrikanischen Feldzugs und der Krieg in Italien 1943 bis 1945," 1100–62, handling all the campaigns from Tunis to the end of the war very briefly. In investigating the German viewpoint of this controversial campaign, a good place to start is with the testimony in the Foreign Military Studies series, available in both German and English at the U.S. Army Heritage and Education Center (USAHEC) in Carlisle, Pennsylvania. It needs to be read with care, of course, but then again, that goes for contemporaneous archival records, as well. See Siegfried Westphal et al., "Der Feldzug in Italien, Apr 1943–Mai 1944" manuscript T-1a, especially the crucial chapter 6 by General Heinrich von Vietinghoff, "Die Kämpfe der 10. Armee in Süd- und Mittelitalien unter besonderer Berücksichtigung der Schlachten bei Salerno, am Volturno, Garigliano, am Sangro und um Cassino." Vietinghoff was commander of the Tenth Army, the formation that opposed the Allied landing.

    Published primary sources abound, and the scholar will need, at the very least, to read the memoirs of the main participants. For the Americans, these include Eisenhower, *Crusade in Europe*, 201–19, and Mark W. Clark, *Calculated Risk* (New York: Enigma Books, 2007), a reprint of the general's memoirs that appeared first in 1950. For the British, see Montgomery, *Memoirs*, and Arthur Bryant, *Triumph in the West, 1943–1946: Based on Diaries and Autobiographical Notes of Field Marshal the Viscount Alanbrooke* (London: Collins, 1959). For the Germans, begin with Kesselring, *Soldat bis zum letzten Tag*, translated into English as *Kesselring: A Soldier's Record* (New York: William Morrow, 1954); Westphal, *Heer in Fesseln*, translated as *The German Army in the West*; and, by the same author, *Erinerrungen*; and Frido von Senger und Etterlin, *Krieg in Europa* (Köln, Ger.: Kiepenhauer & Witsch, 1960), translated into English as *Neither Fear Nor Hope: The Wartime Career of General Frido von Senger und Etterlin, Defender of Cassino* (Novato, CA: Presidio, 1989). See also Warlimont, *Im Hauptquartier der deutschen Wehrmacht 1939–1945*. Italy was an OKW theater, and Warlimont can write on it with authority. For the English translation, see *Inside Hitler's Headquarters*. Helmut Heiber, ed., *Hitlers Lagebesprechungen: Die Protokollfragmente siner militärischen Konferenzen 1942–1945* (Stuttgart, Ger.: Deutsche Verlags-Anstalt, 1962), is also essential for the completely dysfunctional state of the German high command in these days. It too is available in English. See Helmut Heiber and David M. Glantz, eds., *Hitler and His Generals: Military Conferences 1942–1945* (New York: Enigma, 2003). Finally, although it is a secondary source, Josef Schröder, *Italiens Kriegsaustritt 1943: die deutschen Gegenmassnahmen im italienischen Raum: Fall "Alarich" und "Achse"* (Göttingen, Ger.: Musterschmidt-Verlag, 1969), is essential for German plans and operations, both for its incisive analysis and its exhaustive treatment of the German documentary and archival records.

The secondary literature in English is massive, especially if one includes biographies of the principal participants. Begin with Atkinson, *Day of Battle*; Carlo D'Este, *Fatal Decision: Anzio and the Battle for Rome* (New York: Harper Perennial, 1992); Porch, *Path to Victory*; and, as always, the pertinent sections in MacDonald, *Mighty Endeavor*, 190–247. All these works feature meticulous analysis and often inspired writing. See also D'Este's *World War II in the Mediterranean, 1942-1945*, as well as Martin Blumenson's essential biography, *Mark Clark* (London: Jonathan Cape, 1984), a work that serves at least as a partial rehabilitation of this oft-maligned figure. The most useful short summary of the campaign's opening is *Salerno: American Operations from the Beaches to the Volturno, 9 September–6 October 1943* (Washington, D.C.: Center of Military History, 1990), a reprint of a pamphlet originally published by the War Department's Historical Division in 1944.

For the British perspective, see Eric Linklater, *The Campaign in Italy* (London: His Majesty's Stationery Office, 1951); Jackson, *Battle for Italy*; John Strawson, *The Italian Campaign* (New York: Carroll & Graf, 1988); and Bernard Ireland, *The War in the Mediterranean, 1940–1943* (Barnsley, UK: Leo Cooper, 1993). Jackson was a British officer on the staff of General Alexander, and his account of operations is perhaps the most lucid and balanced one available. Both Christopher Buckley, *Road to Rome* (London: Hodder and Stoughton, 1945), and Tregaskis, *Invasion Diary*, offer the perspective of journalists attached to the British and U.S. armies, respectively.

49. For the messy end to Italy's war, see Elena Agarossi, *A Nation Collapses: The Italian Surrender of September 1943* (Cambridge: Cambridge University Press, 2006).

50. For German atrocities against their recent brothers in arms, see Kerstin von Lingen, *Kesselring's Last Battle: War Crimes Trials and Cold War Politics, 1945–1960* (Lawrence: University Press of Kansas, 2009).

51. For the successful German retreat from Calabria in the face of what the Germans saw as a "primitive diversionary maneuver" ("primitives Ablenkungsmanöver"), see Schröder, *Italiens Kriegsaustritt 1943*, 269–74.

52. The best sources for the planning of Operation Avalanche, the "first breach" of German defenses on the European continent, are Jackson, *Battle for Italy*, 81–96, Clark, *Calculated Risk*, 145–51, Blumenson, *Salerno to Cassino*, 16–42, and Molony, *Sicily and Italy*, 230–36.

53. Clark, *Calculated Risk*, 163.

54. Clark, *Calculated Risk*, "a near disaster," 152.

55. For the fighting around the "Tobacco Factory" (*Tabakfabrik*), see the definitive and artful account in Atkinson, *Day of Battle*, 222–27.

56. For a detailed account of the crisis point of the battle, see Blumenson, *Salerno to Cassino*, 112–17.

57. For the role of the burnt bridge, see Vietinghoff, "Die Kämpfe der 10. Armee in Süd- und Mittelitalien," 33–34.

58. Morison, *Sicily—Salerno—Anzio*, 286–94.

59. The only scholarly work to deal with the crucial decision of where to hold the line on the Italian peninsula is Ralph S. Mavrogordato, *Command Decisions: Hitler's Decision on the Defense of Italy* (Washington, D.C.: Center of Military History, 1990).

60. For the standard narrative of U.S. strategy in the Pacific, see the pertinent volume in the U.S. Army's Green Book series *The U.S. Army in World War II*: Louis Morton, *Strategy and Command: The First Two Years* (Washington, D.C.: Center of Military History, 1962), especially chapter 11, "Organization and Command of the Pacific," 240–63.

61. Spector, *Eagle Against the Sun*, 145.

62. Morton, *Strategy and Command*, 250.

63. The early operations on New Guinea, the "Buna campaign," are almost completely absent from the historiography. While discussion of the fighting appears in every history of the war, there is no body of scholarly work dedicated solely to it in the United States. The researcher must begin with the volume in the U.S. Army's Green Book series *The U.S. Army in World War II*: Samuel Milner, *Victory in Papua* (Washington, D.C.: Center of Military History, 1957), but even he is dubious about the strategic value of the campaign, labeling it "a bitter anticlimax." See also Lida Mayo, *Bloody Buna* (New York: Doubleday, 1974), for a useful and engagingly written account.

64. Once again, although Cartwheel is mentioned in every history of the war, it has barely made a dent in the scholarly historiography. The American researcher should begin with the volume in the U.S. Army's Green Book series *The U.S. Army in World War II*: John Miller Jr., *Cartwheel: The Reduction of Rabaul* (Washington, D.C.: Center of Military History, 1959), but will then have to work through various chapters in the vast literature on the Pacific War, biographies of MacArthur, and the various memoirs, including Douglas MacArthur, *Reminiscences* (Annapolis, MD: Naval Institute Press, 1964). Keegan, *Second World War*, 297–307, offers a tight and well-argued synthesis. All in all, it is a shocking situation when one considers the size, scope, and importance of the campaign.

65. Miller, *Cartwheel*, 26. MacArthur went on to specify the stages of the operation: "First by improvement of presently occupied forward bases; secondly, by the occupation and implementation of air bases which can be secured without committing large forces; and then, by the seizure and implementation of successful hostile airdromes."

66. See the pungent commentary by Weinberg, the dean of World War II historians, in *World at Arms*: "Rabaul had been isolated and largely neutralized. This was what the Quadrant Conference of August 1943 in Quebec had called for instead of the direct assault MacArthur had insistently urged. By the end of 1943, MacArthur came to embrace a policy of by-passing strong Japanese garrisons, a policy of which he became the loudest advocate and most successful practitioner (and which he later claimed to have invented)" (646).

67. Spector, *Eagle Against the Sun*, is particularly effective here. See, especially, his description of the conditions on New Guinea (188–89) and Guadalcanal (197–98). See also Drea, *Japan's Imperial Army*, who notes that, based on recent Japanese research, "a majority of Japanese military deaths during the Asia-Pacific War resulted from starvation, not enemy action" (238).

68. Again, Tarawa has had nowhere near the attention paid to it that battles in the European theater have had. Begin with the volume in the U.S. Army's Green Book series *The U.S. Army in World War II*: Philip A. Crowl and Edmund G. Love, *Seizure of the Gilberts and Marshalls* (Washington, D.C.: Center of Military History, 1955). From there, move to more popular literature. Eric M. Hammel is a journalist who weds solid research interviews with the participants to magnificent writing. See *76 Hours: The Invasion of Tarawa* (Pacifica, CA: Pacifica Press, 1985), and *The U.S. Marines in World War II: Tarawa and the Marshalls: a Pictorial Tribute* (Minneapolis: Zenith Press, 2008). The brief account in Joseph H. Alexander, *Storm Landings: Epic Amphibious Battles in the Central Pacific* (Annapolis, MD: Naval Institute Press, 1997), 40–61, is superb in evoking "the classic vulnerability of an opposed amphibious assault" (53).

69. For the social role of photography in wartime, and not just in World War II, see the richly illustrated volume by Anne Wilkes Tucker and Will Michels with Natalie Zelt, *War/Photography: Images of Armed Conflict and its Aftermath* (New Haven, CT: Yale University Press, 2012).

Chapter 4: Victory in Europe

1. The best evocation of the last two years of the war in Europe is still Max Hastings, *Armageddon: The Battle for Germany, 1944–1945* (New York: Alfred A. Knopf, 2004). For a vivid portrait of how Western Europeans experienced "liberation," see William I. Hitchcock, *The Bitter*

Road to Freedom: The Human Cost of Allied Victory in World War II Europe (New York: Free Press, 2009).

2. Erickson, *Road to Berlin*, mentions "twenty-three bridgeheads, ranging in depth from a thousand yards to twenty miles, on the right bank Dnepr" (127).

3. Still the best operational précis for any aspect of the fighting on the Eastern Front is Glantz and House, *When Titans Clashed*. For a discussion of tank armies, see 183. These powerful formations consisted of a tank corps paired with a mechanized corps, and contained 800 to 1,000 tanks apiece. They were, Glantz and House write, "the true stars of the Soviet offensive." For the deployment of the tank armies in the winter of 1943–44, always a good indication of the Soviet *Schwerpunkt* at any given time, see 189.

4. Ziemke, *Stalingrad to Berlin*.

5. For the doctrinal development of deep battle see Richard W. Harrison, *The Russian Way of War: Operational Art, 1904–1940* (Lawrence: University Press of Kansas, 2001).

6. For Soviet skill in employing the "forward detachment," see Glantz and House, *When Titans Clashed*, 183–84.

7. "Irgendeines Dorfes mit aussprechlichen Namen." Wagener, *Heeresgruppe Süd*, 245.

8. There is a mountain of testimony on Hitler's obsession with the *Haltbefehl* (stand-fast order). See especially B. H. Liddell Hart, *The German Generals Talk* (New York: Quill, 1979).

9. The primary source for those arguing on behalf of the maneuver is still Manstein, *Verlorene Siege*, 507–619. The English translation is *Lost Victories*.

10. See the discussion in Johannes Hürter, *Hitlers Heerführer: Die deutschen Oberbefehlshaber in Krieg gegen die Sowjetunion, 1941/42* (Münich, Ger.: R. Oldenbourg, 2006), 348, 609.

11. Weinberg, *World at Arms*, describes Schörner as a man of "extreme National Socialist views" (455), a man who displayed "ruthless fanaticism" (670), who shot "German soldiers after rigged courts martial" (573), whose art of war consisted of "holding fast by having lots of Germans shot" (801), and who at the end of the war "deserted his men to try to evade capture as a civilian" (824).

12. For a meticulous reconstruction of the Battle of the Korsun Pocket (or sometimes "Cherkassy pocket"), see Ziemke, *Stalingrad to Berlin*, 226–38.

13. Glantz and House, *When Titans Clashed*, 192–93. For the epic tale of Leningrad's long nightmare, see Harrison E. Salisbury, *900 Days: The Siege of Leningrad* (New York: Harper & Row, 1969). Anna Reid, *Leningrad: The Epic Siege of World War II, 1941–1944* (New York: Walker, 2011), not only narrates the tale of a great city "falling down the funnel" in compelling fashion, but also brings the account up to the present, showing how various factions have used the siege of Leningrad as a weapon in the memory wars of the Soviet and post-Soviet eras.

14. See *The Soviet Army* (Moscow: Progress Publishers, 1971), 120. Moreover, the partisans controlled some 90 percent of the forests in this heavily forested region. See Hans-Heinrich Nolte, "Partisan War in Belorussia, 1941–1944," in *World at Total War*, 275.

15. Like all the great Soviet offensives, Operation Bagration is tragically underserved in the English-language literature. There are precisely two dedicated volumes: Paul Adair, *Hitler's Greatest Defeat: The Collapse of Army Group Centre, June 1944* (New York: Arms & Armour, 1994), which is brief—overly so—and useful only in a general sense, and Walter S. Dunn Jr., *Soviet Blitzkrieg: The Battle for White Russia, 1944* (Boulder, CO: Lynne Rienner, 2000), a highly detailed account based on the author's own database of Soviet units present in the battle.

For a primary source, see also David Glantz and Harold S. Orenstein, eds., *Belorussia, 1944: The Soviet General Staff Study* (London: Frank Cass, 2001), compiled after the offensive and containing daily situation maps. For a good summary informed by the best available documentation, see the appropriate chapters in Glantz and House, "Operation Bagration: The Death of Army Group Center," in *When Titans Clashed*, 195–215, and Ziemke, "The Collapse of the Center," in *Stalingrad to Berlin*, 313–45. Stephen H. Newton, *Hitler's Commander: Field Marshal Walther Model—Hitler's Favorite General* (New York: Da Capo Press, 2006),

287–302, contains a great deal of useful information. See also Carlo D'Este, "Model," in *Hitler's Generals*, ed. Correlli Barnett (New York: Quill, 1989), 325.

Finally, for a book that stands alone in the literature, see Catherine Merridale, *Ivan's War: Life and Death in the Red Army, 1939–1945* (New York: Picador, 2006), a detailed re-creation of the life of the individual Soviet soldier.

16. Glantz and House, *When Titans Clashed*, 201–2.

17. Gottlob Herbert Bidermann, *In Deadly Combat: A German Soldier's Memoir of the Eastern Front* (Lawrence: University Press of Kansas, 2000), 218–19.

18. For the ease with which the Soviets were able to "peel back" the German defenses in the early stages, ibid., 204–5.

19. For the chaotic situation in and around Minsk, see Ziemke, *Stalingrad to Berlin*, 324–25.

20. "Ein weit grössere Katastrophe als diejenige von Stalingrad." Görlitz, *Zweite Weltkrieg, 1939–1945*, 2:252.

21. Typically, Glantz and House, *When Titans Clashed*, 210–14, is the only English-language source to discuss the Lvov-Sandomierz operation.

22. No historical work on this complex topic rivals Norman Davies, *Rising '44: The Battle for Warsaw* (New York: Viking, 2003).

23. See ibid., 350, where the author speaks of the situation in September, with the Soviets "running out of excuses for not helping Warsaw."

24. See Glantz and House, *When Titans Clashed*, 212–14, which relates the very difficult fight the Soviets had to conduct in August to maintain their Vistula bridgeheads.

25. For Army Group North's retreat to Courland, see Howard D. Grier, *Hitler, Dönitz, and the Baltic Sea: The Third Reich's Last Hope, 1944–1945* (Annapolis, MD: U.S. Naval Institute Press, 2007).

26. For the encirclement, siege, and reduction of the Hungarian capital, see Krisztián Ungváry, *The Siege of Budapest: 100 Days in World War II* (New Haven, CT: Yale University Press, 2005).

27. The best book on the collapse of Germany's allies is Richard L. DiNardo, *Germany and the Axis Powers: From Coalition to Collapse* (Lawrence: University Press of Kansas, 2005). For the immense number of foreign soldiers who fought in and alongside the Wehrmacht in all its campaigns, see Rolf-Dieter Müller, *The Unknown Eastern Front: The Wehrmacht and Hitler's Foreign Soldiers* (London: I. B. Tauris, 2012).

28. Compared with the massive Bagration, the relatively minor and peripheral events in the Italian campaign have received obsessive attention from English-language historians. To begin, see the two volumes in the U.S. Army's Green Book series *The U.S. Army in World War II*: Garland and Smyth, *Sicily and the Surrender of Italy*, and Blumenson, *Salerno to Cassino*. The U.S. Navy's official history is also indispensable: Morison, *Sicily—Salerno—Anzio*. The official British point of view is well represented in Molony, *Mediterranean and Middle East*, vol. 5, *The Campaign in Sicily and Italy*.

Published primary sources abound. They include Eisenhower, *Crusade in Europe*; Clark, *Calculated Risk*; and Montgomery, *Memoirs*. Kesselring, *Soldat bis zum letzten Tag*, translated into English as *Kesselring: A Soldier's Record*, is essential for the German view. For the secondary literature, see Atkinson, *Day of Battle*; D'Este, *Fatal Decision*; and Porch, *Path to Victory*. Finally, the historian must consult the leading German secondary source, Josef Schröder, *Italiens Kriegsaustritt, 1943: Die deutschen Gegenmassnahmen im italienischen Raum: Fall "Alarich" und "Achse"* (Göttingen, Ger.: Musterschmidt-Verlag, 1969).

29. "It was a line built by the famous Nazi Todt Organization on terrain that the Italian War College had used for many years to illustrate to students an area that was ideal for defense against almost anything." Clark, *Calculated Risk*, 211.

30. The Anzio landing has generated a substantial historiography for a corps-sized operation. See the authoritative works by Martin Blumenson, both the official entry in the Green Book series *Salerno to Cassino*, and the monograph *Anzio: The Gamble That Failed* (Philadelphia: Lippincott, 1963). D'Este, *Fatal Decision*, is a typically excellent entry from this master historian.

31. Blumenson, *Anzio*, 56. Quoted in MacDonald, *Mighty Endeavor*, 228.

32. Clark wrote, "My own feeling was that Johnny Lucas was ill—tired physically and mentally— from the long responsibilities of command in battle (he died a few years later)." Clark, *Calculated Risk*, 244.

33. For the struggle for Cassino town and monastery, see the classic by Fred Majdalany, *The Battle of Cassino* (Boston: Houghton Mifflin, 1957).

34. See, for example, Hart, *History of the Second World War*, 529–30.

35. For Operation Diadem, see D'Este, *Fatal Decision*, 334–38.

36. For the Borga Grappa linkup, see Clark, *Calculated Risk*, 283.

37. For an able presentation of the anti-Clark indictment, see D'Este, *Fatal Decision*, 366–82: "Clark's decision on May 25 was a calculated act that was to prove as militarily stupid as it was insubordinate" (366). Williamson Murray and Allan R. Millett, *A War to Be Won: Fighting the Second World War* (Cambridge, MA: Harvard University Press, 2000), are blunt in condemning "Clark's insubordination" and "vainglorious pursuit of publicity and prestige" (385), while Thomas W. Zeiler, *Annihilation: A Global Military History of World War II* (Oxford: Oxford University Press, 2011) references "Clark's showboating" (280).

38. For Clark's own reasonable defense of his decision to go for Rome, see Clark, *Calculated Risk*, 282–91. Senger und Etterlin, *Neither Fear Nor Hope*, 243–58, offers a vigorous refutation of the notion that Tenth Army was in danger of encirclement: "Having been prevented from driving a wedge between the retreating German armies [by a tough defensive stand by Senger's XIV Panzer Corps], the enemy also found it impossible to cut off parts of the 10th Army by blocking their way" (256).

39. For the rest of the war in Italy, a truly forgotten campaign within the literature of World War II, see the belated volume in the Green Book series *The U.S. Army in World War II*, Ernest F. Fisher Jr., *Cassino to the Alps* (Washington, D.C.: Center of Military History, 1977). For a popular history that manages to distill a very complex narrative, see Thomas R. Brooks, *The War North of Rome, June 1944–May 1945* (Edison, NJ: Castle Books, 2001).

40. The Normandy campaign has been the subject of a huge mass of literature. Begin, as always, with the entries in the Green Book series *The U.S. Army in World War II*: Gordon A. Harrison, *Cross-Channel Attack* (Washington, D.C.: Center of Military History, 1951), and Martin Blumenson, *Breakout and Pursuit* (Washington, D.C.: Center of Military History, 1961). The magisterial scholarly account is, and will remain, Russell F. Weigley, *Eisenhower's Lieutenants: The Campaign of France and Germany, 1944-1945* (Bloomington: Indiana University Press, 1981), while the standard popular account—still extremely useful—is Max Hastings, *Overlord: D-Day and the Battle for Normandy* (New York: Simon & Schuster, 1984). See also Antony Beevor, *D-Day: The Battle for Normandy* (New York: Penguin Books, 2010).

    More specialized studies can also be rewarding. Steve R. Waddell, *United States Army Logistics: The Normandy Campaign* (Westport, CT: Greenwood Press, 1994), still the only volume on this crucial area—indeed, the single most important factor in the conduct of the landing and the subsequent operations—is indispensable. Roman Johann Jarymowycz, *Tank Tactics: From Normandy to Lorraine* (Boulder, CO: Lynne Rienner, 2001) is an interesting addition to the literature: a Canadian author highly critical of Allied armored doctrine in general, the U.S. tank destroyer concept in particular, and the British and Canadian preference for the "set piece battle." Two other useful works are James Jay Carafano, *After D-Day: Operation Cobra and the Normandy Breakout* (Boulder, CO: Lynne Rienner, 2000), which looks at the campaign through the lens of the "combat command, regimental and battalion commanders, the 'field-grade' leaders" (4), and argues that "the ability to understand and exploit the full capabilities of the U.S. Army" was the key to the eventual breakout, rather than a magic technological bullet like the Culin hedgerow cutter or the brute firepower of carpet bombing (260); and Russell A. Hart's exhaustive and meticulously researched *Clash of Arms: How the Allies Won in Normandy* (Boulder, CO: Lynne Rienner, 2001), which stresses the "institutional flexibility" and adaptability of the U.S. Army in Normandy compared with its allies, offers controversial argumentation that "the tenacity of the German defense of

Normandy must also be explained in ideological terms," and, a sine qua non for future research into the Normandy campaign, offers full coverage of the Canadian experience.

Another type of literature—now swamping all the others but best avoided by the serious researcher—is the "greatest generation" genre. Best exemplified in the writings of the late Stephen Ambrose, it is an outgrowth of Seymour Lipset's "American exceptionalism," embodying the sense that Americans are somehow unique, touched by fate in a direct way, and endowed with a special mission. It is not scholarly history. Consider the following passage from Ambrose, *Citizen Soldiers: The U.S. Army from the Normandy Beaches to the Bulge to the Surrender of Germany, June 7, 1944–May 7, 1945* (New York: Touchstone, 1997), 159: "There were hundreds of young officers like Fussell, lieutenants who came into Europe in the fall of 1944 to take up the fighting. Rich kids. Bright kids. The quarterback on the championship high school football team. The president of his class. The chess champion. The lead in the class play. The solo in the spring concert. The wizard in the chemistry class. America was throwing her finest young men at the Germans." It is a brilliant passage, of course, but every line could have been written about the soldiers of the Wehrmacht, or the British Army, or the Romanians, for that matter. For a slashing attack on the entire notion of a "greatest generation," united in purpose and quietly following orders, see Kenneth D. Rose, *Myth and the Greatest Generation: A Social History of Americans in World War II* (New York: Routledge, 2008).

41. Eisenhower, *Crusade in Europe*, 220–21.

42. For criticisms of the half-light and joint fire plans, see Lewis, *Omaha Beach*, and Joseph Balkoski, *Omaha Beach: D-Day, June 6, 1944* (Mechanicsburg, PA: Stackpole Books, 2004).

43. For German dispositions in France, see Liddell Hart, *German Generals Talk*, 227–41. For German defensive planning in the early months of 1944, see Warlimont, *Inside Hitler's Headquarters*, 405–21. Samuel W. Mitcham Jr., *Defenders of Fortress Europe: The Untold Story of the German Officers During the Allied Invasion* (Washington, D.C.: Potomac, 2009), is also quite useful on German plans and intentions.

For decades, scholars assumed that Operation Fortitude, the Allied deception operation that placed General George S. Patton Jr. in command of a dummy "1st U.S. Army Group" apparently aimed at an invasion of the Pas de Calais, had frozen the Fifteenth Army in place and prevented it from reinforcing Normandy. Not until 2007 did a scholar actually investigate those claims, performing primary source research in the archives, and find that they were specious. For single-handedly exploding one of the longest-lived myths of World War II historiography, Mary Kathryn Barbier, *D-Day Deception: Operation Fortitude and the Normandy Invasion* (Westport, CT: Praeger Security International, 2007), deserves a careful reading. In the final analysis, Barbier argues, the impact of Operation Fortitude "was minimal" (195). Indeed, Allied bombing of Normandy was so comprehensive and effective that any attempt to redeploy the Fifteenth Army and shift it laterally to the left was probably doomed to failure. "By attacking rail and road bridges across the Seine and Loire Rivers, locomotives, and marshaling yards before and after the invasion, Allied air forces effectively isolated the Normandy area long enough for the Allied invasion forces to establish and reinforce bridgeheads" (194).

44. See Görlitz, *Zweite Weltkrieg*, 2:268–69, and Liddell Hart, *German Generals Talk*, 239.

45. One indispensable source for Omaha is Steven T. Ross, ed., *U.S. War Plans, 1938–1945* (Boulder, CO: Lynne Rienner, 2002), 187–224. Ross reproduces the operational plan, complete with exact numbers of men and vehicles for the assault, follow-up, and buildup forces (201–24).

46. Balkoski, *Omaha Beach*, 189.

47. Bradley, *Soldier's Story*, 270.

48. At 1:30 p.m., Bradley received a terse but reassuring message from V Corps: "Troops formerly pinned down on beaches Easy Red, Easy Green, Fox Red advancing up heights behind beaches." Bradley, *Soldier's Story*, 272. Wheeler, *Big Red One*, 259–91, contains an able retelling and analysis of the division's tough fight at Omaha.

49. For the origins and operations of the Waffen-SS, begin with Gerald Reitlinger, *The SS: Alibi of a Nation 1922–1945* (Englewood Cliffs, NJ: Prentice-Hall, 1981), a reprint of the original work

from 1956; George H. Stein, *The Waffen SS: Hitler's Elite Guard at War, 1939–1945* (Ithaca, NY: Cornell University Press, 1966); and Charles W. Sydnor Jr., *Soldiers of Destruction: The SS Death's Head Division, 1933–1945* (Princeton, NJ: Princeton University Press, 1977). The chapter on the Waffen-SS in Heinz Höhne, *Order of the Death's Head* (New York: Ballantine, 1971), 493–545, is still a useful summary.

50. Both Hastings, *Overlord*, 123–51, and Carlo D'Este, *Decision in Normandy* (New York: Dutton, 1983), 174–98, 231–53, and 298–320, are adequate on Montgomery's serial failures.

51. For the primary source on the planning of Operation Goodwood, see Montgomery, *Memoirs*, 254–62, in which the field marshal recounts his "master plan for the land battle in Normandy" (254).

52. For the primary source on the planning of Operation Cobra, see Bradley, *Soldier's Story*, 326–46. See also Carafano, *After D-Day*; Hart, *Clash of Arms*, especially "A Campaign Overview," 247–64; and Jarymowycz, *Tank Tactics*, 107–202.

53. Omar N. Bradley, *A Soldier's Story* (New York: Modern Library, 1999), 346–48.

54. Both the U.S. 9th and 30th Infantry Divisions were victims of Allied carpet bombing, and the 30th Division had the unhappy distinction of being hit twice. The bombing also killed General Lesley McNair, commander of Army ground forces—the highest-ranking officer killed in Western Europe. See Bradley's discussion, *Soldier's Story*, 348–49. For the Goodwood carpet bombing actually blowing Mark VI Tiger tanks in the air and landing them upside down, see Hans von Luck, *Panzer Commander* (New York: Praeger, 1989), 173.

55. For Patton, begin with a troika of biographies: Ladislas Farago, *Patton: Ordeal and Triumph* (Yardley, PA: Westholme, 1964); Martin Blumenson, *The Patton Papers* (Boston: Houghton Mifflin, 1972); and Carlo D'Este, *Patton: A Genius for War* (New York: Harper, 1995). A summary of Blumenson's work can be found in Martin Blumenson and Kevin M. Hymel, *Patton: Legendary World War II Commander* (Washington, D.C.: Potomac, 2008).

    Stanley P. Hirshson's *General Patton: A Soldier's Life* (New York: Harper Collins, 2002), is a revisionist biography, emphasizing Patton's character failings, his racism and anti-Semitism, and bad generalship throughout. For Patton's ride across northern France, see Blumenson, *Breakout and Pursuit*, still the best and most complete account.

56. Both General Hodges and the First Army are virtually absent from the historiography of the ETO, victims of the general's self-effacing personality as well as the obsessive attention historians have paid to Patton and his antics. The researcher must rely upon one short biography, Stephen T. Wishnevsky, *Courtney Hicks Hodges: From Private to Four-Star General in the United States Army* (Jefferson, NC: McFarland, 2006), as well as one reference work, John T. Greenwood, ed., *Normandy to Victory: The War Diary of General Courtney H. Hodges and the First U.S. Army* (Lexington: University Press of Kentucky, 2008).

57. For a splendidly researched account of the saga of Mortain, see Mark J. Reardon, *Victory at Mortain: Stopping Hitler's Panzer Counteroffensive* (Lawrence: University Press of Kansas, 2002). Alwyn Featherston, *Saving the Breakout: The 30th Division's Heroic Stand at Mortain, August 7–12, 1944* (Novato, CA: Presidio, 1993), provides a readable narrative, although it is much more of a narrowly focused popular history.

58. See Joachim Ludewig, *Der deutsche Rückzug aus Frankreich, 1944* (Freiburg, Ger.: Rombach, 1995), 116. Ludewig's essential book is now available in an English translation: *Rückzug: The German Retreat from France, 1944* (Lexington: University Press of Kentucky, 2012).

59. Beevor, *D-Day*, offers a nuanced view of the Falaise sequence but winds up blaming Montgomery for the "missed opportunity." Weigley, *Eisenhower's Lieutenants*, 208–9, criticizes Bradley, among others, noting "the fragility of Bradley's and other explanations," "the inconsistency of Bradley's positions," and noting that "the fault was also Bradley's" (2098–109).

60. See William B. Breuer, *Death of a Nazi Army: The Falaise Pocket* (New York: Stein and Day, 1985): "However many Germans got out of the pocket, one overriding conclusion emerged: Hitler's armies in France had taken a frightful beating and suffered enormous losses in men and equipment" (294).

61. Operation Market-Garden, with its armada of paratroopers, its daring armored thrust, and its nail-biting ending, continues to generate a great deal of interest. Begin with the popular history by Cornelius Ryan, *A Bridge Too Far* (New York: Simon & Schuster, 1974), and then the scholarly account, based on the most recent archival research, by William F. Buckingham, *Arnhem, 1944* (Stroud, UK: Tempus, 2004).

62. For the Poles at Arnhem, see George F. Cholewczynski, *Poles Apart: The Polish Airborne at the Battle of Arnhem* (London: Greenhill Books, 1993).

63. Arnhem destroyed the 1st Airborne Division as a fighting force. Of its 12,000 men at the start of the battle, nearly 10,000 were killed, wounded, or taken prisoner. Some 2,400, moving in small groups, did manage to escape across a downriver ferry. See Buckingham, *Arnhem 1944*, 226.

64. While the Canadian Army is missing in action in most works on the campaign, a vigorous debate has rippled for years among Canadian scholars, who are divided on the fighting qualities of the First Canadian Army. A good place to start is John A. English, *The Canadian Army and the Normandy Campaign: A Study of Failure in High Command* (New York: Praeger, 1991), a negative assessment, as the title indicates, and its opposite number, Terry J. Copp, *Fields of Fire: The Canadians in Normandy* (Toronto: University of Toronto Press, 2003), a much more positive analysis.

65. For Patton's difficulties getting untracked in front of Metz, see John Nelson Rickard, *Patton at Bay: The Lorraine Campaign, 1944* (Washington, D.C.: Brassey's, 2004).

66. Charles B. MacDonald, *The Battle of the Huertgen Forest* (Philadelphia: Lippincott, 1963), is the classic account, but Robert Sterling Rush, *Hell in Hürtgen Forest* (Lawrence: University Press of Kansas, 2001), is a carefully drawn analysis of what kept soldiers fighting under such terrible conditions.

67. The Battle of the Bulge is arguably the greatest battle ever fought in the history of the U.S. Army and it has generated a literature to match. As always, begin with the appropriate volume in the Green Book series *The U.S. Army in World War II*: Hugh M. Cole, *The Ardennes: Battle of the Bulge* (Washington, D.C.: Center of Military History, 1965), and from there go to the secondary literature, especially Robert E. Merriam, *Dark December: The Full Account of the Battle of the Bulge* (Chicago: Ziff-Davis, 1947); Baldwin, "The Battle of the Bulge—A Case History in Intelligence," in *Battles Lost and Won*, 315–67; Charles B. MacDonald, *A Time for Trumpets: The Untold Story of the Battle of the Bulge* (New York: Morrow, 1984); and Danny S. Parker, *Battle of the Bulge: Hitler's Ardennes Offensive* (New York: Da Capo, 2004). Harold Winton, *Corps Commanders of the Bulge: Six American Generals and Victory in the Ardennes* (Lawrence: University Press of Kansas, 2007), is outstanding in assessing the U.S. Army's fighting power by this point in the war.

68. The blunt-spoken General Josef "Sepp" Dietrich, commander of the Sixth SS Panzer Army, put it even more strongly: "All Hitler wants me to do is to cross a river, capture Brussels, and then go on and take Antwerp. And all this in the worst time of the year through the Ardennes when the snow is waist deep and there isn't room to deploy four tanks abreast let alone armored divisions. When it doesn't get light until eight and it's dark again at four and with re-formed divisions made up chiefly of kids and sick old men—and at Christmas." Quoted in Keegan, *Second World War*, 441.

69. For this horrible story, see Danny S. Parker, *Fatal Crossroads: The Untold Story of the Malmédy Massacre at the Battle of the Bulge* (New York: Da Capo, 2011). See also Cole, *Battle of the Bulge*, 264n5, for the American reaction, a fragmentary order issued by Headquarters, 328th Infantry: "No SS troops or paratroopers will be taken prisoners but will be shot on sight." Cole goes on to point out the isolated nature of the document, admits that some Germans trying to surrender in the immediate wake of Malmédy "ran a greater risk," but concludes that "there is no evidence, however, that American troops took advantage of orders, implicit or explicit, to kill their SS prisoners" (264).

70. For Patton's swift wheel to the north, see John Nelson Rickard, *Advance and Destroy: Patton as Commander in the Bulge* (Lexington: University Press of Kentucky, 2011).

71. Every source on the war mentions the "old men and boys" filling the German ranks by 1945 and gives passing mention to the *Volkssturm*. Only one scholar has yet investigated this incredible phenomenon in any detail: David K. Yelton, *Hitler's Volkssturm: The Nazi Militia and the Fall of Germany, 1944–1945* (Lawrence: University Press of Kansas, 2002), a superbly researched account.

72. The mix of ideological fanaticism, opportunism, and fear is well captured in two edited works by German historian Sönke Neitzel: *Tapping Hitler's Generals: Transcripts of Secret Conversations, 1942–45* (Saint Paul, MN: Frontline, 2007), and *Soldaten: On Fighting, Killing, and Dying; The Secret World War II Transcripts of German POWs* (New York: Alfred A. Knopf, 2012). Both works are based on the secretly recorded conversations of German officers and men in Allied captivity. For morale on the German home front, Martin Kitchen, *Nazi Germany at War* (London: Longman, 1995), is still a fine introduction, especially the section on "Daily Life and Daily Worries" (66–101).

73. The Soviet "Vistula-Oder operation" is no more present in the historical literature than any of the other great post-1942 offensives. As always, begin with the pertinent chapter in Glantz and House, *When Titans Clashed*, 241–47, reading in tandem with Ziemke, *Stalingrad to Berlin*, 410–37. I. S. Konev, *Year of Victory* (Moscow: Progress Publishers, 1966), is the account of the commander of the 1st Ukrainian Front, and remains useful for details of the fighting. Its preservation of a distinctly "Soviet" point of view makes it even more valuable in the post–Cold War world.

74. For the Berlin operation, see Glantz and House, *When Titans Clashed*, 258–72; Ziemke, *Stalingrad to Berlin*, 467–99; and Konev, *Year of Victory*, 79–192.

75. For the ferocity of the fighting inside Berlin, the interested reader can do no better than Cornelius Ryan, *The Last Battle* (New York: Simon & Schuster, 1966): "Marauding gangs of SS men, roving the city in search of deserters, were taking justice into their own hands. They were halting nearly everyone in uniform and checking identities and units" (480). Another vivid account is V. I. Chuikov, *The End of the Third Reich* (Moscow: Progress Publishers, 1978). Chuikov was the commander of Eighth Guards Army during the fight for Berlin, part of Zhukov's 1st Byelorussian Front.

76. The final drive into Germany is less well served than Normandy or the Bulge. Perhaps the sheer size and scope of the broad front advance—with all Allied armies and army groups making rapid forward progress—robs it of the definition that the other battles have. Begin with the appropriate volume in the Green Book series *The U.S. Army in World War II*: Charles B. MacDonald, *The Last Offensive* (Washington, D.C.: Center of Military History, 1973), supplemented by Weigley, *Eisenhower's Lieutenants*, 575–726.

77. The actual exchange has Hodges telling Bradley, "Brad, we've gotten a bridge," and Bradley responding, "Hot dog, Courtney, this will bust him wide open." Bradley, *Soldier's Story*, 510–11.

78. For an interesting work that links operations Market-Garden and Varsity by a discussion of their comparable airborne components, see Lloyd Clark, *Crossing the Rhine: Breaking into Nazi Germany, 1944 and 1945—The Greatest Airborne Battles in History* (New York: Atlantic Monthly Press, 2008).

79. Virtually alone in analyzing the encirclement of Army Group B is Derek S. Zumbro, *Battle for the Ruhr: The German Army's Final Defeat in the West* (Lawrence: University Press of Kansas, 2006).

80. For Jodl's meeting with Eisenhower at Rheims, see Bodo Scheurig, *Alfred Jodl: Gehorsam und Verhängnis* (Berlin: Propyläen, 1991), 331–32. For Jodl's fate—he was condemned to death and hanged at Nuremberg—see the work by his widow, Luise Jodl, *Jenseits des Endes: Leben und Sterben des Generaloberst Aldred Jodl* (Wien, Ger.: Verlag Fritz Molden, 1976). Luise describes hearing the announcement of the unconditional surrender on the radio, "signed by Gustav Jodl." Her first thought was "Gustav"? Her husband's first name was Alfred. Her second thought was of the shame and hatred directed toward those who had signed the treaty of Versailles in World War I (135). General Walter Bedell Smith, chief of staff of the Allied forces in Europe,

describes the curtness of Eisenhower's interview with Jodl in *Eisenhower's Six Great Decisions: Europe, 1944–1945* (New York: Longman, Green, 1956): "He wanted to say a brief, stern word to these representatives of the tyranny against which his great crusade was directed" (211). See also Eisenhower, *Crusade in Europe*, 426, where Eisenhower states that Jodl will be held accountable for any violations of the surrender terms and then dismisses him with an emphatic "That is all."

81. See Richard Overy, *Why the Allies Won* (New York: W. W. Norton, 1995). The title is a declarative, not an interrogatory. Overy's argument is that "Mistakes were obviously made on both sides, but the outcome on the battlefield ultimately depended on as very great improvement in the military effectiveness of Allied forces" (*xiv*) and that "the Allies won the Second World War because they turned their economic strength into effective fighting power, and turned the moral energies of their people into an effective will to win" (325), neither one of which was an inevitable development. In the same vein, see the argument by Mark Harrison, "Why Didn't the Soviet Economy Collapse in 1942?," in *World at Total War*: "Eventually, however, the Allies translated their economic superiority into overwhelming advantage on the battlefield" (141). See also table 7.4 (141), "War Production of the Great Powers, 1942," for just how superior the Allies were. In that fateful year, for example, the Allies produced no fewer than 6,200,000 rifles and carbines (against just 1,800,000 for the Axis), 60,000 tanks (against just 9,000), and 64,000 combat aircraft (against 25,000).

CHAPTER 5: THE DEFEAT OF JAPAN

1. The classic account—based on unparalleled research—is Clark Reynolds, *The Fast Carriers: The Forging of an Air Navy* (repr.; Annapolis, MD: Naval Institute Press, 1992). For a more gripping treatment, also based on impressive research, see William Belote and James A. Belote, *Titans of the Sea* (New York: Harper and Row, 1975). For an essential, albeit dry, study of the Pacific Fleet Amphibious Force, see George C. Dyer, *The Amphibians Came to Conquer: The Story of Admiral Richmond Kelly Turner* (Washington, D.C.: Government Printing Office, 1972). For the life of the senior Marine in the Pacific theater, see Anne C. Venzon, *From Whaleboats to Amphibious Warfare: Lt. Gen."Howling Mad" Smith and the U.S. Marine Corps* (Westport, CT: Praeger, 2003).

2. See Robert Love, *History of the U.S. Navy*, 2 vols. (Harrisburg, PA: Stackpole Books, 1994), 2:213–14.

3. The Fifth Fleet's striking arm included fifteen heavy and light carriers embarking nine hundred aircraft, seven battleships, twenty-one cruisers, and sixty-nine destroyers, and an amphibious force of hundreds of attack transports, cargo ships, and landing craft embarking Smith's V Expeditionary Force. It was supported by an impressive support force of freighters, oilers, and tenders. The distances covered by the invaders were formidable: the Marianas lay thirty-five hundred miles from Pearl Harbor and one thousand miles from the fleet anchorage at Majuro in the Marshalls.

4. A brief, recent overview is Gordon L. Rottman, *Saipan and Tinian: Piercing the Japanese Empire* (Oxford: Osprey, 2004).

5. Toyoda assumed command of the Combined Fleet following the death of his predecessor, Admiral Koga Meinichi, in a plane crash in March 1944. For Ozawa, see Kiyoshi Ikeda, "Vice Admiral Jisaburo Ozawa," chapter 11, in *Men of War: Great Naval Leaders of World War II*, ed. Stephen Howarth (London: St. Martin's Press, 1992). Although none of the Japanese fleet commanders was especially able, as the war progressed, each one showed more ability than his predecessor, despite having fewer forces at his disposal.

6. The Fifth Fleet now included 7 battleships, 21 cruisers, 69 destroyers, and 7 heavy and 8 light carriers operating 956 aircraft.

7. Only one Japanese aviator put a bomb on target, slightly damaging the battleship *South Dakota*. Most of the Japanese pilots were raw trainees.

8. For a balanced overview, see Jack Sweetman, *Great American Naval Battles* (Annapolis, MD: Naval Institute Press, 1998).

9. The best biography—and the only account informed by Chiang's diaries—is Jay Taylor, *The Generalissimo: Chiang Kai-shek and the Struggle for Modern China* (Cambridge, MA: Harvard University Press, 2009). For Stilwell's shabby treatment of one of the masters of tactical air forces, see Claire Lee Chennault, *Way of a Fighter: The Memoirs of Claire Lee Chennault* (New York: G. P. Putnam's Sons, 1949), and Jack Samson, *Chennault* (New York: Doubleday, 1987). "Pop" history at its worst was on display in the well written but thoroughly misleading account by Barbara W. Tuchman, *Stilwell and the American Experience in China, 1911–45* (New York: Macmillan, 1971).

10. From a strength of 65,000, the Fifteenth Army was reduced to 15,000 thanks to Slim's relentless pursuit. The most recent, and readable, life is Robert Lyman, *Slim, Master of War* (London: Constable, 2004).

11. XX Bomber Command was also forced to relocate its bases inland, but General Arnold was about to shut down the command and shift the B-29s to XXI Air Force in the Marianas anyway. Although the Allies wanted to try Nakamura for "war crimes," Chiang Kai-shek so respected his military prowess that he paid him to advise the Republic of China's General Staff during the Chinese Civil War (1945–1949).

12. For a recent summary of the Ichi-gō offensive from a Chinese perspective, see Rana Mitter, *Forgotten Ally: China's World War II, 1937–1945* (New York: Houghton Mifflin, 2013), chapter 17.

13. For the only account of this episode informed by both Chinese and American archives, see Maochun Yu, *Dragon's War: Allied Operations and the Fate of China, 1937–1947* (Annapolis, MD: Naval Institute Press, 2006), 171–73.

14. Albert C. Wedemeyer, *Wedemeyer Reports!* (New York: Henry Holt, 1958). Wedemeyer replaced Stilwell as Chiang's chief of staff and commander of U.S. Army forces in China. Stilwell's other authorities were divvied up by other generals.

15. "China never received more than two percent of the available Lend-Lease" military aid between 1941 and 1944. See Yu, *Dragon's War*, 93. The shortcomings of the Chinese Army were manifold. Most of its best officers and men and modern German and Soviet arms were lost resisting the Japanese invasion long before the United States entered the war. There was little industry and few arsenals in unoccupied China, so the regime depended on imports for most military goods; thus the importance of the prewar Hanoi-Kunming railroad and the Burma Road and the wartime Tenth Air Force airlift over the Hump. For opposing views of Roosevelt's diplomacy, see Frederick W. Marks III, *Wind over Sand: The Diplomacy of Franklin Roosevelt* (Athens, GA: University of Georgia Press, 1988), and Robert Dallek, *Franklin D. Roosevelt and American Foreign Policy, 1932–1945* (New York: Oxford University Press, 1979). Dallek is probably the last of the school known as the "court historians."

16. Too often the Type 93 torpedo, often termed the Long Lance, is confused with the slightly longer, equally lethal Type 95 torpedo carried by Japanese cruisers and destroyers. (The term "Long Lance" was an invention of postwar American historians.) The Type 93 featured the largest warhead and the longest range of any World War II–era torpedo. The secret to the weapon's extraordinary effectiveness was the use of pure oxygen instead of compressed air in the propulsion system.

17. World War II–era U.S. Navy carriers, battleships, and cruisers could make over thirty knots (fifty-six kilometers per hour), and all were defended by robust "sound screens" of two or three destroyers operating sonar and radars and well armed with depth charges, whereas an I-15-class boat, for instance, could make only eight knots (fifteen kilometers per hour) submerged. Although Japanese submarines claimed several American heavy ships, in almost every instance the loss was due to a lucky, very long-range shot, malfunctioning American gear, or a temporary gap in the sound screen.

18. See Mark P. Parillo, *The Japanese Merchant Marine in World War II* (Annapolis, MD: Naval Institute Press, 1993).

19. By contrast, the Allied North Atlantic convoys included between thirty and sixty freighters and tankers defended by an American, British, or Canadian ocean escort group of five to seven destroyer, destroyer escort, or corvette types. During World War I, the British and American navies learned that the success of a passage was highly correlated to the *strength of the escort group* rather than the number of merchantmen in the convoy. This also proved to be true in World War II. Like their American counterparts, most Japanese troop transports were well-defended with strong escort forces until the last year of the conflict.

20. A brief, recent summary of the Japanese shortcomings can be found in H. P. Willmott, "After Midway," in *Pacific War Companion: From Pearl Harbor to Hiroshima*, ed. Daniel Marston (London: Osprey, 2010), 190–91. Not appreciating the dive capabilities of U.S. submarines, the Japanese initially set depth charges to explode too close to the surface. This American advantage evaporated after Congressman Andrew J. May, in June 1943, noted the Japanese error in a press conference and American newspapers reported his remarks. The Japanese also failed to provide merchant ships with sufficient antisubmarine guns, allowing U.S. boats to destroy hundreds of vessels with gunfire instead of scarce torpedoes; failed to develop the equivalent of the Hedgehog depth-charge thrower that proved so effective in the Battle of the Atlantic; frequently broke off antisubmarine attacks too soon in the mistaken belief the target had been sunk; and failed to develop hunter-killer teams based on escort carriers. See chapter 17 of Theodore Roscoe, *United States Submarine Operations in World War II* (Annapolis, MD: Naval Institute Press, 1949), and *Submarine Report: Depth Charge, Bomb, Mine, Torpedo and Gunfire Damage Including Losses in Action, 7 December 1941 to 15 August 1945* (Washington, D.C.: U.S. Hydrographic Office, 1949), sec. 3.

21. The venerable Orange Plan was largely irrelevant to the conduct of the conflict in the Pacific inasmuch as it envisioned a bilateral struggle between Japan and the United States, with neither belligerent aided or burdened by allies. For instance, in its various iterations over four decades, the Orange Plan never envisioned American forces assuming responsibility for the defense of Australia and New Zealand, which formally became an American chore in April 1942, after the British loss of Singapore.

22. Another 228 were completed before Japan surrendered. By comparison, Japan started with 63 and completed 111 more submarines.

23. John Prados, *Combined Fleet Decoded: The Secret History of American Intelligence and the Japanese Navy in World War II* (New York: Random House, 1995). For the "skipper problem" and torpedo malfunctions, see Love, *History of the U.S. Navy*, 2:188–89. The malfunctions of the American torpedo were especially galling inasmuch as the Japanese torpedoes were so effective, one of the very few instances in which the Japanese fabricated a better quality weapon than their opponent.

24. The classic account of the Pacific Fleet Submarine Force is Clay Blair, *Silent Victory: The U.S. Submarine War Against Japan* (Philadelphia: Lippincott, 1975).

25. Quoted in Love, *History of the U.S. Navy*, 2:194.

26. See Parillo, *Japanese Merchant Marine*, and Wilmott, "After Midway," in *Pacific War Companion*, ed. Howarth, 183. On top of the 6 million tons in the merchant fleet at the start of the war, the Japanese had seized some 800,000 tons of shipping and built 3.3 million more. See also Morison, *Two-Ocean War*, 511.

27. A summary of the negotiations among King, Marshall, Nimitz, and MacArthur can be found in Robert Love, "Fleet Admiral Ernest J. King," in *Men of War*, ed. Howarth, chapter 3. For Halsey, see E. B. Potter, *Bull Halsey* (repr.; Annapolis, MD: Naval Institute Press, 2003); and John F. Wukovits, *Admiral "Bull" Halsey: The Life and Wars of the Navy's Most Controversial Commander* (New York: Palgrave Macmillan, 2010). One of the better first person accounts is Daniel Barbey, *MacArthur's Amphibious Navy: Seventh Fleet Amphibious Operations, 1943–1945* (Annapolis, MD: Naval Institute Press, 1969).

28. I. C. B. Dear and M. D. R. Foot, eds., *The Oxford Guide to World War II* (Oxford: Oxford University Press, 1995), 426. Edward J. Drea, *MacArthur's ULTRA: Codebreaking and the War Against Japan, 1942–1945* (Lawrence: University Press of Kansas, 1992), 121.

29. For an excellent account of Kenney's wartime command, see Thomas E. Griffith, *MacArthur's Airman: General George C. Kenney and the War in the Southwest Pacific* (Lawrence: University Press of Kansas, 1998).

30. Although he is widely regarded as one of the most able generals of World War II, the only scholarly biography of Eichelberger is Paul Chwialkowski, *In Caesar's Shadow: The Life of General Robert Eichelberger* (Westport, CT: Greenwood Press, 1993).

31. Walking among the pyramids during a pause in the Big Two Cairo Conference in November 1943, Admiral Charles M. Cooke, King's principal deputy, devised the scheme to use both admirals Halsey and Spruance after the campaign advanced beyond the South Pacific. Halsey and Spruance would change places in command of the Central Pacific Force ships. Halsey, ashore, would plan one operation while Spruance, at sea, would command another. When Halsey was at sea, the command was named the Third Fleet; when Spruance was sea, it was the Fifth Fleet. Subordinate task forces, groups, and units also changed their designations; TF 58 became TF 38, for instance, when Halsey hoisted his flag.

32. General Kenney soon discovered that the captured airstrips were unsuitable for heavy-bomber operations owing to local soil conditions.

33. Neither King nor Nimitz would allow MacArthur to be in the direct chain of command of the fast carriers. Communications between Halsey and Kinkaid were complicated owing to MacArthur's insistence that all of Kinkaid's message traffic be routed through Manus Island, an unwieldy arrangement.

34. King had scant use for "unity of command," which he termed a fruitless "panacea." Marshall pushed the concept relentlessly. Admiral Cooke, who dealt often with Marshall during his three wartime years in Washington and got on well with him, believed the general's approach stemmed from a desire "to command everything." Cooke Oral History, Charles M. Cooke MSS, Hoover Institution, Stanford University.

35. The best biography of a naval figure of World War II is Gerald Wheeler, *Kinkaid of the Seventh Fleet: A Biography of Admiral Thomas C. Kinkaid, U.S. Navy* (Annapolis, MD: Naval Institute Press, 1996).

36. For a concise analysis of the Peleliu operation by a Marine historian who commanded a battalion there, see Gordon D. Gayle, *Bloody Beaches: The Marines at Peleliu* (Washington, D.C.: Marine Corps Historical Center, 1996). For more detail, see Harry A. Gailey, *Peleliu 1944* (Annapolis, MD: Nautical and Aviation, 1983).

37. For an account of Ulithi and similar anchorages by the commanding officer of Service Squadron 10, see Worrall Reed Carter, *Beans, Bullets, and Black Oil: The Story of Fleet Logistics Afloat in the Pacific During World War II* (Washington, D.C.: Government Printing Office, 1953). Also see George Spangler, "Ulithi," *Laffey*, March 1998.

38. The most complete recent account based on primary sources is Thomas Cutler, *The Battle of Leyte Gulf, 23–26 October 1944* (New York: Harper Collins, 1994).

39. They would be supported by the 1st Air Fleet, based on Luzon, which however had only forty aircraft left.

40. For the context of Halsey's decision to head north to confront the Northern Force, based on interviews with some participants, see Love, *History of the U.S. Navy*, 2:242–46.

41. The Center Force still included the superbattleship *Yamato*, three older battleships, eight cruisers, and eleven destroyers.

42. A website is devoted to Taffy 3, www.bosamar.com.

43. The admirals Sprague were unrelated.

44. Quoted Morison, *Two-Ocean War*, 459.

45. *Johnston*'s commanding officer, Commander Ernest E. Evans, received a posthumous Medal of Honor for this action.

46. The Japanese higher command did not accept Kurita's many explanations and he was sent ashore under a dark cloud soon after the battle. After the war, Kurita advanced several, sometimes competing reasons for his decision to retire. The claim that his ships were low on fuel was hokum. In all likelihood, the fury of the air assault from the escort carriers led him to believe that he was being attacked by the heavy carriers of TF 38, that more robust air attacks were impending, and that he had best save his ships. For a detailed account of Kurita's decision from several viewpoints, see the website of Robert Jon Cox, www.bosamar.com/pages/bosc11.

47. For instance, Admiral Chūichi Nagumo failed to launch a third wave during the attack on Pearl Harbor despite the fact that the opposition had been eviscerated. For a brief explanation, see Love, *History of the U.S. Navy*, 2:3. Similar reluctance was exhibited by admirals Isoroku Yamamoto and Chūichi Nagumo off Midway. See Craig Symonds, *The Battle of Midway* (New York: Oxford University Press, 2011). The contradiction between the higher command's dedication to a "decisive battle"—which implied suicidal sacrifices akin to the tactics adopted by the Japanese Army ashore—and the reluctance of the fleet and subordinate commanders to risk their ships and sailors accordingly is striking. Admiral King adopted a contrary approach before the Battle of Midway, when he instructed Admiral Nimitz to adopt "attrition tactics." In effect, King quite expected to lose the three carriers he allowed Nimitz to deploy to challenge the enemy off Midway, but he hoped that the Pacific Fleet would inflict something akin to equivalent damage to the Japanese formation.

48. The Japanese ships sunk totaled some 306,000 tons, compared with 37,000 tons of American warships; this "utterly destroyed Japan's capacity to wage another fleet battle" and thus won for the Allies "uncontested command of the Pacific Ocean." E. B. Potter, *Nimitz* (Annapolis, MD: Naval Institute Press, 1976), 343.

49. The Combined Fleet reported to Tokyo that in actions off Formosa on October 11–14, 1944, its planes had (in addition to other vessels) sunk eleven carriers and damaged eight more. In reality, one carrier had been damaged and no ships sunk. Weinberg, *World at Arms*, 850.

50. For a well-documented account of Krueger's command, see Kevin Holzimmer, *General Walter Krueger: Unsung Hero of the Pacific War* (Lawrence: University Press of Kansas, 2007).

51. When Kenney withdrew promised air cover, Rear Admiral Arthur Struble, commander of the amphibious force, refused to land, a quarrel heated up, and Marshall and King were about to square off when Halsey intervened and offered Third Fleet carrier support. It was ironic that, having crossed swords over Mindoro, when the Korean War erupted, Admiral Struble, known not only for his great ability but also for a rugged pugnacity, found himself in command of Seventh Fleet, which conducted the naval phase of MacArthur's brilliant amphibious hooks at Inchon in September and Wonsan in October and the masterful evacuation of X Corps at Hungnam in December 1950. For the 1944 dispute, see Love, *History of the U.S. Navy*, 2:250.

52. There are no recent, thorough, and reliable accounts of the Philippine campaign or the Battle for Luzon. The best introductory summary remains Spector, *Eagle Against the Sun*, chapter 22. For a brief account by an "official historian," see Dale Andrade, *Luzon* (Washington, D.C.: Government Printing Office, 1996).

53. Between January 4 and 12, 1945, kamikazes sank twenty-four ships and damaged sixty-seven more; among the latter were the three old battleships, a light cruiser, two destroyers, and an Australian cruiser.

54. Hoping—largely in vain, as it turned out—to minimize civilian losses, MacArthur had forbidden use of airstrikes or bombardment with heavy naval guns. Ultimately, field artillery, tanks, and tank destroyers were brought in to blast down one defended building after another, entombing untold numbers of noncombatant citizens along with the defending Japanese riflemen. The fighting is covered in detail in Robert Ross Smith, *Triumph in the Philippines* (Washington, D.C.: Center of Military History, 1961), chapters 15 and 16.

55. For losses, see Andrade, *Luzon*, 29. Totaling Japanese losses in any action in World War II is a vexing proposition. Thanks to the wartime and postwar destruction of Japanese records, the number who perished on Luzon will probably never be known for certain.

56. For the complex amphibious campaigns in the Mindanao group, see Morison, *History of United States Naval Operations in World War II*, vol. 13, *The Liberation of the Philippines—Luzon, Mindanao, the Visayas, 1944–1945* (Boston: Little, Brown, 2002).

57. John T. Mason Jr., *The Pacific War Remembered: An Oral History Collection* (Annapolis, MD: Naval Institute Press, 1986), 310–11.

58. A scrupulously researched account of Arnold's command—with extensive commentary—can be found in John W. Huston, ed., *Airpower Comes of Age: General Henry H. "Hap" Arnold's World War II Diaries*, 2 vols. (Maxwell AFB, AL: Air University Press, 2002–2004). For a broader view of the strategic bombing campaign against Japan, see Kenneth P. Werrell, *Blankets of Fire: U.S. Bombers over Japan During World War II* (Washington, D.C.: Smithsonian, 1996).

59. Thomas R. Searle, " 'It Made a Lot of Sense to Kill Skilled Workers': The Firebombing of Tokyo in March 1945," *Journal of Military History* 66, no. 1 (2002): 115–16; *The Papers of George Catlett Marshall*, vol. 2, ed. Larry I. Bland (Baltimore: Johns Hopkins University Press, 1986), 676–79. The reference to "paper cities" reflects the fact that Japanese buildings were mostly made of wood, with paper partitions inside, and so were far more vulnerable to incendiary attacks than German buildings, which were much more likely to be constructed of brick, stone, or concrete. Nonetheless, General Arnold had assured FDR disingenuously that during the 1942 Tokyo Raid, "we all took care to avoid bombing schools, hospitals, churches, and other non-military objectives." Arnold to FDR, May 3, 1942, File: Arnold, Box 3, PSF, FDR MSS.

60. Curtis E. LeMay, *Superfortress: The Story of the B-29 and American Air Power* (New York: McGraw-Hill, 1988).

61. A treetop raid by Japanese light bombers from Iwo Jima provoked Hansell to order the newly arrived 498th Bombardment Group to retaliate against those bases, but this operation was also ineffective.

62. Colonel John B. Montgomery, Hansell's friend and chief of staff for XXI Bomber Command, tellingly summarized the difference between the two air commanders as follows: "LeMay [from XX Bomber Command] was writing half-page reports telling Arnold what he did yesterday, and Hansell was writing a three-page report explaining why the mission aborted." Moreover, Hansell himself admitted that his principal combat element, the 73rd Bomb Wing, "was openly hostile" to him. Both quoted in Searle, " 'It Made a Lot of Sense to Kill Skilled Workers,' " 131.

63. For losses, see ibid., 123.

64. Because planning for the Iwo Jima invasion was complete before XXI Air Force bombing operations against Japan got under way and the engine problems plaguing the B-29 were fully understood, the island's use as an emergency airfield on the return trip from Japan was an unexpected and important benefit. For a balanced view of the strategy concerning Iwo Jima and Okinawa, see Murray and Millett, *War to be Won*, 510–13.

65. Only 216 Japanese were taken prisoner during the fighting; the rest of the survivors remained hiding in the cave complexes. The best scholarly treatment of the battle and its aftermath is Robert S. Burrell, *The Ghosts of Iwo Jima* (College Station: Texas A&M University Press, 2006); for a shorter narrative, see Colonel Joseph H. Alexander, *Closing In: Marines in the Seizure of Iwo Jima*, a pamphlet in the *Marines in World War II Commemorative Series* (Washington, D.C.: History and Museums Division, Marine Corps Headquarters, 1995).

66. An older but well-written, carefully researched account is James Belote and William Belote, *Okinawa: Typhoon of Steel* (New York: Harper and Row, 1975).

67. Spruance was now in command of the Fifth Fleet, which included the seventeen heavy and light carriers and seven battleships of TF 58 and a recently arrived Royal Navy group of four carriers and a battleship. For an account of the politics surrounding British participation, see

Merrill Bartlett and Robert Love, "Anglo-American Naval Diplomacy and the British Pacific Fleet, 1942–1945," *American Neptune* 42, no. 3 (1982): 203–16.

68. Interview with R. O. Buchanon, November 9, 2004, Veterans History Project, Library of Congress, 5–6 of transcript, http://lcweb2.loc.gov/diglib/vhp/bib/44697.

69. Dear and Foot, eds., *Oxford Guide to World War II*, 642.

70. Love, *History of the U.S. Navy*, 2:260–61. For a detailed account informed by both Japanese and American records, see Mitsuru Yoshida, *Requiem for the Battleship* Yamato (repr.; Annapolis, MD: Naval Institute Press, 1995).

71. Bruce M. Petty, ed., *Voices from the Pacific War* (Annapolis, Maryland: Naval Institute Press, 2004), 116–117.

72. Quoted in Spector, *Eagle Against the Sun*, 539–40.

73. Many of the Japanese who did surrender were Okinawan militiamen. Upon learning that General Buckner was among the dead, MacArthur named the very able General Oscar Griswold to command Tenth Army, but Marshall insisted that his friend General Stilwell, who had been relieved of his command in India-China in October 1944, be given the billet. Tenth Army was slated to be the assault force for the invasion of Honshu in 1946. One can only wonder how long Stilwell would have lasted under MacArthur's orderly, cooperative regime.

74. Recent accounts of Operation Downfall are abundant. The most detailed treatment is Richard B. Frank, *Downfall: The End of the Japanese Empire* (New York: Random House, 1999). A broader perspective is provided in a briefer account by Thomas B. Allen and Norman Polmar, *Code-Name Downfall: The Secret Plan to Invade Japan and Why Truman Dropped the Bomb* (New York: Simon & Schuster, 1995).

75. Owing to their global responsibilities, Admiral King and his key deputy, Admiral Charles M. Cooke, consistently encouraged Admiral Nimitz to assume most of the responsibility for planning Pacific Fleet operations. While Nimitz was in theory a "joint" theater commander, in practice his Pacific Fleet staff planned most operations. This approach worked well overall, especially after Rear Admiral Forrest Sherman, a brilliant strategist, became Nimitz's deputy for plans in late 1943. It backfired on occasion, however, inasmuch as Sherman was far less reluctant than Nimitz to cross Admiral King. Likewise, in the Southwest Pacific, MacArthur's U.S. Army staff planned most operations with little input from the Seventh Fleet.

76. On the one hand, King believed that Nimitz deserved the honor of commanding the invasion of Japan. On the other, allowing MacArthur to command meant that the Navy Department would elude sharing the high costs of a postwar occupation, which in the event were borne almost entirely by the War Department. In a meeting at the White House with Truman on June 18, 1945, King backed Marshall's advocacy of the invasion plan with the rather eccentric assertion that Kyushu afforded more room for American forces to maneuver than they enjoyed on Okinawa. Mins, WH mtg, 18 June 1945, *FRUS: The Conference of Berlin (The Potsdam Conference)*, 2 vols. (Washington, D.C.: Government Printing Office, 1960), 1:903–10. The tangled history of the accuracy and provenance of the notes from this important meeting can be found in Barton J. Bernstein, "Marshall, Leahy, and Casualty Issues—A Reply to Kort's Flawed Critique," *Passport: The Newsletter of the Society for Historians of American Foreign Relations* 35, no. 2 (August 2004): 5–14.

77. MacArthur told Marshall that he would welcome any of the generals from the European theater with the exception of General Omar Bradley, whose shortcomings were well known. For the views of Bradley's contemporaries in the European theater, see D'Este, *Decision in Normandy*. MacArthur was scarcely alone in believing that Bradley had badly mishandled the Battle of the Bulge. See "Text of MacArthur's Statement in Reply to Charges by Truman in Memoir," *New York Times*, February 9, 1956, 25.

78. By contrast, the Royal Navy's Admiral Bertram H. Ramsay, who commanded Operation Neptune, the naval phase of the 1944 invasion of Normandy, had the immense advantage of operating from huge, well-established nearby naval bases, inland facilities, and numerous airfields

in southwestern England. The problems attending shore-to-shore operations in Europe and ship-to-shore operations in the Pacific were largely unrelated. For an intimate account of Ramsay's command problems, see Robert W. Love and John Major, *The Year of D-Day* (Hull, UK: University of Hull Press, 1994).

79. King did not share Nimitz's message with Truman or Marshall. Frank hypothesizes that King planned to wait to spring Nimtiz's critique until an opportunity arose to kill the invasion plan completely. See Frank, *Downfall*, 243. It seems more likely that King, who was more fully informed of the progress of the Manhattan Project than he allowed in his postwar memoir, realized that atomic bombs would be available well before the invasion date, that these weapons would compel Japan to surrender, and that the practicality of MacArthur's Olympic plan was therefore moot.

80. Army and Navy intelligence on Japan, impressive in 1942, declined in quality thereafter. The Pacific Fleet suffered from poor tactical intelligence in the Solomons, the Gilberts, and the Marshalls, all British possessions to which Americans had access before the war. American intelligence failed to identify the major change in Japanese tactics after the fall of the Marianas, but reports on Japanese defenses on Kyushu—based mostly on code breaking—proved to be quite accurate.

81. Frank, *Downfall*, 184. Admiral Kelly Turner, the Pacific Amphibious Force commander, planned to defend the fleet of four hundred ships carrying 500,000 men with a lavish destroyer-cruiser screen and fighters from the fast carriers. In addition, he arranged for a "phantom fleet" with the usual destroyer-cruiser screen and carriers with only fighters but no troops. It would assemble at a line of departure and conduct an offshore bombardment with the object of luring the enemy to "unleash thousands of suicide bombers" two weeks before the real landings. Wayne A. Silkett, "Downfall: The Invasion that Never Was," *Parameters* 24 (1994): 116–17.

82. Concern with Japanese resistance was so great that General Marshall advocated gassing Japanese defenders, but Admiral William Leahy insisted that the Joint Chiefs were bound by Roosevelt's declaration early in the war that the United States would not resort to gas warfare unless the enemy did so first. Marshall also considered the use of a half dozen atomic bombs in a tactical role on the invasion beachheads, which suggests he had little understanding of the weapons' limited availability and did not read the reports on their likely blast and radiation effects. See Dean M. Vander Linde, " 'Downfall': The American Plans for the Invasion of Japan in World War II," MA Thesis, Michigan State University (1987), 12–18. For an overview of Japanese intelligence organization, sources, and achievements, see Ken Kotani, *Japanese Intelligence in World War II*, trans. Chiharu Kotani (Oxford: Osprey, 2009).

83. Moreover, the civilian population was integrated into the island's defense, a policy which had just cost the lives of 100,000 Okinawans.

84. "The battle [for Kyushu] would prove the turning point in political maneuvering," Imperial General Headquarters predicted. Frank, *Downfall*, 235.

85. See messages in *FRUS*, 2:1250–51, 1263, and 1292–93. Vague offers of an "armistice" were also put to American diplomats in Lisbon, Bern, Stockholm, and the Vatican simultaneously. Historians of "surrender diplomacy" often forget that Suzuki and Foreign Minister Togo Shigenor wanted the Soviets to mediate an armistice, *not* a surrender, as the Allied demanded. For one thing, American domestic politics would not tolerate an armistice, even one akin to 1918 that precluded the enemy from renewing the conflict. For another, regardless of the American reaction, opposition from France, China, and the British dominions—especially Australia and New Zealand—surely would have made such talks impossible. See Stephen Ambrose and Brian Villa, "Racism, the Atomic Bomb, and the Transformation of Japanese-American Relations," in *The Pacific War Revisited*, ed. Gunther Bishof and Robert L. DuPont (Baton Rouge: Louisiana State University Press, 1997), 185.

86. "Magic Diplomatic Extracts, July 1945," 1–78, MIS, War Department, SRH-040, Record Group 457, National Archives, College Park, MD (NA). Also see "Russo-Japanese Relations,

(July 28–August 6, 1945)," August 7, 1945, 3–16, SRH-088, RG 457, NA. Stalin understood that his Allies were reading Japanese diplomatic traffic and so made certain that they knew his response. The upshot was to enhance Truman's conviction that Japan would insist on dickering and refused to accept "unconditional surrender" for the moment.

87. "Declaration of Potsdam," *FRUS*, 2: 1280–81. Some American officials wanted to specify that the Japanese could retain the emperor, while others argued that this qualified the longstanding demand for "unconditional surrender." There was surprisingly little discussion about the other aspects of that demand. The wholly unsubstantiated canard that Truman ordered the atomic attacks on Japan to intimidate the Soviet Union rather than to induce the Japanese to surrender is still being repeated. See, for instance, Kai Bird and Martin J. Sherwin, *American Prometheus: The Triumph and Tragedy of J. Robert Oppenheimer* (New York: Alfred A. Knopf, 2005), and the devastating critique by Robert J. Maddox, "The Atomic Bomb and American Prometheus," *Passport* 38, no. 3 (December 2007): 23–26. This specious argument, long accepted by the American Left and nurtured by Japanese apologists, fails to explain why, in the aftermath of the atomic attacks, Truman and Secretary of State James Byrnes refused to exploit this advantage in their dealings with the Soviets. Although Truman took a slightly stiffer line with Moscow after the Japanese surrender, he refrained from threatening the Soviets and remained eager to compromise for at least another year or so.

88. This point is made by Murray and Millett, *War to Be Won*, 522. The nexus between the Soviet overseas intelligence apparatus and the atomic bomb and missile programs is detailed in Stephen Zaloga, *Target America: The Soviet Union and the Strategic Arms Race, 1945–1954* (Novato, CA: Presido Press, 1993).

89. For the thoroughgoing duplicity of the Roosevelt administration on this score, see Graham Farmelo, *Churchill's Bomb: How the United States Overtook Britain in the First Nuclear Arms Race* (New York: Basic Books, 2013).

90. Rather than terrifying America's enemies by advertising a project none could match, General Marshall shrouded it in secrecy, but the bureaucratized security measures failed to thwart a Soviet penetration operation that richly endowed Stalin's postwar nuclear program. Note that $2 billion was a huge sum in the 1940s; in 1939 *all construction in the United States* accounted for only $2.3 billion of the national income of $72.8 billion. *The Statistical History of the United States* (Stamford, CT: Fairfield Publishers, 1965), 140.

91. For a colorful early account of the test, see Lansing Lamont, *Day of Trinity* (New York: Atheneum, 1965). The best recent account of the American atomic bomb project is Jeff Hughes, *The Manhattan Project: Big Science and the Atomic Bomb* (New York: Columbia University Press, 2003).

92. Sadao Asada, "The Shock of the Atomic Bomb and Japan's Decision to Surrender—A Reconsideration," *Pacific Historical Review* 67, no. 4 (1998): 477.

93. Tristan Grunow, "A Reexamination of the 'Shock of Hiroshima': The Japanese Bomb Projects and the Surrender Decision," *Journal of East Asian Studies* 12, nos. 3–4 (Fall–Winter 2003): 155–89.

94. "Statement . . . Hiroshima," 6 Aug 45, *Public Papers of the President: Harry S Truman, 1945* (Washington, D.C.: Government Printing Office, 1961), 197–200; and *FRUS*, 2:1376–77. To dispel the notion that Hiroshima was a unique event, he added that "these bombs are in production and even more powerful forms are in development."

95. Asada, "Shock of the Atomic Bomb," 496.

96. There were two important reasons for accepting the conditional surrender. First, the Allies needed Hirohito to order the overseas Japanese forces to surrender to local Allied authorities. Second, leaving the emperor in place greatly reduced the likelihood of armed or unarmed resistance to American occupation forces in the Home Islands. As for Soviet policy, after meeting Soviet Foreign Minister Vyacheslav Molotov on the tenth, Ambassador W. Averell Harriman reported that it was "clear that the Soviets were in no hurry for the war to end." Quoted in David Mayers, *The Ambassadors and America's Soviet Policy* (New York: Oxford University Press, 1995), 154.

1. President Franklin Roosevelt announced "unconditional surrender" as the terms for ending the war at the Casablanca Conference in January 1943. The text is available online via the Avalon Project, http://avalon.law.yale.edu/wwii/casablan.asp.

2. For histories of the occupation of Germany and Japan, see Frederick Taylor, *Exorcising Hitler: The Occupation and Denazification of Germany* (New York: Bloomsbury Press, 2011); Giles MacDonogh, *After the Reich: The Brutal History of the Allied Occupation* (New York: Basic Books, 2007); Keith Lowe, *Savage Continent: Europe in the Aftermath of World War II* (New York: St. Martin's Press, 2012); John W. Dower, *Embracing Defeat: Japan in the Wake of World War II* (New York: W. W. Norton, 1999); Takemae Eiji, *The Allied Occupation of Japan* (London: Continuum Press, 2002); and Earl F. Ziemke, *The U.S. Army in the Occupation of Germany, 1944–1946* (Washington, D.C.: Center of Military History, 1975).

3. Ziemke, *U.S. Army in the Occupation of Germany, 1944–1946*, 3, and Colonel Irwin I. Hunt, *Military Government of Occupied Germany, 1918–1920* (Washington, D.C.: U.S. Army, 1920), 80. Significantly, the report was reprinted in 1943; a copy of this version is available online via the Haithi Trust, http://babel.hathitrust.org/cgi/pt?id=uiug.30112101024716;view=1up;seq=1.

4. Ziemke, *U.S. Army in the Occupation of Germany, 1944–1946*, 4; U.S. Army, Field Manual (FM) 27-5 *Military Government* (Washington, D.C.: U.S. Army, 1941), 1–2.

5. Ibid., 7.

6. Harry L. Coles and Albert K. Weinberg, *Civil Affairs: Soldiers Become Governors*, in *United States Army in World War II* (Washington, D.C.: Center of Military History, 1964), 13. Recognizing that the School of Military Government would be unable to meet the demand for civil affairs officers, a number of universities and colleges added programs to train CA officers.

7. Ziemke, *U.S. Army in the Occupation of Germany, 1944–1946*, 10. The turf war over who would control military government involved the G-3 operations, G-1 personnel, and the Joint Chiefs of Staff. The combat forces argued that they had to control military government, since it impacted operations, while the G-1 argued it fell within its purview. The creation of the Military Government Division in the Provost Marshal General's Office in August 1942 appeared to settle the issue, but the experience of Operation Torch in North Africa quickly led to changes.

8. Ziemke, *U.S. Army in the Occupation of Germany, 1944–1946*, 17.

9. Waddell, *U.S. Army Logistics: Normandy*, 45–46: The Overlord plan allocated 34,500 tons of supplies for civil affairs for the period of D-Day to D+90. With a planned Omaha Beach capacity of 5,000 tons per day, this meant that civil affairs supplies would require nearly seven of the first ninety days of beach capacity. Furthermore, after D+90, the supply plan included 89,000 pieces of agricultural equipment and 2,625 tons of seeds for distribution on the Continent.

10. S. M. Plokhy, *Yalta: The Price of Peace* (New York: Viking Press, 2010), 107, 330. The text of the agreements reached at the Crimea (Yalta) Conference among President Roosevelt, Prime Minister Churchill, and Generalissimo Stalin, as released by the State Department March 24, 1945, is located online via the Avalon Project, http://avalon.law.yale.edu/wwii/yalta.asp.

11. Jean Edward Smith, *Lucius D. Clay: An American Life* (New York: Henry Holt, 1990), 225. The new organization separated military government from the Army's General Staff. General Clay became the deputy for military government, while General Walter Bedell Smith, Eisenhower's chief of staff, became the deputy for military matters. The division of civilian and military power helped ensure that the occupation worked.

12. Taylor, *Exorcising Hitler*, 313–31. Each of the occupying powers took a slightly different approach to denazification. The Soviet Union took over former German concentration camps and prisons for known or suspected Nazis and seized their properties. The Soviet denazification effort proved to be the harshest of the major powers. The British denazification effort focused on the worst offenders but recognized that to get the economy functioning and the

civil administration working, it would be necessary to work with low-level Nazi party members. The French denazification effort proved to be the most lenient of the major powers. Only thirteen offenders in the French zone were classified as major offenders, while the Americans classified 1,654 as such in their zone.

13. Michael Hirsh, *The Liberators: America's Witnesses to the Holocaust* (New York: Bantam Books, 2010), 89–106.

14. Blumenson, *Patton Papers, 1940–1945*, vol. 2 (Boston: Houghton Mifflin, 1974), 738; Ziemke, *U.S. Army in the Occupation of Germany, 1944–1946*, 384–87.

15. It is interesting to note that the U.S. Army encountered similar issues in its 2003 invasion of Iraq. The wholesale removal of Baathist Party members from their administrative positions caused serious delays in the restoration of public services and contributed to anti-American resistance. "U.S. Vows to Remove Baath Officials in Iraq," CNN, May 15, 2003, and "Policy Easing to Bring Baathist into New Iraq," CNN, April 22, 2004.

16. The Paris Peace Conference, July–October 1946, led to the Paris Peace Treaties, signed on February 10, 1947, which officially ended the Allied war with Italy, Romania, Hungary, Bulgaria, and Finland. The Paris Peace Conference proceedings and documents are available online via the University of Wisconsin Digital Collection, http://digicoll.library.wisc.edu/cgi-bin/FRUS/FRUS-idx?id=FRUS.FRUS1946v03, and http://digicoll.library.wisc.edu/cgi-bin/FRUS/FRUS-idx?id=FRUS.FRUS1946v04.

17. Berlin remained a divided city, with West Berlin located inside the new DDR. East and West Germany finally unified in 1990 following the collapse of the Eastern Bloc.

18. For sources on the occupation of Japan see: Dower, *Embracing Defeat*, and Eiji, *Allied Occupation of Japan*.

19. To gain a more accurate understanding of the emperor's role during the war, see Herbert P. Bix, *Hirohito and the Making of Modern Japan* (New York: Harper Collins, 2000).

20. With the signing of the Treaty of Peace with the Allied powers on September 8, 1951, and its coming into force on April 28, 1952, Japan once again became an independent country. The text of the agreement is available online via the Avalon Project.

21. Mark Wyman, *DPs: Europe's Displaced Persons, 1945–1951* (Ithaca, NY: Cornell University Press, 1998), 17.

22. For a more detailed examination of the DP situation after the war see ibid. For an examination of life and death in Eastern Europe during the years 1933 to 1945 see Timothy Snyder, *Bloodlands: Europe Between Hitler and Stalin* (New York: Basic Books, 2010). Chapter 10, "Ethnic Cleansing," deals specifically with the final months of the war and the immediate postwar period in Eastern Europe.

23. R. M. Douglas, *Orderly and Humane: The Expulsion of the Germans After the Second World War* (New Haven, CT: Yale University Press, 2012), 1. Estimates of German civilians forced out of East Prussia, Poland, and eastern Germany are as high as fourteen million. The Soviet Union did not establish DP camps in its zone, leaving the Americans, British, and French occupying powers responsible for providing food, shelter, and security for the DPs. The Soviets did use former German concentration camps to house suspected former Nazis and enemies of the U.S.S.R.

24. Wyman, *DPs: Europe's Displaced Persons, 1945–1951*, 46–47.

25. The text of the repatriation agreement, signed February 11, 1945, as part of the Yalta agreements, is online via the Avalon Project.

26. U.S. Army Office of the Adjutant General, *Army Battle Casualties and Nonbattle Deaths in World War II: Final Report, 7 December 1941–31 December 1946* (Washington, D.C.: Government Printing Office, 1953), 5.

27. For additional information on World War II POWs, see Brian MacArthur, *Surviving the Sword: Prisoners of the Japanese in the Far East, 1942–45* (New York: Random House, 2005); Daniel Blatman, *The Death Marches: The Final Phase of the Nazi Genocide* (Cambridge, MA: Harvard University Press, 2011); Paul J. Springer, *America's Captives: Treatment of POWs*

from the Revolutionary War to the War on Terror (Lawrence: University Press of Kansas, 2010).

28. The list of Japanese prisoner abuses is long. Each of the Allied powers has its examples of Japanese war crimes toward its POWs. For example, the treatment of British prisoners building the Burma railway and Australian POWs on Ambon Island was particularly bad.

29. MacArthur, *Surviving the Sword*, 295–308; Yuki Tanaka, *Hidden Horrors: Japanese War Crimes in World War II* (Boulder, CO: Westview Press, 1996), 45–46.

30. James Bacque, *Other Losses: The Shocking Truth Behind the Mass Deaths of Disarmed German Soldiers and Civilians Under General Eisenhower's Command* (New York: Prima Publishing, 1991), argues that General Eisenhower was responsible for the death of a large number of German POWs after the war. Gunter Bischof and Stephen E. Ambrose, eds., *Eisenhower and the German POWs: Facts Against Falsehood* (Baton Rouge: Louisiana University Press, 1992), provide a detailed rebuttal to Bacque's argument by leading military historians and demonstrate that Bacque misinterpreted the Army POW records and failed to put them in the proper historical context. The need to feed additional millions in the final weeks of the war and the beginning weeks of the occupation taxed the Allied supply system, but it soon overcame the difficulties. As a short-term solution, many German POWs were transferred to British or French control, while the long-term solution was to screen them quickly, looking for Nazis, and releasing the common soldiers. Many young boys captured in uniform were quickly released and sent home.

31. MacDonald, *Last Offensive*, 478.

32. G. F. Krivosheev, ed., *Soviet Casualties and Combat Losses in the Twentieth Century* (London: Greenhill Books, 1997), 85. This is the first English edition of *Grif Sekretnosti Sniat* (Moscow, 1993), translated from the Russian by Christine Barnard and with a new foreword by John Erickson. The authors provide a detailed examination of the Soviet POW situation during the war on pages 230–38. Utilizing Soviet and German records, the authors place the number of Soviet POWs at 4,059,000 (237).

33. The Defense Prisoner of War/Missing Personnel Office, through DNA testing and further research, continues to search for the missing of World War II and to account for those who could not be identified at the time. See: "World War II," DPMO, www.dtic.mil/dpmo/wwii, for additional information.

34. Of the 78,976 servicemen missing, 32,569 are U.S. Navy personnel, most of whom were lost at sea and were presumed dead. "Service Personnel Not Recovered Following WWII," DPMO, www.dtic.mil/dpmo/wwii/reports.

35. David P. Colley, *Safely Rest* (New York: Caliber, 2004), 191.

36. For additional information on the National Memorial Cemetery of the Pacific, see "National Memorial Cemetery of the Pacific," U.S. Department of Veteran Affairs, www.cem.va.gov /CEM/cems/nchp/nmcp.asp#hi.

37. The best sources on this subject are: Colley, *Safely Rest*; Michael Sledge, *Soldier Dead: How We Recover, Identify, Bury, and Honor Our Military Fallen* (New York: Columbia University Press, 2005); and B. C. Mossman and M. W. Start, *The Last Salute: Civil and Military Funerals, 1921–1969* (Washington, D.C.: Department of the Army, 1971).

38. Useful sources on the Holocaust include: Michael Berenbaum, *The World Must Know: The History of the Holocaust as Told in the United States* (Boston: Little, Brown, 1993); Deborah Dwork and Robert Jan van Pelt, *Holocaust: A History* (New York: W. W. Norton, 2002); Michael Berenbaum and Abraham J. Peck, eds. *The Holocaust and History: The Known, the Unknown, the Disputed, and the Reexamined* (Bloomington: Indiana University Press, 1998); Michael Shermer and Alex Grobman, *Denying History: Who Says the Holocaust Never Happened and Why Do They Say It?* (Berkeley: University of California Press, 2000); and Raul Hilbert, *The Destruction of the European Jews*, 3rd ed., 3 vols. (New Haven, CT: Yale University Press, 2003).

39. The text of the Joint Four Nation Declaration following the Moscow Conference is available online via the Avalon Project, http://avalon.law.yale.edu/wwii/moscow.asp.

40. William Schabas, *Unimaginable Atrocities: Justice, Politics, and Rights at the War Crimes Tribunals* (Oxford: Oxford University Press, 2012).

41. There has been a great deal of debate over the years as to the role played by the German Army in the Holocaust and other war crimes. The publication of the Hamburg Institute for Social Research, *The German Army and Genocide: Crimes Against War Prisoners, Jews, and Other Civilians, 1939–1944* (New York: New Press, 1999), intensified the debate in Germany in the 1990s. Based on a traveling exhibit of German soldier photographs of the Holocaust and war crimes, which opened in 1995, the book highlights the role of the regular German Army in World War II war crimes and atrocities. It forced Germans to reexamine their views of the regular German soldier in World War II.

42. Michael Burleigh, *Moral Combat: Good and Evil in World War II* (New York: HarperCollins, 2011), 543.

43. The Nuremberg Trials took place between October 20, 1945, and October 1, 1946. The Tokyo Trials took place between May 3, 1946, and November 4, 1948.

44. Of the other three, two died before trial and one was deemed mentally unfit. Useful sources on the German War Crimes Trials include: Telford Taylor, *The Anatomy of the Nuremberg Trials: A Personal Memoir* (New York: Alfred A. Knopf, 1992); Patricia Heberer and Jurgen Matthaus, eds., *Atrocities on Trial: Historical Perspectives on the Politics of Prosecuting War Crimes* (Lincoln: University of Nebraska Press, 2008); Hilary Earl, *The Nuremberg SS-Einsatzgruppen Trial, 1945–1958: Atrocity, Law, and History* (Cambridge: Cambridge University Press, 2008); and Christopher J. Dodd, *Letters from Nuremberg: My Father's Narrative of a Quest for Justice* (New York: Crown Publishing, 2007).

45. For additional information on the Tokyo War Crimes Trials and Japanese war crimes, see: Tim Maga, *Judgement at Tokyo: The Japanese War Crimes Trials* (Lexington: University Press of Kentucky, 2001); Allan A. Ryan, *Yamashita's Ghost: War Crimes, MacArthur's Justice, and Command Responsibility* (Lawrence: University Press of Kansas, 2012); Iris Chang, *The Rape of Nanking: The Forgotten Holocaust of World War II* (New York: Basic Books, 1997); Tanaka, *Hidden Horrors*. For additional information on the Japanese treatment of prisoners of war, see: MacArthur, *Surviving the Sword*.

46. Sir Hartley Shawcross, "International Law: A Statement of the British View of Its Role," *American Bar Association Journal* 33 (1947): 32; Schabas, *Unimaginable Atrocities*, 1.

47. Schabas, *Unimaginable Atrocities*, 12–13.

48. John C. Sparrow, *History of Personnel Demobilization in the United States Army* (Washington, D.C.: Center for Military History, 1994), 265.

49. R. Ernest Dupuy and Trevor N. Dupuy, *Military Heritage of America* (New York: McGraw-Hill, 1956), 647.

50. Sparrow, *History of Personnel Demobilization*, 108.

51. Ibid., 112.

52. For an overview of the global effort to understand what happened during the Second World War, see Robin Higham, ed., *Official Histories: Essays and Bibliographies from Around the World* (Manhattan, KS: Kansas State University Library, 1970). The volume includes a number of useful essays on official history in general: Capt. S. W. Roskill's "Some Reasons for Official History" and Martin Blumenson's "Can Official History Be Honest History," are particularly useful for anyone looking to use official histories. The bulk of the book's nearly six hundred pages consists of essays and bibliographies on the official histories produced by forty-six nations to 1970, organized by country. Although the volume covers periods other than World War II, the depth and breadth of official history produced that relates to the Second World War highlights the importance these nations placed on determining what happened and why. Despite the fact that additional material has been produced since 1970, the volume remains an invaluable source on the official histories of the Second World War.

53. Official histories of the U.S. efforts in World War II that are readily available include the following: *The U.S. Army in World War II* series, currently 78 vols.; *The Army Air Forces in World*

War II, 7 vols. edited by W. F. Craven and J. L. Cates; and Morison, *History of United States Naval Operations in World War II*, 15 vols. *The U.S. Army in World War II Readers Guide* and all of the volumes are available online via the U.S. Army Center of Military History, http://history.army.mil/html/bookshelves/collect/usaww2.html. The United States Marine Corps official histories have also been made available online by the Marine Corps History Division, www.mcu.usmc.mil/historydivision/Pages/Staff/Publications.aspx#2001.

54. Unit histories took several forms. Some were published by individual units prior to their deactivation. For example, the Fifth Armored Division Association, *Paths of Armor: The Fifth Armored Division in World War II* (Atlanta: Albert Love, 1950), is a detailed examination of the unit's wartime experience.

55. Higher-level commands, army and army groups, produced reports at war's end. These reports of operations contain a wealth of information. The First Army Report of Operations consists of fourteen volumes in three parts: *First United States Army Report of Operations, 20 October 1943 to 1 August 1944*, 7 vols. (Paris, 1944); *First United States Army Report of Operations, 1 August 1944 to 22 February 1945*, 4 vols. (Washington, D.C.: Government Printing Office, 1946); and *First United States Army Report of Operations, 23 February to 8 May 1945*, 3 vols. (Washington, D.C.: Government Printing Office, 1946). The *Third Army Report of Operations* consists of two large oversized volumes.

56. The Reports of the General Board of the European Theater of Operations are available online via the United States Army Combined Arms Center, http://usacac.army.mil/cac2/cgsc/carl/eto/eto.asp.

57. U.S. Forces, European Theater, "Report 60, Study of Organization, Equipment and Tactical Employment of Tank Destroyer Units," in *Reports of the General Board* (Washington, D.C.: U.S. Army, 1945), 29, or the original typescript report online, http://usacac.army.mil/cac2/cgsc/carl/eto/eto-060.pdf.

58. The Index to the World War II U.S. Strategic Bombing Survey is available online, www.ibiblio.org/hyperwar/AAF/USSBS, and includes links to the summaries of the European and Pacific bombing campaigns. Many of the actual survey volumes are available online, www.angelfire.com/super/ussbs.

59. For the best assessment of the U.S. Strategic Bombing Survey in World War II, see Gentile, *How Effective Is Strategic Bombing?*

60. For a more in-depth examination of why the Allies won World War II, see Overy, *Why the Allies Won*, 1–396. There is no better book to turn to for an explanation of why the Allies won. His analysis remains the best available and has greatly influenced this section of this chapter.

61. Recommended sources for this section include John Ellis, *World War II: The Encyclopedia of Facts and Figures* (New York: Military Book Club, 1995); Mark Harrison, ed., *The Economics of World War II: Six Great Powers in International Comparison* (Cambridge: Cambridge University Press, 1998); R. J. Overy, *War and Economy in the Third Reich* (Oxford: Oxford University Press, 1994); Robert Goralski and Russell W. Freeburg, *Oil & War: How the Deadly Struggle for Fuel in WWII Meant Victory or Defeat* (New York: William Morrow, 1987); Adam Tooze, *The Wages of Destruction: The Making and Breaking of the Nazi Economy* (New York: Viking, 2006); Arthur Herman, *How American Business Produced Victory in World War II* (New York: Random House, 2012); Alan S. Milward, *War, Economy and Society, 1939–1945* (Berkeley: University of California Press, 1979); Paul A. C. Koistinen, *Arsenal of World War II: The Political Economy of American Warfare, 1940–1945* (Lawrence: University Press of Kansas, 2004); John Ellis, *Brute Force: Allied Strategy and Tactics in the Second World War* (New York: Viking, 1990).

62. Goralski and Freeburg, *Oil & War*, 336–47. In 1939 the United States produced on average 3,466,000 barrels of oil per day, compared with Germany's 12,293 and Japan's 7,271 barrels. During the war, German oil production peaked at a daily average of 20,139 barrels in 1940 and never again rose above 17,268 barrels per day. Germany refined 29,120 barrels per day and produced 73,834 barrels per day through synthetic processes in 1940. The 29,120 tons refined

per day included imported crude refined in Germany. The United States, with 62.9 percent of global oil production in 1940, exported 316,606 barrels per day.

63. *The Big Inch and Little Big Inch Pipelines: The Most Amazing Government-Industry Cooperation Ever Achieved* (Houston, TX: Texas Eastern Transmission Corporation, 2000), 18.

64. Mark Harrison, "The Economics of World War II: An Overview," in *Economics of World War II*, ed. Harrison, 10. The percentage GDP increase is based upon wartime GDP of the great powers, 1939–1945, in international dollars and 1990 prices (billions).

65. Ibid., 10.

66. Mark Harrison, "The Soviet Union: The Defeated Victor," in *Economics of World War II*, ed. Harrison, 297.

67. Harrison, "The Economics of World War II," in *Economics of World War II*, ed. Harrison, 10.

68. Werner Abelshauser, "Germany: Guns, Butter, and Economic Miracles," in *Economics of World War II*, ed. Harrison, 160–61.

69. The Japanese wartime economy was in its fifth year of war when the Japanese attacked Pearl Harbor and expanded their war into Southeast Asia. With limited resources and production capacity, Japan was in no position to match Allied production. The war had to end quickly, or the country likely faced a long, slow defeat. For additional information on the Japanese economy, see Akira Hara, "Japan: Guns Before Rice," in *Economics of World War II*, ed. Harrison.

70. Richard Langworth, *Churchill by Himself: The Definitive Collection of Quotations* (New York: Public Affairs, 2008), 12.

71. A large number of World War II Conference documents are available online via the Avalon Project. Recommended document collections include: Washington Conference Documents, http://avalon.law.yale.edu/subject_menus/washconf.asp; Atlantic Conference Documents, http://avalon.law.yale.edu/subject_menus/atmenu.asp; Casablanca Conference Documents, http://avalon.law.yale.edu/wwii/casablan.asp; Quebec Conference Documents, http://avalon.law.yale.edu/subject_menus/quebec.asp; Cairo Conference Documents, http://avalon.law.yale.edu/wwii/cairo.asp; Tehran Conference Documents, http://avalon.law.yale.edu/wwii/tehran.asp; Yalta Conference Documents, http://avalon.law.yale.edu/wwii/yalta.asp; and Potsdam Conference Documents, http://avalon.law.yale.edu/20th_century/decade17.asp.

72. A very good source for the American side of the Joint Chiefs of Staff relationship is Mark A. Stoler, *Allies and Adversaries: The Joint Chiefs of Staff, the Grand Alliance, and U.S. Strategy in World War II* (Chapel Hill, NC: University of North Carolina Press, 2000).

73. When Mussolini launched his invasion of Greece, he unknowingly set in motion a series of events that would deprive Germany of an airborne force for use in Operation Barbarossa. The Italian invasion of Greece brought the British into the Balkans, which put British aircraft in range of Hitler's primary oil supply: the Romanian oil fields at Ploeşti. The German invasion of the Balkans drove the British out of Greece and to Crete. The German airborne assault on Crete succeeded, but its forces suffered such heavy losses that Hitler lost confidence in the effectiveness of airborne forces. An intact German airborne force would not have won the war in the East, but it would have given the German forces an additional option when contemplating its strategy there.

74. Had Japan declared war on Russia in the summer or fall of 1941, the Siberian divisions would not have been available to move west and would not have been available for use in the counterattack at Moscow in December 1941. It would have made the Soviet situation much worse than it already was.

75. The Bretton Woods Conference was held in New Hampshire in July 1944. Delegates from forty-four nations met to outline plans for postwar economic cooperation. They called for the creation of the International Monetary Fund and the International Bank for Reconstruction and Development, now known as the World Bank. The U.S.S.R. refused to attend. The Dumbarton Oaks Conference was held in Washington, D.C., in August–October 1944, with delegates from thirty-nine nations meeting to form the United Nations.

76. Germany was the dominant member of the Axis in Europe. The Axis minor allies, Hungary, Romania, Bulgaria, and Finland, supplied military forces to Germany along with what supplies they could, but never had a role in determining Axis strategy. Italy surrendered in September 1943, and as the Soviet forces advanced westward in 1944–45, the other Axis minor allies surrendered and/or switched sides. Germans and Italians did fight together in North Africa and Sicily and on the Eastern Front. Mussolini supplied an Italian Army, which, along with the Hungarian and Romanian armies, was destroyed by the Soviet counteroffensive at Stalingrad. The surrender of Italy led to a German occupation of northern Italy, the seizure of all military assets, and the arrest of Italian military personnel and their use as forced labor for the remainder of the war. Although Germany and Japan did attempt to share strategic resources once it became clear the war was going badly, the inability to effectively transport materials between the two nations meant that very little was accomplished. Once the Caucasus were lost in the winter of 1942–43, German long-range aircraft could no longer reach Japan; the use of U-boats to transport materials to Japan proved slow and unreliable, and little cargo was actually exchanged. Germany did transfer some scientific information related to jet aircraft at the very end of the war, when it was too late to impact the Japanese war effort. Cooperation among the Axis powers and Axis minor allies was never that of equals.

77. President Franklin Roosevelt put forth the Four Freedoms in his State of the Union speech, January 6, 1941, www.presidency.ucsb.edu/ws/?pid=16092. These were freedoms that all Americans could relate to and understand.

78. The Soviet liberation of Eastern Europe and Manchuria and Northern Korea began with the elimination of the Axis forces and ended with the establishment of pro-Soviet governments.

79. Weinberg, *World at Arms*, 894–920. Peace and freedom in the postwar world depended upon the beholder. Each of the Allies viewed freedom and peace through its own prism. They could agree on the terms to end the war but differed over what victory meant. Peace and freedom for the colonial powers meant one thing; for the Soviet Union, another; and for the United States, another.

80. For an exploration of the moral sentiments of the warring societies in World War II, see Burleigh, *Moral Combat*.

81. Over the course of the war, neutral nations began to join the Allies in increasing numbers. Only countries that had declared war on Germany and Japan as of March 1945 were invited to join the United Nations. While neutral nations continued to trade with the Axis if they could reach them, the majority of their trade was with the Allied powers, since they controlled much of the world's oceans. Some neutrals became Allies early in the war and provided military resources to the fight against the Axis. Mexico declared war on the Axis on May 22, 1942, and provided a fighter squadron that saw service in the Philippines in 1945. Brazil declared war on Germany on August 22, 1942, and provided a division of troops and an air group for service in Italy in 1944. Brazil also played an important role in the Battle of the Atlantic, providing air bases to support air patrols looking for U-boats in the South Atlantic.

82. T. N. Dupuy, *Numbers, Predictions, and War: Using History to Evaluate Combat Factors and Predict the Outcome of Battles* (Indianapolis: Bobbs-Merrill, 1977), 59.

83. The military-effectiveness debate has been ongoing since the end of the war. The debate centers around the effectiveness of each army and its effectiveness relative to other armies. For much of the postwar period, there has been a tendency to overstate the overall effectiveness of the German soldier and to minimize the overall effectiveness of the Allied soldiers. Beginning in the 1990s, a number of new works sought to provide scholarly examinations of the issue. The nature of the debate is illustrated by a *Military Affairs* (now the *Journal of Military History*) article by John Sloan Brown, "Colonel Trevor N. Dupuy and the Mythos of Wehrmacht Superiority: A Reconsideration," *Military Affairs* 50, no. 1 (January 1986): 16–20, and the resulting back-and-forth of letters to the editor by Trevor N. Dupuy and the author. See: Trevor N. Dupuy, "Mythos or Verity? The Quantified Judgment Model and German Combat Effectiveness," *Military Affairs* 50, no. 4 (October 1986): 204–10; John Sloan Brown, "The

Wehrmacht Mythos Revisited: A Challenge for Colonel Trevor N. Dupuy," *Military Affairs* 51, no. 3 (July 1987): 146–47; and Trevor N. Dupuy, "A Response to 'The Wehrmacht Mythos Revisited,'" *Military Affairs* 51, no. 4 (October 1987): 196–97. Michael Doubler, *Closing with the Enemy* (Lawrence: University Press of Kansas, 1994), Keith Bonn, *When the Odds Were Even* (New York: Presidio Press, 1994); and Peter Mansoor, *The GI Offensive In Europe: The Triumph of American Infantry Divisions, 1941–1945* (Lawrence: University Press of Kansas, 1999), each argues that the American soldier in World War II compared well with his German counterpart and that the military effectiveness of the American Army was higher than it had been given credit for.

Chapter 1

1. Copyright Rowan Technology Solutions, 2016.
2. Copyright Rowan Technology Solutions, 2016.
3. *So wie wir kämpfen—Arbeite du für den Sieg!* (Eng. "Like we fight—You too must work for the victory!"), German propaganda poster, 1942.
4. *World War II. German soldiers, bicycle division, tank and lorry transporting soldiers*, Forum, Bridgeman Images.
5. Vadim Volikov, *Sevastopol—Hero City*, 1957, gouache on paper, Gamborg Collection, Bridgeman Images.
6. Copyright Rowan Technology Solutions, 2016.
   Military layer based on Ziemke and Bauer's map, "The Reconquest of Kerch, 8–19 May 1942," *Moscow to Stalingrad: Decision in the East* (Washington, D.C.: Center of Military History, United States Army, 1987).
7. Copyright Rowan Technology Solutions, 2016.
   Military layer based on Ziemke and Bauer's maps, "The Soviet Offensive, Kharkov, 12–19 May 1942" and "The German Counteroffensive, Kharkov, 17–28 May 1942," *Moscow to Stalingrad: Decision in the East.* Washington, D.C.: Center of Military History, United States Army, 1987.
8. German photographer, *An aerial view of the battle of Kharkov-Izium*, twentieth century, black-and-white photograph, copyright SZ Photo, Bridgeman Images.
9. Bundesarchiv, Bild 183-B21845, photo: Wahner.
10. German photographer, *German tanks advancing into the Caucasus mountains, during the Second World War*, 1942, black-and-white photograph, copyright SZ Photo, Bridgeman Images.
11. Copyright Rowan Technology Solutions, 2016.
    Military layer based on Esposito's map 30, "German Summer Offensive of 1942, Plans and Preliminary Operations (8 May–27 June)," *West Point Atlas of American Wars*, vol. 2.
12. Bundesarchiv, Bild 101I-218-0502-32, photo: Lechner.
13. Copyright Rowan Technology Solutions, 2016.
    Military layer based on Esposito's maps 32–34, "German Summer Offensive of 1942, Operations, 23 July 1942–1 January 1943," *West Point Atlas of American Wars*, vol. 2.
14. Bundesarchiv, Bild 183-1991-0221-503, photo: Bauer.
15. Erich Schilling, *Das Zweifrontblitzgespräch*, 1942, Simplicissimus, Heft 43, Seite: 676.
16. Copyright Rowan Technology Solutions, 2016.
    Military layer based on Esposito's map 32, "German Summer Offensive of 1942, Operations, 23 July–23 August 1942," *West Point Atlas of American Wars*, vol. 2.
17. Paske, *Dem Kuhnen allein ist das Gluck hold. CLAUSEWITZ*, 1940, poster courtesy of the Hennepin County Library Special Collections (mpw00603), Minneapolis, Minnesota.
18. Bundesarchiv, Bild 101I-218-0529-07, photo: Thiede.
19. Bundesarchiv, Bild 183-E0406-0022-001, photo: o.Ang.
20. Bundesarchiv, Bild 183-B22478, photo: Rothkopf.
21. Bundesarchiv, Bild 183-R74190, photo: unknown.
22. Kukryniksy, *There Is a Rock on the Volga*, 1943, color lithograph, Tretyakov Gallery, Moscow, Russia, Bridgeman Images.
23. Kukryniksy, *I've lost my ring . . .* , 1943, color lithograph, Tretyakov Gallery, Moscow, Russia, Bridgeman Images.
24. Bundesarchiv, Bild 183-E0406-0022-011, photo: o.Ang.
25. Copyright Rowan Technology Solutions, 2016.
    Military layer based on Esposito's map 75b, "Rommel's Second Offensive (21 January–7 July 1942)," *West Point Atlas of American Wars*, vol. 2.
26. English photographer, *Field Marshal Bernard L. Montgomery during the second battle of El Alamein, Libya, November 1942*, 1942, black-and-white photograph, copyright Galerie Bilderwelt / Bridgeman Images.
27. Bundesarchiv, Bild 101I-443-1574-23, photo: Ernst A. Zwilling.
28. Lute Pease, *Montgomery Africanus*, 1942, The Anne S. K. Brown Military Collection.
29. Copyright Rowan Technology Solutions, 2016.
    Military layer based on Esposito's map 79, "Battle of El Alamein, Operations, 1–4 November 1942," *West Point Atlas of American Wars*, vol. 2.
30. Copyright Rowan Technology Solutions, 2016.
    Military layer based on Esposito's map 132, "Guadalcanal Campaign, The Landing, 7 August 1942, and Concurrent Operations," *West Point Atlas of American Wars*, vol. 2.
31. Copyright Rowan Technology Solutions, 2016.
    Military layer based on Esposito's map 130, "Area Under Japanese Control (6 August 1942), The Allied Reorganization (30 March 1942)," *West Point Atlas of American Wars*, vol. 2.
32. American photographer, *US Marines storm ashore, Battle of Guadalcanal, 7th August 1942*, 1942, black-and-white photograph, private collection, Peter Newark Pictures, Bridgeman Images.
33. Copyright Rowan Technology Solutions, 2016.
    Military layer based on Esposito's maps 133, 135–137, "Guadalcanal Campaign, Initial Landings and Capture of Henderson Field, 7 August 1942–7 February 1943," *West Point Atlas of American Wars*, vol. 2.
34. American photographer, *US Marine operates flamethrower, Battle of Guadalcanal, August 1942*, 1942, photograph, private collection, Peter Newark Military Pictures, Bridgeman Images.

Chapter 2

35. Copyright Rowan Technology Solutions, 2016.
36. Robert Benney, *The Kill*, 1943, 88-159-AP as a Gift of Abbott Laboratories, courtesy of Navy Art Collection, Naval History and Heritage Command.

37. Political Poster Collection, UK 3063, Hoover Institution Archives, courtesy of Hoover Institution Library & Archives, Stanford University.
38. Political Poster Collection, UK 3260, Hoover Institution Archives, courtesy of Hoover Institution Library & Archives, Stanford University.
39. *Convoy WS-12*, 1944, 80-G-464654, courtesy of Navy Art Collection, Naval History and Heritage Command.
40. Admiral Doenitz, *Commander-in-Chief of the German Submarine, at his cartography table. At his right is the lieutenant of the ship*, from *Signal* magazine, no. 3, first edition of February 1943, photograph, private collection, Bridgeman Images.
41. Bundesarchiv, Bild 193-04-1-26, photo: o.Ang.
42. Bundesarchiv, Bild 101II-MW-6816-25A, photo: Tiemer.
43. Political Poster Collection, GE 3855, Hoover Institution Archives, courtesy of Hoover Institution Library & Archives, Stanford University.
44. Copyright Rowan Technology Solutions, 2016.
   Statistical Digest of the War (London: HMSO, 1951), 186–87.
45. Daniel Robert Fitzpatrick, *The Shooting War Has Started*, 1941, Daniel Fitzpatrick Collection, F582 1941-11-01, The State Historical Society of Missouri.
46. European School, *Enigma cipher machine with three rotors viewed from above*, twentieth century, photograph, private collection, Prismatic Pictures, Bridgeman Images.
47. Admiralty, The Anti-Submarine Report, CB 4050/Series, Monthly Losses of Allied and Neutral Shipping by U-boat Action, National Security Agency, *Battle of the Atlantic,* vol. 1, *Allied Communications in Intelligence, December 1942–May 1945.*
48. Edna Reindel, *Calship Burner, Wilmington, California*, 1943, United States Army Center of Military History.
49. National Association of Manufacturers (U.S.), *Making America strong: How American shipyards are winning the race against time to build our Navy*, University of North Texas Libraries.
50. *The Pre-Fabricated Ship*, On the Water, Building Ships for Victory, Smithsonian National Museum of American History, http://americanhistory.si.edu/onthewater/exhibition/6_2.html.
51. *Baltimore, Maryland. A large blower being hoisted into place during the construction of the Liberty ship Frederick Douglass*, Library of Congress Prints and Photographs Division, Washington, D.C.
52. Copyright Rowan Technology Solutions, 2016.
   Stephen W. Roskill, *The War at Sea, 1939–1945: Volume III, Part II* (London, HMSO, 1961), Appendix ZZ.
53. Arthur Douglas Wales-Smith, *Admiral Sir Max Horton*, National Maritime Museum, BHC2783.
54. Frederick Donald Blake, "*The Battle of the Atlantic,*" twentieth century, color lithograph, Museum of New Zealand Te Papa Tongarewa, Wellington, New Zealand, Bridgeman Images.
55. Hitting Germany : where it hurts her most : R.A.F.'s increasing attack : 1943 — the weight of attack grows steadily, 1943, courtesy of World War Poster Collection (msp03154), Literary Manuscripts Collection, University of Minnesota Libraries, Minneapolis, Minnesota.
56. United States Government, *8th Air Force psychological warfare leaflet*, circa 1943-44.
57. United States Government, *8th Air Force psychological warfare leaflet*, circa 1944.
58. Political Poster Collection, UK 3257, Hoover Institution Archives, courtesy of Hoover Institution Library & Archives, Stanford University.
59. Erich Schilling, *Der "Sieger" von Antwerpen*, 1943, Simplicissimus, Heft 16, Seite 239.
60. W. Krogman, "*Britain's Air Offensive: Berlin by Night,*" courtesy of World War Poster Collection (msp04012), Literary Manuscripts Collection, University of Minnesota Libraries, Minneapolis, Minnesota.
61. Stannus (Flying Officer), Royal Air Force official photographer, *The Second World War 1939–1945: Great Britain Personalities*, Imperial War Museums, Air Ministry Second World War Official Collection, copyright IWM (CH 13020).
62. German School, "*The Enemy Sees Your Light! Blackout!*" 1942, color lithograph, private collection, Peter Newark Military Pictures, Bridgeman Images.
63. Thomas Stephens, *Carl A. Spaatz*, Airman Magazine, Creative Commons Attribution NonCommercial 2.0 Generic license.
64. Political Poster Collection, UK 3065, Hoover Institution Archives, courtesy of Hoover Institution Library & Archives, Stanford University.
65. Bundesarchiv, Bild 183-R93452, photo: o.Ang.
66. United States Air Force, *B-24 Flak*, 1944, National Museum of the U.S. Air Force.
67. Copyright Rowan Technology Solutions, 2016.
   Bernhard R. Kroener, Rolf-Dieter Müller, and Hans Umbreit, *Germany and the Second World War, vol. 5, part 2, Wartime Administration, Economy, and Manpower Resources, 1942–1944/5*, ed. Militärgeschichtliches Forschungsamt, trans. Derry Cook-Radmore et al. (Oxford: Clarendon Press, 2003), 708, 712, 610.
68. Military layer based on Esposito's map 23, "German and Russian Dispositions, June 1941, German Gains in Russia (June 1941–May 1942)," *West Point Atlas of American Wars*, vol. 2.
69. Bundesarchiv, Bild 146-1981-157-29, photo: o.Ang.
70. Copyright Rowan Technology Solutions, 2016.
   Richard G. Davis, *Bombing the European Axis Powers: A Historical Digest of the Combined Bomber Offensive, 1939–1945* (Maxwell, AL: Air University Press), 577–80.
71. Copyright Rowan Technology Solutions, 2016.
   Imperial War Museum Archive, S363, Saur papers, "Auszug aus dem Leistungsbericht von Minister Speer, 27.1.1945" [Extract from the Report on Achievements by Minister Speer].
72. The United States Strategic Bombing Survey, *The Effects of Strategic Bombing on German Morale, Volume 1*, 1947, 6.
73. "*You Bet I'm Going Back to Sea,*" circa 1942–1945, National Archives and Records Administration, 516205.
74. Copyright Rowan Technology Solutions, 2016.
   U.S. Bomber Pilot, Chase Stone, 2016.

CHAPTER 3

75. Copyright Rowan Technology Solutions, 2016.

76. Signal Corps Photo: MM-Har-9-3-43-Pl-2 (Harman), *Sicily Invasion, Cartoon on the Jeep of Cpl. Paul F. Janesk, Antrim, Penn., with the face of Mussolini crossed out*, 1943, National Archives and Records Administration, Signal Corps Collection, Record Group #111.

77. "*Snipping Will Never Save the House . . . You Gotta Smash Those Pots!*," 1942, Dr. Seuss Political Cartoons, Special Collection & Archives, University of California, San Diego.

78. Erich Schilling, *Station Salomonen*, 1943, Simplicissimus, Heft 48, Seite: 623.

79. Copyright Rowan Technology Solutions, 2016.
Military layer based on Esposito's map 36, "Russian Winter Offensive of 1943, Operations, 2 February–4 July 1943," *West Point Atlas of American Wars*, vol. 2.

80. Bundesarchiv, Bild 101III-Zschaeckel-190-29, photo: Zschäckel, Friedrich.

81. Copyright Rowan Technology Solutions, 2016.
Military layer based on Esposito's map 30, "German Summer Offensive of 1942, Plans and Preliminary Operations (8 May–27 June)," *West Point Atlas of American Wars*, vol. 2.

82. Bundesarchiv, Bild 101I-698-0038-04, photo: Schmidt-Scheeder, Georg.

83. David M. Glantz and Jonathan M. House, *The Battle of Kursk* (Lawrence, KS: University Press of Kansas, 1999), 283–335.
David M. Glantz, *Companion to Colossus Reborn, Key Documents and Statistics* (Lawrence, KS: University Press of Kansas, 2005), 234–69.

84. Copyright Rowan Technology Solutions, 2016.
Military layer based on Esposito's map 38b, "Russian Summer Offensive of 1943, Operations Around Kursk, July 1943," *West Point Atlas of American Wars*, vol. 2.

85. German photographer, *German infantry men attacking a Russian position during the attack on Kursk*, 1943, black-and-white photograph, copyright SZ Photo, Scherl, Bridgeman Images.

86. Copyright Rowan Technology Solutions, 2016.
Military layer based on Esposito's map 80, "The Pursuit to Tunisia (November 1942–February 1943)," *West Point Atlas of American Wars*, vol. 2.
Military layer based on Esposito's map 81, "The Allied Invasion, General Map," *West Point Atlas of American Wars*, vol. 2.

87. Military layer based on Esposito's map 85, "Battle of Kasserine Pass, Operations, 14–22 February 1943," *West Point Atlas of American Wars*, vol. 2.

88. Military layer based on Esposito's map 85, "Battle of Kasserine Pass, Operations, 14–22 February 1943," *West Point Atlas of American Wars*, vol. 2.

89. *The crew of 105-mm Howitzer, Battery B., 33rd Field Artillery with gun set in Arabic mud-block abode for firing in defense of the Kassserine Pass, North Africa*, 1943, Library of Congress Prints and Photographs Division, Washington, D.C.

90. *Kasserine Pass*, 1943, United States Army Center of Military History.

91. *The Expulsion of Axis forces from North Africa*, 1943, courtesy of World War Poster Collection (msp03274), Literary Manuscripts Collection, University of Minnesota Libraries, Minneapolis, Minnesota.

92. Canadian Government, *Harold Alexander*, circa 1944–1946, Library and Archives Canada, 4233815.

93. Copyright Rowan Technology Solutions, 2016.
Military layer based on Esposito's map 90, "Plan for Landings, 10 July 1943, *West Point Atlas of American Wars*," vol. 2.

94. Mitchell Jamieson, *Invasion Craft—Sicily*, United States Navy, U.S. Navy Art Gallery, Washington, D.C.

95. Bundesarchiv, Bild 102-13805, photo: o.Ang.

96. Copyright Rowan Technology Solutions, 2016.
Paratrooper of the 82nd Airborne Division, Chase Stone, 2016.

97. Copyright Rowan Technology Solutions, 2016.
Military layer based on Esposito's maps 91–93, "Approximate Line, 15 July 1943, and Beachheads Established, 10 July," *West Point Atlas of American Wars*, vol. 2.

98. Sgt John Silverside, No. 2 Army Film & Photographic Unit, *The British Army in Sicily 1943*, 1943, Imperial War Museums, War Office Second World War Official Collection, copyright IWM (NA 5335).

99. Signal Corps, Half-Track Detouring Through a Side Street, SC 184187, *United States Army in World War II, Pictorial Record, The War Against Germany and Italy: Mediterranean and Adjacent Areas*, United States Army Center of Military History, 129.

100. Signal Corps Photo: MM-Bri-7-28-43-R2-6 (Lt. Brin), *Farewell, Gen. Bernard Law Montgomery and Lt. Gen. George S. Patton, Jr.*, 1943, National Archives and Records Administration, Signal Corps Collection, Record Group #111.

101. Political Poster Collection, RU/SU 2520 (OS), Hoover Institution Archives, courtesy of Hoover Institution Library & Archives, Stanford University.

102. *Assault wave, Salerno. Allied troops pour ashore at Salerno, wading through the surf under heavy machine gun and shell fire from hidden enemy positions back of the beaches. One of the landing craft is set aflame by an enemy shell. Another shell just misses an LCVP (landing craft, vehicle personnel) and sends up a plume of smoke and water. Allied cruisers come in close to shore to blast the enemy whose positions are relayed by naval spotters advancing with the landing parties*, Library of Congress Prints and Photographs Division, Washington, D.C.

103. Copyright Rowan Technology Solutions, 2016.
Military layer based on Esposito's map 95, "Salerno Campaign, Plan for Landing at Salerno, 9 September 1943, and Situation at Nightfall, 11 September," *West Point Atlas of American Wars*, vol. 2.

104. *Moving up through Prato, Italy, men of the 370th Infantry Regiment, have yet to climb the mountain which lies ahead*, National Archives and Records Administration, 531277.

105. Copyright Rowan Technology Solutions, 2016.
Military layer based on Martini's map 22, "The Far East and the Pacific, 1942, Status of Forces and Theater Boundaries, 2 July 1942," USMA History Department.

106. *Franklin D. Roosevelt, General MacArthur, and Admiral Nimitz in Pearl Harbor, Hawaii*, National Archives and Records Administration, 196366.
107. Signal Corps Photo: 161-43-4081 (Schuman), *Vella Lavella*, 1943, National Archives and Records Administration, Signal Corps Collection, Record Group #111.
108. Copyright Rowan Technology Solutions, 2016.
    Military layer based on Esposito's map 140, "Operations in the Solomon Islands, August 1942 to December 1943," and "Concurrent Operations in New Guinea and New Britain," *West Point Atlas of American Wars*, vol. 2.
109. Copyright Rowan Technology Solutions, 2016.
    Military layer based on Esposito's map 140, "Operations in the Solomon Islands, August 1942 to December 1943," and "Concurrent Operations in New Guinea and New Britain," *West Point Atlas of American Wars*, vol. 2.
110. Kerr Eby, *Ghost Trail*, 1944, 88-159-DZ as a Gift of Abbot Laboratories, courtesy of Navy Art Collection, Naval History and Heritage Command.
111. United States Navy, Paul T. Barnett, *Rabaul raid*, 1943, Naval Aviation Museum, Robert L. Lawson Photograph Collection, 1996.488.024.021.
112. Copyright Rowan Technology Solutions, 2016.
    Henry I. Shaw, Jr., Bernard C. Nalty, and Edwin T. Turnbladh, *History of U.S. Marine Corps Operations in World War II, Volume III: Central Pacific Drive* (Historical Branch, G-3 Division, Headquarters, U.S. Marine Corps, 1996).
113. Kerr Eby, *Bullets and Barbed Wire*, 1944, 88-159-CN as a Gift of Abbot Laboratories, courtesy of Navy Art Collection, Naval History and Heritage Command.
114. Kerr Eby, *Beachhead Scene, Marines at Tarawa*, 1944, 88-159-DG as a Gift of Abbott Laboratories, courtesy of Navy Art Collection, Naval History and Heritage Command.
115. Kerr Eby, *The Hard Road to Triumph*, 1944, 88-159-CK as a Gift of Abbot Laboratories, courtesy of Navy Art Collection, Naval History and Heritage Command.
116. Kerr Eby, *Marines Fall Forward*, 1944, 88-159-CM as a Gift of Abbot Laboratories, courtesy of Navy Art Collection, Naval History and Heritage Command.
117. Kerr Eby, *March Macabre*, 1944, 88-159-DD as a Gift of Abbot Laboratories, courtesy of Navy Art Collection, Naval History and Heritage Command.
118. Kerr Eby, *Ebb Tide, Tarawa*, 1944, 88-159-DQ as a Gift of Abbot Laboratories, courtesy of Navy Art Collection, Naval History and Heritage Command.
119. Tom Lovell, *Tarawa Landing*, twentieth century, color lithograph, Art Collection, National Museum of the Marine Corps, Triangle, Virginia, Peter Newark Military Pictures, Bridgeman Images.
120. *Roosevelt, Stalin, and Churchill on portico of Russian Embassy in Teheran, during conference—Nov. 28–Dec. 1, 1943*, Library of Congress Prints and Photographs Division, Washington, D.C.

CHAPTER 4

121. Copyright Rowan Technology Solutions, 2016.
122. Political Poster Collection, UK 2898, Hoover Institution Archives, courtesy of Hoover Institution Library & Archives, Stanford University.
123. German photographer, *A type T-34 Soviet tank used in the offensive against Germany*, twentieth century, black-and-white photographer, copyright SZ Photo, Bridgeman Images.
124. Copyright Rowan Technology Solutions, 2016.
    Percy Ernst Scrhamm, ed., *Kriegstagebuch des Overkommandos der Wehrmacht*, vol. 4, pt. 2 (Frankfurt am Main: Bernard & Graefe Verlag für Wehrwesen, 1961), 1515–16
125. USSR, *Pavel Rotmistrov*, circa 1945.
126. Bundesarchiv, Bild 101I-710-0396-18, photo: K. F. Maier.
127. Copyright Rowan Technology Solutions, 2016.
    Military layer based on Martini's map 29, "Eastern Europe, 1941, Russian Leningrad and the Ukraine Offensives, 2 Dec 1943–30 April 1944," USMA History Department.
128. Copyright Rowan Technology Solutions, 2016.
    Military layer based on Esposito's maps 42–43a, "Russian Summer Offensive of 1944, Operations, 23 June–14 September 1944," *West Point Atlas of American Wars*, vol. 2.
129. Bundesarchiv, Bild 183-41636-0002, photo: o.Ang.
130. Copyright Rowan Technology Solutions, 2016.
    Military layer based on Esposito's maps 43a–44a, "Russian Summer Offensive of 1944, Operations, 8 August–15 December 1944, Russian Winter Offensive of 1945, 16 December 1944–15 February 1945," *West Point Atlas of American Wars*, vol. 2.
131. Russian School, *The Red Army forced to cross over the Vistula, 31st July 1944*, 1944, oil on canvas, State Central Artillery Museum, St. Petersburg, Russia, Bridgeman Images.
132. Copyright Rowan Technology Solutions, 2016.
    David M. Glantz and Jonathan M. House, *When Titans Clashed*, 2nd ed. (Lawrence, KS: University Press of Kansas: 2015), Table N.
133. Copyright Rowan Technology Solutions, 2016.
    Military layer based on Esposito's map 97, "Allied Advance to 8 October 1943," *West Point Atlas of American Wars*, vol. 2.
134. Ed Reep, *Bombing the Abbey*, United States Army Center of Military History.
135. Copyright Rowan Technology Solutions, 2016.
    Military layer based on Esposito's map 103, "Cassino-Anzio Campaign, Situation, 31 March 1944, and Major Operations Since 17 January," *West Point Atlas of American Wars*, vol. 2.
136. English photographer, *Allied soldiers in front of Monumento Vittorio Emanuele II, Rome*, 1944, photograph, copyright Galerie Bilderwelt, Bridgeman Images.
137. *Men from the Ghost Army Lifting a Dummy Tank*, Department of Defense image.

138. Copyright Rowan Technology Solutions, 2016.
     Military layer based on Esposito's map 48, "Allied Invasion Force and German Dispositions, 6 June 1944," *West Point Atlas of American Wars*, vol. 2.
139. Bundesarchiv, Plak 003-029-056, photo: Mjölnir; [Schweitzer, Hans].
140. *Bocage Country at Cotentin Peninsula*, Wikimedia Commons.
141. *Sherman Rhino Normandy*, 1944, Wikimedia Commons.
142. Copyright Rowan Technology Solutions, 2016.
     SS Waffen Panzer Grenadier, Chase Stone, 2016.
143. Copyright Rowan Technology Solutions, 2016.
     Military layer based on Esposito's map 54, :The Breakout, Operations, 1–13 August 1944,: *West Point Atlas of American Wars*, vol. 2.
144. Copyright Rowan Technology Solutions, 2016.
     Military layer based on Esposito's map 54, "The Breakout, Operations, 1–13 August 1944," *West Point Atlas of American Wars*, vol. 2.
145. *Dead German troops litter an ambushed convoy in Chambois*, circa 1944, Archives Normandie, p000821.
146. United States Air Force, *Republic P-47D-40-RE in flight firing rockets* (S/N 44-90386).
147. *Omar Nelson Bradley, American General, U.S. Army field commander in both North Africa and Europe during the Second World War. Appointed first Chairman of the Joint Chiefs of Staff, September 1950, by President Truman*, Universal History Archive/UIG, Bridgeman Images.
148. Copyright Rowan Technology Solutions, 2016.
     Military layer based on Esposito's map 58, "General Situation, 15 September 1944, 21st Army Group Operations (15 September–15 December 1944)," *West Point Atlas of American Wars*, vol. 2.
149. *Waves of Paratroops Land in Holland*, 1944, United States National Archives and Records Administration.
150. Harry A. Davis, *The 28th Division in Paris*, United States Army Center of Military History.
151. *Members of the Red Ball Express repair a 2 1/2-ton truck, while a crewman at a machine gun keeps watch*, United States Army.
152. Bundesarchiv, Bild 183-S53854, photo: o.Ang.
153. American photographer, *The capture of Aachen: tanks and trucks of the US First Army enter the shattered city*, 1944, black-and-white photograph, private collection, Peter Newark Pictures, Bridgeman Images.
154. Bundesarchiv, Bild 183-J28303, photo: Jäger.
155. Copyright Rowan Technology Solutions, 2016.
     Military layer based on Esposito's maps 61–63, "The Ardennes Campaign, Operations, 16 December 1944–7 February 1945," *West Point Atlas of American Wars*, vol. 2.
156. Military layer based on Esposito's map 61–63, "The Ardennes Campaign, Operations, 16 December 1944–7 February 1945," *West Point Atlas of American Wars*, vol. 2.
157. American photographer, *Six United States soldiers from the 7th Armored Division patrolling St. Vith during the Battle of the Bulge, also known as the Ardennes Offensive or the Von Rundtstedt Offensive, Belgium*, 1945, photograph, copyright Galerie Bilderwelt, Bridgeman Images.
158. Ben Nason, *Infantry Against Tanks*, United States Army Center of Military History.
159. Howard Brodie, *Malmédy*, 1945, Library of Congress Prints and Photographs Division, Washington, D.C.
160. Copyright Rowan Technology Solutions, 2016.
     Volkssturm, Chase Stone, 2016.
161. Copyright Rowan Technology Solutions, 2016.
     Military layer based on Esposito's map 71, "Final Operations (19 April–7 May 1945)," *West Point Atlas of American Wars*, vol. 2.
162. *Russian and American troops meeting*, Universal History Archive/UIG, Bridgeman Images.
163. P. Baudouin, *Victory, Second World War poster*, 1945, colored engraving, Bibliotheque Nationale, Paris, France, Bridgeman Images.

CHAPTER 5

164. Copyright Rowan Technology Solutions, 2016.
165. *Avenge 7th December American poster after Pearl Harbour attack by Japan*, 1941, Universal History Archive/UIG, Bridgeman Images.
166. Cyrus Leroy Baldridge, *China carries on*, University of North Texas Libraries.
167. Political Poster Collection, JA 89, Hoover Institution Archives, courtesy of Hoover Institution Library & Archives, Stanford University.
168. Copyright Rowan Technology Solutions, 2016.
     Military layer based on Esposito's map 143, "Landings in the Gilbert Islands, 21 November 1943 and Operations in the Central and Southwest Pacific Areas, January–December 1944," *West Point Atlas of American Wars*, vol. 2.
169. Erich Schilling, *Der hungrige Tschunkingdrache*, 1943, Simplicissimus, Heft 25, Seite 341.
170. *World War II Advertisement—Curtiss Wright Corporation*, 1942, Museum of Science and Industry, Chicago, USA, Bridgeman Images.
171. United States Navy, *Alex Vraciu signals six kills following his "Turkey Shoot" mission*, 1944.
172. Copyright Rowan Technology Solutions, 2016.
     Military layer based on Esposito's map 141, "General Situation, 31 December 1944, and Principal Operations in China in 1944," *West Point Atlas of American Wars*, vol. 2.
173. Samuel D. Smith, *Destruction in Liuchow*, United States Army Center of Military History.
174. *Type 93 Torpedo*, U.S. Naval Historical Center.
175. American School, "*See Action Now*," 1944, color lithograph, private collection, copyright Galerie Bilderwelt, Bridgeman Images.
176. Copyright Rowan Technology Solutions, 2016.

The Joint Army-Navy Assessment Committee, *Japanese Naval and Merchant Shipping Losses During World War II By All Causes*, "Chronological List of Japanese Merchant Vessel Losses," February 1947.

177. United States Navy, *Torpedoed Japanese Destroyer Yamakaze Photographed through Periscope of USS Nautilus, 25 June 1942*, 1942.

178. *Official U.S. Navy portrait photograph of Fleet Admiral William F. Halsey, Jr.*, circa late 1945, Official U.S. Navy photograph #80-G-K-15137.

179. J. O'Donohoe, *"Palaus Fall Would Weaken Japs,"* 1944, University of North Texas Libraries.

180. Copyright Rowan Technology Solutions, 2016.
Military layer based on Esposito's maps 143–144, "Landings in the Gilbert Islands, 21 November 1943 and Operations in the Central and Southwest Pacific Areas, January–December 1944," *West Point Atlas of American Wars*, vol. 2.

181. Copyright Rowan Technology Solutions, 2016.
Source for all information except 13th AF is First Marine Division Special Action Report, Palau Operation, appendices C (Logistics), K (Naval Gunfire Support) and L (Air Support). (Library & Records Group, Marine Corps Educational Center, Marine Corps Schools, Quantico VA) 13AF info is from Smith, Approach to the Philippines.

182. Tom Lea, *The 2000-Yard Stare*, 1944, United States Army Center of Military History.

183. Copyright Rowan Technology Solutions, 2016.
Samuel Eliot Morison, *Leyte, June 1944–January 1945,* History of United States Naval Operations in World War II, vol. 12, (Boston: Little, Brown and Company, 1984).

184. Copyright Rowan Technology Solutions, 2016.
Samuel Eliot Morison, *Leyte, June 1944–January 1945,* History of United States Naval Operations in World War II, vol. 12, (Boston: Little, Brown and Company, 1984).

185. Samuel Eliot Morison, *Leyte, June 1944–January 1945,* History of the United States Naval Operations in World War II, vol. 12, (Boston: Little, Brown and Company, 1984), 161, 415–32.

186. Copyright Rowan Technology Solutions, 2016.
Samuel Eliot Morison, *Leyte, June 1944–January 1945,* History of United States Naval Operations in World War II, vol. 12, (Boston: Little, Brown and Company, 1984).

187. Copyright Rowan Technology Solutions, 2016.
Samuel Eliot Morison, *Leyte, June 1944–January 1945,* History of United States Naval Operations in World War II, vol. 12, (Boston: Little, Brown and Company, 1984).

188. Copyright Rowan Technology Solutions, 2016.
Samuel Eliot Morison, *Leyte, June 1944–January 1945,* History of United States Naval Operations in World War II, vol. 12, (Boston: Little, Brown and Company, 1984).

189. Copyright Rowan Technology Solutions, 2016.
Samuel Eliot Morison, *Leyte, June 1944–January 1945,* History of United States Naval Operations in World War II, vol. 12, (Boston: Little, Brown and Company, 1984).

190. Copyright Rowan Technology Solutions, 2016.
Samuel Eliot Morison, *Leyte, June 1944–January 1945,* History of United States Naval Operations in World War II, vol. 12, (Boston: Little, Brown and Company, 1984).

191. Copyright Rowan Technology Solutions, 2016.
Samuel Eliot Morison, *Leyte, June 1944–January 1945,* History of United States Naval Operations in World War II, vol. 12, (Boston: Little, Brown and Company, 1984).

192. United States Navy, *Destroyers Laying Smoke Screen during Battle of Samar 1944*, 1944, United States Navy National Museum of Naval Aviation, photo No. 1996.488.258.003.

193. *Two Coast Guard-manned LSTs open their great jaws in the surf that washes on Leyte Island beach, as soldiers strip down and build sandbag piers out to the ramps to speed up unloading operations*, 1944, National Archives and Records Administration, 513213.

194. Mitchell Jamieson, *Vice Admiral Takeo Kurita*, 1944, NH 63694, Courtesy of Navy Art Collection, Naval History and Heritage Command.

195. Copyright Rowan Technology Solutions, 2016.
Samuel Eliot Morison, *New Guinea and the Marianas, March 1944–August 1944,* History of United States Naval Operations in World War II, vol. 8 (Urbana and Chicago, IL: University of Illinois Press, 2002).
Samuel Eliot Morison, *Coral Sea, Midway and Submarine Actions, May 1942–August 1942,* History of United States Naval Operations in World War II, vol. 4 (Annapolis, MD: Naval Institute Press, 2010).
Samuel Eliot Morison, *Leyte, June 1944–January 1945,* History of United States Naval Operations in World War II, vol. 12 (Boston: Little, Brown and Company, 1984).

196. United States Army, *1st Cav soldiers during the Battle of Leyte*, Wikimedia Commons.

197. Copyright Rowan Technology Solutions, 2016.
Military layer based on Esposito's maps 154–159, "Philippine Campaign, 9 January–15 August 1945," *West Point Atlas of American Wars*, vol. 2.

198. Copyright Rowan Technology Solutions, 2016.
Military layer based on Esposito's maps 154–159, "Philippine Campaign, 9 January–15 August 1945," *West Point Atlas of American Wars*, vol. 2.

199. *General Douglas MacArthur returns to the Philippines with the US landing at Leyte, October 1944*, private collection, Peter Newark Military Pictures, Bridgeman Images.

200. United States Army Signal Corps, *Krueger*, Photo #: 111-SC-183951.

201. Copyright Rowan Technology Solutions, 2016.
George W. Garand and Truman R. Strobridge, *Western Pacific Operations,* History of U.S. Marine Corps Operations in World War II, vol. 4, (Historical Branch, G-3 Division, Headquarters, U.S. Marine Corps, 1971).
Benis M. Frank and Henry I Shaw Jr., *Victory and Occupation,* History of U.S. Marine Corps Operations in World War II, vol. 5, (Historical Branch, G-3 Division, Headquarters, U.S. Marine Corps, 1968).

202. *Jap . . . You're Next! We'll Finish the Job*, National Archives and Records Administration, 513563.

203. Copyright Rowan Technology Solutions, 2016.
I. C. B. Dear and M. R. D. Foot eds. *Oxford Companion to World War II* (Oxford: Oxford University Press, 2001), 113–14

204. *Curtis LeMay,* 1940s, Wikimedia Commons.
205. Copyright Rowan Technology Solutions, 2016.
     Third Report of the Commanding General of the Army Air Forces to the Secretary of War, 12 November 1945, 36–37.
206. Ishikawa Kōyō, *Tokyo Kushu,* 1945, Wikimedia Commons.
207. *Tokyo,* 1945, Wikimedia Commons.
208. Marine Pfc. Stanley A. Parks, then of Allentown, holds a flamethrower on Peleliu. Randolph Peters carries a .30-caliber carbine. Personal photograph, Stanley A. Parks. We would like to thank Barbara E. Parks for her kind permission to reproduce.
209. Copyright Rowan Technology Solutions, 2016.
     Military layer based on Esposito's maps 163–165, "Landings on Adjacent Islands and Operations in Northern Okinawa from 1 to 23 April 1945, Okinawa Campaign, 1 April–21 June 1945," *West Point Atlas of American Wars,* vol. 2.
210. American photographer, *USS St. Lo explodes, Battle of Leyte Gulf,* 1944, black-and-white photograph, private collection, Peter Newark Military Pictures, Bridgeman Images.
211. American photographer, *Ernie Pyle at the Okinawa landing, April 1945,* 1945, black-and-white photograph, private collection/Peter Newark Military Pictures, Bridgeman Images.
212. Copyright Rowan Technology Solutions, 2016.
     Military layer based on Esposito's map 167, "The Invasion of the Mainland, Proposed Plan of Operations for November 1945 and March 1946," *West Point Atlas of American Wars,* vol. 2.
213. *Part of the U.S. Navy Task Force which hammered the heart of the Marshall Is. into submission . . . and then anchored in the Majuro Atoll,* 1944, National Archives and Records Administration, 520645.
214. "*Your Battleship and Her Requirements,*" courtesy of the Historical Museum at Fort Missoula (1986.004)
215. James Turnbull, *Suicide in Pairs,* 1945, 88-159-KI as a Gift of Abbott Laboratories, Courtesy of Navy Art Collection, Naval History and Heritage Command.
216. United States Army Corps of Engineers, *Trinity Test—Oppenheimer and Groves at Ground Zero,* 1945.
217. Sydney Simon, *U.S.S. Missouri,* United States Army Center of Military History.
218. *Firebombing Leaflet,* from Josette Williams, *The Information War in the Pacific, 1945,* CIA Studies in Intelligence vol. 46, no. 3 (2002).

CHAPTER 6

219. Copyright Rowan Technology Solutions, 2016.
220. Thomas Edgar Stephens, *George C. Marshall,* Wikimedia Commons.
221. "*Buy War Bonds,*" circa 1942–1945, National Archives and Records Administration, 514007.
222. Copyright Rowan Technology Solutions, 2016.
     I. C. B. Dear and M. R. D. Foot eds. *Oxford Companion to World War II.* (Oxford: Oxford University Press, 2001), 225.
223. Copyright Rowan Technology Solutions, 2016.
     Military layer based on Esposito's map 72, "Allied Occupation Zones," *West Point Atlas of American Wars,* vol. 2.
224. *Clement Attlee, Harry Truman, and Joseph Stalin, seated outdoors at Potsdam Conference,* 1945, Universal History Archive/UIG, Bridgeman Images.
225. German photographer, *WW II Cologne 1945,* twentieth century, photograph, copyright Galerie Bilderwelt, Bridgeman Images.
226. This picture came from Mr. Kurtz Nakel, Gerstnerstrasse 4, Linos, Austria. It came in a letter to CARE, thanking the nonprofit organization for delivering a food package from a friend in America, © CARE.
227. *A German girl is overcome as she walks past the exhumed bodies of some of the 800 slave workers murdered by SS guards near Namering, Germany, and laid here so that townspeople may view the work of their Nazi leaders,* 1945, National Archives and Records Administration, 531343.
228. Sgt Mapham J., No 5 Army Film & Photographic Unit, *Germany Under Allied Occupation 1945,* Imperial War Museum, War Office Second World War Official Collection, Copyright IWM (BU 7358).
229. United States Army Photographer Lt. Gaetano Faillace, *Emperor Hirohito and General MacArthur, at their first meeting, at the U.S. Embassy, Tokyo, 27 September, 1945,* 1945.
230. Bundesarchiv, Bild 146-1976-137-06A, photo: o.Ang.
231. Stadtarchiv Freiburg M 72 B 271, *Luftbild Freiburg,* 1944.
232. *WWII: German POWs board a train in Boston,* National Archives and Records Administration, 195460.
233. *DP class at Schauenstein Camp,* Wikimedia Commons.
234. Eichler Baden-Baden, "The Marshall Plan Helps Europe," poster, collection of Landesarchiv Baden-Württemberg.
235. Bild 101I-297-1704-10 Bundesarchiv, Bild , photo: Müller, Karl.
236. United States Army, *American tank crews listen as Bernard Herzog (US citizen) who was liberated from the camp of Santo Tomas, Manila, Philippines.*
237. *The endless procession of German prisoners captured with the fall of Aachen marching through the ruined city streets to captivity,* National Archives and Records Administration, 541597.
238. Frank Mechau, *Death by Water,* 1943.
239. Saruman, *Cimetière américain de Colleville-sur-Mer,* 2005.
240. 1st Lt. Arnold E. Samuelson, 167th Signal Photographic Company, *Inside the crematorium at the Ebensee concentration camp on 7 May 1945,* 1945, United States National Archives and Records Administration.
241. American photographer, *Hermann Goering (1893–1946), Rudolf Hess (1894–1987), Joachim von Ribbentrop (1893–1946) and Wilhelm Keitel (1882–1946) at the Nuremberg Trials, 1945–46,* twentieth century, color photograph, private collection, Bridgeman Images.
242. Japanese photographer, *General Hideki Tojo,* 1945, black-and-white photograph, private collection, Peter Newark Pictures, Bridgeman Images.
243. *Bremerton Naval Shipyard, Washington,* circa 1948, NHHC 79051, courtesy of Navy Art Collection, Naval History and Heritage Command.

244. *Happy veterans head for harbor of Le Havre, France, the first to be sent home and discharged under the Army's new point system*, National Archives and Records Administration, 531298.
245. United States Army, *Stars and Stripes*, Issue No. 285 from May 8, 1945, Paris Edition, V-E-Day, 1945.
246. Political Poster Collection, UK 2899, Hoover Institution Archives, courtesy of Hoover Institution Library & Archives, Stanford University.
247. Bundesarchiv, Plak 003-029-043, photo: Mjölnir; [Hans Schweitzer].
248. Political Poster Collection, UK 2226, Hoover Institution Archives, courtesy of Hoover Institution Library & Archives, Stanford University.
249. *A German V-2 rocket fired by the British from a launch pad near Cuxhaven in Germany during Operation Backfire in 1945*, 1945, UK Science Museum.
250. American School, *"Americans All,"* 1942, color lithograph, private collection, copyright Galerie Bilderwelt, Bridgeman Images.
251. Bundesarchiv, Plak 003-028-069, photo: o.Ang.
252. *These are slave laborers in the Buchenwald concentration camp near Jena; many had died from malnutrition when U.S. troops of the 80th Division entered the camp.* Pvt. H. Miller, Germany, April 16, 1945, National Archives and Records Administration, 535560.
253. *This section of Osaka, Japan was levelled by fire-bomb attacks by Superfortresses in a long series of heavy raids during the months that preceded Japan's capitulation*, 1945, Library of Congress Prints and Photographs Division Washington, D.C.
254. Political Poster Collection, RU/SU 2541 (OS), Hoover Institution Archives, courtesy of Hoover Institution Library & Archives, Stanford University.
255. *"The United Nations Fights For Freedom,"* 2nd World War poster, color lithograph, twentieth century, private collection, Photo copyright Barbara Singer, Bridgeman Images.
256. Dwight Shepler, *The Spider and the Fly—USS* Hornet, 1945, 88-199-GN, courtesy of Navy Art Collection, Naval History and Heritage Command.
257. Political Poster Collection, UK 3058, Hoover Institution Archives, courtesy of Hoover Institution Library & Archives, Stanford University.
258. Gary Sheahan, *Buchenwald*, United States Army Center of Military History.
259. United States Office of War Information, Division of Public Inquiries, *The Atlantic Charter*, University of North Texas Libraries.
260. United States Federal Security Agency and Office of Education, *The Four Freedoms, printed in red and black, with President Franklin D. Roosevelt's signature at the bottom. Beneath this is a border of red with white stars*, University of North Texas Libraries.
261. Political Poster Collection, NE 224, Hoover Institution Archives, courtesy of Hoover Institution Library & Archives, Stanford University.
262. Nikol Schattenstein, *"Sacrifice: The Privilege of Free Men,"* University of North Texas Libraries.
263. Russian photographer, *Victory Parade on Red Square, Moscow*, 1945, photogravure, private collection, The Stapleton Collection, Bridgeman Images.

GATEFOLDS

D-Day, June 6, 1944

264. Military layer based on Esposito's map 49, "The Invasion, Operations, 6–12 June 1944," *West Point Atlas of American Wars*, vol. 2.
265. Mitchell Jamieson, *Cold Dawn of D-Day*, 1944, 88-193-HN, Courtesy of Navy Art Collection, Naval History and Heritage Command.
266. Olin Dows, *On the Way to the Assault Boats*, 1943, National Archives and Records Administration, 6384977.
267. Mitchell Jamieson, *LST in Channel Convoy—Invasion Bound*, 1944, 88-193-HK, Courtesy of Navy Art Collection, Naval History and Heritage Command.
268. Mitchell Jamieson, *Naval Demolition Team in Action*, 1944, 88-193-HP, Courtesy of Navy Art Collection, Naval History and Heritage Command.
269. Dwight C. Shepler, *Opening The Attack*, 1944, 88-199-EW, Courtesy of Navy Art Collection, Naval History and Heritage Command.
270. Dwight C. Shepler, *Assault Wave Cox'n*, 1944, 88-199-EN, Courtesy of Navy Art Collection, Naval History and Heritage Command.
271. Dwight C. Shepler, *The Tough Beach*, 1944, 88-199-EU, Courtesy of Navy Art Collection, Naval History and Heritage Command.
272. Dwight C. Shepler, *The Battle for Fox Green Beach, D-Day Normandy*, 1944, 88-199-ET, Courtesy of Navy Art Collection, Naval History and Heritage Command.
273. Gary Sheahan, *Utah Beach*, 1944, United States Army Center of Military History.

Major Allied Operations, June 1944

274. L. F. Ellis, *Victory in the West,* vol. 1, *The Battle of Normandy*, History of the Second World War, United Kingdom Military Series (London: Her Majesty's Stationery Office, 1962).
275. Samuel Eliot Morison, *New Guinea and the Marianas, March 1944–August 1944,* History of United States Naval Operations in World War II, vol. 8, (Urbana and Chicago, IL: University of Illinois Press, 2002), appendices II–IV.
276. "Operations in Support of the Capture of the Marianas," 11 September 1944, Commander, Task Force 58, Record Group (RG) 38, World War II Action and Operational Reports, Box 215, Folder 1, National Archives and Records Administration (NARA) II.
277. "Report of Saipan Operation," 23 August 1944, Commander, Task Group 52.2 (Amphibious Forces), RG 38: World War II Action and Operational Reports, Box 188, Folder 2, National Archives and Records Administration (NARA) II.

Page numbers in *italics* refer to picture captions.

Devers, Jacob L., 184
Dietrich, Josef "Sepp," 334*n*68
displaced persons (DPS) and refugees, 259, 271, 272–74, 308
    in West German camp, *274*
Dnepropetrovsk, 104, 149
Dnieper River, 104, 149
Dniester River, *157*
Donald, William, 68
Donets River, 9, 10, 13, 19, 104, 107
Dönitz, Karl, 53, 58, 59, 66
    biography of, 52
    Hitler and, 52, 59
Don River, 5, 15, *15,* 16, *17,* 19, 21, 29, 103–5
Doolittle, James, 85
Dresden, 75, 89, 312*n*36
Dumbarton Oaks Conference, 301, 350*n*75
Dunkirk, 31, 120
Dutch East Indies, 43
Dzerzhinsky Tractor Works, 28

Eaker, Ira, 80, 82, 85
Ebensee labor camp, *281*
E-boats, 68
Eby, Kerr, *141, 145*
economies, 149, 290
    European
        Marshall Plan and, xii, 261, 274, *275*
        recovery of, 273–74
    of Germany, 5, 45, 294
    gross domestic product (GDP), 291, 293
    of Japan, 199, 205, 242, 350*n*69
    resources and production, 288, 289–94, *290,* 308
    Soviet, 291–92
    total war and, 72–73
Edson's Ridge (Bloody Ridge), 40, *40,* 41
Egypt, 32, *34,* 35
    El Alamein, 1, 4, 31–35, 36, 41, *112*
        First Battle of (Battle of Ruweisat Ridge), *30,* 33
        Second Battle of (Operation Lightfoot), xi, 1, 4, 31, 34–35, *34,* 35, 313*n*49
    Suez Canal, 1, 32, *33,* 35, 164
Eichelberger, Robert, 216, 230, 235
Eindhoven, 181
Einstein, Albert, 251
Eisenhower, Dwight D., 75, 78, 89, 124, *127,* 147, 182, 184, 188, 198, 240, 266–67, 298, 347*n*30
    Normandy campaign and, 169, 180
El Alamein, 1, 4, 31–35, 36, 41, *112, 118*
    First Battle of (Battle of Ruweisat Ridge), *30,* 33
    Second Battle of (Operation Lightfoot), xi, 1, 4, 31, 34–35, *34,* 35, 313*n*49
Elbe River, 192
Elsenborn Ridge, 189
Enigma, 55, *56,* 58, 65, 300
Eniwetok, 206
Enola Gay, 251
Enterprise, U.S.S., 216
Europe:
    Allied victory in, 195–96, *265*
    CARE packages sent to, *267*
    Declaration on Liberated Europe, 191
    demobilization in, 283
    Eastern, Soviet Union and, 269–70, 273, 301
    economies of
        Marshall Plan and, xii, 261, 274, *275*
        recovery of, 273–74
    end of war in, 149, 195, *196,* 283
    restoration of order in, 269
    road to victory in, 149–98

V-E Day, 266, *286*
    Yalta Conference and, xii, 191
European Recovery Program (ERP; Marshall Plan), xii, 261, 274, *275*
European Theater of Operations (ETO), 307
    in 1944, 169–89
    in 1945, 190–95
Ewald von Kleist, Paul Ludwig, 6, 19

Falaise, 179, *179, 182*
Fascism, 80–81, *301*
Feodosia, 7
field equipment, *94*
Finland, 163
Finschhafen, 141
Flak antiaircraft guns, *32, 81*
flamethrowers, *43*
Fletcher, Frank Jack, 39
Florence, 169
Flossenbürg, *268*
Flying Fortress (B-17), 78, 85, 86, 134, 236, *239*
Flying Tigers, *206*
Foggia, 131
food supplies:
    British, 45, *50, 54, 55,* 65–66
    CARE packages and, *267*
    French, 265
    German, 267
    Marshall Plan and, 274
Formosa (Taiwan), 199, 217, *218,* 219, 229, 244, 249
Four Freedoms, 301, *304*
France, 51, 66, 85, 89, 121, 196, 265
    Operation Overlord in,
        Normandy, 45, 149
            bombing of, 332*n*43
            Caen, 170, 174–75
            hedgerows (bocage) in, 174, *174, 175, 178*
            see also Normandy campaign
    Paris liberated, 179, *184*
    Resistance fighters in, 86
    Siegfried Line (West Wall) in, 181, 184, *186*
Franklin, 244
Fredendall, Lloyd R., 114–17, 178, 323*n*25
Frederick Douglass, 64
Freiburg, 272
FUSAG (First U.S. Army Group), 169, *170*
Fusō, 225

Gafsa, 114–15
Galland, Adolf, 87
Gambier Bay, 227
Garth, 68
gas masks, *94*
gas warfare, 343*n*80
Gavutu, 36
Gazala, 31, 44
Geisel, Theodor Seuss, *101*
Gela, 121, 122
General Board of the European Theater, 285
Geneva Convention, *194,* 276
Genoa, 81
Germany, postwar:
    denazification of, 259, 267–69, *269*
    division of, 191, 269–70
    job interviews in, *266*
    occupation of, 259, *264,* 265–69, 271, 308
        Allied Control Council and, 265, 267
Germany, Nazi, xi, 289, 351*n*76
    Allied shipping targeted by, 51
    Allies' "Germany first" strategy, 36, *112,* 199, 253, 261, 300
    in Atlantic war, *see* Atlantic, Battle of

Battle of, 84–89
in Battle of the Bulge, 149, 189, *189,* 190, *190, 191*
Berlin, 81, 101, 102, *184,* 265, 280, 307
    Battle of, 149
    Red Army drive on, 192–93
    war damage to, 267
Blitzkrieg, xi
    against Britain, xi–xii, 72, 75, 78, 91, 124
    against Soviet Union, 5
bombed by Allies, 45, 66–79, *72,* 293–94
    Allied achievements of, 89–95
    Allied expectations vs. reality of, 70, 73
    Battle of Germany, 84–89
    Casablanca Directive in, 79–80
    of cities, 75, *80,* 81, *87,* 91
    civilians and, *72,* 80, 81, *87,* 91, *92*
    Combined Bomber Offensive (CBO), 79–84, *82, 87,* 91, 97, *296,* 298
    daylight, 78–79, 80
    escorts in, *82, 87,* 91–92
    Free Lance tactic in, 85
    German morale and, 91, *92*
    industrial areas targeted in, *69,* 73–76, *74,* 78–79, 82, *82,* 85, 89–91, 97
    in last eight months of war, 89
    at night, *76,* 79, *79,* 80, 97
    Pointblank Directive in, 80, 82–85
    quantity of bombs in, *71, 72*
    restrictions in, 73–75
    survey on effectiveness of, *92,* 285
    tonnage dropped in, *89,* 101
    transportation targeted in, 85, 87, 89, 91
Britain and, 35
    Battle of Britain, 85, 124, 261, 307
    bombing of Britain, xi–xii, *72,* 78, 91, 124
Casablanca conference and, xii
casualties of, by front, *155*
concentration camps of, 268, *268,* 272
    Buchenwald, *294, 302*
    Ebensee, *281*
correlation of forces on the Soviet-German front, *164*
defeat of, 149, 195, *196,* 259, 266
    air contribution to, 85, 89
economy of, 5, 45, 294
    gross domestic product (GDP), 293
at El Alamein, 33–35
in European theater of operations in 1944, 169–89
in European theater of operations in 1945, 190–95
final operations of, *195*
first city to fall to Allies, *187*
Gestapo in, 124
industrial areas of, *69,* 73–76, *74,* 78–79, 82, *82,* 85, 89–91, 97, 181
intelligence in
    B-Dienst, 55, 58
    Operation Blue and, 7
Italy and, 113–14, *130,* 131–32, 269, 351*n*76
Japan and, 300, 351*n*76
Lebensraum and, xi, 289
military (Wehrmacht) of, xi, 48
    antiaircraft guns of, *32, 81,* 86
    Armed Forces High Command (Oberkommando der Wehrmacht; OKW), 5, 21, *54,* 155
    Army High Command (Oberkommando des Heeres; OKH), 5–6, 103
    bicyclists in, 6, *6*
    Bismarck in, 50–51, *53*

German campaigns against, 1, *156,* 196, *288*
  Blitzkrieg, 5
  capture of Red Army soldiers, *12*
  cauldron (Kessel) battles in, 7, 15
  Eastern front in 1944, 149–63
  invasion of 1941 (Operation Barbarossa), xi, 5, 112–13, 196, *290, 291, 292,* 300, 307, 350*n*73
  in January–July 1943, *107*
  Kharkov, 103–7, *103, 104,* 109, *110,* 112, 310*n*17, 322*n*22
  Kursk, 100, 107–13, *107, 109, 110,* 121, 146, 155, 307, 322*n*21
  underestimation of Soviet strength, *4,* 7
German invasion of 1942 (Operation Blue), xi, 1, 13–31, 309*n*1
  Blue I, 13–17, *16*
  Blue II, 15–16, *16,* 19
  Blue III, 16, *16*
  Caucasus campaign in, xi, *13,* 15, 16, *19, 21–25, 31,* 44, 103, 311*n*27
  collapse of, 20
  Crimean campaign and, 5, 7–9, 13, 16
  delayed start of, 7, 9
  dual offensive in, 21
  Hitler and, 5, 9–10, *9, 15,* 17, *17,* 19–21, 25, *27,* 29–31
  Izyum and, 5, 9–12, *10*
  in July 23–August 23, *19*
  Kerch offensive and, 7–9, *9,* 12, 44
  Kharkov campaign and, 9–13, *10,* 13, 21, 44
  non-German Wehrmacht divisions in, 6–7
  oil production and, 21, 25
  planning and preparation for, 5–13, *15, 16*
  resources of, *290*
  Soviet retreat in, 17–18, *17*
  stages of, 13–15
  Stalingrad campaign in, 5, 16, *18, 19,* 20–22, *22,* 25–30, *25, 26, 27, 28,* 36, 41, 44, 100, 103–5, 107, 124, 160, 307, 309*n*1, 310*n*17, 311*n*36, 351*n*76
  underestimation of Soviet strength in, 7
  Volga campaign in , 5, 16, 25, *26,* 29
Germany occupied by, 273
Germany as ally of, 35
horses in, 5
Japan and, 250, 252
Leningrad, 22, 157, *157*
military of, 10–12, 149
  air power of, 10–12, *10*
  Deep Battle doctrine of, 12, 13, *103,* 149, 153, 155, 160, 192, 198
  increasing quality of, 153–55
  Sturmovik attack aircraft of, 155
  submachine guns of, *22*
  tanks of, *6, 153*
  in victory parade, *307*
Moscow, xi, 5
  victory parade in, *307*
oil production in, xi, 5, 21, 25, 31, 103
postwar occupation and, 265
propaganda of, *8*
repatriation and, 275–76
Romania and, *15*
Stalingrad, xi, 1, 4
  grain elevators in, 22, *22,* 28
  Hitler and, *27,* 29–31, 311*n*27, 313*n*45
  in Operation Blue, 5, 16, *18, 19,* 20–22, *22,* 25–30, *25, 26, 27, 28,* 36, 41, 44, 100, 103–5, 107, 124, 160, 307, 309*n*1, 310*n*17, 311*n*36, 351*n*76
  in Operation Uranus, 29, 31, 103, 155
U.S. ideological contest with, xii

Spaatz, Carl "Tooey," 80, 84–85, 87
  biography of, 78
Speer, Albert, 292–93
Sprague, Clifton, 227, *227*
Spree River, 192
Spruance, Raymond, 206, 208, 216, 218, 245, 249, 339*n*31, 341*n*66
Stalin, Josef, 5, 13, *18,* 105, 155, 190, 191, 288–89, 295, 344*n*88
  in Big Three, 295, *296,* 298, *299,* 301
  Japan and, 250
  at Moscow Conference, 280
  Operation Blue counteroffensive and, 9
  Order 227 of, 18
  Poland and, 161, *163*
  at Potsdam Conference, 250, *265*
  POWs and, 276, *276*
  retreat and, 18
  at Tehran Conference, xii, *147,* 298
  Warsaw uprising and, 155
  at Yalta Conference, xii, 265–66
Stalingrad, xi, 1, 4
  grain elevators in, 22, *22,* 28
  Hitler and, *27,* 29–31, 311*n*27, 313*n*45
  in Operation Blue, 5, 16, *18, 19,* 20–22, *22,* 25–30, *25, 26, 27, 28,* 36, 41, 44, 100, 103–5, 107, 124, 160, 307, 309*n*1, 310*n*17, 311*n*36, 351*n*76
  in Operation Uranus, 29, 31, 103, 155
Stalino, 21
Stary Oskol, 17
steel, 292
Stilwell, Joseph "Vinegar Joe," 209, 211, 342*n*71
Strait of Dover, 169
Strategic Air Command, 240
Struble, Arthur, 340*n*51
Sturmgewehr 44, *176*
Sturmovik attack aircraft, 155
submachine guns, *22*
  Thompson, *125*
submarines:
  Allied, commerce-raiding campaign against Japan, 199, 208, 212–16, *214, 215,* 254, 294
  convoy escorts and, *51,* 53, 55, 58, 59, 64, 65, 66, 68, 214, 215, 338*n*19
  Japanese, 212, *212,* 254, 337*n*17
  U.S. Navy, 212, *213, 215,* 338*n*20
submarines, German (U-boats), 1, 45, *48, 50,* 51–66, *53, 54, 56, 59,* 95, 101, 147, 212, 300
  bombing campaigns against, 66–70
  convoy escorts and, *51,* 53, 55, 58, 59, 64, 65, 66, 68
  decline in effectiveness of, 58–59
  depth charges and, 62, 338*n*20
  dimout, 58
  Enigma and, 55, *56,* 58, 65
  radar and, 62–64, *298*
  sonar and, 51, 53–54
  technological advantages in campaign against, 59–65
  in wolf packs, 54, 55, 58, 66
Suez Canal, 1, 32, *33,* 35, 164
Suluan, 221
Superfortress (B-29), 199, 206, 208–9, 210, 236–37, *239,* 240, *240,* 242, 243, 244, *250,* 251, 253, *291, 295*
Supreme Headquarters Allied Expeditionary Force (SHAEF), 75, *170,* 188, 195
Surigao Strait, 221, 225
Suwannee, 228

Suzuki, Kantorō, 235, 249, 250, 252
Sword Beach, 170–72
Syracuse, 121, 122
Szechuan, 210

Taganrog, 7
Taiwan (Formosa), 199, 217, *218,* 219, 229, 244, 249
Tanambogo, 36
tank destroyers, 285
tanks, 107, 109–10, 115, 182
  FUSAG, *170*
  in Normandy, 172
  Rhino, *175*
  Soviet KV-2, *6*
  Soviet T-34, *153*
  Tiger, *107,* 114
  see also Panzer forces
Tarawa, 142–44, *143, 144, 145, 146, 147,* 199
Task Force Stark, 115
Tebessa, 116
Tehran Conference, xii, 97, *147,* 298
Tenaru River, 43
Ten-go, 245
Terek River, 21, 22
Thala, 116
Thorson, Truman, 177
Thunderbolt (P-47), 174, *181*
Tiergarten, 192
Timoshenko, Semyon K., 9, 10
Tinian, *205,* 206, 240, 251
Tirpitz, Alfred von, 53
Tobacco Factory, 133
Tobruk, 32, 44
Tōjō, Hideki, 209, 281, *283,* 300
Tokyo, 102, *102,* 146, 236
  bombing of, 240, *242, 243,* 249
Tokyo Raid, 216
Tokyo War Crimes Tribunal, 281
tommy guns, *125*
Torgau, 192
torpedoes, *48,* 50, 58, 143, *205,* 212, *212,* 215, 300, 337*n*16, 338*n*23
  E-boats, 68
  Japanese submarine-launched, *212*
  torpedoed Japanese destroyer, *215*
total war, *50, 70,* 72–73, 95, *239*
Toyoda, Soemu, 206–8, 221, 229, 336*n*5
Treaty of Versailles, 259
Tregaskis, Dick, 43, 126
Tripoli, 33
Troina, 129
trousers, *94*
Truk, 141, *205,* 206, 208
Truman, Harry S., 78, 250–53, 261, 342*n*74, 344*n*85
  at Potsdam Conference, *265*
Truscott, Lucian K., Jr., 166, 167–69
Tsili Tsili, 140
Tuapse, 22
Tulagi, 36
Tunis, *34,* 101, 113, *118,* 120, 178
Tunisia, 35, 97, 113–19, 131, 134, 178, 196
  Kasserine Pass, 101, 113–19, *114, 115, 116, 117,* 178, 323*n*26
Turin, 81
Turner, Kelly, 343*n*79

U-boats, *see* submarines, German
Ukraine, 13, 100, 153, 157, *157,* 163
Ulithi, 218, 219
Ultra, 120, *170,* 285, 300
Uman, 157
United Kingdom, *see* Great Britain

United Nations, 191, *293*, 301, 350*n*75, 351*n*81
  Relief and Rehabilitation Administration (UNRRA), 273
  War Crimes Commission, 280
United States:
  alliance with Soviet Union and Britain, 190
  Britain as partner of, 190, 300–301
  coastal shipping of, 58
  entry into war, xi, 1, 35, 54, 58, 59, 261, 300
  gross domestic product (GDP) of, 291
  industry in, 5, *63*, 261
  Japan at material disadvantage to, 36, 43
  Pearl Harbor attack on, xi, 43, 59, 199, *202*, 205, 209, 212, 214, 215, 217, *230, 239*, 301, 340*n*47
  Joint Chiefs of Staff in, 36–37, *112, 136*, 137–38, 141, 249, 343*n*80
    War Department Civil Affairs Division of, 264–65
  Lend-Lease program of, 32, 54, 292, 301, 337*n*15
  ships produced by, 59, *62, 63*
  Soviet ideological contest with, xii
  unity in war effort promoted by, *292*
United States military:
  air force, 45, 50, 148
    Air War Plans Division (AWPD), 78
  army, 138, 261, 282, 284
    demobilization of, 282–84
    first European city conquered by, 128
  in Atlantic war, 45, 58, 59; *see also* Atlantic, Battle of
  bomber pilot with gear, *95*
  British naval and air strategies compared with, 92–95
  82nd Airborne Division paratrooper, *124*
  Flying Tigers, *206*
  Germany and
    declaration of war, xi, 54
    undeclared naval war, 54
  Marines in the Pacific, *244*
  Marshall and, 261
  navy, 48, 50, 212, 214
    demobilization of, *284*
    Fifth Fleet, 206, 208, 216, 218, 249, *252*, 336*n*3, 339*n*31, 341*n*66
    submarines of, 212, *213, 215*, 338*n*20
  in Pacific War, *see* Pacific War
  Seabees, 219, 239, 243
University of Virginia, 264
Ural Mountains, 7
Ushijima, Mitsuru, 244, 246
Utah Beach, 170, 171, 178

V-2 rocket, 291
Valmontone, 169
Vandegrift, Alexander, 38
Vasilevsky, Aleksandr, 111
Vella Lavella, 140
Verdun, 179
Verdun, 68
Victor Emmanuel III, King, 131
victory parades, *307*
Victory Program, 73
Villers-Bocage, 175
Vistula River, 155, 160–61, 163, *163*, 192
Vitebsk, 160
V-E Day, 266, *286*
V-J Day, *262*, 274
Vogelkop Peninsula, 216
Volcano Islands, *205*
Volga River, 5, 16, 25, *26*, 29, 104
Volturno River, 135
Voronezh, 15, 16, 17, *103*
Vraciu, Alex, *206*

Waal River, 180
Wake Island, 199, 216
war crimes tribunals, 259, 272, 277, 280–81, 348*n*41
  Nuremberg Trials, 52, 124, 280–81, *282*
  Tokyo War Crimes Tribunal, 281
Warsaw, 149, 161–63, 192
  uprising in, 155, 161, *161, 163*
Wasp, 244
Wedemeyer, Albert, 211
Westphal, Siegfried, 186
West Wall (Siegfried Line), 181, 184, *186*
Wewak, 140, 216
White Plains, 228
Wilhelmina Canal, 180
women:
  in cleaning up damage in Germany, *271*
  in workforce, *62*, 291
Wonsan, 340*n*51
Woodlark Island, 140
workforce, 290–91
  women in, *62*, 291
World War I, xii, 53–54, 66, 72, 73, *94*, 97, 124, *194*, 235, 261
  end of, 259, 266
World War II:
  Allied advantages in, 97, 146–47, 195–96, 253, 259, *286*, 289
  Allied victory in
    in Europe, 195–96
    reasons for, 286–89, *286*, 308
  Allies' gaining of skills in, 196–98, 259
  Allies' "Germany first" strategy in, 36, *112*, 199, 253, 261, 300

Axis nations' loss of initiative in, 100
Axis nations' lack of coordination in, 300, 301
battlefields in, 304–8
coalition warfare in, 97, 120, 198, 259, 294, 295–301, *298, 304*, 308
end of, xii, 259, 266
  in Europe, 149, 195, *196, 265*, 283
  in Japan, 249–53, *257*, 259
first European city conquered by U.S. army in, 128
as global war, 97–148
good vs. evil and the will to win in, 288–89, 301–4, 308
historical assessment of, 259, 284–89
logistics in, 198, *253*, 308
postwar challenges, 259–308
  accounting for the living, dead, and missing, 275–79
  demobilization, 259, 272, 282–84, *284*, 308
  occupation, *see* occupation
  refugees and displaced persons (DPS), 259, 271, 272–74, *274*, 308
  repatriation, 274, 275–76, 277
  war crimes, *see* war crimes tribunals
resources and production for, 288, 289–94, *290*, 308
road to victory in Europe, 149–98
as total war, *50, 70*, 72–73, 95, *239*
turning point of, 1–44, 97
unconditional surrender of Axis powers as Allied goal in, 97, *101*, 131, 191, 199, 259, *298*, 344*n*85
U.S. entry into, xi, 1, 35, 54, 58, 59, 261, 300
victory parades, *307*

Yalta Conference, xii, 191, 265–66, 301
Yamakaze, 215
Yamamoto, Isoroku, *230*, 340*n*47
Yamashiro, 225
Yamashita, Tomoyuki, 229, 231–33, 235
Yamato, 222, 223, 227, 245
Yank, 193
Yap, 208, 218
Yokoyama, Shizuo, 232, 233
Yorktown, 244
Ypres, 31
Yugoslavia, *163*, 300

Zaporozhye, 104
Zeitzler, Kurt, 29, 105
Zhukov, Georgy, 192–93, *307*
Zon, 181
Zuikaku, 226